The Complete Works of
WASHINGTON
IRVING

Richard Dilworth Rust
General Editor

D0169085

General Editor
Henry A. Pochmann (1965–1973)
Herbert L. Kleinfield (1973–1976)
Richard Dilworth Rust

Textual Editor
Edwin T. Bowden

EDITORIAL BOARD
Lewis Leary, Chairman
Ralph M. Aderman   *Walter A. Reichart*
Andrew B. Myers   *Richard Dilworth Rust*
Henry A. Pochmann (1961–1973)
Herbert L. Kleinfield (1965–1976)
Richard Beale Davis (1965–1981)
C. Hugh Holman (1973–1981)

WASHINGTON IRVING

BIBLIOGRAPHY

WASHINGTON IRVING

BIBLIOGRAPHY

Compiled by

Edwin T. Bowden

Twayne Publishers

Boston

1989

Published by Twayne Publishers
A Division of G. K. Hall & Co.

Copyright 1989 by
G. K. Hall & Co.
All rights reserved

The Complete Works of Washington Irving
Volume XXX

Library of Congress Cataloging-in-Publication Data

Bowden, Edwin T.
      Washington Irving bibliography.
      (The Complete works of Washington Irving ; v. 30)
      Includes index.
      1. Irving, Washington, 1783-1859--Bibliography.
I. Title. II. Series: Irving, Washington, 1783-1859.
Works. 1969 ; v. 30.
Z8439.7.B69 1988 [PS2081]   016.818'209   88-31696
ISBN 0-8057-8526-4

Manufactured in the United States of America

Z
8439.7
. B69
1989

CONTENTS

INTRODUCTION   ix

BOOKBINDER'S CLOTHS COMMONLY APPEARING
    ON IRVING'S WORKS   xxi

LIBRARIES MOST FREQUENTLY CITED   xxiii

ORIGINAL WORKS

Salmagundi   3

A History of New York   87

The Poetical Works of Thomas Campbell   115

The Sketch Book   122

Bracebridge Hall   183

Letters of Jonathan Oldstyle, Gent.   205

Charles the Second   208

Tales of a Traveller   216

Oliver Goldsmith   243

The Freyschütz   265

The Beauties of Washington Irving   267

Richelieu   286

The Life and Voyages of Christopher Columbus   288

The Life and Voyages of Christopher Columbus (Abridged)   319

The Conquest of Granada   335

Voyages and Discoveries of the Companions of Columbus   350

The Alhambra   362

WILLIAM F. MAAG LIBRARY
YOUNGSTOWN STATE UNIVERSITY

The Crayon Miscellany   387

    A Tour on the Prairies   387

    Abbotsford and Newstead Abbey   402

    Legends of the Conquest of Spain   410

Astoria   419

The Adventures of Captain Bonneville   433

Biography and Poetical Remains of Margaret Miller Davidson   446

A Book of the Hudson   456

Mahomet and His Successors   460

Wolfert's Roost   475

Life of Washington   485

CONTRIBUTIONS TO OTHER BOOKS

ORIGINAL CONTRIBUTIONS   529

REPRINTED CONTRIBUTIONS   589

WRITINGS IN PERIODICALS   671

COMPLETE WORKS   739

INDEX   749

INTRODUCTION

The number, the variety, and the textual complexity of Irving's publications may surprise many readers -- as they surprised me when I began to sense the full challenge of compiling and writing this bibliography. Irving's final collected works, the Author's Revised Edition of 1848-1859, contains eighteen original books, but that is only the heart of his work. He deliberately omitted from it four of his books, *Letters of Jonathan Oldstyle, Salmagundi, Legends of the Conquest of Spain,* and the *Biography and Poetical Remains of Margaret M. Davidson.* And it reprints none of his poems, plays, reviews, or edited works, and few of his many periodical pieces, some of which have yet to be positively identified.

It should be noted too that since there was no international copyright agreement in the first half of the nineteenth century, the copyright laws of the United States and Great Britain required that an author publish a new work almost simultaneously on both sides of the Atlantic. Irving's common practice, once his reputation and popularity began to be established, was to provide his American and his British publisher each with a separate manuscript. Since he generally continued to revise one of the manuscripts up to the last possible moment, and often to make further revisions in the proofs, the two first editions of a book almost always vary considerably and often provide two quite different works, in text as well as in title page and format. Although Irving generally managed at some later time to unify the two original texts, often the separate lines of textual descent would remain distinct in later reprints of various sorts.

George P. Putnam's title for the collected works, the Author's Revised Edition, suggests one of the other sources of the sheer number of significant items in the bibliography of Irving, his propensity to revise a work after first publication. In particular, the earlier works that he was later willing to recognize publicly, *A History of New York,* for instance, or *The Sketch Book,* underwent revision after revision until the final version was quite different from the original. He gave *A History of New York* five revisions that made significant textual changes, and *The Sketch Book* also five revisions that finally added four new sketches, added a new preface and conclusion, split one of the original sketches into two separate ones, and made greater or smaller changes in them all. And the revisions were not restricted to

American or British editions. He revised *A History of New York* for a Paris edition of 1824, and *The Sketch Book* for a Dresden edition of 1823.

Those later revisions point to still another source of bibliographic richness, the many continental editions both in English and in translation during Irving's lifetime. His work was popular on the continent and often reprinted: in Austria, Czechoslovakia (as it was later to be called), Denmark, France, Germany (in its various parts before unification), Greece, Italy, the Netherlands, Poland, Russia, Spain, Sweden. There were even a few scattered editions of his Spanish works in Latin America. It is revealing that in the 1830's and 1840's, particularly in Germany, Irving's works were sometimes reprinted as school books to be used for the study of English. With James Fenimore Cooper, he was one of the first of the American international authors.

Finally, the reader will notice the eye-opening number of reprints before 1860, whether revised or not. If not literally true it is certainly figuratively true that each of Irving's major works was reprinted somewhere at least once a year during his entire lifetime, and some of them more often. *The Sketch Book*, for instance, appeared in at least seventy-six editions and later impressions of those editions between 1819 and 1859, without counting the translations or selections. (The figure depends to some small extent on how variant states are counted.) *Bracebridge Hall*, a less popular work, was printed thirty-nine times between 1822 and 1859, and *Tales of Traveller*, even as a badly received work, appeared forty-one times between 1824 and 1859. The statistics themselves speak for the demand for his writing. When taken in conjunction with the reprinting of extracts in periodicals, annuals and gift books, anthologies, school readers, and volumes of *Beauties,* the popularity and esteem accorded Irving in his own day is impressive.

The image of Irving as an easy-going author who did not work very hard at his occupation, an image too often held even by biographers and scholars, is clearly false. He may have written easily -- although even that belief ignores the industrious research that went into such books as the four-volume life of Columbus and the five volume life of Washington -- but he wrote continuously and voluminously, and then revised what he had written earlier. Irving supported himself by his pen (and sometimes members of his family too), beginning at a time when that was a major challenge. For him, it was a challenge that could only be met *by* the pen. And he was always willing to help friends, family, even acquaintances with their writing, whether by editing, rewriting, reading and making suggestions, "puffing," or helping to find a publisher. Between times, he kept up a healthy correspondence. If he wrote easily, it was the result of long and constant practice.

From 22 October 1802, when Irving's first identifiable writing appeared in the New York *Morning Chronicle*, to 28 November 1859, the date of his death, is a long time and encompasses a long publication history for such a busy and productive author. A bibliographer attempting that history must be grateful for any prior help, particularly at the beginning of the project. For Irving, there are three previous bibliographies of significance. *Washington Irving: A Bibliography*, by William R. Langfeld with the bibliographic assistance of Philip C. Blackburn (New York: The New York Public Library, 1933) was the first to attempt a full description of the first editions of Irving's books, with other useful information at the end. Langfeld was a collector himself and had the chance to see many of the rarer works in private collections as well as in a few public institutions. Those descriptions are still valuable.   If Langfeld and Blackburn did not solve many of the bibliographical puzzles, at least they called attention to some of the major ones and began to impose order on the history of Irving's first book publications.

A *Bibliography of the Writings of Washington Irving: A Checklist*, by Stanley T. Williams and Mary Allen Edge (New York: Oxford University Press, 1936) made no attempt to duplicate Langfeld and Blackburn's descriptions and discussions, but offered instead a checklist of all of Irving's publications, particularly in book form, from the beginning up to the 1930's. If they missed a number of them, and included a few ghosts, or examples of the same book listed in different fashions by heterogeneous sources, that is only to be expected in a pioneering effort. Stanley T. Williams was, of course, the biographer of Irving, and his *The Life of Washington Irving*, 2 vols. (New York: Oxford University Press, 1935) is a mine of bibliographical information as well as biographical. The two works complement each other. Williams and Edge were careful to note items that they had in fact seen, and the information adds value to their listings.

The section on Irving in *Bibliography of American Literature*, by Jacob Blanck, Vol. 5 (New Haven: Yale University Press, 1969) is by far the most nearly satisfactory of the prior bibliographies. Like the Langfeld and Blackburn, it concentrates on the first editions of the books, although it adds a number of significant later editions and more of Irving's contributions to other books.   Unlike the Williams and Edge, it makes no attempt to list all of the later reprintings, although it does include a few that apparently were caught in the net. Its great contribution is the bibliographical sophistication and skill that it brings to the task. If I disagree with *BAL* in many instances, as I do, and if I go beyond its chosen boundaries in scope and detail, as I do, I still owe it much and am grateful for its aid and reinforcement .

The greatest outside help in my work, however, taking the form of an extra source of information, has been provided by the individual editors of Irving's works in the Twayne edition. That has given me an advantage held by few bibliographers. As a necessary prerequisite of modern editing, each editor has been required to collate the various editions of his or her particular book. Multiple copies of each significant edition were compared on a mechanical collator, and the various editions themselves were collated with each other by eye (since the different settings of type prohibit the use of the Hinman collator or other similar mechanical devices). By that laborious and time-consuming method, the editor discovered the textual variants that appeared through the printing history of the book. In turn, I could use the discovered variants for bibliographical, rather than strictly textual, insight and definition.

Some of the original collation I did myself for the editors. When the collation was performed by someone else, however, I checked it in other available copies of the various editions. But even with that information in hand, I soon found that more collation was needed for my purposes. Some editions, such as the first and second American editions of *A History of New York*, had not turned out to be significant editions in the establishment of the final text and so had not been as heavily collated by the editor. I went back to collate a number of new copies. Some specific elements of a book -- title pages, copyright pages, tables of contents, advertisements, illustrations, paper wrappers -- were not of routine importance in establishing the text but often of considerable bibliographical importance, and so I collated many of those elements, by mechanical collator when possible, by eye when not. In a few instances, such as the discovery of the disguised second London editions of *Bracebridge Hall* and *Columbus*, the discovery sent me back to the collator again. And finally there were those works not included in the Twayne edition, such as the translation of Depons' *Voyage to the Eastern Part of Terra Firma*, or the several plays published under the name of John Howard Payne, which called at least for partial collation.

The relationship between bibliographical studies and textual studies should be a close one. Here in my work it is represented not only in the origins of some of the bibliographical data but also in the presentation of the descriptions. I have stressed in my descriptions of Irving's books the text itself: textual variants in superficially similar states of impressions, and revisions -- particularly revisions by the author -- in new editions. What Irving wrote, and the changes in it, whether by himself or others, is what is finally important to the reader.

Ideally, in editing Irving or any other author a reliable, detailed bibliography should be available for the editor. In compiling a new bibliography, edited texts with reliable, detailed textual notes should be available for the bibliographer. But you can't have it both ways, and in compiling the complete Twayne edition we never had it completely either way. The bibliographer tried to help the editors, the editors tried to help the bibliographer, but inevitably new discoveries by both kept turning up along the way. That will explain why this bibliography, with the advantage of being completed somewhat later in the process, occasionally differs in small ways from the edited volumes, particularly in adding extra information. But still, this final volume of bibliography and the volumes of edited texts are related and complementary. For a full explanation of the textual variants in Irving's books, only defined by representative examples here, the reader can go to the tables in the edited texts; for a full description of the complexities of the printing of Irving's books, merely suggested in the edited texts by the tables of variants that have been found in significant original editions, the reader can come to this bibliography. It should be pointed out, however, that I cover a great deal more of Irving's writing than the editors of the texts needed to struggle with -- the many unrevised impressions or editions, Irving's periodical publication, his original contributions to other books, his reprinted works in books by others, the editions of his collected works -- since my intention is to present a complete account of Irving's published writing. Each new category presented new and different problems in compilation, and to each, except for the reprints of original works, I have devoted a separate section with a brief introduction. For those sections I must accept full responsibility. Of course I must for the account of the original works also. There I had valuable help from the editors of the titles included in the Twayne edition, but the responsibility is mine, and any errors or omissions are mine.

Most of the mechanics of description in this bibliography are fairly conventional and, I hope, are clear to the reader who has any familiarity with bibliography, and to most of those who do not. Still, a few of the methods employed need explanation for some users -- and perhaps defense for those rigorous modern bibliographers who want the minutest details and absolute completeness in description. In adopting the methods here, I have tried to steer a middle course between unreasonable exhaustion of detail and an equally unreasonable, easy simplification that leaves too many details of the physical book untouched and unidentified. My aim has been, on the one hand, to identify unequivocally any book by Irving published before 1860, and, on the other, to describe in sufficient detail all of the known books (and other publications) of Irving in his own lifetime, so that the user of the bibliography will *know* each item even if he or she never has a chance to see the physical object itself. I would like to think that "usefulness" is the key term: for the collector, the book dealer, the librarian and cataloguer, the historian of literature or of the intellectual period or of writing and publishing, and of course, first of all, the reader of Washington Irving, whether as scholar, teacher, student or casual explorer. I want to give information enough to satisfy the many and varied needs, but not to overwhelm.

Before outlining the methods themselves, one related comment seems warranted. Nineteenth-century printing was sometimes careless, hurried, faulty. Even title pages occasionally show typographical errors and often show inconsistencies in form, particularly in the listing of multiple associated publishers. The planning of a book could go astray too, often failing to coordinated the paging or the signing of preliminary matter with the paging or the signing of the body of the text. If such errors and inconsistencies show up in the transcriptions and collations here, it is because they are present in the book being described. It would be awkward and disconcerting to sprinkle the descriptions with "sic's," although that would be one way to indicate that the error is not mine. The reader, I fear, will have to trust my accuracy and care. I hope that the confidence is not misplaced.

The title page of the first impression of each edition is reproduced, although in simplified conventional facsimile. That is, the distinction is made between lower case and upper case, and between roman, italic, or special type such as hollow letters or "fancy" letters (a type derived from the old black letter, often associated today with such "antique" lettering as that on wedding invitations and the like).   No attempt, however, is made to distinguish between sizes of type, whether in separate lines or within the same line. Capitals are simply transcribed as capitals, whether large or small. In the transcription of the title pages of translations there are special and awkward problems.   The various distinct alphabet types that differ widely from the Roman are identified -- Fraktur, modern Greek, Cyrillic -- but transcribed in conventional roman lettering with the necessary accent or other marks.   The less distinctly different alphabets that use, with the exception of occasional individual letters, the roman style with accent or other marks -- French, Scandinavian, Czech and the like -- are reproduced in an approximation of the original lettering. All type is in black ink unless a color is specified.

The title page of the first impression of each edition is reproduced completely. For subsequent impressions of that edition, only the publisher's imprint and the date is usually reproduced, with any new and indicative material that may appear: "Second Edition" (however misleading that term may be), "Newly Revised," and so on. It may be assumed that the complete title, with the imprint, date and additions specified, would approximate with some accuracy that of the first impression.

I try to use the terms "edition" and "impression" with precision. An "edition" includes all of the printings made from a single setting of type, whether directly from standing type or from stereographic plates made from that type. An "impression" of an edition is a distinct, separate printing from that setting. Since few records of early printers have survived, the term "impression" must be a little elastic. Presumably each impression is the result of putting the type (in whatever form) back on the press. But a few books that appear to represent new impressions may in fact be the result simply of stop-press changes or partial reprinting.   The term is still a useful one, however, and generally accurate.

A far more elastic term that I occasionally employ in describing a work is "state." When I say that a book appears in varying states, it simply means that there are detected differences between copies but that the differences do not seem great enough or suggestive enough to define the copies confidently as different impressions. Occasionally, I must admit, it is a weasel word; there are differences between copies, but it is difficult to determine bibliographically exactly what the differences represent. More commonly, I use the term to define superficial differences such as minor variants in title page or text, a different way of handling terminal blank pages, different bound-in advertisements or placing of the advertisements. (Perhaps I should point out here that I consider bound-in advertisements of less significance than some other scholars do; publishers and binders probably used, almost randomly, what they had available, at hand, even left over.   Still, advertisements can create different states of a book.)   The term is particularly useful in describing complex bibliographical situations such as those presented by *Salmagundi* or *The Sketch Book*.   The use of the bibliographical term -- a linguistic parallel to "edition" and "impression" -- will not be confused, I would think, with its use in the non-technical but related sense of a common mode or form, as in "two text states."

The system of reference numbers assigned to each entry is, deliberately, a simple one designed to be in keeping with the general method of reference used by the editors in their textual discussions of individual works in the Twayne edition.   Each of Irving's titles is assigned its own separate numbering, with the edition number given first, the nationality of the edition second, and the particular impression (if more than one is known) third. For example, "2Aa" would identify the second American edition, first impression. "3G" would identify the third German edition (in the English language), of which only one impression has been found. After the first impression of an edition, only the subsequent identifying letters ("b,""c,""d") are actually printed. Translations are not numbered, since detailed information there -- dating, later impressions and so on -- is sometimes not as reliable as I would prefer.

The system, like any system of reference, is open to objections. There is something to be said, for instance, for assigning each and every item through the bibliography a unique reference number so that no one number, whatever the title of Irving's work, duplicates another. But for a prolific author such as Irving, published regularly in a number of countries on the continent as well as in America and Britain, the system would be unwieldy as well as leading to long and possibly confusing reference numbers. Or, for another objection, the use of the capital letter "E" to denote British editions is not the happiest choice. But there I am constrained by history. The editors of the Twayne editions have long used "1E" as a simple shorthand for "first English edition," despite the ambiguity of "English" as a language and as a nation, and the complication offered by the imprecise inclusion of editions published, say, in Edinburgh or in Glasgow under the identification of "E." The Scots, quite properly, can object to that. But the usage is now so standardized in the Twayne editions that I felt I should be faithful to it.

One advantage of the "A" and "E" numbering system is that it does relieve me of the necessity of freezing into a numerical system any collector's-priority of American or British editions. I have presented first in the description of each work either the American editions or the British editions, according to the date on which the first edition of each was published. After *The Sketch Book*, Irving tried to have the American and the British edition appear simultaneously, although he never quite succeeded. As a result, there is considerable question of whether chronological priority has any real significance. Textual priority seems much more significant, and there I have tried to present grounds for conclusions in the brief introduction to each original work and in occasional comments on the text of individual editions. But the order of presentation remains chronological.

Collations of each edition are given in standard form, in a full version for first and other significant editions or a somewhat shortened version for reprinted editions. Page size (properly speaking, leaf sizes) are given in centimeters, as are all measurements. At the end of the collation I list anything originally bound in the book that is not a part of the regular signatures of the book: illustrations, advertisements, special notices and the like. All printing is in black type in conventional format unless specifically described. If the paper is anything other than wove paper in one of the shades of white, it is also specified there.

As part of the full description of a book, this bibliography adds two pieces of information not traditionally given: the name of the printer (and/or the stereotyper), and the lineation of a couple of chosen pages. The printer should be of interest in the history of printing, as well as a means of identification of the particular impression. The lineation is of decided usefulness in determining whether later printings are from the same setting. It is true that a book may occasionally be reset in a line-for-line reproduction, so that the lineation of the two settings is the same for the sample pages, but that does not happen very often, even though the possibility must be considered.

The identification of the printer or stereotyper is taken from the printer's imprint in the book. (To save space, the term "printer's imprint" is shortened to "printer" in my descriptions throughout this work.) If no imprint is present, at least in copies I have seen, the item is simply omitted. I tried several forms for defining lineation and finally settled on the one used here as the simplest and clearest; the page number and the first and last word on that page. Occasional complication arises from a punctuation mark or hyphen following the test word. For precision, I have recorded the mark. But those punctuation marks printed in the text should not be confused with the semicolon used here to divide the lineation of one page from another. A description of the lineation might read, "p. 100, to ... another,; p. 200, so; ... [in footnote] him.". The first word on page 100 is "to", and the last word is "another" followed by a comma. The first word on page 200 is "so" followed by a semicolon, and the last word (appearing in a footnote rather than in the text itself) is "him" followed by a period.

For convenience and utility, the color of bindings is described in familiar everyday terms. There are standardized color charts, I know, that are much more accurate in discriminating between shades. But they are not easily available to many readers, and there is some question of how accurate they would be for the original bindings that have survived from Irving's time. Once in a great while one may be lucky enough to find that pristine copy which has been preserved under ideal conditions, protected from light and handling, but only rarely, and for many of the editions never. Copies in original boards or cloth are scarce enough, and almost always faded or changed in color to one degree or another. Many of the dies used in the first half of the century were quite volatile; sometimes it is difficult now to determine even roughly what the original color must have been. A cloth that is brown today may have been red or purple originally.

For the many cloths used by binders in Irving's day, I have tried to be more exact. It is necessary to be, since publishers and binders routinely used a wide variety. On the first American edition of *Astoria*, 1836, which goes to an extreme, I have identified fifteen different types and textures of cloth, two of them in four different colors, and even then I have probably missed a few. To save the many lines of type that would be necessary to describe the cloths seen or reported on all the many editions and impressions, I have made use of the letter system employed in *Bibliography of American Literature,* a system which was in turn derived from the standard nomenclature used by book cloth manufacturers to identify textures. *BAL* prints, as part of the introductory matter of each volume, photographs of twenty-eight standard nineteenth-century cloths. (Many variants of those standard cloths existed, of course.) Since *BAL* is widely available in libraries, and a photograph is often clearer than a verbal description, I have concurred in describing cloths as "T cloth," "TZ cloth," or whatever. For the reader to whom *BAL* is not readily available, I have included in a table at the end of this Introduction a brief description of the cloths most often encountered on Irving's works.

The date of publication of each major item is identified as accurately as possible from contemporary sources. The most revealing may be private records and letters, some now in print for the scholar, although not as many as we would all like. In a few instances I have been able to draw on the private records of the John Murray company, from information collected by Professor Ben H. McClary, or on the Carey & Lea records printed by David Kaser as *The Cost Book of Carey & Lea,* 1963. Most early publishers' records, unfortunately, are lost or unavailable. One special source has been particularly valuable: Washington Irving himself, cooperating with the Murray firm in fighting a copyright lawsuit, sent John Murray in a letter of 22 September 1850 a detailed account of the American and British publication dates of each of his works with which Murray was associated. Irving's records, or his memory, may not always have been completely accurate, but the dates are still valuable evidence. Then too, there are Irving's other letters, collected in the Twayne *Letters* volumes, as well as his frequent jottings in his *Journals*, again printed in the Twayne edition. In those sources, Irving tended not to mention publication dates specifically, but the sources do offer corroborative evidence.

Public sources for dating may be more accurate or less. Pierre M. Irving in his *The Life and Letters of Washington Irving,* 4 vols., 1862-1864, falls somewhere between the private and the public sector, since he not only knew the older Irving intimately and had access to some of Irving's papers, but he made public in his volumes the information that he cared to give -- and that Washington Irving cared to allow him. One source of dates for French publication seems quite reliable: *Bibliographie de la France,* with its weekly list of publications in France, at least to 1839. But the most common public sources of dating that I have used are the contemporary periodicals. Between publishers' advertisements, occasional columns of literary chitchat, reviews, extracts, and some regular listing of new books, the periodicals do bracket in the dates fairly well. There are problems, of course: some of the information is mistaken or misleading, particularly in promises of future publication. And it must always be remembered that books then as now often circulated before the official day of publication, either in early copies or in the form of proofs or early sheets provided for reviewers. The greatest problem may be not the information itself but the energy of the investigator; there are so many periodicals and so little time to spend with them searching for dates.

I have been particularly fortunate in having available on microfilm -- thanks to my wife Mary Bowden's own research in Irving's publication history -- many of the copyright records (now housed in the Library of Congress) of the District Court of the Southern District of New York during Irving's most creative years. These have not only provided one source of accurate dating, at least for the first deposit of a title page and occasionally for the deposit of a complete volume, but have shown in a number of instances the unreliability of printed copyright dates in the books themselves. Note, for instance, my discussion of the copyright date of Part I of *The Sketch Book,* a date of considerable importance in Irving's life and one that apparently has long been given in error. When publishers in the early 1830's ceased to specify the exact date of copyright, printing only the year, the copyright records can offer the needed specificity.

At the end of the description of each book appears the location of one or more copies. This is in no sense a census but simply a record of the copies that I have examined and used in compiling the entry. For major items -- first editions, revised editions, bibliographically complex books -- I have examined as many copies as I could and have given their locations. For minor items -- late impressions, reprint editions, reprinted contributions and the like -- I have sometimes been content to examine and to locate only a single copy. But those copies located are the ones I have examined. In a very few instances, I have cited (and have said so in the location) copies about which I have received reliable information from reliable informants, particularly librarians, often partially in the form of xerographic copies or microfilms.   I have not listed copies examined by editors of the Irving volumes unless I have seen them myself. (The one exception is in the entry for *Salmagundi*; I discuss that problem in my introduction to the work.) Since I wanted to list and to locate a copy of *every* Irving book, I have occasionally been forced to list unseen books -- with the title always within square brackets. In the location of such a book I have used in the citation the phrase "copy reported in," preceded by the statement that I have not examined the book.

Continental editions and translations have provided a vexing problem, since copies of many of them are very scarce in this country and I have been unable to spend time in continental libraries. But I have wanted to locate at least one copy of each, and two if possible. For French books unlocated in this country I have relied on the printed catalogues of the Bibliothéque Nationale. For German books I have been particularly fortunate in the assistance of Mr. Ingo Stöhr of Wiesbaden who procured for me lists of Irving holdings in many West German libraries, drawn from the admirable system of German Central Catalogues. He has also procured, from the holding libraries, xerographic copies of title pages and other portions of some German printings not known in the United States. It is to him, and to the German library system, that I am indebted for the completeness of the German listings and locations. I should also add that for a few German editions not located and of course not examined, I have relied on Walter A. Reichart's fine article, "The Earliest Translations of Washington Irving's Writings," *Bulletin of the New York Public Library,* 61 (October 1957). For Polish editions I am grateful to the Biblioteka Narodowa in Warsaw. Mrs. Mirosława Kociȩcka, Head of its Reference Service Department, not only answered my questions about known Polish translations but turned up new ones, both in her library and in others.

Whenever possible I have located copies in libraries. In a very few instances when I have been unable to find the book in a library but have seen a copy privately owned, I have entered its location in that vague and infuriating phrase, "private hands." Sometimes too, in listing multiple copies examined, I have also mentioned copies in private hands. But the vast majority of locations are in libraries, sometimes in the rare book collections, sometimes in the stacks. In specifying the location I have used the location symbols employed by the Library of Congress (adding to them *BL* for the British Library in London). A selected list of location symbols is printed on the endpapers of each volume of the National Union Catalogue, and a complete list from time to time in a selected volume. For the convenience of the reader, I have given in a table at the end of this Introduction the symbols for libraries most commonly cited. Most of the citations in this bibliography are, quite expectedly, to the dozen libraries at which I have been able to spend a significant amount of time and so have drawn on most heavily. Among them, all with extensive Irving collections, and all personally helpful in my more extended visits, I would like to mention specifically the British Library, the Library of Congress, the New York Public Library, and the libraries of four universities: Harvard, Yale, Virginia, and my own, The University of Texas at Austin.

BOOKBINDER'S CLOTHS COMMONLY APPEARING ON IRVING'S WORKS

The letter designations are those employed here and in *Bibliography of American Literature,* derived from manufacturers' nomenclature. The initial verbal descriptions -- the thumb-nail terms -- are based in large part upon those of John Carter's *Binding Variants in English Publishing 1820-1900,* 1932, and Michael Sadleir's *XIX Century Fiction,* 2 vols., 1951. Those three works offer photographs of the various cloths.

A.   Pebbled string-grain. A variety of pebbled cloth in which the grains form short "strings" that intersect irregularly but give the impression of generally being in parallel.

AR.   The same pattern but larger and coarser "strings."

C.   Sand-grain. A very fine irregular pebble-grain. In one variety there is a slight suggestion of a parallel movement to the grains.

CM.   The same pattern but somewhat larger grains.

H.   Diaper cloth. Patterned in tiny diamond shapes formed by two angled sets of parallel diagonal lines.

L.   Rope-grain. The rough raised pattern is somewhat reminiscent of short, irregular strands in rope, of varying length, intersecting irregularly, but giving the impression of being arranged more or less in parallel. Similar to string-grain cloth, but coarser and with shorter and less parallel lengths in the pattern.

P.   Pebble-grain. The irregular raised grains do not form discernible patterns. It may be finer or coarser. In one variety, the surface may be morocco-like.

S.   Fine-ribbed. Fine parallel straight lines, relatively smooth.

T.   Bold-ribbed. The parallel straight lines are more heavily raised and further apart.

TB.   Net-grain. Tiny lozenges are arranged side by side to form fine parallel stripes.

TR.   Ripple-grain. Coarse wavy lines are set in parallel.

TZ.   The same pattern but with finer parallel lines, with the lines closer together.

V.   Smooth cloth.   The conventional cloth weave without a raised pattern. Sometimes called calico cloth.

LIBRARIES MOST FREQUENTLY CITED

CSmH   Henry E. Huntington Library, San Marino, Calif.

CtY   Yale University, New Haven, Conn.

DLC   U. S. Library of Congress, Washington.

ICN   Newberry Library, Chicago.

InU   Indiana University, Bloomington.

KU   University of Kansas, Lawrence.

MB   Boston Public Library.

MH   Harvard University, Cambridge, Mass.

NcU   University of North Carolina, Chapel Hill.

NjP   Princeton University, Princeton, N.J.

NN   New York Public Library.

NNC   Columbia University, New York.

NNHi   New-York Historical Society.

OkU   University of Oklahoma, Norman.

OrP   Library Association of Portland, Ore.

TxDaM   Southern Methodist University, Dallas, Tex.

TxFTC   Texas Christian University, Fort Worth, Tex.

TxGeoS   Southwestern University, Georgetown, Tex.

TxU   University of Texas, Austin.

ViU   University of Virginia, Charlottesville.

BL   The British Library, London.

ORIGINAL
WORKS

SALMAGUNDI

1A.   *Salmagundi* presents so many and such varied challenges to complete description that no attempt so far has been wholly satisfactory, and this one is no exception. But each attempt adds that much more to the store of available knowledge and builds a stronger foundation on which analysis can rest. The bibliographical ambiguities are numerous, extending from the question of the most appropriate terminology for description, to the more important questions of the printing history and textual history of the little volumes, to the question of the very reliability of the available evidence. And then there is the added ambiguity of authorship, not a bibliographical question in the strict sense perhaps, but one that is of importance and one that is certainly relevant in considering the history of the text, at the beginning as well as later.

It must be remembered that *Salmagundi* was not originally planned, produced, or thought of as a single work; it was simply a series of short essays, sketches and poems written and published at irregular intervals at the whim of the authors, Washington Irving, William Irving, and James K. Paulding. It apparently began as a casual impulse and ended when the authors wanted to stop. It could have gone on longer, and there is evidence that Washington Irving was indeed thinking of future pieces that were never written. The twenty little individual publications that form the whole, then, are not "parts" in the usual nineteenth-century sense of "publication in parts," in which a planned, unified work is published part by part, allowing the purchaser to acquire the whole in inexpensive installments. But neither is *Salmagundi* a "periodical" or a "magazine," appearing at regular intervals with an advance subscription price and not constituting finally a planned single work. I have used here the term "Number" -- awkward as it occasionally is -- as one that seems appropriate, one that is employed in the Numbers themselves, and the term that Irving used in his letters and in his preface to the Paris edition of 1824.

The general pattern of publication is apparent and may be determined from an examination of the Numbers, with an added dash of commonsense. The growing popularity of the work required continuous reprinting of individual Numbers, particularly of the earlier ones. As new readers discovered the series, no doubt, they wanted the earlier Numbers as well as the current one. With Number XI, Longworth issued a title page and table of contents for the first ten Numbers, treating them as the first volume of a

3

larger work. With Number XI also he began identifying the individual Numbers as belonging to "Vol. II." And finally, he issued bound with Number XX a title page and index for Volume II. The publishing gambit must have increased even more the demand for copies of earlier Numbers. Since the Numbers were hastily printed from set type (and the type probably quickly distributed), reprinting required a new setting of the type in a new edition -- sometimes identified at the head of the Number and sometimes not. Number I finally went through seven distinct editions.

Here again the question of terminology arises. Although each Number appeared in separate editions, the work as a whole is not conveniently defined or referred to by specifying the various separate editions of its twenty original component parts. And there is also the related problem of what to call the subsequent editions of the entire work that were printed in conventional book form. The Twayne edition, with its proper concentration on the history of the text, solves its problem of nomenclature neatly: each edition of a separate Number, even the first edition, is called a "subedition" of that Number, and the sum of the various subeditions may then be called the "first edition" of the work as a whole. For a bibliography, however, that solution does not seem quite so satisfactory. The casual reader is accustomed to and familiar with the conventional term "edition," and the term "subedition" might erroneously suggest "subsequent edition" or an edition somehow subordinate to the first. Therefore, I use the conventional term "edition" when describing the Numbers. But when describing subsequent editions of the work as a whole, I treat the work in Numbers as though the various editions of the Numbers did in fact constitute one, first, edition. That allows the New York edition of 1814 to be called, as it is conventionally, the "second American edition."

With each resetting of a Number, each new edition, new readings were introduced. Some are clearly revisions by the authors; some, particularly the smaller changes in punctuation and spelling, may have been the work of publisher or compositor, as may have been the corrections of various sorts of errors; and, of course, new errors were introduced with new settings. Some revisions were major, as in the second texts of Numbers X and XII, and many were minor, but whatever the source and the degree of the changes, a new edition meant a new revision.

The printing history as well as the textual history, however, is not simply a matter of a series of distinct progressive editions, each set apart and preserved intact like beads on a temporal string. A better metaphor might be a series of waves in the sea, moving generally forward although individual elements move sometimes backwards and sometimes merge with other waves. Stop-press corrections (or at least that is a reasonable assumption) often create variant states in an edition. And in later states of an edition the emendations will sometimes pick up readings that had been abandoned in revisions of an earlier state. For an example, see the term "his readers" on

[21].11f of the first edition of Number II. The same sort of variation can appear in subsequent editions too, when later resettings first change an earlier reading and then return to it again. For an example, see the variations in the spelling of "æther/ether" through the four editions of Number V. Or sometimes whole signatures are reset, to be combined first with the other part of the original setting, and then later added as a part of the next edition. For an example, see Number XII, where gathering B is reset to provide the last signature of State C of the first edition and then employed as the final gathering of the second edition when Signature A is also reset. Sometimes such mixed gatherings may be the result of a desire to improve or correct the text, but sometimes they may simply be the result of thrift. After all, why waste sheets left over, when paper is expensive?

The presence of mixed sheets immediately raises the question of sophistication or perfection of copies -- or, in a simpler word, fraud. *Salmagundi* has long been a scarce, expensive collector's item, and dealers (or perhaps owners) have been known to supply and bind in missing or defective pages, often ones from a different edition. For the scholar, one way to avoid being misled is to limit his investigation to copies in wrappers, copies that show no signs of rebinding or of possible tampering. *BAL* followed such a policy when possible, and there is much to be said for it. But there is also a good deal to be said against it. The chances of finding all existing states in original condition are slim. Numbers in wrappers are scarce and widely scattered. And then too, copies that exhibit mixed states or mixed gatherings, even when rebound, may be the work of the publisher or the original binder rather than that of a sophisticator. Evidence suggests that the early nineteenth-century American publisher did not worry about such matters very much; he used up what he had on hand. The profit was greater and the reader either would not know or would not care. It is even possible that mismatched pagination in mixed gatherings might have occured in original, legitimate issue. As a result, the present-day detection and recording of variants almost certainly is not complete, and those detected may sometimes be open to question. But short of full collation of all known copies, in the hope of duplicating and so reaffirming all the variants, there seems no satisfactory solution to the problem beyond careful, even skeptical, examination of the available evidence. This bibliography establishes a pattern for *Salmagundi*, a bibliographical ordering for the investigation of the many complexities of the original Numbers, but it makes no pretence of offering the last word.

Anyone who works on *Salmagundi* today must be grateful for the efforts of Jacob Blanck in *BAL* and Martha Hartzog in the Twayne edition, and to a large extent must incorporate their examinations and collations. He can attempt to extend and to perfect their work, and he can disagree with them at times (as I have), but he must admit to himself and to others his indebtedness.

The description of the first Numbers is based on examination and collation of a great many copies, drawn from the collections of CtY, DLC, DSI, InU, MB, MBAt, NcU, NN, RPB, TxU, ViU and three private owners. Unlike my practice in the investigation of Irving's other books, I have been willing -- in fact, have felt forced intellectually -- to make use of the collections and descriptions by Jacob Blanck and Martha Hartzog of Numbers in private hands to which I have not had access, and in some public collections which I have not been able to visit. This does not mean, however, that I have accepted their information without confirming it if possible from other copies. And I have always tried to add to it, by my own examination of multiple copies of each Number. In working on a bibliographical problem as complex and challenging as that of the first *Salmagundi,* one accepts as much reliable information as he can find.

AUTHORSHIP

A bibliography of Washington Irving should identify, as accurately and as completely as possible, all of the writing of Irving. And yet, to attempt to identify precisely the authorship of each piece in *Salmagundi* is to attempt the impossible. Perhaps one day some reliable contemporary document will surface, but it has not yet, even in James K. Paulding's own attributions for Numbers I-X, preserved in an 1814 edition in NN. Anyone interested in the question should see the chart and comments on pp. [327]-336 of the Twayne edition of *Salmagundi*; there the editors, Bruce I. Granger and Martha Hartzog, offer an historical summary of previous attributions, specify their own, and defend their conclusions in detail. It is a piece of responsible scholarship that deserves careful study.

I would simply add my own attributions to that list. One preliminary qualification, however, needs to be made forcefully. James K. Paulding in the preface to his edition of *Salmagundi* in 1835 said, "The thoughts of the authors were so mingled together in these essays, and they were so literally joint productions, that it would be difficult, as well as useless, at this distance of time, to assign to each his exact share." His warning should be read literally. Not only were ideas and literary strategies joint efforts, but in many instances the writing itself gives the clear impression of "joint production." It is true that Washington Irving in one of his few comments on the writing says in a letter of 22 June 1807 to Paulding, after expressing dissatisfaction with Number X, "I wrote the greatest part of it myself, and that at hurried moments." But what specifically does that say of the composition of Number X? "The Stranger in Pennsylvania" is traditionally assigned to Irving, and probably is indeed mostly his. The Demi Semiquaver piece, "To Launcelot Langstaff, Esq.," and its introduction, "From My Elbow-Chair," on the other hand, is now generally assigned to Paulding (and was claimed by Paulding himself), although Irving's letter, as well as a close reading of the piece, suggests strongly that it is -- typically -- a joint production of Paulding and Washington Irving.

If a Number for which Irving claimed majority authorship is in part a joint effort, others for which no such claims are made seem to represent even greater mingling of hands.   Even complete agreement by scholars in attributing authorship should be viewed with some skepticism. "Mr. Wilson's Concert" in Number II, for instance, has been universally assigned to Paulding; yet surely those last paragraphs are Washington Irving's? Or, there is almost complete agreement that whatever the authorship of the prose, the poetry is William Irving's.   Washington Irving himself says so in his Publisher's Notice to the Paris edition of 1824.   But even there it is reasonable to suspect some occasional collaboration. The most tempting to suggest is the hand of Washington Irving in the "Tea" in Number XIX; the tone, the verse, the effect are distinguishable from those of the other poems. (Is there any indebtedness to Barlow's "The Hasty Pudding"?) And when the poem was attributed to Washington Irving in several of the "Beauties" volumes in his lifetime, he seems to have made no objection.

The conclusion should be emphasized: although one of the authors may have provided the principal hand in each piece, many -- perhaps even most -- of the pieces are indeed joint efforts. Attribution of individual authorship is not only speculative but may in its very nature be misleading.

In the list that follows, WI stands for Washington Irving, WmI for William Irving, and P for James K. Paulding.   When two authors are suggested, the major hand is given first.

Number I

Untitled introduction	Collaboration by the authors
Publisher's Notice	First paragraph collaboration; second, Longworth
From the Elbow-Chair	P with some WI
Theatrics	WI
New-York Assembly	WI with some P

Number II

From the Elbow-Chair	WI and P
Mr. Wilson's Concert	P and WI

WILLIAM F. MAAG LIBRARY
YOUNGSTOWN STATE UNIVERSITY

[Character of Pindar Cockloft]	P
To Launcelot Langstaff	WmI
Advertisement	P and WI

Number III

From My Elbow-Chair	WI and P
Mustapha Letter	P
Fashions	WI
[The Wise Men of Gotham]	P with some WI
"How now, mooncalf!"	P
Proclamation, by P. Cockloft	WmI

Number IV

From My Elbow-Chair	WI
The Stranger in New-Jersey	P with some WI
From My Elbow-Chair, and Flummery	WmI; introduction and notes by WI
General Remark	P?
Notice	P?
Card	

Number V

From My Elbow-Chair, and Mustapha Letter	WI and WmI; introduction by P
By Anthony Evergreen	WI
To the Ladies	WmI

Number VI

From My Elbow-Chair	WI
Theatrics	WI with some P

Number VII

Mustapha Letter	WmI with some WI?
Mill of Pindar Cockloft	WmI
Notes by William Wizard	P

Number VIII

By Anthony Evergreen	WI
On Style	WI
"Being, as it were"	WI

Number IX

From My Elbow-Chair	WI
From My Elbow-Chair, and Mustapha Letter	WmI; introduction by WI
Mill of Pindar Cockloft	WmI

Number X

From My Elbow-Chair, and To Launcelot Langstaff	P and WI
The Stranger in Pennsylvania	WI

Number XI

Mustapha Letter	WI
From My Elbow-Chair: Mine Uncle John	P; ending by WI

Number XII

From My Elbow-Chair	P and WI
The Stranger at Home	WI and P?
From My Elbow-Chair, and Mill of Pindar Cockloft	WmI

Number XIII

From My Elbow-Chair	WI
Plans for Defending Our Harbour	WI
A Retrospect	P and WI
To Readers and Correspondents	P

Number XIV

Mustapha Letter	WmI
Cockloft Hall	WI and P
Theatrical Intelligence	WI

Number XV

Sketches from Nature	P
On Greatness	WI

Number XVI

Style at Ballston	P
Mustapha Letter	WI and P

Number XVII

Autumnal Reflections   P

By Launcelot Langstaff, and   WI
Chronicles of Gotham

Number XVIII

The Little Man in Black   WI

Mustapha Letter   P with some WI

Number XIX

From My Elbow-Chair, and   WI
Mustapha Letter

By Anthony Evergreen   P

Tea   Wml and WI?

Number XX

From My Elbow-Chair   WI with some P

To the Ladies   P and WI

"How hard it is"   WI

THE INDIVIDUAL NUMBERS

Each Number has the same head-caption and the same comic pseudo-Latin quotation, complete with comic translation, on the first page of the text. The quotation and translation, however, often vary in small details, particularly in the use of contractions and apostrophes and in such spelling variants as folkesez / folksez and smoak'd / smok'd. To avoid unnecessary repetition, the full heading is reproduced only for Number I, although variants from that text are recorded for the first edition of each Number.

The heading in every instance is followed by a line of identification: the Number, the date of publication, and -- from Number XI on -- the place of the Number in the sequence of Volume II. This line is reproduced here for the first edition of each Number.

The first edition of each Number prints no identification of edition in the heading or elsewhere. Subsequent editions usually print an identification (sometimes erroneous) above the heading. Such identification, when present, is specified for each later edition.

The imprint of David Longworth, if present, appears not on the first page but at the foot of the last page of the text in each Number. Since the form of the imprint varies and is often one means of identification of an edition or state, it is reproduced for each state.

A description of the wrappers and of the volume title pages follows the description of the individual Numbers.

Leaves and wrappers are untrimmed. Although individual Numbers may vary somewhat, the usual leaf size is 16.3 x 11.5 cm. All Numbers are printed on white wove paper.

Representative readings for each edition and each state are given in the description. The intent is to offer both identifying variants and a selection of changes that will suggest the sort of textual emendation or revision that appears in all states after the first edition. (Any given variant may be assumed to continue in subsequent states of the text unless a further change is specified.) The list of variants is, of course, not complete but is representative. A much more nearly complete list may be derived from the tables in the Textual Commentary of the Twayne edition of the work.

It should be noted that the printing of the Numbers is often of poor quality; punctuation marks, hyphens, letters occasionally fail to print or, more commonly, are dim and difficult to see. The fact should be borne in mind when examining any copy.

Number I

First Edition.

SALMAGUNDI; | OR, THE | *WHIM-WHAMS AND OPINIONS* | OF | LAUNCELOT LANGSTAFF, ESQ. | AND OTHERS. | [double rule] | In hoc est hoax, cum quiz et jokesez, | Et smokem, toastem, roastem folkesez, | Fee, faw, fum. *Psalmanazar.* | With baked, and broil'd, and stew'd, and toasted, | And fried, and boil'd, and smoak'd, and roasted, | We treat the town. | [double rule].

NO. I.] *Saturday, January* 24, 1807.

Imprint (on p. 20): See the description of the variant states.

[A]^9 . Signed: [A, A$_1$] A$_{2-4}$ [A$_{5-8}$]. A$_4$ is an inserted leaf.

[3]-5. untitled introduction; 5-6, "Publisher's Notice"; 6-14, "From the Elbow-Chair of Launcelot Langstaff, Esq."; 14-16, "Theatrics. ... By William Wizard, Esq."; 17-20, "New-York Assembly. By Anthony Evergreen, Gent."

State A.

Imprint (on p. 20): [rule] | *New-York, Printed and Published by D. Longworth.*

Representative readings:

5.15	notices of epic poems
8.13	think of it
10.1f	or Cambridge
11.9	porcelaine. He is
12.3f	recommend
13.27	honor of his editors
18.17-18	favor with himself,	-- and
19.18-19	they	are going on
20.2	dress he!
20.6	mountebank
20.8f	precaution

State B.

Imprint (on p. 20): [rule] | *New-York, Printed and Published by D. Longworth.* | [rule]. Note that the rule is added.

The sequence, if any, of the first two states is uncertain.

State C.

Imprint (on p. 20): [rule] | *New-York, Printed and Published by D. Longworth.* | [rule].

Quotation: line 2, "folksez."

Representative readings:

20.2	dress! he

State D.

Imprint (on p. 20): [double rule] | *New-York, Printed and Published by D. Longworth.*

Reported by *BAL* as "a reprinting (without reprint notice) from an altered setting." Not seen. The one reading given ("dress! he"), the imprint, and the "altered setting" specified by *BAL* suggest the final leaves of the second edition. If so, the final leaves may have been reset for this state; but an equally likely assumption is that this state was a late issue and employs mixed leaves.

Second edition.

Identification above heading: *(second edition)*

Imprint (on p. 20): [double rule] | *New-York, Printed and Published by D. Longworth.*

State A.

Representative readings:

5.14	exchange of epic
12.3f	commend
19.18	the are going
19.1f	dress! he
20.7f	precautions

State B.

Representative readings:

12.3f	recommend

The sequence of the two states is unknown.

Third edition.

Identification above heading: *(third edition.)*

Imprint (on p. 20): [rule] | *New-York, Printed and Published by D. Longworth.*

Representative readings:

5.15	notices of epic
13.22	honor of his authors
19.18	they are going
20.7f	precaution

Fourth edition.

Identification above heading: *(fourth edition.)*

Imprint (on p. 20): [double rule] | *New-York, Printed and Published by D. Longworth.*

Representative readings:

8.12	think of us
13.22	honor of his editors
19.18	the are going

Fifth edition.

Identification above heading: *(fifth edition.)*

Imprint (on p. 20): [rule] | *Printed by D. Longworth, at the Shakspeare-Gallery.*

Representative readings:

8.11	think of it
11.7	porcclanc, and particularly
13.22	honor of his authors
18.17	favour -- with himself -- and
19.18	they are going

Sixth edition.

Identification above heading: *(fifth edition)*

Imprint (on p. 20): [rule] | *Printed by D. Longworth, at the Shakspeare-Gallery.*

Representative readings:

5.15	notices of epick
8.11	think of us
10.4f	at Cambridge
13.21	honour of his authors
18.17	favour -- with himself, and
20.2	mounteback

Seventh edition.

Identification above heading: *(fifth edition)*

Imprint (on p. 20): [rule] | *Printed by D. Longworth, at the Shakspeare-Gallery.*

Representative readings:

13.17   honor of his authors

20.3   mountebank

Advertisements for Number I by D. Longworth in the New York *American Citizen*, 21 January 1807 (repeated 22, 24, 26, 28 January) and the New York *People's Friend & Daily Advertiser*, 20 January 1807 (repeated 21, 22, 23, 24 January) print as part of the advertisement the untitled introduction and the "Publisher's Notice" of the number. Although the text in the advertisement differs in many instances of punctuation and capitalization, the spelling and word choice are the same as those of the first state of Number I, with five exceptions:

Page & line of Number I	Number I	Advertisement
5.11	neighbor	neighbour
5.22	writer of folios, *Linkum Fidelius*	writer of follies *Linkum Fidelius*
5.25-26	published and sold by D.| Longworth.	published and sold as above.
5.26	hot-prest vellum	hot pressed vellum
6.10	mere hope of	mere hopes of

Although the advertisement probably represents an early version of the text, only the difference on 5.22 seems of particular interest. Did the authors first intend to describe Linkum Fidelius (probably representing DeWitt Clinton) as a writer of follies or as a writer of folios? Perhaps the advertisement merely represents a slip of the hand; in Number XVIII there is a reference to "the invaluable folioes of the sage LINKUM FIDELIUS." The "follies" reading in *People's Friend* appears only in the first advertisement, on January 20, dated January 20 at the foot. All later versions read '"folios." But in *American Citizen*, first appearing January 21, dated January 21 at the foot, the "follies" reading persists through all five advertisements. If the change in *People's Friend* is the work of the authors or of Longworth, why not in *American Citizen* too? Perhaps in *People's Friend* the newspaper itself made the change. We will probably never know. But in considering the puzzle, the historian might consider the political implications of the "misprint."

At the beginning of the advertisement, the comic quotation is given. There the spelling of the word in line 2 is "folksez," a variant of the first spelling in Number I.

The advertisement would explain the paragraph added in Number I after the "Publisher's Notice" -- the paragraph is not included in the advertisement -- in which the authors say that they had not originally intended to publish "the above address" in the work. The "address" was probably written specifically for the advertisement.

New York *American Citizen*, 21, 22, 24, 26, 28 January 1807, "On Saturday will be published ... price twelve and a half cents, No. 1 of SALMAGUNDI." New York *People's Friend*, 20, 21, 22, 23 January 1807, same advertisement; 24 January 1807, "This day will be published"; 7 February 1807, "Yesterday was published the 2nd edition of SALMAGUNDI, *No. 1*"; 19, 20 March 1807, "The third edition of no. 1, is ready for sale March 19 [the advertisement of 19 March reads "March 29"]." New York *Morning Chronicle*, 30 May 1807, "a New Edition of ... 1 (being the fourth) ... is now in the press and will be speedily published." New York *American Citizen*, 27 June 1807, statement repeated.

Number II

First edition.

No. II.] *Wednesday, February* 4, 1807.

Imprint (on p. 38): none.

Quotation: line 2, "folksez."

$[A]^9$. Signed: [A, A$_1$] A$_{2-4}$ [A$_{5-8}$]. A$_4$ is an inserted leaf.

[21]-27, "From the Elbow-Chair of Launcelot Langstaff, Esq."; 27-31, "Mr. Wilson's Concert. By Anthony Evergreen, Gent."; 31-34, untitled, beginning "Sitting late the other evening," signed "Launcelot Langstaff"; 35-37, "To Launcelot Langstaff, Esq."; 37-38, "Advertisement."

State A.

Representative readings:

[21].11f	his readers
22.22	old folks

27.12	*what-d'ye-callums*
27.4f	draining of
27.3f	entirely
27.1f	naiades
28.22	audience,
30.3f-2f	"knight of | of the
34.3	dealt roughly
34.4	passed lightly
37.9	I warrant
38.26	retinues

State B.

Representative readings:

[21].11f	his reader
28.22	audience

State C.

Representative readings:

30.3f-2f	"knight | of the

State D.

Representative readings:

[21].11f	his readers

Second edition.

Identification above heading: (*second edition*)

Imprint (on p. 38): *New-York, Printed and Published by D. Longworth* | [rule].

Representative readings:

27.12	*what-d'ye callums*
28.22	audience,

Third edition.

Identification above heading: (*third edition*)

Imprint (on p. 38): [rule] | *New-York, Printed and Published by D. Longworth.*

Representative readings:

27.13	*What-d'ye-call'ms*
27.2f	intirely
28.22	audience;
37.6	I'll warrant

Fourth edition.

Identification above heading: (*fourth edition*)

Imprint (on p. 38): [rule] | *New-York, Printed and Published by D. Longworth.*

Representative readings:

22.21-22	old	folk
27.4f	drainings of
38.24	retinue

Fifth edition.

Identification above heading: (*fourth edition*)

Imprint (on p. 38): [rule] | *Printed by D. Longworth, at the Shakspeare Gallery.*

Representative readings:

27.14	*what-d'ye-call-'ms*
27.1f	niades
34.4	dealt lightly
34.5	passed roughly

New-York Evening Post, 3, 4 February 1807, "On Wednesday the 4th of February, will be served up at D. Longworth's, a second dish of Salmagundi ... price 12 1-2 cents each." New York *People's Friend*, 3,4,5,6,7 February 1807, same statement; 5,6,7 March 1807, "The second edition of no. 2, is ready for sale." *Salmagundi* Number IV, first state, 24 February 1807, "The second edition of No. II. is now in the press and will be published in a few days." New York *Morning Chronicle*, 30 May 1807, "A New Edition of ... 2 ... is now in the press and will be speedily published." New York *American Citizen*, 26 June 1807, statement repeated.

Number III

First edition.

Imprint (on p. 56): none. In its place appears: [rule] | [three asterisks that form a triangle] *The second edition of* No. I. *is just published.*

Quotation: line 2, "folksez"; line 5, "smok'd."

[A]^9 . Signed: [A, A$_1$] A$_{2-4}$ [A$_{5-8}$]. A$_4$ is an inserted leaf.

[39]-42, "From My Elbow-Chair"; 42-47, "Letter from Mustapha Rub-A-Dub Keli Khan, ... To Asem Hacchem..."; 47-50, "Fashions, by Anthony Evergreen, Gent."; 50-53, untitled, beginning with quotation from Juvenal; 53-54, "'--How now, mooncalf!'"; 54-56, "Proclamation, from the Mill of Pindar Cockloft, esq."

Representative readings:

40.9	antients humorously
40.18	my masters
43.7	necks
50.2	sattin
53.22-23	wool-clad war-	riors
55.5f	the shoe
56. last line of poem	Vhat shmiles ... vhat

Second edition.

Identification above heading: (*second edition*)

Imprint (on p. 56): [rule] | *New-York, Printed and Published by D. Longworth.* | [rule].

Representative readings:

40.4	ancients humorously
53.20-21	wood-clad war	riors
56. last line of poem	What shmiles ... what

Third edition.

Identification above heading: (*third edition.*)

Imprint (on p. 56):   [rule] | *New-York, Printed and Published by D. Longworth.*

Representative readings:

40.4	ancients humourously
53.20-21	wood-clad war-	riours
55.7f	your shoe
56.last line of poem	What smiles ... what

Fourth edition.

Identification above heading: none

Imprint (on p. 56): [rule] | *Printed by D. Longworth, at the Shakspeare-Gallery.*

Representative readings:

40.13	my master
42.31	neck
52.33	wood clad warriours

On p. [39], "VOL I." is added after the identification of the Number.

On pp. 53-54, "'--How now, mooncalf!'" is set in the normal type size of *Salmagundi* rather than in the reduced type size of the earlier editions. So also are pp. 53-54 of the fifth edition.

Although this fourth edition is not so identified above the heading, the sequence is probably correct. In typography and setting it is closely related to the fifth edition, although the substantives of the text are closer to those of the third edition. (The accidentals of the text are close to those of the first edition.) But the identification of the Number and the form of Longworth's imprint are those of the fifth edition.

Fifth edition.

Identification above heading: (*fourth edition*)

Imprint (on p. 56): [rule] | *Printed by D. Longworth, at the Shakspeare-Gallery.*

State A.

Representative readings:

    [39].13   NO. 3] *Friday, February* 31, 1807 [VOL I.

    40.13   my masters

    49.8f   satin

    51.10   Salamagundi

State B.

The typographical error in the heading for the Number is corrected to "*February* 13 1807, "although the comma after 13 is omitted.

New York *American Citizen*, 11, 12 February 1807, "On Friday will be published ... No 3 .... NB. The second edition of the first is also just published." *The Weekly Inspector* [New York], 21 February 1807, reviewed. *The Port Folio*, 21 March 1807, the Mustapha letter extracted. New York *Morning Chronicle*, 30 May 1807, "A New Edition of ... 3 ... is now in the press and will be speedily published." New York *American Citizen*, 26 June 1807, statement repeated.

Number IV

First edition.

NO. IV.] *Tuesday, February* 24, 1807.

Imprint (on p. 82): [rule] | *New-York, Printed and Published by D. Longworth* | [rule].

Quotation: line 2, "folksez"; line 5, "smok'd."

[A^9] A^4. Signed: [A_{1-3}] A_4 A_4 [A_{5-8}] A [A_{2-4}]. The second A_4 in the first gathering, pp. 65-66, is an inserted leaf.

[57]-60, "From My Elbow-Chair"; 61-67, "Memorandums For a Tour ... by Jeremy Cockloft, the Younger"; 67-69, "From My Elbow-Chair"; [70]-80, "Flummery from the Mill of Pindar Cockloft, Esq."; 80, "General Remark"; 81, "Notice"; 81-82, "Card."

On p. 82, below the text and above the imprint: [three asterisks that form a triangle] The second edition of No. II. is now in the|press and will be published in a few days.

State A.

Representative readings:

58.1f	lightening rods
59.5-6	cat, wor- | ried
59.1f	old folks
61.6f	practice
63.12-13	hay ves- | sels?
71.8	Caustic
72.3	poets dray horse
74.3	famed Toney (11
74.24	*I wont*
74.7f	*Louisiana. (ro Lousy anee.)*
75.4f	*hangmen*
77.14	*prospects*
77.23	to out
78.4	hapless town.
80.19	heliconian
81.7	hertofore
82.5	bad english, Will

State B.

Gathering A^4, pp. 75-82, is reset.

Representative readings:

75.4f	*hangman*
77.23	to our
78.4	hapless town,
81.7	heretofore
82.5	bad english. Will

State C.

Representative readings:

74.3	famed Toney (11)
74.7f	*Louisiana. (or Lousy anee.)*

Second edition.

Identification above heading: *(second edition.)*

Imprint (on p. 82): [double rule] | Printed by D. Longworth, at the Shakspeare-Gallery.

On p. 75, the gathering is signed B.

Representative readings:

58.1f	lightning rods
71.8	Costive
74.7f	*Louisiana. (or Lousy-anee.)*
76.6-7	deter-	termine
80.18	heliconean

Third edition.

Identification above heading: *(third edition)*

Imprint (on p. 82): [double rule] | Printed by D. Longworth, at the Shakspeare-Gallery.

NO. 4] *Tuesday, February* 24, 1807. [VOL. I.

State A.

Representative readings:

58.1f	lightning-roads
59.5-6	rat, worri-	ed
59.1f	old folk
61.6f	practise
63.12	hay vessels!
74.24	*I wont or (wunt)*

Only gathering A is reset. Gathering B (pp. 75-82) is that of the second edition. And so, this first state employs mixed gatherings.

State B.

Imprint (on p. 82): [stylized swelled rule] | *Printed by D. Longworth, at the Shakspeare Gallery.* | [rule].

Gathering B is reset also.

Representative readings:

>| 76.p. no. | 67 |
>| 76.6-7 | deter- \| mine |
>| 77.14 | *prospect* |
>| 78.4 | hapless town; |

Fourth edition.

Identification above heading: (*third edition*)

Imprint (on p. 82): [stylized swelled rule] | *Printed by D. Longworth, at the Shakspeare Gallery.* | [rule].

Representative readings:

>| 59.5-6 | rat, wor- \| ried |
>| 63.12 | hay-vessels! |
>| 74.24 | *I wont (or wunt)* |
>| 76.p. no. | 76 |

It could be argued, primarily from the absence of "VOL. I" in the identification of the Number, that this edition is not the fourth but the earlier third edition. The arguments against that position, however, seem stronger, based not only on the text but on the fact that the first state of the third edition makes use of a gathering from the second edition.

New York *American Citizen*, 23 February 1807, "*On Tuesday next will be Published. No 4.*" New York *Morning Chronicle*, 30 May 1807, "A New Edition of ... 4 ... is now in the press and will be speedily published." New York *American Citizen*, 26 June 1807, statement repeated.

Number V

First edition.

NO. V.] *Saturday, March 7, 1807.*

Imprint (on p. 104):   [rule] | New-York, Printed and Published by D. Longworth.

Quotation: line 2, "folksez"; line 5, "smok'd."

[A^9] B^2. Signed: [A, A$_1$] A$_{2\text{-}4}$ [A$_{5\text{-}8}$] B [B$_2$]. A$_4$ is an inserted leaf.

[83], "From My Elbow-Chair"; 84-94, "Letter from Mustapha Rub-A-Dub Keli Khan, to Abdallah Eb'n Al Rahab..."; 94-100, "By Anthony Evergreen, Gent."; 101-104, "To the Ladies. From the Mill of Pindar Cockloft, Esq."

State A.

Representative readings:

[83].11f	November,
[83].8f	in honorable
84.4	*centinal*
87.13	undauntedly,
87.5f	to single combat
88.10	or stun
88.2f	taylor
90.9	*fag rag*
94.9f	surprized
96.4	frizzed
99.4f	have took
101.7f	beauties
103.25	æther
104.6	unhallowed

State B.

Representative readings:

87.13	undauntedly [no comma follows]
88.2f	tailor
90.9	*fag-rag*

State C.

Representative readings:

87.13	undauntedly,
90.9	*fag rag*

99.4f	have taken
99.2f	introducini- |
99.1f-	
100.1	unrg | valled

State D.

Representative readings:

99.2f	introducing |
99.1f-	
100.1	unri- | valled

Second edition.

Identification above heading: (*second edition*)

Imprint (on p. 104): [double rule] \| Printed by D. Longworth, at the Shakspeare Gallery.

Representative readings:

[83].23	in the honourable
96.4	frizzled
103.22	sweelty

Third edition.

Identification above heading: (third edition)

Imprint (on p. 104): [rule] \| *Printed by D. Longworth, at the Shakspeare-Gallery.* \| [rule].

Representative readings:

84.4	*sentinel*
94.27	surprised
101.19	beauty's
103.21	sweetly
103.4f	ether

Fourth edition.

Identification above heading: (third edition)

Representative readings in Gathering [A]:

[83].12f	November;
87.4f	to a single combat
88.10	and stun

This edition appears with three settings of Gathering B.

State A.

Imprint (on p. 104): [double rule] | Printed by D. Longworth, at the Shakspeare-Gallery.

Representative readings in Gathering B:

101.19	beauties
103.22	sweelty
103.4f	æther
104.10	unhallowed

This is Gathering B of the second edition. And so, this state employs mixed gatherings.

State B.

Imprint (on p. 104): [rule] | *Printed by D. Longworth, at the Shakspeare-Gallery.*

Representative readings in Gathering B:

101.17	beauty's
103.22	sweetly
103.4f	æther
104.10	unhallowed
104.23	Still,

State C.

Imprint (on p. 104): [rule] | *Printed by D. Longworth, at the Shakspeare-Gallery.* | [rule].

Representative readings in Gathering B:

| 101.19 | beauty's |
| 103.21 | sweetly |

103.4f	ether
104.10	unhallow'd
104.23	Still [no comma follows]

New York *People's Friend*, 5, 6, 7 March 1807, "On Saturday March 7, will be published, No. 5 of Salmagundi ... *price* 12 1-2 *Cts.*"   *The Observer* [Baltimore], 28 March, extracted. New York *Morning Chronicle*, 30 May 1807, "A New Edition of ... 5 ... is now in the press and will be speedily published." New York *American Citizen*, 26 June 1807, statement repeated.

Number VI

First edition.

NO. VI.] *Friday, March* 20, 1807.

Imprint (on p. 124): See the description of the variant states.

Quotation: line 2, "folksez"; line 5, "smok'd."

[A^9] B^1. Signed: [A, A$_1$] A$_{2-4}$ [A$_{5-8}$] B. A$_4$ is an inserted leaf.

[105]-117. "From My Elbow-Chair"; 117-124, "Theatrics. By William Wizard, Esq."

Representative readings in Gathering [A]:

106.5	rule for
111.27	hates them as he does poison
112.13	unfeelingly
113.3	majority
113.14	to her the son
115.3	half a dozen
122.15	*hen pecked*

This first edition appears with two settings of Leaf B (pp. 123-124), one of them in two states. No sequence determined; the letter-identification is for convenience only.

State [A].

Imprint (on p. 124):   [rule] | *New-York, Printed and Published by D. Longworth.*

Representative readings in Leaf B:

123.7	Philadelphian
123.18	gentleman
123.21	he should
124.12	suspects that he
124.13	mortal blow

State [B].

Imprint (on p. 124):   [rule] | *New-York, printed and published by D. Longworth.*

Representative readings in Leaf B:

123.7	philadelphian
123.18	gentlemen
123.21	she should
124.6	suce
124.12	suspects he that

State [C].

This state is in the setting of State [B], with a typographical error corrected:

124.12	suspects that he

Second edition.

Identification above heading: *(second edition.)*

Imprint (on p. 126):   [double rule] | Printed by D. Longworth, at the Shakspeare Gallery.

In this resetting, the pagination is [105]-126.

Representative readings:

112.13	unreasonably
113.3	majesty

113.14	to be the son
115.3	half dozen
123.20	*hen-pecked*

Third edition.

Identification above heading: (*third edition*)

Imprint (on p. 124): [rule] | New-York, printed and published by D. Longworth. | [rule].

In this resetting, the pagination returns to [105]-124.

State A.

Representative readings:

106.5	rule for
111.27	hates them most cordially for
112.13	unfeelingly
112.23	entirely
113.13-14	tobe the	son
115.3	half a dozen
122.16	*hen pecked*

State B.

Representative readings:

111.27	hates them most cordially, for
113.13-14	to be the	son

Fourth edition.

Identification above heading: (*third edition*)

Representative readings in Gathering [A]:

106.5	rule of
106.27	as is children
112.23	intirely
113.2-3	majes-	ty

This fourth edition appears with two settings of Leaf B (pp. 123-124).

State A.

Imprint (on p. 124): [rule] | New-York, printed and published by D. Longworth. | [rule].

Representative readings in Leaf B:

  123.4f   killing himself,

  124.14   mortal blow

This is Leaf B of the third edition. And so, this state employs mixed gatherings.

State B.

Imprint (on p. 124): [rule] | *Printed by D. Longworth, at the Shakspeare-Gallery.*

Representative readings in Leaf B:

  123.7-6f   killing | himself:

  124.11   mortal wound

In this state, Leaf B is reset.

New York *Morning Chronicle*, 19 March 1807, "On Friday, March 20, will be published, No. VI. ... (Price 12 1/2 cents.)"; 30 May 1807, "A New Edition of ... 6 is now in the press and will be speedily published." New York *American Citizen*, 26 June 1807, statement repeated.

Number VII

First edition.

NO. VII.] *Saturday, April 4, 1807.*

Imprint (on p.142): [rule] | *New-York, Printed and Published by D. Longworth.*

Quotation: line 2, "folksez"; line 5, "smok'd."

$[A^9]$. Signed: $[A, A_1] A_{2-4} [A_{5-8}] A_4$ is an inserted leaf.

[125]-135, "Letter from Mustapha Rub-A-Dub Keli Khan, to Asem Hacchem..." (on 130-131 is a "Note, by William Wizard, Esq."); 136-140,

"From the Mill of Pindar Cockloft, Esq."; 140-142, "Notes, by William Wizard, Esq."

State A.

Representative readings:

126.3f	arabs, who
128.12	accomodated
129.11	excepting
131.13	to find out wisdom
137.2	set
138.11	windings
141.11	extatic

State B.

Representative readings:

129.11	except

Second edition.

Identification above heading: (*second edition*)

Imprint (on p.142): [rule] | *New-York, Printed and Published by D. Longworth.*

Representative readings:

126.3f	arabs, that
128.12	accomadated
131.13	to find wisdom
137.2	sit
141.9-10	ex-	static

Third edition.

Identification above heading: (*second edition*)

Imprint (on p. 142): none

State A.

Representative readings:

    130.28   foliowing

    138.15   winding

    141.22-23   ex- | statick

State B.

Representative readings:

    130.28   following

New York *Morning Chronicle*, 3 April 1807, "On Saturday, April 4 will be published, No VII ... (Price 12 1/2 cents.)." *The Balance* [Hudson, N.Y.], 5 May 1807, Mustapha letter extracted.

Number VIII

First edition.

NO. VIII.] *Saturday, April* 18, 1807.

Imprint (on p. 162): none.

Quotation: line 2, "folksez"; line 5, "smok'd."

[A]^{11}. Signed: [-$_1$][A, A$_1$] A$_{2-4}$ [A$_{5-9}$]. A$_4$ is an inserted leaf.

[i]-[ii], blank, on verso woodcut portrait of Launcelot Langstaff; [143]-151, "By Anthony Evergreen, Gent."; 152-159, "On Style. By William Wizard, Esq."; 159-162, untitled, beginning with a quotation from "Linkum Fidelius": *"Being, as it were...."*

The frontispiece portrait appears in a number of states in the different editions. See the discussion at the end of this entry.

Of all the Numbers of *Salmagundi*, Number VIII in its first edition presents the most complex and puzzling problem of variant textual states. In ten copies examined or reported on in detail, there are six different combinations of readings. Four of the copies are in State A, but the other six show five different combinations. I have no doubt that more copies would present more varieties, particularly so if a greater number of representative readings were checked. Some variant readings are probably the result of a fairly continuous process of change and correction in the standing type, with the changes based on differing pages from earlier printing. Some existing copies, in turn, may be the result of mixed sheets printed from that continuously changing type. The result is that copies that differ from the first state present no consistent logical progression. Two later states, identified here as State E and State F, appear to be the final states, and I have -- with some hesitation -- called them such. But even there, the sequence of those particular two is not certain. State F has been noted in two copies, giving it perhaps some greater validity as a final state. Study of the variant texts that appear to belong somewhere between the first state and what I judge to be the last states leads only to frustration. I have finally, in surrender, listed them simply as "intermediate mixed states" in an order that seems as reasonable as possible. In calling them "states," however, it should be remembered that they are based only on single copies examined and may well not be duplicated in other copies.

Number VIII was published in the last weeks of a state-wide election that may have demanded from the authors more hasty composition than usual, and so more later changes than usual. And it was the first Number to offer an illustration (one with political implications, however hidden) that probably increased its sale, and so increased the number of copies needed. Whether or not the circumstances help to explain the many differing copies, there is no question that Number VIII appeared in a wide and bibliographically frustrating variety of texts.

State A.

Representative readings:

144.2	rise and sink
144.9	tremenduous
146.9	batchelor, for
146.13-14	was | not long ago
146.5f	pointed, and
147.23	poets'
148.2-3	sub- | stantial,
148.7f	heroics, to
149.3	love, and
151.4-3f	of | excellent
153.10	china,
157.27	lodoiska

162.15   satirical and

Intermediate Mixed State B.

Representative readings:

148.2-3	sub- | stantial [no comma]
148.7f	heroics to
149.3	love and
153.10	China,

Intermediate Mixed State C.

Representative readings:

146.9	bachelor; for
146.13-14	was, | not long ago,
146.5f	pointed; and
148.2-3	sub- | stantial,
148.7f	heroics, to
151.4-3f	of most | excellent
157.27	Lodoiska
162.15	satirical, and

Intermediate Mixed State D.

Representative readings:

148.2-3	sub- | stantial [no comma]
148.7f	heroics to
149.3	love, and
153.10	China [no coma]

State E.

Representative readings:

144.9	tremendous
146.9	bachelor, for
146.13-14	was | not long ago

146.5f	pointed, and
151.4-3f	of | excellent
157.27	lodoiska

State F.

Representative readings:

| 148.2-3 | sub- \| stantial, |
| 148.7f | heroics, to |

Second edition.

Identification above heading: (*second edition*)

Imprint (on p. 160): none

In this resetting, the pagination is [i]-[ii], [143]-160.

Representative readings:

144.2	sink and rise
145.8	bachelorisms
146.6	bachelor; for
146.10-11	was, | not long ago,
146.28	pointed; and
147.21	poet's
147.3-2f	sub- | stantial [no comma]
148.26	heroics to
148.35	love and
151.29-30	of most | excellent
153.4	China [no comma]
154.32	time, address
156.29	Lodoiska

Third edition.

Identification above heading: (*second edition*)

Imprint (on p. 160); none

Representative readings:

145.8	bachelorism
148.25	heroicks to
154.32	time address

Frontispiece portrait.

The woodcut portrait of Launcelot Langstaff has been noted or reported in five forms. Additionally, two other forms have been noted, but only in the later editions of 1814 or 1820. All are listed here, since the portraits may have moved about in binding or rebinding. *Form A* is almost certainly the first form, and *Form B* probably the second. They are the only forms noted in the various states of the first edition. *Forms C, D, E* appear in later editions of Number VIII and, like the two earlier forms also, in the bound volumes of 1807, 1808. The sequential relationship of those three is uncertain.

Form A. The portrait is without identifying caption.

Form B. Captioned: Launcelot Langstaff, esq. [fancy]

Form C. Captioned: Launcelot Langstaff   Not seen; reported by *BAL* in a rebound set.

Form D. Captioned: [rule] | LAUNCELOT LANGSTAFF | [rule].

Form E. Captioned: LAUNCELOT LANGSTAFF, ESQ.

Form F. Captioned: Launcelot Langstaff, esq. [fancy] | FROM THE ORIGINAL DRAWING. Seen only in the 1814 edition. There, the page number 181 appears in the upper left corner.

Form G. Captioned: LAUNCELOT LANGSTAFF, Esq. | FROM THE ORIGINAL DRAWING. Seen only in the 1820 edition.

New York *Morning Chronicle*, 18 April 1807, "On Saturday, the 18th inst. will be published ... No. VIII. ... embellished with a *striking* likeness of *one* of the authors, by an artist of *distinction*, and carved on wood by Dr. Anderson. (Price 12 1/2 cents.)" New York *American Citizen*, 18 April 1807, "This day is published ... No. 8." Also advertises the woodcut in the same terms. *New-York Evening Post*, 17 April 1807, "On Saturday the 18th inst. ... No. 8," but a different description of the illustration: "Embellished with a *squalling* likeness...."

Number IX

First edition.

NO. IX.] *Saturday, April* 25, 1807.

Imprint (on p. 188): [rule] | *New-York, Printed and Published by D. Longworth.* | [rule].

Quotation: line 2, "folksez"; line 5, "smok'd."

[A]^9 B^4. Signed: [A, A$_1$] A$_{2-4}$ [A$_{5-8}$] B[B$_{2-4}$]. A$_4$ is an inserted leaf.

[163]-170, "From My Elbow-Chair"; 170-172, "From My Elbow-Chair"; 172-181, "Letter from Mustapha Rub-A-Dub Keli Kahn ... to Asem Hacchem..."; 181-188, "From the Mill of Pindar Cockloft, Esq."

Representative readings:

166.11	finger's
172.25	KAHN
172.4f	departing
175.14	trifle?"
176.21	man was
181.3f	blessing on the land,
182.19	Twas [indented for new paragraph]
185.1	nymphs, alike
185.12	fairy
185.17	timorous

Second edition.

Identification above heading: (*second edition*)

Imprint (on p. 188): [double rule] | *Printed by D. Longworth, at the Shakspeare-Gallery.*

Representative readings:

166.11	fingers'
172.25	KHAN
175.14	trifle!"
176.21	man were
181.3f	blessing on the land.

185.10   faëry

185.15   timid

Page [163], line 15 noted in two states: with, and without, the bracket after the number identification in the heading.

Third edition.

Identification above heading: (*second edition*)

State A.

Imprint (on p. 188): [rule] | *Printed by D. Longworth, at the Shakspeare-Gallery.*

Representative readings:

172.4f   departed

181.3f   blessings on the land.

182.19   Twas [not indented for paragraph]

184.2f   nymphs alike

State B.

Imprint (on p. 188): [rule] | *Printed by D. Longworth, at the Shakspeare-Gallery.* | [rule]. Note that a rule is present below.

The sequence of the two states is not known.

New York *Morning Chronicle*, 25 April 1807, "This day is published ... No. IX. ... (Price 12 1/2 cents.)."

Number X

First edition.

NO. X.] SATURDAY, MAY 16, 1807.

Imprint (on p. 206): See the description of the variant states.

Quotation: line 2, "folksez"; line 5, "smok'd".

[A]^9. Signed: [A, A$_1$] A$_{2-4}$ [A$_{5-8}$]. A$_4$ is an inserted leaf.

[189]-191, "From My Elbow-Chair"; 191-198, "To Launcelot Langstaff, Esq." (Signed at end, "Demy Semiquaver"); 198-206, "The Stranger in Pennsylvania. By Jeremy Cockloft, the Younger."

In the second edition of the Number, "To Launcelot Langstaff, Esq." and "The Stranger in Pennsylvania" are so thoroughly revised that the conventional method of discriminating between editions by defining small variations in representative readings is not satisfactory. This first edition may be identified easily by the first sentence of Demi Semiquaver's description of his musical piece, "Breaking up of the Ice in the North-River" (p. 193), and by the first sentence of "The Stranger in Pennsylvania" (p. 198):

193.26-28. The piece opens with a gentle andante affetuoso, | which ushers you into the assembly-room in the | state-house at Albany,...

198.8-10 Cross the Delaware -- knew I was in Pennsyl- | vania, because all the people were fat and looked | like the statue of William Penn -- ....

State A.

Imprint (on p. 206): [double rule] | *Printed and publised* (sic) *by D.*

Longworth, | at the Shakspeare-Gallery.

State B.

Imprint (on p. 206): the spelling of *publised* is corrected to *published*.

Noted with and without hyphen before "Gallery"; apparently the hyphen was either lost or failed to print in some copies, since the setting is the same in either reading.

Second edition.

Identification above heading: (*second edition, revised and corrected*)

Imprint (on p. 206): none

Gross differences from the first edition:

193.14-16. The piece opens with a gentle andante affetuoso, | soft, sleepy, and monotonous, intended to represent | a discussion in the house of assembly at Albany,....

197.3-2f. The first chapter contains an account of his route | from Trenton to Philadelphia: It is, as usual, much.... (This opening is preceded on the page by an introduction titled "From My Elbow-Chair.")

Representative readings, useful in distinguishing this second edition from the third:

194.21	comes
197.2f	Philadelphia: It
198.7	downwright

201.2f   promenade -- how

206.13   resort, and

Third edition.

Identification above heading: (*second edition, revised and corrected*)

Imprint (on p. 206): none

The text of this third edition differs only in minor ways from that of the second edition. Representative readings:

194.21   come

197.2f   Philadelphia. It

198.7   downright

201.2f   promenade. How

206.14   resort; and

New York *American Citizen*, 15 May 1807, "At Saturday next will be Published ... *NO* X; 16 May 1807, "THIS DAY IS PUBLISHED." New York *Morning Chronicle*, 18 May 1807, "This day is published ... No. X. ... (Price 12 1/2 cents.)." The advertisement is dated May 16 at the foot. *The Port Folio*, 30 May 1807, "The Stranger in Pennsylvania" extracted. New York *American Citizen*, 1 October 1807, "A revised and corrected edition of No. 10 is published for sale."

Number XI

First edition.

NO. XI.] *Tuesday, June 2*, 1807. [NO. I. OF VOL. II.

Imprint (on p. 228): See the description of the variant states.

Quotation: line 2, "folksez"; line 5, "smok'd."

$[A]^9 [B]^2$. Signed: [A, A_1] A_{2-4} [A_{5-8}] [B_{1-2}]. A_4 is an inserted leaf.

[207]-218, "Letter from Mustapha Rub-A-Dub Keli Khan ... to Asem Hacchem..."; 219-227, "From My Elbow-Chair. Mine Uncle John"; 227-228, "Note, by William Wizard Esq."

State A.

Imprint (on p. 228): [double rule] | *Printed & published by D. Longworth*, | at the Shakspeare-Gallery.

Representative readings:

> [207].title   KHAN, captain | of a ketch, to ASEM
>
> 208.11-12   hore- | back
>
> 211.23   puffs about
>
> 212.19   doughty import
>
> 212.2f   horeback -- and they twaddle
>
> 214.5f   *beer barrels* indeed seem
>
> 215.1-2   im- | brued
>
> 215.25   the list
>
> 222.1   Daddy Neptune
>
> 226.17   tradesman
>
> 227.13-14   doubts | had

State B.

Representative readings:

> 214.5f   *beer barrels*, indeed seem

State C.

Imprint (on p. 228): [rule] | *Printed by D. Longworth, at the Shakspeare Gallery*.

Representative readings:

> 226.25   tradesmen
>
> 227.21   doubts, had

In this state, Gathering B is reset and signed.

Second edition.

Identification above heading: (*second edition*)

Imprint (on p. 228): [rule] | *Printed by D. Longworth, at the Shakspeare Gallery*.

Representative readings:

> [207].title   KHAN, | *To Asem*
>
> 211.23   yelps about

212.19   doubty import

212.3f   horseback -- and they hurry

214.5f   *beer barrels*, indeed, seem

221.4f   Father Neptune

226.5f   tradesmen

227.21   doubts, had

Gathering B is that of State C of the first edition. And so, this edition employs mixed gatherings.

Third edition.

Identification above heading: none.

Imprint (on p. 228): none.

In this resetting, the pagination is [207]-226.

Representative readings:

[207].title   KAHN, captain | of a ketch, to ASEM

208.12   horseback

213.4-5   horseback -- and they | twaddle

215.8   imbued

215.3f   a list

225.5f   tradesman

226.19-20   doubts | had

The Twayne edition of *Salmagundi* accepts this setting as the second edition, since the text is derived sequentially from the text of the first edition. Textually, it does indeed fall between the first and the last versions. But bibliographically, there seems little question that this is the third edition. The use in the "*(second edition)*" of Gathering B from the last state of the first edition would argue that the "*(second edition)*" followed the first while either the type was still standing or while the sheets were still available. Additionally persuasive is the fact that some copies, perhaps all, of this setting are signed in 6's to indicate the place of the Number in a bound volume: p. 211 signed A2; p. 219, B; p. 223, B2.

New York *Morning Chronicle*, 30 May, 1 June 1807, "No. XI. ... Will be published ... on Tuesday June 2 (Price 12 1/2 cents.) N.B. A New Edition of

Nos. 1 (being the fourth), 2, 3, 4, 5 and 6 is now in the press and will be speedily published -- Title page and contents will be delivered with No. XI." New York *American Citizen*, 1 June 1807, same advertisement; 2 June 1807, "THIS DAY IS PUBLISHED."

Number XII

First edition.

NO. XII.] *Saturday, June* 27, 1807. [NO. II. OF VOL. II.

Imprint (on p. 254): See the description of the variant states.

Quotation: line 2, "folksez"; line 4, "broiled," "stewed"; line 5, "boiled," "smoked"

$[A]^9 B^4$. Signed: $[A, A_1] A_{2-4} [A_{5-8}] B[B_{2-4}]$. A_4 is an inserted leaf.

[229]-238, "From My Elbow-Chair"; 239-248, "The Stranger at Home; Or, A Tour in Broadway. By Jeremy Cockloft the younger"; 249-250, "From My Elbow-Chair"; 250-254, "From the Mill of Pindar Cockloft, Esq."

On p. 248, at the conclusion of "The Stranger at Home," appears the notation, END OF THE FIRST VOLUME.

In State C of the first edition, as well as in the second and third editions, "From the Mill of Pindar Cockloft, Esq." is thoroughly revised. The first version may be identified easily by the first couplet of the poem (p. 250): "How often I cast my reflections behind, | And call up the days of past youth to my mind!". The second version begins, "Full oft I indulge in reflections right sage, | And ease off my spleen by abusing the age;".

State A.

Imprint (on p. 254): [double rule] | Printed by D. Longworth, at the Shakspeare-Gallery.

Representative readings:

230.8f	favourite
232.6	Old England
232.7	d--n
233.14	them
236.6f	d--d
238.11	young gentlemen

240.6f	toiling, assiduously
241.22	a book
244.10	in being
245.12	this last class
247.21-22	aera	of the Chinese empire
250-254	[first version of the poem]

State B.

Representative readings:

| 240.6f | toiling assiduity |

State C.

Imprint (on p. 254): [rule] | *Printed by D. Longworth, at the Shakspeare-Gallery.*

Representative readings:

236.6f	bullied
250-254	[second version of the poem]
253.8	"lulla-a-by-baby"

In this state, Gathering B is reset.

Second edition.

Identification above heading: (*second edition*)

Imprint (on p. 254): [rule] | *Printed by D. Longworth, at the Shakspeare-Gallery.*

Representative readings:

232.7	condemn
233.14	these articles
236.6f	bullied
240.7f	toiling assiduity
241.22	an essay
244.10	on being
247.21-22	era	of the chinese emperor

250-254   [second version of the poem]

Gathering B is that of State C of the first edition. And so, this edition employs mixed gatherings.

Third edition.

Identification above heading: (*second edition*)

Imprint (on p. 254): [rule] | *Printed by D. Longworth, at the Shakspeare-Gallery.* (In some copies, perhaps all, the final *y* is raised well above the baseline.)

Representative readings:

230.8f   favorite

232.6   Old England

238.11   young men

245.12   this class

253.8   "lull-a-by-baby"

Some copies, perhaps all, signed in 6's to indicated the place of this Number in a bound volume; p. 233 signed C; p. 237, C2; p. 245, D; p. 249, D2.

New York *American Citizen,* 26 June 1807, "*On Saturday, June 27, will be published, ... No. XII.*" "NB. A new edition of No. 1, (being the 4th) 2, 3, 4, 5 and 6, is now in the press, and will be speedily published -- Title page and contents for 1st vol ready for delivery." 27 June 1807, "THIS DAY IS PUBLISHED ... *Price* 12 1/2 *Cents.*"

Number XIII

First edition.

NO. XIII. *Friday, August* 14, 1807. NO. 3 OF VOL. 2.

Imprint (on p. 280): none.

Quotation: line 2, "folksez"; line 4, "broiled," "stewed"; line 5, "boiled," "smoked."

[A]^9 B^4. Signed: [A, A$_1$] A$_{2-4}$ [A$_{5-8}$] B [B$_{2-4}$]. A$_4$ is an inserted leaf.

[255]-259, "From My Elbow-Chair"; 259-267, "Plans for Defending Our Harbour. By William Wizard, Esq."; 268-279, "From My Elbow-Chair. A

Retrospect, Or 'What You Will'"; 279-280, "To Readers and Correspondents."

Representative readings:

260.1	so much in horror
266.8-9	*Bohan* | *upas*
269.5f	atchieved
277.1	publick
280.22	addresses

Second edition.

Identification above heading: none.

Imprint (on p. 280): none.

Representative readings:

260.1	in so much horrour
266.9	*Bohan upus*
269.5f	achieved
277.1	public
280.22	addressed

Some copies, perhaps all, signed in 6's to indicate the place of this Number in a bound volume: p. 257 signed E; p. 261, E2; p. 269, F; 273, F2.

New York *American Citizen*, 13 August 1807, "*THIS DAY IS PUBLISHED, ... NO. XIII ...* (Price 12 1/2 cents)." *New-York Evening Post*, 21 August 1807, "Plans for Defending Our Harbour" extracted.

Number XIV

NO. 14] *Saturday, Sept.* 19, 1807. [No. 4 OF VOL. 2.

Imprint (on p. 306): [rule] | *Printed by D. Longworth, at the Shakspeare-Gallery.*

Quotation: line 2, "folksez"; line 4, "broiled," "stewed"; line 5, "boiled," "smoked."

$[A]^9 B^4$. Signed: [A, A_1] A_{2-4} [A $_{5-8}$] B [B_{2-4}]. A_4 is an inserted leaf.

[281]-291, "From Mustapha Rub-A-Dub Keli Khan, to Asem Hacchem..."; 292-302, "Cockloft Hall. By Launcelot Langstaff, Esq."; 302-306, "Theatrical Intelligence. By William Wizard, Esq.," with a one-paragraph untitled introduction.

State [A].

    289.1f   The last word of the line, "an," is not present.

State [B].

    289.1f   The last word of the line, "an," is present.

The sequence of the two states is uncertain.

Second edition.

BAL reports a second edition reprint signed G and H to indicate the place of this Number in a bound volume. Not seen.

New York Evening Post, 18, 19 September 1807, "To-Morrow, Sept. 19, will be published ... *No*. 14."

Number XV

First edition.

NO. 15] *Thursday, Oct.* 1, 1807. [NO. 5 OF VOL. 2.

Imprint (on p.324): See the description of the variant states.

Quotation: line 2, "folksez"; line 4, "broiled," "stewed"; line 5, "boiled," "smoked."

$[A]^9$. Signed: [A, A_1] A_{2-4} [A_{5-8}]. A_4 is an inserted leaf.

[307]-315, "Sketches from Nature. By Anthony Evergreen, Gent."; 315-324, "On Greatness. By Launcelot Langstaff, Esq."

Six variant states of the first setting of the Number can be identified, but the sequence is ambiguous. Longworth's imprint on p. 324, for instance, is present in only two states, perhaps the first and the last, but an explanation of its presence or absence is not apparent. The variants on p. 320, however, are more understandable. Three or four lines apparently became loose -- the letter t at the beginning of line 13 is lost in one state -- and had to be realigned and adjusted. In the process, commas appear and disappear, presumably as the printer struggled with the problem. The following sequence seems satisfactory but is not certain.

State [A].

Imprint (on p. 324): [rule] | *New-York, Printed and Published by D. Longworth.*

Representative readings:

320.11	meeting [no comma follows]
320.12-13	mor-	tifying
320.13	pimp,

State [B].

Imprint (on p. 324): none. A short swelled rule is present in place of the imprint.

Representative readings: The same as State [A].

State [C].

Imprint (on p. 324): none. Swelled rule present.

Representative readings:

320.11	meeting [no comma follows]
320.12-13	mor-	ifying [A space is present for the missing letter t.]
320.13	pimp,

State [D].

Imprint (on p. 324): none. Swelled rule present.

Representative readings:

320.11	meeting,
320.12-13	mor-	tifying
320.13	pimp,

Line 11 of p. 320 is out of alignment, particularly in the word "notorious."

State [E].

Imprint (on p. 324): none. Swelled rule present.

Representative readings:

320.11	meeting,
320.12-13	mor-	tifying

320.13   pimp [no comma follows]

State [F].

Imprint (on p. 324): [rule] | *New-York, Printed and Published by D. Longworth.*

Representative readings: The same as state [E].

Second edition.

BAL reports a second edition reprint signed I and K to indicate the place of this Number in a bound volume. Not seen.

New York *American Citizen*, 1 October 1807, "*THIS DAY WILL BE PUBLISHED,* ... *NO. XV.*" "A revised and corrected edition of No. 10 is published for sale."

Number XVI

First edition.

NO 16] *Thursday, Oct.* 15, 1807 [NO. 6 OF VOL. 2.

Imprint (on p. 342): none.

Quotation: line 2, "folksez"; line 4, "broiled," "stewed"; line 5, "boiled," "smoked."

[A]^9. Signed: [A, A$_1$] A$_{2-4}$ [A$_{5-8}$]. A$_4$ is an inserted leaf.

[325]-332, "Style at Ballston. By William Wizard, Esq."; 332, untitled prefatory paragraph to Mustapha letter, signed L. Langstaff; 333-342, "From Mustapha Rub-A-Dub Keli Khan, to Asem Hacchem,..." (on pp. 340-341, "Note, by William Wizard, Esq.").

State A

Representative reading

    [325].11f   wits a

    326.5   heart, and

    327.5   dresses, and

    327.20   liveries, carry

    330.1   transferred, bodily, to

    334.18   around;

    336.1f   far

340.1   warrior

State B.

Representative readings:

326.5   heart and

327.5   dresses and

327.20   liveries; carry

340.1   warriour

State C.

Representative readings:

[325].11f   wits, a

330.1   transferred bodily to

334.18   around,

336.1f   Far

Second edition.

BAL reports a second edition reprint signed K2, L, L2 to indicate the place of this Number in a bound volume. Not seen.

New York *American Citizen*, 14 October 1807, "*On Thursday, October* 15, *will be Published, ... NO.* XVI."

Number XVII

First edition.

NO. 17] *Wednesday, Nov.* 11, 1807 [NO. 7 OF VOL. 2.

Imprint (on p. 360): none.

Quotation: line 2, "folksez"; line 4, "broiled," "stewed"; line 5, "boiled," "smoked."

$[A]^9$. Signed: [A, A_1] A_{2-4} [A_{5-8}]. A_4 is an inserted leaf.

[343]-349, "Autumnal Reflections. By Launcelot Langstaff, Esq."; 349-353, "By Launcelot Langstaff, Esq."; 354-360, "Chap. CIX. of the Chronicles of the Renowned and Ancient City of Gotham."

State A.

Representative readings:

    350.22   ancsetors

    352.5-4f   cloud is | is to

State B.

Representative readings:

    350.22   ancestors

Second edition.

BAL reports a second edition reprint signed M, M2, N to indicated the place of this number in a bound volume. Not seen.

New York *American Citizen,* 10 November 1807, *"Tomorrow, November 11, will be published, ...NO. XVII."*

Number XVIII

First edition.

NO. 18] *Tuesday, Nov.* 24, 1807. [NO. 8 OF VOL. 2.

Imprint (on p. 378): New-York, printed and published by D. Longworth. | [rule].

Quotation: line 2, "folksez"; line 4, "broiled," "stewed"; line 5, "boiled," "smoked."

[A]^9. Signed: [A, A$_1$] A$_{2-4}$ [A$_{5-8}$]. A$_4$ is an inserted leaf. In some copies A$_4$ is signed A; no sequence determined.

[361]-370, "The Little Man in Black. By Launcelot Langstaff, Esq."; 371-378, "Letter from Mustapha Rub-A-Dub Keli Khan, to Asem Hacchem...."

State A.

Representative readings:

    374.4   and, so

    374.7f   facinations

    378.5   straight waistcoats

State B.

Representative readings:

> 374.4   and so
>
> 374.7f   fascinations

State C.

Representative readings:

> 378.5   strait waistcoats

Second edition

BAL reports a second edition reprint signed O, O2 to indicate the place of this Number in a bound volume. Not seen.

New York *American Citizen*, 23, 24 November 1807, "*Tuesday, Nov. 24, will be published, ... NO. XVIII.*"

Number XIX

NO. 19] *Thursday, Dec* 31, 1807. [NO. 9 OF VOL. 2. In some copies the punctuation marks, particularly the period after 1807, are so faint as almost to disappear.

Imprint (on p. 404): none.

Quotation: line 2, "folksez"; line 4, "broiled," "stewed"; line 5, "boiled," "smoked."

$[A]^9$. B^4. Signed: [A, A_1] $A_{2\text{-}4}$ [$A_{5\text{-}8}$] B [$B_{2\text{-}4}$]. A_4 is an inserted leaf.

[379]- 380, "From My Elbow Chair"; 380-391, "Letter from Mustapha Rub-A-Dub Keli Khan, to Muley Helim Al Raggi..."; 391-398, "By Anthony Evergreen, Gent."; 399-404, "Tea, A Poem. From the Mill of Pindar Cockloft Esq...." (on p. 401, at foot, a note signed W. Wizard).

State A.

Representative readings:

> 394.6-5f   exclam- | tion

State B.

Representative readings:

394.6-5f   exclam- | ation

It is possible that there exists another, earlier, state. In State B, the first line of p. 386 ends with an unmistakable colon.   In State A, the mark of punctuation is sometimes ambiguous; it may be the colon that is seen clearly in some copies, or it may be a battered semicolon.   An unmistakable semicolon would define an earlier state.   The printer apparently had trouble with that final piece of type in the corner; it moves up and down sharply in various copies, even those in the same state.

Second edition.

BAL reports a second edition reprint, paged [379]-402, signed P, P2, Q, Q2 to indicate the place of this Number in a bound volume. Not seen.

New York *American Citizen*, 31 December 1807, "THIS DAY IS PUBLISHED, ... *NO. XIX*." *New-York Evening Post*, 31 December 1807, "THIS DAY IS PUBLISHED, No. 19. ... price 12 1/2 cents."

Number XX

First edition.

NO. 20] *Monday, Jan.* 25, 1808. [NO. X. OF VOL. II. In some copies the punctuation marks, particularly the period after X, are so faint as almost to disappear.

Imprint (on p. 430): none. In its place appears: [double rule] | END OF VOLUME II.

Quotation: line 2, "folksez"; line 4, "broiled," "stewed"; line 5, "boiled," "smoked."

$[A]^9 B^4$, plus $[-]^2$. Signed: [A, A_1] A_{2-4} [A_{5-8}] B [B_{2-4}], plus 2 unsigned leaves. A_4 is an inserted leaf. The two terminal unsigned leaves consist of a title leaf and an index leaf for Vol. II.

[405]-414, "From My Elbow-Chair"; 415-422, "To the Ladies. By Anthony Evergreen, Gent."; 423-430, untitled, beginning "How hard it is", signed "William Wizard."

For a description of the title leaf and the index leaf for Vol. II, see the following section on "Title Pages for Volumes I and II."

On p. 422, in the blank space after "To the Ladies," appears a large ornament depicting an opening fruit.

State A.

Representative readings

> 415.8   peers
>
> 417.2f   exhibit

State B.

Representative readings:

> 415.8   knights
>
> 417.2f   exhibit

State C.

Representative readings:

> 415.8   knights
>
> 417.2f   exhibits

Second edition.

BAL reports a second edition reprint, paged [403]-424, signed R, R2 to indicate the place of this Number in a bound volume. Not seen.

New York *American Citizen*, 26, 27 January 1808, "SALMAGUNDI No. XX. (*Which completes the Second Volume*) IS THIS DAY PUBLISHED, ... Title Page and Index to the second volume accompanies this number." Dated Jan. 26 at foot.

TITLE PAGES FOR VOLUMES I AND II

By the time of Number XI, Longworth and the authors thought of *Salmagundi* as a multi-volume work. The last ten Numbers were identified on first publication as components of Volume II, and Longworth issued a title page for Vol. I with Number XI and for Vol. II with Number XX. After the completion of the individual twenty Numbers, the work apparently was issued bound in two volumes made up of a random selection of available Numbers, some no doubt produced for the purpose. There is evidence too, derived from the consecutive signature marks, that at some later point Longworth reprinted the last ten Numbers as a single group to provide a new edition of Vol. II.

As so often with the publishing history of *Salmagundi*, however, there is at the beginning some ambiguity. In Number XII at the foot of p. 248

appears the notation, END OF THE FIRST VOLUME. Longworth may have been looking forward to more Numbers than the twenty that were in fact written, planning to divide the Numbers eventually into larger volumes of twelve Numbers rather than the original division into ten Numbers. At the same time and in part for the same reason, he may also have been responding directly to the criticism that survives in Washington Irving's letter of 22 June 1807 to James K. Paulding: "I am much disappointed at your having concluded the first volume at No. 10. Besides making an insignificant baby house volume, it ends so weakly at one of the weakest numbers of the whole." But even before the formal division into volumes, the work seems to have been already thought of by others in terms of volumes. *The Monthly Register, Magazine, and Review of the United States* [New York] in the issue of 3 August 1807 reviewed *Salmagundi* under the heading, "SALMAGUNDI.... New York, printed and published by D. Longworth, at the Shakspeare Gallery -- 1807. -- 1 Vol. 12mo. pp 188." 188 pp. would define the first nine Numbers. Were the Numbers so bound and sold -- with or without the first volume title -- or was *The Monthly Register* simply using the term "volume" loosely?

A title page and table of contents for Vol. I were issued with Number XI on 2 June 1807 but were not bound with the Number. Advertisements in the New York *Morning Chronicle,* 30 May and 1 June 1807, and in the New York *American Citizen,* 1 June 1807, make the distinction: "Title page and contents will be delivered with No. XI." A title page and conjugate index for Vol. II, however, were bound with Number XX as a final doubleton. Here an advertisement for Number XX in the *American Citizen,* 26, 27 January 1808, employs a different term: "Title page and Index to the second volume accompanies this number."

Volume I

The title page for Vol. I has been noted in five forms, three dated 1807 and two dated 1808. Each is in a different setting. It seems likely that the form dated 1807 but without a copyright notice on the verso is the earliest, and the two dated 1808 the latest, but a sequence has not been determined.

Form [A].

SALMAGUNDI; | OR, THE | *WHIM-WHAMS AND OPINIONS* | OF | LAUNCELOT LANGSTAFF, ESQ. | AND OTHERS. | [double rule] | In hoc est hoax, cum quiz et jokesez, | Et smokem, toastem, roastem folksez, | Fee, faw, fum. *Psalmanazar.* | With baked, and broiled, and stewed, and toasted, | And fried, and boiled, and smoked, and roasted, | We treat the town. | [double rule] | *VOL. I.* | [double rule] | NEW-YORK: | PRINTED & PUBLISHED BY D. LONGWORTH, | *At the Shakespeare-Gallery.* | 1807.

Note the spelling of "broiled," "stewed," "boiled," "smoked," "Shakespeare," and the absence of a dotted rule before the date.

No copyright notice on verso.

Form [B].

SALMAGUNDI; | OR, THE | *WHIM-WHAMS AND OPINIONS* | OF | LAUNCELOT LANGSTAFF, ESQ. | AND OTHERS. | [double rule] | [three lines of comic Latin] | With baked, and broiled, and stewed, and toasted, | And fried, and boiled, and smoked, and roasted, | We treat the town. | [double rule] | *VOL. I* | [double rule] | NEW-YORK: | PRINTED & PUBLISHED BY D. LONGWORTH, | *At the Shakspeare-Gallery.* | [dotted rule] | *1807*

Note the spelling of "broiled," "stewed," "boiled," "smoked," "Shakspeare"; the presence of a dotted rule before the date; and the absence of a period after the date.

Copyright notice on verso. The work is listed as: *Salmagundi; or the Whim-Whams and Opinions of* | *Launcelot Langstaff, Esq.* | [double rule]. In some copies, the *f* in *of* is absent; in some copies the hyphen in *Whim-Whams* is absent. The explanation may be faulty press work.

Form [C].

SALMAGUNDI; | OR, THE | *WHIM-WHAMS AND OPINIONS* | OF | LAUNCELOT LANGSTAFF, ESQ. | AND OTHERS. | [double rule] | [three lines of comic Latin] | With baked, and broil'd, and stew'd, and toasted, | And fried, and boil'd, and smok'd, and roasted, | We treat the town. | [double rule] | VOL. I. | [double rule] | NEW-YORK: | PRINTED & PUBLISHED BY D. LONGWORTH, | *At the Shakspeare-Gallery.* | *[dotted rule]* | *1807.*

Note the spelling of "broil'd," "stew'd," "boil'd," "smok'd," "Shakspeare"; the presence of a dotted rule before the date; and the presence of a period after the date

BAL describes this title page with no comma after "smok'd" on line 12. Not seen. A variant? An error by *BAL*?

Copyright notice on verso. The work is listed as: *Salmagundi; or the Whim-Whams & Opinions of Laun-* | *celot, Langstaff, Esq. and others.* | [swelled rule].

Form [D].

SALMAGUNDI; OR, THE | *WHIM-WHAMS AND OPINIONS* | OF | LAUNCELOT LANGSTAFF, ESQ. | AND OTHERS. | [double rule] | three lines of comic Latin] | With baked, and broiled, and stewed, and toasted, | And fried, and broiled, and smoked, and roasted, | We treat the town. | [double rule] | *VOL. I.* | [double rule] | NEW-YORK: | PRINTED & PUBLISHED BY D. LONGWORTH, | *At the Shakspeare-Gallery.* | 1808.

Note the spelling of "broiled," "stewed," "smoked"; the error of "broiled" for "boiled" in line 12; and the period after the date.

Copyright notice on verso. The work is listed as: *Salmagundi; or the Whim-Whams and Opinions of* | *Launcelot Langstaff, esq. & others.* | [stylized swelled rule composed of tapered finials with star-like hollow ornaments at thicker ends and five italic *O*'s at center]. The first line of the notice ends: that | The first line of the citation of the copyright acts ends: Uni- |

Form [E].

SALMAGUNDI; | OR, THE | *WHIM-WHAMS AND OPINIONS* | OF | LAUNCELOT LANGSTAFF, ESQ. | AND OTHERS. | [double rule] | [three lines of comic Latin] | With baked, and broiled, and stewed, and toasted, | And fried, and boiled, and smoked, and roasted, | We treat the town. | [double rule] | *VOL. I.* | [double rule] | NEW-YORK: | PRINTED & PUBLISHED BY D. LONGWORTH, | *At the Shakspeare-Gallery.* | 1808

Note that the spelling is the same; but "boiled" is the correct word in line 12; and the period is absent after the date.

Copyright notice on verso. The listing of the work is the same. The first line of the notice ends: that on | The first line of the citation of the copyright acts ends: United |

Volume II

The title page for Vol. II has been noted in three forms, each dated 1808. Each is in a different setting. On the title page itself, the small differences in text appear only in the imprint. A sequence has not been determined.

Form [A].

SALMAGUNDI; | OR, THE | *WHIM-WHAMS AND OPINIONS* | OF | LAUNCELOT LANGSTAFF, ESQ. | AND OTHERS. | [double rule] | In hoc est hoax, cum quiz et jokesez, | Et smokem, toastem, roastem folksez, | Fee, faw, fum. *Psalmanazar.* | With baked, and broiled, and stewed, and toasted, | And fried, and boiled, and smoked, and roasted, | We treat the town. | [double rule] | *VOL. II.* | [double rule] | NEW-YORK: | PRINTED & PUBLISHED BY D. LONGWORTH, | *At the Shakspeare-Gallery.* | 1808

Note the text of the imprint: an ampersand in line 18; a comma at the end of line 18; and no period after the date.

Copyright notice on verso. The work is listed as: *Salmagundi; or the Whim-Whams and Opinions of* | *Launcelot Langstaff, esq. & others.* | [stylized swelled rule composed of tapered finials with star-like hollow ornaments at thicker ends and five italic *O*'s at center].

Form [B].

NEW-YORK: | PRINTED & PUBLISHED BY D. LONGWORTH | *At the Shakspeare-Gallery.* | 1808.

Note the text of the imprint; an ampersand in line 18; no comma at the end of line 18; and a period after the date.

Copyright notice on verso. The work is listed as: *Salmagundi; or the Whim Whams and Opinions of* | *Launcelot Langstaff, esq. & others.* | [stylized swelled rule composed of tapered finials with star-like hollow ornaments at thicker ends and four (not five) italic O's at center].

Form [C].

NEW-YORK: | PRINTED AND PUBLISHED BY D. LONGWORTH, | *At the Shakspeare-Gallery.* | 1808.

Note the text of the imprint: the word AND spelled out in line 18; a comma at the end of line 18; and a period after the date.

Copyright notice on verso. The work is listed as: *Salmagundi; or the Whim-Whams and Opinions of* | *Launcelot Langstaff, esq & others.* | [stylized swelled rule composed of tapered finials and a small cross-like ornament at center].

THE WRAPPERS

Individual Numbers were issued bound in paper wrappers. But unique wrappers were not produced for each Number; rather, the wrappers were printed in quantity, carrying a general title on the front, without the date (except for the year in the first form) and without identification of the Number, and then tie-bound on the individual Numbers apparently more or less at random. Although a convincing sequence of the wrappers can be established, any individual Number may appear, legitimately, in a wrapper somewhat out of sequence. The binder apparently used whatever wrapper was at hand. No set of Numbers all in sequentially correct wrappers is known or is likely to be found.

(It should be repeated here that *Salmagundi* has been a favorite of collectors for a long time, and unfortunately, just as with the sheets of the Numbers, "restored" or fraudulently sophisticated wrappers are known. The owner and the scholar must be alert to the possibility, but must also be aware of the randomness of original binding.)

The wrappers are printed on wove papers of varying texture, almost all of off-white color with varying shades of yellow or buff applied to the outer side, the inner side being left uncolored. The technique is unusual and one not commonly employed elsewhere. Only a very few *Salmagundi* wrappers have been noted on pulp-dyed paper.

On the outside of the back wrapper appear advertisements by David Longworth, except for the first form which is blank. Fifteen different forms of advertisements have been identified, and more may yet appear. As a general rule, the inner sides of the wrappers are blank, although four have been noted with advertisements printed on the inner sides also. Those four are specifically identified here.

Comparison on the collator of xerographic copies of a number of duplicate examples of many of the forms of the front and back wrappers has revealed no concealed resetting. Although extensive collation of many copies might discover differences not readily apparent to the unaided eye, the probability is slight. It should be noted -- and I have remarked on it in the description of a few forms of the front wrapper -- that David Longworth's printing, on the wrappers as in the contents, falls considerably short of clean competence. Occasionally and irregularly a single type-character will not print clearly, and hyphens in particular will disappear altogether. But such variants do not involve resetting or show any evidence of deliberate change, or even deliberate repair.

The method of presentation followed here calls first for a description of the various forms of the outer front wrapper; then of the forms of the outer back wrapper; and, finally, of the various combinations of the two that have been noted or reported, with a further description of any advertisements appearing on the inner sides of the wrappers. The method is somewhat awkward but does have the advantage of clarity and of avoiding a good deal of repetition.

Any scholar struggling with the puzzle of the *Salmagundi* wrappers today must be indebted to the work of Jacob Blanck, published in its final form in *BAL*. He had the opportunity to compare a great many wrappers, often side by side, and his studied conclusions have stood the test of time and later investigation. Here, without apology, I follow the sequence of wrappers that he established.

The Outer Front Wrapper

The outer front wrapper has been noted in six forms. The first two print no copyright notice. The last four forms do print a copyright notice, all with the same notice, dated "the sixth day of March, in the thirty-first year of the Independence." In addition to this large difference in the forms, each of the two sorts may be distinguished readily by the smaller differences defined in the descriptions here.

It should be remarked that David Longworth took out copyright on the work on 6 March 1807, and that *Salmagundi* Number V is dated Saturday, March 7 on the first page of the text. An advertisement in *People's Friend*, 5-7 March 1807, reaffirms the date for Number V. If the day of publication is correct -- and there is no reason to question it -- Number V is the first Number that could have carried the copyright notice on the wrappers of copies issued in the first days of sale. It should also be remarked, however, that copies of Numbers II and III in the first state of the text have been seen in wrappers carrying the copyright notice, as well as copies of the first four Numbers in later states and later editions of the text. The first Numbers continued to be sold as demand increased, and no doubt some left-over copies of the early states were bound in later wrappers.

Form 1.

[double rule] | SALMAGUNDI, | OR, THE | *WHIM-WHAMS AND OPINIONS* | OF | LAUNCELOT LANGSTAFF, & OTHERS. | [double rule] | In hoc est hoax, cum quiz et jokesez, | Et smokem, toastem, roastem folkesez | Fee, faw, fum. *Psalmanazar.* | With baked, and broil'd, and stew'd and toasted, | And fried, and boil'd, and smoak'd and roasted, | We treat the town. | [double rule] | NEW-YORK: | PUBLISHED BY DAVID LONGWORTH, | *At the Shakspeare Gallery.* | [swelled rule] | 1807

Note the comma after SALMAGUNDI; the spelling of "folkesez" and "smoak'd"; the absence of a comma after "folkesez"; and the absence of a hyphen in *Shakspeare Gallery.*

Form 2.

[double rule] | SALMAGUNDI; | OR, THE | *WHIM-WHAMS AND OPINIONS* | OF | LAUNCELOT LANGSTAFF, & OTHERS. | [double rule] | In hoc est hoax, cum quiz et jokesez, | Et smokem, toastem, roastem folksez, | Fee, faw, fum. *Psalmanazar.* | With baked, and broiled, and stew'd and toasted, | And fried, and boil'd, and smok'd and roasted, | We treat the town. | [double rule] | NEW-YORK: | PUBLISHED BY DAVID LONGWORTH, | *At the Shakspeare-Gallery.* | [swelled rule] | 1807

Note the semicolon after SALMAGUNDI; the spelling of "folksez" and "smok'd"; the presence of a comma after "folksez"; and the presence of a hyphen in *Shakspeare-Gallery*. In some copies the hyphen is so faint as almost to disappear.

Form 3.

District of | New-York. [The two lines are joined by a vertical ligature symbol, followed by the letters *ss.* centered between the two lines. This stylized legality occupies the first third of the space allotted the first two lines of the beginning of the copyright notice. The remainder of the beginning of the notice occupies the last two-thirds of the space allotted, with the initial letter B extending down two lines in height, and then continues in conventional form from margin to margin, beginning with the third line.] BE IT REMEMBERED, that on | the sixth day of March, in | the thirty-first year of the Independence of the United | States of America, *David Longworth*, of the said Dis- | trict, hath deposited in this office, the title of a Book, | the right whereof he claims as proprietor, in the words | and figures following, to wit: | SALMAGUNDI; | OR, THE | *WHIM-WHAMS AND OPINIONS* | OF | LAUNCELOT LANGSTAFF, & OTHERS. | [double rule] | In hoc est hoax, cum quiz et jokesez, | Et smokem, toastem, roastem folksez, | Fee, faw, fum. *Psalmanazar.* | With baked, and broil'd, and stew'd and toasted, | And fried, and boil'd, and smok'd and roasted, | We treat the town. | [swelled rule] | In conformity to the Act of the Congress of the United | States, entitled "An Act for the encouragement of | "Learning, by securing the Copies of Maps, Charts, | "and Books, to the Authors and Proprietors of such | "Copies, during the times herein mentioned;" and al- | "so to an act entitled "An Act supplementary to an | "act entitled, An Act for the encouragement of Learn- | "ing, by securing the copies of Maps, Charts, and | "Books, to the Authors and Proprietors of such Copies, | "during the times therein mentioned, and extending | "the benefits thereof, to the Arts of Designing, Engrav- | "ing and Etching historical and other prints." | EDWARD DUNSCOMB. | Clerk of the District of New-York. | [rule] | NEW-YORK: PUBLISHED BY DAVID LONGWORTH.

In line 3 of the title, the hyphen in "thirty-first" is seen in various degrees of weakness and sometimes disappears altogether. But no sequence should be inferred, since the hyphen is present in the same setting in Form D. The long rule above the imprint often prints irregularly.

One copy has been noted with the hyphen missing from "New-York" in line 3f and the period missing after LONGWORTH in the last line, but the mechanical collator reveals no resetting or redressing. The hyphen in "thirty-first" in line 3 is clearly present. Since the rule above the imprint is missing in large part, it would appear that the lower part of the printer's forme failed to print clearly.

Form 4.

With copyright notice.

From the same setting except for the variant imprint at the foot: [rule] | NEW-YORK: [line of 4 dots] PUBLISHED BY DAVID LONGWORTH. | [rule].

In some copies the period is missing after LONGWORTH. The cause would seem to be faulty printing rather than an omission in the composition, but it is at least possible that a legitimate variant does exist.

Form 5.

With copyright notice.

Above the comic quotation, in place of double rule, appears an elaborated rule composed of two tapered rules divided by a small cross-like ornament.

Imprint: [rule] | NEW-YORK: [line of 4 dots] PUBLISHED BY DAVID LONGWORTH | [rule]. Note the absence of a period after LONGWORTH.

Form 6.

With copyright notice

Above the comic quotation, in place of one of the other rules, appears a stylized swelled rule composed of tapered finials with star-like hollow ornaments at thicker ends and five italic *o*'s at center. The same rule appears below the quotation, in place of the swelled rule.

Imprint: [rule] | NEW-YORK: [line of 4 dots] PUBLISHED BY DAVID LONGWORTH | [rule]. Note the absence of a period after LONGWORTH.

The Outer Back Wrapper

The descriptions of the back of the wrappers consist simply of an identification of the items advertised, with no attempt to reproduce the complete text or the typographical display. The pages are full -- some even crowded -- and a transcription would take entirely too much space. There seems little need for full transcription anyway, since comparison of a number of copies on the mechanical collator (by means of xerographic reproduction) has revealed no resetting or concealed variants within the same forms. My collation was not, of course, complete or even statistically satisfactory, but it did not suggest the need for further such investigation.

Form 1.

Blank.

Form 2.

Just published, ... The Biography and Letters of ... Ninon de l'Enclos.   [3 paragraphs of Extract from the Preface].

Form 3.

Just published, ... The Biography and Letters of ... Ninon de l'Enclos.   [1 paragraph of Extract from the Preface]. Poems, by the late R. B. Davis.

Form 4.

Shakspeare's Plays. [The page is taken up by Proposals by Munroe & Francis of Boston to publish by subscription Samuel Johnson's edition of Shakespeare, and the Conditions of publication, followed by a notice that D. Longworth "will receive subscribers for one hundred copies"; dated at the foot, *Shakspeare-Gallery, April, 1807.*]

In some copies, the hyphen in *Shakspeare-Gallery* has failed to print.

Form 5.

The Shakspeare Gallery is Now in Order to Admit Visitors. The Curfew, a Drama, by John Tobin. False Alarms, a new Comic Opera, by Kenny. Elegant Embost Visiting Cards.

Form 6.

Just published, The Curfew. Margaretta, or The Intricacies of the Heart. The Birds of Scotland, with other poems, by James Grahame. False Alarms. Tekeli, or The Siege of Montgatz [,] a Melo-drame. Elegant Embost Visiting Cards.

Form 7.

The Nun of St. Dominick. Adrian and Orrila, a play, by William Diamond. In the press -- The Rivals. The Critic. Elegant Embost Visiting Cards.

Form 8.

The Novice of St. Dominick. Sully's painting-room is opened at No. 5 Gold-street.

Notice that "The Novice of St. Dominick" has been changed from "The Nun of St. Dominick." And notice the location of the painting-room at "No. 5 Gold-street."

Form 9.

[Advertisements continued from inner wrapper. The first line, continuing a long prose paragraph, reads, "thor, as his own taste, or whim, may dictate --"; that paragraph is followed by two shorter ones, dated at the end, "august 19".] Just published, ... Ethick Diversions, ... by Restore Estlack.

Form 10.

Just Published, ... Town and Country, ... by Thomas Morton. Adrian and Orrila. The most general assortment of the newest and oldest plays. Elegant Embost Visiting Cards.

Form 11.

The Novice of St. Dominick. Sully's painting-room is opened at the Theatre.

Notice the location of the painting-room at "the Theatre."

Form 12.

Subscriptions will be received for ... Munroe & Francis' edition of Shakspeare. Subscriptions will also be received ... for Etheridge and Bliss' ... Rollin. Mrs. Opie's Simple Tales. Birds of Scotland. In the press, Letters from England, translated from the Spanish of don Manual Alvary Espirella. Circulating and social libraries furnished on the most liberal terms and extensive credit.

Form 13.

Subscriptions will be received for ... Shakspeare. Subscriptions will also be received ... for ... Rollin. Just received, Mrs. Opie's Simple Tales. Wild Irish Girl. Birds of Scotland. In the press, Letters from England, translated from the Spanish of don Manual Alvarez Espriella. Circulating and social libraries furnished ...

Form 13 has the same text, reset, as Form 12, except that Wild Irish Girl is added, and the name of the author of Letters from England is changed from Manual Alvary Espirella to Manual Alvarez Espriella.

Form 14.

Just published, a Second Volume of the Miseries of Human Life. Power of Solitude. Dominick. Wild Irish Girl. Lay of the Irish Harp.

Form 15.

For sale by D. Longworth, at the Shakspeare-Gallery   Just Published, a Second Volume of the Miseries of Human Life.

Wrapper Combinations

The six forms of the outer front wrapper and the fifteen forms of the outer back wrapper were issued in a variety of different combinations. The variety was further increased by the occasional use on some of the later wrappers of advertisements printed on the inner sides. When present, such added printing is noticed here in the definitions of the known combinations. Other combinations as yet unnoticed may, of course, exist.

No attempt is made here to list the copies on which each combination has been noted or reported, principally because the definitions of the editions and states of the Numbers offered in this bibliography differ from those offered in earlier bibliographical studies, and so differ from the definitions used by reporters when describing copies that I have not myself examined. The interested reader who wishes such a listing is referred to the extensive one in *BAL*. That seems fitting, since I have accepted the sequence of wrapper combinations established by *BAL*, although in order to maintain consistent and regular designation of combinations -- from Wrapper A to Wrapper T -- I have assigned different letter designations after Wrapper K.

Wrapper A. Front, Form 1. Back, Form 1 [blank].

Wrapper B. Front, Form 2. Back, Form 2.

Wrapper C. Front, Form 2. Back, Form 3.

Wrapper D. Front, Form 3. Back, Form 3.

Wrapper E. Front, Form 3. Back, Form 4.

Wrapper F. Front, Form 3. Back, Form 5.

Wrapper G. Front, Form 3. Back, Form 6.

Wrapper H. Front, Form 3. Back, Form 7.

Wrapper I. Front, Form 4. Back, Form 8.

Wrapper J. Front, Form 3. Back, Form 9. On inner wrappers, front and back, list of English and American Stage. The advertisements continue on the outer back wrapper, as described for Form 9.

Wrapper K. Front, Form 3. Back, Form 10. Inner Wrappers blank.

Wrapper L. Front, Form 3. Back, Form 10. On inner front wrapper, List of Plays, from Blue Beard to Too Many Cooks. On inner back wrapper, the list continued, from Il Bondocani to Douglas.

Wrapper M. The same as Wrapper L, except that the list on the inner back wrapper ends with Adrian and Orrila rather than with Douglas. The sequence of Wrapper L and Wrapper M is uncertain.

Wrapper N. Front, Form 4. Back, Form 11.

Wrapper O. Front, Form 4. Back, Form 12.

Wrapper P. Front, Form 4. Back, Form 13.

Wrapper Q. Front, Form 5. Back, Form 13. On the inner wrappers, front and back, list of French and Spanish Books. At the end of the inner back wrapper, The Miseries of Human Life. Vol. II.

Wrapper R. The same as Wrapper Q, except that the inner wrappers are blank. The sequence of Wrapper Q and Wrapper R is uncertain.

Wrapper S. Front, Form 6. Back, Form 14.

Wrapper T. Front, Form 6. Back, Form 15.

2A. The Second American edition, 1814, the first American version to be designed and printed as a book, is derived from a mixture of editions and variant states of the different Numbers of the first edition. Although a revised edition, it adds few new readings; its larger changes are, rather, deletions, some extensive: "--*How now, mooncalf!*" from Number III; "From My Elbow-Chair," "Flummery," "General Remark," "Notice," and "Card" from Number IV; "The Stranger in Pennsylvania" from Number X. Lesser deletions of a sentence or two -- often satiric remarks -- are made in, for instance, "Theatrics" in Number VI and "The Stranger at Home" in Number XII. Exactly who made the revisions is not known, but Bruce I. Granger and Martha Hartzog in the Twayne edition of *Salmagundi* argue persuasively for the hand of Washington Irving. A letter from Washington Irving to David Longworth, written from Washington, 16 December 1812, seems particularly revealing: "I expect to be home in about eight days, when I will attend to the second edition of Salmagundi." Presumably he was talking about this edition, even though the revised work is copyright in early 1814.

SALMAGUNDI; | OR, THE | *WHIM-WHAMS AND OPINIONS* | OF | LAUNCELOT LANGSTAFF, ESQ. | AND OTHERS. | [double rule] | In hoc est hoax, cum quiz et jokesez, | Et smokem, toastem, roastem folksez, | Fee, faw, fum. *Psalmanazar.* | With baked, and broiled, and stewed, and toasted, | And fried, and boiled, and smoked, and roasted, | We treat the town. | [double rule] | A NEW AND IMPROVED EDITION, WITH TABLES OF | CONTENTS AND A COPIOUS INDEX. | [stylized swelled rule] | VOLUME I. [II.] | [double rule] | NEW-YORK: | PUBLISHED BY DAVID LONGWORTH, | *At the Shakspeare-Gallery.* | [stylized swelled rule] | 1814.

One copy of Vol. II noted with period rather than comma after LONGWORTH in the imprint, but that is apparently the result of faulty printing. No resetting is involved.

(15.5 x 9.5 untrimmed): Vol. I. $[-]^2$, $1-4^6 5^2$, $B-I^6 K-U^6 W^6 X^2$. Not reckoned: four full-page illustrations. Vol. II. $[A]^2 B^4 C-I^6 K-U^6 X-Z^6 Aa-Bb^6 Cc^2$. Not reckoned: Two full-page illustrations.

Illustrations by Alexander Anderson:

Vol. I.

Facing p. 116: Engraving of Will Wizard, signed A. Anderson. Leaf not paged.

Facing p. 173: Engraving of Waltz Dance, signed A. Anderson. Leaf not paged.

Facing p. 181: Woodcut, captioned Launcelot Langstaff, esq. [fancy] | FROM THE ORIGINAL DRAWING. Not signed by artist. Leaf paged 181 in upper left corner.

Facing p. 215: Engraving of Aunt Charity. Not signed by artist. Leaf paged 215 in upper left corner.

Vol. II.

Facing p. 463: Woodcut of The Little man in black, signed A. Leaf paged 463 in upper left corner.

Facing p. 512: Engraving of Malvolio Dubster. Not signed by artist. Leaf not paged.

In addition to the inserted full-page illustrations, there are many printer's ornaments and decorations printed in blank spaces in the text of Vol. I. Vol. II contains only one such printed ornament, on p. 319.

Vol. I. [1]-[2], title, on verso copyright ("twenty first day of January in the thirty eighth year of the Independence" by David Longworth) and printer; [3]-4, table of contents; [iii]-xi, Index; [xii]-liii, "Contents"; [liv], blank; [9]-250, text; [251]-252, "Note, by the Publisher." P. 238 is blank. Vol. II. [253]-[254], title, on verso printer only; [255]-256, table of contents; [261]-304, 307-550, text. P. 353 is mispaged 253. P. 320 is blank. The missing page numbers 305-306 are simply a mistake in pagination.

In Vol. I, the "Contents" section is a summary of each Number in the two vols.

In Vol. II, the heading of Number XI follows accurately the form of the heading of the original Numbers. In Vol. I, the heading of Number I gives the title and comic quotation but does not follow the original form in the Number and date identification. The other Numbers are headed only by numeral and date in upper case.

In the text and in the "Contents" summaries, Arabic numerals are used for the Numbers. In the table of contents, Roman numerals are used.

Printer: N. Van Riper, 194 Greenwich, corner Vesey-st.

Lineation: Vol. I. p. 100, LETTER ... in ; p. 200, they ... par- Vol. II. p. 300, THE ... as ; p. 400, ceremony, ... false.

Binding in two forms, no sequence apparent:

[A]. Drab paper boards. On front, title within decorative border of printer's emblems. On back, table of contents for Vol. I [II] within border of wavy lines. Spine decorated with emblems, titled SALMAGUNDI | VOL. I. [II.]. White endpapers. Flyleaf at front and back of Vol. I, at back only of Vol. II.

[B]. Blue-gray unprinted paper boards with white paper shelfback.

The title page was deposited for copyright 20 January 1814, despite the printed copyright notice for 21 January.

Cty (2), ICN, NN, TxU.

3A.   The third American edition, published in 1820 by David Longworth's son, Thomas Longworth, is for the most part simply a reprint of the text of the second American edition and even retains the 1814 copyright. It corrects a few errors and makes a few minor changes -- such as restoring the full name of Linkum Fidelius where the 1814 edition had shortened it to Linkum -- but shows no signs of authorial revision. By this time, the authors were busy at other concerns, and Washington Irving was beginning to call the work, as he did to Henry Brevoort in 1819, "a juvenile production," "full of errors, puerilities & impertinences." How seriously Irving's condemnation should be taken is open to question (some four years later he is busy revising the work for a Paris edition, and in 1819-1820 he was in England where revision would have been inconvenient, particularly when he was involved with *The Sketch Book* and a new edition of *A History of New York*), but at least it is sure that he made no revisions for this new edition.

SALMAGUNDI; [hollow letters] | OR, THE | *WHIM-WHAMS AND OPINIONS* | OF | LAUNCELOT LANGSTAFF, ESQ. | AND OTHERS. | [rule] | In hoc est hoax, cum quiz et jokesez, | Et smokem, toastem, roastem folksez, | Fee, faw, fum. *Psalmanazar.* | With baked, and broiled, and stewed, and toasted; | And fried, and boiled, and smoked, and roasted, | We treat the town. | [rule] | *THIRD EDITION.* | [stylized swelled rule with three circles at center] | VOLUME I. [II.] | [stylized swelled rule with three circles at center] | *NEW-YORK:* | PUBLISHED BY THOMAS LONGWORTH AND CO. | [rule of 12 dots] | 1820. In Vol. II, added after publisher, on separate line: J. Seymour, Printer.

(14.7 x 9.2): Vol. I. [A]^6 B-I^6 K-U^6 X^6. Last leaf blank. Not reckoned: four illustrations. Vol. II. [A]^6 B-I^6 K-U^6 X-Z^6 2A^6. Not reckoned: two illustrations.

Illustrations by Alexander Anderson:

Vol. I

Before title: Woodcut, captioned LAUNCELOT LANGSTAFF, Esq. | FROM THE ORIGINAL DRAWING. Not signed by artist. Leaf not paged.

Facing p. 112: Engraving of Will Wizard, signed A. Anderson. Leaf paged 112 in upper right corner.

Facing p. 169: Engraving of Waltz Dance, signed A. Anderson. Leaf paged 169 in upper left corner.

Facing p. 211: Engraving of Aunt Charity. Not signed by artist. Leaf not paged.

Vol. II.

Before title: Woodcut of The Little Man in Black, signed A. Leaf not paged.

Facing p. 503: Engraving of Malvolio Dubster. Not signed by artist. Leaf paged 503. The illustration is designed to be viewed with the book turned horizontally. When so viewed, the page number appears in the illustration's upper left corner. When the book is held in the conventional position, the page number is in the lower left corner, running vertically.

Vol. I. [1]-[2], title, on verso copyright ("the twenty-first day of January, in the thirty-eighth year of the Independence" by David Longworth) and printer; [3]-4, table of contents; [5]-246, text; [247]-249, "Note by the Publisher"; [250], blank. Vol. II. [253]-[254], title, verso blank; [255]-256, table of contents; [257]-540, text.

Printer: J. Seymour, 49 John-street.

Lineation: Vol. I. p. 100, they ... were ; p. 200, manifestly ... wrong, Vol. II. p. 300, CHAPTER II. ... single ; p. 400, table. ... about

Drab paper boards. Sides blank. On spines, only the volume number: 1 [2]. In Vol. I, there is a fly-leaf only at the front; the integral blank leaf at the end serves the same purpose. In Vol. II, there are fly-leaves at the front and the back.

Also issued in what is presumably a remainder binding, probably some years after original issue. 2 vols. in 1. Tan T cloth. Sides blank. Paper label on spine: SALMAGUNDI | [rule] | TWO VOLS. IN ONE. All within border of small o's. All printing in brown. Red-brown endpapers. Fly-leaves. The blank leaf at the end of the original Vol. I is preserved. In this issue, only the two preliminary illustrations, before the two title pages, are retained.

DLC, NNC, TxU (2), Private hands (2).

4A.   In 1834, James K. Paulding wrote Irving, proposing a new edition of *Salmagundi* and agreeing to use, for the joint effort, Irving's Paris revision of 1824. Paulding's son William says that Irving agreed but added that he was "disinclined to any additions or modifications that may appear to give it the sanction of our present taste, judgment and opinions" (*Literary Life of James Kirk Paulding,* pp. 40-41). If Irving made no revisions for the new edition, Paulding certainly did. Perhaps that is understandable, since the edition was a part of his own *Works.* He used Irving's Galignani text of 1824, as promised, but he replaced the Mustapha letter in Number XI with one of his own, replaced the essay "On Greatness" in Number XV with one of his on a man who married four times, added seven paragraphs following Malvolio Dubster's letter in Number XIX, and deleted scattered political references. In his Preface, Paulding -- modeling his remarks on the Publisher's Notice of Irving's Paris edition -- implies that all the authors agreed on the new revisions: "The present edition has been submitted to the revision of the authors, who at first contemplated making essential alterations. On further consideration, however, they have contented themselves with correcting or expunging a few of what they deemed the most glaring errors and flippancies..." In the narrowest sense, I suppose, that is correct, at least in regard to Washington Irving. But the fact is that Irving made no *new* revisions for this edition. The edition is of interest, since it represents a revision by one of the original authors, but it is not the work of Washington Irving.

SALMAGUNDI; | OR, THE | WHIM-WHAMS AND OPINIONS | OF | LAUNCELOT LANGSTAFF, ESQ. | AND OTHERS. | In hoc est hoax, cum quiz et jokesez. | Et smokem, toastem, roastem folksez, | Fee, faw, fum. PSALMANAZAR. | With baked, and broil'd, and stew'd, and toasted, | And fried, and boil'd, and smoked, and roasted, | We treat the town. | FIRST SERIES. | IN TWO VOLUMES. | VOL. I. [II.] | A NEW EDITION, CORRECTED BY THE AUTHORS. [in Vol. II, the article A is omitted] | NEW-YORK: | HARPER & BROTHERS -- 82 CLIFF-STREET. | [rule] | 1835.

These are the first two volumes of a four-volume set of James K. Paulding's works.

(18.7 x 11.5): Vol. I. [-]^4 [A]^6 B-I^{12}. Vol. II. [1]^6 2-22^6. Also signed (but not bound) [A]^{12} B-I^{12} K-L^{12}. The last leaf is a blank.

Vol. I. [i]-[ii], title, on verso copyright (1835); [1]-2, "Publishers' Advertisement"; [3]-[4], table of contents; [5]-[6], Preface, dated New-York, April, 1835, verso blank; [13]-215, text; [216], blank. Vol. II. [i]-[ii], title, verso blank (but see description below of variant state); [iii]-iv, table of contents; [5]-262, text.

Lineation: Vol. I. p. 100, loop-hole ... these ; p. 200, And, ... stock, Vol. II. p. 100, varieties ... me,; p. 200, to ... their

In two states, probably representing two impressions:

State A.

> Vol. I. Sheets bulk 1.6 cm.

> Vol. II. Sheets bulk 1.8 cm. No copyright notice on verso of title page.

State B.

> Vol. I. Sheets bulk 1.3 cm.

> Vol. II. Sheets bulk 1.5 cm. Copyright notice on verso of title page.

Noted in brown cloth embossed with overall flower design. Sides blank. Spines titled in gilt: at head, PAULDING'S [in curved line] | WORKS. | I [II]; at foot, SALMAGUNDI | FIRST SERIES | VOL 1 [2]. Vols. III, IV of Paulding's Works noted in same cloth in blue; were some copies of Vols. I, II also bound in blue?

Knickerbocker, February 1835, "forthcoming"; July 1835, the two vols. reviewed. *New-York Mirror*, 20 June 1835, "will shortly appear." Vol. I deposited 24 June 1835; Vol. II, apparently after publication, 11 September 1835.

DLC, TxU.

5Aa. SALMAGUNDI; | OR, THE | WHIM-WHAMS AND OPINIONS | OF |
      LAUNCELOT LANGSTAFF, ESQ., | AND OTHERS. | [rule] | [6-line
      comic quotation] | [rule] | NEW YORK: | G. P. PUTNAM & CO., 321
      BROADWAY. | [rule] | 1857.

"Putnam's Railway Classics" series.

(16.5 x 10.7): [i]-x, 7-243 [244]. Reckoned in pagination: preliminary title
with the original drawing of Launcelot Langstaff, Esq., and illustration of The
Little Man in Black, identified as *"Engraved by* ANDERSON, *from the
original Drawing."*

The text is derived from the unrevised British editions, which in turn were
derived from the American edition of 1820. The Introduction is attributed to
proof sheets of the article on Irving in "Allibone's forthcoming '*Critical
Dictionary of Authors.'*"

Printer: R. Craighead, Caxton Building, 81, 83, and 85 Centre Street.

Lineation: p. 100, justice ... companion ; p. 200, rusty, ... and

Issued in paper boards and in cloth:

Light green paper boards. On front, cover-title and identification of this as
"PUTNAM'S RAILWAY CLASSICS.   Price 50 cents."   On back,
advertisements for Putnam editions of Irving, including *Life of Washington* in
4 vols. 12mo., 4 vols. 8vo., and illustrated in numbers (14 nos. to each vol.).

Purple V cloth. On sides, in blind, Putnam's | Railway | Classics within oval.
Spine titled in gilt: Salmagundi [in curved line] with small decoration below.
Manila endpapers with Putnam advertisements imprinted.

Purple V cloth. Same design. Buff endpapers with no advertisements
imprinted.

American Publishers' Circular, 2 May 1857, "Next week"; 9 May 1857, "Now
ready," "In cloth, 60 cents. In paper boards, 50 cents." Copy deposited 7 May
1857.

CtY, DLC (copyright copy), NjP, TxU (2).

  b. NEW YORK: | G. P. PUTNAM, 115 NASSAU-STREET. | 1859.

Green cloth embossed with fine round dots. Blind border on sides. Spine
titled in gilt.

MH.

1E.   In 1811, John Lambert, who had first introduced the British public to
       selections from *Salmagundi* in his *Travels Through Lower Canada and the
       United States of North America, in the Years 1806, 1807, and 1808,* 1810,
       brought out the first British edition of the full work, with notes and an
       appreciative introduction. Somewhat ironically, as Stanley T. Williams points
       out in the *Life,* this was the first printing of *Salmagundi* in conventional book
       form.

              Lambert says in his preface, "Just before my departure from the United
       States the essays were discontinued, and I had an opportunity of procuring a
       complete copy of the whole." That is probably accurate enough, for his text is
       derived from a mixture of later revised texts of the various Numbers, typical
       of the sort of collected volumes that were being sold by Longworth in 1808
       and after. In Number X, for instance, Lambert prints the revised versions of
       "Breaking Up of the Ice in the North-River" and "The Stranger in
       Pennsylvania," and in Number XII the revised version of "From the Mill of
       Pindar Cockloft, Esq." He also corrected misprints and misreadings that he
       detected in the particular text state of the Number that he was using.
       Lambert's edition, however, was a dead end in the history of the text except
       for the contents of his notes to the work; later British editions turned to the
       American edition of 1820 as the source of their texts.

SALMAGUNDI; | OR, THE | WHIM-WHAMS AND OPINIONS | OF |
LAUNCELOT LANGSTAFF, ESQ. | AND OTHERS. | [double rule] | In
hoc est hoax, cum quiz et jokesez, | Et smokem, toastem, roastem folksez, |
Fee, faw, fum. *Psalmanazar.* | With baked, and broiled, and stewed, and
toasted, | And fried, and boiled, and smoaked, and roasted, | We treat the
town. | [double rule] | REPRINTED FROM THE AMERICAN EDITION,
| WITH | AN INTRODUCTORY ESSAY | *And Explanatory Notes,* | BY
JOHN LAMBERT. | [swelled rule] | VOL. I. [II.] | [swelled rule] |
LONDON: | PRINTED FOR J. M. RICHARDSON, 23, CORNHILL, |
OPPOSITE THE ROYAL EXCHANGE. | [wavy rule] | 1811.

(16.1 x 12.4): Vol. I. [-]^2 a-d^6 e^3 B-I^6 K-T^6. Presumably Sig. e, at the end of
the Introductory Essay, was originally a gathering of 4, with the last leaf
excised. The leaves are signed e, e2, e3. The copy in boards examined is too
fragile and too tightly bound for certainty. Vol. II. [A]^2 B-I^6 K-U^6 X^1.

Vol. I. [a]-[b], title, on verso printer; [c]-[d], table of contents; [i]-iv, Preface
by John Lambert, dated London, April 8th, 1811; [v]-liv, Introductory Essay;
[1]-211, text, printer at foot of last page; [212], blank. Vol. II. [i]-[ii], title, on
verso printer; [iii]-[iv], table of contents; [1]-230, text, printer at foot of last
page.

In Vol. II, p. 110, the page number uses a Roman number I for the second number 1.

Printer: Galabin and Marchant, Ingram-court, London.

Lineation: Vol. I. p. 100, the ... whim ; p. 200, music ... bundles Vol. II. p. 100, affection ... mar-; p. 200, MR. ... It

Noted in three bindings:

A.   In two vols. Blue-gray paper boards with drab-tan paper shelfback. Sides blank. On spines, white paper labels: [rule of small ovals] | SALMAGUNDI; | OR, THE | *WHIM-WHAMS* | AND | *OPINIONS* | OF | *Launcelot Langstaff.* [in Vol. II, spelled *Lanncelot*] | [rule] | VOL. I. [II.] | [rule of small ovals]. White endpapers.

B.   In two vols. Red A cloth. Sides decorated in blind with border of three rules, ornaments within corners, and semi-rectangular design at center. Spine titled in gilt: WHIM WHAMS | & OPINIONS | [rule] | *Price 6/6*. Yellow endpapers. Leaf size slightly taller and narrower: 16.5 x 10.2.

C.   Two vols. in one. Red V cloth. Sides decorated in blind. Spine titled in gilt: WHIM WHAMS | & OPINIONS | [rule] | *Price 6/6* . In decorated box. The style of binding suggests a later date of issue.

Critical Review, July 1811, reviewed. *Monthly Review,* August 1811, reviewed.

2 vols in boards: CtY. 2 vols in cloth, and 1 vol. in cloth boxed: *BL.*

A Note on Later British Editions

From 1823 through 1855, *Salmagundi* was published regularly by a number of different British publishers. At first, Irving expressed annoyance at this reprinting; in response, he revised the text for Galignani in Paris in 1824 and that same year planned a revised edition for John Murray that was never published. But the reprinting continued at a good pace. The text commonly used by the various publishers, however, was not that of Lambert's edition of 1811, but -- following the lead of Richard Griffin's Glasgow edition of 1823 -- that of the American edition of 1820, often with informative notes derived from Lambert.

The one exception, and the one edition providing a text of possible significance, was the curious one published by Thomas Tegg in 1824, described as "Corrected and Revised by the Author." In December of 1823, Tegg had brought out a routine edition, dated 1824 on the title page and derived ultimately from the American edition of 1820. In August of 1824, he brought out another edition of the same text, a line-for-line resetting. Irving saw this edition in the press, near its day of publication, and described the sight amusingly in his Journal for 7 August 1824: "After breakfast, go down to Mr. Davidsons (sic). Find a man there whom I suspect to be Tegg -- who was busy with Davidson about a book which I see to be Salmagundi -- Takes up the book in confusion [.]" Then in early October, only two months later, Tegg published a third edition dated 1824, "Corrected and Revised by the Author." This new edition takes the "Publisher's Notice" from the Galignani Paris edition (with an added brief paragraph on *Tales of a Traveller*) but only a very few of the textual changes. In the untitled opening of Number I, for instance, the first two sentences of the next-to-last paragraph ("We beg the public particularly to understand, that we solicit no patronage. We are determined, on the contrary, that the patronage shall be entirely on our side.") are moved to the third paragraph of "From the Elbow-Chair of Launcelot Langstaff," as they are in the Galignani text. But, on the other hand, the third sentence ("We have nothing to do with the pecuniary concerns of the paper ....") is retained, as it is not in the Galignani edition. In fact, most of the changes in the Galignani text do not appear here. The attacks on Thomas Moore in "To the Ladies" in Number V, for instance, are retained. If Tegg had simply reprinted the Paris text, that would be understandable enough. But why would he take the "Publisher's Notice" and a small handful of the changes, ignoring the others? To identify those few changes that he accepted would in fact have required collation of the two texts and then a deliberate choice -- and that by a busy publisher of inexpensive editions.

One hypothesis is very tempting: Irving, catching Tegg at reprinting the work again, but too late to stop publication, furnished him with the preface and a few of the textual changes that Irving remembered from his recent revision. That, from Irving's point of view, would at least improve matters a little. And Tegg might have been willing to pay for the right to advertise another edition as "Corrected and Revised by the Author" -- a payment that Irving would not have discussed publicly. We will probably never know how the text of this curious edition did come into being, but it is difficult to find another satisfying explanation.

2E. SALMAGUNDI: | OR, THE | Whim-Whams and Opinions [fancy] | OF | *LAUNCELOT LANGSTAFF, ESQ.* | AND OTHERS. | [swelled rule] | [six-line comic quotation] | [swelled rule] | Glasgow : [fancy] | PRINTED FOR RICHARD GRIFFIN & CO. | E. West & Co., Edinburgh; W. Scott, D. Weir, and | J. Hislop, Greenock; M. Currie, Port Glasgow; | T. Dick, and G. Cuthbertson, Paisley; | J. Dick, Ayr; H. Crawford, Kilmarnock; and | T. Tegg, London. | [rule] | 1823. | [*Reprinted from the latest American Edition.*]

(14.5 x 8.5 untrimmed): [i]-[iv], [1]-369 [370]. Signed in 8's.

Lineation: p. 100, for ... would ; p. 200, a ... not

Tan paper boards. On front, cover-title within ornamental border. On back, advertisement for *Literary Coronal* for 1823. Spine titled in black:

Salmagundi [fancy] | BY WASHINGTON | IRVING, ESQ. White endpapers.

NN.

3E.   SALMAGUNDI: | OR, | The Whim-Whams and Opinions [fancy] | OF | LAUNCELOT LANGSTAFF, ESQ. | AND OTHERS. | BY THE | AUTHOR OF KNICKERBOCKER'S HISTORY OF NEW YORK, SKETCH | BOOK, AND BRACEBRIDGE HALL. | [rule] | [six-line comic quotation] | [rule] | LONDON: | PRINTED BY T. DAVISON, WHITEFRIARS; | FOR THOMAS TEGG, CHEAPSIDE; AND RODWELL AND MARTIN, | BOND-STREET: ALSO R. GRIFFIN AND CO. GLASGOW. | [rule] | 1824.

(18.8 x 11.8): [i]-viii, [l]-389 [390]. Signed in 8's.

The "Prefatory Notice" is dated London, November, 1823.

Printer: Thomas Davison, Whitefriars.

Lineation: p. 100, manufactory ... on ; p. 200, youth, ... contemplate

Literary Chronicle and Weekly Review, 13 December 1823, reviewed, listed, advertised: "This day is published ... uniform with the Author's other works, price 7s 6d boards."

TxU (2), ViU.

4E.   SALMAGUNDI: | OR, | The Whim-Whams and Opinions [fancy] | OF | LAUNCELOT LANGSTAFF, ESQ. | AND OTHERS. | BY THE | AUTHOR OF KNICKERBOCKER'S HISTORY OF NEW YORK, | SKETCH BOOK, AND BRACEBRIDGE HALL. | [rule] | [six-line comic quotation] | [rule] | NEW EDITION. | LONDON: | PRINTED BY T. DAVISON, WHITEFRIARS; | FOR THOMAS TEGG, 73, CHEAPSIDE; RODWELL AND MARTIN, | BOND-STREET: ALSO R. GRIFFIN AND CO. GLASGOW. | [rule] | 1824.

A new edition, generally a line-for-line resetting, of Tegg's earlier edition. But on p. 12, lines 14-15 are divided *Flam;* | (*English* [rather than (*En- / glish*].

(19.2 x 11.9): [i]-viii, [1]-389 [390]. Signed in 8's.

Lineation: p. 100, manufactory ... on ; p. 200, youth, ... contemplate

Literary Gazette, 7 August 1824, mentioned in "Sights of Books," apparently as new.

CtY, MH, TxU, ViU.

5E.   SALMAGUNDI: | OR, | The Whim-Whams and Opinions [fancy] | OF |
        LAUNCELOT LANGSTAFF, ESQ. | AND OTHERS. | BY | THE
        AUTHOR OF KNICKERBOCKER'S HISTORY OF NEW YORK, |
        SKETCH BOOK, | BRACEBRIDGE HALL, TALES OF A |
        TRAVELLER, &c. | [rule] | [six-line comic quotation] | [rule] | NEW
        EDITION, | CORRECTED AND REVISED BY THE AUTHOR. |
        LONDON: | PRINTED BY T. DAVISON, WHITEFRIARS; | FOR
        THOMAS TEGG, 73, CHEAPSIDE; RODWELL AND MARTIN, |
        BOND-STREET: ALSO R. GRIFFIN AND CO. GLASGOW. | [rule] |
        1824.

        Revised by Irving? See the discussion in the prefatory remarks to these later
        British editions.   The "Publisher's Notice" is that written by Irving for
        Galignani's Paris edition of 1824. A few of the revisions made by Irving for
        the Paris edition also appear here.

        (19.9 x 12.4 untrimmed): [i]-viii, [1]-391 [392]. Signed in 8's.

        Printer: Thomas Davison, Whitefriars.

        Lineation: p. 100, them, ... were ; p. 200, boxes, ... of

        Drab tan paper boards. Sides blank. Paper label on spine.

        Literary Gazette, 9 October 1824, advertised under "Books Published This
        Day": "Price 7s. 6d. in extra bds." "A new Edition, corrected and revised by
        the Author."

        CtY.

6Ea.   SALMAGUNDI: | OR, THE | WHIM-WHAMS AND OPINIONS | OF |
        LAUNCELOT LANGSTAFF, ESQ. | AND OTHERS. | [double rule] | [six-
        line comic quotation] | [double rule] | London: [fancy] | PRINTED AND
        PUBLISHED BY J. LIMBIRD, 143, STRAND, | *(Near Somerset House.)* |
        [rule] | 1824. All within double frame lines.

        (20.8 x 13.3): [i]-viii, [1]-144. Not reckoned: engraved portrait of Irving
        before title. In double columns. Signed in 8's.

        Lineation: p. 50, increase ... of ; p. 100, universally ... outrage

        DLC.

   b.   LONDON: | PRINTED AND PUBLISHED BY J. LIMBIRD, 143,
        STRAND. | (Near Somerset House.) | [rule] | 1833.

        CtY.

7E.   SALMAGUNDI: | OR, THE | WHIM-WHAMS AND OPINIONS | OF |
       LAUNCELOT LANGSTAFF, ESQ. | AND OTHERS. | BY | THE
       AUTHOR OF KNICKERBOCKER'S HISTORY OF NEW YORK, |
       SKETCH BOOK, AND BRACEBRIDGE HALL. | [rule] | [six-line comic
       quotation] | [rule] | NEW EDITION. | LONDON: | WILLIAM
       CHARLTON WRIGHT, | 65, PATERNOSTER-ROW. | [rule] | 1825.

       The Publisher's preliminary "Note" is dated 1st January, 1825.

       (15.3 x 9.6): [i]-vii [viii], [1]-285 [286]. Not reckoned: preliminary engraved
       title with illustration by H. Corbould. Signed in 6's.

       Printer: T. White, Johnson's Court, Fleet Street.

       Lineation: p. 100, but ... keep ; p. 200, south. ... bench,

       Paper boards. On front, cover-title with designation of this as THIRD
       EDITION; series identification: "Charlton Wright's Cabinet Edition." On
       back, advertisements for Goldsmith's *History of the Earth*, and *The Literary
       Magnet*. Spine missing in copy examined.

       BL.

8E.   SALMAGUNDI: | OR, | THE WHIM-WHAMS AND OPINIONS | OF |
       LAUNCELOT LANGSTAFF, ESQ. | AND OTHERS. | BY
       WASHINGTON IRVING, ESQ. | AUTHOR OF KNICKERBOCKER'S
       HISTORY OF NEW YORK, | SKETCH BOOK, | AND BRACEBRIDGE
       HALL. | [rule] | [six-line comic quotation] | [rule] | LONDON: | JOHN
       BUMPUS, 85, NEWGATE STREET. | [rule] | 1825.

       The "Prefatory Notice," dated London, November, 1823, is taken from one of
       the Tegg unrevised editions of 1824.

       (15.1 x 9.5 untrimmed): [a]-[b], [i]-[vi], [1]-315 [316]. Not reckoned:
       engraved illustration of The Little Man in Black by Heath, with publisher's
       identification of John Bumpus, 1825. Signed in 6's.

       Printer: J. Starke.

       Lineation: p. 100, *Notes*, ... conclu-; p. 200, ancients ... of

       Drab gray boards. Sides blank. Paper label on spine (with price at foot of
       label, 3s. 6d.).

       CtY.

9Ea. SALMAGUNDI; | OR, | THE WHIM-WHAMS AND OPINIONS | OF | Launcelot Langstaff. | [fancy] | BY WASHINGTON IRVING, | AUTHOR OF "THE SKETCH BOOK," "KNICKERBOCKER'S HISTORY OF NEW YORK," | "THE PRAIRIES," & C. | A NEW EDITION, ABRIDGED. | [engraving, titled The Little Man in Black.] | GLASGOW: | PUBLISHED BY RICHARD GRIFFIN & CO. | [rule] | MDCCCXXXVI.

Contains selections from 19 Numbers.

(17.6 x 10.9): [1]-72. Signed in 6's. The title page (with table of contents on verso) and pp. 11-12 [that is, the outer leaves of the first gathering] are on a parchment type of heavier paper; the engraving is clear and sharp, but the printing is weak and gray.

Printer: George Brookman, Glasgow.

Lineation: p. 50, The ... *hay*."

BL.

b. FIVE HUNDRED | CURIOUS AND INTERESTING | NARRATIVES AND ANECDOTES. | COMPRISING | THE WONDERFUL BOOK, THE ANECDOTE BOOK, | SAILORS' YARNS, SALMAGUNDI, | AND THE | DOMESTIC MANNERS OF THE AMERICANS. | [rule] | Embellished with numerous Engravings. [fancy] | [cut of city scene] | GLASGOW: | PUBLISHED BY RICHARD GRIFFIN AND CO | [rule] | 1838.

(18.4 x 10.7): [a]-[b], [1]-72, [1]-72, [1]-60, [1]-72, [1]-60. Each work is paged separately; *Salmagundi* is the fourth work and is in the same setting as the Griffin edition of 1836. Preliminary fold-out set of illustrations. Signed in 6's.

NN.

c. [Glasgow: Richard Griffin, 1839.]

Not seen. Copies reported in DLC, ICU.

d. GLASGOW: | PUBLISHED BY RICHARD GRIFFIN AND CO. | [rule] | MDCCCXLIV.

NN.

e. THE | POPULAR LIBRARY: | A MISCELLANY | OF | AMUSEMENT AND INSTRUCTION. | [rule] | Embellished with Numerous Engravings. [fancy] | [rule] | [engraved illustration] | LONDON: | PUBLISHED BY JOHN J. GRIFFIN & COMPANY. | 53 BAKER-STREET, PORTMAN SQUARE; | AND RICHARD GRIFFIN & CO., GLASGOW.

One of the selections in the volume is dated 1850.

(16.0 x 11.1): The volume contains various selections, paged separately. *Salmagundi* is in the same setting as the Griffin edition of 1836 and has its own sub-title: SALMAGUNDI; | OR, | THE WHIM-WHAMS AND OPINIONS | OF | Launcelot Langstaff. [fancy] | [engraving, titled The Little Man in Black.] | BY WASHINGTON IRVING, | AUTHOR OF THE SKETCH BOOK.

Brown cloth impressed to resemble crushed morocco. On sides, decorations in blind. On spine, volume title in gilt.

BL.

10E.   SALMAGUNDI: | OR, | THE WHIM-WHAMS AND OPINIONS | OF | LAUNCELOT LANGSTAFF, ESQ. | AND OTHERS. | [rule] | BY THE AUTHOR OF | "KNICKERBOCKER'S HISTORY OF NEW YORK," "SKETCH BOOK, | "BRACEBRIDGE HALL," "TALES OF A TRAVELLER," &c. | [engraving by Cruikshank of Cockloft Hall in what is clearly a London street scene] | NEW EDITION, | CORRECTED AND REVISED BY THE AUTHOR. | [rule] | LONDON: | PRINTED FOR THOMAS TEGG, 73, CHEAPSIDE; | TEGG AND CO., DUBLIN; R. GRIFFIN AND CO., GLASGOW; | ALSO, J. AND S.A. TEGG, SYDNEY AND HOBART TOWN. | [rule] | MDCCCXXXIX.

Title page in two states:

    A.   Line 9, no quotation mark after BOOK,

    B.   Line 9, quotation mark present

The preliminary "Publisher's Notice" and the text are reprinted from the Tegg edition of 1824, "Corrected and Revised by the Author."

(15.4 x 10.1): [i]-x, [1]-378. Not reckoned: one leaf of advertisements at end. Cruikshank illustrations in blank spaces in the text. Signed in 8's.

Printer: Balne Brothers, Gracechurch Street, London.

Lineation: p. 100, was ... there ; p. 200, great ... cele-

Red A cloth. On sides, in blind, intertwined decorative design within ruled border. Spine decorated in blind, titled in gilt simply SALMAGUNDI . Cream endpapers.

TxU (2).

11Ea. SALMAGUNDI; | OR THE | Whim-Whams and Opinions [fancy] | OF | LAUNCELOT LANGSTAFF, ESQ. | AND OTHERS. | BY THE | AUTHOR OF "KNICKERBOCKER'S HISTORY OF NEW | YORK," "SKETCH BOOK," AND | "BRACEBRIDGE HALL." | [rule] | [six-line comic quotation] | [rule] | LONDON: | PUBLISHED BY C. DALY, RED LION SQUARE. | 1841.

(11.9 x 7.6): [i]-xii, [1]-363 [364]. Not reckoned: preliminary engraved title page with "View in the Lake of Llangollen," and anonymous engravings through the text; eight pages of advertisements at end.

Printer: C. Daly, Red Lion Square.

Lineation: p. 100, mortal ... ago.; p. 200, CHAPTER V. ... in

Dark green cloth. Sides decorated in blind. Spine titled in gilt.

DLC, TxU.

b. LONDON: | PUBLISHED BY C. DALY, | 17, GREVILLE STREET, HATTON GARDEN. | 1845.

Green H-like cloth (embossed with small diamonds). Sides decorated in blind. Spine titled and decorated in heavy gilt that almost covers the area. AEG.

CtY.

12Ea. SALMAGUNDI; | OR, | THE WHIM-WHAMS AND OPINIONS | OF | LAUNCELOT LANGSTAFF, ESQ. | And Others. [fancy] | BY | WASHINGTON IRVING. | [rule] | [six-line comic quotation] | [rule] | LONDON: | GEORGE ROUTLEDGE & CO. SOHO SQUARE. | 1850.

"Popular Library" series.

The preface is the same as that in the Daly edition of 1841.

(16.0 x 10.0): [i]-v [vi]-[viii], [1]-232. Not reckoned: one page of preliminary advertisements. Signed in 8's.

Lineation: p. 100, For, ... way;; p. 200, This ... wilt

Other volumes in the series noted in boards printed in colors, or in brown AR cloth, sides decorated in blind with series name at center, spine titled in gilt.

Also issued in the Popular Library series bound with *A History of New York*. The volume has a common title page but no individual titles:

KNICKERBOCKER'S | HISTORY OF NEW YORK: | AND | SALMAGUNDI. | [rule] | BY WASHINGTON IRVING. | [rule] | LONDON: | GEORGE ROUTLEDGE & CO. SOHO SQUARE. | 1850.

Royal blue L cloth.   On sides, in blind, elaborate border and decoration;
POPULAR LIBRARY in circle at center.   Spine decorated in blind, titled in
gilt: WASHINGTON | IRVING'S | WORKS. | KNICKERBOCKER'S |
NEW YORK. | AND SALMAGUNDI | ROUTLEDGE [in blind].   Yellow
endpapers.

Individual form: *Athenæum*, 8 June 1850, listed, 1*s*. bds.

Individual form: *BL*. Works form: CtW.

b.   [Individual form].   LONDON: | GEORGE ROUTLEDGE & CO.
FARRINGDON STREET. | 1855.

Michael Sadleir in *XIX Century Fiction* describes the binding as yellow
pictorial boards; cover drawing by Crowquill.

NjP.

13Ea.   SALMAGUNDI; | OR, | THE WHIM-WHAMS AND OPINIONS | OF |
LAUNCELOT LANGSTAFF, ESQ., | AND OTHERS. | BY |
WASHINGTON IRVING. | [rule] | [six-line comic quotation] | rule] |
LONDON: | HENRY G. BOHN, YORK STREET, COVENT GARDEN. |
[rule] | 1850.

The Preface is the same as that in the Routledge edition of 1850 and the Daly
edition of 1841.

(18.1 x 11.4): [i]-vi, [1]-269 [270].   Signed in 8's.

Issued individually as "Bohn's Shilling Series"; bound with *A History of New
York* as Vol. I of "Bohn's Library Edition."

Printer: George Woodfall and Son, Angel Court, Skinner Street.

Lineation: p. 100, skip ... she ; p. 200, would ... he

Seen only in "Bohn's Library Edition."   Gray T cloth.   Sides decorated in
blind.   Spine titled in gilt as Irving's Works, Vol. I, Bohn's Library Edition.
Endpapers white with advertisements in blue.   Portrait of Irving before title.
(No works title in volume.)

NN, TxU.

b.   [London: Henry G. Bohn, 1854.]

"Bohn's Library Edition." With a portrait of Irving.

Not seen. Copy reported in Staats- und Universitätsbibliothek Hamburg.

1Fa. On 8 February 1824, Irving wrote his friend Charles R. Leslie, "I am sorry to see that Salmagundi is published at London with all its faults upon its head. I have corrected a copy for Galignani, whom I found bent upon putting it to press...." His journal through January and into February is full of references to his correcting and revising. In particular, he enters on 12 February, "Write preface to Salmagundi," and on 26 February, "Receive proof of introduction to Salmagundi."

Although on 7 January he had asked John H. Payne for a copy of the 1811 London edition of *Salmagundi,* it would seem that in fact he used a copy of the American 1814 or 1820 edition for his text. The description of his revisions that he gives in his "Publishers' Notice" is accurate enough: "The present edition has been submitted to the revision of one of the authors, who, at first, contemplated making essential alterations. On further consideration, however, he contented himself with correcting merely a few of what he termed the most glaring errors and flippancies, and judged it best to leave the evident juvenility of the work to plead its own apology." He followed the 1814 text with all of its excisions, but further cut a number of remarks and phrases that seemed , seventeen years after their first composition, crude or cruel or no longer in keeping with his feelings: slurs on Thomas Jefferson, for instance, or lines harshly critical of Thomas Moore in "To the Ladies" in Number V. He also added a few explanatory notes: one on p. 59 of Vol. I, for instance, on Tripolitan prisoners taken by an American squadron and brought to New York; or one on p. 66 of Vol. I explaining the allusion to "the primitive habits of Mr. Jefferson" in dressing plainly and riding his horse alone, even when on state business in Washington.

SALMAGUNDI: | OR, THE | Whim-Whams and Opinions [fancy] | OF | LAUNCELOT LANGSTAFF, ESQ. | AND OTHERS. | [rule] | In hoc est hoax, cum quiz et jokesez, | Et smokem, toastem, roastem folksez, | Fee, faw, fum. *Psalmanazar.* | With baked, and broil'd, and stew'd, and toasted, | And fried, and boil'd, and smoked, and roasted, | We treat the town. | [rule] | IN TWO VOLUMES. | VOL. I. [II.] | [emblem: D in star within wreath with pendant medal] | PARIS: | PRINTED BY JULES DIDOT, SEN. | FOR | A. AND W. GALIGNANI, RUE VIVIENNE, N° 18. | [rule] | M DCCC XXIV.

(16.5 x 10.4): Vol. I. [-]^8 1-11^{12}. First two leaves missing in copies examined; series title? Last leaf missing in copies examined; advertisements? Vol. II. [-]^4 1-13^{12} 14^8. First leaf missing in copies examined; series title? Laid paper.

Vol. I. [i]-[ii], half-title, on verso printer; [iii]-[iv], title, verso blank; [v]-viii, Publisher's Notice; [ix]-xi, table of contents; [xii], blank; [1]-262, text. Vol. II. [i]-[ii], half-title, on verso printer; [iii]-[iv], title, verso blank; [v]-vi, table of contents; [1]-328, text.

Printer: Jules Didot, Senior, Printer to His Majesty.

Lineation: Vol. I. p. 100, LETTER ... mush-; p. 200, and ... like Vol. II. p. 100, assured, ... they ; p. 200, No. ... lapse

Bibliographie de la France, 20 March 1824, # 1501, listed with the Baudry impression.

OrP, ViU.

b. PARIS: | PRINTED BY JULES DIDOT, SEN. | FOR BAUDRY, RUE DU COQ, N° 9. | M DCCC XXIV.

Bibliographie de la France, 20 March 1824, # 1501, listed with the Galignani impression.

BL.

TRANSLATIONS

German

Eingemachtes | von | Washington Irving. | [rule] | Aus dem Englischen. | [ornament: flower urn on flat base] | [quintuple rule] | Frankfurt am Main, 1827. | Gedruckt und verlegt bei Johann David Sauerländer. [in fraktur]

"Washington Irving's sämmtliche Werke," Neunzehntes Bändchen. "Uebersetzt von Mehreren und herausgegeben von Christian August Fischer."

A translation of 13 selections from *Salmagundi*: "Das Vorwort," "Theater-Kritik," "Moden," "Ein Brief," "Der Ball," "Die Familie Cockloft," "Mein Oheim John," "Ballston," "Christopher Cockloft's Gesellschaft," "Miss Charity Cockloft," "Cockloft-Hall," "Die Bibliothek in Cockloft-Hall," "Die Chronik."

(14.7 x 10.5 untrimmed): [1]-108 [109]-[110]. Not reckoned: three leaves of terminal advertisements (the first is integral). Signed in 8's. Laid paper.

Lineation: p. 50, Forellenfischen ... ge-; p. 100, gemittelt ... wäre.

Tan paper wrapper. On front, series identification and volume title within ornamental border. On back, ornaments of two lions couchant with urn between, within same ornamental border. Spine blank.

TxU. Copy reported in Universitätsbibliothek Würzburg.

A HISTORY OF NEW YORK

Little is known in detail of Irving's composition of *A History of New York,* although fragments of manuscript have survived. It would appear that in early 1808 Washington and his brother Peter began gathering information and making notes for the burlesque in Book I. On 30 April 1808, Peter wrote Washington, presumably about the *History,* urging him to "whip your imagination into a gallop.... If you do not, I shall have to give the thing such a hasty finish as circumstances may permit, immediately on my return...." In effect, Peter had dropped out of the project. Between that time and October of 1809 when Washington went to Philadelphia to see the book through the press, he completed a first draft of the work, apparently doing all of the writing himself, although accepting occasional suggestions and small revisions from friends and family. Pierre M. Irving in the *Life and Letters* (I, 235-236) says that in Philadelphia Irving continued to revise and to add, as it is known he did in so many of his works: "Though the author had carried the manuscript in a complete state to Philadelphia, yet he afterwards made some additions, as was not unusual with him, as the work was going through the press. It was here that he wrote the voyage of Peter Stuyvesant up the Hudson, and the enumeration of the army." On 6 December 1809, St. Nicholas day and the day of the anniversary meetings of the New-York Historical Society, the *History* was published.

The first edition had been hastily and carelessly printed. In 1812, Irving revised the work extensively, not only correcting the errors but reworking the entire text. Stanley Williams and Tremaine McDowell in the preface to their edition of the *History,* 1927, note that about ten thousand words were cut and about the same number added, to leave the second edition approximately the same length as the first. Comparison reveals that Irving dropped some of the comic material, particularly the repetitive discussions of Knickerbocker's problems as a historian. But in the most significant revision, he added important new sections: the continuation of the Account of the Author at the beginning; the recounting of the voyage of exploration and Oloffe's dream in Book Two, Chapters Four and Five; the satiric story of the growth of political parties, under the guise of the history of the Long Pipes and the Short Pipes, in Book Four, Chapter Six. The last three Books, the Peter Stuyvesant section, were revised less heavily, although the first third of Chapter Six of Book Six was almost entirely rewritten.

In 1819, by now in England and busy with *The Sketch Book*, Irving revised the *History* again for a third edition to be published by Moses Thomas in Philadelphia. The revision was less extensive than he had made for the second edition, but nevertheless he still changed almost every chapter to one degree or another. Most of the revisions took the form of deletions: a word here, a sentence there, a short paragraph occasionally. The dedication to the New-York Historical Society was omitted. Irving also arranged personally in England for the illustrations by two friends, Charles R. Leslie, the English artist, and Washington Allston, the American. Once the drawings were engraved, Irving ordered two thousand copies for Thomas's use in the new edition and three hundred proof impressions suitable for framing.

In February of 1820, a favorable notice of the *History* in *Blackwood's Magazine* called the British public's attention to that earlier work by the author of *The Sketch Book*. Irving was beginning to make a reputation in Great Britain with *The Sketch Book,* not published in London until that same February but already becoming known through the appearance of selections in various British periodicals. The time was right for a British edition of the *History*, and others as well as Irving knew it. On 15 August 1820 he wrote to Walter Scott, "These Eulogiums will oblige me to publish an edition of the work in this country; Murray has repeatedly mentioned the thing; but I have always felt affraid of the work as being local, crude and juvenile. I find however that the notices in Blackwood have put one of the Booksellers in the American trade on the scent; and I shall, I fear, be obliged to publish in my own defence, to prevent a spurious & incorrect republication." On 30 September John Murray published the new edition, and on 26 October Irving wrote to him from Paris to thank him for hurrying it out "to prevent a spurious edition from being thrown into circulation."

The edition that so alarmed Irving was one by W. Wright of London that did appear in 1820. Its exact date of publication is yet to be determined --it may have been out before Murray's edition -- but whatever the sequence of the two, Murray's was the one that Irving approved and authorized. Its text was taken from Moses Thomas's Philadelphia edition of 1819, without revision by Irving. In fact, when Irving wrote Murray in October about the edition, he even added, "I should have liked to have made some corrections and alterations." His opportunity in a British edition did not come until the Author's Revised Edition, although he did "correct and alter" in a French edition for Galignani in 1824 and an American edition for Carey, Lea & Carey in 1829.

The revision for the Paris edition of 1824 was a relatively minor one. It was apparently based on one of the earlier London editions; Irving wrote Murray from Paris on 22 December 1823 asking for a copy of the *History.* (Since the Murray editions were, in turn, based on the American 1819 text, Irving was in effect giving the latest American edition a facelifting.) Little is known of Irving's work on the revision, beyond a comment in the Journal for 5 March 1824, "In morng. correct Knickerbocker."

Irving was not then to let that Paris text of 1824 stand for long. On 31 August 1828, he wrote Henry Carey in Philadelphia, "I send you a Parisian edition of Knickerbocker, with a few trifling corrections -- should you reprint that work I wish you to do it from this copy." The sentence is ambiguous: he may simply have been sending a copy of the Paris edition for which he had made "a few trifling corrections," or -- and the likelihood is greater of the second meaning -- he was sending the actual copy (now in the Franklin Institute in Philadelphia) from which the 1829 Philadelphia edition by Carey, Lea & Carey was in fact printed. That printer's copy, whether sent by Irving in August of 1828 or later, contained cancellations or revisions on thirty pages of Vol. I and twenty-eight pages of Vol. II. With it came also two pages of holograph manuscript now bound between pp. 270-271 of Vol. I.

With the Philadelphia edition of 1829, Irving's revising hand seems to have been withheld until his major revision for the Author's Revised Edition, published by George P. Putnam in 1848. For that, the first volume in the new collected works, Irving rewrote extensively and particularly reworked Books Five, Six and Seven, the section on Peter Stuyvesant. For copy-text, oddly enough, he used a Vol. I of the 1824 edition published in New York by C. S. Van Winkle, and a Vol. II of the 1824 edition published in Paris by A. and W. Galignani. He also added "The Author's Apology" at the beginning. But the new text was still not completed until Putnam's edition of 1849 in which appears on p. 122 a paragraph that had been printed in earlier editions but which was omitted from the manuscript for the 1848 edition. Smaller and larger corrections and attempts to regularize the text continued to appear in the plates until 1859, but they do not suggest the hand of the author.

1A.   A HISTORY | OF | NEW YORK, | FROM THE BEGINNING OF THE WORLD TO THE | END OF THE DUTCH DYNASTY. | CONTAINING | Among many Surprising and Curious Matters, the Unutterable Ponderings of WALTER THE DOUBTER, the Disastrous | Projects of WILLIAM THE TESTY, and the Chivalric | Achievments of PETER THE HEADSTRONG, the three | Dutch Governors of NEW AMSTERDAM; being the only | Authentic History of the Times that ever hath been, or ever | will be Published. | [double rule] | BY DIEDRICH KNICKERBOCKER. | [double rule] | De waarheid die in duister lag, | Die komt met klaarheid aan den dag. [quotation in fraktur] | [swelled rule] | IN TWO VOLUMES. | [swelled rule]| VOL. I. [II.] | [double rule] | PUBLISHED BY INSKEEP & BRADFORD, NEW YORK; | BRADFORD & INSKEEP, PHILADELPHIA; WM. M'IL- | HENNEY, BOSTON; COALE & THOMAS, BALTIMORE; | AND MORFORD, WILLINGTON, & CO. CHARLESTON. | [rule of 13 dots] | 1809.

(19.5 x 11.7 in boards, untrimmed): Vol. I. [a]^6 A-I^6 K-U^6 X-Z^6 Aa^2. The first leaf is a blank. Vol. II. In leather, [A]^1 B^4 C-I^6 K-U^6 X-Z^6. The last leaf is commonly excised. Copies in boards are too rare and too fragile for complete collation; presumably, the first signature is [A]^2, including a preliminary blank leaf, and the last blank leaf is not excised.

In Vol. I, an engraved fold-out view of New Amsterdam is inserted before the title. Most commonly, the view is inserted by its right edge (so, for instance, in the ViU copy in original boards). Also noted with lower edge trimmed to privide a stub and so bound.

Vol. I. [i]-[ii], blank; [iii]-[iv], title, on verso only the statement "Copy-right secured according to Law"; [v]-[vi], dedication to The New York Historical Society, verso blank; [vii]-xiv, "Account of the Author"; [xv]-xxiii, "To the Public" (with running head for "Preface"); [xxiv], blank; [1]-268, text. Vol. II. [i]-[ii], title, on verso same copyright notice; [1]-258, text.

Three deliberate textual changes, presumably representing stop-press corrections rather than separate impressions, appear in the volumes. For those three, the sequence would appear to be certain. Two other changes are more ambiguous in sequence: the presence or absence of a period at the end of a footnote may be a matter of accidental loss or of deliberate addition, or -- reasoning from the movement of the period when present -- a matter of displacement and loss with subsequent replacement; a missing letter (or in one noted instance letters) from the end of a line is surely the result of accidental loss during printing, although one is never entirely certain. Given these five changes, particularly when coupled with occasional slight type-shifts, it should be possible to define a chronological sequence among copies. But the varying combinations in the many copies examined are such that no clear sequence emerges. The three deliberate changes do suggest an order in the individual signatures in which they appear (Vol. I., sigs. I, X; Vol. II, Sig. B), but it is probable that the signatures were bound in random combinations. No copy has yet been examined in which the apparent first state of each of the signatures is present.

Vol.	Sig.	P. & Line	Variant	Remarks
I	B	7.12f	t present or missing in bucket	In one copy noted, both "e" and "t" missing.
I	E	39.ftnte	period or no period at end	In one copy noted, the period is raised well above the baseline. In only one copy noted is the period accurately placed.

I	I	89.10f	Weinant or Winant	The second and subsequent editions read "Winant."
I	X	238.7f	continue. | or continues |	"continues" is the correct reading.
II	B	3.11	John, Doe or John Doe	"John Doe" is the correct reading.

For those interested in pursuing the investigation further, movement of type resulting in "split" words occurs in some copies in the following lines: I, 48.1f; I, 157.10; I, 254.1; II, 6.9; II, 63.4. Obvious textual errors, uncorrected in all copies examined, occur in I, 207.12f ("rivier" for "river"); II, 31.13 (parenthesis before "eschew" rather than after); II, 239.2f ("ther" for "their").

Lineation: Vol. I. p. 100, of ... in ; p. 200, new ... Hoop. Vol. II. p. 100, and ... veracity,; p. 200, down ... uproar.

Slightly greenish blue laid paper boards with white paper shelfbacks. Sides blank. On spines, only the numbers 1 or 2; the numbers appear to have been printed but may have been added by hand. In Vol. I, a preliminary integral blank leaf, and a terminal flyleaf. In Vol. II, a preliminary and a terminal blank leaf, probably integral. More commonly seen in full calf, and apparently so issued.

The work was copyright 29 November 1809 in the District Court of Pennsylvania. In the copyright records it is described as two volumes, but the title page of Vol. I only was deposited. Somewhat puzzlingly, the work was copyright in the name of Charles Nicholas as proprietor. Nicholas was a Philadelphia publisher and a friend of Irving, but why Irving chose him as proprietor is not known.

New York *American Citizen* , 4 December 1809, "in the press"; 6 December 1809, "Is This Day Published." *New-York Evening Post,* 29 November 1809, "in the press"; 7 December 1809, "This Day Is Published" (The later advertisement-notice-spoof was, in fact, a day late).

CtY, DLC (3), KU, NN, TxGeoS, TxU (6), ViU.

2A.   A HISTORY | OF | NEW-YORK, | FROM THE BEGINNING OF THE WORLD | TO THE END OF THE | DUTCH DYNASTY. | CONTAINING | Among many Surprising and Curious Matters, the Unutterable | Ponderings of WALTER THE DOUBTER, the Disastrous Projects | of WILLIAM THE TESTY, and the chivalric achievements of | PETER THE HEADSTRONG, the three Dutch Governors of NEW- | AMSTERDAM; being the only Authentic History of the Times | that ever hath been published. | [elaborated swelled rule] | *The Second Edition with Alterations.* | [double rule] | De ... lag, | Die ... dag. [quotation in fraktur] | *IN TWO VOLUMES.* | VOL. I. [II.] | [elaborated swelled rule] | *NEW-YORK:* | PUBLISHED BY INSKEEP AND BRADFORD, AND | BRADFORD AND INSKEEP, PHILADELPHIA. | [rule] | 1812.

(17.2 x 10.3): Vol. I. [-]^2 1-24^6 25^2. Vol. II. [-]^2 1-20^6 21^4.

In Vol. I, inserted before the title, is an engraved view of "NEW AMSTERDAM (NOW NEW-YORK)" "Copied from an ancient Etching of the same size, Published by Justus Danckers at Amsterdam."

Vol. I. [a]-[b], title, on verso copyright ("the third day of June, in the thirty-sixth year of the Independence" by Inskeep and Bradford, New-York); [c]-[d], dedication to The New-York Historical Society, verso blank; [i]-xiv, "Account of the Author"; [xv]-xxii, "To the Public" (with running head for "Preface"); [1]-270, text. Vol. II [a]-[b], title, verso blank; [c]-[d], blank; [1]-248, text.

No evidence has been found to suggest more than one impression. A single noted variant, almost certainly a stop-press correction, appears in the running head of Vol. I, p. 95: the incorrect HISTORY OF is corrected to NEW-YORK. A number of errors remain uncorrected in all copies examined:

Vol.	*P. &Line*	
I	xvii.3f	with with
I	xix.16	jealousy (for jealously)
I	xxi.11-12	and / and
I	xxii.3-4	at / at
I	126.RH	NEW-YORK (rather than HISTORY OF)
II	31.5-6	of / of
II	106.RH	HISTORY FO
II	154.title	Book VI (rather than VII)
		Chapter VI (rather than I)

| II | 168.title | Chapter VII (rather than II) |
| II | 227 | mispaged 527 |

Lineation: Vol. I. p. 100, transparent ... the ; p. 200, what ... manner Vol. II. p. 100, men ... of ; p. 200, back ground ... empty

Some copies probably issued in paper boards, like the first edition, but no such copy located. Commonly noted in full calf, and probably so issued.

The Port Folio, July 1812, "The ingenious author of Diedrick Knickerbocker, is said to be preparing a new edition for the press ...."; October 1812, reviewed.

ArU, CtY, MB, MH, NN (2), TxGeoS, TxU.

3A.   A HISTORY | OF | NEW YORK, [hollow letters] | FROM THE | BEGINNING OF THE WORLD | TO THE | END OF THE DUTCH DYNASTY. | CONTAINING | AMONG MANY SURPRISING AND CURIOUS MATTERS, THE UNUTTER- | ABLE PONDERINGS OF WALTER THE DOUBTER, THE DISASTROUS | PROJECTS OF WILLIAM THE TESTY, AND THE CHIVALRIC | ACHIEVEMENTS OF PETER THE HEADSTRONG, THE THREE | DUTCH GOVERNORS OF NEW AMSTERDAM; BEING THE ONLY | AUTHENTIC HISTORY OF THE TIMES THAT EVER HATH BEEN | PUBLISHED. | THE THIRD EDITION. | BY DIEDRICH KNICKERBOCKER. | De ... lag, | Die ... dag. [quotation in fraktur] | IN TWO VOLUMES. -- VOL. I. [II.] | PHILADELPHIA: | PUBLISHED BY M. THOMAS. | J. MAXWELL, PRINTER. [in Vol. II: Wm. Fry, Printer.] | 1819.

(19.9 x 11.7 untrimmed): Vol. I. [A]^6 B-I^6 K-U^6 X-Z^6 Aa-Bb^6. The last two leaves are blank. Vol. II. [A]^6 B-I^6 K-U^6 X-Y^6 Z^2. The last leaf is blank.

In Vol. I, an engraving by Charles R. Leslie is inserted before the title: "Dutch Courtship." In Vol. II, an engraving by Washington Allston is inserted before the title: "A Schepen Laughing at a Burgomasters Joke."

In some copies of Vol. II, six leaves of advertisements by Moses Thomas are inserted before the half-title: 12 pp., unpaged, undated. The first page is headed REMOVAL in hollow letters; the first item announces Thomas's move of his "Book and Stationary Establishment" from No. 52 to No. 108 Chesnut Street.

Vol. I. [i]-[ii], half-title, verso blank; [iii]-[iv], title, on verso copyright ("the fifth day of March, in the forty-third year of the independence ... A.D. 1819," by Moses Thomas); [v]-xviii, "Account of the Author"; [xix]-xxvi, "To the

Public" (with running head for "Preface"); [27]-296, text. Vol. II. [i]-[ii], half-title, verso blank; [iii]-[iv], title, on verso same copyright; [5]-265, text; [266], blank.

In all copies of Vol. II examined, Book VI is misnumbered IV.

Lineation: Vol. I. p. 100, CHAPTER II. ... Am-; p. 200, from ... nap- Vol. II. p. 100, The ... perchance ; p. 200, But ... candy.

Drab paper boards. Sides blank. White paper label on spines: [double rule of small ornaments] | KNICKERBOCKER'S | NEW-YORK | [rule] | VOL. I. [II.] | THIRD EDITION. | *Fine Paper*, $3.50. | [double rule of small ornaments].

Flyleaf at the front of the volumes; the integral blank leaves serve as flyleaves at the back. White endpapers.

The edition was issued on two grades of paper, not identified but advertised as "fine paper" at $3.50 and "coarse paper" at $3.00. Did the bindings differ also, particularly in the identification of the paper in the last line of the label?

Henry Brevoort to Irving, 9 November 1819, "The Edit: you know consisted of 1500 copies --"

Analectic Magazine, June 1819 (back cover), M. Thomas "will publish on Saturday next, the 5th of June, a third edition, elegantly printed ...." *Philadelphia Register, and National Recorder,* 19 June 1819, listed. *New-York Evening Post,* 23 June 1819, "Just published ... with plates, fine paper, $3 50; do. do. coarse paper, $3." *The Villager* [Greenwich Village, N.Y.], 2nd no. for June 1819, listed.

TxU, ViU.

4Aa.   A | HISTORY | OF | NEW YORK, | FROM THE | BEGINNING OF THE WORLD | TO THE | END ... DYNASTY. | CONTAINING, | AMONG ... MATTERS, | THE ... DOUBTER, | THE ... TESTY, | AND ... PETER | THE HEADSTRONG. | THE ... AMSTERDAM: | *Being the only Authentic History of the Times that ever hath been | published.* | IN TWO VOLUMES. | *FOURTH AMERICAN EDITION.* | [stylized swelled rule] | BY DIEDRICH KNICKERBOCKER. | [stylized swelled rule] | VOL. I. [II.] | [rule] | De ... lag, | Die ... dag. [quotation in fraktur] | [rule] | NEW-YORK: | PRINTED BY C. S. VAN WINKLE, | No. 2 Thames-street. | [rule of 10 dots] | 1824.

(19.6 x 11.5 untrimmed): Vol. I. [i]-xxx, [31]-300. Vol. II. [i]-[viii], unpaged, [9]-268. Signed in 6's. Crude laid paper.

In Vol. II, Book V is misnumbered Book I.

Copyright November 21, in the forty-eighth year of the Independence [1823], by C. S. Van Winkle.

Lineation: Vol. I. p. 100, swimming ... [in footnote] river.; p. 200, frowns ... innovation -- Vol. II. p. 100, -- the ... Hudson.; p. 200, gle pen ... trumpeter

NN, copy reported in ViU.

b.   *FIFTH AMERICAN EDITION.* | ... | *NEW-YORK:* |PRINTED BY C. S. VAN WINKLE, | No. 48 Pine-street.| [rule] | 1826.

In Vol. II, Book V is still misnumbered Book I, but pp. vi, vii, viii are now paged.

MH.

5Aa.   A | HISTORY | OF | NEW-YORK, | FROM THE | BEGINNING OF THE WORLD | TO THE | END OF THE DUTCH DYNASTY. | CONTAINING, | AMONG MANY SURPRISING AND CURIOUS MATTERS, | THE UNUTTERABLE PONDERINGS OF WALTER THE DOUBTER, | THE DISASTROUS PROJECTS OF WILLIAM THE TESTY, | AND THE CHIVALROUS ACHIEVEMENTS OF PETER | THE HEADSTRONG, | THE THREE DUTCH GOVERNORS OF NEW-AMSTERDAM: | *Being the only Authentic History of the Times that ever hath been published.* | IN TWO VOLUMES. | SIXTH AMERICAN EDITION. | [rule] | BY DIEDRICH KNICKERBOCKER. | [rule] | VOL. I. [II.] | [rule] | De ... lag, | Die ... dag. [quotation in fraktur] | [rule] | Philadelphia: [fancy] | CAREY, LEA & CAREY. -- CHESNUT - STREET. | [rule of 13 dots] | 1829.

(16.3 x 10.2): Vol. I. [A]^6 B-I^6 K-U^6 X-Z^6. Vol. II. [A]^6 B-I^6 K-T^6 U^4. (Collation derived from later impression)

Vol. I. [i]-[ii], title, on verso copyright ("the twenty-first day of November, in the forty-eighth year of the independence," by C.S. Van Winkle); [iii]-vi, table of contents; [vii]-xviii, "Account of the Author"; [xix]-xxv, "To the Public" (with running head for "Preface"); [xxvi], blank; [27]-276, text. Vol. II. [i]-[ii], title, on verso copyright?; [iii]-vi, table of contents; [7]-235, text; [236], blank.

In Vol. II, Book V misnumbered Book I.

Lineation: Vol. I. p. 100, their ... cherished ; p. 200, CHAPTER VIII. ... lament, Vol. II. p. 100, be ... "secret ; p. 200, He ... coun-

NN, copy reported in ViU.

b.   SEVENTH AMERICAN EDITION. | ...| Philadelphia: [fancy] | CAREY & LEA -- CHESNUT-STREET. | [rule of 17 dots] | 1830.

NN.

c.   SEVENTH AMERICAN EDITION. | ... | Philadelphia: [fancy] | CAREY
     & LEA -- CHESNUT-STREET. | [rule of 16 dots] | 1831.

     NN.

d.   SEVENTH AMERICAN EDITION. | ... | Philadelphia: [fancy] | CAREY
     & LEA -- CHESNUT-STREET. | [rule of 16 dots] | 1832.

     NN (2).

e.   SEVENTH AMERICAN EDITION. | ... | Philadelphia: [fancy] | CAREY
     & LEA -- CHESNUT-STREET. | [rule of 16 dots] | 1834.

     NN.

f.   SEVENTH AMERICAN EDITION. | ... | Philadelphia: [fancy] | CAREY
     & LEA -- CHESNUT-STREET. | [rule of 16 dots] | 1835.

     Drab-tan paper boards. Sides blank. Paper label on spines.

     CtY, NN.

g.   A NEW EDITION. | ... | Philadelphia: [fancy] | CAREY, LEA, &
     BLANCHARD. | [rule of 21 dots] | 1835.

     Still copyright the twenty-first day of November, in the forty-eighth year of
     the independence.

     Drab-tan paper boards. Sides blank. Paper label on spines: [double rule] |
     Knickerbocker's | HISTORY | OF | NEW-YORK. | [rule] | VOL. I. [II.] |
     [double rule]. White endpapers. Flyleaves.

     TxU.

h.   A NEW EDITION. | ... | Philadelphia: [fancy] | CAREY, LEA, &
     BLANCHARD. | [rule of 21 dots] | 1836.

     Copyright 1836 by Washington Irving.

     Purple cloth embossed in vine and branch design. Sides blank. Spine titled
     in gilt within gilt framing design: IRVING'S | WORKS | [rule] | 1 [2] |
     [stylized swelled rule] | KNICKER | BOCKER | VOL. 1 [2].

     New-York Mirror, 14 May 1836, in "Literary Notices of the Week": "has just
     been issued"; "It is, we suppose, the first of a collected and uniform series of
     the works of Washington Irving, published under that gentleman's
     supervision."

     NN, TxU (2).

i.   A NEW EDITION. | ... | Philadelphia: [fancy] | CAREY, LEA, &
     BLANCHARD. | [rule of 21 dots] | 1836.

In this later impression of 1836, line 16 of the title page is divided into two lines and expanded to its full original version: *"Being the only Authentic History of the Times that ever hath been | or ever will be published."*

NN.

j.   A NEW EDITION. | ... | Philadelphia: [fancy] | CAREY, LEA, & BLANCHARD. | [rule of 21 dots] | 1837.

In the full, expanded version of lines 16-17 of the title page.

Green V cloth. Sides blank. Paper label on spines.

CtY, DLC.

k.   A NEW EDITION. | ... | Philadelphia: [fancy] | CAREY, LEA, & BLANCHARD. | [rule of 21 dots] | 1838.

NN.

l.   A NEW EDITION. | ... | PHILADELPHIA: | LEA & BLANCHARD, | SUCCESSORS TO CAREY & CO. | [rule of 27 dots] | 1839.

NN.

m.   A NEW EDITION. | ... | PHILADELPHIA: | LEA & BLANCHARD. | [rule of 27 dots] | 1840.

Dark green V cloth. Sides blank. White paper label on spines: [double rule] | *Knickerbocker* | NEW-YORK. | BY THE | Author of the | "SKETCH BOOK" | &c. &c. | [rule] | *In Two Vols.* | VOL. I. [II.] | [double rule]. White endpapers.

CtY, TxU.

n.   A NEW EDITION. | ... | PHILADELPHIA: | LEA & BLANCHARD. | [rule of 27 dots] | 1842.

In Vol. II, Book V is still misnumbered Book I.

Blue-green V cloth. Sides blank. White paper label on spines.

CtY, NN (Vol. II only, rebound).

6Aa. A | HISTORY OF NEW-YORK, | FROM THE | BEGINNING OF THE WORLD TO THE END OF | THE DUTCH DYNASTY; | CONTAINING, | AMONG MANY SURPRISING AND CURIOUS MATTERS, | The Unutterable Ponderings of Walter the Doubter, the | Disastrous Projects of William the Testy, and the | Chivalric Achievements of Peter the Head- | strong -- the three Dutch Governors | of New Amsterdam: | Being the only Authentic History of the Times that ever hath been or | ever will be published. | BY | Diedrich Knickerbocker. [fancy] | [rule] | De waarheid die in duister lag, | Die komt met klaarheid aan den dag. [quotation in fraktur] | [rule] | THE AUTHOR'S REVISED EDITION. | COMPLETE IN ONE VOLUME. | NEW-YORK: | GEORGE P. PUTNAM, 155 BROADWAY | And 142 Strand, London. | 1848.

(18.6 x 12.8): $[-]^2$ $2\text{-}3^{12}$ $[4]^{12}$ $5\text{-}18^{12}$ 19^6 $[20]^4$.

For distinctions from the second impression, see the description of the later impression. Three easily identified differences may be useful. On the title page of the first impression, line 6 consists of the single word CONTAINING, and the principal description of those contents is set in lower case. In the preliminary matter, page xiv is unpaged.

[i]-[ii], Works title for Vol. I, dated 1848, verso blank; [iii]-[iv], title, on verso copyright (1848) and printer; [v]-x, table of contents; [xi]-[xiv], "The Author's Apology," dated 1848; [xv]-xvi, original advertisements; [13]-22, "Account of the Author"; [23]-28, "To the Public"; [29]-452, text.

Printer: Leavitt, Trow & Co., 49 Ann-street, New York.

Lineation: p. 100, open ... Zee.; p. 200, dar, ... often ; p. 300, Netherlands; ... heaven

Noted in light blue T cloth. On sides, in gilt, geometric design within wide-rule border. Spine decorated in gilt in leaf and flower design, titled in gilt: KNICKERBOCKER'S | NEW YORK | [slightly swelled rule] | IRVING Cream-white endpapers. AEG. Flyleaves.

Literary World, 19 August 1848, "Will be published on Friday, September 1st"; 26 August 1848, listed; 2 September 1848, "Just published."

TxU.

b. A | HISTORY OF NEW-YORK, | FROM THE | BEGINNING OF THE
WORLD TO THE END OF | THE DUTCH DYNASTY; |
CONTAINING, AMONG MANY SURPRISING AND CURIOUS
MATTERS, THE UNUTTERABLE | PONDERINGS OF WALTER THE
DOUBTER, THE DISASTROUS PROJECTS OF WILLIAM | THE
TESTY, AND THE CHIVALRIC ACHIEVEMENTS OF PETER THE
HEADSTRONG | -- THE THREE DUTCH GOVERNORS OF NEW
AMSTERDAM: BEING THE ONLY | AUTHENTIC HISTORY OF THE
TIMES THAT EVER HATH BEEN OR EVER WILL | BE PUBLISHED.
| BY | Diedrich Knickerbocker. [fancy] | [rule] | De ... lag, | Die ... dag.
[quotation in fraktur] | [rule] | THE AUTHOR'S REVISED EDITION. |
COMPLETE IN ONE VOLUME. | NEW-YORK: | GEORGE P.
PUTNAM, 155 BROADWAY, | And 142 Strand, London. | 1848.

(19.0 x 12.8): $[-]^8 \ 1^{*4} \ [*]^2 \ 2\text{-}3^{12} \ 5\text{-}18^{12} \ 19^8 \ [20]^2$.

A terminal publisher's catalogue is unreckoned: 24 pp., paged [1]-[2], 3-22,
[23]-[24], dated *Sept.*, 1848. On p. [2], the Works of Washington Irving are
advertised "*In Twelve elegant duodecimo volumes*"; also, THE
ILLUSTRATED SKETCH-BOOK, "In October will be published," and THE
ILLUSTRATED KNICKERBOCKER, "in preparation." At the foot of the
page, MR. IRVING'S NEW WORKS, "Now nearly ready for the press,"
include "The Life of Mohammed," "The Life of Washington," and "new
volumes of Miscellanies, Biographies, &c."

From the same setting as the first impression, although p. xiv is now paged.

Blue-green TB cloth. On sides, ornament with publisher's initials at center.
Spine titled in gilt: IRVING'S | WORKS | [rule] | KNICKERBOCKER'S |
NEW YORK || PUTNAM Cream-white endpapers.

On pp. 12-13 of the terminal catalogue, *A History of New York* is offered in
cloth at $1 25; cloth gilt, $1 75; half calf, $2; half morocco, top edge gilt, $2
25; calf extra, $2 50.

The standard cloth binding, matching that of Irving's later works in the
Author's Revised Edition, suggests that this second impression was produced
specifically as a volume of the projected Works rather than as a volume
designed to be sold separately as well.

Literary World, 30 September 1848, "Second Edition" advertised under "New
Publications." The copy in TxU is dated by the owner 1848.

MH, TxU, ViU.

c. NEW-YORK: | GEORGE P. PUTNAM, 155 BROADWAY. | And 142
Strand, London. | 1849.

Works title, dated 1849.

Pagination: [i]-xvi, [13]-454.

A new paragraph is added on p. 222, necessitating some repaging and alterations in the following pages. Page 256 is left blank. Running heads are shifted. The table of contents is also adjusted to the new pagination. But the basic setting remains unchanged.

Lineation: p. 100, open ... Zee.; p. 200, dar, ... often ; p. 300, physicians, ... England!

Dark green TB cloth. On sides, in blind, ornament with publisher's initials at center. Spine not seen.

Literary World, 2 December 1848, "THIRD EDITION" advertised; 9 December 1848, "Published this week." Is that the impression described here? Contemporary advertisements in *The Literary World* suggest the existence of more impressions than have been identified: 3 February 1849, "The third impression of Knickerbocker, on Wednesday"; 17 March 1849, "5th edition" advertised under "New Publications."

KU (original cloth, spine replaced), NN (rebound).

d.   [Illustrated form]. A | HISTORY OF NEW-YORK, | FROM THE | BEGINNING OF THE WORLD TO THE END OF | THE DUTCH DYNASTY; | CONTAINING, AMONG MANY SURPRISING AND CURIOUS MATTERS, THE UNUTTERABLE | PONDERINGS OF WALTER THE DOUBTER, THE DISASTROUS PROJECTS OF | WILLIAM THE TESTY, AND THE CHIVALRIC ACHIEVEMENTS OF PETER | THE HEADSTRONG -- THE THREE DUTCH GOVERNORS OF NEW | AMSTERDAM: BEING THE ONLY AUTHENTIC HISTORY | OF THE TIMES THAT EVER HATH BEEN OR | EVER WILL BE PUBLISHED. | BY | Diedrich Knickerbocker. [fancy] | [rule] | De ... lag, | Die ... dag. [quotation in fraktur] | [rule] | WITH ILLUSTRATIONS | BY FELIX O. C. DARLEY, | ENGRAVED BY EMINENT ARTISTS. | NEW-YORK: | GEORGE P. PUTNAM, 155 BROADWAY, | M.DCCC.L. All within single frame lines.

The Works title is omitted and a table of illustrations is added on p. [iii]. The impression is printed from the same setting of the text (with p. 256 blank and the text ending on p. 454) with single frame lines added around all pages.

Seventeen illustrations added, including an engraved title, a fold-out illustration at the end from a drawing by William Heath, and one illustration pasted in a blank space on p. 163. All are listed in the table of illustrations.

Printer: John F. Trow, 49 Ann-street, New York.

Noted in dark green full morocco. On both sides, elaborate decoration in gilt; at center, a drawing of Knickerbocker within an inset purple oval. Spine decorated and titled in gilt: Knickerbocker [fancy] | [rule] | IRVING. | ILLUSTRATED | BY | DARLEY AEG. Light cream endpapers. Another copy noted rebound but with goffered gilt edges preserved.

Advertised in *Literary World,* 14 July 1849 (before publication), "in cloth, $3 50; extra dark cloth, gilt edges, $4; dark calf, unique style, $5; morocco extra, $6." Advertised 10 November 1849 (at time of publication) as available in "Cloth, $3 50; Cloth, extra gilt, $4 00; Turkey morocco extra, $6 00; Papier Maché -- unique -- $7 00."

Williams and Edge mention "Fifty copies printed on large paper." Not identified or located; the largest copy seen is 21.1 x 14.6, notably larger than the Works impression.

Although the first illustrated impression was apparently published in 1849, no copy dated 1849 on the title page has been located. It is likely that the impression of 1849 was dated 1850.

Literary World, 22 September 1849, "in press"; 20 October 1849, "on Oct. 25"; 10 November 1849, "Now ready."

MH, NN, Copy in hands of dealer.

e. [Works form].   NEW-YORK: | GEORGE   P.   PUTNAM,   155 BROADWAY, | And 142 Strand, London. | 1850.

Works title, dated 1850.

Six pp. of terminal advertisements, undated, paged 17A-22. On p. 19, Irving's Works are listed as published through *Mahomet,* Vols. XII-XIII; later vols. "not yet ready."

KU.

f. [Works form].   NEW-YORK: | GEORGE   P.   PUTNAM,   155 BROADWAY, | And 142 Strand, London. | 1851.

Works title, dated 1851.

Brown TB cloth. On sides, in blind, ornament with publisher's initials at center. Spine titled in gilt. Tan endpapers printed with publisher's advertisements.

TxU, ViU.

g. [Illustrated form]. [New York: George P. Putnam, 1852.]

Not seen. Copy reported in KMK.

h. [Works form]. NEW-YORK: | G. P. PUTNAM & COMPANY, 10 PARK PLACE. | 1853.

Works title, dated 1853.

ViU.

i. [Illustrated form]. NEW-YORK: | G.P. PUTNAM & COMPANY, 10 PARK PLACE, | 1854. All within single frame lines.

Five small Darley illustrations, pasted down in blank spaces, added to the original 17 illustrations. The new illustrations are not listed in the table of illustrations.

Noted in full black morocco. On sides, gilt decoration and triple borders. Spine titled in gilt: KNICKERBOCKER | [rule] | IRVING AEG. White endpapers.

TxU.

j. [Works form]. [New York: George P. Putnam, 1856.]

Not seen. Listed by Williams and Edge, but not seen by them.

k. [Works form]. New York: [fancy] | G. P. PUTNAM & CO., 321 BROADWAY. | 1857.

Works title, dated 1857.

Green TB cloth. On sides, in blind, ornament with publisher's initials at center, within wide-rule border. Spine titled in gilt: IRVING'S | WORKS | [stylized swelled rule] | KNICKERBOCKER'S | NEW YORK || Putnam Buff endpapers.

TxU.

l. [Works form]. NEW YORK: | G. P. PUTNAM, 115 NASSAU STREET. | 1859.

Works title, dated 1859.

Two preliminary engraved illustrations, with imprint of Childs & Peterson, Philadelphia.

Green BD cloth. On sides, blind elaborated border only. Spine titled in gilt: IRVING'S | WORKS | [rule] | KNICKERBOCKER [all within gilt decoration]; at foot, G. P. Putnam Green endpapers.

TxU.

m. [Works form]. NEW YORK: | G P PUTNAM (for the Proprietor), 506 BROADWAY. | 1859.

Two preliminary engravings, with imprint of Childs & Peterson, Philadelphia.

NjP.

7A. A | HISTORY OF NEW YORK, | FROM THE | BEGINNING ... OF | THE ... DYNASTY; | CONTAINING, ... UNUTTERABLE | PONDERINGS ... WILLIAM | THE ... HEADSTRONG -- | THE ... AUTHEN- | TIC ... PUBLISHED. | BY | Diedrich Knickerbocker. [fancy] | [rule] | De ... lag, | Die ... dag. [quotation in fraktur] | [rule] | THE AUTHOR'S REVISED EDITION. | COMPLETE IN ONE VOLUME. | NEW YORK: | G. P. PUTNAM, 115 NASSAU STREET. | 1859.

(19.6 x 12.8): [1]^{12} 2-19^{12} 20^8. Two engravings (by Allston and Leslie), with imprint of Childs & Peterson, Philadelphia, inserted before title.

[1]-[2], Works title for Vol. 1, dated 1859, verso blank; [3]-[4], title, on verso copyright (1848) and printer; [5]-10, table of contents; [11]-14, The Author's Apology; [15]-16, Notices; [17]-27, Account of the Author; [28], blank; [29]-34, To the Public; [35]-472, text.

This new edition may be identified readily by its 472 pages and by the Roman numerals used in paging the preliminary matter. Although the edition offers twenty changes in substantive words and hundreds of changes in accidentals, there is no evidence of authorial revision. The edition may have been produced for immediate use in the new "Sunnyside Edition" of collected works, but in succeeding years it replaced the earlier edition in reprints of the standard Author's Revised Edition.

Printer: John F. Trow, Printer, Stereotyper, and Electrotyper, 377 and 379 Broadway, Cor. White Street, New York.

Lineation: p. 100, they ... handsaw.; p. 200, CHAPTER IX. ... more.

Seen only in binding for the Sunnyside Edition. Brown A cloth. On sides, frame line in blind around edges. On spine, in gilt, IRVING'S | WORKS | 1 [within an oval] | KNICKERBOCKER [all within a box of single frame lines]; at foot, SUNNYSIDE EDIT. Brown endpapers. Single flyleaf at front and back.

MoU.

1E. A | HISTORY | OF | NEW YORK, | FROM THE | BEGINNING OF THE WORLD | TO THE | END OF THE DUTCH DYNASTY. | CONTAINING, | AMONG MANY SURPRISING AND CURIOUS MATTERS, | THE UNUTTERABLE PONDERINGS OF WALTER THE DOUBTER, | *THE DISASTROUS PROJECTS OF WILLIAM THE TESTY,* | AND THE CHIVALRIC ACHIEVEMENTS OF PETER THE HEADSTRONG, | THE THREE DUTCH GOVERNORS OF NEW AMSTERDAM: | *Being the only authentic History of the Times that ever hath been published.* | [rule] | BY DIEDRICH KNICKERBOCKER, |

(AUTHOR OF THE SKETCH BOOK.) | [swelled rule] | A NEW EDITION. | [rule] | De waarheid die in duister lag, | Die komt met klaarheid aan den dag. [quotation in fraktur] | [rule] | LONDON: | JOHN MURRAY, ALBEMARLE-STREET. | [rule] | 1820.

(23.2 x 14.4 untrimmed): [-]^8 C^8 *C^4 D-I^8 K-U^8 X-Z^8 AA-II^8 KK^8 LL^4. Copy in contemporary leather noted with Sig. *C inserted in Sig. [-]; another with Sig. *C following Sig. LL. Not reckoned: terminal or preliminary advertisements in some copies.

Noted or reported in three states of the publisher's advertisements; the sequence, if any, is unknown:

[A]. 8 pp. of advertisements inserted at end, dated October 1820, unpaged. The first page begins with *A History of New York*. The last page is given to *The Quarterly JOURNAL,* published on the first of October.

[B]. 4 pp. of advertisements tipped onto the front flyleaf. Not seen.

[C]. No advertisements.

[i]-[ii], half-title, on verso, notice of a new edition of *The Sketch Book,* just published, and printer; [iii]-[iv], title, verso blank; [v]-xxi, "Account of the Author"; [xxii], blank; [xxiii]-xxxii, "To the Public" (with running head for "Preface"); [8 unnumbered pages], table of contents; [33]-520, text, printer at foot of last page.

Printer: Thomas Davison, Whitefriars.

Lineation: p. 100, up ... day ; p. 200, But, ... which

Light blue paper boards with drab paper shelfback. Sides blank. White paper label on spine: [rule] | KNICKERBOCKER'S | NEW | YORK. | [rule] | *New Edition*. | [rule] | 12*s*. | [rule]. Flyleaves. Also reported in pink paper boards.

Literary Gazette, 30 September 1820, advertised under "Books Published This Day": "printed uniformly with the above [*The Sketch Book,* Vol. I], a new edition of Knickerbocker's History ... 8vo. 12*s*." *Literary Chronicle,* 7 October 1820, reviewed.

NjP, TxU (2).

2Ea. This unauthorized edition published by W. Wright in at least three impressions in 1820-21 is somewhat ambiguous in status in its later printing history. Irving in 1820 called it "a spurious edition," and Langfeld and Blackburn in the twentieth century called it flatly "a pirated edition." But the fourth impression from the setting, 1824, appeared under the imprint of John Murray, the authorized publisher.

A | HUMOUROUS HISTORY | OF | NEW YORK, | FROM THE
BEGINNING OF THE WORLD, | TO THE END OF | The Dutch
Dynasty; [fancy] | *CONTAINING, AMONG MANY SURPRISING AND*
CURIOUS MATTERS, | THE UNUTTERABLE PONDERINGS OF |
WALTER THE DOUBTER, | THE DISASTROUS PROJECTS OF |
WILLIAM THE TESTY, | AND THE |CHIVALRIC ACHIEVEMENTS
OF | PETER THE HEADSTRONG; | THE THREE DUTCH
GOVERNORS OF NEW AMSTERDAM; | BEING THE ONLY
AUTHENTIC HISTORY OF THE TIMES THAT | EVER HATH BEEN
PUBLISHED. | [swelled rule] | *A NEW EDITION.* | [rule] | BY
DIEDRICH KNICKERBOCKER, | AUTHOR OF "THE SKETCH
BOOK." | [rule] | LONDON: | PRINTED FOR W. WRIGHT, 46, FLEET-
STREET. | [rule] | 1820.

(23.1 x 14.1 untrimmed): [a]-[d], [i]-xvi, [1]-495 [496]. Signed in 8's.
Unreckoned: inserted before the title, an engraved illustration of
Knickerbocker is imprinted *Published by W, Wright, 46. Fleet Street.*

For distinctions from the second impression, see the discussion of the second
impression.

Printer: J. M'Creery, Tooks-Court, Chancery-Lane, London.

Lineation: p. 100, *How* ... [in footnote] d'Enfer.; p. 200, an ... pur-

Noted only in leather, but it is probable that, like the second impression, it
was issued in paper boards with paper label on the spine.

NN.

b.   LONDON: | PRINTED FOR W. WRIGHT, 46, FLEET-STREET. | [rule]
      | 1820.

In this second impression, the leaves paged vii-viii and xiii-xiv are cancels,
with a number of textual variants:

Page & Line	First Impression	Second Impression
vii.5	vain-glory	vainglory
vii.8f	library,	library
xiv.6	epicures, I	epicures -- I
xiv.16	| die d o	| died to

The frontispiece illustration appears in two states of the imprint:

[A]. *Published by W, Wright, 46. Fleet Street.*

[B]. *Published by J. Wright, 46, Fleet Street.*

The first impression has been noted only with the illustration in the [A] state, but it is always possible that copies may exist in the [B] state also. Hesitation in assigning a sequence should be exercised, since the third impression of the volume (the so-called "Second Edition") has been noted only with the illustration in the [A] state.

Brown paper boards. White paper label on spine: [double rule] | KNICKERBOCKER'S | *HUMOUROUS* | HISTORY | OF | NEW YORK | [rule] | WITH AN | ORIGINAL PLATE. | [rule] | *Price* 10s. 6d. *bds.* | [double rule].

CtY, NN, TxU.

c.   SECOND EDITION. | ... | PRINTED FOR W. WRIGHT, 46, FLEET-STREET. | [rule] | 1821.

Despite the identification as "Second Edition" on the title page, the impression is printed by the same printer from the same setting. The readings on pp. vii-viii and xiii-xiv, now integral leaves, are those of the second impression. The frontispiece imprint is in the [A] state.

NN.

d.   A | HISTORY | OF | NEW YORK, | ... | A NEW EDITION. | ... | LONDON: | JOHN MURRAY, ALBEMARLE STREET.| [rule] | 1824.

Despite the change of publisher and the identification as "A New Edition," the impression is printed by the same printer from the same setting. The readings on pp. vii-viii and xiii-xiv are those of the second and third impressions. The frontispiece imprint is in the [A] state. One engraved illustration by Washington Allston and five by Charles R. Leslie are added: "Published by John Murray, Albemarle Street, February 1, 1823."

NN.

3E.   A | HISTORY | OF | NEW-YORK, | FROM ... WORLD | TO ... THE | DUTCH DYNASTY; | CONTAINING, | AMONG ... MATTERS, | THE ... DOUBTER, | *THE ... TESTY,* | AND | THE ... HEADSTRONG, | *The ... New-Amsterdam;* | BEING ... PUBLISHED. | [double rule] | BY DIEDRICH KNICKERBOCKER. | [double rule] | De ... lag, | Die ... dag. [quotation in fraktur] | [rule] | A NEW EDITION. | [stylized swelled rule] | GLASGOW: | PRINTED FOR JOHN WYLIE & CO. | By Robert Chapman. [fancy] | [wavy rule] | 1821.

(21.0 x 12.7 untrimmed): [i]-xxviii, [1]-372. Signed in 4's. Laid paper, watermarked large elaborate shield.

Printer: R. Chapman, Glasgow.

Lineation: p. 100, main ... your ; p. 200, the ... [in footnote] Blome.

Gray-blue paper boards with brown paper shelfback. Sides blank. Paper label on spine: [double rule] | History [fancy] | OF | NEW-YORK | [rule] | *Price* 8/, *Boards* | [double rule]. Right edge of label missing on copy examined.

NN, TxGeoS, TxU.

4Ea.   A | HISTORY | OF | NEW YORK, | FROM THE | BEGINNING ... WORLD | TO THE | END ... DYNASTY. | CONTAINING, | AMONG ... MATTERS, | THE ... DOUBTER, | *THE ... TESTY,* | AND ... PETER | THE HEADSTRONG. | THE ... AMSTERDAM: | *Being ... published.* | IN TWO VOLUMES. | [rule] | BY DIEDRICH KNICKERBOCKER. | (AUTHOR OF THE SKETCH BOOK.) | [swelled rule] | A NEW EDITION. | VOL. I. [II.] | [rule] | De ... lag, | Die ... dag. [quotation in fraktur] | [rule] | LONDON: | JOHN MURRAY, ALBEMARLE STREET. | [rule] | 1821.

(18.9 x 11.5): Vol. I. [a]-[f], unpaged, [i]-xxxi [xxxii], [33]-341 [342]. Five illustrations not reckoned. Vol. II. [i]-[vi], unpaged, [1]-282. One illustration not reckoned. Signed in 8's.

Printer: C. Roworth, Bell-yard, Temple-bar.

Lineation: Vol. I. p. 100, send ... it ; p. 200, Tammany ... eter- Vol. II. p. 100, CHAPTER III. ... longer,; p. 200, lands ... premises.

NN, NNHi.

b.   [London: John Murray, 2 vols., 1823.]

Not seen. Presumably a later impression of Murray's edition of 1821, although it may be a new edition.

Advertised in *Literary Gazette,* 6 December 1823, at 14*s.* Also in same advertisement: "Ten Plates to illustrate the above, including a Portrait of the Author, 1*l.* 11*s.* 6*d.*"

5E.   A | HISTORY OF NEW-YORK, | FROM THE | BEGINNING ... WORLD | TO THE | END ... DYNASTY. | CONTAINING, | AMONG ... MATTERS, | THE ... DOUBTER, | THE ... TESTY, | AND | THE ... HEADSTRONG, | THE ... NEW-AMSTERDAM; | BEING THE ONLY | Authentic ... published. [fancy] | [rule] | BY DIEDRICH KNICKERBOCKER. | [engraving by Cruikshank of men in boat] | LONDON: | PRINTED FOR THOMAS TEGG, 73, CHEAPSIDE; | RODWELL AND MARTIN, BOND STREET: ALSO, R. GRIFFIN AND CO. GLASGOW. | [rule] | 1824.

(20.1 x 12.3 untrimmed): [i]-xxx, [1]-368. Signed in 8's. Laid paper.

One rebound copy noted with the one engraving by Allston and the five by Leslie published by Murray February 1, 1823. Some copies so issued? Not in copy seen in original boards.

Printer: C. Whittingham, College House, Chiswick.

Lineation: p. 100, your ... hun-; p. 200, those ... entered

Drab brown paper boards. Sides blank. Paper label on spine: [double rule] | KNICKERBOCKER'S | HISTORY | OF | NEW-YORK| [rule] | *Price* 8*s.* | [double rule].

TxGeoS, TxU (2).

6E.   A | HISTORY OF NEW-YORK, | FROM THE | BEGINNING ... WORLD | TO THE | END ... DYNASTY. | CONTAINING, | AMONG ... MATTERS, | THE ... DOUBTER, | THE ... TESTY, | AND ... HEADSTRONG, | THE ... NEW-AMSTERDAM; | Being ... Times [fancy] | THAT ... PUBLISHED. | BY DIEDRICH KNICKERBOCKER. | [rule] | LONDON: | JOHN BUMPUS, 85, NEWGATE STREET; | AND R. GRIFFIN & CO., GLASGOW. | [rule] | 1825.

(14.6 x 9.2): [i]-xx, [1]-340. Not reckoned: preliminary engraving by Heath of Peter Stuyvesant, published by Bumpus, 1825. Signed in 6's.

Printer: J. Starke, Glasgow.

Lineation: p. 100, untried ... so ; p. 200, But ... him

DLC.

7Ea.   Engraved title, in a variety of styles: A | HISTORY OF NEW YORK. | from the | *BEGINNING OF THE WORLD.* | By | DIEDRICH KNICKERBOCKER. | *Author of the Sketch Book. Tales of a Traveller. &c.* | [engraving of Knickerbocker, identified beneath: *Corbould, del. I. Stewart, sc.* Vide Preface.] | *LONDON.* | WILLIAM CHARLTON WRIGHT. | 65. Pater Noster Row. | 1825. | Fenner, sc.

Printed title missing in copy examined.

"Charlton Wright's Cabinet Edition."

(15.0 x 9.5): [i]-xxx (mispaged xx), [1]-312. Signed in 6's. Laid paper.

Printer: W. Sears, 45, Gutter Lane, Cheapside.

Lineation: p.100, Such ... other.; p. 200, choler ... there-

NN.

b. London: [fancy] | ROBERT THURSTON, FLEET STREET. | [rule] | 1828.

TxU.

c. LONDON: | PRINTED FOR T. T. & J. TEGG, 73, CHEAPSIDE; | AND RICHARD GRIFFIN AND CO., GLASGOW. | [rule] | MDCCCXXXIII.

Preliminary engraving of Peter Stuyvesant by William Heath.

Blue-gray cloth.

NN.

d. LONDON: | PRINTED FOR T. T. & J. TEGG, 73, CHEAPSIDE; | AND RICHARD GRIFFIN AND CO., GLASGOW. | [rule] | MDCCCXXXIV.

Kelly green cloth with small irregular pattern. Sides blank. On spine, black paper label titled in gilt; at foot of label: "6s. Cloth Boards".

NNHi.

e. LONDON: | PRINTED FOR T. T. & J. TEGG, 73, CHEAPSIDE; | AND RICHARD GRIFFIN AND CO., GLASGOW. | [rule] | MDCCCXXXV.

Red T cloth. Sides decorated in blind. Spine titled in gilt.

MH, NN.

8Ea. A | HISTORY OF NEW-YORK, | FROM | The ... World [fancy] | TO | THE ... DYNASTY. | CONTAINING, | AMONG ... MATTERS, | THE ... DOUBTER, | THE ... TESTY, | AND | THE ... HEADSTRONG, | THE ... NEW-AMSTERDAM: | BEING ... ONLY | Authentic ... Published. [fancy] | [stylized swelled rule] | BY DIEDRICH KNICKERBOCKER. | LONDON: | PRINTED FOR THOMAS TEGG AND SON, | 73, CHEAPSIDE. | [rule] | MDCCCXXXVI.

The Library of Congress lists this edition as "Family Library," No. 55.

(14.7 x 9.5): [i]-xxvi, [1]-397 [398]. Not reckoned: four engravings by Cruikshank, published by Tegg, February 1, 1836. Signed in 8's.

Printer: Bradbury and Evans, Whitefriars.

Lineation: p. 100, and ... was ; p. 200, spirit ... amusing

MB, MH, TxU.

b. LONDON: | PRINTED FOR THOMAS TEGG, 73, CHEAPSIDE; | TEGG AND CO., DUBLIN; R. GRIFFIN AND CO., GLASGOW; | ALSO, J. AND S.A. TEGG, SYDNEY AND HOBART TOWN. | [rule] | MDCCCXXXIX.

Printer: Balne Brothers, Gracechurch Street, London.

MB.

9E.   Cover-title: Smith's Standard Library. [hollow fancy letters] | [cut of British arms] | KNICKERBOCKER'S | HISTORY OF NEW YORK. | BY | WASHINGTON IRVING. | [emblem of William Smith] | LONDON: | WILLIAM SMITH, 113, FLEET STREET. | Bradbury & Evans, [closing square bracket] MDCCCXXXIX. [opening square bracket] Printers, Whitefriars. | [opening square bracket] PRICE TWO SHILLINGS AND THREE-PENCE. [closing square bracket]. Two sets of double frame lines around and within title.

Apparently issued without conventional inner title.

(23.2 x 15.0): [i]-v [vi], [1]-113 [114]. Text in double columns. Double frame lines around all pages. Signed in 8's.

Lineation: p. 50, from ... gate ; p. 100, his ... [in footnote] is

Light buff paper wrapper. Back and spine missing on copy examined.

MB.

10E. [London: George Routledge & Co., 1850.]

Routledge's "Popular Library." Issued individually, and also bound with *Salmagundi* as a volume of the Works. Seen only in the Works form. There, the individual title page is omitted and replaced with a combined title: KNICKERBOCKER'S | HISTORY OF NEW YORK: | AND | SALMAGUNDI. | [rule] | BY WASHINGTON IRVING. | [rule] | LONDON: | GEORGE ROUTLEDGE & CO. SOHO SQUARE. | 1850.

(16.9 x 10.6): [1]-256. Signed in 8's.

The text is not that of the Author's Revised Edition.

Lineation: p. 100, crawl ... with ; p. 200, the ... Brin-

Other individual volumes in the series noted in boards printed in colors, or in brown AR cloth, sides decorated in blind with series name at center, spine titled in gilt. The works form (bound with *Salmagundi*) is in royal blue L cloth. On sides, elaborate border and decoration in blind with POPULAR LIBRARY in circle at the center. Spine decorated in blind, titled in gilt: WASHINGTON | IRVING'S | WORKS. | KNICKERBOCKER'S | NEW YORK. | AND SALMAGUNDI | ROUTLEDGE [in blind]. Yellow endpapers.

Athenæum, 1 June 1850, in "List of New Books," 1*s*.; 31 August 1850, advertised, "Washington Irving's complete Works, in 16 vols." "All sold scparatc at Onc Shilling each." It is not clear whether the later entry refers to combined volumes or to a collection of the individual volumes.

Combined volume, CtW.

11Ea.   A | HISTORY OF NEW-YORK, | FROM THE | BEGINNING ... THE | DUTCH DYNASTY; | CONTAINING, | AMONG ... MATTERS, | The ... the | Disastrous ... the | Chivalric ... Head- | strong -- ... Governors | of New Amsterdam: | Being ... been | or ever will be published. | BY | DIEDRICH KNICKERBOCKER. [fancy] | [rule] | De ... lag, | Die ... dag. [quotation in fraktur] | [rule] | THE AUTHOR'S REVISED EDITION. | COMPLETE IN ONE VOLUME. | LONDON: | HENRY G. BOHN, YORK STREET, COVENT GARDEN. | 1850.

(18.1 x 11.4): [i]-xxiv, [1]-280. Signed in 8's.

Issued individually as "Bohn's Shilling Series"; bound with *Salmagundi* as Vol. I of "Bohn's Library Edition."

Printer: Spottiswoodes and Shaw, New-street-Square.

Lineation: p. 100, waves, ... bad ; p. 200, robe ... [in footnote] greedily."

Noted in original binding only in "Bohn's Library Edition." Gray T cloth. Sides decorated in blind. Spine titled in gilt as Irving's Works, Vol. I, Bohn's Library Edition. White endpapers with advertisements in blue. (No works title in volume.)

Shilling Series. *Athenæum*, and *Literary Gazette*, 29 June 1850, listed, at 1*s*.6*d*. Library Edition. *Athenæum*, and *Literary Gazette*, 2 November 1850, the set of 10 vols. at 35*s* listed.

NN, in Library Edition, original cloth; TxU (2), in Library Edition.

b.   [London: Henry G. Bohn, 1854.]

"Bohn's Library Edition." With a portrait of Irving.

Not seen. Copy reported in Staats- and Universitätsbibliothek Hamburg.

1Fa.   A | HISTORY | OF | NEW-YORK, | FROM THE | BEGINNING OF THE WORLD TO THE END OF THE | DUTCH DYNASTY. | CONTAINING, AMONG MANY SURPRISING AND CURIOUS MATTERS, THE | UNUTTERABLE PONDERINGS OF WALTER THE DOUBTER, THE DIS- | ASTROUS PROJECTS OF WILLIAM THE TESTY, AND THE CHIVALRIC | ACHIEVEMENTS OF PETER THE HEADSTRONG, THE THREE DUTCH | GOVERNORS OF NEW-AMSTERDAM: BEING THE ONLY AUTHENTIC | HISTORY OF THE TIMES THAT EVER HATH BEEN OR EVER WILL BE | PUBLISHED. | IN TWO VOLUMES. | [rule] | BY DIEDRICH KNICKERBOCKER. | (AUTHOR OF THE SKETCH BOOK.) | VOL. I. [II.] | De ... lag, | Die ... dag. [quotation in fraktur] | [emblem: D in star within wreath with pendant medal] | PARIS: | PRINTED BY JULES DIDOT, SEN. | FOR A. AND W. GALIGNANI, N° 18, RUE VIVIENNE. | [rule] | M DCCC XXIV.

(17.1 x 10.1 rebound): Vol. I. [i]-xxxix [xl], [1]-344. Vol. II. [i]-viii, [1]-318. Signed in 12's. Laid paper.

Lineation: Vol. I. p. 100, and ... this ; p. 200, full ... by   Vol. II. p. 100, CHAPTER II. ... of ; p. 200, be ... bulwark

Bibliographie de la France, 22 May 1824, # 2787, listed.

NN.

b.   [emblem: D in star within wreath with pendant medal] | PARIS: | PRINTED BY JULES DIDOT, SEN. | FOR BAUDRY, RUE DU COQ, N° 9. | [rule] | M DCCC XXIV.

ViU.

TRANSLATIONS

French.

HISTOIRE | DE | NEW-YORK, | DEPUIS LE COMMENCEMENT DU MONDE | JUSQU'À LA FIN DE LA DOMINATION HOLLANDAISE, | CONTENANT, ENTRE AUTRE COSES CURIEUSES ET SURPRENANTES, LES INNOMBRABLES HÉSITATIONS | DE WALTER-L'INDÉCIS, LES PLANS DÉSASTREUX DE WILLIAM-LE-BOURRU, ET LES EXPLOITS | CHEVALERESQUES DE PIERRE-FORTE-TÊTE, LES TROIS GOUVERNEURS DE NEW-AMSTERDAM: SEULE | HISTOIRE AUTHENTIQUE DE CES TEMPS QUI AIT JAMAIS ÉTÉ OU PUISSE ÊTRE JAMAIS PUBLIÉE. | PAR DIEDRICK KNICKERBOCKER, | AUTEUR DU SKETCH BOOK. | OUVRAGE TRADUIT DE L'ANGLAIS. | [rule] | TOME PREMIER. [SECOND.] |

[stylized swelled rule] | PARIS, | A. SAUTELET ET Cie, LIBRAIRES, | PLACE DE LA BOURSE. | [wavy rule] | M DCCC XXVII.

(20.2 x 12.6): Vol. I. [i]-[iv], [1]-351 [352]. Vol. II. [i]-[iv], [1]-290. Signed in 8's.

Printer: H. Fournier, Rue de Seine, n. 14.

Lineation: Vol. I. p. 100, met ... PREMIER.; p. 200, procurent ... s'éta- Vol. II. p. 100, qu'il ... ou ; p. 200, vaster ... proportion.

Bibliographie de la France, 14 July 1827, # 4633, listed.

CtY, TxU.

German

Humoristische | Geschichte von New-York, | von | Anbeginn der Welt bis zur Endschaft der | holländischen Dynastie, | worin, unter vielen erstaunlichen und merkwürdigen Din- | gen, abgehandelt sind die unaussprechlichen Erwägungen | Walters des Zweiflers, die vom Unstern verfolgten Pro- | jecte Wilhelms des Eigensinnigen, und die ritterlichen | Thaten Peters des Starrköpfigen, der drei holländischen | Gouverneure von New-Amsterdam: -- als die einzige | authentische Historie dieser Zeiten, so jemals an's Licht | gestellt worden oder werden wird. | [rule] | In sieben Büchern. | Von | Dietrich Knickerbocker. | (Verfasser des Skizzenbuchs.) | Aus dem Englischen übersetzt. | [rule] | De ... lag, | Die ... Dag. | [double rule] | Frankfurt am Main, 1829. | Gedruckt und verlegt bei Johann David Sauerländer. [in fraktur]

"Washington Irving's sämmtliche Werke," Bändchen 38-40.

(14.6 x 10.8 untrimmed): [1]-298 [299]-[304]. Signed in 8's. Laid paper.

Lineation: p. 100, über's ... Mäd-; p. 200, sterdam. ... starr-

Light gray paper wrapper. Sides blank. On spine, paper label: Irving's | Werke. | 38-40. | New-York.

CtY, NN, TxU (in wrapper).

Dietrich Knickerbocker's | humoristische | Geschichte von New-York, | von | Anbeginn der Gründung der Colonie | durch | Hendrick Hudson, | bis zur Endschaft der holländischen Dynastie. | Von | Washington Irving. | [rule] | De ... lag, | Die ... Dag. | [rule] | New-York: | Druck und Verlag von Koch & Co., | 160 William-Strasse. [in fraktur]

Not dated. Not copyright. 1851?

(18.5 x 11.1):   [i]-[iv], 11-164, 1-11, [page numbered both 12 and 1] -7, 1-53 [54], [I]-XVIII (out of order in this copy). Signed in 12's.

The volume also includes, after *History of New York*, translations of "Rip Van Winkle" from *The Sketch Book*, "The Bold Dragoon," "The Adventure of the German Student," "Kidd the Pirate," and "The Devil and Tom Walker" from *Tales of a Traveller*, and "The Adventure of the Mason" from *The Alhambra*. A few pages of writing not by Irving, "Die aristokratischen Einwanderer," appear at the end.

Lineation: p. 100, heisst ... oder

Brown T cloth. Sides decorated in blind. Spine decorated and titled in gilt. The binding is signed on the sides: KOCH & CO. | BINDERS, N.Y. The identification is upside down on the back. Cream endpapers.

CtY.

Swedish

NEW-YORK'S HISTORIA | FRÅN VERLDENS BEGYNNELSE | INTILL HOLLÄNDSKA VÄLDETS SLUT. | AF | WASHINGTON IRVING. | [rule] | Öfversättning | AF | JOHAN ER. RYDQVIST. | [rule] | Första Delen. | [rule] | STOCKHOLM. | BERNH. MAGN. BREDBERG, 1827.

A second volume apparently not published.

(20.2 x 12.0): [I]-XXXIX [XL], [1] -261 [262]. Errata slip at end. Signed in 4's. Laid paper.

Lineation: p. 100, att ... Öfvers.; p. 200 ögon, ... byxfic-

MH, NN.

THE POETICAL WORKS OF
THOMAS CAMPBELL

On 24 June 1810 Irving spent part of the day with Archibald Campbell, brother of Thomas Campbell the British poet. Perhaps it was at that time that Archibald convinced Irving to undertake help in America for Thomas Campbell's poems. At any rate, Irving apparently passed the request on to Charles Nicholas, the Philadelphia publisher and husband of Irving's friend Ann Hoffman, who in turn, according to Pierre M. Irving in the *Life and Letters*, suggested that Irving compose an introduction to a collection of selected poems. Whatever the specific details of the origin and composition of the work, by 26 September 1810 Irving -- having seen the printed work -- could write to John E. Hall that he had to struggle "to check and keep down an itching propensity to scribble." "This excellent determination I confess I broke through lately, in writing a queer and rather anamolous biography of Campbell -- and as a punishment therefore, I had the misery of seeing my delectable sketch most horribly misprinted, with outrages on grammar & good language that made my blood run cold, to look at them -- but let these offences lay at the printer's door, I swear myself innocent of them." Obviously, Irving did not read proof on the first edition!

The work was published by Philip H. Nicklin of Baltimore, and others (what happened to Charles Nicholas?), in both a two-volume and a one-volume edition. No sure sequence has been determined, but it is suggestive that the copy belonging to Irving's friend John Howard Payne, now in the New York Public Library, is the two-volume Nicklin edition. And it was the two-volume edition that was first listed in the periodicals of the day. It would also seem significant that Nicklin chose the one-volume edition to reprint in a later impression in 1811. The two-volume edition is here listed first.

Both original editions appear with two variant imprints on the title page. Other variant imprints may exist -- and earlier bibliographies suggest that they do -- but none has been located.

Some four and a half years after its first publication, Irving revised the text of the "Biographical Sketch" of Campbell for publication in *The Analectic Magazine* for March 1815. In that year the revised text of the Sketch also appeared in two editions of *The Poetical Works* published by Edward Earle of Philadelphia. The sequence of the two editions is unknown and no sure grounds have been discovered for preferring one before the other. The edition in 261 pages of text is more common in public collections and is arbitrarily listed first here, as the third edition. The fact that the edition in 234 pages of text was also shared, in one state, with another publisher, Eastburn, Kirk of New York, may be a relevant argument in establishing a sequence.

The revised 1815 text of the "Biographical Sketch" may be distinguished from the original text of 1810 by the opening sentences of the first and last paragraphs.

First sentence, first paragraph:

1810: "It has long been admitted as a lamentable truth, that authors seldom receive impartial justice...."

1815: "It has long been deplored by authors as a lamentable truth, that they seldom receive impartial justice...."

First sentence, last paragraph:

1810: "But whatever may be the subject he may choose, we feel confident that modern literature...."

1815: "We hope therefore, soon to behold Mr. Campbell emerging from those dusty labours...."

The Poetical Works with the Biographical Sketch by Irving continued to appear in America until 1845. The Biographical Sketch itself also appeared during Irving's lifetime in William L. Stone, *The Poetry and History of Wyoming*, 1841 and 1844. Williams and Edge say, apparently mistakenly, that the Sketch also appears in Thomas Campbell's *Specimens of the British Poets*, London, 1819; in Campbell's *The Pleasures of Hope and Other Poems*, New York, 1822; and in *Life and Letters of Thomas Campbell*, ed. William Beattie, New York, 1841. A copy of Campbell's *Specimens of the British Poets* in the library of The University of Texas is inscribed in the first volume, "Washington Irving Esqre | From his friend | The Publisher | London | August 16. 1820"; Volumes 2-7 are inscribed (with minor variations), "Sarah Van Wart, | From her Brother W. Irving." Irving's biographer may have been misled by references to the double gift of the work. No 1841 American edition of Beattie's *Life and Letters of Thomas Campbell* has been located; it apparently does not exist. The 1850 New York edition does not contain the Biographical Sketch, but it does print a long letter by Irving commenting on Campbell; that is probably the cause of the confusion.

1A.   THE | POETICAL WORKS | OF | THOMAS CAMPBELL. | INCLUDING | Several Poems from the Original Manuscript, never | before published in this country. | To which is prefixed | A BIOGRAPHICAL SKETCH OF THE AUTHOR, | BY A GENTLEMAN OF NEW-YORK. | IN TWO VOLUMES. | VOL. I. [II.] | [double rule] | PRINTED FOR PHILIP H. NICKLIN & Co., BALTIMORE. | Also, for D. W. Farrand and Green, Albany; D. Mallory and Co., | Boston; Lyman and Hall, Portland; and E. Earle, | Philadelphia. | Fry and Kammerer, Printers. | 1810.

(Boards, 19.2 x 11.7; leather, 17.4 x 10.5): Vol. I. [a]^6 b-d^6 A-I^6 K-M^6. Vol. II. [a]^6 A-I^6 K-0^6.

Vol. I. [i]-[ii], title, verso blank; [iii]-[iv], table of contents, verso blank; [v]-[vi], divisional title for "A Biographical Sketch of Thomas Campbell," on verso copyright ("the sixteenth day of August, in the thirty fifth year of the Independence," by William P. Farrand & Co.); [vii]-xliii, the Biographical Sketch; [xliv], blank; [xlv]-[xlvi], divisional title, verso blank; [1]-146, text. A half-title noted in a rebound copy in MB; so issued in some copies? If so, not integral with Sig. [a]. Vol. II. [i]-[ii], half-title, verso blank; [iii]-[iv], title, verso blank; [v]-[vi], table of contents, verso blank; [vii]-[viii], divisional title, verso blank; [ix]-[x], Advertisement, verso blank; [1]-170, text.

Lineation: Vol. I. p. xxx, little, ... Wyoming ; p. 100, Say, ... gore! Vol. II. p. 50, Upris'n, ... share?; p. 100, children, ... for

Reported in printed paper boards. (See the description below of the boards on a copy with the variant imprint.) Seen in contemporary calf; probably so issued.

MB, NN, ViU. CtW in reproduction.

Variant imprint: PRINTED FOR D. W. FARRAND & GREEN, ALBANY. | Also, for E. Earle, Philadelphia; D. Mallory and Co. Boston; Lyman | and Hall, Portland; and Philip H. Nickilin [correctly spelled Nicklin in Vol. II.] and Co., Baltimore. | Fry and Kammerer, Printers. | 1810.

Langfeld and Blackburn state that copies exist with the misspelling of Nicklin corrected, although they have seen only copies with the misspelling. No copy located with the correct spelling in Vol. I.

Also, Langfeld and Blackburn reproduce a photograph of the title of Vol. I of a copy in Langfeld's collection. There, A BIOGRAPHICAL SKETCH OF THE AUTHOR is followed by a period rather than a comma. If the reproduction is accurate, no such copy has been located.

Tan paper boards. On front, cover-title within single fancy frame lines. The imprint differs from the title page of the volume: PUBLISHED BY | EDWARD EARLE, PHILADELPHIA. | Also, by | D. Mallory & Co., Boston; P. H. Nicklin & Co., Baltimore; | Lyman, Hall & Co., Portland; and Swift and | Chipman, Middlebury, Vt. | Fry and Kammerer, Printers. | 1810. On back, advertisement for books lately published by Edward Earle. On spine, at top, [wavy rule] | CAMPBELL'S | POEMS [space for possible period missing on copy examined] | [wavy rule]; at center, [wavy rule]; in lower portion of spine, [wavy rule] | VOL. I. [II.] | [wavy rule]. Were all the variants so issued? Probably also issued in calf.

Monthly Anthology, and Boston Review, October 1810, listed: "In two volumes. Boston; D. Mallory, &c."

DLC, ViU (Vol. I only, in boards).

2Aa.   THE | POETICAL WORKS | OF | THOMAS CAMPBELL. | INCLUDING | Several Pieces from the Original Manuscript, never | before published in this country. | To which is prefixed | A BIOGRAPHICAL SKETCH OF THE AUTHOR. | BY A GENTLEMAN OF NEW-YORK. | [double rule] | PRINTED FOR PHILIP H. NICKLIN & Co., BALTIMORE. | Also, for D. W. Farrand and Green, Albany; D. Mallory and Co., | Boston; Lyman and Hall, Portland; and E. Earle, | Philadelphia. | Fry and Kammerer, Printers. | 1810.

(17.2 x 10.5): [A]^6 B-I^6 K-U^6 X-Z^6 2A^6 2B$^{4.}$

[1]-[2], title, verso blank; [3]-[4], table of contents; [5]-[6], divisional title, on verso copyright ("the sixteenth day of August, in the thirty fifth year of the Independence," by William P. Farrand & Co.); [7]-41, the Biographical Sketch; [42], blank; [43]-296, text.

Lineation: p. 30, unite ... he ; p. 100, Thrice ... tears!

Reported in boards. Seen only in contemporary calf; probably so issued.

DLC.

Variant imprint: PRINTED FOR D. W. FARRAND & GREEN, ALBANY. | Also, for E. Earle, Philadelphia; D. Mallory and Co. Boston; Lyman | and Hall, Portland; and Philip H. Nicklin and Co., Baltimore. | Fry and Kammerer, Printers. | 1810.

NN.

b.   *Second American Edition*. | BALTIMORE: | PUBLISHED BY PHILIP H. NICKLIN, | Also, by E. Sargeant, New-York; A. Finley, Philadelphia; D. Mallory, & co. | Boston; Joseph Cushing, Baltimore; Joseph Milligan, Georgetown; | James Kennedy, sen. Alexandria; John R. Jones, Rich- | mond, (V.) and Caleb Emerson, Marietta, Ohio. | Fry and Kammerer, Printers. | 1811.

Leaf size: 19.7 x 11.5 untrimmed.

Tan paper boards. On front, cover-title (with same imprint as inner title) within elaborated border. On back, advertisements for Philip Nicklin within elaborated border. Spine missing on copy examined. White endpapers.

TxU.

3A. THE | POETICAL WORKS | OF | THOMAS CAMPBELL. | Comprising | SEVERAL PIECES NOT CONTAINED IN ANY FORMER | EDITION. | To which is prefixed | A REVISED AND IMPROVED BIOGRAPHICAL | SKETCH OF THE AUTHOR, | BY A GENTLEMAN OF NEW-YORK.

A preliminary engraved title adds the publisher: *Philadelphia | Published by Edward Earle | W.* Fry Printer

Copyright "the seventeenth day of March, in the thirty-ninth year of the Independence," 1815, by Edward Earle.

(Boards, 15.0 x 7.9 untrimmed; 13.0 x 7.1 trimmed): $[-]^4$ A-I^{12} K-L^{12}. First leaf a blank. Last leaf excised in copy collated. Engraved title not reckoned.

[i]-[ii], title, on verso copyright; [iii]-v, table of contents; [vi], blank; [vii]-[viii], fly-leaf for the Biographical Sketch, verso blank; [1]-24, Biographical Sketch; [25]-[26], fly-leaf for "The Pleasures of Hope," verso blank; [27]-261, text; [262], blank

Contains the revised 1815 text of the Biographical Sketch.

Lineation: p. 20, at ... forests,; p. 100, Lake ... last.

Gray unprinted paper boards with white paper shelfback. White endpapers. Leaves untrimmed. Also, apparently a publisher's binding, unprinted black boards impressed to give a watered effect, with leather shelfback titled in gilt. Marbled endpapers. All edges trimmed. Probably also issued in calf.

Analectic Magazine, April 1815, noted: "E. Earle, of Philadelphia, has just published a handsome pocket edition of *Campbell's Poetical Works*. This very neat edition ... contains the biographical sketch of his life and literary character, which appeared in the March number of this Magazine."

DLC, calf. TxU, black boards. ViU, gray boards.

4A. THE | POETICAL WORKS | OF | THOMAS CAMPBELL. | Comprising | SEVERAL PIECES NOT CONTAINED IN ANY FORMER | EDITION. | To which is prefixed | A REVISED AND IMPROVED BIOGRAPHICAL | SKETCH OF THE AUTHOR, | BY A GENTLEMAN OF NEW-YORK. | [double rule] | PHILADELPHIA: | PUBLISHED BY EDWARD EARLE. | William Fry, Printer. | 1815.

(13.2 x 7.6): $[-]^2$ a^{12} [A]12 B-I^{12} K^6 L-M^4. Does not contain an engraved title.

[i]-[ii], title, on verso copyright ("the seventeenth day of March, in the thirty-ninth year of the Independence," 1815, by Edward Earle); [iii]-iv, table of contents; [v]-xxvii, Biographical Sketch; [xxviii], blank; [1]-[2], fly-title for

"The Pleasures of Hope," verso blank; [3]-234, single blank leaf, [235]-242, text.

Contains the revised 1815 text of the Biographical Sketch.

Page 95 in two states: [A]. Mispaged 59. [B]. Correctly paged.

Seen only in contemporary calf.

CtY, both states of p. 95. ICN, mispaged.

Variant imprint: PHILADELPHIA: | PUBLISHED BY EDWARD EARLE; | AND | EASTBURN, KIRK, AND CO., NEW-YORK. | William Fry, Printer. | 1815.

It is not certain whether this is a separate impression or simply a variant state of the title page. Located only in a portion of a single copy, consisting of pp. [i]-xxvii [xxviii].

NN.

5A.   THE | POETICAL WORKS | OF | THOMAS CAMPBELL [hollow letters] | TO WHICH IS PREFIXED, | A BIOGRAPHICAL SKETCH | OF | THE AUTHOR. | *First complete American Edition.* | [double rule] | PHILADELPHIA: | PUBLISHED BY EDWARD PARKER. | William Brown, Printer. | 1821.

(14.2 x 8.5): [i]-xxxiii [xxxiv]-[xxxvi], [1]-243 [244]. Signed in 6's.

Lineation: p. xx, improving ... never ; p. 100, One ... sire

Contains the revised 1815 text of the Biographical Sketch. A long footnote referring to the current war with Great Britain is omitted.

TxU.

6A.   THE | POETICAL WORKS | OF | THOMAS CAMPBELL, | COMPLETE: | WITH | A MEMOIR OF THE AUTHOR | BY | WASHINGTON IRVING, | AND | REMARKS UPON HIS WRITINGS | BY | LORD JEFFREY. | WITH ILLUSTRATIONS. | [wavy rule] | PHILADELPHIA: | LEA AND BLANCHARD. | 1845.

(21.7 x 13.3): [i]-xxiv, [25]-434. Two pages of advertisements bound at end. Signed in 6's.

Printer: T.K. & P.G. Collins, No. 1 Lodge Alley.

Lineation: p. x, theories ... so ; p. 100, But ... veins!

In the "Memoir," pp. [v]-[25], a new concluding paragraph is substituted, within square brackets, for the original conclusion. The paragraph was apparently furnished by Rufus W. Griswold and is not the work of Irving. The Memoir itself is a version of the original 1810 text, taken from the corrupt text in William L. Stone's *The Poetry and History of Wyoming*, 1841.

Red LI-like cloth. On sides, cruciform design in gilt within border and rules in blind. Spine decorated and titled in gilt. Top edges stained green. Cream endpapers.

CtY.

THE SKETCH BOOK

From the spring of 1819 to the summer of 1820, Washington Irving, then in England, sent to his brother Ebenezer in New York the manuscripts that were to form the original seven parts of the first American edition of *The Sketch Book*. Washington's friend Henry Brevoort, at Irving's request, acted as literary agent, dealing with the printer, C. S. Van Winkle, and reading proof on the first four parts. Apparently Ebenezer took over the role for the last three parts. Irving sent manuscripts on these dates: Part I, 1 March 1819; Part II, 1 April 1819; Part III, 13 May 1819; Part IV, 2 August 1819 (the manuscript of "Rural Funerals" was sent 16 August as a substitute for "John Bull," which later appeared in Part VI); Part V, 28 October 1819; Part VI, 29 December 1819; Part VII, much later, probably 28 June 1820. As Irving received printed copies of those original parts, he revised each part and sent a marked copy back to America as text for the second edition. The only change in selections that he made for the second edition in parts was to divide "Christmas Day" in Part V into two separate sketches, "Christmas Morning" and "Christmas Dinner."

Unlike *Salmagundi*, the individual parts of *The Sketch Book* apparently were never issued bound together, and no common title page was furnished. That was so in spite of the fact that the first six parts were thought of as the first volume of a longer work, at least until the appearance of the seventh and last part nearly six months after the publication of Part VI. On the day of publication of Part VI, Haly & Thomas advertised *The Sketch Book* in "Complete sets in 6 Nos. price 4 50," the first advertising for such a set. Or more revealing, another advertisement appeared in the *New-York Evening Post* on the same day, 16 March 1820: "NOTICE. One volume of the SKETCH BOOK being completed, those persons who are desirous of having their numbers bound, are informed that they can procure them done in every variety of binding, on application to L. & F. LOCKWOOD."

Before completion of publication in parts in America, Irving made arrangements with John Miller of London to bring out a volume of *The Sketch Book*, its text made up of revised versions of the sketches of Parts I-IV and a new "Prospectus." It was published in February 1820. When Miller's firm failed shortly after the publication, Irving with the help of Walter Scott (a story that Irving tells in his "Preface to the Revised Edition" of 1848) prevailed upon John Murray of London to take over the Miller imprint of Volume I and to bring out a second volume made up of revised versions of the sketches of Parts V-VI, the forthcoming Part VII, and some new material. For that volume, Irving revised the order of the sketches and added the "Advertisement," "L'Envoy," and two more sketches, "Traits of Indian Character" and "Philip of Pokanoket," both previously published in *The Analectic Magazine*. Murray brought out the second volume in mid-July, some two months before Part VII was published in America.

That flurried beginning of its printing history was the introduction to a long and broad series of subsequent editions and revisions in America, in Britain, and on the Continent. In 1822, Irving made a number of small revisions for a new edition by John Murray, and in 1823 another set of small revisions for an edition by A. Montucci in Dresden. For the Montucci edition, somewhat oddly, Irving used for his basic text a Murray London edition of 1821 and so did not incorporate all of the changes he had already made for Murray. In 1824, C.S. Van Winkle's "Fourth American Edition" used, essentially, the text of Murray's revised edition of 1822, and so established the contents and the order of the sketches of the early London editions as the basic text of *The Sketch Book* until Irving's major revision and expansion for Putnam's Author's Revised Edition of 1848. In that final revision, Irving added seventeen pages of new material and made numerous specific changes. To the text he added "Preface to the Revised Edition," "A Sunday in London," and "London Antiques," as well as adding a postscript to "Rip Van Winkle" and notes to "Westminster Abbey." He seems to have used the text of the Baudry-Galignani Paris edition of 1823 as the basis for his revisions, careless as that seems. But since the Paris edition had been reprinted from the text of Murray's revised London edition of 1822, Irving continued even in his last revision the textual tradition he had established in the first London version.

CONTENTS OF THE ORIGINAL PARTS AND LATER MAJOR REVISIONS

In this compressed table, the term "same" indicates the repetition of a sketch from the first American edition, whether individually revised or not. New sketches added in the London edition or in the Author's Revised Edition are indicated by title. Titles within parentheses indicate the repetition of the sketch from the first American edition, but in a different position in the order of sketches. The term "repeated" indicates the repetition in the Author's Revised Edition of a sketch first added to the London edition. A horizontal line divides the two volumes of the first London edition.

Part	First American Edition, 1819-20	First London Edition, 1820	Author's Revised Edition, 1848
I	Prospectus		
		Advertisement	
			Preface to the Revised Edition
	The Author's Account	[same]	[same]
	The Voyage	[same]	[same]
	Roscoe	[same]	[same]
	The Wife	[same]	[same]
	Rip Van Winkle	[same]	[same]
II	English Writers on America	[same]	[same]
	Rural Life in England	[same]	[same]
	The Broken Heart	[same]	[same]
	The Art of Book Making	[same]	[same]
III	A Royal Poet	[same]	[same]
	The Country Church	[same]	[same]
	The Widow and Her Son	[same]	[same]
			A Sunday in London
	The Boar's Head Tavern, East Cheap	[same]	[same]
IV	The Mutability of Literature	[same]	[same]

Rural Funerals	[same]	[same]
The Inn Kitchen	[same]	[same]
The Spectre Bridegroom	[same]	[same]

V	(Westminster Abbey)	(Westminster Abbey)
Christmas	[same]	[same]
The Stage Coach	[same]	[same]
Christmas Eve	[same]	[same]
Christmas Day		
In second edition divided and titled:		
Christmas Morning	Christmas Day (a new title for Christmas Morning)	[repeated]
The Christmas Dinner	[same as second American edition]	[repeated]
VI		London Antiques
	(Little Britain)	(Little Britain)
	(Stratford-on-Avon)	(Stratford-on-Avon)
	Traits of Indian Character	[repeated]
	Philip of Pokanoket	[repeated]
John Bull	[same]	[same]
The Pride of the Village	[same]	[same]
	(The Angler)	(The Angler)

The Legend of Sleepy Hollow	[same]	[same]

VII	Westminster Abbey
	The Angler
	Stratford-on-Avon
	Little Britain

	L'Envoy	[repeated]

1A-3A. The first three American editions of *The Sketch Book*, each published in parts, are most conveniently described by considering each part individually rather than by considering the work as a whole. That method is especially desirable for the incomplete third edition, of which only the first three parts seem to have been published. C. S. Van Winkle must have considered the three first parts of that third edition significant, however, since he called his next edition, the first published in conventional book form, the Fourth American Edition.

The Sketch Book, like *Salmagundi*, has long been a favorite of collectors, and sophisticated or fraudulently made-up copies have sometimes satisfied the demand. Since *The Sketch Book* is bibliographically less complex than *Salmagundi*, however, one can hope that careful investigation will be more successful in detecting fraud. C. S. Van Winkle appears to have been a generally competent and careful printer, and any appearance of the mixed sheets (and even mixed editions) that characterize *Salmagundi* should arouse immediate skepticism in *The Sketch Book*. The descriptions here are taken from copies in original wrappers. Necessarily, I often used rebound copies in making the many comparisons on the mechanical collator -- copies in wrappers are generally considered too fragile for such handling -- but whenever possible I then checked the results against copies in original condition.

Part I

First edition.

THE | SKETCH BOOK | OF | *GEOFFREY CRAYON, Gent.* | [swelled rule] | No. I. | [rule] | "I have no wife nor children, good or bad, to provide for. A mere spectator of | other men's fortunes and adventures, and how they play their parts; which me- | thinks are diversely presented unto me, as from a common theatre or scene." | BURTON. | [rule] | *NEW-YORK:* | PRINTED BY C. S. VAN WINKLE, | No. 101 Greenwich-street. | [rule of 11 dots] | 1819.

For distinctions from the second edition, see the description of the second edition and the table of variants there.

(23.3 x 14.9 untrimmed, the maximum dimensions noted; different copies and individual leaves vary considerably, as in all the parts): [1]^4 2-12^4. The last leaf is a blank.

[i]-[ii], title, on verso copyright ("the fifteenth day of May, in the forty-third year of the Independence" by C. S. Van Winkle); [iii]-iv, Prospectus, dated London, 1819; [5]-94, text. See also the description of variant State [B] below.

Lineation: p. 25, ROSCOE. ... in ; p. 50, est ... strongly

Noted in three states. A discussion of the sequence follows the brief definitions.

[A]. Pagination as described: [i]-iv, [5]-94.

[B]. The last five pages incorrectly paged 82-85, 78. The second p. 85 (the misnumbering for p. 93) is in a different setting of the same text.

[C]. Correctly paged as described. Signature 8 is in a different setting of a slightly different text than in State [A] or [B]; for identification, page [57], line 9 has no comma after "lore." Other identifying readings appear in the table of variants in the description of the second edition. All the other signatures, as well as p. 93, are in the same setting as State [A].

An acceptable explanation and a sure definition of sequence for the three different states is not readily apparent. The text and the setting of State [B] are those of State [A] throughout, except for the second p. 85 which is a unique setting: the text of the page is the same as that in all other states and editions, but the type has been reset and corresponds to no other state or edition. This variant setting may easily be identified by the line division of the first two lines: "time | he" rather than "every | time".

State [B] has been noted only in a single rebound copy, in TxFTC. But the unique setting of p. "85" and the standard first edition setting of the other four mispaged pages deny the possibility of sophistication or tampering with the copy; no other known state or edition could have supplied those pages.

If State [B] represents a few early copies that escaped from Van Winkle's shop before the careless mispaging was discovered -- the most tempting of the possible sequences -- why would one page need to be reset? If it is a later state than State [A], produced after p. 93 had to be reset for some unknown reason, why would the other four pages be renumbered incorrectly? Furthermore, if State [B] falls between State [A] and State [C] -- and State [C] from other evidence would appear to be a late state -- why does State [C] not show the resetting on p. 93? In turn, if for some reason it followed State [C], why does it not show the reset Sig. 8 of State [C]? Unless further evidence appears, State [B] should be considered an odd variant of the common State [A], perhaps earlier but one whose sequential relationship to State [A] finally is unknown.

Although a specific explanation of State [C] is also lacking -- that is, a reason why Sig. 8 was reset and three commas dropped from the text -- the sequence of the state would not appear to be quite such a puzzle. The second edition restores the commas to the text; the second edition was printed from a copy of the first edition revised by Irving; Irving received early copies and presumably used one of them to mark up for the printer; therefore, State [C] must have been produced after early copies were sent to Irving. The argument is not beyond challenge but does present the probability that State [C] is later than State [A].

Brown-tan paper wrapper. On front, within a box of double frame lines: No. I....Price 75 cents. | [rule] | THE SKETCH BOOK. [hollow letters] | [rule] | C. S. VAN WINKLE, PRINTER, | 101 Greenwich-street. On back: [double rule] | No. II. | OF | *THE SKETCH BOOK*, [in left-slanting italic] | WILL BE PUBLISHED | ON THE FIRST OF AUGUST NEXT. | [double rule]. Spine blank. White endpapers.

Pierre M. Irving in the *Life and Letters* (I, 416-17) says that 2000 copies were printed, published simultaneously in New York, Boston, Baltimore, Philadelphia.

A title page for Part I was apparently deposited for copyright on 15 April 1819. The printed copyright notice in the Part itself gives the date as 15 May 1819, but the Copyright Record Book of the Southern District Court of New York (Vol. 134, p. 294) gives 15 April. As was customary in the Record Book, the copyright document itself provides the record. It is a printed legal form with blank spaces in which the required data were entered by pen. Here is the pertinent section (with the pen entries indicated by italics):

Be it Remembered, that on the *Fifteenth* day of *April* in the *43rd* year of the Independence of the United States of America, *C. S. Van Winkle* of the said District, *hath* deposited in this office the title of a *Book* the right whereof he claims as *Proprietor* in the words following, to wit: *The Sketch Book of Geoffrey Crayon, Gent. -- No. I. -- I have no wife nor children....*

The form is signed at the foot by James Dill. No other dating appears on the document.

There is no evidence in the Record Book itself to raise questions about the given date. The three copyright forms that precede this one are dated 15 April, 15 April, 21 April; the three that follow are dated 21 April, 28 April, 28 April. This document is paged by hand 294, in the sequence in which the forms appear. The sequence, it will be noted, is not strictly chronological; the forms were probably paged and filed at intervals.

Outside information is not conclusive but offers no evidence to deny the earlier date. On 1 March 1819, Washington Irving wrote from London to his brother Ebenezer in New York that he was sending a small parcel of manuscript of a new work. About 3 March, Irving began his next letter to Ebenezer, "I have sent by Capt. Merry, of the Rosalie, the first number of a work which I hope to be able to continue from time to time." On 16 April 1819, *The New-York Evening Post* and the New York *Commercial Advertiser* reported in their maritime news, under the heading "ARRIVED LAST EVENING," "Ship Rosalie, Merry, 36 days from London," followed by a list of freight consignees and first-class passengers. But that was simply *Rosalie*'s docking time. The newspapers regularly reported three categories in their maritime news of New York: arrivals, departures, and the category headed "BELOW," that is, ships that had arrived but were not yet docked and not discharging full cargo. On Wednesday, 14 April 1819, the *Commercial Advertiser*, under "BELOW," lists "Ship Rosalie, Merry, from London, to J. U. & W. F. Coles." *Rosalie* had arrived and, as I interpret the entry, had immediately sent on by packet boat express cargo to the Coles. With it would have gone the mail. That means that C. S. Van Winkle probably received Irving's manuscript on 14 April. If so, and particularly if Irving had provided copy for a title page -- as he almost certainly did -- Van Winkle would have had plenty of time to set a title page and take our copyright on the fifteenth.

New-York Evening Post, 21 June 1819, "C. WILEY & CO. No. 3 Wall-street, have this day published The Sketch Book ... No. 1. Price 75 cents." *Philadelphia Register, and National Recorder*, 26 June 1819, listed. *Villager* (Greenwich Village, N.Y.), 2nd number for June 1819, listed.

State [A], in wrapper: CtY, NN (4), TxFTC, ViU. State [B]: TxFTC. State [C]: ViU.

Second edition.

101 Greenwich Street. | [rule of 10 dots] | 1819.

Most of the revisions in the second edition were provided by Irving in correspondence from England, primarily in a marked copy of the first edition.

Collation: $[1]^4$ $2\text{-}12^4$. The last leaf is not a blank.

Pagination: [i]-iv, [5]-93, [blank page], 94, [blank page]. That is, p. 95 is mispaged 94.

Light gray paper wrapper. On front, within a box of double frame lines: SECOND EDITION. | [rule of 13 dots] | No. I....Price 75 cents. | [rule] | THE SKETCH BOOK. [hollow letters] | [rule] | C. S. VAN WINKLE, PRINTER, | 101 Greenwich-street. Back and spine blank. White endpapers.

Representative and identifying variants in Part I, First and Second Edition:

Page & line	First edition, State [A]	First edition, State [C]	Second edition
Title	No. 101 Greenwich-street.		101 Greenwich Street.
Copyright, last line	| "of designing		| "ving, and
[5]. 3f	town-crier		town crier
13.8f	said that		said, that
21.7f	war, that prowled		war, prowling like
31.2f	awakening		awaking
45.9	but feels undervalued		but will feel undervalued
[57].9	lore,	lore	lore,
[57].14	bookworm		book-worm
58.4	now,	now	now,
58.5	memory, to	memory to	memory, to
60.6-7	va- | pours	gray | vapours	va- | pours
64.12	do. So		do; so
74.8	sugarloaf		sugar-loaf
80.3-4	not one of which he | recognized for his old acquain-tances		none of which he | recognized for his old acquaintances

82.7f	none that	none whom
88.6f	pedlar	peddler
92.3	torpor. How	torpor; how

Henry Brevoort to Irving, 9 September 1819, "The 2d Edit. of No. 1 will be put to press in a few days."

CtY (in wrapper), NN, NNC, TxU (2).

Third edition.

101 Greenwich Street. | [rule] | 1822.

The text is derived from Vol. I of the first London edition.

Collation: $[1]^4 2\text{-}12^4$.

Pagination: [i]-iv, [5]-93 [94] 95 [96].

Light gray paper wrapper. On front, within a box of double frame lines: THIRD EDITION. | [rule of 11 dots] | No. I.....Price 75 cents. | [rule] | THE SKETCH BOOK. [hollow letters] | [rule] | C. S. VAN WINKLE, PRINTER, | 101 Greenwich Street. Back and spine blank. White endpapers.

The text may be identified by a few representative changes from the first and second editions:

45.9   it feels undervalued

80.3-4 not one of which he | recognized for an old acquaintance

CtY (in wrapper), NjP, TxU, ViU.

Part II

First edition.

THE | SKETCH BOOK | OF | *GEOFFREY CRAYON, Gent.* | [swelled rule] | No. II. | "I have no wife nor children, good or bad, to provide for. A mere spectator | of other men's fortunes and adventures, and how they play their parts; which | methinks are diversely presented unto me, as from a common theatre or scene." | BURTON. | [rule] | *NEW-YORK:* | PRINTED BY C. S. VAN WINKLE, | 101 Greenwich Street. | [rule of 10 dots] | 1819.

(22.9 x 14.0 untrimmed, the maximum dimensions noted): $[13]^4\ 14\text{-}15^4\ [16]^4\ 17\text{-}19^4\ [20]^4\ 21^4\ [22]^2$. The last leaf is a blank.

[97]-[98], title, on verso copyright ("the twenty-sixth day of July, in the forty-third year of the Independence" by C. S. Van Winkle); [99]-[100], divisional

fly-title for "English Writers on America," verso blank; [101]-169, text; [170], blank.

In some copies a slip, approximately 12.7 x 2.1 cm, is tipped onto the flyleaf facing the title page: SEVERAL Editors of Magazines and Newspapers having reprinted | entire articles from the first number of the Sketch Book, the proprie- | tor expects they will, in future, desist from any farther infringement | of his copy-right. *BAL* reports two different settings of the slip; not identified.

Lineation: p. 125, for ... has,; p. 150, vain ... however,

In paper wrapper (for colors, see below). On front, within a box of double frame lines: No. II....Price 50 cents. | [rule] | THE SKETCH BOOK. [hollow letters] | [rule] | C. S. VAN WINKLE, PRINTER, | 101 Greenwich-street. On back: [double rule] | No. III. | OF | *THE SKETCH BOOK.* [in left-slanting italic] | WILL BE PUBLISHED | ON THE TENTH OF SEPTEMBER. | [double rule]. Spine blank. White endpapers.

Noted on gray, tan, and chocolate brown stock. No sequence is apparent.

The wrapper has been noted in at least two, and probably more, states of the cover-title and three or more states of issue.

Printed State 1. At head of title, as described, "No. II....Price 50 cents."

In a second state of issue, the printed price of 50 cents is changed by pen to 62 1/2 cents. One copy in TxU has the price changed once more by pen to 75 cents. Pasted to the front of that copy is a printed bookseller's label of M. Thomas, Philadelphia, the Philadelphia publisher of *The Sketch Book.* Whether the second price change represents a publisher's state is not certain.

Printed State 2. At head of title, "No. II....Price 62 1/2 cents."

Most, although not all, copies are printed on waste stock. On the recto of the back wrapper, concealed by the pasted-down endpaper, appears the cover-title for State 1, with the printed price of 50 cents. It is apparent that Van Winkle used up the remaining copies of the first wrapper for printing the new state when the price was changed to 62 1/2 cents. When held against a strong light, the cancelled cover-title can generally be observed, although dimly.

The dimensions of the cover-title of printed State 2 vary so noticeably that it is possible, perhaps even probable, that there are two settings. Since copies are relatively scarce in wrappers, widely scattered, and invariably classed as "rare" and "non-circulating," they cannot be compared on the mechanical collator. Comparison of a number of xerographic copies yields ambiguous results, in part because of the small amount of type in the cover-title, in part because of the tendency of individual copying machines to distort and to change the dimensions. Unfortunately, there is no clear evidence of shifting of type on the page to indicate resetting. But measurement of original wrappers (not the copies of the wrappers) shows them falling into two general groups, represented here by the smallest and the largest. A wet-printing technique might, of course, produce some variation, but probably not that great.

Width between inner frame lines at center:

16.6 x 9.0   17.0 x 9.2

Length of title, from edge of T to edge of shading in period:

7.8   7.95

2000 copies, published simultaneously in New York, Boston, Baltimore, Philadelphia.

Title deposited for copyright 26 July 1819. The notice on the back of the wrapper of Part I names "First of August Next" as publication date. *New-York Evening Post*, 31 July 1819, "C. Wiley & Co. ... have this day published No. 2 ... price 62 1/2 cts." *National Recorder* [Philadelphia], 7 August 1819, reviewed.

In wrappers: CtY, NN (4), TxU (2), ViU (2). Wrappers examined in xerographic copy: CSmH, InU, TxFTC.

Second edition.

101 Greenwich Street. | [rule of 10 dots] | 1820.

Most of the revisions in the second edition were provided by Irving in a copy of the first edition sent from England.

Collation: $[13]^4$ $14\text{-}19^4$ $[20]^4$ 21^4 $[22]^2$. The last leaf is a blank.

Pagination: the same.

Wrapper not located. Presumably it is generally similar to that of the second edition of Part I.

Representative and identifying textual variants in Part II, First and Second Edition. A number of pages vary in lineation; see, for instance, p. 109.

Page & line	First edition	Second edition
103.7f	oracles respecting America	information respecting a coun-/
105.13	Where	where
107.5	test	examine

119.3	to be affected	[line 6] to be influenced
131.1	pervert. In	pervert, or
147.6-7	it / would be in vain to describe.	no / tongue nor pen could describe.
148.3	grave! -- so	grave! so
150.11	touching -- it	touching, it
155.7f	advances in life	[line 6f] jogs on in life

Henry Brevoort to Irving, 9 November 1819, "The printer will put the 2 edits. to press on Friday." Despite the ambiguity of the entry and the plural of "edition" -- a slip of the pen? -- the context suggests that Brevoort is referring to the second edition of Part II.

CtY (2), ICN, MB, NjP, NN (2), TxU.

The Langfeld and Blackburn bibliography reports a variant second edition of Part II in a different setting. Despite a diligent search over a number of years, in which sixteen copies of the second edition were checked in twelve libraries, no copy similar to the one there described has been discovered. It is possible that William Langfeld was describing a copy in his own collection; unfortunately, his collection was dispersed by auction in 1942.

Since Langfeld and Blackburn are so specific and detailed in description, however, they must have examined such a copy. They describe the title page as having double rules in place of the swelled rule, and a single rule in place of the rule of dots above the date, 1820. On their pp. 19-20 they list thirty-eight specific differences in text or setting between the first edition and this variant second edition. I reproduce here a few that differ in text both from the first edition and from the common second edition.

Page & line	First edition	Second edition
103.6	But it has been	It has been
105.8	Or, perhaps, they	They may, perhaps,
106.1	Or, perhaps	Perhaps
107.17	Nay, what is worse, they	Nay, they

A study of the few given textual variants suggests that this edition would fall textually somewhere between the common second edition and what is now considered the third edition, described below. If so, it would constitute the true third edition of Part II, and the so-called third edition below would be in fact a fourth edition.

Third edition.

101 Greenwich Street. | [rule] | 1822.

The text is derived from Vol. I of the first London edition.

Collation: $[13]^4$ 14-15^4 $[16]^4$ 17-21^4 22^2. The last leaf is a blank.

Pagination: the same.

Light gray paper wrapper. On front, within a box of double frame lines: THIRD EDITION. | [rule of 11 dots] | No. II.....Price 62 1/2 cents. | [rule] | THE SKETCH BOOK. [hollow letters] | [rule] | C. S. VAN WINKLE, PRINTER, | 101 Greenwich Street. Back and spine blank. White endpapers.

The text may be identified by a few representative changes from the first and second editions:

119.5 (the equivalent of line 3 of the first edition and line 6 of the second edition) to retaliate the

131.1 pervert, and

CtY (in wrapper), TxU, ViU.

Part III

First edition.

THE | SKETCH BOOK | OF | *GEOFFREY CRAYON, Gent.* | [swelled rule] | "I have no wife nor children, good or bad, to provide for. A mere spectator | of other men's fortunes and adventures, and how they play their parts; which | methinks are diversely presented unto me, as from a common theatre or scene." | BURTON. | [rule] | *NEW-YORK:* | PRINTED BY C. S. VAN WINKLE, | 101 Greenwich Street. | [rule of 10 dots] | 1819.

(23.5 x 15.0 untrimmed, the maximum dimensions noted): $[23]^4$ 24-32^4.

[171]-[172], title, on verso copyright ("the eleventh day of August, in the forty-third year of the Independence" by C. S. Van Winkle); [173]-[174], divisional fly-title for "A Royal Poet," verso blank; [175]-210, 203-242 (i.e., pp. 211-250 are mispaged 203-242), text.

Lineation: p. 200, laced, ... pran-; p. 225, song ... which

Page 240, line 12 occurs in two states; sequence not determined.

[A].   ont he

[B].   on the

Tan paper wrapper. On front, within a box of double frame lines: No. III....Price 62 1/2 cents. | [rule] | THE SKETCH BOOK. [hollow letters] | [rule] | C. S. VAN WINKLE, PRINTER, | 101 Greenwich-street. Back and spine blank. White endpapers.

The wrapper has been noted in at least two, and probably more, states of the cover-title and three or more states of issue.

Printed State 1. At head of title, as described, "No. III....Price 62 1/2 cents."

In a second state of issue, the printed price of 62 1/2 cents is changed by pen to 75 cents. Henry Brevoort wrote to Irving, 9 September 1819, "The price is printed 62 1/2 Cents on the cover, instead of 75 Cents -- this error was corrected after a few copies had been struck off." No uncorrected copy has been located. When Brevoort said "this error was corrected," however, he probably meant a correction in the type itself, the Printed State 2, rather than correction by pen.

It is possible that none of the copies in Printed State 1 escaped the printing house before correction by pen; if so, there would finally be only one "issue" of Printed State 1. But what if the pen corrections were made by one of the publishers? To pursue the question of terminology even further into the thicket, if the wrappers corrected by pen were mingled with wrappers in Printed State 2 and applied indiscriminately to copies of the part, and then the whole lot distributed to the publishers as one, there would be, in strict definition of the term, only one issue of the entire edition. But in considering the wrappers, the term "state of issue" is a convenient one for lack of a better and will serve usefully here, particularly since we know so little of the process followed in correcting the wrappers, application of the wrappers, or in distribution and issuance of the edition.

Printed State 2. At head of title, "No. III....Price 75 cents."

Some, although not all, copies are printed on waste stock. On the recto of the back cover, concealed by the pasted-down endpaper, appears the cover-title for the first printed state, with the printed price of 62 1/2 cents. See the discussion of the similar state of Part II.

The dimensions of the cover-title of Printed State 2 suggest the possibility, perhaps even the probability, of two settings. See the discussion of the similar condition of Part II. The two sets of extreme dimensions are as follows.

Width between inner frame lines at center:

    16.8 x 9.1   17.13 x 9.3

Length of title, from edge of T to edge of shading in period:

7.65   7.9

Length of top line, from edge of serif on N to edge of period:

4.3   4.15

2000 copies, published simultaneously in New York, Boston, Baltimore, Philadelphia.

Title deposited for copyright 11 August 1819. The notice on the back of the wrapper of Part II names the tenth of September as publication date. Henry Brevoort to Irving, 9 September 1819, "The 3d number will be published on Monday the 13th." *New-York Evening Post,* 13 September 1819, "C. WILEY & CO. ... have this day published, No. 3 ... price 75 cents"; also advertisements of Part 3 for sale by three booksellers.

In wrappers: CtY, NN (3), TxU (2), ViU (2). Wrappers examined in xerographic copy: CSmH, DLC, InU, TxFTC.

Second edition.

101 Greenwich Street. | [rule of 10 dots] | 1820.

Most of the revisions in the second edition were provided by Irving in a marked copy of the first edition sent from England.

Collation: $[1]^4$ $2\text{-}11^4$ 12^2.

Pagination: [1]-[5] 6-92.

[Tan paper wrapper. On front, within box of double frame lines: SECOND EDITION. | [rule of dots] | No. III....Price 75 cents. | [rule] | THE SKETCH BOOK. [hollow letters] | [rule] | C. S. VAN WINKLE, PRINTER, | 101 Greenwich-street. Back and spine blank. White endpapers. Wrapper not examined; description from secondary sources.]

In addition to the variations in title, collation, and pagination, the revised text shows a number of changes. The first three lines of the first page of the text, p. [175] in the First Edition and p. [5] in the Second Edition, are representative.

First Edition: On a soft sunny morning, in the month of | May, I made an excursion to Windsor, to visit | the castle. It is a proud old pile, stretching its |

Second Edition: On a soft sunny morning in the genial month | of May, I made an excursion to Windsor Castle. | It is a place full of storied and poetical associa- |

ICN, MB, MH, NjP, NN (2), NNC, TxU, ViU. MWA (in wrapper) not seen.

Third edition.

1823.

The text is derived from Vol. I of the first London edition.

The title and the wrapper, although not seen, are presumably similar to those of the third edition of Parts I and II.

Not located. William R. Langfeld owned a copy. It is listed under # 466 in the auction catalogue of his collection sold by City Book Auction, New York, 23-25 April 1942, Sale No. 193.

Part IV

First edition.

THE | SKETCH BOOK | OF | *GEOFFREY CRAYON, Gent.* | [swelled rule] | No. IV. | [rule] | "I have no wife nor children, good or bad, to provide for. A mere spectator of | other men's fortunes and adventures, and how they play their parts; which me- | thinks are diversely presented unto me, as from a common theatre or scene." | BURTON. | [rule] | *NEW-YORK:* | PRINTED BY C. S. VAN WINKLE, | 101 Greenwich Street. | [rule of 10 dots] | 1819.

(23.2 x 14.4 untrimmed, the maximum dimensions noted): [33]^4 34-44^4.

[243]-[244], title, on verso copyright ("the twelfth day of October, in the forty-fourth year of the Independence" by C. S. Van Winkle); [245]-[246], divisional fly-title for "The Mutability of Literature," verso blank; [247]-301 [302] [1 leaf unpaged] [303] 304-335, text; [336], blank.

One copy, at ViU, noted with a leaf of advertisements pasted between the front endpapers. On recto, advertisement for New Works by M. Carey & Son: *Fredolfo, A Tragedy,* by C. R. Maturin; *Oakwood Hall,* a Novel, by Catherine Hutton; *The Diverting History of John Bull and Brother Jonathan,* by Hector Bull-Us, Third edition. On verso, advertisement for Dubois on the Character, Manners, and Customs of the People of India; *Clarentine,* a Novel, by Miss Burney; *Llewellen, or The Vale of Phlinlimmon;* also a list of fourteen books for sale and two to be published. Presumably the leaf was inserted by Carey. Did it appear in all of the copies issued in Philadelphia?

Lineation: p. 250, bell ... painful ; p. 300, which ... and

Pages 286 and 320 appear each in two variant states. The relationship between the two states of the two individual pages is so variable that it does not define clearly a chronological series in the part as a whole: copies have been seen containing State [A] of p. 320 and both State [A] and State [B] of p. 286; but also copies with State [B] of p. 320 and both State [A] and State [B] of p. 286. Mixed sheets, or an occasional example of sophistication in rebound copies, would account for the random combinations, but perhaps these variant states should be considered only in terms of the individual page.

Page & line	State [A]	State [B]
286.5	open --	open,
320.10	corslets	corselets
320.17	bridegroom	Bridegroom

As a matter of information, the equivalent readings in the Second Edition, apparently set from an early copy of the First Edition revised by Irving, are all three those of State [A].

Page 313, line 1 has been noted with the reading "when" or "hen." Presumably that is the result of an accidental loss of the initial letter, in contrast to the changes on pp. 286 and 320 which had to be deliberate. But was the dropped "w" replaced later in the printing run?

Tan paper wrapper. On front, within a box of double frame lines: No. IV....Price 75 cents. | [rule] | THE SKETCH BOOK. [hollow letters] | [rule] | C. S. VAN WINKLE, PRINTER, | 101 Greenwich-street. Back and spine blank. White endpapers.

Published simultaneously in New York, Boston, Baltimore, Philadelphia.

Title deposited for copyright 12 October 1819. Henry Brevoort to Irving, 9 November 1819, "will be published tomorrow -- I have given Ebenezer 5 copies of it...." *New-York Evening Post,* 10 November 1819, "C. WILEY & CO. ... have this day published No. 4 ... price 75 cts"; 11 November 1819, advertisement by L. & F. Lockwood, "No 4 is just received for sale, and for the use of our Library subscribers."

In wrappers: CtY, NN (3), ViU (2).

Second edition.

101 Greenwich Street. | [rule of 10 dots] | 1820.

The revisions in the second edition were provided by Irving in a marked copy of the first edition sent from England.

Collation: [1]^4 2-12^4. The last leaf is a blank; in some copies it forms the pasted-down endpaper.

Pagination: [1]-[5] 6-93 [94].

In addition to the variations in title, collation, and pagination, the revised text shows a number of changes. Line 4f of the first page of the text, p. [247] in the First Edition and p. [5] in the Second Edition, is representative.

First Edition: reveries and

Second Edition: reveries, and

Tan paper wrapper. On front, within box of double frame lines: SECOND EDITION. | [rule of 15 dots] | No. IV.....Price 75 cents. | [rule] | THE SKETCH BOOK. [hollow letters] | [rule] | C. S. VAN WINKLE, PRINTER, | 101 Greenwich-street. Back and spine blank. White endpapers.

CtY (in wrapper), NjP, NN (in wrapper), TxU, ViU.

Part V

First edition.

THE | SKETCH BOOK | OF | *GEOFFREY CRAYON, Gent.* | [swelled rule]| No. V. | [rule] | "I have no wife nor children, good or bad, to provide for. A mere spectator of | other men's fortunes and adventures, and how they play their parts; which me- |thinks are diversely presented unto me, as from a common theatre or scene." | BURTON. | [rule] | *NEW-YORK:* | PRINTED BY C. S. VAN WINKLE, | 101 Greenwich Street. | [rule of 10 dots] | 1819.

Title in two states, no sequence determined.

[A]. In the fourth line, all letters are on baseline and evenly spaced.

[B]. The *O* in *GEOFFREY* is raised above the baseline and there is a slight gap between the *O* and the preceding *E*.

(23.3 x 14.6 untrimmed, the maximum dimensions noted): $[45]^4\ 46^4\ [47]^4\ 48^4$ $[49]^4\ 50\text{-}57^4\ 58^2$.

[337]-[338], title, on verso copyright ("the sixteenth day of December, in the forty-fourth year of the Independence" by C. S. Van Winkle); [339]-[340], divisional fly-title for "Christmas," verso blank; [341]-443, text; [444], blank.

Inserted at the front of some copies is a leaf of advertisements by M. Thomas, Philadelphia. On recto, a proposal to publish by subscription the Poetical Works of John Trumbull. On verso, advertisement for, among other items, 11 Late Publications, including *Salmagundi: Second Series* in 8 numbers, and *Knickerbocker's New York*, a new edition with elegant plates. Presumably the leaf was inserted by Moses Thomas. Did it appear in all of the copies issued in Philadelphia? A copy in InU with the advertising leaf bears on the front cover Thomas's bookseller's label.

Lineation: p. 350, as ... time ; p. 400, train, ... was

In paper wrapper (for colors, see below). On front, within a box of double frame lines: No. V.....75 cents. | [rule] | THE SKETCH BOOK [hollow letters] | [rule] | C. S. VAN WINKLE, PRINTER, | 101 Greenwich-street. Back and spine blank. White endpapers.

Noted on tan and on light gray stock; no sequence apparent.

The wrapper appears in two states; sequence not determined.

[A]. Line 1f of the cover title as described, with a period at the end.

The dimensions of the cover-title of State [A] suggest the possibility of two settings. See the discussion of the similar condition of Part II. The two sets of this wrapper, however, differ markedly only in a single measurement.

Vertical width between rules above and below title, at center;

    4.2   4.0

There seems to be no clear correlation between the two sets of dimensions, the two colors of the wrapper, and the two states of the title page.

[B]. Line 1f of the cover-title has no period at the end.

Located only in a single copy, in InU. The vertical width between rules is 4.0; the title page is in State [B].

Published simultaneously in New York, Boston, Baltimore, Philadelphia.

Title deposited for copyright 17 December 1819, despite the printed copyright notice for 16 December. *New-York Evening Post,* 31 December 1819, "C. WILEY & CO...will this day publish, ... No. 5"; also advertisements of Part 5 for sale by three booksellers. *Analectic Magazine,* January 1820, listed.

In wrappers: CtY, InU, NN (3), TxU, ViU (2). Wrappers examined in xerographic copy: DLC, TxFTC.

Second edition.

101 Greenwich Street. | [rule of 10 dots] | 1820.

Most of the revisions in the second edition were provided by Irving in a marked copy of the first edition sent from England. "Christmas Day" is divided into two sketches, "Christmas Morning" and "The Christmas Dinner," with basically the same text.

Collation: [1]⁴ 2-13⁴ 14².

Pagination: [1]-[5] 6-108.

Tan paper wrapper. On front, within box of double frame lines: SECOND EDITION. | [rule of 15 dots] | No. V.....Price 75 cents. | [rule] | THE SKETCH BOOK. [hollow letters] | [rule] | C. S. VAN WINKLE, PRINTER, | 101 Greenwich-street.   On back: [double rule] | *KNICKERBOCKER'S NEW-YORK.* [in left-slanting italic] | [swelled rule] | An arrangement having been made, by which the | remainder of the last edition of this work has passed | into the hands of the author's agent, the trade can be | supplied with copies, on application to EBENEZER | IRVING, 142 Pearl Street, New-York. | [double rule]. Spine blank. White endpapers.

In addition to the variations in title, collation, and pagination, and the division of "Christmas Day" into two separate sketches, the revised text shows a number of changes. Lines 4-6 of the first page of the text, p. [341] in the First Edition and p. [5] of the Second Edition, are representative.

First Edition: They recal the fond | picturings of an ideal state of things, which I | was wont to indulge in the May morning of |

Second Edition: They recal the | pictures my fancy used to draw in the May morn- | ing of life, when as yet I only knew the world |

Note: In all copies examined, the middle S in CHRISTMAS in the sketch-title on p. [5] of the Second Edition is set in the wrong font: a larger and more elaborate letter.

CtY (in wrapper), ICN, NN (2), NNC, TxU, ViU. DLC reports a copy in wrapper.

Part VI

First edition.

THE | SKETCH BOOK | OF | *GEOFFREY CRAYON, Gent.* | [swelled rule] | No. VI. | [rule] | "I have no wife nor children, good or bad, to provide for. A mere spectator of | other men's fortunes and adventures, and how they play their parts; which me- | thinks are diversely presented unto me, as from a common theatre or scene." | BURTON. | [rule] | *NEW-YORK:* | PRINTED BY C. S. VAN WINKLE, | 101 Greenwich Street. | [rule of 10 dots] | 1820.

To distinguish this first edition from the second, see the table of variant readings in the description of the second edition. The two title pages are the same.

(23.4 x 14.6 untrimmed, the maximum dimensions noted): $[1]^4$ $2\text{-}15^4$.

[1]-[2], title, on verso copyright ("the tenth day of February, in the forty-fourth year of the Independence" by C. S. Van Winkle); [3]-[4], divisional fly-title for "John Bull," verso blank; [5]-120 text.

Page 19 and page 108 appear in variant states, presumably the result of stop-press corrections.

Page & line	State A (incorrect)	State B (correct)
19.8f	gaze	graze
108.1	pedagouge	pedagogue

Lineation: p. 50, blank; p. 75, From ... beset ; p. 100, shaded ... to

Tan paper wrapper. On front, within box of double frame lines: No. VI.....Price 87 1/2 cents. | [rule] | THE SKETCH BOOK. [hollow letters] | [rule] | PUBLISHED BY HALY AND THOMAS, NEW-YORK, | AND M. THOMAS, PHILADELPHIA. On back: [double rule] | JUST PUBLISHED, | BY HALY AND THOMAS, NEW-YORK, | *AND M. THOMAS, PHILADELPHIA,* | GIOVANNI SBOGARRO, [hollow letters] | A VENETIAN TALE, | *BY PERCIVAL GORDON.* | In 2 vols. -- Price $2 00. | A WELL WRITTEN AND VERY INTERESTING TALE. | ALSO, | A THIRD EDITION OF THAT POPULAR AND AMUSING WORK, THE | *HISTORY OF NEW-YORK,* [in left-slanting italic] | BY DIEDRICH KNICKERBOCKER. | [double rule]. Spine blank. White endpapers.

Some, although not all, copies of the wrapper are printed on waste stock. On the recto of the back cover, concealed by the pasted-down endpaper, appears a cancelled cover-title for Part VI with the imprint: C.S. VAN WINKLE, PRINTER | 101 Greenwich-street. See the discussion of the similar state in Parts II and III. Presumably the original wrapper was cancelled after Haly and Thomas assumed the publication rights in New York -- and wanted their imprint on the wrapper. Note that the wrapper of the second edition, however, bears the imprint of C. S. Van Winkle.

Published simultaneously in New York, Boston, Baltimore, Philadelphia.

Title deposited for copyright 10 February 1820. *New-York Evening Post,* 10 March 1820, "Is in press, and will be published about the middle of this month, by HALY & THOMAS, No. 142 Broadway, New-York, and by M. THOMAS, 103 Chesnut-street, Philadelphia"; 16 March 1820, "Haly & Thomas ... have this day published the 6th number.... Complete sets in 6 Nos. price 4 50," individually priced 87 1/2 cents; also advertisements of Part 6 for sale by a number of booksellers.

In wrappers: CtY, DLC, NN (3), ViU (2).

Second edition.

Title, collation, and pagination unchanged.

The revisions in the second edition were provided by Irving in a marked copy of the first edition sent from England.

Tan paper wrapper. On front, within box of double frame lines: SECOND EDITION. | [rule of 15 dots]| No. VI.....Price 87 1/2 cents. | [rule] | THE SKETCH BOOK. [hollow letters] | [rule] | C. S. VAN WINKLE, PRINTER, | 101 Greenwich Street. Back and spine blank. In copy examined, white endpapers at front but no endpapers at back.

Representative and identifying variants in Part VI, First and Second Edition:

Page & line	First Edition	Second Edition
title	The U of BURTON under the "c" of "scene"	The U of BURTON under the period after "scene"
copyright	The B of BE under the *e* of *Southern*	The B of BE under the space between *Southern District*
19.8f	gaze (or graze)	gaze
33.1f	flowers; a	flowers -- a
47.12	lover!	lover.
55.5f	known, at	known at
59.2	voices conning	voices, conning
81.10	redoutable	redoubtable
85.8	green,	green
91.14	eel-skin	eelskin
109.7	lopping	loping
117.7f	schoolhouse	school-house

CtY (in wrapper), MB, MH (2), NN, TxU, ViU.

Part VII

First edition.

THE | SKETCH BOOK | OF | *GEOFFREY CRAYON, Gent.* | [swelled rule] | No. VII. | [rule] | "I have no wife nor children, good or bad, to provide for. A mere spectator of | other men's fortunes and adventures, and how they play their parts; which me- | thinks are diversely presented unto me, as from a common theatre or scene." | BURTON. | [rule] | *NEW-YORK*: | PRINTED BY C. S. VAN WINKLE, | 101 Greenwich Street. | [rule of 10 dots] | 1820.

To distinguish this first edition from the second, see the table of variant readings in the description of the second edition. The two title pages are the same.

(23.2 x 14.7 untrimmed, the maximum dimensions noted): $[1]^4$ 2-15^4 16^2.

[1]-[2], title, on verso copyright ("the twelfth day of August, in the forty-fifth year of the Independence" by C. S. Van Winkle); [3]-[4], divisional fly-title for "Westminster Abbey," verso blank; [5]-123, text; [124], blank.

Inserted at the front of some copies is a leaf of advertisements by M. Thomas. On recto, advertisement for *The Analectic Magazine*. On verso, advertisement for "Books, Stationery and Fancy Articles," and for publications by Thomas. Presumably the leaf was inserted by Moses Thomas, the Philadelphia publisher. Did it appear in all of the copies issued in Philadelphia?

Lineation: p. 50, blank; p. 75, air ... wor-; p. 100, customers, ... workshop!

Tan or brown-tan paper wrapper. On front, within box of double frame lines: No. VII.....Price 87 1/2 cents. | [rule] | THE SKETCH BOOK. [hollow letters] | [rule] | PUBLISHED BY HALY AND THOMAS, NEW-YORK, | AND M. THOMAS, PHILADELPHIA. On back: [double rule] | *KNICKERBOCKER'S NEW-YORK.* [in left-slanting italic] | [swelled rule] | An arrangement having been made, by which the | remainder of the last edition of this work has passed | into the hands of the author's agent, the trade can be | supplied with copies, on application to EBENEZER | IRVING, 142 Pearl Street, New-York. | [double rule]. Spine blank. White endpapers.

Published simultaneously in New York, Boston, Baltimore, Philadelphia.

Title deposited for copyright 12 August 1820. Irving to John Murray, 22 September 1850, "published ... Septr 13, 1820." *Analectic Magazine,* September 1820, "in press and will be published about the middle of the present month." *New-York Evening Post,* 11 September 1820, "Haly & Thomas ... will publish on Wednesday next, the Seventh Number"; 13 September 1820, "Haley & Thomas ... have this day published ...," at 87 1/2 cents; also advertisements of Part 7 for sale by a number of booksellers. *Literary and Scientific Repository,* 1 October 1820, listed.

In wrappers: CtY, NjP, NN (3), ViU.

Second edition.

Title, collation, and pagination unchanged.

The revisions in the second edition were provided by Irving from England, probably in a marked copy of the first edition, although sections of two sketches follow the text of the first London edition.

Tan paper wrapper. On front, within box of double frame lines: SECOND EDITION. | No. VII....Price 87 1/2 cents. | [rule] | THE SKETCH BOOK. [hollow letters] | [rule] | C. S. VAN WINKLE, PRINTER, | 101 Greenwich Street. Back and spine blank. White endpapers.

Representative and identifying variants in Part VII, First and Second Edition:

Page & line	*First Edition*	*Second Edition*
title	Width between straight rules 1.75 cm.	Width between straight rules 2.1 cm.
copyright	Last line begins: "etching	Last line begins: "and etching
7.10f	cloud, and	cloud; and
13.3f	Sepul- |	sepul- |
21.5f	notes, and piling	notes, piling
37.10	| tlemen's	| tleman's
46.1f	cage. The scene	cage. He had
[53].5f	may -- let	may; let
61.3	girl; and	girl, and
74.5f	footpath	foot-path
88.1	path -- and	path; and
104.11	apothecary: it	apothecary: It

CtY (in wrapper), MB, MH (2), NjP, NNC, TxU (3), ViU (in wrapper).

4A.   THE | SKETCH BOOK | OF | GEOFFREY CRAYON, GENT. | [rule] |"I ... of | other ... methinks, | are ... scene." | BURTON. | [rule] | FOURTH AMERICAN EDITION. | *IN TWO VOLUMES.* | VOL. I. [II.] | [double rule] | *NEW-YORK:* | PRINTED BY C. S. VAN WINKLE, | No. 2 Thames-street. | [rule] | 1824.

(19.6 x 11.7): Vol. I. [1]^2 2-24^6. Vol. II. [1]^2 2-26^6 27^4.

The Order of Sketches is essentially that of 1E, although the edition contains an "Advertisement" to *both* the American and the English edition. Vol. I ends with "Westminster Abbey."

Vol. I. [1]-[ii], title, on verso copyright ("the fifteenth day of May, in the forty-third year of the Independence" [i.e., the date of the original Part I] by C. S. Van Winkle), [iii]-[iv], table of contents, verso blank; [v]-[vi], dedication to Sir Walter Scott, verso blank; [vii]-viii, Advertisement to First American Edition; [ix]-x, Advertisement to First English Edition; [11]-280, text. Vol. II. [1]-[2], title, on verso same copyright; [3]-[4], table of contents, verso blank; [5]-312, text.

Lineation: Vol. I. p. 100, He ... suddenly ; p. 200, "Softly, ... might Vol. II. p. 100, many ... ges.; p. 200, feelings ... men

Drab paper boards with paper label.

CtY (2), ViU.

5A.   THE | SKETCH BOOK | OF | GEOFFREY CRAYON GENT. [Vol. II has comma after CRAYON] | [rule] | "I ... mere | spectator ... their | parts, ... common | theatre or scene." -- *Burton.* | [rule] | FIFTH AMERICAN EDITION. | *IN TWO VOLUMES.* | VOL. I. [II.] | [double rule] | *NEW-YORK:* | PRINTED BY C. S. VAN WINKLE, | No. 48 Pine-street. | [rule] | 1826.

(18.0 x 10.2 rebound):   collation, pagination, and lineation unchanged. Although the type is reset, the setting of this edition reproduces the Fourth American Edition, often line for line.

Lineation: the same as the Fourth Edition.

ViU.

6Aa.   THE | SKETCH-BOOK | OF | GEOFFREY CRAYON, GENT. | [rule] | "I ... mere | spectator ... play | their ... a | common ... scene." -- *Burton.* | [rule] | IN TWO VOLUMES. | VOL. I. [II.] | SIXTH AMERICAN EDITION. | [double rule] | Philadelphia: [fancy] | CAREY, LEA & CAREY -- CHESNUT-STREET. | [rule of dots] | 1828.

Still copyright "the fifteenth day of May, in the forty-third year of the Independence" by C. S. Van Winkle.

(17.5 x 10.8 rebound): Vol. I. [i]-x, [11]-236. Vol. II. [i-vi unpaged], [7]-264. Signed in 6's.

The Order of Sketches reproduces that of the Fourth and Fifth American editions.

Lineation: Vol. I. p. 100, THE | ART ... to ; p. 200, embroider ... wonderfully Vol. II. p. 100, butcher ... that ; p. 150, hardships; ... the ; p. 200, blank.

The Cost Book of Carey & Lea lists 1000 copies @ 1.00; 1000 copies @ 1.40; 75 copies, "Fine copy paper," @ 5.00. That suggests two standard bindings (boards and cloth?) and a more elegant paper and binding. Seen only rebound.

PPL.

b. SEVENTH AMERICAN EDITION. | [double rule] | Philadelphia: [fancy] | CAREY, LEA & CAREY -- CHESNUT-STREET. | [rule of 12 dots] | 1829.

Despite the identification on the title page, this is an impression of the Sixth American Edition.

NN.

c. SEVENTH AMERICAN EDITION. | [double rule] | Philadelphia: [fancy] | CAREY & LEA -- CHESNUT-STREET. | [rule of dots] | 1830.

BL.

d. SEVENTH AMERICAN EDITION. | [double rule] | Philadelphia: [fancy] | CAREY & LEA -- CHESNUT-STREET. | [rule of 17 dots] | 1831.

NN, ViU.

e. Philadelphia: [fancy] | CAREY & LEA -- CHESNUT-STREET. | [rule of 16 dots] | 1832.

Identification of edition omitted.

Noted in green, and in pink-tan, paper boards.

CtY, NN, ViU.

f. Philadelphia: [fancy] | CAREY & LEA -- CHESNUT-STREET. | [rule of 16 dots] | 1833.

NN.

g. Philadelphia: [fancy] | CAREY & LEA -- CHESNUT-STREET. | [rule of 16 dots] | 1834.

Tan paper boards.

CtY.

h. A NEW EDITION. | [rule] | Philadelphia: [fancy] | CAREY, LEA, & BLANCHARD. | [rule of 21 dots] | 1835.

Copyright "the twenty-first day of November, in the forty-eight (sic) year of the independence."

Tan paper boards with white paper label on spines.

CtY, NN.

i. A NEW EDITION. | [rule] | Philadelphia: [fancy] | CAREY, LEA, & BLANCHARD. | [rule of 21 dots] | 1836.

Copyright 1836 by Washington Irving.

Noted only in drab paper boards with white paper label on spines: [double rule] | THE | SKETCH BOOK | [rule] | VOL. I. [II.] | [double rule].

As two volumes in the Collected works being published by Carey, Lea & Blanchard, the impression must certainly have been issued also in cloth with a Works identification on the spines.

Copyrighted and title pages deposited 20 July 1836. Each volume was copyrighted separately. In the copyright records, there is also a single copyright entry for the work on 12 August 1836, but the entry is canceled. It is possible that a complete copy of the impression was deposited on that day and incorrectly entered until the error was discovered. If so, a notation recording the deposit of a copy was not made on the original entries, a notation that was sometimes made in the records and sometimes not.

TxU, ViU.

j. A NEW EDITION. | [rule] | Philadelphia: [fancy] | CAREY, LEA & BLANCHARD. | [rule of 21 dots] | 1837.

Dark green V cloth. Sides blank. White paper label on spines: [rule] | THE | SKETCH BOOK | [rule] | VOL. I. [II.] | [rule].

NN.

k. A NEW EDITION. | [rule] | PHILADELPHIA: LEA & BLANCHARD, | SUCCESSORS TO CAREY & CO. | [rule of 27 dots] | 1839.

Dark green V cloth with white paper label on spines.

NN.

l. A NEW EDITION. | [rule] | PHILADELPHIA: | LEA & BLANCHARD. | [rule of 27 dots] | 1840.

Green V cloth with white paper label on spines.

NNU (Vol. II only).

m. A NEW EDITION. | [rule] | PHILADELPHIA: | LEA & BLANCHARD. | 1842.

Purple V cloth with white paper label on spines: [double rule] | THE | *Sketch Book*. | BY THE | Author of the | "ALHAMBRA," | &c. &c. | [rule] | *In Two Vols.* | VOL. I. [II.] | [double rule].

CtY, NN.

7Aa, THE | SKETCH BOOK | OF | GEOFFREY CRAYON, GENT. | THE
b. AUTHOR'S REVISED EDITION. | COMPLETE IN ONE VOLUME. | NEW-YORK: | GEORGE P. PUTNAM, 155 BROADWAY, | And 142 Strand, London | 1848.

Noted in two states:

A. (18.6 x 12.6): $[1]^{12}$ ($[A]^2$ bound between first two leaves) $2\text{-}19^{12}\ 20^6$. The last leaf is a blank. No advertisements.

B. (18.9 x 12.6): $[1]^{12}$ ($[A]^2$ bound between first two leaves) $2\text{-}19^{12}\ 20^4\ [21]^1$. Not reckoned: terminal catalogue of 24 pp., paged [1]-[2] 3-19 [20]-[21] 22 [23]-[24], dated *Sept.*, 1848. On p. [2] of the catalogue, *The Sketch Book* "Will be published on the first of October"; the illustrated *Sketch Book*, "in October will be published."

The two states apparently represent two impressions. If so, State A precedes State B. State B shows more type batter than State A: see, for example, the wear on p. 129. In State B, on p. [v] of the table of contents, the fourth dot between "Rural Funerals" and its page number is missing; on p. vi, the last dot between "L'Envoy" and its page number is missing. (In both states, on p. [v] a comma incorrectly appears in place of the second dot after "English Writers on America.") State B has been seen only bound in dark green TB cloth to match the other volumes of the collected Works.

Order of Sketches: ARE.

[i]-[ii], Works title, Vol. II, 1848, verso blank; [iii]-[iv], title, on verso copyright (1848) and printer; [v]-vi, table of contents; [vii]-xii, Preface to the Revised Edition, dated Sunnyside, 1848; [9]-465, text; [466], blank.

Printer: Leavitt, Trow & Co., Printers and Stereotypers, 49 Ann-street, N. Y.

Lineation: p. 100, throng, ... to ; p. 200, count ... and

Noted in two bindings:

Dark green T cloth with horizontal lighter green stripes in "watered" effect. On sides, in gilt, interlocked geometrical design within single broad line of border. On spine, in gilt, interlocked geometrical design; titled: SKETCH BOOK | [rule] | IRVING . AEG. White endpapers flowered with small green cross-and-dot design. Fly leaves.

Dark green TB cloth.   On sides, in blind, publisher's initials within ornamental design.   Spine decorated in blind, titled in gilt: IRVING'S | WORKS | [rule] | SKETCH BOOK | PUTNAM . Endpapers manila-buff. Flyleaves.

Advertised in *Literary World,* 30 September 1848, as available in "Cloth Extra, $1 25; Cloth Extra Gilt, $1 75; Half-Calf, $2 00; Half Morocco, top edge Gilt, $2 25; Calf Extra, $2 50." That may not include the dark green cloth to match the other volumes in the ARE collected Works.

Literary World, 2 September 1848, "Will be published on the first of October"; 30 September 1848, advertised under "New Publications"; 7 October 1848, listed, reviewed, advertised as "Published this day." *Knickerbocker,* October 1848, extract printed "from the early sheets of the volume."

Literary World, 2 December 1848, "THIRD EDITION, To be published this week"; 9 December 1848, "Published this week." Does this represent State B? (The illustrated form of 1848 may have been considered the "second edition.")

TxU, ViU, Private hands.

c,d.   [Illustrated form].   THE | SKETCH BOOK | OF | GEOFFREY CRAYON, GENT^N. [with 2 dots beneath the raised N] | AUTHOR'S REVISED EDITION, | WITH ORIGINAL DESIGNS BY F. O. C. DARLEY, | ENGRAVED BY CHILDS, HERRICK, ETC. | NEW-YORK: | GEORGE P. PUTNAM, 155 Broadway. | 1848. All within single frame lines.

In two states of the title page, probably representing two impressions of the work:

State 1. Title as described, without quotation from Burton.

State 2.   Title page: THE | SKETCH BOOK | OF | GEOFFREY CRAYON, GENT^N. [with 2 dots beneath the raised N] | "I ... spectator | of ... parts; | which ... or | scene." -- *Burton.* | AUTHOR'S REVISED EDITION. | WITH ORIGINAL DESIGNS BY F. O. C. DARLEY, | ENGRAVED BY CHILDS, HERRICK, ETC. | NEW-YORK: | GEORGE P. PUTNAM, 155 BROADWAY. | 1848. All within single frame lines.

(21.5 x 15.5):   collation and pagination the same as the Works form. Illustrations not reckoned.

The text is from the same plates as the Works form, with single frame lines added around each page. The Works title is replaced by the regular title, and a table of illustrations is substituted as p. [iii].

The table of illustrations lists 17 engravings: a vignette title, a preliminary portrait of Irving, and 15 other illustrations through the text, some inserted on extra leaves, some pasted down in appropriate blank spaces in the text. Some copies, however, have five or six additional engravings pasted down; the full six extra appear on pp. vi, 187, 191, 279, 422, 460.

Later impressions of the illustrated form, after 1848, print the quotation on the title page and list 22 engravings, rather than 17, in the table of illustrations, taking into account at least five of the added pasted-down illustrations.

Printer: Leavitt, Trow & Co., Printers and Stereotypers, 49 Ann-street, N. Y.

State 1 noted in three cloths: [A]. Blue S-like heavily ribbed cloth. On sides, in gilt, vignette of Rip Van Winkle asleep with gun and dog, within blind border of large geometrical decorations, all within triple frame lines. Spine "hand lettered" in gilt. AEG. Manilla endpapers. [B]. Blue A cloth. Sides decorated in gilt with stylized rectangle of vine, leaves, flowers, within border of triple frame lines. On spine in gilt, THE | SKETCH | BOOK | [rule] | IRVING within box of double frame lines; below, three ornaments (the central one a female figure holding vase with flowers above her head) within box of double frame lines. AEG. White endpapers. [C]. Purple TB-like cloth. On sides, the same decoration as [B], except in blind. Spine the same as [B]. No edges gilt. White endpapers.

Advertised in *Literary World*, 14 October 1848, and in the publisher's catalogue found in some copies of the Works form, dated 1848, as available in cloth extra, $3.50; cloth gilt, $4.00; morocco extra, $6.00; or, proofs on India paper, morocco super extra (only 50 printed), $7.50.

Literary World, 30 September 1848, advertised under "New Publications"; 7 October 1848, "To be published Monday, October 16th"; 14 October 1848, "Published this week."

State 1: NN, NjP, TxU, ViU. State 2: NN.

e. [Works form].   NEW-YORK: | GEORGE P. PUTNAM, 155 BROADWAY, | And 142 Strand, London. | 1849.

Quotation from Burton added on title.

Works title, dated 1849.

In the copy seen, four pages of advertisements are bound at the beginning, dated July, 1849; six pages of advertisements are bound at the end, undated, paged 5-10. On p. 10 of the terminal advertisements, *Mohammed and His Successors* (sic) is marked *In October*.

It is highly probable that there were two impressions dated 1849. The preliminary advertisements in the copy seen suggest a publication date close to July 1849. But there is an advertisement in *Literary World*, 3 February 1849, for "The new impression (7th thousand) ... now ready."

DLC.

f. [Illustrated form].   NEW-YORK: | GEORGE   P.   PUTNAM,   155 BROADWAY. | MDCCCXLIX.

Quotation from Burton on title.

Noted in the binding state that the advertisements for (or at least presumably for) an 1848 impression call "morocco super extra," with proof illustrations. That advertisement in 1848 specifies fifty copies. Was such a limited state issued again in 1849, or was the original limited state issued with an 1849 title page? Full morocco. On sides, in gilt, outer border of double frame lines, inner floral border, and floral design at center. Spine heavily corded, decorated in gilt, titled: IRVING'S | SKETCH BOOK | | ILLUSTRATED | BY DARLEY AEG.

Literary World, 10 November 1849, "A New Edition," "Now ready," "Cloth extra, $3 50; cloth gilt, $4; morocco extra, $6; papier mache, $7." *Albion*, 17 November 1849, "Now ready."

NN. "Morocco super extra" in Sleepy Hollow.

g. [Works form].   NEW-YORK: | GEORGE   P.   PUTNAM,   155 BROADWAY, | And 142 Strand, London. | 1850.

Works title, dated 1850.

Dark green TB cloth with publisher's initials within ornament on sides in blind. White endpapers. One copy noted with cream endpapers printed with publisher's advertisements.

DLC, ViU.

h. [Illustrated form].   NEW-YORK: | GEORGE   P.   PUTNAM,   155 BROADWAY. | MDCCCL.

Dark blue vertical A cloth. On front, in gilt, vignette of Rip Van Winkle asleep with gun and dog, within blind border of large geometrical decorations, within triple frame lines. Repeated on back, entirely in blind. Spine "hand lettered" in gilt. TEG.

ViU.

i. [Works form].   NEW-YORK: | GEORGE   P.   PUTNAM,   155 BROADWAY, | And 142 Strand, London. | 1851.

Works title, dated 1851.

TxU.

j. [Works form]. NEW-YORK: | GEORGE P. PUTNAM, 10 PARK PLACE, | And 142 Strand, London. | 1852.

Works title, dated 1852.

MB.

k. [Works form]. NEW-YORK: | G. P. PUTNAM & COMPANY, 10 PARK PLACE. | 1852.

Works title, dated 1852.

Private hands.

l. [Illustrated form]. NEW-YORK: | GEORGE P. PUTNAM, 10 PARK PLACE. | 1852.

The illustration for "Rural Life in England" replaces the portrait of Irving before the title. The portrait is placed in the text, as one of the twenty in the text, some pasted down. The list of illustrations is changed to correspond. The setting of the text remains the same.

NN.

m. [Works form]. NEW-YORK: | G. P. PUTNAM & COMPANY, 10 PARK PLACE. | 1853.

Works title, dated 1853.

Blue-green TB cloth with publisher's initials on sides in blind. Spine titled in gilt. White endpapers.

NN, MH (With works title only).

n. [Works form]. NEW YORK: | G. P. PUTNAM & COMPANY, 10 PARK PLACE. | 1854.

Works title, dated 1854.

Preliminary engraved illustration and engraved title added.

DLC.

o. [Illustrated form]. NEW-YORK: | G. P. PUTNAM & COMPANY, 10 PARK PLACE. | 1854.

Printer: John F. Trow, 49 Ann-street, N. Y.

Royal blue AR cloth. On sides, in gilt, Rip Van Winkle asleep with gun and dog within oval frame, all within border in blind. Spine decorated in gilt and titled in fancy individual lettering. Yellow endpapers.

Also reported by bookseller in black morocco, extra gilt, AEG.

NNHi.

p. [Works form]. NEW-YORK: | G. P. PUTNAM & COMPANY, 10 PARK PLACE. | 1855.

Works title, dated 1855.

DLC.

q. [Works form]. NEW YORK: | G. P. PUTNAM & CO., 321 BROADWAY. | 1857.

Works title, dated 1857.

MH.

r. [Works form]. NEW YORK: | G. P. PUTNAM (for the Proprietor), 506 BROADWAY. | 1859.

Preliminary portrait of Irving and engraved title for *Irving Vignettes* added, published by Childs & Peterson, Philadelphia.

NjP.

8A. THE | SKETCH BOOK | BY | WASHINGTON IRVING. | [rule] | "I ... mere | spectator ... their | parts; ... com- | mon ... scene." -- BURTON. | [rule] | NEW YORK: | G. P. PUTNAM & CO., 321 BROADWAY. | [rule] | 1857.

"Putnam's Railway Classics" series.

(16.5 x 10.7): [-]^8 1-16^8. The first leaf is a blank. Not reckoned: preliminary engraved portrait of Irving and vignette title.

Order of Sketches: ARE.

[i]-[ii], half-title, verso blank; [iii]-[iv], title, on verso copyright (1848) and printer; [v]-xii, Preface; [xiii]-xiv, table of contents; [1]-256, text.

Printer: R. Craighead, Printer & Stereotyper, Caxton Building, 81, 83, and 85 Centre Street.

Lineation: p. 100, the ... [in footnote] arm.; p. 200, who ... [in footnote] Island.

Noted in pink paper boards. On front, cover-title, dated 1857, and identification of series, price 50¢ . On back, advertisements for Irving's

Works: "15 vols. Cloth, $19.00; sheep, $20.00; half calf, $30; half calf extra, $33; half calf ant. $33; calf extra, $37; calf ant. $40. Morocco ed. $48." On inner covers, advertisements.

Contemporary advertisements list the edition as available in paper boards, 50 cents; in cloth, 60 cents.

American Publishers' Circular, 2 May 1857, "Next week"; 9 May 1857, "Now ready."

TxU. NNU, rebound.

9A.   NEW YORK: | G. P. PUTNAM, 115 NASSAU STREET. | 1859.

(18.5 x 12.6 rebound): [1]-465 [466]. Not reckoned: preliminary portrait of Irving by Jarvis and engraved title for *Irving Vignettes*, published by Childs & Peterson, Philadelphia. Signed in 12's.

Decorations and a few illustrations printed in blank spaces in the text.

Order of Sketches: ARE.

Printer: John F. Trow, 377 and 379 Broadway, Cor. White Street, New York.

Lineation: p. 100, the ... Whether ; p. 200, entranced; ... mingled

Seen only rebound. Other volumes in the same set of complete Works are bound in green BD cloth.

DLC.

1E,   Since the first complete London edition, in two volumes, was issued by two
2E.   different publishers (with the first volume bearing two different title pages), and since the second complete edition bears a different identification of edition on the title page of Vol. I and Vol. II, it seems not only convenient but finally less confusing to describe the first two London editions volume by volume rather than complete edition by complete edition.

Volume I

First edition, first issue.

THE | SKETCH BOOK | OF | GEOFFREY CRAYON, Gent. | [rule] | "I have no wife nor children, good or bad, to provide for. A mere | spectator of other men's fortunes and adventures, and how they play | their parts; which methinks are diversely presented unto me, as from | a common theatre or scene." | BURTON. | [rule] | [ornament of Athena's head within an elaborate wreath of oak leaves and acorns] | London: [fancy] | JOHN MILLER, BURLINGTON ARCADE. | [rule] | 1820.

(21.2 x 12.6 rebound): $[A]^4$ $B-I^8$ $K-U^8$ $X-Z^8$.

Langfeld and Blackburn describe the volume as containing a preliminary gathering of 6 pp. of advertisements, with leaves smaller in size than those of the complete volume. Not seen. One copy is reported by a correspondent to contain 4 pp. of advertisements, paged [1] 2-3 [4]; pp. [1]-3 are given to a prospectus for *Annals of Oriental Literature*, p. [4] to works recently published by Longman, Hurst, Rees, Orne, and Brown of London.

[i]-[ii], half-title, on verso printer; [iii]-[iv], title, verso blank; [v]-vi, "Advertisement," dated February, 1820; [1]-[2], table of contents, verso blank; [3]-354, text, printer at foot of last page.

Printer: W. Pople, 67, Chancery Lane, London.

Lineation: p. 100, one ... con-; p. 200, blank; p. 250, English ... depo-

Printed in an impression of 1000 copies, of which 500 were issued as described. When Miller fell into financial difficulties, the remaining 500 were sold in sheets to John Murray who issued them, with a cancel title page, under his own imprint. See the description of the Murray issue below.

Probably issued in paper boards with paper label on spine.

Literary Gazette, 15 January 1820, advertised by John Miller: "preparing for publication..., and will appear early in February," described as "The first American Edition with alterations and additions, by the Author. In one handsome vol. 8vo."; 8 April 1820, reviewed. Irving to John Murray, 22 September 1850, "published in Feby 1820."

NcU, TxU (2), WU-Ex.

First edition, second issue.

THE | SKETCH BOOK | OF | GEOFFREY CRAYON, GENT. | [RULE] | "I have no wife nor children, good or bad, to provide for. | A mere spectator of other men's fortunes and adventures, and | how they play their parts; which, methinks, are diversely pre- | sented unto me, as from a common theatre or scene." | BURTON. | [rule] | *SECOND EDITION.* | [double rule] | LONDON: | JOHN MURRAY, ALBEMARLE-STREET. | [rule] | 1820.

(21.7 x 13.0 rebound): the same sheets as the John Miller issue, with a cancel title page.

The identification of "Second Edition" should not mislead; this is simply an issue by John Murray of the John Miller first edition.

Literary Gazette, 22 July 1820, advertisement for Vol. II of *The Sketch Book* by John Murray, "of whom may be had, a new Edition of the First Volume, 12*s*."

OkU, ViU.

Second edition.

THE | SKETCH BOOK | OF | GEOFFREY CRAYON, GENT. | [rule] | "I ... A | mere ... how | they ... unto | me, ... scene." | BURTON. | [rule] | VOL. I. | *THIRD EDITION.* | [double rule] | LONDON: | JOHN MURRAY, ALBEMARLE-STREET. | [rule] | 1820.

(21.4 x 13.3 rebound): $[A]^4$ $B-I^8$ $K-U^8$ $X-Y^8$ Z^4.

Order of Sketches: 1E.

[i]-[ii], title, on verso printer; [iii]-[iv], dedication, verso blank; [v]-vi, Advertisement; [vii]-[viii], table of contents, verso blank; [1]-343, text, printer at foot of last page; [344], advertisement for A New Edition of *A History of New York*, just published.

Printer: C. Roworth, Bell-Yard, Temple-Bar. (Y and B in lower case on last page.)

Lineation: p. 100, I ... and ; p. 200, headed ... gate,

This second edition of Vol. I (even though called "Third Edition" on the title page) was intended to be paired with the matching second edition of Vol. II, correctly called "Second Edition" on its title page.

Literary Gazette, 30 September to 14 October 1820, Third Edition of Vol. I advertised under the heading of "Published This Day."

NN, TxGeoS, TxU.

Volume II

First edition.

THE | SKETCH BOOK | OF | GEOFFREY CRAYON, GENT. | [rule] | "I have no wife nor children, good or bad, to provide for. A | mere spectator of other men's fortunes and adventures, and how | they play their parts; which, methinks, are diversely presented unto | me, as from a common theatre or scene." | BURTON. | [rule] | VOL. II. | [double rule] | LONDON: | JOHN MURRAY, ALBEMARLE-STREET. | [rule] | 1820.

(21.6 x 13.4 rebound): [A]^4 B-I^8 K-U^8 X-Z^8 AA-DD^8 EE^2.

In two states, sequence probable.

A. Page [ii], the verso of the half-title, blank. On p. [2], the verso of the
    divisional fly-title, printer's imprint.

B. On p. [ii], the printer's imprint. Page [2], blank.

[i]-[ii], half-title, verso either blank or with printer's imprint; [iii]-[iv], title
verso blank; [v]-[vi], dedication to Sir Walter Scott, verso blank; [vii]-[viii],
table of contents, verso blank; [1]-[2], divisional fly-title for "Westminster
Abbey," on verso either printer's imprint or blank; [3]-419, text, printer at
foot of last page; [420], blank.

Printer: C. Roworth, Bell-yard, Temple-bar.

Lineation: p. 100, something ... deplorable ; p. 200, which ... the

Washington Irving to Ebenezer Irving, 15 August 1820, "a thousand were
printed." The first London edition of Vol. II was sold as a separate volume
but was intended to be paired with the first London edition of Vol. I issued
earlier, first by John Miller and then by John Murray.

Issued in paper boards with paper label on spines. Not seen. Langfeld's
private collection, now dispersed, contained two copies in boards, apparently
of different colors.

Literary Gazette, 22 July 1820, reviewed, advertised at 12*s*. Irving to John
Murray, 22 September 1850, "published by Mr. Murray 15th July."

State A: ViU. State B: NN, OkU.

Second edition.

THE | SKETCH BOOK | OF | GEOFFREY CRAYON, GENT. | [rule] |
"I ... A | mere ... how | they ... unto | me, ... scene." | BURTON. | [rule] |
VOL. II. | *SECOND EDITION.* | [double rule] | LONDON: | JOHN
MURRAY, ALBEMARLE-STREET. | [rule] | 1820.

(21.4 x 13.3 rebound): [A]^4 B-I^8 K-U^8 X-Z^8 AA-DD^8 EE^2.

Order of Sketches: 1E.

[i]-[ii], (half-title, on verso printer?); [iii]-[iv], title, verso blank; [v]-[vi],
dedication, verso blank; [vii]-[viii], table of contents, verso blank; [1]-419, text,
printer at foot of last page; [420], advertisement for A New Edition of *A
History of New York*, just published.

Printer: C. Roworth, Bell-yard, Temple-bar.

Lineation: p. 100, something ... deplorable ; p. 200, was ... the

Despite the same pagination and lineation, this edition is reset, generally in a line-for-line reproduction of the previous edition.

This second edition of Vol. II was intended to be paired with the matching second edition of Vol. I, misleadingly called "Third Edition" on its title page.

Literary Gazette, 21 October 1820, advertised under the heading of "Published This Day": "a second edition" of The Sketch Book, Vol. 2.

NN, TxGeoS, TxU.

3E.   With the third complete London edition, John Murray began printing *The Sketch Book* in conventional form: two volumes with the same title page. To give both volumes the same identification of edition, he called this third edition the "Fourth Edition" on the title page.

THE | SKETCH BOOK | OF | GEOFFREY CRAYON, GENT. | [swelled rule] | "I ... A | mere ... how | they ... unto | me, ... scene." | BURTON. | [swelled rule] | FOURTH EDITION. | *IN TWO VOLUMES*. | VOL. I. [II.] | [double rule] | LONDON: | JOHN MURRAY, ALBEMARLE STREET. | [rule] | 1821.

(17.8 x 11.0 rebound): Vol. I. Not seen. Vol. II. $[A]^2$ B-I^8 K-U^8 X-Y^8 Z^4. Paged [i]-[iv], [1]-343 [344].

Order of Sketches: 1E, although Vol. I ends with "Westminster Abbey."

Printer: C. Roworth, Bell-yard, Temple-bar.

Lineation: Vol. II. p. 100, gether, ... preservation ; p. 200, cloud, ... trunks

DLC, Vol. II only.

4E.   THE | SKETCH BOOK | OF | GEOFFREY CRAYON, GENT. | [rule] | "I ... mere | spectator ... play | their ... from | a ... scene." | BURTON. | [rule] | FIFTH EDITION. | *IN TWO VOLUMES*. | VOL. I. [II.] | [rule] | LONDON: | JOHN MURRAY, ALBEMARLE-STREET. | MDCCCXXI.

(18.5 x 11.1 rebound): Vol. I. [i]-viii, [1]-326 [327]-[328]. Vol. II. [i]-[iv], [1]-343 [344]. Signed in 8's.

Order of Sketches: 1E. Vol. I ends with "Westminster Abbey."

Printer: Thomas Davison, Whitefriars.

Lineation: Vol. I. p. 100, blank; p. 150, The ... [in note] Buchanan.; p. 200, blank; p. 250, itself ... gloves. Vol. II. p. 100, sovereign ... preservation ; p. 200, cloud, ... trunks

TxU.

5E. THE | SKETCH BOOK | OF | GEOFFREY CRAYON, GENT. | [swelled rule] | "I ... A | mere ... how | they ... unto | me ... scene." | BURTON. | [swelled rule] | A NEW EDITION. | *IN TWO VOLUMES.* | VOL. I. [II.] | [double rule] | LONDON: | JOHN MURRAY, ALBEMARLE STREET. | [rule] | 1821.

(18.9 x 11.5 rebound): Vol. I. [i]-vi [vii]-[viii], [1]-298. Vol. II. [i]-[iv], [1]-310. Signed in 8's.

Order of Sketches: 1E. Vol. I ends with "Westminster Abbey."

Printer: C. Roworth, Bell-Yard, Temple Bar.

Lineation: Vol. I. p. 100, Such ... nature ; p. 200, gaze, ... [in note] then, Vol. II. p. 100, his ... of ; p. 200, low, ... trifles,

MH.

6E. THE | SKETCH BOOK | OF | GEOFFREY CRAYON, GENT. | [rule] | "I ... A | mere ... how | they ... unto | me, ... scene." | BURTON. | [rule] | NEW EDITION. | *IN TWO VOLUMES.* | VOL. I. [II.] | [double rule] | LONDON: | JOHN MURRAY, ALBEMARLE-STREET. | 1822.

Irving made a number of small revisions in this edition, perhaps as many as a hundred.

(21.7 x 13.6 rebound): Vol. I. [A]^4 B-I^8 K-U^8 X-Z^8 AA^8 BB^2. (Last leaf missing in copy examined). Not reckoned: preliminary portrait of Irving and one illustration in the text. Vol. II. [A]^2 B-I^8 K-U^8 X-Z^8 AA-BB^{8}CC^6. (Last leaf missing in copy examined). Not reckoned: one illustration in the text.

Vol. I. [i]-[ii], engraved portrait of Irving by Newton, apparently counted in the pagination; [iii]-[iv], title, on verso printer; [v]-vi, "Advertisement"; [vii]-[viii], dedication, verso blank; [ix]-[x], table of contents, verso blank; [1]-370, text, printer at foot of last page. Vol. II. [i]-[ii], title, on verso printer; [iii]-[iv], table of contents, verso blank; [1]-393, text, printer at foot of last page; [394], advertisement for *Knickerbocker's History* and *Bracebridge Hall.*

Order of Sketches: 1E. Vol. I ends with "Westminster Abbey."

Printer: C. Roworth, Bell Yard, Temple Bar.

Lineation: Vol. I. p. 100, I ... moral ; p. 200, headed ... the Vol. II. p. 100, When ... church ; p. 200, whelming ... talons;

TxU.

7Ea. THE | SKETCH BOOK | OF | GEOFFREY CRAYON, GENT. | [swelled rule] | "I ... A | mere ... how | they ... unto | me, ... scene." | BURTON. | [swelled rule] | NEW EDITION. | *IN TWO VOLUMES.* | VOL. I. [II.] | [double rule] | LONDON: | JOHN MURRAY, ALBEMARLE STREET. | [rule] | 1823.

(18.4 x 11.5 rebound): Vol. I. [i]-viii, [1]-326. Vol. II. [i]-[iv], [1]-341 [342]. Signed in 8's.

Order of Sketches: 1E. Vol. I ends with "Westminster Abbey."

Printer: C. Roworth, Bell Yard, Temple Bar.

Lineation: Vol. I. p. 100, blank; p. 150, detained ... tastes,; p. 200, blank; p. 250, itself ... gloves. Vol. II. p. 100, Corner, ... Here ; p. 200, whatever ... inso-

Literary Gazette, 6 December 1823, advertised, "price 16*s*. a New Edition."

DLC, TxU.

b. NEW EDITION. | ... | LONDON: | JOHN MURRAY, ALBEMARLE STREET. | MDCCCXXIV.

TxU

8E. THE | SKETCH-BOOK | OF | GEOFFREY CRAYON, GENT. | [rule] | "I ... A | mere ... how | they ... presented | unto ... scene." | BURTON. | [rule] | NEW EDITION. | *IN TWO VOLUMES.* | VOL. I. [II.] | [rule] | LONDON: | JOHN MURRAY, ALBEMARLE-STREET. | [rule] | MDCCCXXVI.

(19.0 x 11.5 rebound): Vol. I.[i]- [viii], [1]-326. Not reckoned: three engravings. Vol. II. [i]-[iv], [1]-341 [342]. Not reckoned: two engravings. Signed in 8's.

Order of Sketches: 1E. Vol. I ends with "Westminster Abbey."

Printer: Thomas Davison, Whitefriars.

Lineation: Vol. I. p. 100, blank; p. 200, blank; p. 250, itself ... of Vol. II. p. 100, above ... [in footnote] Fair.; p. 200, possessed ... inso-

ICN.

9Ea. THE | SKETCH-BOOK | OF | GEOFFREY CRAYON, ESQ. | A NEW EDITION. | [rule] | IN TWO VOLUMES. | VOL. I. [II.] | [rule] | LONDON: | JOHN MURRAY, ALBEMARLE STREET. | MDCCCXXXIV.

"Murray's Family Library," Vols. 39, 40.

(14. 7 x 9.5 rebound): Vol. I. [i]-vi [vii]-[viii], [1]-298. Not reckoned: preliminary engraving by C. R. Leslie, dated Feb. 1, 1834. Vol. II. [i]-[iv], [1]-316. Not reckoned: preliminary engraving by C. R. Leslie, dated Feb. 1, 1834. Signed in 8's.

Order of Sketches: 1E. Vol. I ends with "Westminster Abbey."

Printer: A. Spottiswoode, New-Street-Square, London.

Lineation: Vol. I. p. 100, but ... of ; p. 200, by ... sea-coal Vol. II. p. 100, pents, ... the ; p. 200, bow ... struggle.

The English Catalogue of Books, 1801-1836 lists January 1834 as the publication date.

TxU.

b.   [London: John Murray, 2 vols., 1838.]

"Murray's Family Library" series.

Not seen. Copy reported in NjP.

10E.   THE | SKETCH BOOK | OF | GEOFFREY CRAYON, ESQ. | A NEW EDITION. | IN TWO VOLUMES. | VOL. I. [II.] | LONDON: | JOHN MURRAY, ALBEMARLE STREET; | AND | THOMAS TEGG, 73, CHEAPSIDE. | [rule] | MDCCCXLV.

(15.2 x 10.2): Vol. I. [i]-[viii], [1]-296. Not reckoned: preliminary engraving by C. R. Leslie, published by William Tegg & Co. Vol. II. [i]-[iv], [1]-316. Not reckoned: preliminary engraving by C. R. Leslie, published by William Tegg & Co. Signed in 8's.

Order of Sketches: 1E. Vol. I ends with "Westminster Abbey."

Printer: Bradbury and Evans, Whitefriars.

Lineation: Vol. I. p. 100, of ... and ; p. 200, gaze ... [in footnote] on Vol. II. p. 100, the ... which ; p. 200, blank; p. 250, cruelties ... and

Red A cloth. On sides, in blind, circular design within elaborate border. Spines decorated in blind, titled in gilt: SKETCH | BOOK. | VOL. 1. [II.]. Cream endpapers.

BL, Private hands.

11E.   THE | SKETCH BOOK | OF | GEOFFREY CRAYON, GENT^N . | "I have no wife nor children, good or bad, to provide for. A mere spectator | of other men's fortunes and adventures, and how they play their parts; | which methinks are diversely presented unto me, as from a common theatre | or scene." -- *Burton.* | WITH A NEW INTRODUCTION BY THE AUTHOR. | ILLUSTRATED WITH ORIGINAL DESIGNS. | LONDON: | JOHN MURRAY, ALBEMARLE STREET. | 1849. All within single frame lines.

(Approx. 21.2 x 15.2): Printed from the plates of the Illustrated Form of the Author's Revised Edition, New York, 1848, with the same collation and the same illustrations. Single frame lines around each page.

Order of Sketches: ARE.

Lineation: p. 100, throng, ... to ; p. 200, count ... and

BL.

12E.   THE | SKETCH BOOK | OF | GEOFFREY CRAYON, ESQ. | A New Edition in One Volume. [fancy] | LONDON: | SIMMS AND M'INTYRE, | PATERNOSTER ROW, AND DONEGALL STREET, BELFAST. | [rule] | 1850. All within single frame lines.

"The Parlour Library," No. XLI.

(16.4 x 10.0): [1]-272. Signed in 8's.

Order of Sketches: ARE.

Printer: T. Constable, Printer to Her Majesty, Edinburgh.

Lineation: p. 100, mical ... CHURCHYARD.; P. 200, convenience. ... enforced.

Described by Michael Sadleir in *XIX Century Fiction* as (1) bright green glazed boards. On front, pictorially and decoratively printed in brown. On back, advertisements. Spine decorated and titled. Endpapers white, printed with series. Or, (2) dark green ribbed cloth. Sides blocked in blind, with series title on front. Spine scroll blocked, and titled in gilt. Endpapers white, printed with series.

Examiner and *Literary Gazette*, 27 April 1850, "Now ready."

BL.

13E.   THE | SKETCH BOOK. | BY | WASHINGTON IRVING. | [rule] | "I ... spectator | of ... which, | methinks, ... scene." -- | *Burton.* | [rule] | LONDON: | GEORGE ROUTLEDGE AND CO., SOHO SQUARE. | 1850.

Routledge's "Popular Library."

(16.5 x 10.1 rebound): [i]-viii, [1]-280. Signed in 8's.

Order of Sketches: ARE.

Printer: Reynell and Weight, Little Pulteney Street, Haymarket.

Lineation: p. 100, man, ... of ; p. 200, same ... build-

Seen only rebound. Other volumes in the series noted in boards printed in colors, or in brown AR cloth, sides decorated in brown with series name at center, spine titled in gilt.

Athenæum, 13 April 1850, advertised as "New volume," 1*s*. "in fancy cover," 1*s*. 6*d*. in cloth gilt; 4 May 1850, in "List of New Books."

IaU.

14Ea.   THE | SKETCH BOOK. | BY | WASHINGTON IRVING. | [rule] | "I ... of | other ... which, | methinks, ... scene." | -- BURTON. | [rule] | LONDON: | HENRY G. BOHN, YORK STREET, COVENT GARDEN. | MDCCCL.

In two states of the printer's imprint on the verso of the title page, sequence not determined:

[A]. J. & H. Cox (Brothers), 74 & 75 Great Queen Street, Lincoln's-Inn Fields.

[B]. Cox (Brothers) and Wyman, Great Queen Street, Lincoln's-Inn Fields.

Order of Sketches: ARE.

Issued individually as "Bohn's Shilling Series"; bound with *Life of Goldsmith* as Vol. II of "Bohn's Library Edition."

Lineation: p. 100, over ... corse.; p. 200, cottage ... shadowes."

Seen in original binding only in "Bohn's Library Edition." Gray T cloth. Sides decorated in blind. Spine titled in gilt as Irving's Works, Vol. II, Bohn's Library Edition. White endpapers with advertisements in blue. Portrait of Goldsmith at beginning of volume. (No works title in volume.)

Shilling Series. *Athenæum*, 11 May 1850, listed, 1*s*. 6*d*. *Literary Gazette*, 11 May 1850, "Ready this day." Library Edition. *Athenæum* and *Literary Gazette*, 2 November 1850, the set of 10 vols. at 35*s*. listed.

Library Edition: NN. Shilling Series: TxU, *BL*.

b.   [London: Henry G. Bohn, 1854.]

"Bohn's Library Edition." With a portrait of Goldsmith.

Not seen. Copy reported in Staats- und Universitätsbibliothek Hamburg.

c.   LONDON: | HENRY G. BOHN, COVENT GARDEN. | MDCCCLIX.

"Bohn's Shilling Series."

ViU.

1Fa.   THE | SKETCH BOOK | OF | GEOFFREY CRAYON, GENT. [in Vol. II, no period after GENT] | [rule] | "I have no wife nor children, good or bad, to provide for.   A mere spectator of other | men's fortunes and adventures, and how they play their parts; which, methinks, are | diversely presented unto me, as from a common theatre or scene." | BURTON. | [rule] | NEW EDITION. | IN TWO VOLUMES. | VOL. I. [II.] | [emblem: D in star within wreath with pendant medal] | PARIS: | PUBLISHED BY BAUDRY, 9, RUE DU COQ; | AND JULES DIDOT, SENIOR, 6, RUE DU PONT-DE-LODI. | [rule] | M DCCC XXIII.

(16.7 x 9.8): Vol. I. [a]^4 1-15^{12} 16^4. Vol. II. [a]^4 1-16^{12}. Laid paper.

Order of Sketches: 1E. Vol. I ends with "Westminster Abbey."

The text of this first French edition in English is derived from Murray's London "New Edition" of 1823, and so includes Irving's revisions made for the London edition of 1822.   There is no evidence of further revision by Irving for this edition.

Vol. I. [i]-[ii], half-title, on verso printer; [iii]-[iv], title, verso blank; [v]-[vi], table of contents, verso blank; [vii]-viii, Advertisement; [1]-368, text. Vol. II. [i]-[ii], half-title, on verso printer; [iii]-[iv], title, verso blank; [v]-[vi], table of contents, verso blank; [vii]-[viii], dedication, verso blank; [1]-383, text; [384], blank. Another rebound copy noted with the dedication to Scott correctly inserted in Vol. I rather than Vol. II; so issued?

Printer: Jules Didot, Senior, Printer to His Majesty.

Lineation: Vol. I. p. 100, blank; p. 200, noble ... all ; p. 300, strew ... and Vol. II. p. 100, on ... fa-; p. 200, last ... in

Bibliographie de la France, 27 September 1823, # 4109, listed.

CtY, DLC.

b.   PARIS: | PUBLISHED BY A. AND W. GALIGNANI, | AT THE ENGLISH, FRENCH, ITALIAN, GERMAN AND SPANISH LIBRARY, | 18, RUE VIVIENNE. | [rule] | 1824.

Blanks apparently substituted for half-titles. No printer given, but the title carries the D emblem.

CtY, NN.

c.   PARIS: | PUBLISHED BY A. AND W. GALIGNANI, | AT THE
     ENGLISH, FRENCH, ITALIAN, GERMAN, AND SPANISH LIBRARY,
     | N°. 18, RUE VIVIENNE. | [rule] | 1825.

     Blanks apparently substituted for half-titles. No printer given, but the title
     carries the D. emblem.

     BL.

d.   PARIS: | PUBLISHED BY L. BAUDRY, | AT THE ENGLISH,
     FRENCH, ITALIAN, GERMAN, AND SPANISH LIBRARY, | NO. 9,
     RUE DU COQ-ST-HONORÉ. | [rule] | 1825.

     Half-titles present, with printer on versos: Jules Didot, Senior, Printer to His
     Majesty, Rue du Pont de Lodi, No. 6. The title page carries a Baudry
     emblem: L. B. within a wreath.

     TxU.

e.   [Paris: Baudry, 1831. "Seventeenth Edition."]

     Paged [i]-xii, [1]-486. 12mo.

     Printer: J. Smith, Paris.

     Not seen. Listed in *Bibliographie de la France*, 29 January 1831, # 514. Copy
     reported in Bibliothèque Nationale.

2F. THE | SKETCH BOOK | OF | GEOFFREY CRAYON, GENT. | [rule] |
     "I ... spectator | of ... parts: | which, ... common | theatre ... scene." |
     BURTON. | [rule] | Eighteenth Edition. [fancy] | [rule] | IN TWO
     VOLUMES. | VOL. I. [II.] | [emblem: L. B. within a wreath] | PARIS, |
     BAUDRY, BOOKSELLER IN FOREIGN LANGUAGES, | 9, Rue du
     Coq-Saint-Honoré. | A. & W. GALIGNANI, 18, RUE VIVIENNE. | [rule]
     | 1831.

     (16.5 x 9.8): Vol. I. [i]-viii, [1]-360. Vol. II. [i]-[iv], [1]-371 [372].

     Order of Sketches: 1E. Vol. I ends with "Westminster Abbey."

     Printer: J. Smith, rue Montmorency, No. 16.

     Lineation: Vol. I. p. 100, blank; p. 200, humble ... wealthy Vol. II. p. 100, of
     ... mer-

     BL.

3Fa. [Paris and Lyons: B. Cormon and Blanc, 1834. 2 vols.]

     Printer: G. Rossary, Lyons.

Not seen.   Listed in *Bibliographie de la France*, 16 August 1834, # 4519. Copy reported in Bibliothèque Nationale. See the description of the second impression below.

b.   THE | SKETCH BOOK | OF | GEOFFREY CRAYON, | GENT. | [rule] | "I ... provide | for ... adventu- | res, ... methinks, | are ... theatre | or scene." | BURTON. | [swelled rule] | VOLUME I. [II.] | [swelled rule] | B. CORMON AND BLANC, [period in Vol. II] | BOOKSELLERS. | [In two parallel columns, divided by two vertical rules. In first column: PARIS. | 70, MAZARINE STREET.   In second column: LYONS. | 1, ROGER STREET.] | 1835.

(13.6 x 8.5): Vol. I. [1]-180. Vol. II. [1]-177 [178]. Signed in 12's and 6's.

Order of sketches: 1E.   Vol. I ends with "Westminster Abbey." "Advertisement" omitted.

Printer: G. Rossary, Saint Dominique street, No 1. [Lyons].

Lineation: Vol. I. p. 100, parents ... again.; p. 150, it ... from Vol. II. p. 100, muskets; ... retrieve ; p. 150, formed ... a

NN.

4F.   THE | SKETCH BOOK | OF | GEOFFREY CRAYON, GENT. | [rule] | "I ... A | mere ... and | how ... diversely | presented ... scene." | BURTON. | [rule] | VOL. I. [II.] | [emblem: L. B. within wreath] | PARIS, | BAUDRY, BOOKSELLER IN FOREIGN LANGUAGES, | 9, RUE DU COQ-SAINT-HONORÉ. | [elaborated swelled rule] | 1834.

(14.6 x 9.7): Vol. I. [i]-[viii] [v]-1, [1]-280. Vol. II. [i]-[iv], [1]-290. Signed in 12's and 6's.

Vol. I contains an anonymous "Memoir of Washington Irving."

Order of sketches: 1E. Vol. I ends with "Westminster Abbey."

Printer: Casimir, 12, rue de la Vieille-Monnaie.

Lineation: Vol. I. p. 100, To .. farm-; p. 200, chance ... Eng- Vol. II. p. 100, Lamb, ... along ; p. 200, least ... world,

Bibliographie de la France, 23 August 1834, # 4657, listed.

TxU.

5F. THE | SKETCH-BOOK | OF | GEOFFREY CRAYON, ESQ. | (WASHINGTON IRVING.) | [emblem: intertwined elaborated letters, apparently BEL] | PARIS, | BAUDRY'S EUROPEAN LIBRARY, | RUE DU COQ, NEAR THE LOUVRE. | SOLD ALSO BY AMYOT, RUE DE LA PAIX; TRUCHY, BOULEVARD DES ITALIENS; | THEOPHILE BARROIS, JUN., RUE RICHELIEU; LIBRAIRIE DES ÉTRANGERS, | RUE NEUVE-SAINT-AUGUSTIN; AND HEIDELOFF AND CAMPE, | RUE VIVIENNE. | [rule] | 1836.

"Collection of Ancient and Modern British Authors," Vol. XCIX.

(22.4 x 14.2): [i]-xxxiv, [1]-365[366]. Signed in 8's.

Pp. [xi]-xxxiv contain an anonymous "Memoir of Washington Irving."

Order of sketches: 1E.

Printer: J. Smith, 16, rue Montmorency.

Lineation: p. 100, sisters, ... whirlwind.; p. 200, From ... thee.

A tiny remaining fragment of the original wrapper suggests the general appearance: gray paper wrapper; on front, probably cover-title with elaborated black printed border.

Bibliographie de la France, 12 March 1836, # 1295, listed.

TxU (2).

6F. THE | SKETCH-BOOK | OF | GEOFFREY CRAYON. ESQ. | (WASHINGTON IRVING) | [emblem: intertwined elaborated letters, apparently BEL] | PARIS | BAUDRY'S EUROPEAN LIBRARY | 3, QUAI MALAQUAIS, NEAR THE PONT DES ARTS | AND STASSIN ET XAVIER, 9, RUE DU COQ | SOLD ALSO BY AMYOT, RUE DE LA PAIX; THÉOPHILE BARROIS, QUAI VOLTAIRE | TRUCHY, BOULEVARD DES ITALIENS; | LEOPOLD MICHELSEN, LEIPZIG; AND | BY ALL THE PRINCIPAL BOOKSELLERS ON THE CONTINENT | [rule] | 1846

"Collection of Ancient and Modern British Authors," Vol. XCIX.

(21.2 x 18.2): [i]-[xviii], [1]-336. Signed in 8's.

Order of sketches: 1E.

Printer: Crapelet, 9, rue de Vaugirard.

Lineation: p. 100, THE ... produces ; p. 200, and ... ob-

NN.

1G.   THE | SKETCH BOOK | OF | GEOFFREY CRAYON, GENT. | WITH
      THE | LAST CORRECTIONS OF THE AUTHOR. | [rule] | "I have no
      wife nor children, good or bad, to provide for. A mere | spectator of other
      men's fortunes and adventures, and how they play | their parts; which
      methinks are diversely presented unto me, as from | a common theatre or
      scene." | BURTON. | [rule] | EIGHTH EDITION | COMPLETE IN ONE
      VOLUME AND EMBELLISHED | WITH THREE LITHOGRAPHIC
      PRINTS. | [rule] | DRESDEN: | PRINTED FOR THE EDITOR A.
      MONTUCCI LL. D. | SOLD BY HIM NO. 8, ALT-MARKT -- AND |
      FRIEDRICH   FLEISCHER,   BOOKSELLER,   IN   LEIPSIC. |
      MDCCCXXIII.

      (22.6 x 13.2): [i]-[iv], [1]-457 [458]. Not reckoned: three illustrations. Signed
      in 8's. Laid paper.

      Order of Sketches: 1E.

      Irving revised the work in a minor fashion specifically for this first German
      edition, using as the basis for his text a Murray London edition of 1821.

      Printer: C. C. Meinhold and Sons, Printers to His Majesty, Dresden.

      Lineation: p. 100, and ... fiction.; p. 200, in ... her-

      In his Journal for 12 May 1823, Irving writes, "Went to Montuccis &
      corrected proof &c."

      Tan paper wrapper. On sides and spine, typographic ornaments in black.
      Spine lettered with title only, without author or publisher.

      CtY, NN. Copy reported in Universitätsbibliothek Kiel.

2G.   THE | SKETCH BOOK | OF | GEOFFREY CRAYON, GENT. | [rule] |
      ,"I ... for. | A ... adven- | tures, ... methinks, | are ... common | theatre ...
      scene." | BURTON. | [rule] | A NEW EDITION. | IN THREE
      VOLUMES. | VOL. I. [II., III.] | [wavy rule] | ZWICKAU, | PRINTED
      FOR BROTHERS SCHUMANN. | 1829.

      "Pocket Library of English Classics," Nos. 211-213.   "The Works of
      Washington Irving," Vols. I-III.

      (10.4 x 8.1): Vol. I. [i]-[xii], [1]-227[228]. Vol. II. [i]-[viii], [1]-198. Vol. III.
      [i]-[viii], [1]-248.

      Order of Sketches: 1E.

      Lineation: Vol. I. p. 100, dearer ... check- Vol. II. p. 100, after ... [in footnote]
      Brown. Vol. III. p. 100, of ... applause

      ViU. Copy reported in Universitätsbibliothek Heidelberg.

3G.   THE | SKETCH BOOK | OF | WASHINGTON IRVING. | [double rule] | Für | Schulen und zum Privatunterrichte | in der englischen Sprache. | [rule] | Mit | Erläuterungen und einem ausführlichen Wörterbuche | versehen | von | I. H. Lohmann. | [rule] | Quedlinburg. | Druck und Verlag von G. Basse. [all except title in fraktur]

Undated. Since the Advertisement to the first English edition, on p. [v], is dated *Juli*, 1838 (although it is the original version), presumably this edition was published in 1838.

(19.5 x 12.1): [i]-[vi], [1]-310, [blank leaf], [1]-13 [14] 15-123 [124]-[126].

Vorwort, pp. [iii]-iv, in German; Advertisement, table of contents, and text, pp. [v]-[vi], [1]-310, in English; Erläuterungen, pp. [1]-13, and Worterbuch, pp. [14]-123, in German. Three pages of advertisements, pp. [124]-[126], in German. Order of sketches: 1E.

Lineation: p. 100, ture ... from ; p. 200, solicitous ... prede-

Stadtbibliothek Wuppertal.

4G.   Washington Irving's | SKETCH BOOK. | [rule] | Mit einer Einleitung | über | Irving's Leben und Schriften | und | erklärenden Anmerkungen| herausgegeben | von | Dr. *E. A. Toel*, | Lehrer an der Ritter-Akademie in Lüneburg. | [rule with decorations at ends] | Lüneburg. | Im Verlage der Herold-und Wahlstab'schen Buchhandlung. | [rule] | 1840.

(16.9 x 10.6): [I]-LII, [1]-506 [507]-[508]. Signed in 12's.

The text itself is in English. The other matter is in German: introduction by the editor, a translation of the anonymous "Memoir of Washington Irving" that appears in the Baudry Paris editions of 1834, 1836, notes at the foot of many pages, and a list of errata at the end. Order of sketches: 1E.

Printer: Königl. Hofbuchdruckerei der Gebrüder Jänecke, Hannover.

Lineation: p. 100, poured ... and ; p. 200, struggling, ... arm.

Noted in pebbled brown cloth. Sides blank. Spine titled in gilt. Pink endpapers. Probably a publisher's binding.

TxU. Copy reported in Landesbibliothek Kassel.

5G.   THE | SKETCH BOOK | OF | GEOFFREY CRAYON, GENT. | (WASHINGTON IRVING.) | [rule] | VOL. I. [II.] | [double rule of heavy and light line] | HAMBURGH: | PUBLISHED BY J. P. ERIE. | [rule] | 1840.

(17.0 x 10.1): Vol. I. [1]-179 [180]. Vol. II. [1]-192.

Lineation: Vol. I. p. 100, They ... the Vol. II. p. 100, ancients, ... with

Probably issued as two volumes in one, since the table of contents for both
Vol. I and Vol. II appear on p. [180] of Vol. I.

Hessische Landesbibliothek, Wiesbaden; Universitätsbibliothek Mainz.

6G. THE | SKETCH BOOK | OF | GEOFFREY CRAYON, GENT. | [rule] |
"I ... for. | A ... and | how ... pre- | sented ... scene." | BURTON. | [rule] |
[triple rule] | BREMEN, | printed and published by CARL
SCHÜNEMANN. | [rule] | 1840.

(20.3 x 11.9): [I]-XXXII, [1]-312. Signed in 8's.

Contains the anonymous "Memoir of Washington Irving" from the Baudry
Paris editions of 1834, 1836.

Order of sketches: 1E. "Advertisement" omitted.

Lineation: p. 100, Mine ... 2.; p. 200, dies, ... up

TxU. Copy reported in Universitätsbibliotek Bremen.

7G. THE | SKETCH BOOK | OF | GEOFFREY CRAYON, ESQ. |
(WASHINGTON IRVING.) | WITH THE PORTRAIT OF THE
AUTHOR. | [elaborated swelled rule] | LEIPZIG | BERNH.
TAUCHNITZ JUN. | 1843.

(15.0 x 10.4): [i]-x, [1]-338. Preliminary portrait by A. H. Payne not reckoned.
Signed in 8's.

Order of the sketches: 1E.

"Collection of British Authors," Vol. XXXIII.

Printer: Bernh. Tauchnitz jun.

Lineation: p. 100, THE ... obscurity ; p. 200, tained ... confusion.

It is probable that the above description is not that of the first printing. The
earliest copies should, if in parallel with early copies of the first titles in the
Tauchnitz series, have an ornament above the imprint on the title page. But
such a copy has not been located.

NN, TxU.

8G. THE | SKETCH BOOK | OF | GEOFFREY CRAYON, ESQ. |
(WASHINGTON IRVING.) | AUTHORIZED EDITION. | WITH THE
PORTRAIT OF THE AUTHOR. | LEIPZIG | BERNHARD
TAUCHNITZ | 1843.

(15.5 x 11.7): [i]-x, [1]-361 [362]. Preliminary portrait not reckoned. Signed
in 8's.

"Collection of British Authors."

Order of sketches: 1E.

Printer: Printing Office of the Publisher.

Lineation: p. 100, issued ... suffering!; p. 200, a ... accustomed

In paper wrapper. On front, title; on verso, advertisements. On back, advertisements on recto and verso. The advertisements for Irving titles are for *Sketch Book, Mahomet, Sucessors of Mahomet, Goldsmith, Wolfert's Roost, Life of Washington* in 5 vols.

The advertisement on the wrapper for *Life of Washington* in 5 vols. would date the wrapper, if not the edition itself, in the late 1850's or later.

BL.

A still later edition, almost certainly after Irving's lifetime, carries the title: THE | SKETCH BOOK. | BY | WASHINGTON IRVING. | *AUTHORIZED EDITION.* | LEIPZIG | BERNHARD TAUCHNITZ | 1843.

Copies examined vary from 15.2 x 11.0 with trimmed edges to 16.4 x 12.0 with untrimmed edges. Pagination: [1]-446 [447]-[448].

The order of sketches is still that of the first English edition rather than that of the Author's Revised Edition of 1848.

On the verso of the series title, a list of Tauchnitz editions of Irving includes *Wolfert's Roost* and *Life of Washington*, 5 vols., defining the edition as one of 1859 or later.

Lineation: p. 100, bald ... upon ; p. 200, week; ... path

Noted in several different paper wrappers as well as in red cloth. Copies examined in wrappers carry advertisements that define those states as issued in the twentieth century.

TxU, Private hands (3).

TRANSLATIONS

Danish.

Gotfred Crayons | Skidsebog. | [double rule] | Jeg har ingen Kone og ingen Bern, gode eller | onde, at sørge for. Jeg er blot en Jagttager af an- | dre Folks Hændelser og Eventyr, og seer til, hvorledes | de spille deres Roller, saa at det ret kommer mig for, | som om jeg stod foran et almindeligt Theater eller | en Fjellebod. | Burton. | [double rule] | Af | Washington Irving. | Oversat | af | Ph. Wallich. | Første [Anden] Deel. | [swelled rule] |

Kjöbenhavn. | Trykt i L. J. Jacobsens Bogtrykkerie. | [rule] | 1827. [in fraktur]

(Vol. I: 20.0 x 11.9. Vol. II: 19.3 x 12.3 untrimmed): Vol. I. [i]-[iv], [1]-320. Vol. II. [i]-[iv], [1]-356. Signed in 8's. Laid paper.

Order of sketches: 1E.

Lineation: Vol. I. p. 100, England, ... vanskelige Vol. II. p. 100, lærd ... [in footnote] Historie.

MH, ViU.

Dutch.

SCHETSEN EN PORTRETTEN, | IN | *ENGELAND EN AMERIKA* | naar het leven geteekend | DOOR | GEOFFREY CRAYON, | (WASHINGTON-IRVING.) | [swelled rule] | *Ik heb noch vrouw, noch kinderen. Als een | eenvoudig aanschouwer van het woelen, wroeten, | sloven en zwoegen mijner medemenschen, poog ik, | zoo veel mogelijk, nut en leering te trekken uit | de wijze, waarop ik elk op het groote tooneel | der wereld zijne rol zie spelen.* | BURTON. | [swelled rule] | UIT HET ENGELSCH. | [flowered rule] | *Te LEEUWARDEN,* | *bij* STEENBERGEN VAN GOOR. | [elaborated swelled rule] | 1823. The title of Vol. II adds TWEEDE EN LAATSTE DEEL after UIT HET ENGELSCH. There are also other minor differences.

Translator's Preface signed S. V. G. [Steenbergen Van Goor].

(21.0 x 11.7): Vol. I. [I]-XI [XII], [1]-236. Vol. II. [I]-[IV], [1]-253 [254]. Signed in 8's. Laid paper.

Order of the sketches: 1E. Several sketches omitted.

Lineation: Vol. I. p. 100, talen, ... FALSTAFF.; p. 200, hebben. ... aankoop Vol. II. p. 100, "moeds ... moed ; p. 200, vond, ... Nu

DLC (Vol. I only), NN.

French.

VOYAGE | D'UN AMÉRICAIN | A LONDRES, | OU | ESQUISSES SUR LES MOEURS | ANGLAISES ET AMÉRICAINES; | TRADUIT DE L'ANGLAIS | DE M. IRWIN WASHINGTON. | TOME PREMIER. [SECOND.] | [emblem: letters and wreath] | A PARIS, | CHEZ PONTHIEU, LIBRAIRE, | PALAIS-ROYAL, GALLERIE DE BOIS, N^O 252. | [wavy rule] | 1822.

(19.6 x 12.0): Vol. I. [i]-[viii], [I]-VII [VIII], [1]-352. Vol. II. [i]-[iv], [1]-375 [376]. Signed in 8's. Laid paper.

Some sketches omitted; the others reordered.

Printer: P. Dupont, Hôtel des Fermes.

Lineation: Vol. I. p. 100, et ... les ; p. 200, près ... chancelant. Vol. II. p. 100, bes ... porte ; p. 200, qui ... avait

Bibliographie de la France, 13 October 1821, listed, #4122.

DLC, NN.

TRADUIT DE L'ANGLAIS | de M. Washington Irving. [fancy] | ... | Deuxième Edition. [fancy] | ... | A Paris, | CHEZ PONTHIEU ET COMPAGNIE, LIBRAIRES, | PALAIS-ROYAL, GALERIE DE BOIS, N^O 252. | 1827.

(21.3 x 13.5 untrimmed). Eight pages of preliminary advertisements in Vol. I.

Printer: C. J. Trouvé, Paris.

Pink paper wrappers. On front, cover-title with decorative border. On back, decorative border around printer's devices of anchors, flowers, wings, snakes, etc. in a group.

Bibligraphie de la France, 20 January 1827, listed, # 394.

ViU.

ESQUISSES | MORALES ET LITTÉRAIRES, | OU | OBSERVATIONS | SUR LES MOEURS, LES USAGES ET LA LITTÉRATURE | DES ANGLOIS ET DES AMERICAINS; | PAR M. WASHINGTON IRVING. | Traduites de l'anglois sur la quatrième édition, par MM. DELPEUX | et VILLETARD; et ornées de six jolis sujets lithographiés et de | vignettes. | [rule] | Je n'ai ni femme ni enfants; simple | spectateur de la fortune et des aventures | des autres hommes, j'examine, comme | sur un théâtre, la manière dont chacun | joue son rôle. | (BURTON) | TOME PREMIER. [SECOND.] | A PARIS, | CHEZ CONSTANT LE TELLIER FILS, LIBRAIRE, | BOULEVART SAINT-ANTOINE, N^O 71. | [double rule] | 1822. The quotation is to the right of center of the page.

(20.7 x 12.4): Vol. I. [i]- viii , [1]-300. Illustrations not reckoned. Vol. II. [i]-[vi], [1]-331 [332]. Illustrations not reckoned. Signed in 8's. Laid paper.

Order of sketches: 1E.

Printer: J. Gratiot, Paris.

Lineation: Vol. I. p. 100, elle ... antique.; p. 200, dans ... [in footnote] bière. Vol. II. p. 100, "Que ... la ; p. 200, bord ... donc

Bibliographie de la France, 23 February 1822, listed, # 898.

DLC.

SECONDE ÉDITION. | ... | A PARIS, | CHEZ CONSTANT LE TELLIER FILS, LIBRAIRE, | RUE TRAVERSIÈRE SAINT-HONORÉ, N^O 25. | [double rule] | 1827.

NN.

German.

Gottfried Crayon's | Skizzenbuch. | [rule] | Ich habe keine Frau und keine Kinder, gut' oder böse, für | die ich sorgen musste. Ich bin ein blosser Beobachter der | Schicksale und Abenfeuer anderer Leute, und sehe zu, wie sie | ihre Rollen spielen, so, dass es mir gerade vorkommt, als stände | ich vor einem gewöhnlichen Theater oder einer Schaubühne. | Burton. | [rule] | Aus dem Englischen | des Washington Irving | übersetzt | von | S. H. Spiker. | Erster [Zweiter] Band. | [swelled rule] | Berlin, | verlegt bei Duncker und Humblot. | [rule] | 1825. [in fraktur]

(17.5 x 10.5): Vol. I. [I]-XII, [1]-336. Vol. II. [I]-VI [VII]-[VIII], [1]-376. Two pages of terminal advertisements. Signed in 12's.

Order of sketches: 1E. Vol. I ends with "Westminster Abbey."

Printer: A. W. Schade, Berlin.

Lineation: Vol. I. p. 100, länders ... Uebers.; p. 200, chen ... ihn, Vol. II. p. 100, die ... vorzüg-; p. 200, er ... und

Noted in brown V cloth. Sides blank. Spines titled in gilt. Probably a publisher's binding.

TxU. Copy reported in Universitätsbibliothek Bonn.

[Gottfried Crayon's Skizzenbuch, von Washington Irving. Aus dem Englischen übersetzt von S. H. Spiker. 3 vols. Wien: Chr. Fr. Schade, 1825.]

[Apparently issued also in a second state: "Classische Cabinett-Bibliothek oder Sammlung auserlesener Werke der deutschen und Fremd-Literatur," 51, 52, 53 Bändchen. Wien: Schade, 1825.]

Not located.   Listed by Walter A. Reichart in "The Earliest German Translations of Washington Irving's Writings," *Bulletin of the New York Public Library*, 61 (October 1957), 491-498.

Gottfried Crayon's | Skizzenbuch. | Von | Washington Irving. | [rule] | Aus dem Englischen übersetzt | von | S. H. Spiker. | Erster [Zweiter] Theil. | [swelled rule] | Wien, 1826. | Gedruckt und verlegt bei Chr. Fr. Schade. [in fraktur]

(14.5 x 9.7): Vol. I. [II]-VIII, [9]-190. Front of wrapper apparently counted. Vol. II. [I]-[II], [1]-200. Signed in 8's.

A third volume must have been published, since the final sketches, from "Stratford-on-Avon" to "L'Envoy, " are missing in the two volumes examined. (Although it should be noted that the sketches from "The Mutability of Literature" to "The Spectre Bridegroom" are missing in Vol. II.) It is likely that this 1826 printing is a second impression of the 3-vol. Vienna edition of 1825, although no such indication appears on the title page or on the wrappers.

Order of sketches: 1E.

Printer: Christian Friedrich Schade, Wien.

Lineation: Vol. I. p. 100, grosse ... uebers.; p. 150, Nächsten ... mich Vol. II. p. 100, so ... thun,; p. 150, neueres ... alte

Light gray paper wrapper. On front, cover-title. On back, identification of series, "Sammlung auserlesener Werke der deutschen und fremden Literatur," No. 3, 4. "Pränumeration des ersten Semesters 1826."

TxU.

Gottfried Crayon's | Skizzenbuch | von | Washington Irving. | [rule] | Ich habe weder Weib noch Kinder, gute oder böse, | für die ich zu sorgen habe. Ein blosser Beobachter | der Schicksale und Abentheuer Anderer und wie sie | ihre Rollen spielen; diese, dünkt mich, stellen sich mir | manchfaltig dor, wie von einem gewöhnlichen Theater | oder einer Bühne. | Burton. | [rule] | Aus dem Englischen. | [double rule] | Erstes [Zweites - Sechstes] Bändchen. | [quintuple rule] | Frankfurt am Main, 1826. | Gedruckt und verlegt bei Johann David Sauerländer. [in fraktur]

"Washington Irving's sämmtliche Werke," Erstes - Sechstes Bändchen.

(13.5 x 10.0): Part I. [1]-126 [127]-[128]. Part II. [1]-110 [111]-[112]. Part III. [1]-110 [111]-[112]. Part IV. [1]-102 [103]-[104]. Part V. [1]-93 [94]-

[96]. Part VI. [1]-96, plus terminal advertisements paged [1]-8. Signed in 8's. Laid paper.

Some sketches are omitted, the others reordered.

Lineation: Part I. p. 50, nur ... Nachdenkens. Part II. p. 50, Die ... er Part III. p. 50, etwas, ... allmähligen Part IV. p. 50, und ... [in footnote] habe. Part V. p. 50, und ... ei- Part VI. p. 50, der ... Windstoss

In the only original binding seen, the work is bound in 3 vols.: unprinted light blue-gray paper boards. It is possible that the work was also issued bound in 2 vols., or in the 6 parts in paper wrappers.

NN, TxU. Copy reported in Stadtbibliothek Mainz.

Gottfried Crayon's | Skizzenbuch | von | Washington Irving. | [rule] | Ich habe weder Weib noch Kinder, gute oder | böse, für die ich zu sorgen hätte. Ein blosser | Beobachter der Schicksale und Abenteuer Anderer | und wie sie ihre Rollen spielen; diese, dünkt mich, | stellen sich mir mannichfaltig dar, wie von einem | gewöhnlichen Theater oder einer Bühne. | Burton. | [rule] | Zweite, sorgfältig verbesserte Auflage. | Mit 2 Stahlstichen. | [stylized swelled rule] | Frankfurt am Main. | Druck und Verlag von Johann David Sauerländer. | 1846. [in fraktur]

The preliminary series title identifies this as "Washington Irving's | ausgewählte Schriften. | Herausgegeben | von | Dr. [in Roman letters] J. V. Adrian | [rule] | Erster Theil. | Gottfried Crayon's Skizzenbuch. | Zweite, sorgfältig verbesserte Auflage."

(15.2 x 11.2): [i]-xiv, [3]-471 [472]. Not reckoned: preliminary engraving and one between pp. 264-265. Signed in 8's.

Order of sketches: 1E, with "L'Envoy" omitted.

Lineation: p. 100, Untergange ... Lebens-; p. 200, Während ... Graf

Universitätsbibliothek Marburg.   Copies reported in Stadtbibliothek München, Stadtbibliothek Nürnberg.

Polish.

RYSY [shaded letters] | MORALNOŚCI I LITERATURY [hollow letters] | ALBO | POSTRZEŻENIA | WE WZGLEDZIE OBYCZAJÓW, ZWYCZA- | JÓW I LITERATURY | ANGLIKÓW I AMERYKANÓW | PRZEZ | *Waszyngtona Irwinga* [in script] | AMERYKANINA | PO ANGIELSKU NAPISANE, A S CZWARTEGO WYDANIA | NA POLSKI JĘZYK PRZELOŻONE. | [rule] | 4-line quotation] | *Burton.* | [rule] |

TOM PIÉRWSZY. [DRUGI.] | WILNO. [fancy] | DRUKIEM B. NEUMANA. | [rule] | 1830.

This translation is probably derived from the French translation of *The Sketch Book* by Mm. Delpeux and Villetard, first published in Paris by Constant Le Tellier Fils, 1822. That French edition uses a similar title, *Esquisses Morales et Littéraires*, and is similarly identified on the title page as a translation of the fourth edition.

(9.5 x 16.5): Vol. I. [16 pp. unpaged], [298 pp. paged]. Vol. II. [6 pp. unpaged], [326 pp. paged]. 8vo.

Not examined. Information based on copy in Biblioteka Narodowa, Warsaw.

EDITIONS OF INDIVIDUAL SKETCHES

Rip Van Winkle.

ILLUSTRATIONS [in red] | OF | RIP VAN WINKLE | DESIGNED AND ETCHED [in red] | BY | FELIX O C DARLEY | FOR THE MEMBERS OF | THE AMERICAN ART-UNION [in red] | MDCCCXLVIII. All within single frame lines.

Copyright 1849. A note on the copyright page by The Committee of Management of The American Art-Union says that this edition is presented to the Subscribers of 1848.

(32.1 x 37.8): [1]-11 [12]. Not reckoned.: 6 plates at end. Unsigned.

Text of "Rip Van Winkle," pp. 3-11. In double columns. Single frame line around each page.

Printer: Leavitt, Trow & Company, New York.

Lineation: p. 10 (first column), "I ... stout

Tan paper wrapper. On front, in gray, lithographed title with illustrations, within gravestone-shaped border. On back, in white, PUBLISHED | BY THE | AMERICAN ART-UNION | FOR THE | SUBSCRIBERS | OF | 1848 [in intaglio raised letters] within wreath. Flyleaves.

Literary World, 11 November 1848, reviewed from unfinished state, "nearly ready," "to be distributed in December," "an edition of some twenty thousand"; 4 November - 16 December 1848, an advertisement by the Art-Union for the annual meeting of 22 December points out that "This year, each member will be entitled to a copy," but does not promise them at the meeting; 30 December 1848, an account of the meeting of 22 December describes the sketches, in future tense, as "to be given to each member"; 7 April 1849, "now ready in sufficient numbers to warrant the entire distribution to all members commencing with the first of May." Did members present at the meeting of 22 December receive their copies then?

TxU, ViU.

[*Rip Van Winkle*. Illustrated with six etchings on steel, by Charles Simms, from drawings by Felix Darley. London: Joseph Cundall, 21, Old Bond-street, 1850.]

Crown 8vo.

A review in *The Athenæum*, 4 May 1850, suggests the original technique as well as the source of this edition: "These [illustrations], as the English publisher warns us in his 'advertisement,' have been reduced by the agency of the daguerreotype from originals, on a large scale, 'which have lately been issued by the American Art-Union.'"

Athenæum, 13 April 1850, "Just published" at 5s.; 4 May 1850, listed, reviewed, advertised.

Not located.

The Legend of Sleepy Hollow.

ILLUSTRATIONS [in red] | OF THE | LEGEND OF SLEEPY HOLLOW | DESIGNED AND ETCHED [in red] | BY | FELIX O C DARLEY | FOR THE MEMBERS OF | THE AMERICAN ART-UNION [in red] | MDCCCXLIX All within single frame lines.

Copyright 1850. A note on the copyright page by The Committee of the American Art-Union says that this edition is presented to the Subscribers of 1849.

(31.3 x 37.9): [1]-16. Not reckoned: 6 plates at end. Unsigned.

Text of "The Legend of Sleepy Hollow," pp. 3-16. In double columns. Single frame line around each page.

Printer: John F. Trow, 49, 51 & 53 Ann-st.

Lineation: p. 10 (first column), master's, ... Indian

Light brown paper wrapper. On front, cover-title within double frame lines. On back, classical medallion within double frame lines. Flyleaves.

Literary World, 15 December 1849, the annual meeting of the Art-Union will take place "at Niblo's, on the evening of December twenty-first," "Each Member is entitled to a copy"; 29 December 1849, in "The Fine Arts" column,

"18,960 members from all parts of the country," "Each member of the present year receives [a copy]." Did members present at the meeting receive their copies then? Presumably, the majority of the copies were distributed later.

TxU, ViU.

Roscoe.

SKETCH | OF | WILLIAM ROSCOE, | BY | WASHINGTON IRVING. | LIVERPOOL: | PRINTED BY HARRIS AND COMPANY. All within double frame lines.

(20.1 x 13.2): [1]-15 [16], [i]-iv. One gathering of 12, unsigned.

Following the text of "Roscoe" is an Appendix, paged [i]-iv: From The Life of Roscoe, by His Son.

Lineation: p. 10, an ... by

Deep bright blue paper wrapper. On front, in gilt, engraved cover-title within gilt frame; at foot, PRINTED & PRESENTED BY | MESS^{RS}. HARRIS & Co. | *Successors to M^r McCreery* [with comma under the raised c] | at the [fancy] | Celebration of the Centenary of W^m. Roscoe. [elaborated fancy lettering in an undulating line] | 8TH. MARCH. 1853. On back, in gilt within gilt frame, medallion of Roscoe with identification below (repeated from front cover-title). AEG. Flyleaves.

TxU, ViU.

EDITIONS OF INDIVIDUAL SKETCHES:
TRANSLATIONS

The Legend of Sleepy Hollow.

Sagan | om | *Sofdalen* | af | DIDRICK KNICKERBOCKER. | *Efter hans död utgifven* | af | WASHINGTON IRVING. | [rule] | öfversättning | af | VITALIS. | [rule] | [long rule] | STOCKHOLM, | BERNH. MAGN. BREDBERG, | 1827.

(19.9 x 12.0): [i]-[ii], [1]-49 [50].

Lineation: p. 25, skade ... larmande

Gray-blue unprinted paper wrapper.

TxU.

Philip of Pokanoket and *Traits of Indian Character.*

Drag | af | *Indianernes Charakter.* | Af | WASHINGTON IRVING. | [rule] | Ofversättning | af | VITALIS. | [rule] | [long rule] | STOCKHOLM, | BERNH. MAGN. BREDBERG, | 1827.

(16.4 x 10.6): [i]-[ii], [1]-43 [44]. Signed in 8's. Light gray laid paper.

Lineation: p. 20, colonisterna ... belägenhet i [the i above baseline]

NN.

The Spectre Bridegroom.

Andebruden. | Berättelse | af | Washington Irving. | [rule] | Öfversättning. | [rule] | [elaborated rule] | Upsala, | tryckt hos Em. Bruzelius, | 1827. [in fraktur]

(14.1 x 8.9): [i]-[ii], [1]-30. Signed in 6's. Crude laid paper.

NN.

BRACEBRIDGE HALL

In July 1821, as Irving was to tell John Murray many years later in a letter of 22 September 1850, Washington Irving returned to England from France with "the rough manuscript" of *Bracebridge Hall*. By 29 January 1822 he had produced a still-hasty manuscript of Volume I that he felt was sufficiently completed to send to his brother Ebenezer in New York, following it with Volume II on 25 February. Irving's letter of 29 January, accompanying the first installment of the manuscript, makes clear that he was primarily interested in hurrying out an edition, however imperfect, to establish copyright in America. That first edition could be followed by a second, revised, better edition, to be derived from the proof sheets of the planned London edition, "in which there will doubtless be many alterations, as I have not had time to revise some parts of the work sufficiently, and am apt to make alterations to the last moment." He followed his plans exactly. By 11 May 1822, when Irving returned the last proof of the London edition to John Murray, he had rewritten many sections, added five pieces, and altered the order of presentation. When the American edition was published on 21 May 1822, and the London edition on 23 May, the two texts varied widely. The second American edition, however, published later in 1822, was derived from one of the text states of the first London edition, and Irving's plan was completed.

After the second American edition, Irving seems to have left the text unchanged until his revision for the Author's Revised Edition in 1849. The continental editions and translations (and *Bracebridge Hall* apparently proved not quite as popular on the continent as some of Irving's other works) simply followed the text of the London edition. In 1849, Irving published a new text, aimed more directly at the American audience and derived from the American second edition or one of its immediate descendants. For this Author's Revised Edition, he made a number of revisions, primarily stylistic, but retained the contents and the order of presentation of the second American and first London edition. The first half of the work was somewhat more carefully and heavily revised than the second.

CONTENTS

It should be noted that the first American edition, 1822 -- but only that edition -- lacks "The Rookery," "Family Misfortunes," "Lovers' Troubles,"

"The Storm-Ship," and "The Author's Farewell." "Gentility" is there titled
"True Gentlemen."

The Author

The Hall

The Busy Man

Family Servants

The Widow

The Lovers

Family Reliques

An Old Soldier

The Widow's Retinue

Ready-Money Jack

Bachelors

Wives

Story Telling

The Stout Gentleman

Forest Trees

Literary Antiquary

The Farm-House

Horsemanship

Love-Symptoms

Falconry

Hawking

St. Mark's Eve

Gentility

Fortune Telling

Love-Charms

The Library

The Student of
    Salamanca

English Country
    Gentlemen

A Bachelor's Confessions

English Gravity

Gipsies

May-Day Customs

Village Worthies

The Schoolmaster

The School

A Village Politician

The Rookery

May-Day

The Manuscript

Annette Delarbre

Travelling

Popular Superstitions

The Culprit

Family Misfortunes

Lovers' Troubles

The Historian

The Haunted House

Dolph Heyliger

The Storm-Ship

The Wedding

The Author's Farewell

1A.   BRACEBRIDGE HALL, | OR | THE HUMOURISTS. [hollow letters] | A Medley, [fancy] | BY | GEOFFREY CRAYON, GENT. | [rule] | Under this cloud I walk, Gentlemen. I am a traveller, who, having | surveyed most of the terrestrial angles of this globe, am hither arri- | ved, to peruse this little spot. | CHRISTMAS ORDINARY. | [rule] | IN TWO VOLUMES. | VOL. I. [II.] | [double rule] | NEW-YORK: | PRINTED BY C. S. VAN WINKLE, | No. 101 Greenwich Street. | [rule] | 1822.

(23.8 x 13.3 untrimmed): Vol. I. $[1]^4$ 2-43^4 44^2. Vol. II. $[1]^4$ 2-44^4.

Vol. I. [1]-[2], half-title, verso blank; [3]-[4], title, on verso copyright ("the fifth day of April, in the forty-sixth year of the Independence" by C. S. Van Winkle); [5]-[6], table of contents, verso blank; [7]-[8], fly-title, verso blank; [9]-348, text. Vol. II. [1]-[2], half-title, verso blank; [3]-[4], title, on verso copyright ("the ninth day of May, in the forty-sixth year of the Independence" by C. S. Van Winkle); [5]-[6], table of contents, verso blank; [7]-[8], fly-title, verso blank; [9]-351, text; [352], blank.

Lineation: Vol. I. p. 100, extracts, ... agreeable;; p. 200, bound ... was Vol. II. p. 100, A VILLAGE ... The ; p. 200, teously ... and

Drab brown paper boards. Sides blank. On spines, white paper label: [double rule] | BRACEBRIDGE | HALL. | [rule] | VOL. I. [II.] | [rule] | PUBLISHED BY | *M. & S. Thomas.* | Philadelphia. | [double rule]. White endpapers. Flyleaves.

Copies in boards with surviving labels on the spines are very scarce, but all labels seen or reported name M. & S. Thomas as publisher. Verification of the Thomases as the publishers appears in a letter of 29 January 1822 from Irving to his brother Ebenezer, accompanying the American manuscript for Vol. I: "*I wish, expressly, Moses Thomas to have the preference over every other publisher.*" Irving's explanation is significant for the history of his publications: "Whatever may have been his embarrassments and consequent want of punctuality, he is one who shewed a disposition to serve me, and who did serve me in the time of my necessity, and I should despise myself could I for a moment forget it."

Ebenezer Irving, paraphrased by Pierre M. Irving in the *Life and Letters*, reported 1000 copies printed.

Title page for Vol. I deposited 5 April 1822; for Vol. II, 9 May 1822. *New-York American*, 21 May 1822, "This day is published"; "price in boards $5." *Literary and Scientific Repository*, May 1822, reviewed. Irving to John Murray, 22 September 1850, gives 21 May as the publication date.

TxU (4), rebound. ViU, in boards.

2Aa.   BRACEBRIDGE HALL, | OR | THE HUMOURISTS. [hollow letters] |
A Medley, [fancy] | BY | GEOFFREY CRAYON, GENT. | [rule] | Under
this cloud I walk, gentlemen; pardon my rude as- | sault. I am a traveller,
who, having surveyed most of the | terrestrial angles of this globe, am hither
arrived to peruse | this little spot. | CHRISTMAS ORDINARY. | [rule] |
IN TWO VOLUMES. | VOL. I. [II.] | [stylized swelled rule with oblong in
center] | NEW-YORK: | PRINTED BY C. S. VAN WINKLE, | No. 101
Greenwich Street. | [rule] | 1822.

No identification of second edition is printed on the title page, but on page
[3] of the first volume appears, ADVERTISEMENT TO THE SECOND
EDITION: "The manuscript for the first edition of this work was transmitted
to America at a time when the author was suffering under a long and
obstinate indisposition, and much depression of spirits. He was conscious of
the imperfections of the work, but he was advised by his physician to commit
it to the press.... In the course of publication in England, however, an
improved state of health and spirits enabled him to make considerable
alterations and additions; which will account for the material difference that
will be perceived between the first and second editions of the work, as
published in America."

Whatever the validity of the claims of the ADVERTISEMENT, the text of
this second American edition is derived from that of the first London edition
in its first or second text state (a paragraph added near the end of the second
text state appears here as well). Irving did not read proof. There are minor
textual differences from the first London edition, but with the possible
exception of the insertion at Vol. I, p. [13], line 14 of "to my European
readers," the changes appear to be the work of the publisher. The
Advertisement itself, however, must surely have been added by Irving.

(19.5 x 11.5 untrimmed): Vol. I. $[1]^4$ $2\text{-}26^6$. The last leaf is a blank. Vol. II.
$[1]^2$ $2\text{-}26^6$ 27^2. (Examined only in rebound copies).

Vol. I. (8 pp. preliminary matter unpaged): [first leaf], title, on verso
copyright ("the fifth day of April, in the forty-sixth year of the Independence"
by C. S. Van Winkle); [second leaf], "Advertisement to the Second Edition,"
verso blank; [third leaf], table of contents, verso blank; [fourth leaf], fly-title,
verso blank; [13]-309, text; [310], blank. Vol. II. (4 pp. preliminary matter
unpaged): [first leaf], title, on verso copyright ("the ninth day of May, in the
forty-sixth year of the independence" by C. S. Van Winkle); [second leaf],
table of contents, verso blank; [13]-316, text. The contents are these in the
rebound copies examined, one untrimmed and apparently complete.
Originally issued with half-titles?

Lineation: Vol. I. p. 100, make ... technically ; p. 200, acquainted ... of Vol. II.
p. 100, the ... dream."; p. 200, new ... the

North American Review, January 1823, in "Quarterly List of New Publications."

MH, TxU.

b. THIRD AMERICAN EDITION. | ... | *NEW-YORK*: | PRINTED BY C.S. VAN WINKLE, | No. 48 Pine-street. | [rule of 14 dots] | 1826.

Despite the identification on the title page of "Third American Edition," this is simply a new impression of Van Winkle's second edition of 1822 with a few minor corrections, such as "gaols" for "goals" at II, 42.13.

North American Review, January 1827, in "Quarterly List of New Publications."

NN.

3Aa. BRACEBRIDGE HALL: | OR, | THE HUMOURISTS. [hollow letters] | A MEDLEY. | BY | GEOFFREY CRAYON, GENT. | [rule] | Under ... a | traveller ... am | hither ... spot. CHRISTMAS ORDINARY. | [rule] | IN TWO VOLUMES. | VOL. I. [II.] | [rule] | FOURTH AMERICAN EDITION. | [rule] | Philadelphia: [fancy] | CAREY & LEA -- CHESNUT-STREET. | [rule of 16 dots] | 1830.

(17.9 x 10.9): Vol. I. [i]-xii, [13]-261 [262]. Vol. II. [i]-[iv], [5]-259 [260]. Signed in 6's.

Copyright "the fifth day of April, in the forty-sixth year of the Independence" by C. S. Van Winkle.

The text is derived from Van Winkle's second edition of 1822-26 with a number of careless errors.

Lineation: Vol. I. p. 100, parts ... than ; p. 200, burning ... and Vol. II. p. 100, he ... lover's ; p. 200, or ... rest

NN.

b. FOURTH AMERICAN EDITION. | [rule] | Philadelphia: [fancy] | CAREY & LEA -- CHESNUT-STREET. | [rule of 16 dots] | 1831.

CtY, MH (Vol. II only).

c. FOURTH AMERICAN EDITION. | [rule] | Philadelphia: [fancy] | CAREY & LEA -- CHESNUT-STREET. | [rule of 16 dots] | 1835.

CtY, NN, TxU.

d. A NEW EDITION. | [rule] | Philadelphia: [fancy] | CAREY, LEA, & BLANCHARD. | [rule of 21 dots] | 1835.

Copyright 1836 by Washington Irving.

Despite the claim of "A New Edition" and the new copyright date, this is simply a new impression of the edition of 1830.

Blue-green V cloth. Sides blank. Paper label on spines: [double rule] | BRACEBRIDGE | HALL. | [rule] | *VOL. I. [II.]* | [double rule]. White endpapers.

Is the date on the title page a misprint? The new copyright was taken out and a copy deposited on 5 December 1836.

TxU.

e. A NEW EDITION. | [rule] | Philadelphia: [fancy] | CAREY, LEA, & BLANCHARD. | [rule of 21 dots] | 1836.

Blue-green V cloth. Sides blank. Same paper label on spines. White endpapers.

CtY, TxU.

f. [Advertisement in *National Gazette and Literary Register*, 21 and 31 January 1837, "Carey, Lea & Blanchard have just published ... the 5th and 6th volumes of the New and Uniform edition of Irving's works, containing Bracebridge Hall...." This impression has not been identified. It may be dated 1836 or 1837 on the title page, with a "Works" label on the spines.]

g. A NEW EDITION. | [rule] | Philadelphia: [fancy] | CAREY, LEA, & BLANCHARD. | [rule of 21 dots] | 1838.

CtY, NN.

h. A NEW EDITION. | [rule] | PHILADELPHIA: | LEA & BLANCHARD, | SUCCESSORS TO CAREY & CO. | [rule of 30 dots] | 1839.

Green V cloth. Sides blank. Paper label on spines. White endpapers.

CtY.

i. [A New Edition. Philadelphia: Lea & Blanchard, 1841.]

Not located. Listed in *BAL*.

4Aa- BRACEBRIDGE HALL, | OR | THE HUMORISTS. | A Medley. [fancy]
d. | BY | GEOFFREY CRAYON, GENT[N]. [with 2 dots beneath the raised N] | "Under this cloud I walk, Gentlemen; pardon my rude assault. I am a traveller, who, | having surveyed most of the terrestrial angles of this globe, am hither arrived, to peruse this | little spot." | CHRISTMAS ORDINARY. | AUTHOR'S REVISED EDITION. | COMPLETE IN ONE VOLUME. | NEW-YORK: | GEORGE P. PUTNAM, 155 BROADWAY, | And 142 Strand, London. | 1849.

(18.6×12.8): $[1]^{12}$ $2\text{-}20^{12}$ 21^4. The first leaf is blank, but reckoned in the pagination. Some copies 21^6 with two integral leaves of terminal advertisements.

In two text states. No sequence established, if one exists.

[A].   Page viii is mispaged vii. On page 201, line 8f, the word "fathers" is complete.

[B].   Page viii is correctly paged. On page 201, line 8f, the "f" is missing in "fathers."

A probable explanation of the variant states is not that of plate damage or plate correction, but rather of duplicate plates. In the later impressions, copies have been noted in State [A] in 1851, 1853, 1854; in State [B] in 1856, 1859.

In two collation states, no sequence established.

[A].   Collation as described, with Sig. 21 in 4. No terminal advertisements.

[B].   Sig 21 is in 6. The last two leaves carry advertisements, dated November, 1848, paged 1-4.

In the limited number of copies examined, all copies in Collation State [A] contain Text State [A], all copies in collation State [B] contain Text State [B].

In relation to the several states of the volume, it should be noted that advertisements in *Literary World* suggest four impressions dated 1849:   2 December 1848, "Published this week"; 10 February 1849, "New edition ... next week"; 17 March 1849, under the heading of "New Publications," "4th edition." The four impressions have not been identified.

[i]-[ii], blank; [iii]-[iv], Works title for Vol. VI, dated 1849, verso blank; [v]-[vi], title, on verso copyright (1848) and printer; [vii]-viii (misnumbered vii in Text State [A]), table of contents; [9]-487, text; [488], blank.

Printer: Leavitt, Trow & Co., Printers and Sterotypers, 49 Ann-street, N.Y.

Lineation: p. 100, tice-window ... Norman ; p. 200, chivalry ... King

Blue-green TB cloth. On sides, in blind, publisher's initials within ornament. Spine titled in gilt: IRVING'S | WORKS | [rule] | BRACEBRIDGE | HALL | | PUTNAM Flyleaf at end; integral blank leaf at front. Also noted in red AR cloth. On sides, in gilt, triple-rule straight border around ivy-like design forming a rectangle. Spine decorated and titled in gilt. AEG. Light manilla endpapers.

Within the next few years, advertisements for the Works offer them in cloth, cloth extra, sheep extra, half calf, half calf extra, calf extra, calf antique, half morocco, morocco extra. Presumably *Bracebridge Hall* was also available in some or all of these bindings.

Deposited 15 December 1848. *Literary World*, 2 and 9 December 1848, "Published this week," "cloth, $1 25; cloth gilt, $1 75"; 16 December 1848, listed. *Albion*, 9 December 1848, in "Notice of New Works."

States [A]: MH, TxU, ViU. States [B]: CtY, ViU.

e.   NEW-YORK: | GEORGE P. PUTNAM, 155 BROADWAY, | And 142 Strand, London. | 1851.

Works title, dated 1851.

Noted in State [A], with p. viii mispaged vii.

TxU, ViU.

f.   NEW-YORK: | G. P. PUTNAM & COMPANY, 10 PARK PLACE. | 1852.

Works title, dated 1852.

Private hands. Copy reported in PPGi.

g.   NEW-YORK: | G. P. PUTNAM & COMPANY, 10 PARK PLACE. | 1853.

Works title, dated 1853.

Noted in State [A], with p. viii mispaged vii.

Green TB cloth. On sides, in blind, publisher's initials within design.

Spine titled in gilt.

DLC, MH.

h.   NEW-YORK: | G. P. PUTNAM & COMPANY, 10 PARK PLACE. | 1854.

Works title, dated 1854.

Noted in State [A], with p. viii mispaged vii.

Noted in purple fine T cloth. On sides, in blind, publisher's initials within design. Spine titled in gilt, with gilt leaf designs within blind panels. Yellow endpapers.

CtY.

i.   [NEW YORK: GEORGE P. PUTNAM, 1855.]

Works title, dated 1855.

Not seen. Copy reported in OCI.

j. NEW YORK: [fancy] | G. P. PUTNAM & CO., 321 BROADWAY. | 1856.

Works title, dated 1856.

Noted in State [B], with p. viii correctly paged.

MH.

k. New York: [fancy] | G. P. PUTNAM & CO., 321 BROADWAY. | 1857.

Works title, dated 1857.

CtY.

l. BRACEBRIDGE HALL. | BY | WASHINGTON IRVING. | "Under ... who | having ... peruse | this ... spot." | CHRISTMAS ORDINARY. | Illustrated [fancy] | WITH FOURTEEN ORIGINAL DESIGNS BY SCHMOLZE, | ENGRAVED ON STEEL BY GREATBACH AND OTHERS. | NEW YORK: | G. P. PUTNAM, No. 321 BROADWAY. | 1858 .

(21.1 x 15.5): [1]-[2]^{12} 3-19^{12} 20^6 First and last leaf blank. Not reckoned: preliminary engraved illustration and engraved title, and thirteen other engravings through the volume.

[i]-[ii], title, on verso copyright (1857) and printer; [iii]-[iv], table of illustrations, verso blank; [v]-vi, table of contents; [9]-465, text; [466], blank.

Printer: John F. Trow, 377 & 379 Broadway, Cor. White Street, N.Y.

Lineation: p. 100, She ... seemed ; p. 200, to ... splendid

Noted in two bindings. [A]. Blue CM-like cloth on extra-thick boards. On sides, elaborate border in gilt and blind. [Spine missing on this copy]. AEG. Manila endpapers. [B]. Brown morocco. On sides, geometric design in blind and darker brown. Spine titled in gilt. AEG. Noted with brown endpapers and also with marbled endpapers.

MH, TxU (2).

m. [Works form]. NEW YORK: | G. P. PUTNAM (for the Proprietor), 506 BROADWAY. | 1859.

Two preliminary engraved illustrations, with the imprint of Childs & Peterson, Philadelphia.

Noted in State [B], with p. viii correctly paged.

NjP.

n. [Works form]. NEW YORK: | G. P. PUTNAM, 115 NASSAU STREET. | 1859.

Two preliminary engraved illustrations, with the imprint of Childs & Peterson, Philadelphia.

Green BD cloth. Identified on the spine as Vol. VI of the Works.

TxU.

1E- The first two London editions of *Bracebridge Hall* masquerade as one, the
2E. second being a fairly faithful line-for-line resetting in the same type style and with the same title page. But comparison on the mechanical collator proves that both volumes were reset from cover to cover in the disguised second edition. Since the two are so similar in appearance, however, and make use of the same text with minor corrections and changes, it is useful and convenient to describe both in one entry. The publisher must have considered them as a unit since he did not identify the second edition on the title page; that edition, in fact, may even be the "run-on" of 1000 copies of the first edition that appears in the Murray records.

For distinctions in collation, setting, and text between the first and the second edition, see the discussion that follows.

BRACEBRIDGE HALL; | OR, | THE HUMORISTS. | [rule] | BY GEOFFREY CRAYON, GENT. | [rule] | Under this cloud I walk, gentlemen; pardon my rude assault. I | am a traveller, who, having surveyed most of the terrestrial angles of | this globe, am hither arrived to peruse this little spot. | CHRISTMAS ORDINARY. | IN TWO VOLUMES. | VOL. I. [II.] | LONDON: | JOHN MURRAY, ALBEMARIE-STREET. | [rule] | 1822.

(22.9 x 14.3 untrimmed): Vol. I. $[A]^2$ B-I^8 K-U^8 X-Z^8 AA-BB^8 CC$^{6.}$ In the first edition, leaf G$_7$ is a cancel. The last leaf is a blank. Vol. II. $[A]^2$ B-I^8 K-U^8 X-Z^8 AA-CC^8 DD^2.

Vol. I. [i]-[ii], title, on verso printer; [iii]-iv, table of contents; [1]-[2], fly-title, verso blank; [3]-393, text; [394], printer. Vol. II. [i]-[ii], title, on verso printer; [iii]-iv, table of contents; [1]-[2], fly-title, verso blank; [3]-403, text; [404], printer. From the second text state of the first edition through the second edition, the text extends to p. 404.

Printer: Thomas Davison, Whitefriars.

Lineation: Vol. I p. 100, exemplified ... young ; p. 200, the ... of Vol. II. p. 100, lovely ... country ; p. 200, of ... several

The printing history of the first two London editions is one of constant textual changes, some perhaps the work of Irving himself, some certainly the work of the publisher or compositor attempting to regularize and to correct. Four successive text states can be defined, three in the first edition and the fourth in the second edition. Whether the three text states of the first edition represent three distinct impressions is open to question, since it cannot now be known with certainty which changes may have been made during a press run and which were made during a time between separate printings. The difficulty is compounded by the known practice of the day -- which may well appear here -- of using up old sheets before substituting new corrected ones. Apparent intermediate states are known. Despite the ambiguities and exceptions, a textual and chronological pattern is clear:

Text State 1 (first edition). The text ends on p. 403 of Vol. II.

This Text State appears in the two minor collation states:

A. Vol. I. leaf G_7, pp. 93-94, a cancelled leaf, is pasted to the stub of the old leaf.

B. The cancelled leaf is bound in. The leaf is in the same setting as in State A.

The situation insists upon the existence at one time of an earlier state in which the original uncancelled leaf contained something that needed changing. (Since the text here concerns men flirting with young women, and indecent jests, it is not difficult to imagine the problem.) But since no original leaf has been found, the survival of a copy of the earlier uncancelled state must for the present be considered only in the realm of the possible. Perhaps for once a publisher caught and corrected all copies before they escaped.

Text State 2 (first edition). A new paragraph ("I am sure ... study.") is added on pp. 402-403 of Vol. II, requiring the resetting of the last three pages. The expanded text ends on p. 404 of Vol. II. No other changes detected. Cancelled leaf G_7 is bound in Vol. I. An unusual copy in the University of Kansas library shows the stub of the excised leaf G_7 with the new cancelled leaf inserted and bound beside it.

Text State 3 (first edition). A number of textual changes and corrections appear (see the chart below), a few possibly the result of stop-press correction. Cancelled leaf G_7 is bound in Vol. I.

Text State 4 (second edition). The two volumes are entirely reset. (Leaf G_7 of Vol. I is now reset and integral). In the resetting, a number of new corrections appear, as well as a few new errors. Most of the changes previously made in text state 3 are incorporated, although in a few instances the text returns to that of Text States 1 or 2. The compositor may have been working from a copy of the second state; that at least would explain the repetition of some earlier readings. See the table below for some examples and for unique readings that will identify the edition.

Representative variants in the first and second editions:

Vol., page and line	First edition, Text State 1	First edition, Text State 2	First edition, Text State 3	Second Edition, Text State 4
I, title	Rule under author 2.9 cm.			Rule under author 2.7 cm.
I, [ii]	DAVSION		DAVISON	
I, 54.4f	old fashioned			old-fashioned
I, 62.19	ladies		ladies'	ladies
I, 162.7f	Tibbets			Tibbetses
I, 204.2	Remigius			Remegius
I, 311.19	chrystal			crystal
I, 323.12	woods			wood
I, 383.11	intellects, A		intellects. A	
II, title	Rule above date does not extend to period after date			Rule extends to period after date
II, 5.5	| the trees, from		| trees, from	| the trees from
II, 42.13	goals		gaols	
II, 75.11f	me, as			me as
II, 106.1f	Cobbet		Cobbett	
II, 165.4	Tibbets's		Tibbetses	
II, 185.16	Heirarchie		Hierarchie	
II, 223.15	called			call'd
II, 307.7	haunted house		Haunted House	
II, 354.6	Vander Spiegle		Vander Spiegel	Vander Speigle

II, 402-403		Paragraph
		added
II, 403-404	Text ends on	Text ends on
	p. 403	p. 404

Three bindings seen or reported; no sequence, if any, determined.

[A]. Slate-blue paper boards with brown paper shelfbacks. Sides blank. White paper label on spines: BRACEBRIDGE | HALL. | BY | GEOFFREY CRAYON. | [rule] | TWO VOLS. -- 24s. | [rule] | VOL. I. [II.] At extreme head and foot of labels, a fine line across (to mark dividing line between multiple printings?). White endpapers. Noted on a copy in Text State 1.

[B]. Brown paper boards with matching brown paper shelfbacks. Sides blank. Same paper label on spines. White endpapers. Noted on a copy in Text State 2.

[C]. Brown paper boards with green cloth shelfbacks. Sides blank. Paper label on spines. Not seen. Reported by *BAL*. State not determined.

The account book of the Murray firm records payment to Thomas Davison on 30 May 1822 for 4000 copies. A letter to *BAL* from the Murray family reports 4000 copies printed, made up of 3000 plus a run-on of 1000 copies. The "run-on" may be the second edition but is more likely one or both of the later states.

Deposited and registered at Stationers' Hall 17 May 1822. *Literary Gazette*, 25 May 1822, "issued"; 1 June 1822, reviewed. *Edinburgh Magazine*, July 1822, reviewed. Irving to John Murray, 22 September 1850, "The London edition appeared 23rd May 1822." *Literary Gazette*, 22 February 1823, advertised under "New Editions": "Bracebridge Hall, 2 vols. 8vo. 24s. Ditto, 2 vols. small 8vo. 16s." Is the full 8vo. at 24s. the second edition?

State 1: TxGeoS, TxU (2), ViU. State 2: KU, MH, ViU. State 3: TxU; copy in CLU reported on. Second edition: NN, TxU.

3Ea.   BRACEBRIDGE HALL: | OR | THE HUMORISTS. | [swelled rule] | BY GEOFFREY CRAYON, GENT. | [rule] | Under ... I | am ... angles | of ... spot. | CHRISTMAS ORDINARY. | [rule] | A NEW EDITION. | *IN TWO VOLUMES.* | VOL. I. [II.] | [double rule] | LONDON: | JOHN MURRAY, ALBEMARLE STREET. | [rule] | 1823.

The text of this new edition is derived from Text State 3 of the first London edition. There are a few additional changes.

(18.0 x 11.2 rebound):   Vol. I. [i]-iv, [1]-336. Vol. II. [i]-iv, [1]-347 [348]. Signed in 8's.

Printer: C. Roworth, Bell Yard, Temple Bar.

Lineation: Vol. I. p. 100, the ... a ; p. 200, love ... this Vol. II. p. 100, to ... the ; p. 200, a ... to

Literary Gazette, 22 February 1823, advertised under "New Editions": "2 vols. small 8vo. 16*s*."

TxU.

b. A NEW EDITION. | ... | LONDON: | JOHN MURRAY, ALBEMARLE STREET. | MDCCCXXIV.

DLC, TxU.

4E. BRACEBRIDGE HALL: | OR | THE HUMORISTS. | [stylized swelled rule with diamond in center] | BY GEOFFREY CRAYON, GENT. | [rule] | Under ... I | am ... angles | of ... spot. | CHRISTMAS ORDINARY. | [rule] | A NEW EDITION. | *IN TWO VOLUMES.* | VOL. I. [II.] | [double rule] | LONDON: | JOHN MURRAY, ALBEMARLE STREET. | MDCCCXXV.

(19.5 x 12.0): Vol. I. [i]-iv, [1]-336. Vol. II. [i]-iv, [1]-347 [348]. Signed in 8's.

For the most part, a line-for-line reprint of the 1824 edition, but reset.

Printer: C. Roworth, Bell Yard, Temple Bar.

Lineation: Vol. I. p. 100, the ... a ; p. 200, love ... ceremony, Vol. II. p. 100, to ... the ; p. 200, a ... to

Brown paper boards with green S cloth shelfbacks. Sides blank. Paper label on spines, with price, TWO VOLS. -- 16s.

TxU (2).

5E. BRACEBRIDGE HALL; | OR | THE HUMORISTS. | [rule] | BY | GEOFFREY CRAYON, GENT. | [rule] | Under ... am | a ... this | globe ... spot. | CHRISTMAS ORDINARY. | [rule] | LONDON: | JOHN MURRAY, ALBEMARLE STREET. | [rule] | 1845.

(17.9 x 12.0): [i]-iv, [1]-375 [376]. Signed in 8's.

"Murray's Colonial and Home Library," No. 11.

Printer: W. Clowes and Sons, Stamford Street.

Lineation: p. 100, ST. MARK'S ... church.; p. 200, ENGLISH ... sup-

Red L cloth. On sides, in blind, design with MURRAY'S COLONIAL & HOME LIBRARY at center. Spine titled in gilt. Yellow endpapers with printed advertisements in red.

TxU.

6E.   BRACEBRIDGE HALL, | OR, | THE HUMORISTS. | A Medley. [fancy] | BY | GEOFFREY CRAYON, GENT^N. [with two dots under the raised N] | "Under ... a | traveller, ... am | hither ... spot." -- CHRISTMAS ORDINARY. | AUTHOR'S REVISED EDITION. | COMPLETE IN ONE VOLUME. | LONDON: | GEORGE ROUTLEDGE AND CO., SOHO SQUARE. | 1850.

Routledge's "Popular Library."

(16.3 x 10.2 rebound): [i]-iv, [1]-292. Signed in 8's.

Printer: Cox (Brothers) and Wyman, Great Queen Street, Lincoln's-Inn Fields.

Lineation: p. 100, auspicious; ... stone!; p. 200, window ... as

Seen only rebound. Other volumes in the series noted in boards printed in colors, or in brown AR cloth, sides decorated in blind with series name at center, spine titled in gilt.

Athenæum, 13 April 1850, advertised as "New volume": 1*s*. "in fancy cover," 1*s*. 6*d*. in cloth gilt.

IaU.

7E.   [London: Simms and M'Intyre, 1850.]

"The Parlour Library."

The text is that of the Author's Revised Edition.

Not located. Advertised *Examiner* and *Literary Gazette*, 27 April 1850, "Just ready."

8Ea.   BRACEBRIDGE HALL; | OR, | THE HUMORISTS. | A Medley. [fancy] | BY GEOFFREY CRAYON. | "Under ... traveller, | who, ... arrived, | to ... spot." -- CHRISTMAS ORDINARY. | AUTHOR'S REVISED EDITION. | LONDON: | HENRY G. BOHN, YORK STREET, COVENT GARDEN. | 1850.

(18.1 x 11.5): [i]-iv, [1]-320. Signed in 8's.

Issued individually as "Bohn's Shilling Series"; bound with *Abbotsford* and *Newstead Abbey* as Vol. III of "Bohn's Library Edition." The Shilling Series issue has four pages of terminal advertisements in blue.

Printer: Harrison and Son, St. Martin's Lane.

Lineation: p. 100, "As ... pur- ; p. 200, Whoever ... eyes.

Noted in original binding only in "Bohn's Library Edition." Gray T cloth. Sides decorated in blind. Spine titled in gilt as Irving's Works, Vol. III, Bohn's Library Edition. White endpapers with advertisements in blue. Portrait of Scott before title. No works title. Noted also in a later issue, bound with *Abbotsford* and *Newstead Abbey* dated 1853, with a works title dated 1854.

Shilling Series. *Athenæum*, 7 September 1850, in "List of New Books," at 1s.6d. Library Edition. *Athenæum* and *Literary Gazette*, 2 November 1850, the set of 10 vols. at 35s listed.

NN in Library Edition, original cloth. MB, in Library Edition, later issue. *BL*, in Shilling Series.

b.   [London: Henry G. Bohn, 1854.]

"Bohn's Library Edition." With a portrait of Scott.

Not seen. Copy reported in Staats- und Universitätsbibliothek Hamburg.

1Fa.   [*Bracebridge Hall*: *or The Humorists*. New Edition. In Two Volumes. Paris: Baudry, 1823.]

For description, see the impression below by A. and W. Galignani, 1824, from the same setting.

Not seen. Listed *Bibliographie de la France*, 15 November 1823, # 4989 (misnumbered 4999).

Copy reported in Bibliothèque Nationale.

b.   BRACEBRIDGE HALL; | OR | THE HUMORISTS. | [swelled rule] | BY GEOFFREY CRAYON, GENT. | [rule] | Under this cloud I walk, gentlemen; pardon my rude assault. I am | a traveller, who, having surveyed most of the terrestrial angles of this | globe, am hither arrived to peruse this little spot. | CHRISTMAS ORDINARY. | [rule] | NEW EDITION. | IN TWO VOLUMES. | VOL. I. [II.] | [emblem: D in star within wreath with pendant medal] | PARIS: | PUBLISHED BY A. AND W. GALIGNIANI, [sic] | AT THE ENGLISH, FRENCH, ITALIAN, GERMAN AND SPANISH LIBRARY, | 18, RUE VIVIENNE. | [rule] | 1824.

(16.2 x 10.2): Vol. I. [-]^4 1-15^{12} 16^{10}. Last leaf a blank. Vol. II. [-]^4 1-16^{12} 17^2. Last leaf a blank. Laid paper.

Vol. I. [i]-[ii], half-title, on verso printer (?); [iii]-[iv], title, verso blank; [v]-vi, table of contents; [1]-377, text; [378], blank. Vol. II. [i]-[ii], half-title, on verso printer (?); [iii]-[iv], title, verso blank; [v]-vi, table of contents; [1]-386, text.

Printer: Jules Didot, Sen.

Lineation: Vol. I. p. 100, may ... distin-; p. 200, What ... no- Vol. II. p. 100, was ... their ; p. 200, Morning. ... hunters.

TxU.

c. PARIS: | PUBLISHED BY A. AND W. GALIGNANI, | AT THE ENGLISH, FRENCH, ITALIAN, GERMAN, AND SPANISH | LIBRARY, N° 18, RUE VIVIENNE. | [rule] | 1827.

Bibliographie de la France, 16 June 1827, # 4095, listed.

CtY.

d. [*Bracebridge Hall*. 2 vols. Paris: Baudry, 1834.]

Not seen. Copy reported in Bibliothèque Nationale.

1G. [*Bracebridge-Hall*. Mit crklärcndcn Anmcrkungcn hcrausgcgcbcn von E. A. Toel. Lüneburg: Im Verlage der Herold- und Wahlstab'schen Buchhandlung, 1841.]

The text itself is in English; the other matter in German.

Not seen. Listed in Wilhelm Heinsius, *Allgemeines Bücher-Lexicon 1835-1841* and Christian G. Kayser, *Vollständiges Bücher-Lexicon 1841-1846*. Copy reported in Stadtbibliothek Braunschweig.

TRANSLATIONS

Danish.

[*Bracebridge-Hall eller Karakterene*.   Oversat af Ph. Wallich.   2 vols. København: Schubothe, 1829.]

8vo.

Not located. Listed in *Bibliotheca Danica*, Vol. IV.

Dutch.

[*Mijn Verblijs op het Kasteel Bracebridge*.   Naar het Engelsch, door Steenbergen van Goor. 2 vols. Amsterdam: C.L. Schleyer, 1828.]

8vo.

Not located. Listed in *Alphabetische Naamlijst van Boeken*. Supplement, 1790-1832.

French.

[*Le château de Bracebridge,* par Geoffroy-Crayon. Traduit de l'anglais par M. Jean Cohen. 4 vols. Paris: Hubert, 1822.]

Printer: Cordier, Paris.

Bibliographie de la France, 6 September 1823, # 3766, listed.

Not seen. Copy reported in Bibliothèque Nationale.

[*Les humoristes, ou, Le château de Bracebridge,* par Washington Irving. Traduit de l'anglais par Gustave Grandpré. 2 vols. Paris: Corbet aîné, quai des Augustins, n. 61, 1826.]

Some chapters omitted.

Printer: Cosson, Paris.

Bibliographie de la France, 15 November 1826, # 7060, listed.

Not seen. Copy reported in Bibliothèque Nationale.

German.

Bracebridge-Hall | oder | die Charaktere. | [rule] | Aus dem Englischen | des | Washington Irving | übersetzt | von | S.H. Spiker. | Erster [Zweiter] Band. | [swelled rule] | Berlin, | Im Verlage von Duncker und Humblot. | [rule] | 1823. [in fraktur]

(17.5 x 10.5): Vol. I. [I]-XVI [XVII]-[XVIII], [1]-372 [373]-[374]. Four pages of advertisements at end. Vol. II. [I]-[IV], [1]-405 [406]. Two pages of advertisements at end. Signed in 12's.

Printer: Johann Friedrich Starcke.

Lineation: Vol. I. p. 100, Leb' ... erscheinst ; p. 200, seres ... [in footnote] Uebers. Vol. II. p. 100, Der ... die ; p. 200, man ... auf

Noted in red boards with impressed cross-hatching. Original binding?

TxU. Copy reported in Stadtbibliothek Hannover.

Bracebridge-Hall | oder | die Charaktere. | [rule] | Aus dem Englischen | des Washington Irving | übersetzt | von | S.H. Spiker. | Erster [Zweiter] Band. | [rule] | Zweite verbesserte Auflage. | [swelled rule] | Berlin, | im Verlage von Duncker und Humblot. | [rule] | 1826.

(17.6 x 10.4): Vol. I. [I]-XVI, [1]-283 [284]. Vol. II. [I]-[IV], [1]-292. Eight pages of advertisements at end. Signed in 8's. Crude laid paper.

Printer: Trowitzsch und Sohn.

Lineation: Vol. I. p. 100, edlen ... [in footnote] Uebers.; p. 200, abermals ... [in footnote] Uebers. Vol. II. p. 100, an ... zusam-; p. 200, lag ... um-

Noted in orange boards with impressed crosshatching. Original binding?

TxU. Copy reported in Stadtbibliothek Braunschweig.

Bracebridge-Hall, | oder | die Humoristen. | Von | Washington Irving. | Uebersetzt | von | Henriette Schubart. | [rule] | *Erster* [*Zweyter, Dritter, Vierter*] *Theil.* | [wavy rule] | Zwickau, | im Verlage der Gebrüder Schumann. | 1826.

"Taschenbibliothek der ausländischen Klassiker, in neuen Verdeutschungen," Nos. 159, 160, 161, 161 (the last number is repeated, although the series title says "Vierter Theil" at the foot).

(10.1 x 8.2): Vol. I. [i]-[viii], [1]-184. Vol. II. [i]-[viii], [1]-178. 6 pp. terminal ads not reckoned. Vol. III. [i]-[iv] (2 leaves missing in this copy?), [1]-213 [214]. Vol. IV. [i]-[viii], [1]-140.

Lineation: Vol. I. p. 100, Wie ... ich Vol. II. p. 100, Bey ... Schrift- Vol. III. p. 100, von ... das Vol. IV. p. 100, beym ... beschöni-

CtY. Copy reported in Staatsbibliothek Bamberg.

Bracebridge-Hall | oder | die Charaktere | von | Washington Irving. | [rule] | Aus dem Englischen. | [double rule] | Erstes [- Sechstes] Bändchen. | [quintuple rule] | Frankfurt am Main, 1827. | Gedruckt und verlegt bei Johann David Sauerländer. [in fraktur]

"Washington Irving's sämmtliche Werke," Bändchen 13-18.

Translated by Christian August Fischer.

(14.1 x 10.9 untrimmed): Vol. I. [1]-110 [111]-[112]. Vol. II. [1]-94 [95]-[96]. Vol. III. [1]-130 [131]-[132]. Vol. IV. [1]-97 [98]-[100]. Vol. V. [1]-101 [102]-[104]. Vol. VI. [1]-126 [127]-[128]. Signed in 8's. Crude laid paper.

Lineation: Vol. I. p. 100, Ticken ... dicke Vol. II. p. 50, ganze, ... Reit- Vol. III. p. 100, gern ... Stim- Vol. IV. p. 50, Der ... freundlichen Vol. V. p. 100, innere ... der Vol. VI. p. 100, Krächzen ... belohnt,

Tan paper wrappers. On front, cover-title with ornamental border. On back, ornamental border with design of lions and urn in center. Spine blank.

NN, TxU (in wrappers).

Bracebridge-Hall | oder | die Charaktere. | [swelled rule] | Aus dem
Englischen | des | Washington Irving | übersetzt | von | S. H. Spiker. |
Erster [Zweiter, Dritter] Theil. | [swelled rule] | Wien, 1828. | Gedruckt und
Verlegt bei Chr. Fr. Schade. [in fraktur]

"Classische Cabinets-Bibliothek," Nos. 152-154.

(13.0 x 9.3): Vol. I. [I]-XVI, [17]-175 [176]. Vol. II. [I]-[IV], [1]-160 [161]-
[162]. Vol. III. [I]-[IV], [1]-149 [150]. Signed in 8's.

Lineation: Vol. I. p. 100, unterscheidet ... suchen." Vol. II. p. 100,
hinkollerten. ... Vertheidiger Vol. III. p. 100, Fertigkeit ... unver-

Off-white flexible boards. On front, cover-title and decorations in black. On
back, "Pränumeration des ersten Semesters 1828. $N^{ro.}$ 8. [9., 10.]" and series
description.

TxU. Copy reported in Stadtbibliothek Mainz.

[Bracebridge-Hall, oder die Charaktere, 2., sorgfältig verbesserte Auflage.
Frankfurt am Main: Johann David Sauerländer, 1846.]

Two engraved illustrations.

"Ausgewählte Schriften," No. 2.

Not seen. Copy reported in Stadtbibliothek Braunschweig.

Polish

GALERYA [in hollow letters] | OBRAZÓW ŻYCIA LUDZKIEGO |
CZYLI | CHARAKTERY. | PRZEZ | AMERYKANINA
WASHINGTONA IRWINGA. | PRZEKŁADAŁ | JOZEF BYCHOWIEC.
| [wavy rule] | TOM I. [II.] | [wavy rule] | [double rule] | WILNO | W
DRUKARNI B. NEUMANA. | [rule] | 1829.

(17.8 x 10.5): Vol. I. [i]-xvii [xviii]-[xxii], [1?]-171 [172]. Vol. II. [i]-[vi], [1?]-
144. 8vo.

Not examined. Information based on copy in Biblioteka Narodowa, Warsaw.

Swedish.

BRACEBRIDGE HALL, | ELLER | EN VÅR PÅ LANDET I
ENGLAND; | AF | WASHINGTON IRVING. | [rule] | *Mina Herrar!*
Förlåten min oartighet, att jag spatse- | *rar under dessa moln. -- Jag är en*
resande, | *som besett de flesta vinklar och vrår i verlden,* | *och är nu*
hitkommen, för att betrakta denna | *lilla jordfläk.* | CHRISTMAS
ORDINARY. | [rule] | *FÖRRA [SEDNARE] DELEN.* | [rule] | [elaborated

rule composed of a number of small ornaments] | STOCKHOLM, 1828, | hos *Zacharias Haeggström.*

(19.0 x 12.2 untrimmed): Vol. I. [i]-[iv], [1]-272. Vol. II. [i]-[iv], [1]-272. Not reckoned: thirteen leaves of terminal advertisements. Signed in 8's. Laid paper.

The thirteen leaves of terminal advertisements, Vol. II, are made up of five groups of separate advertisements variously dated: the first is undated; second, 1 June 1827; third, 1827; fourth, 1 February 1827; fifth, 1 February 1827. The fifth includes, as the last item, this edition as forthcoming, "Under utgifning åro."

Lineation: Vol. I. p. 100, dertryckta, ... och ; p. 200, ta ... tillfäl- Vol. II. p. 100, bedjerskan: ... regioner,; p. 200, förbi ... beslöt

Blue-gray unprinted heavy paper wrappers. On spines of copy examined, paper labels with handwritten title, probably the work of an owner.

NN, TxU (in wrappers).

EDITIONS OF INDIVIDUAL SKETCHES

Dolph Heyliger.

ILLUSTRATIONS [in red] | OF | WASHINGTON IRVING'S | DOLPH HEYLIGER [in red] | DESIGNED AND ETCHED | BY | JOHN W. EHNINGER | NEW-YORK [in red] | GEORGE P PUTNAM 155 BROADWAY | M DCCC LI All within single frame lines.

Copyright 1850. The dedication to Washington Irving is dated New-York, December, 1850.

(28.5 x 36.7): [1]-32. Not reckoned: ten plates.

Text of "Dolph Heyliger," pp. 5-32. In double columns. Single frame line around each page.

The text is taken from the Author's Revised Edition.

Printer: John F. Trow, 49, 51 & 53 Ann-st., New-York.

Light blue T cloth. In copy examined, the original binding is obscured by a book cover that cannot be removed.

Literary World, 21 December 1850, "Published this week," "On Saturday," advertised at $4 in cloth gilt. *American Whig Review,* January 1851, reviewed.

NNC.

[Advertised in *The Athenæum*, 13 December 1851, by Addey & Co. (*late* Cundall & Addey), 21, Old Bond-street, [London]: "DOLPH HEYLIGER. By WASHINGTON IRVING. With Ten Original Illustrations, designed and sketched by J. W. EHNINGER, of New York. Oblong folio, cloth, 1*l.* 1*s.*" "Have Just Ready."]

Not located.

LETTERS OF JONATHAN OLDSTYLE, GENT.

The nine letters to the editor that constitute the full version of this work appeared first, without formal title, in the New York *Morning Chronicle,* edited by Washington Irving's brother Peter: 15 November 1802, 20 November 1802, 1 December 1802, 4 December 1802, 11 December 1802, 17 January 1803, 22 January 1803, 8 February 1803, and 23 April 1803. Each letter was quickly reprinted in the New York *Chronicle Express*, a semi-weekly version of the *Morning Chronicle,* except for the first letter (which had appeared before the first issue of the *Chronicle Express*) and the short first paragraph of the second letter (which referred to the first letter). In 1824, the New York printer William H. Clayton published the letters for the first time in book form, without the supervision and probably without the consent of Irving. The text is derived from the letters in the *Chronicle Express* and omits the first letter and the opening paragraph of the second. In the same year, Effingham Wilson of London published a pirated edition that took its text from Clayton's edition. He reprinted the text four times during that year. Except for a German translation of that edition in 1824, the work did not appear again in book form during Irving's lifetime, and the first letter was not reprinted at all.

1A.   LETTERS | OF | JONATHAN OLDSTYLE, GENT. | BY THE AUTHOR OF | THE SKETCH BOOK. | WITH A | BIOGRAPHICAL NOTICE. | [elaborated swelled rule] | New-York: [fancy] | PUBLISHED BY WILLIAM H. CLAYTON. | Clayton & Van Norden, Printers. | [rule] | 1824.

The text of the letters is derived from those in the New York *Chronicle Express*: the first Oldstyle letter is omitted, as well as the first paragraph of the second letter. In further changes appearing here, the editorial introductions to the original sixth and eighth letters are omitted, the letters are numbered I-VIII (beginning with the original second letter), and a number of minor revisions are introduced, apparently the result of house-styling by William Clayton. Even the title itself was furnished by the publisher. Washington Irving, according to Pierre Irving, had nothing to do with the revision or the publication.

(23.1 x 14.5 untrimmed): [A]^4 B^2 2-9^4.

[i]-[ii], title, on verso copyright ("the nineteenth day of February, in the forty-eighth year of the Independence" by J. L. Buckingham); [iii]-x, "Biographical Notice"; [1 leaf unpaged], fly-title, verso blank; [5]-67, text; [68], blank.

Lineation: p. 20, other ... a ; p. 50, LETTER VII. ... with

Drab brown paper wrapper. On front, cover-title within double frame lines: Price 50 Cents. | [double rule] | LETTERS | OF | JONATHAN OLDSTYLE, GENT. | BY THE AUTHOR OF | THE SKETCH BOOK. | WRITTEN IN 1802. | New-York: [fancy] | CLAYTON AND VAN NORDEN, PRINTERS, | No. 64 Pine-street. | [rule] | 1824. Back and spine blank. White endpapers. Fly leaves seem to occur randomly at front or at back or neither.

Title deposited 19 February 1824. *North American Review*, April 1824, listed.

In wrappers, DLC (2), NN, ViU.

1Ea. LETTERS | OF | JONATHAN OLDSTYLE, GENT. | BY THE AUTHOR OF | THE SKETCH BOOK. | WITH A | Biographical Notice. [fancy] | [double rule] | LONDON: | EFFINGHAM WILSON, ROYAL EXCHANGE. | [rule] | 1824.

The text is taken from that of the New York 1824 edition with a few minor changes in accidentals.

(22.0 x 14.2 untrimmed): $[A]^8$ B-E^8. The last leaf is a blank.

[i]-[ii], title, on verso printer; [iii]-x, "Biographical Notice"; [1]-[2], fly-title, verso blank; [3]-68, text, printer at foot of last page.

Printer: J. M'Creery, Tooks Court, London.

Lineation: p. 20, formation, ... the ; p. 50, LETTER VII. ... free-

Dark brown unprinted paper wrapper. White endpapers.

Literary Gazette, 10 April 1824, advertised for Monday [12 April]; 17 April 1824, listed.

In wrapper, ViU.

b. SECOND EDITION. | [double rule] | LONDON: EFFINGHAM WILSON, ROYAL EXCHANGE. | [rule] | 1824.

Literary Gazette, 24 April 1824, Second Edition advertised.

BL.

c. THIRD EDITION. | [double rule] | LONDON: EFFINGHAM WILSON, ROYAL EXCHANGE. | [rule] | 1824.

Literary Gazette, 22 May 1824, Third Edition advertised.

BL.

d. [Fourth Edition. London: Effingham Wilson, 1824.]

Not located, not recorded. Presumably it was published, since a "Fifth Edition" follows.

2E. LETTERS | OF | JONATHAN OLDSTYLE, GENT. | BY THE AUTHOR OF | THE SKETCH BOOK. | WITH A | Biographical Notice. [fancy] | [swelled rule] | *FIFTH EDITION.* | [double rule] | LONDON: |EFFINGHAM WILSON, ROYAL EXCHANGE. | [rule] | 1824

(17.5 x 11.2 rebound): [i]-xi [xii], [1]-71 [72]. Signed in 8's.

Printer: J. M'Creery, Tooks Court, London.

Lineation: p. 25, was ... OLDSTYLE.; p. 50, The ... end

DLC.

TRANSLATIONS

German.

Jonathan Oldstyle's | Briefe. | [swelled rule] | Aus dem Englischen | des | Washington Irving | übersetzt | von | S. H. Spiker. | [swelled rule] | Berlin, | Im Verlage von Duncker und Humblot. | [rule] | 1824. [in fraktur]

(18.1 x 10.7): [i]-x, [1]-92. Two pages of advertisements bound at end. Signed in 8's.

Printer: Johann Friedrich Starcke.

Lineation: p. 50, sieht, ... Be-

TxU. Copy reported in Universitätsbibliothek Heidelberg.

CHARLES THE SECOND

A study of Irving's Journal for 1823-1824, and especially his correspondence with John Howard Payne during those years, reveals his major hand in the composition of *Charles the Second*, founded on Alexandre Duval's *La jeunesse de Henri V*. In the initial composition of the play as well as in the later revisions, Irving certainly deserves, at the least, equal billing with Payne, and the impartial observer would say that he deserves top billing. On 5 November 1823 he wrote Payne, "I have nearly rewritten La Jeunesse, but have made no songs for it." On receipt of a manuscript of the play in November 1823, as Pierre M. Irving reports in the *Life and Letters* (II, 171), Payne wrote Irving, " I consider it one of the best pieces of the kind I ever read ...," hardly the exclamation of an author whose manuscript had been touched up by a friend. But typically, Irving carefully preserved his anonymity in the work. (He even withdrew from consideration for production another play on which he had been working, *Azendai*, when his authorship became known. See his letter to Payne from Paris, 29 December 1823.)

On 26 November 1823, he wrote to Payne, "I wish you would present the piece either in your own name or if you would prefer it, fabricate a name, as of a friend resident near Paris, which name we may afterwards make use of, but at all events do not let my name be implicated in the thing." On 29 December 1823, he repeated the injunction, "As to Richelieu & Rochester [*Charles the Second*], let them appear in your own name, and, to save your conscience, say that they have been revised and occasionally touched up by a literary friend." On 31 January 1824, he repeated the instructions a third time, revealing also something of his generous intentions toward Payne in this insistence on anonymity:

Richelieu & Rochester if tolerably performed will do you credit & operate favorably for you, in future dealings -- You must not hesitate to claim them as your productions; though to satisfy scruples & obviate cavilling you may say they have been revised & occasionally touched up by a literary friend -- I wish however, my name to be kept completely out of sight.

After three warnings, Payne could hardly have misunderstood, and in his printed Preface to the play, dated London, June 5, 1824, he faithfully followed instructions, saying only, "My manuscript has been revised by a literary friend to whom I am indebted for invaluable touches...." It was not until his dedication of *Richelieu* to Irving in 1826 that he was to reveal the name of his literary friend.

The question of text in the various printed editions of the play is a vexed and puzzling one. When Irving saw the play, on 28 May 1824, the day on which he arrived in London upon returning from France, he was disappointed in the performance, particularly of the first act. On 31 May, he wrote his bother Peter of his disappointment, and added, "I shall assist Payne in pruning the piece to-day, and I have no doubt it will have a good run." It was that pruned version that apparently was published in the second edition. On 3 January 1826, when Payne was preparing to send a manuscript to America, Irving wrote him, "The printed copy has the first act in the mutilated state in which it was published in consequence of my disgust at the barbarous performance of Lady Clare & the coarse manner in which what was intended for polite dialogue was played. If you can restore [it,] do so." On 7 February 1826, he wrote again, telling Payne to send copy to America "with the passages restored, which I cut out in London."

Irving's letters suggest two printed versions of the play, particularly of the first act. But an examination of the various editions themselves reveals a situation much more complex than that. In fact, the very reference to "the first act" is itself ambiguous, since some editions divide the play into three acts (1E, 1-2A) and some into two (2-4E, 3A). In further fact, the earlier portion of the play remains relatively unchanged in all editions, with greater changes appearing as the play progresses, until the very end where five distinctly different endings appear (although the final curtain speeches remain the same).

The text needs detailed study. But three representative sets of variants will illustrate the complexities. Differences in spelling and punctuation are ignored, and stage directions if present are not reproduced. The order of listing within each set is arbitrary.

1. Captain Copp's song in Act II, sc. 1 of 1E, 1-2A; Act I, sc. 2 of 2-4E, 3A.

[A].   (This is the version that Irving sent to Payne in a letter of 26
             November 1823.)

             And his crew of Tenbreeches.
             Those Dutch sons of ------

         (In 1E, 1-2A)

[B].   And his crew of Bigbreeches.
             Those Dutch sons of ------

         (In 2-4E, 3A)

2. Beginning of Act III in 1E, 1-2A; Act II of 2-4E, 3A.

[A]. EDW.   I've had a hard scramble of it,... The king must arrive presently,... Hark! a noise in the king's private stair-case -- Softly, then, softly.

   (In 1E, 4E)

[B]. EDW.   I've had a hard scramble of it,... The king must arrive presently,... Ha! ha! ha! I cannot help laughing, tho' I do it with fear and trembling, to think of the confounded prank that mad wag, Rochester, has played off upon her majesty. Hark! a noise in the king's private staircase. Softly, then, softly.

   (In 2-3E, 1-3A)

3. The ending, beginning about a page before the curtain.   Only the beginning of each character's lines is given here. The final curtain lines, which are generally the same in all editions, are omitted.

[A].   COPP. Thunder and lightning!

   MARY. What, can he be that hard-hearted man?

   COPP. Come along, girl, come along.

   ROCH. One moment, Captain Copp. --

   COPP. Dead!

   MARY. That's my own uncle!

   CHAS. I have pardoned you, Rochester;

   ROCH. And I, my liege,

   (In 1E)

[B].   COPP. Thunder and lightning!

   CHAS. What say you, Captain Copp?

   COPP. Fair and softly, your majesty --

   CHAS. You are right, captain --

   COPP. Your majesty has fathomed my own wishes.

   (In 2-3E)

[C].   COPP. Thunder and lightning!

    ROCH. One moment, Captain Copp --

    COPP. Dead!

    MARY. That's my own uncle!

    CHAS. I have pardoned you, Rochester.

    ROCH. And I, my liege,

    (In 4E)

[D].   COPP. Thunder and lightning!

    ROCH. One moment, Captain Copp.

    COPP. Dead!

    CHAS. I have pardoned you, Rochester;

    ROCH. I shall not attempt my liege,

    (In 1-2A)

[E].   COPP. Thunder and lightning!

    ROCH. Hold, Captain Copp.

    COPP. Dead!

    CHAS. What say you, Captain Copp?

    COPP. Fair and softly, your majesty --

    CHAS. You are right, Captain --

    (In 3A)

1E.   CHARLES THE SECOND; | OR, | THE MERRY MONARCH. | A COMEDY, | *IN THREE ACTS,* | (WITH SOME SONGS): | FIRST PERFORMED AT THE THEATRE ROYAL, COVENT GARDEN, | ON THURSDAY EVENING, MAY 27, 1824. | [rule] | BY | JOHN HOWARD PAYNE, | *Author of Brutus, Clari, Therese, Accusation, Adeline, Ali Pacha,* | *The Two Galley Slaves, Love in Humble Life, Mrs. Smith,* | *and various other Pieces.* | [rule] | LONDON: | PRINTED FOR | LONGMAN, HURST, REES, ORME, BROWN, AND GREEN, | PATERNOSTER-ROW. | [rule] | 1824.

(22.6 x 14.0 untrimmed): [A]^4 B-I^4 K^2.

[i]-[ii], title, on verso printer; [iii]-[iv], dedication to Charles Kemble, verso blank; [v]-[viii], untitled introduction, dated London, June 5, 1824; [1]-47, text; [48], blank; [49]-66, text, printer at foot of last page; [67], list of characters; [68], blank.

Printer: Thomas Davison, Whitefriars, London.

Lineation: p. 20, EDW. ... dart ; p. 40, COPP. ... with

Issued in paper wrapper?

The English Catalogue of Books, 1801-1836 gives June 1824 as the publication date.

CtY. On microcard in *Three Centuries of Drama: American*, source not identified.

2Ea. Dolby's British Theatre. [fancy] | [swelled rule] | CHARLES THE SECOND; | OR, | THE MERRY MONARCH. | *A COMEDY,* | IN TWO ACTS, | (WITH SOME SONGS) | BY JOHN HOWARD PAYNE. | [rule] | Printed from the Acting Copy, with Remarks. | TO WHICH ARE ADDED, | DESCRIPTION OF THE COSTUME, CAST OF THE | CHARACTERS, SIDES OF ENTRANCE AND EXIT, | RELATIVE POSITIONS OF THE PERFORMERS | ON THE STAGE, AND THE WHOLE OF THE | STAGE BUSINESS, | AS NOW PERFORMED AT THE | THEATRE ROYAL, COVENT-GARDEN. | [rule] | Embellished with a Wood Engraving, from an original Drawing | made expressly for this Work, by Mr. I. R. CRUIKSHANK, | and executed by Mr. WHITE. | [embellished swelled rule] | London: [fancy] | PRINTED AND PUBLISHED BY T. DOLBY, BRITANNIA | PRESS, 17 CATHERINE STREET, STRAND; | And Sold by HODGSON and Co. 10, Newgate Street. | [rule] | *Price Sixpence.*

(14.1 x 8.6 rebound): [A]⁶ B-D⁶. Last leaf missing in copy examined; blank? Preliminary leaf of illustration not reckoned.

Preliminary matter unpaged. [First leaf], blank, on verso illustration; [Second leaf], title, verso blank; [Third leaf], dedication to Charles Kemble, verso blank; [Fourth leaf], introduction, dated London, June 5, 1824 (verso paged iv); [Fifth leaf], Costume, on verso Stage Directions; [9]-45, text; [46], blank.

Lineation: p. 20, son ... here--; p. 40, *Lady C.* ... you

MH.

b. AS PERFORMED AT THE | THEATRE-ROYAL, COVENT GARDEN. | ... | LONDON: | THOMAS DOLBY, CATHERINE-STREET, STRAND | [rule] | 1825.

(Note that NOW is omitted before PERFORMED on the title page.)

CtY.

3Ea. CHARLES THE SECOND; | OR, THE MERRY MONARCH: | A COMEDY, | In Two Acts, [fancy] | BY JOHN HOWARD PAYNE, ESQ. | *Author of Brutus, The Lancers, Love in Humble Life, Ali Pacha, &c.* | [rule] | PRINTED FROM THE ACTING COPY, WITH REMARKS, | BIOGRAPHICAL AND CRITICAL, BY D--G. | To which are added, | A DESCRIPTION OF THE COSTUME, -- CAST OF THE CHARACTERS, | ENTRANCES AND EXITS, -- RELATIVE POSITIONS OF THE PER- | FORMERS ON THE STAGE, -- AND THE WHOLE OF THE STAGE | BUSINESS. | As now performed at the | THEATRES ROYAL, LONDON. | [rule] | EMBELLISHED WITH A FINE ENGRAVING, | By Mr. WHITE, from a Drawing taken in the Theatre by | MR. R. CRUIKSHANK. | [rule] | LONDON: | JOHN CUMBERLAND, 2, CUMBERLAND TERRACE, | CAMDEN NEW TOWN.

D--G. has been identified as George Daniel, editor of Cumberland's British Theatre.

(14.0 x 9.0 rebound; reported 16.5 x 10.5 approx. in original untrimmed condition): [A]^6 (third leaf signed B3) B-D^6.

[1]-[2], blank, on verso illustration; [3]-[4], title, verso blank; [5]-9, Remarks, signed D--G., Stage Directions at foot of p. 9; [10], Costume and Cast of Characters at the Theatre Royal, Covent Garden; [9]-45, text; [46], blank.

Lineation: p. 20, *Roch.* ... put ; p. 40, *Lady C.* ... you

Brown paper wrapper. Not examined. Copy in MH reported with cover-title that specifies this as "Cumberland's British Theatre," No. 59. The imprint adds eleven publishers, ending with G. Berger, 42, Holywell street, Strand.

TxU.

b. A variant title page, presumably representing a separate impression, sequence unknown, identifies the illustration as a wood engraving by Mr. Bonner (rather than Mr. White) from a drawing taken in the theatre by Mr. R. Cruikshank.

Not examined. Copy reported in NN.

c. [London: Davidson, n.d.]

Included in later editions of Cumberland's British Theatre, ca. 1840.

Not seen. Copy reported in InU, 00, ScU.

4E.   CHARLES THE SECOND; | OR, | THE MERRY MONARCH. | A Comedy, [fancy] | IN TWO ACTS, | *Adapted from "La Jeunesse de Henri V."* | BY | JOHN HOWARD PAYNE, | AUTHOR OF | *"Brutus," "Clari," "Therese," "Accusation," "Adeline," "Ali | Pacha," "The Two Galley Slaves," "Love in Humble Life, " | "'Twas I," "Lancers," "Mrs. Smith,"* &c. | THOMAS HAILES LACY, | 89, STRAND, | *(Opposite Southampton Street, Covent Garden Market,)* | LONDON.

(18.1 x 10.8): [A]^4 B-C^6 D^4. Preliminary illustration of "Mr. C. Kemble as Charles the 2nd." not reckoned.

[1]-[2], title, on verso Characters, Costumes, and the statement, *First performed at the Theatre Royal Covent Garden, on Thursday, May 27th,* 1824.; [3]-40, text, Stage Directions at foot of last page.

Lineation: p. 20, CHARLES. ... explosion?; p. 30, ACT II. ... dress?

Lacy's Acting Editions were issued in volumes in the 1850's. Individual editions were probably published earlier.

TxU (in Vol. 30 of Acting Editions).

1A.   CHARLES THE SECOND; | OR, | *THE MERRY MONARCH.* | A COMEDY, | IN THREE ACTS. | [stylized swelled rule with rectangle at center] | BY JOHN HOWARD PAYNE, | *Author of Brutus, Clari, Therese, Adeline, &c.* | [same rule] | AS PERFORMED AT THE | CHESTNUT-STREET THEATRE. | [square bracket] From the Prompt-Book. [square bracket] | [double rule] | PHILADELPHIA: | NEAL & MACKENZIE, No. 201 CHESTNUT-STREET: | & No. 4 Chambers-Street, NEW-YORK | Mifflin & Parry, Printers. | [rule] | 1829.

See below for a description of a variant edition.

(15.4 x 9.5 approx.): [A]^2 B-D^6 E^4.

[1]-[2], title, on verso Dramatis Personae; [3]-47, text; [48], cut of military officer in full dress.

Note that this American edition lacks the dedication and the author's introduction.

Lineation: p. 20, *ROCH* ... lass?; p. 40, two ... up.

PU, seen in microprint.

2A.   A variant edition has the same title page except for the presence of a period after NEW-YORK in the imprint. The sequence is unknown.

(15.4 x 9.5 untrimmed): same collation and pagination. P. [48] is blank.

Lineation: p. 20, secretary. ... creatures ; p. 40, very ... ACT.

MB.

3Aa. No. XIX. | MODERN STANDARD DRAMA. | EDITED BY EPES
       SARGENT, | AUTHOR OF "VELASCO, A TRAGEDY, " &c. | [stylized
       swelled rule] | CHARLES THE SECOND: | OR, | THE MERRY
       MONARCH. | A Comedy [fancy] | IN TWO ACTS. | BY JOHN
       HOWARD PAYNE, ESQ. | THE STAGE EDITION: | WITH THE
       STAGE BUSINESS, CAST OF CHARACTERS, COS- | TUMES,
       RELATIVE POSITIONS, &c. | [wavy rule] | NEW YORK: | WILLIAM
       TAYLOR & CO., No. 2 ASTOR HOUSE. | PHILADELPHIA -- 73 DOCK
       STREET, OPPOSITE EXCHANGE BUILDING. | BALTIMORE --
       JARVIS BUILDINGS, NORTH STREET. | 1846. | PRICE 12 1-2 CENTS.

       (18.2 x 11.7): collation ambiguous; p. 13 signed B.

       [i]-[ii], title, verso blank; [iii]-iv, Author's Preface, dated London, June 5,
       1824; [v]-[vi], Editorial Introduction (which reprints the original dedication to
       Charles Kemble), on verso Cast of Characters, Costumes, Exits and
       Entrances, Relative Positions; [7]-44, text.

       Lineation: p. 20, *Edw.* ... music.; p. 40, *Copp.* ... book.

       TxU.

b.   [New York: J. Douglas, 1848.]

       "Modern Standard Drama," No. 19.

       Not seen. Copy reported in MH.

TALES OF A TRAVELLER

On 25 March 1824 Irving wrote to John Murray from Paris, "I have the materials for two volumes nearly prepared, but there will yet be a little rewriting & filling up necessary." On 31 May, he told his brother Peter that he had met Murray on 29 May in London and "arranged the business in two minutes." On 10 June he wrote Peter again, saying that John Howard Payne had copied part of the manuscript and had got other parts copied by others; on the fifteenth he hoped to send a complete manuscript to America *via* Liverpool, but that he would wait a few days before putting the work to press in London, since "I wish the American edition to have a little chance for a start." Accordingly, he began sending the manuscript for the London edition to John Murray on 18 June, and promised more as fast as Murray wanted it. On 7 July he wrote Peter that he was adding material to fill out two volumes. On 5 August, he told Murray, "I have been at work half the night to make additions & alternations which might obviate the impression some parts of the story has (sic) made upon your friends." On 14 August he wrote Murray again, apparently returning the final corrected proofs. On 25 August 1824 the London edition was published; on 23 August, Part I of the American edition, although Part IV did not appear until October.

The letters explain why there are such marked differences between the text of the London edition and that of the American. After sending the manuscript for the American edition, Irving added to the London text (including five additional pieces) and emended the proofs to a considerable degree. When the full second edition was published in America by C. S. Van Winkle in 1825, the extra material of the first London edition was added from some early state of the proofs. And then, in turn, the Author's Revised Edition of 1849 was based upon the second American edition. So the first London edition established the full contents that were to remain constant, except for the first appearance in America, through the printing history of the work.

These are the contents of the first editions (with differences in punctuation of the titles ignored):

First London edition   *First American Edition*

PART I. STRANGE STORIES, BY   [same]
A NERVOUS GENTLEMAN

To the Reader [not in table of contents]	[not present]
The Great Unknown	[present but untitled]
The Hunting Dinner	A Hunting Dinner
The Adventure of My Uncle	[same]
The Adventure of My Aunt	[same]
The Bold Dragoon; or, The Adventure of My Grandfather	[same]
The Adventure of the German Student	[not present]
The Adventure of the Mysterious Picture	[same]
The Adventure of the Mysterious Stranger	[same]
The Story of the Young Italian	[same]
PART II. BUCKTHORNE AND HIS FRIENDS	[same]
Literary Life	[same]
A Literary Dinner	[same]
The Club of Queer Fellows	[same]
The Poor-Devil Author	[same, with additional paragraph at end]
Notoriety	[not present]
A Practical Philospher	[not present, although the matter appears as a single short paragraph at the end of "The Poor-Devil Author"]
Buckthorne; or, The Young Man of Great Expectations	[same]
Grave Reflections of a Disappointed Man	[same]
The Booby Squire	[same]
The Strolling Manager	[same, with two additional paragraphs on the Fantadlins]

PART III. THE ITALIAN BANDITTI	[same]
The Inn at Terracina	[same]
The Adventure of the Little Antiquary	[same]
The Belated Travellers	[not present]
The Adventure of the Popkins Family	[same]
The Painter's Adventure	[same]
The Story of the Bandit Chieftain	[same]
The Story of the Young Robber	[same]
The Adventure of the Englishman	Titled, The Route to Fondi
PART IV. THE MONEY-DIGGERS	[same]
Hell-Gate	[same]
Kidd the Pirate	[same]
The Devil and Tom Walker	[same]
Wolfert Webber, or Golden Dreams	[same]
The Adventure of the Black Fisherman	Titled, The Adventure of Sam, the Black Fisherman, commonly denominated Mud Sam

Between the first American edition of 1824 and the full second American edition of 1825, published in two volumes by C. S. Van Winkle, appeared a second American edition of Part I only, published by Carey & Lea of Philadelphia. It added from the London text the five pieces missing from the original four parts of the American edition, thus providing, when combined with the remaining three parts of the first American edition, a complete text, even though not in the correct order.

The work was quickly reprinted in Paris by Baudry and Galignani, probably from some state of the London proofs, and within five years had been translated into Danish, Dutch, French (in two translations), German (in two translations), Polish, and Swedish, all derived from the London text.

In 1849 Irving revised the work for the Author's Revised Edition, making numerous small changes but retaining the contents and the order of the second American edition, including the two extra paragraphs in "The Strolling Manager."

1A. TALES | OF | A TRAVELLER, | PART 1. [2., 3., 4.] | [stylized swelled rule with diamond at center] | BY GEOFFREY CRAYON, GENT. | AUTHOR OF "THE SKETCH BOOK," "BRACEBRIDGE HALL," | "KNICKERBOCKER'S NEW-YORK." &c. [Parts 2, 3, 4 have comma rather than period after NEW-YORK] | [stylized swelled rule with rectangle at center] | *PHILADELPHIA:* | H. C. CAREY & I. LEA, CHESNUT-STREET. | [rule of 10 dots] | 1824.

Issued in four separate paper-wrappered parts.

Printer for all parts: C. S. Van Winkle, No. 2 Thames-street, New-York.

Part 1.

The title appears in two states:

A. With the publishers incorrectly spelled: H. C. Cary & I. Lee.

B. With the publishers correctly spelled: H. C. Carey & I. Lea.

(23.3 x 14.5): $[1]^2$ 2-21^4 22^2. The last leaf is a blank.

[1]-[2], title, on verso copyright ("the twenty-second day of July. A. D. 1824, in the forty-ninth year of the Independence" by C. S. Van Winkle) and printer; [3]-[4], table of contents, verso blank; [5]-[6], fly-title for "Strange Stories, by a Nervous Gentleman," verso blank; [7]-8, untitled preface, with square bracket at beginning and end; [9]-165, text; [166], blank.

Page 43, line 13 appears in two states, presumably the result of a stop-press correction:

A. counteuance

B. countenance

Tan paper wrapper. On front, cover-title within double rules: TALES | OF | A TRAVELLER, | PART 1. | [stylized swelled rule with diamond at center] | BY GEOFFREY CRAYON, GENT. | AUTHOR OF "THE SKETCH BOOK," "BRACEBRIDGE HALL," | "KNICKERBOCKER'S NEW-YORK," &c. | [stylized swelled rule with rectangle at center] | *PHILADELPHIA:* | H. C. CAREY & I. LEA, CHESNUT-STREET. | [rule of 10 dots] | 1824. Back and spine blank. White endpapers.

The cover-title appears in two settings. No sequence has been determined.

[A]. As described, with comma in line 8 after NEW-YORK.

[B]. As described, except for period in line 8 after NEW-YORK.

Some copies of the wrapper are printed on the blank side of salvaged wrappers on which the name of the publishers had been incorrectly spelled

H. C. CARY & I. LEE. The original incorrect title is concealed beneath the white pastedown endpaper, on the verso of the back wrapper in the copies examined. Generally the original incorrect printing can be discerned, even though not very distinctly, if the opened wrapper is held before a strong light. Not all copies are printed on a salvaged wrapper; some are on otherwise unprinted stock.

An unused example of the original incorrect wrapper is laid into a copy of Part 1 in ViU, apparently as a curio. The absence of the pastedown allows a close examination of the incorrect title. It has the period in line 8 after NEW-YORK, but is in a different setting.

Note that the wrapper of Part 4 also is printed on a salvaged wrapper for Part 1 in some copies, but with the imprint of C. S. VAN WINKLE. The cancelled wrapper of H. C. CARY & I. LEE has been noted only on Part 1, and the cancelled wrapper of C. S. VAN WINKLE only on Part 4.

Title page deposited 22 July 1824. *National Gazette and Literary Register*, 24 August 1824, advertisement by bookseller, dated 23 August, "Just received and for sale." *United States Literary Gazette*, 15 September 1824, reviewed. Irving to John Murray, 22 September 1850, "lst part published Aug 24th 1824."

In wrappers. CtY, title B, cover-title [B], salvaged wrapper. CSmH, title B, cover-title [A]. NN, title A, cover-title [A]; title B, cover-title [B] (3), two in salvaged wrappers. ViU, title B, cover-title [B] (2), laid in one, a blank wrapper with incorrect imprint on verso. Not in wrappers. NN, title A.

Variant Publisher's Imprint.

NEW-YORK: | PRINTED BY C. S. VAN WINKLE. | No. 2 Thames-street. | [rule of 10 dots] | 1824.

This variant impression with the publisher's imprint of C. S. Van Winkle, the printer of the Carey & Lea impression in State B of the text, has been located only in Part 1, and that in a rebound copy lacking the wrapper. Note, however, that some copies of Part 4 of the Carey & Lea impression appear in wrappers printed on the verso of salvaged wrappers for Part 1 carrying the imprint of C. S. Van Winkle. Those original wrappers were probably produced for this impression of Part 1 by Van Winkle.

The variant impression raises a number of unanswered questions. Were Parts 2-4 also so issued, constituting a distinct impression of the entire work? If so, the later parts have yet to be discovered. Did Van Winkle originally intend to publish Part 1 but for some reason passed the publishing rights for the entire work to Carey & Lea after producing a few copies of Part 1? Or did he simply want his imprint on some copies of Part 1, perhaps for copyright purposes (and it is interesting that the located copy is in the Library of Congress), perhaps so that a complete set for sale would show his imprint on the first title? Did he intend to produce a second impression of the whole work but for some reason gave up the plan after Part 1? Does this impression of Part 1, then, precede or follow the Carey & Lea impression? The fact that the cancelled wrapper for this impression of Part 1 appears only on Carey & Lea's wrapper for Part 4 suggests that the Van Winkle impression might have come later in the printing history of Part 1.

Another of the tantalizing questions is whether this impression of Part 1 in 1824 by Van Winkle is directly related to Carey & Lea's later revised second edition of Part 1 -- and again Part 1 only -- in 1825, the same year that Van Winkle brought out a revised second edition of the complete work in two volumes. (See below for a description of those second editions.) As early as 1 January 1825, Carey & Lea were advertising in *The United States Literary Gazette,* *"Have in Press,* ... Tales of a Traveller. Second edition." But they brought out only Part 1 of that new edition. The entire problem of the relationship of the two firms of C. S. Van Winkle and Carey & Lea to the publication of the early editions of *Tales of a Traveller* needs further investigation.

DLC.

Part 2.

(23.3×14.5): $[1]^2$ $2\text{-}27^4$.

[1]-[2], title, on verso copyright ("the fourteenth day of August, A. D. 1824, in the forty-ninth year of the Independence" by C. S. Van Winkle) and printer; [3]-[4], table of contents, verso blank; [5]-[6], fly-title for "Buckthorne and His Friends," verso blank; [7]-212, text.

Page 99, line 13 appears in two states; the order is probable, although not certain:

> [A].   at housand

> [B].   a thousand

Lineation: p.50, It ... bosom ; p. 100, would ... to

Tan paper wrapper. On front, cover-title within double rules: TALES | OF | A TRAVELLER, | PART 2. | [stylized swelled rule with diamond at center] | BY GEOFFREY CRAYON, GENT. | AUTHOR OF "THE SKETCH BOOK," "BRACEBRIDGE HALL," | "KNICKERBOCKER'S NEW-YORK." &c | [stylized swelled rule with rectangle at center] | *PHILADELPHIA*: | H.C. CAREY & I. LEA, CHESNUT STREET | [rule of 10 dots] | 1824. Back and spine blank. White endpapers. One copy noted without endpapers.

In the cover-title, minute shifts of type in line 3 and line 6 of some copies appear when reproductions are compared by mechanical collator. The two simultaneous shifts appear to be the result of slight horizontal repositioning, perhaps merely slippage of the type, rather than of resetting. The movement is too slight to be easily measured or defined, and no sequence can be inferred.

Title page deposited 14 August 1824. *New-York American*, 8 September 1824, "Just published." *National Gazette and Literary Register*, 11 September 1824, extracted; 1 October 1824, reviewed. Irving to John Murray, 22 September 1850, "2d part published Sept 7 1824."

In wrappers. CSmH. CtY. NN (4). ViU (2).

Part 3.

(23.3 x 14.5): $[1]^2$ 2-17^4 18^2.

[1]-[2], title, on verso copyright ("the thirtieth day of August, A. D. 1824, in the forty-ninth year of the Independence" by C. S. Van Winkle) and printer; [3]-[4], table of contents, verso blank; [5]-[6], fly-title for "The Italian Banditti," verso blank; [7]-135, text; [136], blank.

In some copies a prospectus is inserted before the title: a single sheet folded to make two leaves, 4 pp. Page 1 is headed: PROSPECTUS [hollow letters] | OF A | COLLECTION | OF | ENGLISH LITERATURE, | EDITED BY | WASHINGTON IRVING, ESQ. | AND | NOW PUBLISHING BY SUBSCRIPTION, | BY | A. & W. GALIGNANI, AND JULES DIDOT, SENIOR, PARIS, | AND | H. C. CAREY & I. LEA, | PHILADELPHIA. The first paragraph reads: "This Collection will contain the best works of the most emi- | nent English authors, in every department of literature, com- | mencing with GEOFFREY CHAUCER, and coming down to the | present day." At the foot of p. 2: "N. B. The works of OLIVER GOLDSMITH will form the first | four volumes. They are now in press and will be published | shortly." On pp. 2-4 appears the list of authors to be published, including 6 vols. of "Miscellanies of English Literature," and a list of booksellers receiving subscriptions across the country. The text of the prospectus also appears in advertisements by Carey & Lea in *The United States Literary Gazette*, 15 October 1824, repeated 1 November 1824.

Lineation: p. 50, the ... looks.; p. 100, fore ... words.

Tan paper wrapper. On front, cover-title within double rules: TALES | OF | A TRAVELLER, | PART 3. | [stylized swelled rule with rectangle at center] | BY GEOFFREY CRAYON, GENT. | AUTHOR OF "THE

SKETCH BOOK," "BRACEBRIDGE HALL," | "KNICKERBOCKER'S NEW-YORK." &c. | [stylized swelled rule with rectangle at center] | *PHILADELPHIA;* | H. C. CAREY & I. LEA, CHESNUT STREET | [rule of 10 dots] | 1824. Back and spine blank. White endpapers.

BAL reports a variant cover-title with a hyphen in CHESNUT STREET in line 3f. Not located. Is there confusion here with Part 4?

One copy noted with a period rather than a comma after TRAVELLER in line 3. The mark is somewhat fuzzy but seems definite. When a reproduction is placed on the collator and compared with reproductions of other copies that have the usual comma, the two marks of punctuation coincide exactly. It is probably, then, that the variant period is created by the faulty imprint of a comma. Since, however, one state of the cover-title of Part 4 does have a period rather than a comma, the possibility of a variant state of the wrapper of Part 3 should be entertained.

One copy noted without the colon after *PHILADELPHIA* in line 4f, but the mark appears to have been erased.

Title page deposited 30 August 1824. *New-York American,* 24 September 1824, "Chas. Wiley ... will publish on Saturday, the 25th inst." *National Gazette and Literary Register,* 28 September 1824, "This day is published." Irving to John Murray, 22 September 1850, "3d part published Sept 25 1824."

In wrappers. CSmH. CtY, with variant period. DLC. MWA. NN (3). ViU (2), one with prospectus.

Part 4.

(23.3 x 14.5): [1]^2 2-21^4. The last leaf is a blank.

[1]-[2], title, on verso copyright ("the thirtieth day of August, A. D. 1824, in the forty-ninth year of the Independence" by C. S. Van Winkle) and printer; [3]-[4], table of contents, verso blank; [5]-[6], fly-title for "The Money Diggers," verso blank; [7]-161, text; [162], blank.

Lineation: p. 50, sed ... jumbled ; p. 100, the ... the

Tan paper wrapper. On front, cover-title within double rules: TALES | OF | A TRAVELLER. | PART 4. | [stylized swelled rule with diamond at center] | BY GEOFFREY CRAYON, GENT. | AUTHOR OF "THE SKETCH BOOK," "BRACEBRIDGE HALL," | "KNICKERBOCKER'S NEW-YORK." &c. | [stylized swelled rule with rectangle at center] | *PHILADELPHIA:* | H. C. CAREY & I. LEA, CHESNUT STREET | [rule of 10 dots] | 1824. Back and spine blank. White endpapers.

The cover-title appears in two settings. No sequence has been determined.

[A]. As described, with period after TRAVELLER in line 3; no hyphen in
CHESNUT STREET in line 3f, and no mark of punctuation following.

[B]. With comma after TRAVELLER in line 3; hyphen in CHESNUT-
STREET in line 3f, and period following.

Some copies of the wrapper are printed on the blank side of salvaged
wrappers. The cancelled cover-title is for Part 1, has a comma rather than a
period after NEW-YORK in line 8, and bears the imprint of C. S. Van
Winkle. See the discussion of a parallel salvaged wrapper on Part 1, and the
discussion of the variant impression of Part 1 by Van Winkle for which this
cancelled wrapper was probably originally designed.

The two examples noted of wrapper State [B] are on salvaged wrappers.
State [A] has been noted both on salvaged wrappers and on otherwise
unprinted stock.

Title page deposited 30 August 1824. *New-York American*, 9 October 1824,
"C. Wiley ... will publish on Monday next, the 11th inst." *National Gazette
and Literary Register,* 12 October 1824, "This day is published." *United States
Literary Gazette*, 15 October 1824, listed as "in press". Irving to John Murray,
22 September 1850, "4th part published Octr 9 1824."

In wrappers. CSmH, wrapper State [A]. CtY, State [A], salvaged wrapper.
DLC, State [A]. NN, State [A]; State [B], salvaged wrappers (2). ViU, State
[A] (2), one in salvaged wrapper.

Revised Part 1.

[Part 1 only]. TALES | OF | A TRAVELLER, | PART 1 | [stylized swelled
rule with diamond at center] | I am neither your minotaure, nor your
centaure, nor your satyr, nor your | hyæna, nor your babion, but your meer
traveller, believe me. | BEN JONSON. | [stylized swelled rule with
rectangle at center] | BY GEOFFREY CRAYON, GENT. | AUTHOR OF
"THE   SKETCH   BOOK,"   "BRACEBRIDGE   HALL," |
"KNICKERBOCKER'S NEW-YORK," &c. | [stylized swelled rule with
rectangle at center] | SECOND EDITION. | [rule] | *PHILADELPHIA:* |
H. C. CAREY & I. LEA, CHESNUT-STREET. | [rule of 10 dots] | 1825.

The new edition retains the titles from Part 1 of the first American edition
but adds to them the titles that appear in the first London edition of the
complete work: from the London Part 1, "To the Reader" (although it is not
listed in the table of contents) and "The German Student" (in the London
edition called "The Adventure of the German Student"); from Part 2,
"Notoriety" and "A Practical Philosopher"; and from Part 3, "The Belated
Travellers." In keeping with the first American edition of Part 1, "The Great
Unknown" is still untitled, and "A Hunting Dinner" is not given the title from

the London edition, "The Hunting Dinner." The quotation from Ben Jonson on the title page is also added.

Some pages are entirely reset, others altered to one degree or another. In all, hundreds of changes appear -- apparently taken in a cursory fashion from proofsheets of the first London edition sent by Washington Irving to his brother Ebenezer -- including a dozen substantive changes.

Located in Part 1 only. In both instances of the copies located, this second edition of Part 1 is bound with the first American editions of Parts 2-4, although not in original binding. It is probable that the new Part 1 was produced to be so combined, and the later parts were not issued in a new edition. With the new material added here, a mixed set of the second edition of Part 1 and the original edition of Parts 2-4 would offer, essentially, the complete contents of the full London edition. The set would also offer competition to C. S. Van Winkle's fully revised second edition that followed immediately.

(21.0 x 13.2): $[1]^2$ 2-30^4.

[i]-[ii], half-title, verso blank; [iii]-[iv], title, on verso copyright ("the twenty-second day of July, A. D. 1824, in the forty-ninth year of the Independence" by C. S. Van Winkle) and printer; [v]-x, "To the Reader"; [xi], table of contents; [xii], blank; [13]-[14], fly-title for "Strange Stories by a Nervous Gentleman," verso blank; [15]-235, text; [236], blank.

Printer: C. S. Van Winkle, No. 2 Thames-street, New-York.

Lineation: p. 100, In ... the ; p. 200, would ... A

United States Literary Gazette, 1 January 1825 and 15 January 1825, advertised by Carey & Lea: "*Have in Press*, ... Tales of a Traveller. Second edition."

CoU, TxU.

2A.   TALES | OF | A TRAVELLER. [hollow letters] | BY | GEOFFREY CRAYON, GENT. | AUTHOR OF "THE SKETCH BOOK," "BRACEBRIDGE HALL," | "KNICKERBOCKER'S NEW-YORK," &c. | [stylized swelled rule with rectangle at center] | I am neither your minotaure, nor your centaure, nor your satyr, nor your | hyæna, nor your babion, but your meer traveller, believe me. | BEN JONSON. | [swelled rule: Vol. I, rising to diamond shape at center; Vol. II, conventional swelled rule] | SECOND AMERICAN EDITION. | *IN TWO VOLUMES.* | VOL. I. [II.] | [stylized swelled rule with rectangle at center] | *NEW-YORK:* | PRINTED BY C. S. VAN WINKLE, | No. 2 Thames-street. | [rule of 10 dots] | 1825.

The text of this revised and expanded American edition is derived from various states of the proofs of the first London edition, many of them early enough to precede some of the final changes of the printed London text. It contains the same titles (with some minor changes in punctuation) in the same order.

(20.0 x 12.0 untrimmed): Vol. I. [1]^6 2-25^6. Vol. II. [1]^4 2-27^6 28^1. The first leaf is a blank. Wove paper, watermarked eagle within hollow oval.

Vol. I. [ii]-[ii], half-title, verso blank; [iii]-[iv], title, on verso copyright ("the twenty-second day of July, A. D [period after D in Vol. II] 1824, in the forty-ninth year of the Independence" by C. S. Van Winkle); [v]-[vi], table of contents, verso blank; [vii]-xii, "To the Reader"; [13]-[14], fly-title for "Strange Stories by a Nervous Gentleman," verso blank; [15]-300, text.   Vol. II. Preliminary matter unpaged. [i]-[ii], half-title, verso blank; [iii]-[iv], title, on verso copyright (the same); [v]-[vi], table of contents, verso blank; [13]-[14], fly-title for "Buckthorne and His Friends," verso blank; [15]-326, text.

Lineation: Vol. I. p. 100, sought ... hands --; p. 200, Mr. ... sufficient- Vol. II. p. 100, The ... prince!"; p. 200, blank   ; p. 250, the ... windows.

Drab tan paper boards. Paper label on spines: [double rule] | TALES | OF | A TRAVELLER. | [rule] | *VOLUME I.* [*II.*] | [rule] | SECOND EDITION. | *Fine Paper*, $3 00. | [double rule]. Flyleaves in Vol. I, and at the beginning of Vol. II (in addition to the blank leaf) but not at the end.

In *The North American Review*, April 1825, in "Quarterly List of New Publications," there is a "Second Edition" listed, no publisher nor place given. Presumably that is this edition.

In boards: TxU. Rebound: DLC, MH, NN.

3Aa.   TALES [hollow letters] | OF | A TRAVELLER. | BY | GEOFFREY CRAYON, GENT. | AUTHOR OF THE "SKETCH BOOK," "BRACEBRIDGE HALL," | "KNICKERBOCKER'S NEW-YORK," &c. | [rule] | I ... your | hyæna, ... me. | BEN JONSON. | [rule] | THIRD AMERICAN EDITION. | IN TWO VOLUMES. | VOL. I. [II.] | [swelled rule slightly hollow in center] | Philadelphia: [fancy] | CAREY & LEA. -- CHESTNUT STREET. | [rule of 17 dots] | 1832.

The contents and the text are derived from C. S. Van Winkle's "Second American Edition," with a number of minor changes, primarily in punctuation and spelling.

(17.4 x 10.6): Vol. I. [A]^6 B-I^6 K-U^6. Last two leaves missing in copy examined; blank? advertisements? Vol. II. [A]^6 B-I^6 K-V^6. Last two leaves missing in copy examined.

Vol. I. [i]-[ii], missing in copy examined; half-title?; [iii]-[iv], title, on verso copyright ("the twenty-second day of July, A. D. 1824, in the forty-ninth year of the Independence" by C. S. Van Winkle) and printer; [v]-[vi], table of contents, verso blank; [vii]-xii, "To the Reader"; [1]-235, text; [236], blank.

Vol. II. [i]-[ii], half-title, verso blank; [iii]-[iv], title, on verso copyright (the same) and printer; [v]-[vi], table of contents, verso blank; [7]-247, text; [248], blank.

Printer: Stereotyped by J. Howe.

Lineation: Vol. I. p. 100, reigned ... Her ; p. 200, For ... they Vol. II. p. 100, THE ... earth.; p. 200, giving ... said

NNC.

b. THIRD AMERICAN EDITION. | IN TWO VOLUMES. | VOL. I. [II.] | [rule] | A NEW EDITION. | [rule] | Philadelphia: [fancy] | CAREY, LEA, & BLANCHARD. | [rule of 21 dots] | 1835.

NN.

c. A NEW EDITION. | [rule] | Philadelphia: [fancy] | CAREY, LEA, & BLANCHARD. | [rule of 21 dots] | 1835.

TxU.

d. A NEW EDITION. | [rule] | Philadelphia: [fancy] | CAREY, LEA, & BLANCHARD. | [rule of 21 dots] | 1836.

(18.7 x 11.3 trimmed, in original cloth. Another copy 19.3 x 11.9 untrimmed but rebound; this apparently represents a different original binding.

Noted in blue V cloth. Sides blank. White paper label on spines.

NN, Vol. I only, untrimmed, rebound. TxU, trimmed, in original cloth.

e. A NEW EDITION. | [rule] | Philadelphia: [fancy] | CAREY, LEA, & BLANCHARD. | [rule of dots] | 1837.

An impression produced for the Complete Works by Carey, Lea, & Blanchard. A new copyright notice appears, 1837 by Washington Irving. The copyright was taken out 8 April 1837 and a title page deposited. The complete book was deposited 10 May.

National Gazette and Literary Register, 15 April 1837, "This day, volumes 7 and 8 of the new and uniform edition of Washington Irving's Works, containing Tales of a Traveller...."

ViU.

f. A NEW EDITION. | [rule] | Philadelphia: [fancy] | CAREY, LEA, & BLANCHARD. | [rule of 21 dots] | 1838.

Printer: T. K. and P. G. Collins.

NN.

g.   [A New Edition. Philadelphia: Lea & Blanchard, 1840.]

Not seen. Copy reported in ViU.

h.   A NEW EDITION. | [rule] | PHILADELPHIA: | LEA & BLANCHARD. | 1841.

NN, Vol. I only.

4Aa. TALES OF A TRAVELLER. | BY | GEOFFREY CRAYON, GENT^N. | AUTHOR OF "THE SKETCH BOOK," "BRACEBRIDGE HALL," "KNICKERBOCKER'S | NEW-YORK," ETC. | I am neither your minotaure, nor your centaure, nor your satyr, nor your hyæna, nor | your babion, but your meer traveller, believe me. | BEN JONSON. | AUTHOR'S REVISED EDITION. | COMPLETE IN ONE VOLUME. | NEW-YORK: | GEORGE P. PUTNAM, 155 BROADWAY. | And 142 Strand, London. | 1849.

The revised text is derived from C. S. Van Winkle's "Second American Edition" with numerous small changes, some authorial, some probably the result of Putnam's house styling.

(18.7 x 12.7): [1]^{12} 2-19^{12}.

[i]-[ii], Works title for Vol. VII, dated 1849, verso blank; [iii]-[iv], title, on verso copyright (1849) and printer; [v]-vi, table of contents; [vii]-xi, "To the Reader"; [xii], blank; [13]-[14], fly-title for "Strange Stories by a Nervous Gentleman," verso blank; [15]-456, text.

Printer: Leavitt, Trow & Co., Printers and Stereotypers, 49 Ann-street, N. Y.

Lineation: p. 100, vent, ... was ; p. 200, poetry. ... wis-

Blue-green TB cloth. Sides decorated in blind with publisher's initials at center. Spine decorated in blind, titled in gilt: IRVING'S WORKS | [rule] | TALES OF A | TRAVELLER || PUTNAM Buff endpapers. Flyleaves.

Literary World, 3 February 1849, "To be published on the 1st of March"; 10 March 1849, "new volume of Irving's works"; 17 March 1849, listed.

CtY, MH, TxU.

b.   [Illustrated form]. TALES OF A TRAVELLER | BY | GEOFFREY CRAYON GENT^N. | I ... hyæna, | nor ... me. | BEN JONSON. | WITH ILLUSTRATIONS | BY FELIX O. C. DARLEY, | ENGRAVED BY EMINENT ARTISTS. | NEW-YORK: | GEORGE P. PUTNAM, 155 BROADWAY. | M.DCCC.L. All within single frame lines.

(21.5 x 14.5): [1]^{12} 2-19^{12}. Not reckoned: preliminary engraved illustration and engraved title, and seven other engravings on separate leaves inserted through the text. The text is printed from the same plates as the Works form, with single frame line added around all pages.

In addition to the nine engravings on separate leaves, there are eight more printed in the blank spaces at chapter endings, making seventeen in all.

[i]-[ii], title, on verso copyright (1849) and printer; [iii]-[iv], table of illustrations, verso blank; [v]-vi, table of contents; [vii]-xi, "To the Reader"; [xii], blank; [13]-[14], fly-title for "Strange Stories by a Nervous Gentleman," verso blank; [15]-456, text.

In the table of illustrations, "The Death of Filippo," engraved by Leslie, opposite p. 112, is listed out of order, appearing between an illustration on p. 156 and one on p. 206.

Printer: John F. Trow, 49 Ann-street, N. Y.

Noted in dark blue morocco. Ornate gilt decoration on sides and spine. Spine titled in gilt: TALES | OF A | TRAVELLER. | [rule] | IRVING || ILLUSTRATED | BY | DARLEY AEG. Yellow endpapers.

Advertised in *Literary World,* 24 November 1849, as available in "Cloth, $ 3 50; Cloth, extra gilt, $4; Morocco extra, $6; Papier maché, unique, $ 7 50." A copy in DLC has the plates and engraved title in the form of mounted proofs.

Albion, 17 November 1849, "Ready on the 20th." *Literary World,* 22 September 1849, "in press"; 20 October 1849, "on November 1"; 10 November 1849, "on the 20th," "Same style and prices as the Knickerbocker."

NN, TxU.

c. [Works form].   NEW-YORK: | GEORGE P. PUTNAM, 155 BROADWAY, | And 142 Strand, London. | 1850.

Works title, dated 1850.

Printer: John F. Trow, Printer and Stereotyper, 49 Ann-street, N. Y.

Blue-green TB cloth. Sides decorated in blind with publisher's initials at center. Spine decorated in blind, titled in gilt.

TxU.

d. [Works form].   NEW-YORK: | GEORGE P. PUTNAM, 155 BROADWAY, | And 142 Strand, London. | 1851.

Works title, dated 1851.

DLC.

e. [Works form]. NEW-YORK: | GEORGE P. PUTNAM, 10 PARK PLACE. | 1852.

Works title, dated 1852.

Private hands. MH, without volume title.

f. [Works form]. NEW-YORK: | G. P. PUTNAM & COMPANY, 10 PARK PLACE. | 1853.

Works title, dated 1853.

ViU.

g. [Works form]. NEW-YORK: | G. P. PUTNAM & COMPANY, 10 PARK PLACE. | 1854.

Works title, dated 1854.

Preliminary engraved illustration and engraved title.

DLC.

h. [Illustrated form]. The title page follows the format and text of the Works form rather than that of the first illustrated form. NEW-YORK: | G. P. PUTNAM & COMPANY, 10 PARK PLACE. | 1854.

Table of illustrations omitted, although the illustrations themselves are present.

Noted in morocco. Full gilt decoration on sides and spine. Spine titled in gilt. AEG. Marbled endpapers.

NN.

i. [Works form]. New York: [fancy] | G. P. PUTNAM & CO., 321 BROADWAY. | 1856.

Works title, dated 1856.

ViU.

j. [Works form]. New York: [fancy] | G. P. PUTNAM & CO., 321 BROADWAY. | 1857.

Works title, missing in this copy.

MH.

k. [Works form]. NEW YORK: | G. P. PUTNAM, 115 NASSAU STREET. | 1859.

Works title, dated 1859.

Two preliminary illustrations added, published by Childs & Peterson, Philadelphia.

Green BD cloth. Sides with frame in blind. Spine titled in gilt with gilt decoration around title.

TxU.

I. [Works form]. NEW YORK: | G. P. PUTNAM (for the Proprietor), 506 BROADWAY. | 1859.

Works title, dated 1859.

Two preliminary illustrations before title.

NjP, TxU.

5A. TALES OF A TRAVELLER. | BY | WASHINGTON IRVING. | [rule] | "I ... satyr, nor | your ... me." | JONSON. | [rule] | NEW YORK: | G. P. PUTNAM & CO., 321 BROADWAY. | [rule] | 1857.

"Putnam's Railway Classics."

(16.4 x 10.8): [i]-x, [1]-258. Signed in 8's.

Printer: R. Craighead, Printer and Stereotyper, Caxton Building, 81, 83, and 85 Centre Street.

Lineation: p. 100, law, ... about ; p. 200, brow ... Eng-

Purple V cloth. On sides, in blind, "Putnam's Railway Classics" in ornamental oval. Spine titled in gilt. Buff endpapers; the pasted-down endpapers have advertisements for Putnam books. Also issued in paper boards, at 50 cents.

American Publishers' Circular, 2 May 1857, "Next week"; 9 May 1857, "Now ready."

TxU, in cloth.

1Ea. TALES | OF | A TRAVELLER. | [rule] | BY GEOFFREY CRAYON, GENT. | [rule] | I am neither your minotaure, nor your centaure, nor your | satyr, nor your hyæna, nor your babion, but your meer tra- | veller, believe me. | BEN JONSON. | IN TWO VOLUMES. | VOL. I. [II.] | LONDON: | JOHN MURRAY, ALBEMARLE-STREET. | [rule] | 1824.

(22.5 x 14.2 untrimmed) : Vol. I. [A]^8 B-I^8 K-U^8 X-Z^8 AA^4 BB^2. Vol. II. [A]^4 B-I^8 K-U^8 X-Z^8 AA-BB^8 CC^6. The first leaf is a blank. Wove paper watermarked 1824 with bar below.

Vol. I. [i]-[ii], half-title, on verso printer; [iii]-[iv], title, verso blank;[v]-xiv, "To the Reader"; [xv]-xvi, table of contents; [1]-[2], fly-title for "Strange Stories by a Nervous Gentleman," verso blank; [3]-364, text, printer at foot of last page. Vol. II. [i]-[ii], half-title, on verso printer; [iii]-[iv], title, verso blank; [v]-vi, table of contents; [1]-[2], fly-title for "Buckthorne and His Friends," verso blank; [3]-394, text; [395], "Notice"; [396], printer.

Vol. II, p. [395] reads: NOTICE. | [rule] | Several spurious Works have issued from the | press, alleged to be by the AUTHOR OF THE SKETCH | BOOK, but published without his knowledge or appro- | bation. Among these is an incorrect Edition of | SALMAGUNDI, a work in which he was but partially | concerned, and at a juvenile age. An edition of this | work, revised and corrected, with several papers | originally intended for it, but never published, is | about to appear in America. The Author hopes he | may be judged by such works as appear under his | own sanction....

The "Notice" appears only in the first impression. For distinctions in the text between the first impression and the second, see the discussion of the second impression.

Printer: Thomas Davison, Whitefriars.

Lineation: Vol. I. p. 100, mysterious ... the ; p. 200, to ... circum- Vol. II. p. 100, numbers ... entered ; p. 200, however, ... alone,

Drab paper boards, and tan paper boards with green cloth shelfback. White paper label on spines: [rule] | TALES | OF A | TRAVELLER | [rule] | VOL. I. [II.] | [rule] | 24s | [rule].

Literary Gazette, 10, 17, 24 July 1824, "In the Press. On the lst of August"; 14 August 1824, in editorial note, "We do not think Mr. Washington Irving's new work will be published so early as was anticipated: perhaps a few weeks..."; 21 August 1824, advertised for August 25; 28 August 1824, listed, reviewed, advertised.   Irving to John Murray, 22 September 1850, "published collectively in London in two volumes August 25th 1824."

TxFTC, rebound. TxU (4), rebound. ViU, in boards, incomplete, first or second impression.

b.   The second impression has the same title page. It may be identified by the absence of the "Notice" from Vol. II, p. [395], and by the resetting of individual pages, resulting in changes in the text. These are a few:

Page & Line	First impression	Second impression
I, 91.10	clothes' press	clothes-press
I, 247.3	beings:	beings;
I, 347.19	handwriting	hand-writing
II, 39.1	daggers-drawings	daggers-drawing
II, 96.16	with various	with the various

II, 338.15   neve rheeding   never heeding

TxU.

2E.   TALES | OF | A TRAVELLER. | [rule] | BY GEOFFREY CRAYON,
       GENT. | [rule] | I ... satyr, nor | your ... me. | BEN JONSON. | *NEW
       EDITION.* | IN TWO VOLUMES. | VOL. I. [II.] | LONDON: | JOHN
       MURRAY, ALBEMARLE-STREET. | [rule] | 1825.

       A few variant readings appear, some probably authorial.

       (18.0 x 11.0): Vol. I. [i]-xii, [1]-305 [306]. Vol. II. [i]-iv, [1]-329 [330]. Not
       reckoned in each vol.: a preliminary illustration, and one also in the text.
       Signed in 8's.

       Printer: Thomas Davison, Whitefriars.

       Lineation: Vol. I. p. 100, the ... story. --; p. 200, one's ... I Vol. II. p. 100, that
       ... poor ; p. 200, all ... authenticity.

       NN, TxU.

3E.   [London: John Murray, 1829. 2 vols.]

       Not located. Listed by Williams and Edge, as seen. They also list as seen,
       apparently as part of the same entry, "Another issue with a notice, 1 leaf, at
       end."

4E.   TALES OF A TRAVELLER. | BY GEOFFREY CRAYON, GENT. |
       [wavy rule] | I ... satyr, | nor ... traveller, | believe me. -- BEN JONSON. |
       [wavy rule] | *NEW EDITION.* | LONDON: JOHN   MURRAY,
       ALBEMARLE STREET. | [rule] | 1848.

       The British Library assigns this edition to "Murray's Colonial and Home
       Library." The identification would appear on the binding.

       Printer: William Clowes and Sons, Stamford Street.

       Lineation: p. 100, disappear ... by ; p. 200, It ... com-

       Athenæum, 4 November 1848, advertised as "Lately published."

       BL.

5E.   TALES | OF | A TRAVELLER. | BY | GEOFFREY CRAYON, GENT[N].
       | "I ... hyæna, | nor ... me." -- *Ben Jonson.* | ILLUSTRATED WITH
       ORIGINAL DESIGNS. | LONDON: | JOHN MURRAY, ALBEMARLE
       STREET. | 1850. All within single frame lines.

       (21.3 x 14.9): from the plates of the illustrated form of the Author's Revised
       Edition, New York, Putnam, 1850. Preliminary engraved illustration and

engraved title, and 15 engraved illustrations within the text. Single frame line around all pages.

Noted in black morocco. Sides decorated with elaborate gilt border. Spine decorated and titled in gilt. AEG. Marbled endpapers.

MH.

6E. TALES OF A TRAVELLER, | BY | WASHINGTON IRVING. | [rule] | LONDON: | GEORGE ROUTLEDGE & CO. SOHO SQUARE. | 1850.

The text is that of the Author's Revised Edition.

"The Popular Library."

(16.9 x 10.6): [i]-viii, [1]-255 [256]. Signed in 8's

Printer: R. Clay, Bread Street Hill.

Lineation: p. 100, heaven ... fought ; p. 200, PART IV. ... unruly

Noted in blue boards. On front, title and identification as "The Popular Library," price One Shilling. Advertisements on endpapers. Back and spine missing from this copy. Also issued in cloth.

Athenæum, 13 April 1850, "New volume," 1*s*. in "fancy cover," or 1*s*.6*d*. in cloth gilt; 4 May 1850, in "List of New Books."

MH, rebound but part of original boards preserved.

7Ea. TALES OF A TRAVELLER. | BY | WASHINGTON IRVING. | [rule] | I ... satyr, nor | your ... me. | BEN JONSON. | [rule] | LONDON: | HENRY G. BOHN, YORK STREET, COVENT GARDEN. | 1850.

The text is that of the Author's Revised Edition.

Issued individually as "Bohn's Shilling Series"; bound with *The Alhambra* as Vol. IV of "Bohn's Library Edition."

(18.1 x 11.5): [i]-[viii], [1]-296. Signed in 8's.

Printer: Whiting, Beaufort House, Strand.

Lineation: p. 100, trials ... among ; p. 200, There ... they

Noted in original binding only in "Bohn's Library Edition." Gray T cloth. Sides decorated in blind. Spine titled in gilt: IRVING'S | WORKS | [rule] | VOL. IV. | [rule] | ALHAMBRA | TALES OF A TRAV^R. | BOHN'S | LIBRARY | EDITION. Endpapers white with advertisements in blue. One illustration at beginning of volume. (No works title in volume.)

Shilling Series. *Literary Gazette*, 11 May 1850, "Ready this day." Library Edition. *Athenæum* and *Literary Gazette*, 2 November 1850, the set of 10 vols. at 35*s*. in "List of New Books."

NN, in Library Edition. TxU, in Shilling Series.

b. [London: Henry G. Bohn, 1854.]

"Bohn's Library Edition." With frontispiece.

Not seen. Copy reported in Staats- und Universitätsbibliothek Hamburg.

8E. TALES OF A TRAVELLER. | BY | GEOFFREY CRAYON, GENT. | [rule] | I ... satyr, nor | your ... me. -- | BEN JONSON. | [rule] | LONDON: | SIMMS AND M'INTYRE, | PATERNOSTER ROW, AND DONEGAL STREET, BELFAST. | [rule] | 1850. All within single frame lines.

The text is that of the Author's Revised Edition.

"The Parlour Library," No. XLII.

(16.4 x 10.0): [i]-x, [1]-288. Signed in 8's.

Lineation: p. 100, furnish ... and ; p. 200, They ... assured

Described by Michael Sadleir in *XIX Century Fiction* as (1) bright green glazed boards. On front, pictorially and decoratively printed in brown. On back, advertisements. Spine decorated and titled. Endpapers white, printed with series. Or, (2) dark green ribbed cloth. Sides blocked in blind, with series title on front. Spine scroll blocked, and titled in gilt. Endpapers white, printed with series.

Literary Gazette, 27 April 1850, "Just ready." *Athenæum*, 18 May 1850, listed, 1*s*. in boards, 1*s*. 6*d*. in cloth.

BL.

1Fa. TALES | OF | A TRAVELLER. | [swelled rule] | BY GEOFFREY CRAYON, GENT. | [rule] | I AM neither your minotaure, nor your centaure, nor your satyr, nor | your hyæna, nor your babion, but your meer traveller, believe me. | BEN JONSON. | [rule] | IN TWO VOLUMES. | VOL. I. [II.] | [emblem: D in star within wreath with pendant medal] | PARIS: | PUBLISHED BY L. BAUDRY, | AT THE ENGLISH, FRENCH, ITALIAN, GERMAN, AND SPANISH LIBRARY, | RUE DU COQ SAINT-HONORÉ. | [rule] | 1824.

The text of this first French edition is derived from that of the first English edition, 1824, perhaps from some penultimate state of the proof. As a result, it is complete in contents. There is no evidence of further revision by Irving.

(17.1 x 10.0): Vol. I. [i]-xiv, [1]-358. Vol. II. [i]-vi, [1]-383 [384]. Signed in 12's. Laid paper.

Printer: Jules Didot, Senior, Paris.

Lineation: Vol. I. p. 100, picture; ... began. --; p. 200, Buckthorne ... career. Vol. II. p. 100, from ... again ; p. 200, for ... I

Bibliographie de la France, 30 October 1824, # 5523, listed.

NcD.

b.   [emblem: D in star within wreath with pendant medal] | PARIS: | PUBLISHED BY A. AND W. GALIGNANI, | AT THE ENGLISH, FRENCH, ITALIAN, GERMAN, AND SPANISH LIBRARY, | 18, RUE VIVIENNE, | [rule] | 1824.

From the same setting as the Baudry impression.

Printer: Jules Didot, Senior, Paris.

KU.

c.   [emblem: L.B. within wreath] | PARIS. | BAUDRY, AT THE FOREIGN LIBRARY, | N^O 9, RUE DU COQ-SAINT-HONORÉ. | [rule] | 1829.

In Vol. I, twelve pages of preliminary advertisements, headed LIBRARIE POUR LES LANGUES ÉTRANGÈRES, including Irving's *Sketch Book, Bracebridge Hall, Tales of A Traveller, Salmagundi, Knickerbocker's History;* also, "Portrait" at 2 francs.

Printer: Jules Didot, Senior, Rue du Pont-de-Lodi, No. 6.

Yellow paper wrapper. On front, cover-title within elaborated border of stars. On back, within same border, advertisements for new Baudry publications, including Irving's *Granada* in 2 vols., *Columbus* in 4 vols., *Works* in 10 vols.

Bibliographie de la France, 10 October 1829, # 6023, listed.

TxU.

2F.   TALES | OF | A TRAVELLER. | BY GEOFFREY CRAYON, GENT. | [rule] | I AM neither ... your | satyr, ... traveller, | believe me. BEN JONSON. | [rule] | VOL. I. [II.] | [emblem: L.B. within wreath] | PARIS, | BAUDRY, BOOKSELLER IN FOREIGN LANGUAGES, | 9, RUE DU COQ-SAINT-HONORÉ. | [elaborated swelled rule] | 1834.

(14.5 x 9.6): Vol. I. [i]-x, [v]-l, [1]-259 [260]. Vol. II. Not seen. Signed in 6's.

Printer: Casimir, 12, Rue de la Vieille-Monnaie.

Lineation: Vol. I. p. 100, I ... and ; p. 200, the ... and

NN, Vol. I only.

3F.   TALES | OF | A TRAVELLER. | BY | GEOFFREY CRAYON, GENT. |
       (WASHINGTON IRVING.) | [rule] | I am ... satyr, nor | your ... me. | BEN
       JONSON. | [rule] | [emblem: intertwined elaborated letters, apparently
       BEL] | PARIS: | BAUDRY'S EUROPEAN LIBRARY, | 3, QUAI
       MALAQUAIS, NEAR THE PONT DES ARTS; | AND STASSIN AND
       XAVIER, 9, RUE DU COQ. | SOLD ALSO BY AMYOT, RUE DE LA
       PAIX; THÉOPHILE BARROIS, QUAI VOLTAIRE; TRUCHY,
       BOULEVARD | DES ITALIENS; FRANK, RUE RICHELIEU;
       LEOPOLD MICHELSEN, LEIPZIG; | AND BY ALL THE PRINCIPAL
       BOOKSELLERS ON THE CONTINENT. | [rule] | 1846.

       "Collection of Ancient and Modern British Authors," Vol. CCCXCVIII.

       (20.8 x 12.5): [I]-XII, [1]-313 [314]. Signed in 8's.

       Printer: Fain and Thunot, 28, Rue Racine.

       Lineation: p. 100, of ... me ; p. 200, When ... complete.

       NN.

1G.   Tales of a Traveller | by | Washington Irving. | [rule] | Mit erklärenden
       Anmerkungen | herausgegeben | von | Dr E. A. Toel. | [rule] | Lüneburg, |
       Verlag der Herold und Wahlstab'schen Buchhandlung. | [rule] | 1841.

       (16.9 x 10.5): [i]-x, [1]-518. Signed in 12's.

       The full text in English, with notes in German at foot of pages.

       Lineation: p. 100, beauty ... and ; p. 200, itinerant ... cities.

       TxU. Copy reported in Landesbibliothek Hannover.

TRANSLATIONS

Danish .

[*En Reisendes Fortæøllinger.* Oversat af Ph. Wallich. 2 vols. København:
Schubothe, 1827-28.]

Not located. Listed in *Bibliotheca Danica*, Vol. IV.

Dutch.

[*Verhalen van eenen Reiziger.* Uit het Engelsch Vertaald, door Steenbergen
van Goor. 2 vols. Amsterdam: C.L. Schleyer, 1827.]

8vo.

Not located. Listed in *Alphabetische Naamlijst van Boeken,* 1790-1831.

French.

[*Contes d'un Voyageur.* Traduits de l'anglais par Mme. Adèle Beaurgard. 4 vols. Paris: Lecointe et Durey, et Hubert, 1825.]

Bound in 12's.

Bibliographie de la France, 1 January 1825, # 68, listed.

Not seen. Copy reported in Bibliothèque Nationale.

[*Historiettes d'un Voyageur.* 4 vols. Paris: Carpentier-Méricourt, 1825.]

Translated by Lebègue.

Bound in 12's.

Bibliographie de la France, 1 January 1825, # 69, listed.

Not seen. Copy reported in Bibliothèque Nationale.

OEUVRES COMPLÈTES | DE | M. WASHINGTON IRVING, | TRADUITES DE L'ANGLAIS | SOUS LES YEUX DE L'AUTEUR, | PAR M. LEBÈGUE D'AUTEUIL. | TOME PREMIER. [SECOND. TROISIÈME. QUATRIÈME.] | [rule] | CONTES D'UN VOYAGEUR. | PREMIÈRE [SECONDE, TROISIÈME, QUATRIÈME] PARTIE. | [elaborated rule with asterisk in center] | PARIS, | CHÉZ BOULLAND ET Ce, LIBRAIRES, | Palais-Royal, N° 254. | [double rule] | JANVIER 1825. Minor variations on the three other title pages.

Irving's Journal entries for 27, 28 November 1824 prove that he did at least "look over" the translation.

(15.5 x 9.8): Vol. I. [i]-[iv], [1]-246 [247]-[248]. Vol. II. [i]-[vi], [1]-280. Vol. III. [i]-[vi], [1]-199 [200]. Vol. IV. [i]-[iv], 1-326 [327]-[328]. Laid paper. In 12's, signed in 4's and 8's.

Printer: Imprimerie de J.-L. Chanson, rue des Grands-Augustins, no. 10.

Lineation: Vol. I. p. 100, tous ... fa- Vol. II. p. 100, elles ... à Vol. III. p. 100, portefeuilles ... ses Vol. IV. p. 100, proie. ... tirant

The preface promises future editions of *History of New York, Bracebridge Hall, Sketch Book,* and *Salmagundi* but apparently they were never published.

Bibliographie de la France, 15 January 1825, # 270, Vol. I listed; 9 July 1825, # 3835, the four vols. listed.

TxU.

German.

Erzählungen eines Reisenden. | Von | Washington Irving. | Ich ... Centaur, | noch ... ein | Pavian, ... glaubt | mir nur. | Ben Jonson (Cynthia's Fest). | Aus dem Englischen übersetzt | von | S. H. Spiker. | Erster [Zweiter] Band. | [swelled rule] | Berlin, | verlegt bei Duncker and Humblot. | [rule] | 1825. [in fraktur]

Walter A. Reichart, "The Earliest Translations of Washington Irving's Writings," *Bulletin of The New York Public Library*, 61 (October 1957), reports that the original edition of Vol. I is dated 1824 and has a different pagination than the volume dated 1825.

(16.8 x 10.3): Vol. I. [I]-XVI, [1]-362. Two pages of advertisements at end. Vol. II. [I]-VI, [1]-381 [382]. Signed in 12's.

Printer: U. W. Schade, Berlin.

Lineation: Vol. I. p. 100, ebenfalls ... ge-; p. 200, auf ... [in footnote] Uebers. Vol. II. p. 100, Seitenkapellen ... Impro-; p. 200, Es ... surcht-

MH. Copy reported in Stadtbibliothek Hannover.

Erzählungen eines Reisenden. | Von | Washington Irving. | [rule] | Aus dem Englischen übersetzt | von | S. H. Spiker. | Erster [Zweiter, Dritter] Theil. | [swelled rule] | Wien, 1825. | Gedruckt und verlegt bei Chr. F. Schade. [in fraktur]

"Classische Cabinets-Bibliothek oder Sammlung auserlesener Werke der deutschen und Fremd-Literatur," vols. 25-27.

(12.9 x 9.0): Vol. I. [i]-xiv [xv]-[xvi], 18-208. Vol. II. [i]-[iv], [5]-200. Vol. III. [i]-[iv], [5]-200.

Lineation: Vol. I. p. 100, vermehren ... ergriffen Vol. III. p. 100, ser ... werden

Description from copy in CtW, not examined. Copy reported in Stadtbibliothek Mainz.

[*Erzählungen eines Reisenden.* Aus dem Englischen übersetzt von S. H. Spiker. Wien: Kraulfuss und Krammer, 1825.]

"Hundert und ein Abend. Eine Sammlung vorzüglicher ausgewählter Erzählungen, Mährchen, Volkssagen und Novellen."

Not located. Listed by Walter A. Reichart, "The Earliest Translations of Washington Irving's Writings."

[*Erzählungen eines Reisenden.* Aus dem Englischen übersetzt von S. H. Spiker. 4 vols. Wien: Michael Lechner, 1826.]

Not located   Listed by Walter A. Reichart, "The Earliest Translations of Washington Irving's Writings."

Erzählungen eines Reisenden | von | Washington Irving. | [rule] | Ich bin weder euer Minotaure, noch euer Centaur, | noch euer Satyr, noch eure Hyäne, noch euer Pavian, | sondern euer blosser Reisender: glaubt mir das. | Ben Jonson (Cynthia's Fest.) | [rule] | Aus dem Englischen. | [double rule] | Erstes [Zweites ... Sechstes] Bändchen. | [heavy rule of multiple lines] | Frankfurt am Main, 1827. | Gedruckt und verlegt bei Johann David Sauerländer. [in fraktur]

"Washington Irving's sämmtliche Werke. Uebersetzt von Mehreren und herausgegeben von Christian August Fischer." Bändchen 7-12.

(13.6. x 10.0): Vol. I. [1]-108 [109]-[110]. Vol. II. [1]-118 [119]-[120]. Vol. III. [1]-118 [119]-[120]. Vol. IV. [1]-116 [117]-[118]. Vol. V. [1]-126 [127]-[128]. Vol. VI. [1]-110 [111]-[112]. Signed in 8's.

Lineation: Vol. I. p. 100, warum ... Nähe   Vol. II. p. 100, nehmen, ... [in footnote] (Sp.)   Vol. III. p. 100, und .. [in footnote] (Sp.)   Vol. IV. p. 100, seiner ... Liqueurs   Vol. V. p. 100, Boote, ... Eigen-   Vol. VI. p. 100, "Ich ... seyn

Issued in paper wrappers. Seen only rebound.

Cty (2). Copy reported in Universitätsbibliothek Würzburg.

[*Erzählungen eines Reisenden.* Zweite, verbesserte Auflage. Frankfurt am Main: gedruckt und verlegt bei Johann David Sauerländer, 1846.]

"Ausgewählte Schriften. Herausgegeben von J. V. Adrian." Theil 3.

Not seen.   Copies reported in Stadtbibliothek Braunschweig and in Universitätsbibliothek Marburg.

Italian

[Lo Straniero Misterioso, novella del Signor Irving. Traduzione dall'originale Inglese, di G. B.   Milano, 1826.]

8vo. G. B. is probably Gaetano Barbieri.

Not seen. Copy reported in *BL*.

Polish.

A Polish translation of *Tales of a Traveller* in four separate parts was planned, but apparently only two parts were published.

Nadzwyczajne [in semi-script] | PRZYGODY | CZLOWIEKA | *Oslabionych Nerwów.* [script] | Z DZIEŁ | P. Washington Irving Amerykanina [in semi-script] | *wyjęte.* | z Portretem Autora. | [ornament: cut of Greek lamp, snake, sword, · and branch] | W WARSZAWIE, | W DRUKARNI ŁĄTKIEWICZA PRZY ULI: SENATORSKIEY N. 467. | [double rule] | 1826.

This volume, published as a separate entity, is a translation by Ksawery Bronikowski of the section, "Strange Stories by a Nervous Gentleman."

(16.5 x 9.7 rebound): [i]-xii, [1?]-184. Preliminary portrait of Irving. 8 vo.

Issued in paper wrapper.

Not examined. Information based on copy in Biblioteka Narodowa, Warsaw.

Cover-title: ROZBÓJNICY | we [in semi-script] | WŁOSZECH. | Z DZIEŁ | P. Washingtona-Irving [in semi-script] | Amerykanina. [in script] | [ornament: cut of wolf] | W WARSZAWIE, | W DRUKARNI ŁĄTKIEWICZA PRZY ULI: SENATORSKIEY N. 467. | [double rule] | 1826.

This volume, published as a separate entity, is a translation by Ksawery Bronikowski of the section, "The Italian Banditti."

(16.6 x 10.3 untrimmed): [1]-179 [180]. 8vo.

In paper wrapper. On front, cover-title.

Not examined. Information based on copy in the Warsaw University Library.

Swedish.

EN RESANDES | BERÄTTELSER | AF | WASHINGTON IRVING. | [rule] | *Jag är hvarken en Minotaur, eller en Centaur,* | *eller en Satyr, eller en Hyena, eller en Babian,* | *men helt enkelt en Resande; tro mig!* | BEN JONSON. | ÖFVERSÄTTNING, | AF | LARS ARNELL. | [rule] | *FÖRRA [SEDNARE] DELEN.* | [rule] | [elaborated rule of small ornaments] | STOCKHOLM, 1829, | hos *Zacharias Hæggström.*

(17.8 x 11.2): Vol. I. [I]-IV, [1]-251 [252]. Vol. II. [1]-263 [264]. Signed in 8's. Laid paper.

Lineation: Vol. I. p. 100, lekens ... borde ; p. 200, bölada ... och Vol. II. p. 100, att ... öfverdrifna ; p. 200, ne ... värden

Light gray-blue unprinted heavyweight paper wrappers.

MH, NN.

EDITIONS OF INDIVIDUAL TALES

The Devil and Tom Walker.

THE DEVIL | AND | TOM WALKER: | TOGETHER WITH | DEACON GRUBB | AND THE | OLD NICK. | [rule] | WOODSTOCK, VT. | PRINTED AND PUBLISHED BY | R. & A. COLTON. | [rule of 16 dots] | 1830.

(11.0 x 7.0): [1]-32. Signed in 8's.

Text of Irving's "The Devil and Tom Walker," pp. [3]-20.

Lineation: p. 10, licly. ... might ; p. 20, shortly ... WALKER."

Gray-blue unprinted paper wrapper.

ViU.

Wolfert Webber.

WOLFERT WEBBER; | OR, | GOLDEN DREAMS. | BY WASHINGTON IRVING. | LONDON: | HENRY LEA, WARWICK LANE. | [rule] | 1856.

(12.1 x 8.2): [1]-90. Six pages of terminal advertisements. Signed in 12's.

The text of Irving's "Wolfert Webber," pp. [3]-62, is followed by another tale, "The Patriot Slave," not by Irving.

Lineation: p. 40, A ... haunted ; p. 70, might ... conversation

Buff-yellow paper wrapper. On front, within brown-red elaborated border, title for "The Fireside Library," Vol. IX, WOLFERT WEBBER and THE PATRIOT SLAVE (with the S in SLAVE reversed). On back, advertisements for teas by Phillips and Company.

ViU.

OLIVER GOLDSMITH

Irving published three distinct biographies of Oliver Goldsmith: in 1824, a 78-page biographical introduction to a collection of miscellaneous works of Goldsmith; in 1840, a 178-page introduction to a collection of selected works of Goldsmith; and in 1849, a full book-length life designed to stand on its own. The later versions drew on the earlier, of course, but can hardly be called "revised and expanded" versions in the usual sense of that familiar phrase.

On 14 March 1824, Irving contracted with A. and W. Galignani and W. (sic) Didot of Paris to edit a Collection of English Literature that was planned to expand to two hundred volumes. The agreement in Irving's hand, now in the Barrett collection of manuscripts in the University of Virginia library, specified that Irving was to select the authors and the parts of their works to be published. "He is to collate and correct the Biographies and notes [the 'and notes' added between the lines]; making such alterations and additions as he may think proper; but it is expressly understood that he does not obligate himself to contribute any original matter. That is to be left entirely to his own discretion."

In July of 1824, a Prospectus was issued describing the collection, listing the authors to be published, and saying that the first four volumes, "now in the press," would be the works of Goldsmith. The series was to be edited by Washington Irving, was to include a biography of each author, and was to be published at the rate of two volumes a month by Galignani and Didot of Paris, and by H. C. Carey and I. Lea of Philadelphia. The Prospectus was apparently written, in part at least, by Irving.

As far as can be discovered, the one product of this grandiose scheme was *The Miscellaneous Works of Oliver Goldsmith* with its introductory "Memoirs of the Life and Writings of Oliver Goldsmith." Over the next few years Galignani did publish similar collections of Byron, Scott, and Thomas Moore -- all authors of particular interest to Irving -- but the introductions are by J. W. Lake, show no observable hand of Irving, and the editions apparently did not belong to the projected series. Carey and Lea must have dropped out of the plan early, since they brought out no edition under their imprint, and on 10 September 1824 Irving entered in his journal, "Receive a very forward letter from an impudent Bookseller in America named Coleman who has assumed the Agency of Galignanis Edition of British Authors." (It should be noted, however, that as late as 1 November the

Prospectus appears in the *United States Literary Gazette*, and the phrase "assumed the Agency" might have meant, in fact, "has become an agent.")

On 20 September 1824, Irving wrote his sister Catherine Paris of his pleasure at their brother Peter's staying with him, and then added, "I undertook a literary enterprize, of which you have no doubt heard, the editing of a Collection of English literature, it was for the purpose of yielding him an income and occupation--" And in his journal for 23 February 1824 he had earlier written, "Galignani & Didot call to engage me as Editor of their Edition of British Classics. Refer them to Peter--" What exactly was Peter Irving's role in the project? Perhaps, like Pierre M. Irving in later years, he was to gather and order the necessary material for Washington to write up or "correct." Or perhaps he was to select for Washington the works of the author under consideration. Did Peter select the Goldsmith works for this edition?

By 22 March 1824, according to his journal, Irving was writing at the life of Goldsmith. On 16 April he delivered part of the manuscript to Galignani. And on 5 May he could enter in his journal, probably with some satisfaction, "Wrote conclusion to Goldsmith life." On 27 October he received a copy of the work. Some six years later, in 1830, Crissy and Grigg of Philadelphia brought out an American edition in one volume, keeping it in print until the 1850's, well after the publication of Irving's two later versions.

In 1840, nearing the end of his occasional pieces for *The Knickerbocker*, Irving rewrote and expanded his original sketch, drawing heavily for new material on James Prior's recent life of Goldsmith. Again the life was intended as an introduction to a collection of Goldsmith's writings, this time in the Harpers' "Family Library" series.

Although the Harpers' Family Library edition of 1840 was never reprinted as such in Britain, Irving's prefatory Biography appeared in an edition of Goldsmith's *History of the Earth and Animated Nature* in 1848, reprinted until 1856, and was "epitomized" for a selection of Goldsmith's works in the 1850's. The latter work was picked up and reprinted in America also. The description given of the "epitome" is amusing: "Stripped of all the superfluous matter, it contains all that is of interest; and has been rendered only less bulky, less wearisome, and more convenient."

In the late spring of 1849, Irving proposed to George P. Putnam a volume on Goldsmith. Putnam encouraged the suggestion and, in the words of Putnam's Recollections in the *Atlantic* for November 1860, "within sixty days the first sheets of Irving's 'Goldsmith' were in the printer's hands. The press (as he says) was 'dogging at his heels,' for in two or three weeks the volume was published." Since the work, Vol. XI of the Author's Revised Edition, was advertised on 14 July as "in press" and was published by the end of August, it would follow that Irving spent most of the summer of 1849 working on the volume, perhaps drawing on earlier preparation, since the volume is long and well written. The manuscript, now in the Seligman

Collection of the New York Public Library, consists of 512 pp., of which about two-thirds are in Irving's hand and about one-third in printed pages taken from the 1840 edition, from John Forster's life of Goldsmith, and from other sources. The manuscript itself will speak for the extent of the expansion of the new version. Some of the proof sheets have survived also, showing both that Irving read proof on the volume and that he took the opportunity to make a number of changes in proof. Some two months after the publication in America, John Murray brought out an edition in London from duplicate plates of the New York edition.

1825 TEXT OF MEMOIRS

1Fa.   THE | MISCELLANEOUS WORKS | OF | OLIVER GOLDSMITH, | WITH AN | ACCOUNT OF HIS LIFE AND WRITINGS. | A NEW EDITION, IN FOUR VOLUMES. | EDITED BY | WASHINGTON IRVING, ESQ. | VOLUME I. [II., III., IV.] | | [Publisher's emblem: intertwined letters within wreath formed by two joined cornucopias; pendant medal below, halo-like circle suggesting a snake swallowing its tail above] | PARIS: | PUBLISHED BY A. AND W. GALIGNANI, 18, RUE VIVIENNE; | AND JULES DIDOT, SEN. 6, RUE DU PONT-DE-LODI. | [rule] | 1825.

"Collection of English Literature" series.

(22.0 x 14.1 trimmed): Vol. I. $[-]^4$ A-H^8 1-18^8 19^4. First and last leaf missing in copies examined; blank? Vol. II. $[-]^4$ 1-27^8 28^6. First leaf blank? Vol. III. $[-]^6$ 1-30^8 31^2. First leaf blank? Vol. IV. $[-]^4$ 1-26^8 27^4. First leaf blank? In Vol. I, preliminary engravings of Irving (dated 1824; from a portrait by F. Sieurac; in a high stock and fur collar) and Goldsmith (dated 1824; from a portrait by Sir Joshua Reynolds) are not reckoned. Laid paper watermarked MONTGOLFIER ANNONAY and a variety of numbers, predominantly 190.

The Prospectus (see below) offers the work in paper of three qualities: "1. On fine paper at two dollars per volume. 2. On vellum paper, with a proof impression of the portrait, at two dollars and seventy-five cents per volume. 3. On large superfine vellum paper, with a proof impression of the portrait, and the etching on India paper, at four dollars per volume. Only fifty copies will be printed." The three papers are described in *Bibliographie de la France*, 15 October 1824, as "papier fin"; "papier vélin carré"; "papier jésus-vélin." No copy in vellum paper has been located.

Vol. I. [a]-[b], half-title and identification of series, on verso printer; [c]-[d], title, verso blank; [e]-[f], table of contents, verso blank; [i]-cxxviii, Irving's "Memoirs of the Life and Writings of Oliver Goldsmith"; [1]-294, the

Miscellaneous Works, beginning with *The Vicar of Wakefield*. Vol. II. [i]-[ii], half-title, on verso printer; [iii]-[iv], title, verso blank; [v]-vi, table of contents; [1]-445, the Miscellaneous Works; [446], blank. Vol. III. [i]-[ii], half-title, on verso printer; [iii]-[iv], title, verso blank; [v]-x, table of contents; [i]-[ii], fly-title for *Letters from a Citizen of World*, verso blank; [iii]-vi, "The Editor's Preface" (by Goldsmith); [7]-481, *The Citizen of the World*; [482], blank. Vol. IV. [i]-[ii], half-title, on verso printer; [iii]-[iv], title, verso blank; [v]-vi, table of contents; [1]-424, the Miscellaneous Works.

Printer: Jules Didot, Senior. Printer to His Majesty. No. 6, Rue du Pont-de-Lodi.

Lineation: Vol. I. p. l, times ... fretful ; p. c, Beauclerk ... intercourse ; p. 100, CHAPTER XXVIII. ... miles Vol. II. p. 100, POSTSCRIPT ... Advertiser.; p. 200, ment ... hither Vol. III. p. 100, was ... of ; p. 200, now ... Their Vol. IV. p. 100, but ... partner ; p. 200, praise ... not

Boards? Paper wrappers? At least one contemporary Galignani volume noted in boards.

Bibliographie de la France, 15 October 1824, # 5268, listed. *United States Literary Gazette*, 15 October 1824, "in the press." *National Gazette and Literary Register* [Philadelphia], 29 January 1825, "Just received and for sale by H. C. Carey and I. Lea." The three papers are described in the advertisement, but copies on "large superfine vellum paper" are now priced at $4.25 per volume. The advertisement is dated 27 January at the foot.

BL, MH, Private hands. 2 copies reported in Bibliothèque Nationale.

A Prospectus for the entire projected collection is bound in some copies of Part 3 of *Tales of a Traveller*, Philadelphia, Carey & Lea, 1824, and reprinted as an advertisement by Carey & Lea in *United States Literary Gazette*, 15 October and 1 November 1824. It was probably also issued separately in America and in France. In *Bibliographie de la France*, 10 July 1824, a Prospectus is listed in English, # 3704, and in French, # 3654, as "Chefs-d'OEuvre de la littérature anglaise. (Prospectus)." Both entries describe the form as "In-8° d'une demi-feuille." Issued in both languages?

The four pages in *Tales of a Traveller* are headed PROSPECTUS OF A COLLECTION OF ENGLISH LITERATURE, EDITED BY WASHINGTON IRVING, ESQ. AND NOW PUBLISHING BY SUBSCRIPTION, BY A. & W. GALIGNANI, AND JULES DIDOT, SENIOR, PARIS, AND H. C. CAREY & I. LEA, PHILADELPHIA. It describes the collection and lists the authors to be published. A note points out that the Works of Goldsmith "will form the first four volumes. They are now in the press, and will be published shortly." (Although Carey & Lea are credited as second publishers, apparently the firm acted only as distributor and seller in the United States. No copy of the edition has been located with the Carey & Lea imprint.) The Prospectus may well have been written in part by Irving, who entered in his journal for 14 March 1824, "Write Prospectus & terms for Collection of British Literature."

[*BAL* item 10118 mentions a reprinting by Baudry in 1834. Not located. Is this the Baudry impression of 1837, which *BAL* does not list?]

b. PARIS: | PUBLISHED BY A. AND W. GALIGNANI, AND Co., | 18, RUE VIVIENNE. | [rule] | 1837.

DLC.

c. PARIS, | BAUDRY'S EUROPEAN LIBRARY, | RUE DU COQ, NEAR THE LOUVRE. | SOLD ALSO BY AMYOT, RUE DE LA PAIX; TRUCHY, BOULEVART DES ITALIENS; | THÉOPHILE BARROIS, JUN., RUE RICHELIEU; LIBRAIRIE DES ÉTRANGERS, | RUE NEUVE-SAINT-AUGUSTIN; AND HEIDELOFF AND CAMPE, | RUE VIVIENNE. | 1837.

"Collection of Ancient and Modern British Authors," Vols. CL-CLIII.

Printer: Julius Didot, Senior, 4, Boulevart d'Enfer.

Brown coarse T cloth. Sides decorated in blind. Spine titled in gilt: THE | WORKS | OF | OLIVER GOLDSMITH | [rule] | VOL. I. [II., III., IV.].

BL, NN (Vols. III, IV only), NNU.

1Aa. THE | MISCELLANEOUS WORKS [hollow letters] | OF | OLIVER GOLDSMITH, | WITH AN | Account of his Life and Writings. [fancy] | STEREOTYPED FROM THE PARIS EDITION, | EDITED BY | WASHINGTON IRVING. | COMPLETE IN ONE VOLUME. | [double rule] | Philadelphia: [fancy] | PUBLISHED BY J. CRISSY AND J. GRIGG. | [rule] | 1830.

The statement on the title, "Stereotyped from the Paris edition," should not mislead. This is a new edition of the work, in a different setting, although it reprints the text of the Paris edition of 1824. The reprinting, however, is not exact. Minor variants in spelling and punctuation do appear, apparently deliberately so, and some fifteen minor changes in words, probably the work of the compositor. "The" is changed to "this," for instance, and words occasionally dropped. There is no evidence of authorial revision.

(21.1. x 13.3 rebound): $[1]^8$ 2-33^8. Not reckoned: engraving of portrait of Goldsmith by Reynolds before title. In double columns.

[i]-[ii], title, on verso printer; [iii]-vi, table of contents; [7]-56, Irving's "Memoirs"; [57]-527, the Miscellaneous Works; [528], advertisement for publications of J. Grigg.

Printer: Stereotyped by J. Crissy & G. Goodman, Philadelphia.

Lineation: p. 50, 'London ... others,; p. 100, ty ... habitation.

Seen only rebound. Issued in paper boards, and in leather?

North American Review, October 1830, in "Quarterly List of New Publications."

NN, OkU.

b. Philadelphia: [fancy] | PUBLISHED BY J. CRISSY AND J. GRIGG. | [rule] | 1832.

    MiU.

c. Philadelphia: [fancy] | PUBLISHED BY J. CRISSY. | [rule] | 1833.

    Noted in full calf with black leather label on spine. Apparently so issued.

    ViU.

d. Philadelphia: [fancy] | PUBLISHED BY J. CRISSY. | [rule] | 1834.

    P. [528] blank.

    DLC.

e. Philadelphia: [fancy] | J. CRISSY, No. 4, MINOR STREET, | AND DESILVER, THOMAS, AND Co., No. 247, MARKET STREET. | [rule] | 1835.

    Noted in black hard-pressed boards. Sides decorated in blind and gilt. Spine decorated in gilt, with black leather label titled GOLDSMITH in gilt. Marbled endpapers. All edges marbled.

    TxU.

f. Philadelphia: [fancy] | J. CRISSY, No. 4, MINOR STREET, | AND DESILVER, THOMAS, AND Co., No. 247, MARKET STREET. | [rule] | 1836.

    Noted in full calf with black leather label on spine.

    DLC.

g. Philadelphia: [fancy] | J. CRISSY, No. 4, MINOR STREET, | AND DESILVER, THOMAS, AND Co., No. 247, MARKET STREET. | [rule] | 1837.

    Noted in full calf with black leather label on spine.

    ViU.

h. Philadelphia: [fancy] | J. CRISSY, No. 4, MINOR STREET, | AND
    THOMAS, COWPERTHWAIT & Co., No. 253 MARKET STREET. |
    [rule] | 1838.

    MH.

i. Philadelphia: [fancy] | J. CRISSY, No. 4, MINOR STREET, | AND
    THOMAS, COWPERTHWAIT & Co., No. 253 MARKET STREET. |
    [rule] | 1839.

    NN.

j. Philadelphia: [fancy] | J. CRISSY, No. 4, MINOR STREET, | AND
    THOMAS, COWPERTHWAIT & Co., No. 253 MARKET STREET. |
    [rule] | 1841.

    ViU.

k. Philadelphia: [fancy] | J. CRISSY, No. 4, MINOR STREET, | AND
    THOMAS, COWPERTHWAIT & Co., No. 253 MARKET STREET. |
    [rule] | 1844.

    MiDW

l. Philadelphia: [fancy] | J. CRISSY, No. 4, MINOR STREET, | AND
    THOMAS, COWPERTHWAIT & Co., No. 253 MARKET STREET. |
    [rule] | 1845.

    NN, ViU.

m. PHILADELPHIA: | CRISSY & MARKLEY, No. 4 MINOR ST. | 1847.

    NN.

n. PHILADELPHIA: | CRISSY & MARKLEY, No. 4 MINOR ST. | 1849.

    Red V cloth. Sides decorated in blind and gilt. Spine decorated and titled in
    gilt: GOLDSMITH'S | WORKS. AEG. Endpapers cream.

    TxU.

o. PHILADELPHIA: | CRISSY & MARKLEY, No. 4 MINOR ST. | 1850.

    Brown T cloth. Sides decorated in blind. Spine decorated in blind and titled
    in gilt.

    CtY.

p. PHILADELPHIA: | PUBLISHED BY CRISSY & MARKLEY, |
    GOLDSMITH'S HALL, LIBRARY STREET. | 1852. All within double
    frame lines.

Purple T cloth. Sides decorated in blind. Spine decorated in blind and titled in gilt: [double rule] | GOLDSMITH'S | WORKS. | [double rule] || PHILADELPHIA | CRISSY & MARKLEY White endpapers.

Private hands.

q. PHILADELPHIA: | PUBLISHED BY CRISSY & MARKLEY, | GOLDSMITH'S HALL, LIBRARY STREET. All within double frame lines.

[No date of publication].

TxU, ViU.

r. E. C. MARKLEY & SON, | 422 Library Street, | PHILADELPHIA. All within double frame lines.

[No date of publication].

Information reported by KyU, but copy not examined.

1840 TEXT OF BIOGRAPHY

1Aa- THE | LIFE | OF | OLIVER GOLDSMITH, | WITH | SELECTIONS
 b.   FROM HIS WRITINGS. | BY | WASHINGTON IRVING. | IN TWO VOLUMES. | VOL. I. [II.] | NEW-YORK: | HARPER & BROTHERS, 82 CLIFF-STREET. | [rule] | 1840.

"Harpers' Family Library," Nos. CXXI-CXXII.

(15.3 x 9.4): Vol. I. $[A]^4$ B-I^6 K-U^6 X-Z^6 AA-DD^6. Not reckoned: preliminary engraving of portrait of Goldsmith by Sir Joshua Reynolds.

Vol. II in two collation states, probably representing two impressions:

State A: $[-]^2$ A-I^6 K-U^6 X-Z^6 AA-CC^6 DD^2. First and last leaf blanks.

State B: $[-]^2$ A-I^6 K-U^6 X-Z^6 AA-BB^6 CC^8. First and last leaf blanks. Superfluous signature mark DD retained on p. 313.

Although not certain, the suggested sequence is probably correct. The impression of 1842 is in Collation State B.

Vol. I. [v]-[vi], title, on verso copyright (1840); [vii]-viii, table of contents; [9]-186, "Biography of Oliver Goldsmith"; [187]-323, selections from Goldsmith; [324], blank. Vol. II. [a]-[b], title, on verso copyright (1840); [i]-v, table of contents; [vi], blank; [7]-313, selections from Goldsmith; [314], blank.

Lineation: Vol. I. p. 50, How ... per-; p. 100, Several ... temper ; p. 200, Vain, ... tree: Vol. II. p. 100, for, ... to ; p. 200, pany. ... the

Issued in two bindings:

[A]. Tan V cloth printed in black. On front, title within double frame lines; at head, HARPERS' | FAMILY LIBRARY. | N^O. CXXI. [CXXII.]. On back, advertisement for "Harpers' Family Library" with 129 numbers, plus "Classical Series" with 36 numbers. (Some titles require more than one number.) On spine, within rules: IRVING'S | LIFE AND WRITINGS | OF | OLIVER GOLDSMITH | [rule] | IN TWO VOLS. | VOL. I. [II.]. At foot: FAMILY | LIBRARY. | N^O. CXXI. [CXXII.].

[B]. Dark brown irregularly-grained CM-like cloth. Sides blank. On spine, in gilt, within elaborated panel: THE | FAMILY | LIBRARY. In panel below: N^O. 121 [122]. At foot: IRVING'S | GOLDSMITH | IN TWO VOLS. | VOL. 1. [2.]. White endpapers.

Both bindings have been noted on collation State A. Only Binding [B] has been noted on collation State B, although Binding [A] on State B may also exist. Bindings on the impressions of 1842 and 1847 are imprinted in State [B].

Knickerbocker, November 1840, discussed in "Editors' Table": "now passing through the press," "will be given to the public in all the present month (sic)"; extracts from proofsheets published. *Arcturus*, December 1840, listed. *New World*, 6 February 1841, reviewed.

CtY, State A, Binding [A], 2 copies. NNHi, State A, Binding [A]. ViU, State B, Binding [B]. Reported in MWA, State A, Binding [B].

c. Also issued as Harpers' "School District Library," Nos. 109-110.

For a description of a later binding, but one probably similar, see the description below of the impression of 1844.

New York Review, January 1841, reviewed.

Not examined. Copy reported in DLC.

d. NEW-YORK: | HARPER & BROTHERS, 82 CLIFF-STREET. | [rule] | 1842.

Vol. I, p. [324] imprinted with advertisement for Harper & Brothers books.

In Vol. II, the last gathering is CC^8. The superfluous signature mark DD is retained on p. 313.

In the binding of State [B] of the first edition.

ViU.

e. NEW-YORK: | HARPER & BROTHERS, 82 CLIFF-STREET. | [rule] | 1844.

In Vol. II, the last gatherings are CC^6 DD^4. DD$_1$ is integral with 3 leaves of advertisements, paged [1]-6.

Black textured V cloth with black leather shelfbacks. Sides blank. On spines, in gilt, SCHOOL | DISTRICT | LIBRARY | N^O. 109 [110] within elaborate frame; HARPER & BROTHERS a part of the frame at the top. At foot: IRVING'S | GOLDSMITH | IN TWO VOLS [.?] | VOL. 1. [2.].

TxU, Vol. II only.

f. NEW-YORK: | HARPER & BROTHERS, 82 CLIFF-STREET. | [rule] | 1847.

In Vol. II, the last gatherings are CC^6 DD^4. DD$_1$ is integral with 3 leaves of advertisements for Harpers' Family Library, dated at the end 1846.

Brown gray cloth with small interlocked "squiggles." The imprinting is that of binding State [B] of the first edition.

NjP.

g. NEW-YORK: | HARPER & BROTHERS, PUBLISHERS, | 329 & 331 PEARL STREET | FRANKLIN SQUARE. | 1855.

MB, Vol. II only.

1Ea. A HISTORY | OF THE | EARTH AND ANIMATED NATURE, | BY | OLIVER GOLDSMITH. | With an Introductory View of the Animal Kingdom, Translated from the French of | Baron Cuvier, [the two lines in fancy type] | AND COPIOUS NOTES | EMBRACING ACCOUNTS OF NEW DISCOVERIES IN NATURAL HISTORY; | A LIFE OF THE AUTHOR, | BY WASHINGTON IRVING; | AND | A CAREFULLY PREPARED INDEX TO THE WHOLE WORK. | IN TWO VOLUMES. | VOL. I. [II.?] | LONDON, EDINBURGH, AND DUBLIN. | A. FULLARTON AND CO. | [rule] | 1848. All within double frame lines.

The title page for Vol. II is missing in the copy examined. So issued? An engraved title is present for both vols. See the discussion of the impression of 1856 below.

(25.4 x 16.3 rebound): Vol. I. [i]-liv, [1]-536. Not reckoned: engraved title and numerous illustrations. Vol. II. [1]-541 [542]. Not reckoned: engraved title and numerous illustrations. In double columns. Double frame lines around each page. Signed in 8's.

Irving's "Biographical Sketch of Oliver Goldsmith," I, [3]-53.

Printer: Fullarton and Co., Printers, Leith Walk, Edinburgh.

Lineation: Vol. I. p. 50, This (col. 1) ... him (col. 2) ; p. 300, the ... in Vol. II. p. 100, length, ... short ; p. 300, scrutable ... reckoned

NjP.

b. LONDON, EDINBURGH, AND DUBLIN: | A. FULLARTON AND CO. | [rule] | 1852.

Printed title present for Vol. II.

NjP.

c. LONDON, EDINBURGH, AND DUBLIN: | A. FULLARTON AND CO. | [rule] | 1853.

Printed title present for Vol. II.

NN.

d. [LONDON, EDINBURGH, AND DUBLIN: | A. FULLARTON AND CO. | [rule] | 1854.]

Not seen. Reported in NcU.

e. LONDON, EDINBURGH, AND DUBLIN: | A. FULLARTON & CO. | 1856.

In slightly larger size, apparently untrimmed: 26.1 x 17.1.

The copy seen is composed of bound parts, each still in its original pink paper wrapper. The work itself is divided into 9 "Divisions," and each Division constitutes a part. A prospectus on the back of the wrapper for Part I, however, offers the edition in 18 parts at 2/ each; also in 36 monthly parts at 1/.

No printed dated title for Vol. II. A set of title pages for both volumes, undated, is bound at the end of the last part: A | HISTORY | OF | THE EARTH | AND | ANIMATED NATURE, | BY | Oliver Goldsmith. [fancy] | WITH AN INTRODUCTORY VIEW OF THE ANIMAL KINGDOM BY | BARON CUVIER: | COPIOUS NOTES OF DISCOVERIES IN NATURAL HISTORY: | And a Life of the Author; [fancy] | BY WASHINGTON IRVING. | VOL. I. [II.] | [publisher's decorative monogram] | A. FULLARTON AND CO., | EDINBURGH, LONDON, AND DUBLIN.

Although earlier impressions have not been noted in original parts, it is possible that the first impression at least was also so issued. The missing title for Vol. II would suggest the possibility.

BL.

(EPITOMIZED VERSION)

2Ea.   OLIVER GOLDSMITH'S | WORKS: | Poems, Comedies, Essays, [fancy] |
       VICAR OF WAKEFIELD: | WITH LIFE | BY | WASHINGTON
       IRVING: | AND | Illustrations. [fancy] | LONDON: | CHARLES DALY,
       GREVILLE STREET, | HATTON GARDEN.

       No date. 1851?

       (16.0 x 10.0): [i]-[xii] unpaged, [v]-lxiv, | leaf unpaged, [1]-425 [426]. Signed
       in 6's.

       Irving's "Life of Oliver Goldsmith," [v]-lxiv. At the end appears a note: "The
       'Life of Oliver Goldsmith,' by Washington Irving, has been epitomised in the
       foregoing biographical sketch.   Stripped of all the superfluous matter, it
       contains all that is of interest; and has been rendered only less bulky, less
       wearisome, and more convenient."

       Lineation: p. l, had ... musing ; p. 100, *Croaker.* ... it.

       NjP.

   b. THE WORKS | OF | OLIVER GOLDSMITH: | COMPRISING HIS |
       Poems, Comedies, Essays, [fancy] | AND | VICAR OF WAKEFIELD. |
       [rule] | WITH ILLUSTRATIONS. | [rule] | PHILADELPHIA: | WILLIS
       P. HAZARD, 190 CHESTNUT ST. | 1857. All within single frame lines.

       (17.5 x 11.4): [i]-[xii] unpaged, [v]-lxiv, 1 leaf unpaged, [1]-425 [426].   Not
       reckoned: preliminary illustration and engraved title.   Single frame line
       around all pages. Signed in 6's.

       In the same setting as the London edition by Charles Daly, [1851?], with the
       same note on the "epitomised" life by Irving.

       Lineation: p. xl, aristocratic ... her ; p. 100, *Croaker.* ... it.

       ViU.

   c. [Philadelphia: Davis, Porter & Co.].

       No date. 185-?

       Not seen. Reported in MH.

   d. [Philadelphia: James B. Smith & Co., 1859].

       Not seen. Reported in MtU.

       An 1856 edition by James B. Smith & Co. has been examined. The copy
       seen, in original brown T cloth, is from the same setting but lacks the Life by
       Irving, even though the preliminary engraved title calls for it. Do some states
       contain the Life? The copy with engraved title but without the Life is in
       FTaSU.

1849 TEXT OF AUTHOR'S REVISED EDITION

1Aa.   OLIVER GOLDSMITH: | A BIOGRAPHY. | BY | WASHINGTON IRVING. | NEW-YORK: | GEORGE P. PUTNAM, 155 BROADWAY. | LONDON: JOHN MURRAY. | 1849.

(19.0 x 12.9): [1]^{12} 2-16^{12}. Terminal catalogue; see description below.

[i]-[ii], Works title for Vol. XI, dated 1849, verso blank; [iii]-[iv], title, on verso copyright (1849) and printer; [v]-xiii, table of contents; [xiv], blank; [xv]-xvi, Preface, dated August 1, 1849; [17]-382, text; [383], notice that the publisher "Has in press, and will shortly publish," *The Miscellaneous Works of Oliver Goldsmith*, uniform with Irving's Works "now in course of publication"; [384], blank.

(For a discussion of *The Miscellaneous Works* advertised on p. [383], see the note at the end of the listing of Putnam impressions of the Author's Revised Edition.)

The first impression may be distinguished from a later one also dated 1849 by the textual changes defined below in the entry [c] for that impression.

The terminal catalogue has been noted in four states. The sequence, if any, is unknown.

[A].   36 pp., paged 1-36. Dated July, 1849. On p. 15, *Goldsmith* is marked "not yet ready, June, 1849."

[B].   24 pp., paged 1-24. Dated July, 1849. On p. 15, *Goldsmith* is marked "not yet ready, June, 1849."

[C].   16 pp., paged 25-36, followed by 4 pp. unpaged, of which the first is dated July, 1849.

[D].   No catalogue.

State [D], with no catalogue, has been noted only in a copy in publisher's "fine binding" or "cloth extra gilt," probably designed, without advertising, for use as a gift.

Printer: John F. Trow, Printer and Stereotyper, 49 Ann-street, New-York.

Lineation: p. 100, cannot ... of ; p. 200, powerful ... but

Blue-green TB cloth. Sides decorated in blind with publisher's initials at center. Spine titled in gilt: IRVING'S | WORKS | [rule] | GOLDSMITH || Putnam Cream endpapers. Fly-leaves. Also noted in red A cloth. Sides decorated in gilt with bust of Goldsmith at center. Spine decorated and titled in gilt: GOLDSMITH | [rule] | Irving AEG. White endpapers.

The advertisement on p. 15 of the catalogue present in some copies offers the work in half calf, half morocco, or full calf, as well as in "dark cloth."

Pierre M. Irving, *Life and Letters*, "On the 19th of September [1849], I stopped in at Putnam's, who told me he had already disposed of the first edition of Goldsmith of 2,500, and was now busy on a second of 2,000."

Literary World, 14 July 1849, "in press"; 25 August 1849, "new publication"; 1 September 1849, listed and reviewed.

Catalogue State [A]: DLC, ViU. State [B]: TxU. State [C]: MH, ViU. State [D]: TxU.

b.   [Illustrated form]. OLIVER GOLDSMITH: | A BIOGRAPHY. | BY | WASHINGTON IRVING. | [cut of bust of Goldsmith] | WITH ILLUSTRATIONS. | NEW-YORK: | GEORGE P. PUTNAM, 155 BROADWAY. | LONDON: JOHN MURRAY. | 1849. All within single frame lines.

On 25 August 1849, Irving requested ten small changes in the text of the work; they were made in this impression.   Representative examples are: 162.6, "most" to "almost"; and 360.3f, "made wrong" to "made weary." Two other corrections may have been the work of the publisher: 154.9f, "*un-ideal*" to "*un-idea'd*"; and 242.19, "Shannon" to "Channel."

(21.5-22.4 x 15.0-15.5): [1]^{12} 2-16^{12}. Not reckoned: frontispiece and eleven illustrations on single leaves inserted through the volume.

In the publisher's catalogue found in some copies, the advertisement for this illustrated form describes it, "With about 40 illustrations selected by the publisher from FORSTER'S LIFE OF GOLDSMITH, beautifully engraved on wood by W. Roberts." In addition to the eleven illustrations on separate leaves, smaller ones are added in appropriate blank spaces in the text.

[1]-[2], title, on verso copyright (1849) and printer; [3]-[4], Preface; [5]-12, table of contents; 13-15, facsimile of Goldsmith letter; 16, illustration; [17]-382, text; [383], advertisement for *The Miscellaneous Works of Oliver Goldsmith*; [384], blank.

The table of contents is reset, with illustrations added on six of the pages. Single frame lines added around each page.

A terminal catalogue has been noted in some copies: 32 pp., paged 1-32, dated July, 1849. On p. 20, this illustrated edition is marked "*in August.*"

Printer: John F. Trow, Printer and Stereotyper, 49 Ann-street, New-York.

The volume was issued in a wide variety of bindings, although contemporary advertisements list them simply as, "Cloth, $2 50; cloth, extra gilt, $3; morocco extra, $5." Five have been noted:

Dull blue A cloth, and dark blue coarse diagonal T cloth. On front, gilt bust of Goldsmith within decorative arabesque border in blind. On back, the border in blind without the bust. On spine, in gilt, three cherubs with trumpets, a baptismal font, and an ornament, all within double frame; titled at top: Oliver | Goldsmith [fancy] | A BIOGRAPHY | [rule] | Irving | [rule] | *ILLUSTRATED* [in left-tilted italic]. White endpapers. One copy noted with endpapers gold-figured on white.

Royal blue T cloth. On sides, all in gilt, elaborate border with bust of Goldsmith within oval at center. On spine, same design and titling. AEG. Endpapers gold-figured on white.

Bright blue AR cloth. On sides, in blind, single rule border with elaborated corners; gilt bust of Goldsmith at center within elaborate frame that suggests a Victorian picture frame. Spine decorated over the entire area with gilt arabesques; titled: Goldsmith | [rule] | Irving | [rule] | Illustrated AEG. Yellow endpapers.

Dark blue full morocco. On sides, elaborate border in gilt, center blank. Spine decorated and titled in gilt. AEG. White endpapers. In this state, the publisher's advertisement on p. [383] is omitted.

Three other cloth bindings have been reported but not examined:

Blue pebbled cloth. Sides decorated in gilt and blind. Spine decorated in gilt, titled: Goldsmith | Irving | [rule] | Illustrated TEG.

Red, and also green, pebbled cloth. Sides decorated in gilt. Spine decorated and titled in gilt.

Literary World, 14 July 1849, "in August"; 22 September 1849, "in press"; 20 October 1849, "now ready"; 10 November 1849, advertised in various bindings. *Albion*, 17 November 1849, "now ready."

CtY, MH, TxU (2), ViU, Private hands.

c. [Works form]. NEW-YORK: | GEORGE P. PUTNAM, 155 BROADWAY. | LONDON: JOHN MURRAY. | 1849.

Works title, dated 1849.

This concealed impression may be distinguished from the first impression by the changes made in the text: those made in the first illustrated impression, above, plus one more on 298.2, "conversational" to "conventional."

CtY, copy reported on but not examined.

d. [Works form]. NEW-YORK: | GEORGE P. PUTNAM, 155 BROADWAY. | LONDON: JOHN MURRAY. | 1850.

Works title, dated 1850.

Terminal catalogue: 18 pp., with one page blank and others repeated, undated.

On first page of advertisements, publisher's notice that *The Miscellaneous Works of Goldsmith*, 4 vols., uniform with Irving's Works, is "just published."

A number of small new corrections or changes appear in the text. Representative examples are: 149.2f, "were arrived" to "had arrived"; 162.9f, "solitary" to "melancholy"; and 373.6-5f, "Wharton" to "Warton."

DLC.

e.   [Works form].   NEW-YORK: | GEORGE P. PUTNAM, 155 BROADWAY. | LONDON: JOHN MURRAY. | 1851.

Works title, dated 1851.

Three further changes appear in the text: 45.6, "Elfin" to "Elphin"; 98.16, comma added after "school"; and 105.5, comma added after "Yet."

TxU.

f.   [Works form]. NEW-YORK: | G. P. PUTNAM & COMPANY, 10 PARK PLACE. | 1852.

Works title, dated 1852.

Private hands. Copy reported in PPGi.

g.   [Works form]. NEW-YORK: | G. P. PUTNAM & COMPANY, 10 PARK PLACE. | 1853.

Works title, dated 1853.

ViU.

h.   [Illustrated form]. NEW-YORK: | GEORGE P. PUTNAM & CO., 10 PARK PLACE. | M.DCCC.LIII.

A number of small changes appear in the text. A representative example is: 45.5, "time was" to "time had."

MH.

i.   [Works form]. NEW-YORK: | G. P. PUTNAM & COMPANY, 10 PARK PLACE. | 1854.

Works title, dated 1854.

Engraved title added.

DLC.

j. [Works form]. NEW-YORK: | G. P. PUTNAM & COMPANY, 10 PARK PLACE. | 1855.

Works title, dated 1855.

DLC.

k. [Works form]. New York: [fancy] | G. P. PUTNAM & CO., 321 BROADWAY. | 1856.

Works title, dated 1856.

ViU.

l. [Works form]. New York: [fancy] | G. P. PUTNAM & CO., 321 BROADWAY. | 1857.

Works title, dated 1857.

MH.

m. [Works form]. NEW-YORK: | G. P. PUTNAM, 115 NASSAU STREET. | 1859.

Works title, dated 1859; same imprint.

Green BD cloth. On sides, elaborated double border in blind. Spine titled in gilt within gilt decorative framing on three sides: IRVING'S | WORKS | [rule] | GOLDSMITH || G. P. Putnam Green endpapers.

TxU.

n. [Works form]. NEW YORK: | G. P. PUTNAM (for the Proprietor), 506 BROADWAY. | 1859.

Works title, dated 1859; same imprint.

Two preliminary engravings added, with imprint of Childs & Peterson, Philadelphia.

Green BD cloth. On sides, elaborated double border in blind. Spine titled in gilt within gilt decorative framing on three sides. Green endpapers.

MH.

Note: In *The Literary World*, 20 October 1849, appears an advertisement by G. P. Putnam for *The Miscellaneous Works of Oliver Goldsmith*, edited by James Prior, to be completed in four volumes. The work is described as, "Published under the supervision of Washington Irving, and uniform with his Life of Goldsmith." Whether there is any validity to the claim of "supervision" by Irving is uncertain but doubtful. An advertisement in the issue of 24 November 1849 describes the edition more simply, and perhaps more accurately, as "Published uniform, and in connexion with 'Irving's Life of Goldsmith.'" That is the same information conveyed in the advertisement in the Putnam impressions of 1849-50. In the review of Vol. 1 in *The Literary World*, 1 December 1849, nothing is said of supervision by Irving, although the volume is described as "printed uniformly with the series of Washington Irving." Apparently the binding itself was not in fact uniform, at least in all copies, since the review ends, "The binding by Middlebrook is something of a novelty, and quite successful as a matter of taste."

1E.   OLIVER GOLDSMITH: | A BIOGRAPHY. | BY | WASHINGTON IRVING. | [wavy rule] | LONDON: | JOHN MURRAY, ALBEMARLE STREET. | 1849.

"Murray's Home and Colonial Library."

(17.8 x 11.9 in one vol. in cloth; 17.1 x 11.7 in two vols. in paper): [a]^8 B-I^8 K-U^8 X-Z^8 2A^8.

[i]-[ii], half-title, verso blank; [iii]-[iv], title, on verso printer; [v]-vi, Preface, dated Sunnyside, August 1, 1849; [vii]-xv, table of contents; [xvi], blank; [17]-382, text; [383], printer; [384], blank.

Printed from duplicate plates of the New York Author's Revised Edition. Murray rearranged the preliminary matter and made a number of small changes in the text before issuance. Four changes were unique, such as 272.9f, "the book" to "the work," and 313.7-8, "more dif- | ficulties" to "greater | difficulties"; nine were corrections that were also corrected in one later Putnam impression or another. It is reassuring to report that both publishers failed to correct a number of misprints.

Printer: William Clowes and Sons, Stamford Street.

Lineation: p. 100, cannot ... of ; p. 200, powerful ... but

Issued in two binding states:

[A].   In two volumes. The volumes are paged continuously, divided between pp. 208-209, signatures N-O. In paper wrappers. On fronts, title within triple frame lines: No. LXXV. [LXXVI.] | CHEAP LITERATURE FOR ALL CLASSES. | [double rule] | MURRAY'S | HOME AND COLONIAL LIBRARY. | [double rule] | LIFE OF OLIVER GOLDSMITH. | BY WASHINGTON IRVING. | PART I. [II.] | [wavy rule] | LONDON: | JOHN MURRAY, ALBEMARLE STREET. | *Price Half-a-Crown*. Within frame at foot: W. CLOWES AND SONS, STAMFORD STREET. Advertisements on back and on inside of wrappers.

[B]. In one volume. Red L-like cloth. On sides, in blind, decorative designs; in circle at center: MURRAY'S COLONIAL & HOME LIBRARY. Spine decorated in blind, titled in gilt: IRVING'S | LIFE OF | GOLDSMITH | MURRAY Light yellow endpapers imprinted with advertisements in red.

Literary Gazette, 6 and 20 October 1849, "On November 1st, will be published, -- forming the 37th Volume of the HOME and COLONIAL LIBRARY"; 10 November 1849, the two-vol. edition, designated (mistakenly?) as Nos. 85, 86 of the Home and Colonial Library, noticed. *Athenæum*, 27 October 1849, the one-vol. edition listed; 17 November 1849, reviewed. *Literary Gazette*, 8 December 1849, the Home and Colonial Library series advertised, "price 2*s*. 6*d*. each Part, or (Two Parts as a Volume) price 6*s*. in cloth."

One vol.: MH, TxU (2). Two vols.: *BL*.

2Ea.   OLIVER GOLDSMITH: | A BIOGRAPHY. | BY | WASHINGTON IRVING. | [wavy rule] | LONDON: | H. G. CLARKE & CO., 4, EXETER CHANGE. | [rule] | 1850.

In the terminal advertisements, this edition is listed as "Clarke's Cabinet Library," No. 5. Price 2*s*.

(12.3 x 8.4): [i]-xv [xvi], [17]-428. Not reckoned: preliminary portrait of Goldsmith, and four pages of integral terminal advertisements. (An engraved titled is counted.) Signed in 8's.

Printer: H. Willerson, 39, Fleet Lane, Farringdon Street.

Lineation: p. 100, at ... know ; p. 200, author. ... dis-

Blue AR cloth. On front, in gilt, elaborated border, two muses at center. On back, the border in blind. Spine decorated and titled in gilt: GOLDSMITH | [rule] | IRVING AEG. Yellow endpapers.

Publishers' Circular, 15 December 1849, listed.

TxU.

b.   OLIVER GOLDSMITH, | A BIOGRAPHY. | BY | WASHINGTON IRVING. | [rule] | LONDON: | PUBLISHED BY W. TWEEDIE, STRAND. | [rule] | MDCCCLIII.

Lithographed title and portrait of Goldsmith. Four pages of terminal advertisements.

Red V cloth. Sides decorated with star and dot design in blind. Spine decorated in blind, titled in gilt: LIFE OF | GOLDSMITH | [rule] | IRVING

TxU.

3Ea-   OLIVER GOLDSMITH: | A Biography. [fancy] | BY | WASHINGTON
  b.   IRVING. | [rule] | LONDON: | GEORGE ROUTLEDGE & CO., 36,
        SOHO SQUARE. | 1850.

"The Popular Library."

(17.0 x 10.5): [i]-xi [xii], [5]-213 [214]. Not reckoned: two pages of terminal
advertisements. Signed in 8's.

Printer: Savill and Edwards, 4, Chandos Street, Covent Garden. (Printer
identified only in impression in boards).

Lineation: p. 100, nesses ... [in note] Goldsmith.; p. 200, Garrick, ... task

Noted in two bindings, apparently representing two impressions:

[A]. Brown AR cloth. On sides, in blind, elaborate border; at center, within
     circle and rosette, POPULAR LIBRARY. Spine decorated and titled
     in gilt: WASHINGTON | IRVING'S | WORKS. || OLIVER |
     GOLDSMITH || ROUTLEDGE Yellow endpapers.

[B]. Cream paper boards printed in blue. On front, title: The | Popular
     Library. [in elaborated lettering] | OLIVER GOLDSMITH: | A |
     Biography. [fancy] | [wavy rule] | BY | WASHINGTON IRVING. |
     [wavy rule] | ONE SHILLING. | LONDON: | GEO. ROUTLEDGE
     & CO. | SOHO SQUARE. Background of intertwined leaves and
     vines. On back, advertisements for "The Railway Library." On spine,
     decorative design and vertical title: OLIVER GOLDSMITH. White
     endpapers printed in black. Advertisements on front endpapers,
     including ones for "The Popular Library." On back endpapers, a single
     long advertisement for "Completion of the Walpole Memoirs."

Also advertised as available in "extra cloth, gilt edges, 3s. 6d."

Publishers' Circular, 15 January 1850, listed. *Athenæum*, 23 March 1850,
advertised as "New volume": 1s.; in cloth gilt, 1s. 6d.

In boards: TxU. In cloth: Private hands.

4Ea.   OLIVER GOLDSMITH: | A BIOGRAPHY. | BY | WASHINGTON
        IRVING. | [rule] | LONDON: | HENRY G. BOHN, YORK STREET,
        COVENT GARDEN. | 1850.

Issued individually as "Bohn's Shilling Series"; bound with *The Sketch Book* as
Vol. II of "Bohn's Library Edition."

(18.0 x 11.5): [i]-xii, [1]-242. Signed in 8's.

Printer: Harrison and Son, St. Martin's Lane, London.

Lineation: p. 100, sellers' ... for ; p. 200, "*For* ... as

Seen only in "Bohn's Library Edition." Gray T cloth. Sides decorated in blind. Spine titled in gilt as Irving's Works, Vol. II, Bohn's Library Edition. Endpapers white with advertisements in blue. Preliminary portrait of Goldsmith. (No works title in volume).

Shilling Series. *Athenæeum*, 27 April 1850, listed, 1*s*. in boards, 1*s*. 6*d*. in cloth gilt. Library Edition. *Athenæum* and *Literary Gazette*, 2 November 1850, the set of 10 vols. at 35*s*. in "List of New Books."

Library Edition: NN. Shilling Series: Reported in *BL*.

b. [London: Henry G. Bohn, 1854.]

"Bohn's Library Edition." With a portrait of Goldsmith.

Not seen. Copy reported in Staats- und Universitätsbibliothek Hamburg.

1G. OLIVER GOLDSMITH: | A BIOGRAPHY. | BY | WASHINGTON IRVING. | *Published for the Continent of Europe by contract with the Author.* | LEIPZIG | BERNH. TAUCHNITZ JUN. | 1850.

"Collection of British Authors," Vol. 193.

(15.6 x 12.6): [i]-xiv, [1]-356 [357]-[358]. Signed in 8's.

Lineation: p. 100, two ... poor.; p. 200, early ... ran;

White paper wrapper. On front, title and identification of series. On back, advertisements. In the advertisements for Irving's books, the presence of *Wolfert's Roost* and *Life of Washington* in 4 vols. defines this impression seen as one of about 1857-1858.

BL, with wrapper leaves bound in.

TRANSLATIONS

German.

Oliver Goldsmith. [in red] | Eine Lebensbeschreibung | von | Washington Irving. [in red] | Aus dem Englischen. | [elaborated swelled rule] | Berlin, 1858. | Verlag von G. Mertens. [in fraktur] Portrait of Goldsmith above title. All within double frame lines, the inner one red.

A translation of the text of the Author's Revised Edition.

(18.4 x 11.7 untrimmed): [a]-[b], [i]-x, [1]-365 [366]. Signed in 8's. The half-title and title are printed on a doubleton of a variant wove paper.

Printer: Julius Sittenfeld, Berlin.

Lineation: p. 100, zeigen; ... [in footnote] Brief IV.; p. 200, „Doctor" ... Gegenstände

Noted in two bindings. [A]. Tan paper wrapper. On front, cover-title within ornamental border. On back, printer's imprint within ornamental border. On spine, title, publisher, price (1 thaler). One leaf of advertisements inserted at front. [B]. Blue T cloth. On sides, decorations in blind. Spine titled in gilt. Yellow endpapers. Leaves trimmed to 17.3 x 11.1.

MH, TxU (2).

THE FREYSCHÜTZ

This translated and reworked version of Weber's opera *Der Freischütz* is the product of active collaboration between Irving and Barham John Livius. For a detailed account of the collaboration, see the discussion in the *Miscellanies* volume of the Twayne edition. As usual in all of Irving's work as a playwright, he carefully concealed his name from the public, and the adaptation was published in the name of Livius alone. Livius did, however, give some public hint of credit in the "Prefatory Remarks" (which Irving helped to write also): "The author indulges himself in the opportunity of stating the obligation he is under to another friend, whose name, were he permitted, it would be his pride and his pleasure to declare, for various valuable hints and emendations."

1Ea. THE FREYSCHÜTZ; | OR, THE | WILD HUNTSMAN OF BOHEMIA. | A ROMANTIC OPERA, | IN THREE ACTS, | ALTERED FROM THE GERMAN BY | BARHAM LIVIUS, Esq. | [stylized swelled rule] | THE MUSIC COMPOSED BY | The Chevalier CARL MARIA DE WEBER, | Maître de Chapelle to the King of Saxony, and Director of | the Opera at Dresden. | [stylized swelled rule] | FIRST PERFORMED | AT THE | Theatre Royal Covent Garden. [fancy] | THURSDAY, OCTOBER 14, 1824. | [rule] | London: [fancy] | PRINTED FOR JOHN MILLER, NEW BRIDGE STREET, | BLACKFRIARS. | [rule] | 1824. | (*Two Shillings and Six-pence.*)

(21.1 x 12.6): [A]⁴ B-H⁴.

[i]-[ii], title, on verso printer; [iii]-[iv], Dramatis Personae, verso blank; [v]-viii, Prefatory Remarks, dated Paris, 10th October, 1824; [1]-55, text; [56], printer.

Printer: William Molineux, Bream's Buildings, Chancery Lane.

Lineation: p. 25, *Adagio.* ... power.; p. 50, CAVATINA. ... all.

Issued unbound?

NNC.

b.   SECOND EDITION. | [rule] | London: [fancy] | PRINTED FOR JOHN
     MILLER, NEW BRIDGE STREET, | BLACKFRIARS. | [rule] | 1825. |
     (*Two Shillings and Six-pence .*)

     ICN.

THE BEAUTIES OF WASHINGTON IRVING

When Richard Griffin of Glasgow published *The Beauties of Washington Irving* in 1825, he began a tradition of "Selections from Irving" that was to continue under various titles from that day to this. His volume did more than begin the tradition and illustrate the wide-spread popularity of Irving; its specific selection of excerpts almost defined the choice in subsequent collections, in America as well as in Britain, for the next twenty years and more, and influenced the choice in the collections published in Irving's last years. The second, third and fourth British editions either duplicate the selections of the first edition exactly or repeat them with minor variations of selection and order. Carey, Lea & Blanchard's first American edition, 1835, extensively reprinted through the rest of Irving's life, is based upon a collection derived from the 1825 edition and admits as much in a publisher's notice printed in another of Irving's books. In 1837 a miniature London edition by Charles Tilt did make its own set of selections, but it was not until 1849 and the 1850's in America that several volumes of selections began to choose new excerpts and to make choices from some of Irving's later works.

There is no evidence that Irving took any part in making the selections -- the early volumes seem in fact to have been something close to piracies -- and the Carey, Lea & Blanchard notice specifically exempts him from any charge of "the indelicacy of selecting and pointing out any portions of his writings as 'beauties.'" (Although it should be noted that if Irving had objected strongly to the choices, his own publishers, Carey, Lea & Blanchard, or George P. Putnam, would probably not have accepted them.) It is not known who made Richard Griffin's first, influential selection. Contemporary advertisement (one of which is quoted here in the description of the first British edition) suggests the possibility of one Alfred Howard who was compiling the "Beauties" of other authors, but that must remain speculation unless other evidence appears.

It seems desirable to list the contents of these volumes of selections, for the evidence they offer in literary and cultural history as well as for bibliographical completeness. To save space and to make comparison easier, each selection that appears in any one of the British or American collections is listed at the end of this section. It might have been desirable also to list the contents of the continental volumes, but they are scarce (one has been located in a single copy only, and I have been unable to obtain much information about it), tend generally to repeat the selections in British or

American collections even when newly selected, and would have had little influence on literary history. In the listing, the various titles are grouped alphabetically under the Irving book from which they are taken, with identification of the collection in which each appears. The titles of many of the selections are not Irving's titles but rather were supplied by the various compilers.

1Ea. THE | BEAUTIES | OF | WASHINGTON IRVING, ESQ. | AUTHOR OF | "THE SKETCH BOOK," "BRACEBRIDGE HALL," | "TALES OF A TRAVELLER," &c. | ILLUSTRATED WITH SIX ETCHINGS, | BY WILLIAM HEATH, ESQ. | Glasgow: [fancy] | PRINTED FOR RICHARD GRIFFIN & CO. | 75, HUTCHESON STREET. | [rule] | MDCCCXXV.

(14.9 x 9.3 untrimmed): $[-]^4$ A-I^6 K-U^6 X-Z^6 Aa-Cc^6 Dd^2. Not reckoned: six inserted etchings, with imprint GLASGOW: GRIFFIN & Co. 1825.

[i]-[ii], title, on verso printer; [iii]-iv, Introduction; [v]-vii, table of contents; [viii], blank; [1]-316, text.

Printer: J. Starke, Glasgow.

Lineation: p. 100, temporaries, ... imme-; p. 200, One ... thieves!"

Tan paper boards with large paper label on front: title with elaborated border and emblem of tree on shield. Else blank. White endpapers.

MH.

b. *London impression*: London: [fancy] | PRINTED FOR JOHN BUMPUS, | 85, NEWGATE STREET. | [rule] | MDCCCXXV.

Light brown paper wrappers. On front, title within border of frame lines with ornaments in corners. On back, advertisements within elaborated border.

DLC.

In *John Bull*, 27 February 1825, there appears an advertisement for "The BEAUTIES OF LITERATURE, consisting of Classic Selections from the most eminent British and Foreign Authors, by ALFRED HOWARD, Esq." "A volume will issue from the press every month, and the whole be comprised in 40 volumes. Each volume will form a complete work.... London: Printed by T. Davison, for Thomas Tegg, No. 73, Cheapside; also R. Griffin and Co. Glasgow; and J. Cumming, Dublin." Except for those of the first two volumes, the authors to be presented in the advertised series are not identified. It is likely that this first *Beauties of Washington Irving* is related to the series (which seems not to have been fully carried out in its projected form), although no such listing or advertisement has been found.

2E. THE | BEAUTIES | OF | WASHINGTON IRVING, ESQ. | AUTHOR OF | "THE SKETCH BOOK," "BRACEBRIDGE HALL," | "TALES OF A TRAVELLER," &c. | ILLUSTRATED WITH SIX ETCHINGS, | BY WILLIAM HEATH, ESQ. | A NEW EDITION. | Glasgow: [fancy] | PRINTED FOR RICHARD GRIFFIN & CO. | 64, HUTCHESON STREET. | [rule] | MDCCCXXX.

(15.1 x 9.6 untrimmed): [-]^4 A-I^{6}K-U^6 X-Z^6 Aa-Cc^6 Dd^2. Not reckoned: five inserted etchings, with imprint GLASGOW: GRIFFIN & C^O. 1829.

[i]-[ii], title, on verso printer; [iii]-v, table of contents; [vi], blank; [vii]-viii, Preface; [1]-316, text, printer at foot of last page.

Printer: Robert Malcolm.

Lineation: p. 100, accents ... gra-; p. 200, lediction ... his

In light green paper boards, or in tan-yellow paper boards. On front, title within ornamental border. On back, advertisements within ornamental border. Spine titled in black (including price, *4s. Boards*). White endpapers.

Although a new setting, this edition prints the same selections as the first edition.

BL, CtY, DLC, TxU.

3E. THE | BEAUTIES | OF | WASHINGTON IRVING, | AUTHOR OF | "THE SKETCH BOOK," "BRACEBRIDGE HALL," | "TALES OF A TRAVELLER," &c. | [double rule] | ILLUSTRATED WITH SIX ENGRAVINGS. | BY WM. HEATH, ESQ. | [rule] | LONDON: | PUBLISHED BY BALDWIN, CRADOCK, AND JOY, | 47, PATERNOSTER-ROW. | [rule] | 1831.

(15.7 x 8.5 untrimmed): [i]-viii, [9]-264. Not reckoned: six inserted etchings. Signed in 6's.

Lineation: p. 100, Manhattoes ... [in footnote] New-York.

In drab boards. Front and back blank. Spine titled.

Although there is some small rearrangement and substitution of selections, particularly at the beginning and end of the volume, the selections are in great part still those of the first edition.

InU.

4E.   THE | BEAUTIES | OF | WASHINGTON IRVING, ESQ. | AUTHOR
      OF THE SKETCH BOOK, BRACEBRIDGE HALL, TALES OF A
      TRAVELLER, | KNICKERBOCKER'S HISTORY OF NEW YORK,
      SALMAGUNDI, ETC. | [rule] | ILLUSTRATED WITH| WOOD CUTS,
      ENGRAVED BY THOMPSON; | FROM DRAWINGS | BY GEORGE
      CRUIKSHANK, ESQ. | [illustration of man being knocked over as he fires
      gun in boat] | THE FOURTH EDITION. | [rule] | LONDON: | PRINTED
      FOR THOMAS TEGG AND SON, CHEAPSIDE; | R. GRIFFIN AND
      CO. GLASGOW; AND TEGG, WISE, AND CO. DUBLIN. | 1835.

      (15.5 x 8.8): [i]-viii, [1]-291 [292]. Six pages of advertisements at end. Signed
      in 6's.

      The publisher's terminal advertisements indicate that this volume was a part
      of "The Family Library."

      Printer: C. Whittingham, Chiswick.

      Lineation: p. 100, found ... true ; p. 200, The ... guns,

      Reddish-brown highly figured cloth.

      Except for a few omissions, the selections in this edition duplicate those of
      the first edition; they are even in the same order.

      Literary Gazette, 19 and 26 December 1835, advertised.

      MH, *BL*.

5Ea. ESSAYS AND SKETCHES. | [rule] | BY | WASHINGTON IRVING, |
      AUTHOR OF "THE SKETCH BOOK," "BRACEBRIDGE | HALL," ETC.
      | [stylized swelled rule] | LONDON: | CHARLES TILT, FLEET STREET.
      | [rule] | MDCCCXXXVII.

      (10.3 x 6.4): [i]-viii, [1]-222. Not reckoned: one leaf of illustration before
      title; six pages of advertisements at end.

      The half-title identifies this as a volume of "Tilt's Miniature Classical
      Library."

      Printer: Bradbury and Evans, Whitefriars.

      Lineation: p. 100, COMMISSARY ... fort ; p. 200, These ... they

      Noted in brown morocco, decoration in gilt and blind. AEG. See the
      discussion below of bindings available on later impressions.

      Although the selections repeat some of those in earlier collections, this
      appears to be an original compilation.

      Athenæum, 1 July 1837, listed.

DLC, *BL.*

b.   LONDON: | DAVID BOGUE, FLEET STREET. | [rule] | MDCCCXLIV.

A new preliminary title in red and black replaces the half-title with its series identification.

Printer: the same.

An advertisement in the catalogue bound in *Life and Poetical Remains of Margaret M. Davidson*, London, 1843 (both the Tilt and Bogue and the David Bogue impressions) offers the set of "Tilt's Miniature Classics" in "Ornamented cloth, gilt edges" at 1*s*. 6*d*. each, "Prettily bound in silk" at 2*s*., and "Very handsome in morocco" at 3*s*. As one of the thicker volumes, this one cost 6*d*. per volume extra. Also advertised is a Rosewood Cabinet with glass door and lock for the entire set, and a Morocco Box with glass door to hold ten or twelve volumes.

Since one state of the Tilt and Bogue catalogue is dated 1841, it is obvious that the three bindings were available on the volume before David Bogue's impression of 1844. There is a probability too of earlier unlocated impressions perhaps issued by Tilt and Bogue.

CtY.

1Aa.   THE | BEAUTIES [hollow letters] | OF | WASHINGTON IRVING, | AUTHOR OF | "THE SKETCH-BOOK," "KNICKERBOCKER," | "CRAYON MISCELLANY," &c. | [swelled rule] | Philadelphia: [fancy] | CAREY, LEA, & BLANCHARD. | [rule of 20 dots] | 1835.

(15.3 x 9.4): $[1]^6$ $2\text{-}22^6 23^4$. 23_4 is a blank.

[i]-[ii], half-title, verso blank; [iii]-[iv], title, verso blank [see additional information below]; [v]-viii, table of contents; [9]-270, text.

In some copies, a copyright notice (1835, in the name of Washington Irving) printed on a slip is pasted down on the blank verso of the title.

Lineation: p. 100, Manhattoes. ... [in footnote] New-York.; p. 200, will ... yet

Noted in green and in purple cloth figured with design of intertwined branches. Sides blank. Spine titled in gilt: B E A U T I E S [forming a half-circle] | OF | IRVING. White endpapers.

In the preliminary matter of *Legends of the Conquest of Spain*, Philadelphia: Carey, Lea & Blanchard, 1835 there appears a notice by the publisher:

BEAUTIES OF WASHINGTON IRVING.

The selection bearing the foregoing title was not made by Mr. Irving. It originally appeared in England, and was the piratical act of some English bookseller. A copy was stereotyped by some American publisher, and was about to be put to press in this country, when he was informed that he would be liable to prosecution for infringing the copyrights of the works selected from. Mr. I. purchased the plates to destroy them. He was afterwards induced to permit us to issue an edition for our own benefit. The copyright was taken out and advertised by Mr. Irving's agent, without his knowledge.

This explanation is due to Mr. I., that he may not stand chargeable with the indelicacy of selecting and pointing out any portions of his writings as "beauties."

The selections and the order of presentation are essentially those of the London edition of 1831.

The *Cost Book of Carey & Lea* specifies 1000 copies, finished 31 August 1835. *New-York Mirror*, 3 October 1835, noticed. *New-England Magazine*, November 1835, reviewed. A copy in TxU is dated by the owner September 1835.

TxU (with pasted-down copyright slip), ViU (without copyright slip).

b.   Philadelphia: [fancy] | CAREY, LEA, & BLANCHARD. | [rule of 20 dots] | 1837.

Without copyright notice.

Noted in green cloth with large raised embossed dots. Spine titled in gilt.

ViU.

c.   Philadelphia: [fancy] | CAREY. LEA, & BLANCHARD. | [rule of 20 dots] | 1838.

Noted in two green cloths: H-like cloth with small diamond design; and LI-like lightly textured cloth. Spine titled in gilt.

MH, ViU.

d.   [Philadelphia: Lea & Blanchard, 1839.]

Not seen. DLC attributes copy to CtY. See also *BAL* #10314.

e.   PHILADELPHIA: | LEA & BLANCHARD. | 1841.

Noted in purple coarse T cloth. Spine titled in gilt.

CtY.

f. THE | IRVING GIFT: | BEING | Choice Gems [fancy] | FROM | THE WRITINGS OF | WASHINGTON IRVING. | ILLUSTRATED. | BUFFALO: | PUBLISHED BY PHINNEY & CO. | 1853. All surrounded by double frame lines.

Despite the new title and publisher, printed from the same plates. Double frame lines added around pages.

Copyright 1852 by George P. Putnam.

Added: colored lithographed half-title and title; preliminary portrait and five engraved illustrations.

Purple (?) AR cloth. On sides, in gilt, title and drawing of Diedrich Knickerbocker within triple frame lines with flower-and-leaf decorations inside the four corners. Spine decorated and titled in gilt. AEG. Manila endpapers.

On p. [iii] appears a Publisher's Note:

It is due to Mr. Irving to state, that although the publication of this volume is permitted, through an arrangement with Mr. Putnam, the publisher of the revised edition of Irving's works, the author has had nothing to do with its preparation, and waives all pecuniary interest in it. The selection was made in England.

MH, ViU.

g. BUFFALO: | PUBLISHED BY PHINNEY & CO. | 1857.

Red LI-like cloth in "bark impression." Decorated and illustrated in lavish gilt. All edges marbled. Yellow endpapers.

NjP, TxU.

h. BUFFALO: | PUBLISHED BY PHINNEY & CO. | 1858.

KMK.

2A. THE | BEAUTIES | OF | WASHINGTON IRVING, | AUTHOR OF | "THE SKETCH-BOOK," "KNICKERBOCKER," "CRAYON | MISCELLANY," "LIFE OF COLUMBUS," &c. | [rule] | PHILADELPHIA: | CAREY, LEA & BLANCHARD, | FOR | GEORGE W. GORTON. | 1838.

(18.0 x 10.5 rebound): [i]-viii, [1]-307 [308]. Not reckoned: one page of advertisements at front. Signed in 6's.

No statement of copyright.

Lineation: p. 100, ings ... [in footnote] Brooklyn.; p. 200 [2 missing in page number], body ... me.

Although reset, the contents are the same as those in the first Carey, Lea & Blanchard edition.

The *Cost Book of Carey & Lea* specifies 3000 copies, finished February 1838, I. Ashmead printer.

DLC.

3A.   THE | BEAUTIES | OF | WASHINGTON IRVING. | AUTHOR OF | "THE   SKETCH-BOOK,"   "KNICKERBOCKER,"   "CRAYON | MISCELLANY,"   "LIFE   OF   COLUMBUS,"   &c. | [rule] | PHILADELPHIA: | LEA & BLANCHARD, | SUCCESSOR TO CAREY & co. | FOR | GEORGE W. GORTON. | [rule of 12 dots.] | 1839.

(18.8 x 11.4):   [i]-viii, [13]-349 [350].   Not reckoned: two pages of advertisements at end. Signed in 6's.

No statement of copyright.

Lineation: p. 100, Now ... [in footnote] vol. 1.; p. 200, waves. ... others.

The contents, reset, are the same as those in the 1838 Carey, Lea, & Blanchard edition, the first American edition, with five new selections added at the end.

ViU.

4A.   THE | CRAYON READING BOOK: | COMPRISING | SELECTIONS FROM THE VARIOUS WRITINGS | OF | WASHINGTON IRVING. | Prepared for the Use of Schools. [fancy] | NEW-YORK: | GEO. P. PUTNAM, 155 BROADWAY. | 1849.

(18.4 x 11.8):   [i]-viii, [9]-255 [256].   Not reckoned: eight pages of advertisements at end, paged 24-29, 32-33. Signed in 12's.

Printer: John F. Trow, Printer and Stereotyper, 49 Ann-street, New-York.

Lineation: p. 100, agreed ... to ; p. 200, the ... and

Gray T cloth with black leather shelfback. Sides blank. Spine titled in gilt: CRAYON | READER | [swelled rule] | IRVING

The collection prints a new, original selection of excerpts.

Literary World, 26 May 1849, "In press," "on 1st August"; 7 July 1849, in "Literary Intelligence" column, "in August"; 18 August 1849, listed, and noticed as "just issued."

DLC (2).

5Aa.   Irving Vignettes.   [fancy] | [stylized swelled rule] | VIGNETTE ILLUSTRATIONS | OF THE | WRITINGS | OF | WASHINGTON IRVING, | ENGRAVED ON STEEL BY SMILLIE, HALL. AND OTHERS. | WITH A SKETCH OF HIS LIFE AND WORKS, FROM ALLIBONE'S FORTHCOMING | "DICTIONARY OF AUTHORS," AND PASSAGES FROM THE WORKS | ILLUSTRATED. | [rule] | NEW YORK: | G. P. PUTNAM, No. 321 BROADWAY. | 1857.

(22.0 x 15.9): $[1]^{12}$ $2-12^{12}$. Not reckoned: preliminary engraved portrait and vignette title (undated); twenty-six engraved illustrations through the volume. *BAL* reports the vignette title dated 1858, but no such copy has been located.

[1]-[2], half-title?   [missing in copies examined]; [3]-[4], title, on verso copyright (1857) and printer; [5]-[6], table of contents, verso blank; [7]-[8], table of illustrations, verso blank; [9]-64, "Sketch of Irving's Works"; [65]-80, "Sunnyside and Its Proprietor"; [81]-287, text; [288], blank.

Printer: John F. Trow, 377 & 379 Broadway, Cor. White Street, New York.

Lineation: p. 100, tlemen ... nei-; p. 200, deal ... "It

In *American Publishers' Circular*, 8 August 1857, a Putnam catalogue advertises the volume: "To be published in two sizes, viz.: 1. In square octavo. Cloth extra, $3; gilt edges, $3 50; Turkey morocco extra, $6; Turkey morocco antique, $6. 2. Duodecimo Edition, *uniform with Irving's Works*. Cloth, $1 50; morocco extra, $3 50; morocco antique, $3 50."

No Copy in octavo located. The term in the advertisement is almost certainly the equivalent of "large paper." But no "small paper" copy dated 1857 has been located. (The 1858 impression, in duodecimo, is smaller: 18.9 x 12.5.) Since the "smaller and cheaper edition," as the publisher called it in an advertisement in *American Publishers' Circular*, 26 December 1857, was not published until almost the last day of 1857, it was probably dated 1858.

The collection prints a new, original selection of excerpts.

American Publishers' Circular, 19 September 1857, "soon to be published"; 21 November 1857, "to be published early in December"; 19 December 1857, listed

TxU.

b.   NEW YORK: | G. P. PUTNAM, No. 321 BROADWAY. | 1858.

(18.9 x 12.5). See the discussion under 5Aa of the large paper and small paper format. *BAL* reports both for 1858, but no large paper copy dated 1858 has been located.

The vignette title is dated 1858.

Noted in brown T cloth, decorated and titled in gilt and blind. See the advertisement quoted under 5Aa for other publisher's bindings.

American Publishers' Circular, 26 December 1857, "to be published on Wednesday ... smaller and cheaper edition."

TxU (2).

c. Illustrated Beauties of Irving. [fancy] | [stylized swelled rule] | VIGNETTE ILLUSTRATIONS | OF THE | WRITINGS | OF | WASHINGTON IRVING, | ... | PHILADELPHIA: | CHILDS & PETERSON, 602, ARCH STREET, | 1858.

(21.1 x 12.1).

The vignette title is undated but carries the imprint of Childs & Peterson.

Noted in bright royal blue AR cloth. Front decorated in blind and titled in gilt. Back the same design but all in blind. Spine decorated and titled in gilt. Dark brown endpapers.

CtY.

1F. EXTRACTS | FROM THE | COMPLETE WORKS | OF | WASHINGTON IRVING. | COMPRISING | SELECTIONS FROM EACH OF HIS WRITINGS, | INTERSPERSED WITH EXPLANATORY NOTICES, | [rule] | BY | CHARLES OLLIFFE, | AUTHOR OF THE *Waverley Sketch Book*, etc. | [rule] | ... | PARIS | BAUDRY'S EUROPEAN LIBRARY, | QUAI MALAQUAIS, 3. | [rule] | 1843

(15.9 x 10.0 approx.): pp. xxxii, 328. Bound in 18's.

Pp. [319]-328 constitute an Appendix of poetic quotations "with which several of Irving's tales and essays are elegantly and appositely studded."

Printer: A. René et Ce., Rue de Seine, 32.

Lineation: p. 322, Whose ... were

Not examined. Information from xerographic reproduction of title page and Appendix of the single located copy, in Bibliothèque Nationale.

1G. [*Essays and Sketches*. Carlsruhe: Crauzbauer, 1839.]

222 pp.

Not seen. Copies reported in Badische Landesbibliothek, Karlsruhe, and Staats- und Seminarbibliothek Eichstätt.

Hessischer Landes- und Hochschulbibliothek, Darmstadt reports a copy dated 1834. A typographical error?

2G.   SELECTIONS | FROM THE WORKS | OF | WASHINGTON IRVING. | [rule] | ILLUSTRATED | BY | HENRY RITTER | AND | WILLIAM CAMPHAUSEN. | [rule] | WITH THE PORTRAIT OF HENRY RITTER. | [flowered rule] | LEIPZIG: | F.A. BROCKHAUS. | [rule] | 1856.

(27.0 x 18.5): [-]^4, **^{4}, 1-34^4 35^2. Not reckoned: illustration by Ritter before title.

[i]-[ii], half-title, verso blank; [iii]-[iv], title, verso blank; [v]-xiv, Preface; [xv]-[xvi], table of contents, verso blank; [1]-276, text, printer at foot of 276.

Printer: F.A. Brockhaus, Leipzig.

Lineation: p. 100, ments, ... innocence.; p. 200, of ... along

Noted in salmon-pink P-like rough grain cloth. Decorated in blind, titled in gilt. AEG. Yellow endpapers.

The collection prints an original selection of excerpts.

TxU, *BL*.

3G.   SKETCHES OF A TRAVELLER. | [rule] | AUS DEM | SKETCH-BOOK UND BRACEBRIDGE HALL | VON | WASHINGTON IRVING. | MIT ANMERKUNGEN HERAUSGEGEBEN | VON | DR. H. ROBOLSKY. | [rule] | LEIPZIG, | WOLFGANG GERHARD. | 1859.

Series title: Bibliothek | der | Englischen Literatur | für | Schule und Haus. | Herausgegeben | von | Dr. [in roman] H. Robolsky. | Viertes Heft. | Sketches of a Traveller. [in roman] | [rule] | Leipzig, | Wolfgang Gerhard. | 1859. [in fraktur]

This book of selections is the fourth work in a single volume that also includes *Benjamin Franklin's Autobiography; The Life of Benjamin Franklin*, by Jared Sparks; and *Jacobite Plots Against the Person of William the Third*, from Macaulay's *History of England*. The text is in English, with "Einleitung" and notes in German.

(18.6 x 11.6): [i]-[vi], [1]-2 [3]-[4], 3-102 (text), [103]-[104]. In the text, every other page is blank and not reckoned in the printed pagination. Preliminary and terminal matter is here described in the conventional manner.

Printer: C. P. Melzer, Leipzig.

Lineation: p. 100, the ... comfort!"

Of the eleven selections included, ten are from *The Sketch Book* and one from *Bracebridge Hall*.

Stadtbibliothek München.

TRANSLATIONS

German

[*Washington Irving. Auswahl aus seinen Schriften*. Illustriert von Henry Ritter und Wilhelm Camphausen. Mit dem Bildniss Henry Ritter's (in Stahlst.). Leipzig: F. A. Brockhaus, 1856.]

Paged xv, 291. Illustration by Ritter. Signed in 4's.

A German version of the selections published in English by Brockhaus in 1856.

Not seen. Copy reported in Bayerischer Staatsbibliothek, München.

EXTRACTS FROM IRVING'S WORKS
IN THE VOLUMES OF *BEAUTIES*

Salmagundi

"Absent Friends." (No. XV). A4.

"Autumnal Reflections." (No. XVII). E1-2, 3, 4, 5. A1-3.

"The Cockloft Family." (No. VI). E1-2, 3, 4, 5. A1-3.

"Frenchmen." (No. I). E1-2, 3, 4. A1-3.

"Influences of Nature on the Heart." (No. XIV?). A4.

"Letter from Mustapha Rub-A-Dub Keli Khan to Asem Hacchem...." (No. III). E1-2, 3, 4.

"Letter from Mustapha ... to Asem...." (No. IX). E1-2, 3, 4. A1-3.

"Letter from Mustapha ... to Asem...." (No. XVIII). E1-2, 3, 4. A1-3.

"Letter from Mustapha ... to Muley Helim al Raggi...." (No. XIX). E3. A1-3.

"The Little Man in Black." (No. XVIII). E1-2, 3, 4, 5. A1-3.

"Love of Fame." (No. XVI). A4.

"Mine Uncle John." (No. XI). E1-2, 3, 4, 5.

"My Aunt Charity." (No. IX). E1-2, 3, 4. A1-3.

"On Greatness." (No. XV). E1-2, 4, 5. A3.

"On Modern Fame." (No. XVI). E5.

"Poetry, from Salmagundi." (No. IX). E1-2, 3.

"Style." (No. VIII). E1-2, 3, 4. A1-3

"A Summer Evening in America." (No. XVII). A4.

"Tea, a Poem." (No. XIX). E1-2, 3, 4.

"To Anthony Evergreen, Gent." (No. XIX). E1-2, 3, 4. A1-3.

"Tom Straddle." (No. XII). E1-2, 3, 4, 5. A1-3.

"The Waltz." (No. VII). E1-2, 3, 4. A1-3.

"Will Wizard." (No. V). E1-2, 3, 4. A1-3.

A History of New York

"The Author's Account of His History of New York." E1-2, 3, 4. A1-3.

"Burgomasters of New Amsterdam. " A5.

"Commissary Jacobus Van Curlet." E5.

"Conversion of the Americans." E1-2, 3, 4. A1-3.

"Cosmogony." E1-2, 3, 4. A1-3.

"Description of the Powerful Army that Assembled at the City of New-Amsterdam...." E1-2, 3, 4. A1-3.

"The Dignified Retirement and Mortal Surrender of Peter the Headstrong." E1-2, 3,4. A1-3.

"Dirk Schuiler and the Valiant Peter." E1-2, 3, 4, 5. A1-3.

"Doleful Disaster of Anthony the Trumpeter." E1-2, 3, 4. A1-3.

"Dutch Beaux and Belles." E5.

"Dutch Courtship and Other Customs." A5.

"A Dutch Household of the Olden Time." E5.

"Dutch Legislators." E1-2, 3, 4. A1-3.

"A Dutch Settler's Dream." E1-2, 3, 4. A1-3.

"Dutch Tea Parties." E1-2, 3, 4. A1-3.

"A Dutch Voyage of Discovery." E1-2, 3, 4. A1-3.

"Economy." E5.

"Fate of William the Testy." E5.

"General Von Poffenburgh." E5.

"Governor Peter Stuyvesant." E5.

"The Grand Council of New-Amsterdam -- with Reasons Why an Alderman Should be Fat." E1-2, 3, 4, 5. A1-3.

"The Grief of Peter Stuyvesant." E1-2, 3, 4. A1-3.

"How Peter Stuyvesant Relieved the Sovereign People from the Burden of Taking Care of the Nation...." E1-2, 3, 4, 5. A1-3.

"How the People of New-Amsterdam Were Thrown into a Great Panic...." E1-2, 3, 4. A1-3.

"Master Henry Hudson." E1-2, 3, 4. A1-3.

"Master Robert Juet." E1-2, 3, 4. A1-3.

"A Militia Review." E5.

"Modern Accomplishments." E5.

"Morning." E1-2, 3, 4. A1-3.

"New York As It Is." E5.

"Of Peter Stuyvesant's Expedition Into the East Country." E1-2, 3, 4. A1-3.

"Perseverance." E1-2, 3, 4. A1-3.

"Peter Stuyvesant; His Voyage Up the Hudson." E5.

"Peter Stuyvesant; How He Defended the City of New Amsterdam Against the British for Several Days." E5.

"Portrait of a Dutchman." A4.

"Showing the Great Difficulty Philosophers Have Had in Peopling America...." E1-2, 3, 4. A1-3.

"Showing the Nature of History in General, -- Furthermore, the Universal Acquirements of William the Testy...." E1-2, 3, 4. A1-3.

"The Situation of New-York." A4.

"The Troubles of New-Amsterdam Appear to Thicken...." E1-2, 3, 4. A1-3.

"Varieties of Female Character." E5.

"Voyage Up the Hudson." A4.

"War." E1-2, 3, 4. A1-2.

"A Warlike Portrait of the Great Peter." E1-2, 3, 4. A1-3.

"William the Testy." E5.

"Wouter Van Twiller." E1-2, 3, 4, 5. A1-3.

"A Yankee Squatter." E5.

The Sketch Book

"The Angler." E3. A1-3.

"Blindman's Buff." ("The Christmas Dinner"). E3. A1-3.

"Book Making." ("The Art of Book-Making"). E1-2, 3, 4. A1-3.

"The Broken Heart." E1-2, 3, 4. A1-3.

"Christmas." A4.

"A Contrast." ("The Country Church"). E1-2, 3, 4. A1-3.

"Death." ("Rural Funerals"). A4.

"A Desirable Match." ("The Legend of Sleepy Hollow"). E1-2, 3, 4. A1-3.

"Domestic Scene." ("Christmas Eve"). E1-2, 3. A1-3.

"A Dutch Entertainment." ("The Legend of Sleepy Hollow"). E1-2, 3, 4. A1-3.

"English Stage Coachmen." ("The Stage Coach"). E1-2, 3, 4. A1-3.

"The Family of the Lambs." ("Little Britain"). E1-2, 3, 4. A1-3.

"Genius." ("Roscoe"). E1-2, 3, 4. A1-3.

"Ichabod Crane." ("The Legend of Sleepy Hollow"). E1-2, 3, 4. A1-3.

"Ichabod Crane and the Galloping Hessian." ("The Legend of Sleepy Hollow"). E1-2, 3, 4. A1-3.

"The Inn Kitchen." E1-2, 3. A1-3.

"An Invitation." ("The Legend of Sleepy Hollow"). E1-2, 3, 4. A1-3.

"James I. of Scotland." ("A Royal Poet"). E3. A1-3.

"John Bull." E1-2, 3, 4. A1-3.

"Land." ("The Voyage"). E1-2, 3, 4. A1-3.

"Master Simon." ("Christmas Eve"). E1-2, 3. A1-3.

"Mutability of Literature." E3. A1-3.

"An Obedient Hen-pecked Husband." ("Rip Van Winkle"). E1-2, 3, 4. A1-3.

"Philip of Pokanoket." A4.

"The Pride of the Village." E1-2, 3, 4. A1-3.

"A Rival." ("The Legend of Sleepy Hollow"). E1-2, 3, 4. A1-3.

"Rural Life in England." E3. A1-3.

"Sleepy Hollow." ("The Legend of Sleepy Hollow"). E1-2, 3, 4. A1-3.

"The Spectre Bridegroom." E1-2, 3. A1-3.

"Storm at Sea." ("The Voyage"). E1-2, 3, 4. A1-3.

"Superstition." ("The Legend of Sleepy Hollow"). E1-2, 3, 4. A1-3.

"Traits of Indian Character." A4.

"The Voyage." A4

"Westminster Abbey." E1-2, 3, 4. A1-3, 4.

"The Widow and Her Son." E1-2, 3, 4. A1-3, 4.

"The Wife." E1-2, 3, 4. A1-3, 4, 5.

"A Wreck at Sea." ("The Voyage"). E1-2, 3, 4. A1-3.

Bracebridge Hall

"Consequence." ("Dolph Heyliger"). E1-2,3,4. A1-3.

"Invisible Companions." ("St. Mark's Eve"). A4.

"The Lovers." A5.

"Ready Money Jack." A5.

"The Storm Ship." A4.

"A Thunderstorm on the Hudson." ("Dolph Heyliger"). A4.

"A Wet Sunday in a Country Inn." ("The Stout Gentleman"). E1-2, 3. A1-3.

"Wives." A4, 5.

Tales of a Traveller

"The Adventure of the Englishman." E1-2.

"The Bold Dragoon." A5.

"Buckthorne and the Shopkeeper's Daughter." ("Buckthorne"). A5.

"Filial Affection." ("Grave Reflections of a Disappointed Man"). A4.

"Italian Scenery." ("The Italian Banditti"). A4.

"Kidd the Pirate." A3.

"A Practical Philosopher." A4.

Oliver Goldsmith

"Character of Goldsmith." A4, 5.

"Dr. Johnson Reading the 'Vicar.'" A5.

Life and Voyages of Columbus

"Americus Vespucius." A5.

"Arrival at Court in Irons." A4.

"The Character of Columbus." A4.

"Christopher Columbus." A5.

"Columbus at the Convent of La Rabida." A4.

"Columbus Before the Council at Salamanca." A4.

"Columbus in Irons." A4.

"Convent of La Rabida." A4, 5.

"Departure of Columbus on His Second Voyage." A4.

"Discovery of the Mines of Hayna." A4.

"Embarcation of Columbus at Palos." A5.

"Ferdinand and Isabella of Spain." A4.

"First Landing of Columbus in the New World." A4.

"First Voyage of Columbus, Discovery of Land." A4, 5.

"A Gold Mania in Hispaniola in 1503." A4.

"Reception of Columbus by the Spanish Court." A4.

The Conquest of Granada

"Boabdil el Chico." A3.

"Boabdil's Return to Granada." A4.

"The Christian Army at the City of Cordova." A4.

"How King Ferdinand Foraged the Vega...." A3.

"How the Castilian Sovereigns Took Possession of Granada." A4.

"Isabella of Arragon." A5.

"Lamentations of the Moors for the Battle of Lucena." A4.

"Morn, Noon, and Evening at Granada." A4.

"Surrender of Granada." A5.

The Companions of Columbus

"Discovery of the Pacific Ocean." A4.

"Execution of Vasco Nuñez." A4.

"Vasco Nuñez on the Shores of the South Sea." A4.

The Alhambra

"The Alhambra by Moonlight." A3, 4.

"The Court of Lions." A4.

"Palace of the Alhambra." A5.

A Tour on the Prairies

"A Bee Hunt." A4.

"Crossing the Arkansas." A4.

"A Night Scene on the Prairies." A4.

"Picturesque March on the Prairies." A4.

"Thunder Storm on the Prairies." A4.

Abbotsford

"Scottish Music." A4.

"Some Traits of Sir W. Scott's Character." A4.

"Visit to Abbotsford." A5.

Newstead Abbey

"Parliament Oak, Sherwood Forest." A4.

"Visit to Newstead Abbey." A5.

Astoria

"The Black Mountains." A4.

"Climate and Productions of Oregon." A4.

"Domestic Life of an Indian." A4.

"Flight of Pigeons." A4.

"An Indian Council Lodge." A4.

"The Mouth of the Columbia." A4.

"Prairie Hunting Grounds." A4.

"Return of a War Party." A4.

"Settlement at Astoria." A5.

"The Wilderness of the Far West." A4.

Adventures of Capt. Bonneville

"Wind River Mountains." A5.

Mahomet and His Successors

"The Faith of Islam." A5.

"Nocturnal Journey from Meccah." A5.

Wolfert's Roost

"Birds of Spring." A4.

Life of George Washington

"The Fate of André." A5.

"Washington's Courtship, 1758." A5.

RICHELIEU

Close reading of Irving's Journal for 1823-1826 and his correspondence with John Howard Payne during the same period proves his primary authorship of *Richelieu*. Even after the first composition, he continued to revise and work at the play. On 23 October 1825, for instance, he enters in his Journal, "Wrote all [day] at Richelieu, completely alterd the character of Mad Fleurey -- Sent this alteration to Payne by post." Before the play was produced, George Colman, the Examiner of Plays, objected to the text, and the Lord Chamberlain withheld the necessary license. As Irving explains the reason in a letter to Payne, 27 January 1826, with a good deal of irony, "It certainly did not enter into my brain that it could be considered applicable to the English court & English statesmen of the present day." After revision -- "garbled by the theatrical play wrights," as Irving described it in a letter of 7 February 1826 -- the play was allowed to be produced, on 11 February 1826 at the Covent Garden Theatre, with Richelieu renamed Duke de Rougemont. An unfortunate title, *The French Libertine*, was chosen for the production. But Irving had his way finally in the printed text: it offers the original uncensored version under the original title. And that too was at his direction; on 7 February 1826, he wrote Payne, "I think you had better let Richelieu appear in America in the original form & state in a notice prefixed to it, that alterations have been made in it in England without your privity in compliance with objections of the licensers, for some political reasons which could not prevail in America." His suggested statement is repeated almost verbatim in Payne's "Advertisement" to the volume.

As with the earlier play of *Charles the Second*, Irving insisted that his name not be associated publicly with this play. (See his letters to Payne of 29 December 1823 and 31 January 1824, quoted in the introduction to the discussion of *Charles the Second*.) Again, his name does not appear on the title page. But in the dedication to Irving in the printed edition, published in America, Payne finally revealed the name, if not the full extent of authorship:

> In the little comedy of Charles the Second I have referred to the assistance you gave me, without venturing to violate your injunction with regard to the concealment of your name. But that aid has been repeated to such an extent in the present work, as to render it imperative upon me to offer you my thanks publicly, and to beg you will suffer me to dedicate it to one from whose pen it has received its highest value.

The revelation, however, was hardly a surprise to Irving. On 2 October 1825 he had written Payne, "Do not send the dedication without letting me see it -- I want it to be as simple as possible & free from all puffing & praising." On 3 January and 27 January 1826 he wrote his approval of Payne's draft. The dedication by Payne is dated 13 February 1826.

1A. RICHELIEU: | A | *DOMESTIC TRAGEDY,* | FOUNDED ON FACT. | [As accepted for performance at the Theatre Royal, Covent Garden, London; before it was altered by order of the | Lord Chamberlain, and produced under a new name.] | IN FIVE ACTS. | *BY JOHN HOWARD PAYNE,* | AUTHOR OF "THERESE," "BRUTUS," "ADELINE," | "CHARLES THE SECOND," &c. &c. &c. | [rule] | *Now first Printed from the Author's Manuscript.* | [rule] | *NEW-YORK:* | PUBLISHED BY E. M. MURDEN, | At the Dramatic Repository and Circulating Library, | No. 4 Chamber-street. | [rule] | 1826.

(17.0 x 10.9; in untrimmed copy examined, last gathering 14.3 x 10.9): [A]^6 B-F^{6}G^4.

[1]-[2], title, on verso copyright ("twenty-seventh day of May, A. D. 1826, in the fiftieth year of the Independence" by C. S. Van Winkle); [3]-4, dedication to Washington Irving, dated Paris, February 13, 1826; [5]-6, Advertisement, dated Paris, February 13, 1826; [7]-[8], characters, verso blank; [9]-79, text; [80], blank.

Lineation: p. 25, *Rich.* ... are ; p. 50, band's ... in

Something of the history of the American publication can be deduced from scattered pieces of information:

Irving to Payne, Bordeaux, 3 January 1826 (misdated 1825), "You need not send it [the manuscript] to me, as there is no opportunity of forwarding it hence to New York -- Send it ... directed to Mr. E. Irving New York. I inclose you a letter to be forwarded with it, which will perhaps explain all that is necessary."

The New-York Mirror, 28 October 1826, "*Richelieu.* -- The manuscript of a new tragedy, by John Howard Payne, Esq. with this title, has been forwarded by the author to Mr. E. M. Murden of this city, for publication." "The author will receive the whole profits arising from the sale of this publication."

Ebenezer Irving to Washington Irving, 15 March 1827, "The publisher had one thousand copies printed at this own expense, seven hundred of which are in my hands. The other three hundred he has to repay him his expenses." (*Life and Letters,* II, 175-176)

MB, NNHi (untrimmed), PU (seen in microprint).

THE LIFE AND VOYAGES OF
CHRISTOPHER COLUMBUS

The Life and Voyages of Columbus has a prolonged and complicated textual history of manuscript revisions, although a fairly simple printing history. The text of the first London edition, published by John Murray in 1828, was taken from a manuscript, still extant, that was itself a copy by five scribes in Spain, later partially revised by Irving. On 29 July 1827, Irving wrote from Madrid to his friend and future literary agent in London, Colonel Thomas Aspinwall, "The Manuscript I send you contains the first nine books or Seventy three Chapters, making 716 pages. There are nine more books containing fifty chapters, together with notes and illustrations and a few documents." The first manuscript bundle in fact left Madrid on 9 August 1827; the second, or remainder of the text, was sent on 20 August; the third, or "illustrations," was planned for 15 October but apparently sent on 18 October. Characteristically, Irving continued to send small changes up to, and beyond, the last chance of having them included in the printed text. There are, however, noticeable variations between the manuscript and the printed version, the work of an editor or proofreader now unknown. Irving did not read proof for the edition.

The first American edition, 1828, was printed from a separate manuscript, now lost, which Irving sent from Spain in two bundles dispatched a week apart, in September 1827. That manuscript was seen through the press by Irving's brother Ebenezer who had the book printed up and then sold the sheets to the New York publishers, G. and C. Carvill. Again, Irving did not read proof. The two printed editions, London and New York, vary in text.

When Irving received copies in Spain of the first London edition, in May 1828, he immediately set to work industriously on revisions for a proposed second edition. But that revised second London edition was never to appear, despite Irving's numerous requests to Murray, and even though Murray did in fact bring out a second edition, although one corrected only by his own firm and masquerading as the original edition. Although Irving's revisions for a second edition were never published by Murray, some of them found their way into the second American edition, 1831. The manuscript sources for those American revisions are now lost. Again, Irving did not read the proof.

In the Author's Revised Edition, published by George P. Putnam, 1848-49, Irving at last saw all of his own revisions in print, and, for the first time, read and revised proof for the edition. John H. McElroy, in his Textual Commentary to the Twayne edition, estimates that for this new edition Irving introduced something like one new word in every ten words of text and made substantive change to perhaps sixty percent of the sentences that had existed in the second American edition. The manuscript that served as printer's copy, now at ViU, is made up of a revised copy of the second London edition, with added pages of manuscript, shifted pages of printed text, and added pages from the second American edition (the Carey, Lea & Blanchard impression of 1835), all loosely interleaved. (Some of the changes in the original London printed text, it is interesting to note, were made by a scribe some years before 1848.) By now, the work was recast, re-thought and re-documented. With the revised version of *The Companions of Columbus* added at the end of *Columbus*, and the expanded "Appendix: Containing Illustrations and Documents" added after *Companions*, Irving had produced, in effect, a new work and one presumably satisfying his final desires for his final audience. The London printing of the Author's Revised Edition, accordingly, is simply an impression from duplicate plates of the American edition.

The work was popular on the continent, being reprinted in English a number of times by Galignani and Baudry in Paris. Soon after its first publication it was translated into Dutch, French, German, Italian, Polish, Russian, and Spanish. All of those reprints and translations seem to have been derived from the first London edition.

The four texts of the work for which Irving was responsible may be quickly and conveniently distinguished, in the body of the work, by the two opening sentences of Book I, Chapter II.

First London edition: "Columbus left the university of Pavia while yet extremely young, and returned to his father's house in Genoa. It has been asserted by Guistimani, a contemporary writer, in his annals of that republic...."

First American edition: [First sentence the same]. It has been asserted by Giustiniani, a contemporary writer, in his Annals of that Republic...."

Second American edition: "Columbus left the university of Pavia while he was yet extremely young and returned to his father's house in Genoa. Here, according to a contemporary historian, he remained for some time...." [In a footnote, the historian is identified as Giustiniani.]

Author's Revised Edition: Neither sentence appears. Some of the content appears in Book I, Chapter I.

1-2E.   The first and second English editions are so nearly alike in appearance that
         they are more easily described, and the distinctions between them defined, in
         one entry than in two separate ones.

         In past bibliographical work on Irving, the two editions have been
thought one edition or treated as one. But, in fact, they are clearly two, both
in the strict sense of the term-- they are printed from two different settings of
type--and in the popular sense of a separate printing, particularly one that
makes some changes. The second edition of Volumes II, III and IV are
completely reset, from first to last page. Volume I does preserve the original
setting almost intact for signatures B-I, K-U, and X, but is completely reset in
title and preliminary matter (signatures [A], a, b) and in the ten final
signatures, Y-Z, 2A-2H. The resetting is in the same type style and generally
line-for-line. A good many textual changes appear as well, although none
bears the mark of authorial revision. Although there are a few substantive
changes ("uncultured" and "uncultivated" at I, 329.10; or "the ships" and "their
ships" at III, 211.5) they are very few and are almost certainly the work of a
compositor or editor. The vast majority of the changes are in punctuation,
spelling and capitalization, either to correct errors in the first edition or to
impose a more nearly "correct" house style on the text. It is perhaps a
comment on the demands of printing that if the typographical errors of the
first edition are generally corrected, a number of new ones are made in the
second. Since copies with mixed sheets have been seen (at ViU, for
instance, there is a copy of Vol. I in original binding that contains signature
[A] and leaf D_6 from the first edition although the rest of the volume is
second edition) , and rebound sophisticated copies either noted or suspected,
an identification of each reset signature in the four volumes is offered here.
         Why the early chapters of Volume I were reprinted from the first
setting may never be known. The text of the early retained chapters seems
no more "correct" than that of the first setting of the later chapters of Volume
I or of the text of the last three volumes. There is little doubt, however, that
the second edition follows after the first and is set from it. Internal textual
evidence is strong. Although there are possible exceptions, the text in
general moves toward the accepted conventions of the time in spelling and
punctuation. It is on this fact that the principal argument must rest. Spot
checks of the two texts with the manuscript from which the text was derived
are inconclusive, since not only was the house styling imposed heavily on the
manuscript text, but it is also apparent that some person or persons made
pervasive changes in the text, presumably at the proof stage. But one other
piece of evidence is suggestive at least. The text of the first American
edition, set from a manuscript now lost, is often close in details to the English
manuscript. A check of the thirteen representative variants listed here for
Vol. I of the English editions reveals that of the ten readings that appear in
the American edition, seven of the first English edition readings correspond

to the American text, and only three of the second English edition readings correspond to the American text--and one of those may be a misprint.

Internal bibliographical evidence of an absolute nature is missing. I can find no citable, clear instances of type batter or wear in the retained signatures of Volume I. Perhaps that is why the setting was retained. Subjectively, the early parts of the first edition copies of Volume I seem more crisp in type impression than those of the second edition; and they are occasionally more nearly perfect in margin alignment. That is, at best, complementary information. The paper is not dated or watermarked in either edition. External evidence is unfortunately not much greater. Perhaps the strongest that I can cite is that I have not seen a second edition copy with an early date of acquisition recorded in it. The copy that I used for primary collation and as a control for checking other copies [TxU, E111.I86.1828.Vol.1-4] is a prize book given at Trinity College, Dublin, Paschal term, 1830, two years after the publication of the first edition. The second edition also is noticeably scarcer in public collections than the first, suggesting that it represents a smaller printing.

One is tempted to suspect that John Murray, badgered by Washington Irving for an enlarged revised second edition (see the discussion in Professor John McElroy's edition of *Columbus*), deliberately omitted from the actual second edition any identification of it as a new edition; he needed more copies for sale but did not want to undertake the expensive, time-consuming and bothersome job of an enlarged revision. It is more probable, however, that the printer had already printed off as many more second edition copies as Murray needed for sale, simply not bothering with an identification of the second edition, before Irving, then in Spain, became importunate for still another edition. Irving did not send copy for the desired revisions until August of 1828. Whatever the specific circumstances, Murray put off Irving with vague discussion of a "second edition" that as far as Irving ever knew he never produced, but that in fact he did, whether knowingly or not. It should be noted, however, that both he and Irving were probably using the term "edition" not in the present bibliographical sense of a resetting but in the popular sense of a revision. And the very minor revisions of the concealed second edition would not have satisfied Washington Irving's demands.

The Four Volumes, Both Editions, in Common.

A | HISTORY | OF THE | LIFE AND VOYAGES | OF | CHRISTOPHER COLUMBUS. | BY | WASHINGTON IRVING. | Venient annis | Sæcula seris, quibus Oceanus | Vincula rerum laxet, et ingens | Pateat tellus, Typhisque novos | Detegat Orbes, nec sit terris | Ultima Thule. | *Seneca, Medea.* | IN FOUR VOLUMES. | VOL. I. [II., III., IV.] | LONDON: | JOHN MURRAY, ALBEMARLE-STREET. | [rule] | MDCCCXXVIII.

(22.3 x 14.4 untrimmed): Vol. I. $[A]^2$ a^4 b^2 B-I^8 K-U^8 X-Z^8 2A-2G^8 2H^6. One copy, in original boards, seen with b^2 inserted between A_3 and A_4. One copy, in original boards, seen with the last leaf pasted down to form the endpaper. Vol. II. [a]-b^2 B-I^8 K-U^8 X-Z^8 2A-2H^8 2I^6. Vol. III. [a]-b^2 B-I^8 B-I^8 K-U^8 X-Z^8 2A-2D^8. Vol. IV. $[A]^4$ B-I^8 K-U^8 X-Z^8 AA-HH^8 II^4 KK^2.

Issued with two fold-out charts, inserted at apparent random in Vols. I and II; either chart may appear in either volume, or both in Vol. I. The charts remain unchanged in the second edition.

Printer: Vols. I, II, III, W. Clowes, Stamford-Street. Vol. IV, Thomas Davison, Whitefriars.

Lineation: Vol. I. p. 100, Perez ... Castile.; p. 300, the magnificent ... [in footnote] cap. 29. Vol. II. p. 100 , falls ... [in footnote] 90. MS.; p. 300, Columbus ... and Vol. III. p. 100, CHAPTER II. ...supposed ; p. 300, them ... made Vol. IV. p. 100, and ... intercession ; p. 300, that ... [in footnote] tower.

Copies of the first and second edition have been seen or (more often) reported in a wide variety of bindings that together constitute the common, frequently seen form of binding: brown, drab, dark rose, and light blue-green paper boards; blue paper boards with gray paper shelfbacks, tan or drab paper boards with purple cloth shelfbacks, gray-green paper boards with maroon cloth shelfbacks, gray paper boards with figured green cloth shelfbacks; gray-blue cloth. All are unprinted, with a white paper label on the spines.

The label has been noted in two states:

[A]. [rule] | LIFE | AND | VOYAGES | OF | COLUMBUS. | BY | WASHINGTON IRVING. | [rule] | £2 2s. | [rule].

[B]. Only fragments remain in the single copy seen, but enough to indicate that the lower portion showed only title | volume number | double rule.

State [A] is, in overwhelming numbers, the standard or common state. The single copy seen in State [B] is a first edition, bound in light blue-green paper boards.

One copy of the second edition has been seen in a different form of binding: brown H-like cloth. Sides decorated in blind with vine and flower design. Spine titled in gilt: IRVING'S | VOYAGES | OF | COLUMBUS | VOL. I [II, III., IV]. Cream endpapers. A late form?

Volume I

Contents of both editions: [two pages, unpaged], half-title, on verso printer; [i]-[ii], title, verso blank; [iii]-viii, Preface, dated Madrid, 1827; [ix]-xii, table of contents; [xiii]-[xiv], fly-title, verso blank; [1]-473, text; [474], blank; [475]-[476], printer, verso blank. One copy, in original boards, seen with pp. [475]-[476] missing; apparently so issued.

In the second edition, signatures [A], a, b, and Y-Z, 2A-2H are reset, with the basic text taken from that of the first edition. The resetting is generally faithful to a line-for-line reproduction, although there are a few exceptions [see, for instance 337.2-4, 389.2-4, 433.6-8, 465.12-14]. Representative identifying changes, at least one for each signature, are offered in the table below, chosen from textual differences rather than differences in lineation or type justification.

Page & Line	First Edition	Second Edition
Title page	Date 1.9 in extent; same length as rule above it.	Date 1.8- cm. in extent; slightly shorter than the rule above it.
iv.8f	manuscript,	manuscript
vii.1	Antonio with	Antonio, with
x.3f	Cruize	Cruise
329.10	uncultured	uncultivated
349.10f	Providence	Providence!
353.3f	anything he	than any he
381.7	to think, that	to think that,
385.4f	rope;	rope:
402.5f	Still, the king	Still the King
421.6	providence	Providence
441.1f	seniors	seigniors
451.7	expedition, was	expedition was
472.footnote	Vasconcelos	Vasconceles

In both editions, the footnote on p. 92 appears in two states: lines 6-7 read "from/from", or (correctly) "Hope,/from". This appears to be a stop-press correction, oddly enough in both editions.

In the first edition, leaf D$_6$ (pp. 43-44) appears in two forms and more than two states:

Form A. Page 43: The first line begins "to the coast. . ."; line 4 ends with "strict"; the identification "VOL. I." is present at the foot of the page; and an

asterisk is present below the footnote, set under the first N in N. Mundo".
Page 44: Line 14 of the footnote reads "Terroto por Cofino."

Form B. Page 43: the first line begins "like Columbus..."; line 5 ends with
"strict"; the identification "VOL. I." is not at the foot of the page; and there is
no asterisk below the footnote. Page 44: Line 14 of the footnote reads
"Derroto por Tofino."

Form A has been noted, in copies in original condition, both on a cancelled
leaf and on an integral leaf. Form B has been noted only on a cancelled leaf.

In the second edition, a third form of the leaf appears:

Form C. Page 43: The first line begins "to the coast..."; line 4 ends with "eco-";
the identification "VOL. I." is present at the foot of the page; and an asterisk
is present below the footnote, set under the d of "del". Page 44: Line 11 of
the footnote reads "Venet. 1606).", with the period outside of the closing
parenthesis; and line 14 of the footnote reads "Terroto por Cofino."

The leaf of Form C has been noted as a cancel in one rebound copy of the
second edition. In other loosely rebound copies, the leaf gives every
appearance of being integral. No copy located in original binding. Unless
further evidence appears, the leaf should be considered as existing both in the
cancelled and in the integral state.

Signature [A], the half-title with the imprint of the printer on the verso, also
occurs in two impressions in the first edition: identifiable by the presence or
absence of a colon in the printer's imprint. Since copies with a genuine half-
title are not common, a definitive statement should be avoided. The colon is
not present in the copies of the second edition examined.

Volume II

Contents of both editions: [i]-[ii], half-title, on verso printer; [iii]-[iv], title,
verso blank; [v]-[viii], table of contents; [1]-490, text; [491]-[492], printer,
verso blank.

In the second edition, all signatures are reset. The resetting is fairly faithful
to a line-for-line reproduction, although not so faithful as the later signatures
of Vol. I. Representative identifying changes, as least one for each signature,
are offered in the table below, chosen from textual differences in all but a few
instances.

Page & Line	First Edition	Second Edition
Title page	The *S* of *Seneca* is directly beneath the space between rr of "terris" above, and the comma is to the right of any of the type in the quotation	The *S* is beneath the t of "terris", and the comma is beneath the second o of "novos" above it.
[v].1f	Three dots before page number.	Four dots before page number.
15.3f	and, straying	and straying
19.10	commanded, that,	commanded that,
37.3	exertions, but	exertions; but
51.5	arrived with	arrived, with
66.3f	natives |	natives, |
89.3f	| facts; and	| of facts, and
111.4	blood, |	[111.5] blood; |
114.9f	caciques	cicaques
133.10f	father Boyle	Father Boyle
147.7f	| Asia,	| Asia;
169.12	Cuba it	Cuba, it
181.3	every thing	everything
193.footnote.1	p. 24.)	p. 24)
209.8f	island, |	island |
225.5	sister |	sister, |
243.1	them as	them, as
257.3	weapons and	weapons, and
275.7	made	make
292.7	East	east
309.3-2f	cause | with	[309.2f] cause, with
334.7f	employed, for	employed for

337.12	cavarels	caravels
367.9	justify		jnstify	
371.3	freshness and	freshness, and
394.1	when once		when	
407.2	atmosphere, and	atmosphere; and
428.11	fellow-caciques	follow-caciques
433.5	posts thus	posts, thus
463.8	a messenger	a message
469.2	cacique, Maconiatex	cacique Maconiatex
489.13	disasterous	disastrous

In the first edition, p. [v] appears in two states: in line 4f, the third dot before the page number (93) is a comma, or (correctly) is a dot. This appears to be a stop-press correction.

In the second edition, two pages demonstrate variant states. On p. 50, one state shows no period after "VI" in the heading and no comma after "Escobido" on line 7f; the other, a period after "VI" in the heading and a comma after "Escobido" on line 7f. No sequence is suggested. On page 490, one state (presumably the earlier, although not necessarily) is mispaged 460; the other is correctly paged.

As in Vol. I, the printer's imprint on the verso of the half-title of the first edition appears in two settings: with or without a colon. The same warning should apply. Again, the colon is not present in the copies of the second edition examined.

On pp. 288-289 of both editions, in all copies examined, a hiatus in the text occurs between pages, so that they read, " . . . under the supervision of the admiral, or, | absence, in the presence of those in authority . . ."

Volume III

Contents of the first edition: [i]-[ii], half-title, on verso printer; [iii]-[iv], title, verso blank; [v]-viii, table of contents; [1]-413, text; [414], blank; [415]-[416], printer, verso blank.

Contents of the second edition: the same, except [414], printer; [415]-[416], blank.

In the second edition, all signatures are reset. The resetting is fairly faithful to a line-for-line reproduction, although not so faithful as the later signatures of Vol. I. Representative identifying changes, at least one for each signature, are offered in the table below, chosen from textual differences rather than differences in lineation or type justification.

Page & Line	First Edition	Second Edition
Title page	The s of "novos" is only slightly to the right of the s of "ingens" above it.	The second o of "novos" is directly under the s of "ingens" above it, and the s of "novos" is well to the right of the s above it.
vi.14	Supersede	supersede
15.3	that until	that, until
17.7	Sovereigns	sovereigns
37.8f	Columbus, |	Columbus |
53.5f	life: |	life. |
66.7f	| serted;	| serted,
78.page no.	87	78
90.2f	Alpuxarra in	Alpuxarra, in
97.4f	shewn	shown
113.5	letter-patent	letters patent
129.7	he mournfully,	he, mournfully,
145.5f	| bus:	| bus;
162.7f	were	where
179.4	this, Columbus	this Columbus
195.11f	day, |	day |
211.5	the ships	their ships
227.8	and sea |	and sea- |
251.5f	Antiquities	antiquities
270.13	manner in	manner, in
273.5	river |	river, |
289.footnote.2	de Diego	por Diego
317.footnote	collec.,	collec.

327.footnote	c. 102.	cap. 102.
341.13	San Domingo	San domingo
356.9	them, and	them; and
373.11f	Isabella,	Isabella;
387.5f	concurring	concuring
405.1	bloodthirstiness	blood-thirstiness

Note: In the first edition, p. 60 has been noted both with and without the page number; no other differences on the page.

Title pages of the first edition show minute type shifts in two lines when compared on the mechanical collator, but so slight as to leave open question of whether resetting has occurred or simply some slight tightening of the type in the lines.

Volume IV

Contents of both editions: [i]-[ii], half-title, on verso printer; [iii]-[iv], title, verso blank; [v]-vii, table of contents; [viii], blank; [1]-439, text; [440], blank; [441]-489, Index; [490], blank; [491], blank; [492], printer.

In the second edition, all signatures are reset. The resetting is generally faithful to a line-for-line reproduction, although there are a number of exceptions [see, for instance, 5.1-4, 189.1-3, 318.6-7, 448.1-2]. Representative identifying changes, at least one for each signature, are offered in the table below, chosen from textual differences in all but a few instances.

Page & Line	First Edition	Second Edition
Title page	The comma of "Seneca," is well to the right of any of the type in the quotation.	The comma is beneath the space between vo in "novos".
vii.6	Of the	On the
6.1	| ble massacre	| massacre
18.10	Morales |	Morales, |
38. heading	Book XVIII.	Book XVIII
57.3f	distin- |	di- |
77.1	it was	is was
88.5	Cuba in	Cuba, in

100.11	1825	1525
114.footnote	Anales	Annales
131.footnote.1	Spotorno.	Sportono,
147.footnote.1	partizan	partisan
169.5f	&c*."	&c.*"
185.1f	extre- |	ex- |
196.9f	teconding	seconding
210.11	inserted into	inserted in
235.9f	decades	Decades
242.9f	whereas,	whcrcas
266.5f	head-land	headland
278.1f	all |	all, |
289.9f	and, with	and with
[313].3	island, Atalantis	island Atalantis
325.9	testified, having	testified having
351.4	licenses	licences
354.11f	with a	with the
379.6f	World and	World, and
385.3f	| cation,	| cation
401.2	OF THE	ON THE
421.10	inherit this	inherit his
435.7	Diego, my	Diego my
450.9f	| bus' indignation	| bus's indignation
469.11f	introduced to	introduced into
486.17f	introduced to	introduced into

Note: On p. [393] of the first edition, the chapter heading appears as "XXXII." or as "No. XXXII." (which matches the other chapter headings); presumably a stop-press correction.

A letter from the modern publisher to *BAL*, 2 December 1964, specifies 4000 copies, made up of 3000 plus a run-on of 1000 copies printed without taking the type off the machine.

First Edition. *Literary Gazette*, 8, 15 December 1827, "In the press," "In December"; 2 February 1828, reviewed, with opening comment, "This work will appear in the course of the ensuing month"; 9 February 1828, announced for "Monday, the 11th instant"; 16 February 1828, listed at *2l. 2s.* in boards. *Athenæum*, 12 February 1828, listed; 12, 19, 26 February 1828, reviewed. *Literary Chronicle*, 16 February 1828, "We are not anxious to make up *reviews* from *proof sheets*." Irving to John Murray, 22 September 1850, "published in London Feby 8th 1829 [1828]."

Second Edition (although not so identified in advertisements). *Athenæum*, 1 April 1828, advertised for "This day," with extracts from two reviews, "4 vols., 8vo, with a chart, *2l. 2s.*" *Literary Gazette*, 5 April 1828, advertised under "Books Published This Day," with extract from one review, number of charts not stated.

First Edition: MH, NN, TxU (4), Private hands. Second Edition: CtY, MH, TxU (2), ViU.

3E. THE LIFE AND VOYAGES | OF | CHRISTOPHER COLUMBUS; | TOGETHER WITH | THE VOYAGES OF HIS COMPANIONS. | BY WASHINGTON IRVING. | Venient annis | Sæcula seris, quibus, Oceanus | Vincula, rerum laxet, et ingens | Pateat tellus, Typhisque novos | Detegat Orbes, nec sit terris | Ultima Thule. | SENECA: *Medea*. | A NEW AND REVISED EDITION. | IN THREE VOLUMES. -- VOL. 1. [II., III.] | LONDON: | JOHN MURRAY, ALBEMARLE STREET. | 1849. All within single frame lines. In a variant state, the volume number of Vol. I is in Roman.

Printed from duplicate plates of the New York Author's Revised Edition with new half-titles and titles, rules added around all pages, preliminary matter rearranged, and in a different collation.

(22.3 x 14.2): Vol. I. a^8 B-I^8 K-U^8 X-Z^8 AA-DD^8 EE^4. Vol. II. $[A]^4$ B-I^8 K-U^8 X-Z^8 AA-HH^8 II^4. Vol. III. $[A]^8$ B-I^8 K-U^8 X-Z^8 AA-HH^8 II^2. Not reckoned: chart inserted in Vols. I, II; varying states of advertisements.

In two states; the sequence is probable.

A. *Vol. I.* On title page, the volume number is an Arabic numeral. One page of preliminary advertisements, dated June, 1849. EE_4 is a blank.

   Vol. II. One page of preliminary advertisements, dated June, 1849. II_4 is a blank.

   Vol. III. One page of preliminary advertisements, dated June, 1849.

B. *Vol. I.* On title page, the volume number is a Roman numeral. No preliminary advertisements. EE_4 has one page of advertisements, RECENT BIOGRAPHICAL WORKS, verso blank.

Vol. II. No preliminary advertisements. II$_4$ has one page of advertisements, STANDARD HISTORICAL WORKS, verso blank.

Vol. III. No preliminary advertisements. Terminal catalogue of eight leaves, unsigned, MR. MURRAY'S LIST OF FORTHCOMING WORKS, paged [1] 2-16.

Vol. I. [First leaf], half-title, verso blank; [Second leaf], title, on verso printer; [vii]-xii, Preface; [xiii]-xvi, table of contents; [xvii]-[xviii], fly-title, verso blank; [19]-437, text; [438], printer. Vol. II. [i]-[ii], half-title, verso blank; [iii]-[iv], title, on verso printer; [v]-viii, table of contents; [9]-493, text; [494], printer. Vol. III. [i]-[ii], half-title, verso blank; [iii]-[iv], title, on verso printer; [v]-x, Introduction; [xi]-xvi, table of contents; [17]-470, text; [471]-492, Index, printer at foot of last page.

Printer: Bradbury and Evans, Whitefriars.

Lineation: Vol. I. p. 100, to ... hope;; p. 300, leagues ... [in footnote] vi. Vol. II. p. 100, Nothing ... mind.; p. 300, Columbus. ... seven   Vol. III. p. 100, against ... that,; p. 300, now ... [in footnote]12.

State B noted in red AR cloth. On sides, elaborate border in blind. Spines decorated in blind, titled in gilt: VOYAGES | OF | COLUMBUS | AND HIS | COMPANIONS | [rule] | VOL. I. [II., III.] | IRVING || JOHN MURRAY. Yellow endpapers.

Athenæum, 28 April 1849, advertised as "nearly ready"; 17 November 1849, as "forthcoming"; 10 November and 1 December 1849, for December; 8 December 1849, as "ready"; 15 December 1849, listed.

State A: *BL*. State B: CtY, TxU.

4E.   [London: George Routledge, 2 Vols., 1850.]

In Routledge's "Popular Library" series.

Issued as two separate vols. and also as two vols.-in-one.

The two-vol. form listed in *Athenæum*, 11 May 1850, at 2*s*. in boards. The one-vol. form listed in *Athenæum* and in *Literary Gazette*, 18 May 1850, at 2*s*. 6*d*. in cloth.

Not located.

5Ea.   THE LIFE AND VOYAGES | OF | CHRISTOPHER COLUMBUS. | BY | WASHINGTON IRVING. | [cut of galley] | [six-line quotation] | SENECA: *Medea*. | AUTHOR'S REVISED EDITION. | VOL. I. [II.] | LONDON: | HENRY G. BOHN, YORK STREET, COVENT GARDEN. | 1850.

(17.4 x 10.9 rebound): Vol. I. [i]-viii, [1]-280. Not reckoned: one page of
terminal advertisements in blue for the "Shilling Series." Vol. II. [i]-xi [xii],
281-607 [608]. Not reckoned: two pages of terminal advertisements,
including one for Irving's Works, "Uniform with the Standard Library"; two
pages between pp. [xii]-281, including one for "Works of Washington Irving
Published in the Present Series, and Printed Uniformly." Signed in 8's.

Issued individually in two vols. as "Bohn's Shilling Series"; bound with *The
Companions of Columbus*, with a new title page, all in two vols., as Vols. VII,
VIII of "Bohn's Library Edition." See the next entry for a description of the
"Library Edition."

Printer: Harrison and Son, London Gazette Office, St. Martin's Lane; and
Orchard Street, Westminster.

Lineation: Vol. I. p. 100, be ... trans-; p. 200, poisoned ... Chanca. Vol. II. p.
400, him; ... [in footnote] 9.; p. 500, domestic ... [in footnote] i.

Athenæum, 1 June 1850, Vol. I listed; 15 June 1850, Vol. II listed, each at 1*s.*
6*d.*, apparently in boards.

BL.

[a].   THE LIFE AND VOYAGES | OF | CHRISTOPHER COLUMBUS; |
TOGETHER WITH | THE VOYAGES OF HIS COMPANIONS. | BY |
WASHINGTON IRVING. | [cut of galley] | [six-line quotation; ending of
last line: SENECA: *Medea*.] | AUTHOR'S REVISED EDITION,
COMPLETE   IN   TWO   VOLUMES. | WITH   AN   INDEX   OF
HISTORICAL DOCUMENTS, AND A GENERAL INDEX. | VOL. I. [II.]
| LONDON: | HENRY G. BOHN, YORK STREET, COVENT GARDEN.
| 1850.

"Bohn's Library Edition," Vols. VII, VIII.

(18.1 x 11.4): Vol. I. [a]-[b], [i]-viii, [1]-481 [482]. Vol. II. [i]-[ii], 481-607
[608]; [i]-x, [609]-962. At the break in pagination in Vol. II, there is a
separate title page for *The Companions of Columbus*. Not reckoned:
illustration before title in each vol. Signed in 8's.

Printer: Harrison and Son, St. Martin's Lane, London.

Both *Columbus* and *The Companions of Columbus* are from the same
settings as those of the "Shilling Series."

Gray T cloth. Sides decorated in blind. Spines titled in gilt as Irving's Works,
Vols. VII, VIII, Bohn's Library Edition. Endpapers white with
advertisements in blue.

Athenæum, and *Literary Gazette*, 29 June 1850, listed, at 3*s.* 6*d.* in cloth.

NN, *BL*.

b. [London: Henry G. Bohn, 1854.]

"Bohn's Library Edition." Illustration before title in each vol.

Not seen. Copy reported in Staats- und Universitätsbibliothek Hamburg.

c. [London: Henry G. Bohn, 1859.]

"Bohn's Library Edition."

Not located. Listed by Williams and Edge, as seen.

1A. A | HISTORY | OF THE | LIFE AND VOYAGES | OF | CHRISTOPHER COLUMBUS. | [rule] | BY WASHINGTON IRVING. | [rule] | Venient annis secula seris, | Quibus Oceanus vincula rerum | Laxet, et ingens pateat tellus, | Tiphysque novus detegat orbes, | Nec sit terris ultima Thule. -- *Seneca. Medea*. | [rule] | IN THREE VOLUMES. | VOL. I. [II., III.] | [rule] | G. & C. CARVILL, 108 BROADWAY, NEW-YORK. | [rule] | 1828.

(23.1 x 14.1 untrimmed): Vol. I. [A]^4 B^4 1-5^4 [6]^4 7-50^4. Sig. mark 6 (on p. 41) present in some copies. Fold-out map inserted, generally before title, occasionally before half-title. Vol. II. [1]^4 2-46^4. Vol. III. [-]^4 1-51^4.

Vol. I. [i]-[ii], half-title, verso blank; [iii]-[iv], title, on verso copyright (January 24, 1828 by Washington Irving) and printer; [v]-xi, Preface, dated Madrid, October 18th, 1827; [xii], blank; [xiii]-xvi, table of contents; [1]-399, text; [400], blank. Vol. II. [i]-[ii], half-title, verso blank; [iii]-[iv], title, on verso copyright and printer; [v]-viii, table of contents; [9]-367, text; [368], blank. Vol. III. [i]-[ii], half-title, verso blank; [iii]-[iv], title, on verso copyright; [v]-viii, table of contents; [13]-420, text.

Two pages noted with minor variants.

Vol. I, p. 41. [A], without Sig. mark 6; [B], with Sig. mark 6.

Vol. III, p. 420. [A], with complete page number; [B], with the O only; [C], with no page number.

The sequence of the minor variants is conjectural only. It is suggestive that a copy in TxU, with both pages in State [A], has the original owner's signature of John S. Popkin, dated 1827. (The date appears only in Vol. III.)

Printer: Elliott and Palmer. Printer's imprint in Vols. I, II only.

Lineation: Vol. I. p. 100, fort ... to ; p. 200, Puerto ... admi- Vol. II. p. 100, The ... [in footnote] Cap. 60 ; p. 200, that ... humanity. Vol. III. p. 100, helpless ... [in footnote] 102.; p. 200, and ... Chersonesus

Light brown boards with purple cloth shelfbacks. (Copies have been seen with brown cloth shelfbacks, but the color appears to be a result of the degeneration of the original dye.) Sides blank. White paper label on spines: [double rule] | IRVING'S | LIFE | AND | VOYAGES | OF | COLUMBUS. | [rule] | VOL. I. [II., III.] [Vol. II lacks the period after VOL] | [double rule].

Title deposited 24 January 1828. New York *Evening Post*, 20 February 1828, repeated 3-8 March 1828, "In the press and will shortly be published." *American Quarterly Review*, March 1828, reviewed (publishers named as Elliot and Palmer; Elliott and Palmer were the printers of Vols. I, II). Irving to John Murray, 22 September 1850, "published in London Feby 8th 1829 [a mistake for 1828] and in New York March 15th of the same year."

NN, TxU (3).

2Aa. HISTORY | OF THE | LIFE AND VOYAGES | OF | CHRISTOPHER COLUMBUS. | [double rule] | BY WASHINGTON IRVING. | [double rule] | Venient annis | Sæcula seris, quibus Oceanus | Vincula rerum laxet, et ingens | Pateat tellus, Typhisque novos | Detegat Orbes, nec sic terris | Ultima Thule. | *Seneca Medea*. | [rule] | A NEW EDITION REVISED AND CORRECTED BY THE AUTHOR. | [rule] | IN TWO VOLUMES. | VOL. I. [II.] | [emblem: GCHC intertwined within wreath] | G. & C. & H. CARVILL, No. 108 BROADWAY, NEW-YORK. | [rule] | 1831.

(24.0 x 14.6): Vol. I. Signed unconventionally, and in the instance of the first Sig. 3 erroneously. $[A]^2 B^4$ $1-2^4$ 2^4 4^43-25^8 26^6. Fold-out map inserted before text. Not reckoned: eight-page preliminary catalogue of Grigg & Elliot, undated, unpaged. Vol. II. $[1]-22^8$ 23^6.

Vol. I. [i]-[ii], half-title, verso blank; [iii]-[iv], title, on verso new copyright ([March 9], 1831) and printer; [v]-viii, Preface; [ix]-xii, table of contents; [1]-411, text; [412], blank. Vol. II. [i]-[ii], half-title, verso blank; [iii]-[iv], title, on verso copyright and printer; [v]-vii, table of contents; [viii], blank; [1]-205, text; [206], blank; [207]-356, Appendix.

Printer: G. F. Bunce.

Lineation: Vol. I. p. 100, the ... beheld ; p. 300, and ... as- Vol. II. p. 100, CHAPTER V. ... [in footnote] L. 4.; p. 300, credit ... [in footnote] Ch. 3.

Purple V cloth. Sides blank. Brown leather label on spines, titled in gilt: IRVING'S | COLUMBUS | [rule] | 1. [2.], the numbers within decorative gilt border. Also noted in full calf that appears to be a publisher's binding. Two red leather labels on each spine. Upper label, in gilt: [double rule] | IRVING'S | COLUMBUS | [double rule]. Lower label, in gilt: [double rule] | VOL. | 1 [2] | double rule].

New-York American, 23 March 1831, "Just published and for sale."

TxU (2).

b. A NEW EDITION REVISED AND CORRECTED BY THE AUTHOR. | [rule] | IN TWO VOLUMES. | VOL. I. [II.] | [rule] | Philadelphia: [fancy] | CAREY, LEA, & BLANCHARD. | [rule of 21 dots] | 1835.

Although issued by a new publisher, this is an impression from the plates of the Carvill edition of 1831.

The original signature marks are retained, but a second set is added that corresponds to the collation of this impression: Vol. I. $[A]^2 B^4 A\text{-}I^6 K\text{-}Z^6$ (U and V are present) $2A\text{-}2I^6 2K^2$. Fold-out map inserted. Vol. II. $[\text{-}]^4 A\text{-}I^6 K\text{-}Z^6 2A\text{-}2D^6 2E^4$.

Green cloth, titled in gilt on spines. A copy described in a bookseller's catalogue has *The Companions of Columbus*, Carey, Lea & Blanchard, 1835, bound as a third volume and so numbered on the spine.

The Cost Book of Carey & Lea specifies 500 copies in cloth, "finished" June 1835, with I. Ashmead as printer.

New-York Mirror, 15 August 1835, noted as "A new edition ... revised and improved by the accomplished author."

TxAM, TxU.

c. Philadelphia: [fancy] | CAREY, LEA, & BLANCHARD. | [rule of 21 dots] | 1837.

MB.

d. PHILADELPHIA: | CAREY, LEA, & BLANCHARD, | FOR | GEORGE W. GORTON. | [rule of 26 dots] | 1838.

The Cost Book of Carey & Lea specifies 500 copies, "finished" February 1838, with I. Ashmead as printer.

DLC.

e. PHILADELPHIA: | LEA & BLANCHARD, | SUCCESSORS TO CAREY & CO. | FOR | GEORGE W. GORTON. | [rule of 28 dots] | 1839.

ViU.

f. [Philadelphia: Lea & Blanchard for George W. Gorton, 1840.]

Not seen. Copy reported in OCIW.

g. PHILADELPHIA: | LEA & BLANCHARD. | FOR | GEORGE W. GORTON. | 1841.

Brown T cloth. Sides blank. Spines titled in gilt.

TxU.

3Aa.   The Author's Revised Edition of *The Life and Voyages of Christopher Columbus* added the revised edition of *The Companions of Columbus* as a third volume of the work. Since each volume was first issued separately, each differs in title page, and each occurs in several states, the three volumes are here described separately.

Sets of the three volumes may occur in different combinations of the various states.   An analogy recurs in impressions of later years when a set -- apparently bound and sold as a set -- may be made up of impressions of different dates.

Volume I.

THE | LIFE AND VOYAGES | OF | CHRISTOPHER COLUMBUS; | TO WHICH ARE ADDED THOSE OF | HIS COMPANIONS. | BY | WASHINGTON IRVING. | Venient annis | Sæcula seris, quibus Oceanus | Vincula rerum laxet, et ingens | Pateat tellus, Typhisque novos | Detegat Orbes, nec sit terris | Ultima Thule. | SENECA: *Medea.* | AUTHOR'S REVISED EDITION. | VOL I. | NEW-YORK: | GEORGE P. PUTNAM, 155 BROADWAY, | And 142 Strand, London | 1848.

(19.0 x 12.8): $[1]^{10}$ $2\text{-}19^{12}$.

Tipped in before the Works title is a notice that the maps will be given in Vol. II, to be published on the first of January, 1849.

In two states, sequence not determined:

[A]. On the title page, a period is present after London in the imprint.

Sig. 19 is in 6.

The catalogue at the end of Sig. 19, dated *November*, 1848, is paged 1-4.

[B]. On the title page, a period is not present after London in the imprint.

Sig. 19 is in 12.

The catalogue at the end of Sig. 19, dated *November*, 1848, is paged 1-6, 1-9, followed by a blank page.

[i]-[ii], Works title, Vol. III, dated 1848, verso blank; [iii]-[iv], title, on verso copyright (1848) and printer; [ix]-xii, table of contents; [xiii]-xviii, Preface; [19]-437, text; [438], blank. Between pp. 56-57 is an illustration of Part of a Terrestrial Globe, description on verso, not counted in pagination.

Printer: Leavitt, Trow & Co., Printers and Stereotypers, 49 Ann-street, N. Y.

Lineation: p. 100, to ... [in footnote] sup.; p. 300, leagues ... [in footnote] vi.

For bindings, see the description at the end of the entry.

Literary World, 30 September 1848 (and repeated several times), "Volume I will be published on the first of November"; 4 November 1848, "Published this week"; 11 November 1848, listed and reviewed. In *Literary World*, 9 December 1848, a "Second Edition" is advertised as "Published this week"; is this one of the original states, or is it the impression dated 1849 on the title page?

State [A]: CtY. State [B]: CtY, MH, TxU.

Volume II.

THE | LIFE AND VOYAGES | OF | CHRISTOPHER COLUMBUS; | TO WHICH ARE ADDED THOSE OF | HIS COMPANIONS. | BY | WASHINGTON IRVING. | Venient annis | Sæcula seris, quibus, Oceanus | Vincula rerum laxet, et ingens | Pateat tellus, Typhisque novos | Detegat Orbes, nec sit terris | Ultima Thule. | SENECA: *Medea.* | AUTHOR'S REVISED EDITION. | VOL. II. | NEW-YORK: | GEORGE P. PUTNAM, 155 BROADWAY. | And 142 Strand, London. | 1849.

(19.0×12.8): $[1]^{12}$ $2\text{-}21^{12}$.

Some copies have tipped in before the title a notice that the present volume contains 100 pages more than originally estimated, that the price is necessarily increased to $1 50, and that the next volume will contain the "Companions of Columbus" and Appendix. The slip has been noted only in State [A] described below.

The final five leaves of Sig. 21 contain a publisher's catalogue. The catalogue has been noted in three states, sequence not determined:

[A]. Catalogue dated *November,* 1848, paged 1-6, 1-4.

[B]. Catalogue undated, paged 3-12.

[C]. Catalogue undated, paged 2-11.

[i]-[ii], Works title, Vol. IV, dated 1849, verso blank; [iii]-[iv], title, on verso copyright (1848) and printer; [v]-viii, table of contents; [9]-493, text; [494], blank.

Printer: Leavitt, Trow & Co., Printers and Stereotypers, 49 Ann-street, N. Y.

Lineation: p. 100, Nothing ... mind.; p. 300, Columbus. ... seven

For bindings, see the description at the end of the entry.

Literary World, 2 December 1848, "Will be published on the 1st January"; 6 January 1849, "Recently published"; 13 January 1849, listed.

State [A]: MH, TxU. State [B]: MH. State [C]: MH.

Volume III.

THE | LIFE AND VOYAGES | OF | CHRISTOPHER COLUMBUS; | TO WHICH ARE ADDED THOSE OF | HIS COMPANIONS. | BY | WASHINGTON IRVING. | Venient annis | Sæcula seris, quibus, Oceanus | Vincula, rerum laxet, et ingens | Pateat tellus, Typhisque novos | Detegat Orbes, nec sit terris | Ultima Thule. | SENECA: *Medea.* | AUTHOR'S REVISED EDITION. | VOL. III. | NEW-YORK: | GEORGE P. PUTNAM, 155 BROADWAY. | And 142 Strand, London. | 1849.

(19.0 x 12.8): [1]^{12} 2-21^{12}. Fold-out chart of Tracks Across the North Atlantic Ocean inserted before title.

The final six leaves of Sig. 21, if present, contain a publisher's catalogue. The catalogue has been noted in three states, sequence not determined.

[A]. Catalogue dated *November*, 1848, paged 1-6, 1-6.

[B]. Catalogue undated, paged 3-14.

[C]. No catalogue present. Sig. 21 in 6.

[i]-[ii], Works title, Vol. V, dated 1849, on verso quotation from P. Martyr, Lok's translation; [iii]-[iv], title, on verso copyright (1848) and printer; [v]-x, table of contents; [xi]-xvi, Introduction to *The Companions of Columbus*; [17]-288, text of *The Companions of Columbus*; [289]-[290], divisional fly-title for Appendix, verso blank; [291]-470, Appendix; [471]-492, Index.

Printer: Leavitt, Trow & Co., Printers and Stereotypers, 49 Ann-street, N. Y.

Lineation: p. 100, against ... that,; p. 300, now ... [in footnote] 12.

For bindings, see the description at the end of the entry.

Literary World, 3 February 1849, "On Wednesday, February 7"; 10 February 1849, "This week."

State [A]: MH, TxU. State [B]: MH. State [C]: MH.

The three volumes noted in the standard binding: green TB cloth. On sides, in blind, design with publisher's initials. Spines decorated in blind and titled in gilt: IRVING'S | WORKS | [rule] | COLUMBUS | VOL. I. [II., III.]. Endpapers buff-yellow.

The publisher's catalogue in Vol. I of the Octavo Edition offers the complete work, "3 vols., 12 mo., green cloth, uniform with the new edition of Irving's Works, $4; half calf, $6; half morocco, top edge gilt, $6.75; full calf, gilt, $7.50." An advertisement in *Literary World*, 10 February 1849, lists the same variety and prices.

b. The Author's Revised Edition was also issued in a large-paper impression called the "Octavo Edition."

The title page of Vol. I has no period after VOL and has a period after London in the imprint.

(23.0 x 14.3 rebound): Vol. I. [-]^2 [1]^8 2-18^8 19^4. In copy examined, the first leaf is missing; blank? Portrait of Columbus inserted before title; so issued? Vol. II. [1]^8 [-]^4 2-21^8. Last leaf missing in copy examined; blank? Fold-out map inserted. Vol. III. [1]^8 [-]^4 2-20^8 21^6. Fold-out map inserted.

Vol. I has two terminal catalogues, not integral. The first is dated at the beginning *March*, 1849, and is paged [1] 2-16. The second is dated at the end *November*, 1848, is paged 1-16, and is on a different wove paper. No catalogues in Vols. II, III.

Printer: Leavitt, Trow & Co., Printers and Stereotypers, 49 Ann-street, N. Y.

The first catalogue at the end of Vol. I advertises, "The OCTAVO EDITION, in 3 vols., on superfine paper, uniform with Prescott's Ferdinand and Isabella, $6."

Pierre M. Irving in the *Life* (IV, 189) quotes a letter from George Putnam to Irving, 11 January 1855, "You are aware we printed an edition of Columbus in octavo, ... but of these we have never sold but two hundred and fifty copies; while about eleven thousand have been sold of the duodecimo."

Literary World, 21 April 1849, advertised as published 16 April 1849, 3 vols., in cloth at $6.

TxAM.

c. NEW-YORK: | GEORGE P. PUTNAM, 155 BROADWAY, | And 142 Strand, London. | 1849. 3 vols. In 12's.

Works title, dated 1849.

Vol. I has been noted in two states of the catalogue: dated 1849, paged 9-16; and undated, paged 13-16..

Vols. II and III are the same as State [C] of the original impressions, and may in fact be the same impression. In Vol. II, Sig. 21 is in 12, and the catalogue is undated, paged 2-11. In Vol. III, Sig. 21 is in 6, and there is no catalogue. Both have the same inserted map, and both, like Vol. I, are printed by Leavitt, Trow & Co.

The standard binding is that of the original impressions: green TB cloth.

ViU, TxU.

d,e. NEW-YORK: | GEORGE P. PUTNAM, 155 BROADWAY, | And 142 Strand, London. | 1850.

Works title, dated 1850.

Vols. I, III have been noted in two states: with the imprint of Leavitt, Trow & Co.; and with the imprint of John F. Trow. Vol. II seen only with the imprint of Leavitt, Trow & Co., but both states probably exist.

ViU: the 3 vols 1850. MH: Vol. I, 1850; Vols. II, III, 1849. TxU: Vols. I, III, 1850; Vol. II, 1851.

f. NEW-YORK: | GEORGE P. PUTNAM, 155 BROADWAY, | And 142 Strand, London. | 1851.

Works title, dated 1851.

Printer: John F. Trow, 49 Ann-street, N. Y.

DLC.

g. NEW-YORK: | G. P. PUTNAM & COMPANY, 10 PARK PLACE, | AND 142 STRAND, LONDON. | 1852.

Works title, dated 1852.

Private hands. ViU: Vol. I, 1852; Vols. II, III, 1853.

h. NEW-YORK: | G. P. PUTNAM & COMPANY, 10 PARK PLACE, | AND 142 STRAND, LONDON. | 1853.

Works title, dated 1853.

MH: the 3 vols., Works titles present but regular titles missing. ViU: Vol. I, 1852; Vols. II, III, 1853.

i. NEW-YORK: | G. P. PUTNAM & COMPANY, 10 PARK PLACE, | AND 142 STRAND, LONDON. | 1854.

Works title, dated 1854.

Seen only in Vols. I, II.

CtY: Vols. I, II, 1854; Vol. III, 1855.

j. NEW-YORK: | G. P. PUTNAM & COMPANY, 10 PARK PLACE, | AND 142 STRAND, LONDON. | 1855.

Works title, dated 1855.

Seen only in Vol. III.

CtY: Vols. I, II, 1854; Vol. III, 1855. Copy of 1855 reported in NjP.

k. New York: [fancy] | G. P. PUTNAM & CO., 321 BROADWAY. | 1856.

Works title, dated 1856.

Seen only in Vol. III.

ViU: Vol. III.

l.   New York [fancy] | G. P. PUTNAM & CO., 321 BROADWAY | 1857.

Works title, dated 1857.

MH.

m.   NEW YORK: | G. P. PUTNAM, 115 NASSAU STREET | 1859. In Vols. II, III, period after STREET. In quotation, Typhisque changed to Tethysque.

Works title, dated 1859.

Two engraved illustrations added before each title, but maps omitted from Vols. II, III.

Green BD-like heavily-pebbled cloth. On sides, line decoration in blind. Spines titled in gilt with gilt semi-framing decoration at top. Green endpapers.

TxU.

n.   NEW YORK: | G. P. PUTNAM (for the Proprietor), 506 BROADWAY. | 1859.

Works title, dated 1859.

Two engravings before each title. No maps.

NjP, TxU.

lFa.   A | HISTORY | OF THE | LIFE AND VOYAGES | OF | CHRISTOPHER COLUMBUS. | BY | WASHINGTON IRVING. | [swelled rule with stars in center] | Venient annis | Sæcula seris, quibus Oceanus | Vincula rerum laxet, et ingens | Pateat tellus, Typhisque novos | Detegat Orbes, nec sit terris | Ultima Thule. | SENECA: *Medea.* | [rule] | IN FOUR VOLUMES. | VOL. I. [II., III., IV.] | [emblem: D in star within wreath with pendant medal] | PARIS: | PUBLISHED BY A. AND W. GALIGNANI, | AT THE ENGLISH, FRENCH, ITALIAN, GERMAN, AND SPANISH | LIBRARY, N° 18, RUE VIVIENNE. | [rule] | 1828.

(16.9 x 10.2 approx.): Vol. I. [i]-xv [xvi], [1]-472. Two charts by H. Toquet inserted, dated 1828, printed by Raban. Vol. II. [i]-viii, [1]-517 [518]. Vol. III. [i]-viii, [1]-434. Vol. IV. [i]-vii [viii], [1]-513 [514]. Signed in 12's. Crude laid paper.

Printer: Jules Didot, Senior, Rue du-Pont-de-Lodi, No. 6.

Lineation: Vol. I. p. 100, and ... Castile.; p. 200, science ... appa- Vol. II. p. 100, prodigious ... [in footnote] MS.; p. 200, came ... times Vol. III. p. 100, nuance ... appointed ; p. 200, obedience ... [in footnote] 3. Vol. IV. p. 100, and ... [in footnote] 9.; p. 200, open ... nature.

Bibliographie de la France, 22 March 1828, # 1868, listed. Listed in same entry with the Baudry impression.

DLC. Copy reported in CtY.

b. [emblem: L. B. within wreath] | PARIS: | BAUDRY, AT THE FOREIGN LIBRARY, | N° 9, RUE DU COQ-SAINT-HONORÉ. | [rule] | 1828.

Bibliographie de la France, 22 March 1828, #1868, listed. Listed in same entry with the Galignani impression.

DLC, TxU (Vols. II-IV).

c. PARIS: | PUBLISHED BY A. AND W. GALIGNANI, | AT THE ENGLISH, FRENCH, ITALIAN, GERMAN, AND SPANISH | LIBRARY, N° 18, RUE VIVIENNE. | [rule] | 1829.

Bibliographie de la France, 23 May 1829, #3269, listed. Listed in same entry with the Baudry impression of 1829.

NN, *BL*.

d. [Paris: Baudry, 1829.]

Bibliographie de la France, 23 May 1829, #3269, listed. Listed in same entry with the Galignani impression of 1829.

Not seen. Copy reported in Bibliothèque Nationale.

2F. [Paris: A. and W. Galignani, 1839. 4 vols.]

Possibly a later impression, although this may well be a new edition.

Not located. Reported by Williams and Edge as seen. Listed in Antonio Palau y Dulcet, *Manual del Librero Hispanoamericano*, 2nd ed.

TRANSLATIONS

Dutch.

HET LEVEN | EN | DE REIZEN | VAN | CHRISTOFFEL COLUMBUS, | DOOR | *WASHINGTON IRVING*. | Venient annis | Sæcula ... oceanus | Vincula ... ingens | Pateat ... novos | Detegat orbes. | SENECA, *Medea*. [The quotation is off-center to the right] | [rule] | Uit het Engelsch. | [rule] | EERSTE [TWEEDE, DERDE, VIERDE EN LAATSTE] DEEL. | Met eene Kaart. [Vol. II: Met een Portret van

COLUMBUS gevolgd naar | de oorspronkelijke schilderij toebehooren- | de aan Z. K. M.] [Vol. III: Met een Facsimile.] [Vol. IV: Met een Register.] | [cut of West Indies scene with barrels, anchors, ships, etc.] | TE HAARLEM, BIJ | DE WED. A. LOOSJES, PZ. | MDCCCXXVIII. Vols. III, IV dated MDCCCXXIX.

Translated by Jan Willem Jacobus Steenbergen van Goor.

(21.6 x 12.7): Vol. I. [I]-XXI [XXII], [1]-359 [360]. Vol. II. [I]-IX [X], [1]-392. Vol. III. [I]-X, [1]-357 [358]. Vol. IV. [I]-VIII, [1]-366 [367]-[368]. Maps and illustrations, produced for this edition, not reckoned. Signed in 8's. Laid paper.

Printer: Gedrukt te *Gorinchem* bij JACOBUS NOORDUYN.

Lineation: Vol. I. p. 100, tot ... [in footnote] *c.* 7.; p. 200, dat ... [in footnote] I. Vol. II. p. 100, voor ... boomen,; p. 200, den ... Yagui, Vol. III. p. 100, Men ... [in footnote] 6.; p. 200, teren, ... [in footnote] voren. Vol. IV. p. 100, andere ... [in footnote] COLUMBUS.; p. 200, verzoeken, ... zij

DLC. Copy reported in NNH.

French.

HISTOIRE | DE | LA VIE ET DES VOYAGES | DE | CHRISTOPHE COLOMB, | PAR M. WASHINGTON IRVING, | TRADUITE DE L'ANGLAIS | PAR C. A. DEFAUCONPRET FILS, | TRADUCTEUR DE L'HISTOIRE D'ÉCOSSE PAR SIR WALTER SCOTT, ETC. | [six-line quotation] | SENECA, *Medea.* | TOME PREMIER. [DEUXIÈME., TROISIÈME., QUATRIÈME.] | PARIS, | CHARLES GOSSELIN, | LIBRAIRE DE SON ALTESSE ROYALE MONSEIGNEUR LE DUC DE BORDEAUX, | RUE SAINT-GERMAIN-DES-PRÉS, N° 9. | MAME ET DELAUNAY-VALLÉE, LIBRAIRES, | RUE GUÉNÉGAUD, N° 25. | MDCCCXXVIII.

(20.4 x 12.9): Vol. I. [I]-XVI, [1]-381 [382]. Vol. II. [I]-VIII, [1]-402. Vol. III. [I]-VIII, [1]-364. Vol. IV. [I]-VI, [1]-425 [426]. Signed in 8's. Laid paper.

Printer: Imprimerie de Cosson, rue Saint-Germain-des-Prés, No. 9, Paris.

Lineation: Vol. I. p. 100, Genèse, ... plai- Vol. II. p. 100, spiré ... [in footnote] heremito. Vol. III. p. 100, quelques ... [in footnote] 9. Vol. IV. p. 100, dans ... [in footnote] 7.

Bibliographie de la France, 19 April 1828, # 2273, Vol. I listed; 24 May 1828, # 3071, Vol. II listed; 21 June 1828, # 3797, Vols. III, IV listed.

ViU. Copy reported in NNC.

HISTOIRE | DE | LA VIE ET DES VOYAGES | DE | CHRISTOPHE COLOMB, | PAR WASHINGTON IRVING, | Auteur de l'*Histoire des Compagnons de Colomb*, | TRADUITE DE L'ANGLAIS | PAR C. A. DEFAUCONPRET FILS. | [six-line quotation] | SENECA, *Medea*. | Deuxième Edition, revue et corrigée. [fancy] | [rule] | TOME PREMIER. [DEUXIÈME, TROISIÈME., QUATRIÈME.] | PARIS, | LIBRAIRIE DE CHARLES GOSSELIN, | RUE SAINT-GERMAIN DES PRÉS, N° 9. | [rule] | M DCCC XXXVI.

(19.6 x 12.0): Vol. I. [I]-XVI, [1]-381 [382]. Vol. II. [I]-VIII, [1]-406. Vol. III. [I]-VIII, [1]-364. Vol. IV. [I]-VII [VIII], [1]-422. Fold-out map inserted in Vol. IV. Signed in 8's. Laid paper.

Printer: Sézanne. -- Imprimerie de David.

Lineation: Vol. I. p. 100, Genèse, ... confon- Vol. II. p. 100, spiré ... [in footnote] heremito. Vol. III. p. 100, quelques ... [in footnote] 9. Vol. IV. p. 100, gnano ... [in footnote] 7.

DLC.

German.

Die Geschichte | des | Lebens und der Reisen | Christoph's Columbus | von | Washington Irving. | [rule] | Aus dem Englischen übersetzt. | [double rule] | Späte Jahrhunderte | Sehen die Zeit, wo der Ocean | Lüs't die Bande Der Dinge, wo grosser | Erdstrich sich aufhut, ein Tiphus | Neue Welten entdeckt, nicht der Länder | Letztes ist Thule. | Seneca's Medea. | [rule] | Erstes bis drittes [Viertes bis sechstes, Siebentes bis neuntes] Bändchen. | [quintuple rule] | Frankfurt am Main, 1828. | Gedruckt und verlegt bei Johann David Sauerländer. [in fraktur]

"Washington Irving's sämmtliche Werke," Bändchen 20-28.

(13.3 x 9.8): Vol. I. [1]-404. Fold-out map inserted. Vol. II. [1]-418. Vol. III. [1]-408. Fold-out map inserted. Signed in 8's.

Lineation: Vol. I. p. 200, Delphine ... [in footnote] Dollars. Vol. II. p. 200, im ... [in footnote] IV. Vol. III. p. 200, Fünftes ... [in footnote] Almirante.

Also issued in a four-vol. set, with Vol. IV, "Zehntes bis zwölftes Bändchen," containing a translation of *The Companions of Columbus* and of the Appendix. The Fourth vol. expands the title slightly, "Aus dem Englischen übersetzt und mit | Anmerkungen begleitet," and is dated 1829. Paged [i]-[ii], [1]-424 [425]-[426]. Lineation: p. 200, gewöhnlichen ... tranken

In 3 vols.: ViU. In 4 vols.: CtY.

[Aus dem Englischen übersetzt von Ph. A. G. von Meyer. Neue Ausgabe. 12 Bändchen. Frankfurt am Main: Johann David Sauerländer, 1832.]

"Washington Irving's sämmtliche Werke," Bändchen 20-31.

Is this a later impression or, as claimed, a new edition?

Not located. Listed in W. Heinsius, *Allgemeines Bücher-Lexicon, 1828-1834.*

[Des Christoph Columbus Leben und Reisen. Aus dem Englischen von F. H. Ungewitter. 4 Bändchen. Frankfurt am Main: Wesché, 1828-1829.]

Bound in 8's.

Not seen.   Copies reported in Universitätsbibliothek Giessen, and Landesbibliothek Kiel.

Italian.

STORIA [hollow letters] | DELLA VITA E DE | VIAGGI | DI | CRISTOFORO COLOMBO | SCRITTA | DA WASHINGTON IRVING [hollow letters] | AMERICANO | Prima versione Italiana [fancy] | Corredata di Note, adorna di Carte geografiche, | e Ritratto. | Venient annis | Sæcula ... Oceanus | Vincula ... ingens | Pateat ... novos | Detegat ... terris | Ultima Thule... | SENECA: *MEDEA*. | GENOVA | Dalla Tipografia dei Fratelli Pagano [fancy] | 1828. Vols. II-IV add before imprint: [swelled rule] | VOL. II. [III., IV.] | [swelled rule].

Issued in 12 parts.

(20.0 x 12.8): Vol. I. [I]-VI, [7]-315 [316]. Vol. II. [1]-320. Vol. III. [1]-288. Vol. IV. [1]-288. Not reckoned: Preliminary engraving of Columbus in Vol. I, fold-out map in Vols. I, IV. Signed in 8's.

Lineation: Vol. I. p. 100, nuovo ... Medina Vol. II. p. 100, stieri ... *IV.* Vol. III. p. 100, tronche ... [in footnote] II. Vol. IV. p. 100, affine ... [in footnote] scrittore

ViU.

STORIA | DELLA VITA E VIAGGI | DI CRISTOFORO COLOMBO [hollow letters] | SCRITTA | DA WASHINGTON IRVING | *AMERICANO* | TRAD. DALL'INGLESE | [six-line quotation, in italic] | SENECA. MEDEA *At.* II. | [rule] | TOMO PRIMO [SECONDO, TERZO, QUARTO] | [rule] | Firenze [fancy] | DALLA TIPOGRAFIA COEN E COMP. | 1829. Vols. III, IV are dated 1830.

(14.4 x 8.9): Vol. I. [1]-468. Vol. II. [1]-480. Vol. III. [1]-420. Vol. IV. [1]-440. Signed in 6's.

Lineation: Vol. I. p. 100, mico ... oltre, Vol. II. p. 100, dagl' ... [in footnote] MS. Vol. III. p. 100, Oltre ... [in footnote] 7. Vol. IV. p. 100, dato ... [in footnote] 443.

A copy in NN is bound in twelve fascicles, each in a paper wrapper. On front, in black type, title and identification of volume and fascicle, within decorative border.

MB, NN.

Russian.

[Translated title:] A History | of | the Life and Voyages | of Christopher Columbus. | by | Washington Irving. | Translated from the French, | by Nicolai Bredikin. | [Quotation from Seneca, *Medea*, in Roman lettering] | Volume One. [Two., Three, Four.] | [stylized swelled rule] | Saint Petersburg, | Published by the K. Ginda Press. | 1836. Vols. II-IV dated 1837. [in Cyrillic]

(19.5 x 12.3): Vol. I. [I]-XVI [XII]-[XX], [1]-438. Map. Preliminary engraving of Columbus not reckoned. Vol. II. [I]-VIII, [1]-458. Map. Vol. III. [I]-IX [X], [1]-504. Vol. IV. [I]-VIII, [1]-337 [338]. Signed in 8's.

Lineation: Vol. I. p. 100, zanost ... [in footnote] voynee. Vol. IV. p. 100, nee ... offisair;

MH.

Spanish.

Historia [fancy] | DE LA VIDA Y VIAJES | DE | CRISTÓBAL COLON, [hollow letters] | ESCRITA EN INGLES POR EL CABALLERO | WASHINGTON IRVING, [elaborated letters] | Y TRADUCIDA AL CASTELLANO | por Don José Garcia de Villalta. [script-like letters] | [elaborated swelled rule] | MADRID: Diciembre de 1833. | *Imprenta de* D. JOSÉ PALACIOS, *calle del Factor.* Vols. II-IV substitute for the swelled rule of Vol. I: [rule] | TOMO II. [III., IV.] | [rule]. Vol. II dated Enero de 1834; Vol. III, Febrero de 1834; Vol. IV, Marzo de 1834.

(14.6 x 10.0): Vol. I. [1]-637 [638]. Vol. II. [1]-629 [630]. Vol. III. [1]-535 [536]. Vol. IV. [1]-560. Signed in 8's. Laid paper.

Lineation: Vol. I. p. 100, de ... [in footnote] II. Vol. II. p. 100, La ... vereda Vol. III. p. 100, tó ... Gue- Vol. IV. p. 100, últimos ... no

TxU.

BIBLIOTECA DE GASPAR Y ROIG. | [rule] | VIDA Y VIAGES | DE | CRISTOBAL COLON | POR WASHINGTON IRVING. | [rule] |

Adornada con sesenta grabados | [cut of Indian] | MADRID | GASPAR Y ROIG, EDITORES | calle del Principe, núm. 4. | 1851

(25.5 x 16.0 rebound): [i]-[ii], [1]-251 [252]-[260]. In double columns. Signed in 12's.

Lineation: p. 100 (first column), segun ... Cuan- ; p. 200 (first column), "tros ... pros-

MB.

[Same title, except cut of three ships, and a period after "grabados."]

(25.8 x 13.7 rebound): [i]-[ii], [1]-251 [252]-[262]. In double columns. Signed in 12's.

In part, or entirely, reset, predominantly line-for-line.

Lineation: p. 100 (first column), estos, ... isla.; p. 200 (first column, "tros ... pros-

ViU.

BIBLIOTECA DE GASPAR Y ROIG. | [rule] | VIDA Y VIAJES | DE | CRISTOBAL COLON | POR WASHINGTON IRVING. | [rule] | Adornada con sesenta grabados. | [cut of native house] | MADRID. | GASPAR Y ROIG, EDITORES. | Calle del Principe núm. 4. | 1852.

Pagination and lineation the same.

NN.

[Vida y viajes de Cristobal colon. 3. edición. Madrid: Gaspar y Roig, 1854.

At head of title: Biblioteca illustrada de Gaspar y Roig. Title vignette.]

251 pages, in double columns.

Translated by José García de Villalta.

Not examined. Copies reported in ICN, NNH.

VIDA Y VIAJES | DE | CRISTOBAL COLON, | POR | Washington Irving. | [vignette] | MEXICO. -- 1853. | IMPRENTA DE BOIX, BESSERER Y COMPAÑIA, | callejon del Espíritu Santo núm. 8.

2 volumes.

At the end of Vol. II, pp. [1]-32: Elogio de Cristóbal Colon, por Eulalio Maria Ortega, presentado y premiado en el concurso del Ateneo mexicano de 20 de julio de 1845.... México: Andres Boix, [1]853.

Not seen. Information from copy in NNHi.

VIDA I VIAJES | DE | CRISTOBAL COLON | POR | WASHINGTON
IRVING. [shaded letters] | REIMPRESO | PARA LAS BIBLIOTECAS
POPULARES. | [emblem of Republic of Chile] | SANTIAGO. | Imprenta
del FERROCARRIL. | [rule] | Febrero de 1859. Vols. II-IV substitute for
the emblem of Vol. I: [double rules] | TOMO II. [III., IV.] [hollow letters]|
[double rules]. Vols. II-IV are dated simply 1859.

(16.9 x 10.9): Vol. I. [1]-504. Vol. II. [1]-438. Vol. III. [1]-235 [236]. Vol.
IV. [1]-250. Signed in 4's.

Lineation: Vol. I. p. 100, pues ... opinion. Vol. II. p. 100, CAPITULO VI.
... favorita, Vol. III. p. 100, él ... revela Vol. IV. p. 100, principal ... mismo

MH.

THE LIFE AND VOYAGES OF
CHRISTOPHER COLUMBUS (ABRIDGED)

In November 1828 Washington Irving received word from his brother Peter that someone in America was planning to publish an abridgment of the full *Columbus*. Irving promptly began work on his own abridgment. A letter to Peter from Seville, December 13, 1828, describes the results:

> I have finished the Abridgment, and shall send it off to America by the brig Francis, which sails from Cadiz for New York about the 22d inst. I have had it copied, that I might forward a copy to Murray. It will make about five hundred pages of the Sketch Book, or four hundred good full pages of ordinary printing. I finished it in nineteen days--hard work, but I think it will be all the better for being written off at a heat. I have no doubt that it will prove a work of extensive and durable sale. All the passages and scenes of striking interest are given almost entire, and the other parts are compressed with clearness and fluency, and without losing in language, I think they gain in spirit by conciseness. The vessel by which it goes to America was originally advertised for the 15th, and to enable me to forward the MSS., man, woman, and child of my acquaintance here that understood English, volunteered to assist in copying it, so that I had it copied in the course of a very few days.

It should be noted that the abridgment was printed from two manuscripts, the original sent by Irving to America (or so the letter to Peter seems to say), and the other, a copy made in Spain, sent to John Murray in London. It is of human interest as well as bibliographical that Irving asked of Murray only the cost of copying. According to a letter from Washington Irving to Peter, 29 October 1830, Murray quickly sold out an edition of ten thousand copies.

The two versions of the abridgment differ in text, most noticeably in the number of chapters. The London text contains forty-six chapters and an Appendix: "Obsequies of Columbus." The American text contains forty-four chapters and is without the Appendix; Chapter XXI, "Customs and Characteristics of the Natives," and Chapter XXIV, "Return Voyage," do not appear as separate chapters in the American text, although some of the material itself is retained. In further differences, the London edition contains at the end a last-minute "Note" on the Duke of Veraguas, not included in the

American edition, and the American edition contains at the beginning an "Advertisement" that is not included in the London edition.

In a New York edition of 1834 published by N. and J. White, described on the title page as "Abridged and Arranged by the Author, Expressly for the Use of Schools," a third distinct text appears. Although it contains the forty-six chapters and the Appendix of the London text, the length is somewhat shortened and the style decidedly simplified for the use of school children. Chapter I of the American and London text begins, "Christopher Columbus, or Columbo, as the name is written in Italian, was born in the city of Genoa, [London text: was a native of Genoa, born] about the year 1435, of poor but reputable and meritorious parentage." Chapter I of the American school text begins, "Christopher Columbus, or Columbo, as the name is written in Italian, was a native of Genoa, and born about the year 1435." Similarly, the Introduction of the American and the London text begins, "Whether in old times beyond the reach of history or tradition, and at some remote period when, as some imagine, the arts may have flourished to a degree unknown to those whom we term the ancients, there existed an intercourse between the opposite shores of the Atlantic;...." The Introduction of the American school text begins, "Whether in old times beyond the reach of history or tradition, there existed an intercourse...." It is possible that Irving did make the further condensation, as the title page claims. The text was copyright in his name (by Irving himself?) on 16 August 1834. It can certainly be said with confidence that he approved the text, in part because of the copyright, in part because a copy of the 1834 edition at TxU bears the inscription, "Lewis Irving | From his uncle | Washington | Decr. 25, 1837." He would hardly make a Christmas present of a text he did not approve.

1A. THE | LIFE AND VOYAGES | OF | CHRISTOPHER COLUMBUS, | BY | WASHINGTON IRVING. | (ABRIDGED BY THE SAME.) | [rule] | Venient annis | Sæcula seris, quibus Oceanus | Vincula rerum laxet et ingens | Pateat tellus, Typhisque novos | Detegat orbes, nec sit terris | Ultima Thule. | *Seneca. Medea.* | [rule] | STEREOTYPED BY JAMES CONNER, FOR | G. & C. & H. CARVILL, 108 BROADWAY, NEW-YORK. | [rule] | 1829.

The American text.

(17.9 x 10.9): [1]^6 2-26^6. Not reckoned: terminal catalogue.

The terminal catalogue is dated June 1, 1829, paged [1] 2-12. On p. 11, this edition of the Abridged *Columbus* is listed as Number XLIV.

[1]-[2], title, on verso copyright ("the 4th day of April, A. D. 1829, in the 53d year of the Independence" by Washington Irving) and printer; [3]-4, Advertisement, dated Seville, December, 1828; [5]-8, Introduction; [9]-311, text; [312], blank.

Printer: Sleight, No. 3 Chatham Square.

Lineation: p. 100, that ... the ; p. 200, this ... one

Publisher's full calf. Sides blank. On spine, red leather label titled in gilt: [double rule] | IRVING'S | COLUMBUS | (ABRIDGED) | [double rule].

Title page deposited 4 April 1829. *New-York American*, 8 June 1829, "Will be published and ready for delivery on Tuesday, the 9th instant." *Critic*, 13 June 1829, reviewed. *Albion*, 20 June 1829, noticed as "just published."

TxU (2).

2A.   THE | LIFE AND VOYAGES | OF | CHRISTOPHER COLUMBUS, | BY | WASHINGTON IRVING. | (ABRIDGED BY THE SAME.) | [rule] | [6-line quotation] | *Seneca. Medea.* | [rule] | STEREOTYPED BY JAMES CONNER, FOR | G. & C. & H. CARVILL, 108 BROADWAY, NEW-YORK. | [rule] | 1830.

The American text.

Copyright 4 April 1829.

(14.9 x 8.9): [i]-[iv], [5]-252.

Lineation: p. 100, other ... the

Not examined. Description from Xerox of title and other information supplied by NRU.

3Aa.   THE | LIFE AND VOYAGES | OF | CHRISTOPHER COLUMBUS, | BY | WASHINGTON IRVING. | (ABRIDGED BY THE SAME.) | [rule] | [6-line quotation] | *Seneca. Medea.* | [rule] | A NEW EDITION, | WITH ADDITIONS AND IMPROVEMENTS, | BY THE AUTHOR. | [rule] | STEREOTYPED BY JAMES CONNER, FOR | G. & C. & H. CARVILL, 108 BROADWAY, NEW-YORK. | [rule] | 1831.

Essentially the London text, but with the Advertisement of the American text retained. Two chapters are numbered XXI.

On 2 September 1831, G. & C. & H. Carvill took out a new copyright, in their own name as proprietors, for the new abridged text. They also deposited a copy on that day.

(15.5 x 10.0): [i]-iv, [5]-267 [268]. Not reckoned: four pages of terminal notices of the first edition of the work. Signed in 6's.

Lineation: p. 100, other ... the ; p. 200, at ... privi-

Copy in MH reported in cloth with leather label on spine.

DLC.

b. PRINTED BY J. & J. HARPER, | 82 CLIFF-STREET. | [rule] | 1833.

Place of publication (New York) not named.

Four pages of preliminary advertisements; twelve pages of terminal advertisements.

Publisher's full calf with black leather label on spine.

NNC.

c. [New York: N. and J. White, 1833.]

Printed by J. & J. Harper.

Not seen. Copy reported in WaS.

4A. THE | LIFE AND VOYAGES | OF | CHRISTOPHER COLUMBUS, | BY | WASHINGTON IRVING. | (ABRIDGED BY THE SAME.) | [rule] | [6-line quotation] | *Seneca. Medea.* | [rule] | A NEW EDITION, | WITH ADDITIONS AND IMPROVEMENTS, | BY THE AUTHOR. | [rule] | NEW-YORK: | PRINTED AND PUBLISHED BY J. & J. HARPER, | NO. 82 CLIFF-STREET, | AND FOR SALE BY THE PRINCIPAL BOOKSELLERS THROUGHOUT | THE UNITED STATES. | [rule] | 1833.

Essentially the London text, but with the Advertisement of the American text retained.

Copyright 1831.

(20.0 x 11.6): [1]-327 [328]. Bound at front, not reckoned, two pages of recommendation of the book to the legislature by John A. Dix, Superintendant of Common Schools, New York, dated 30 May 1833. Signed in 6's.

Lineation: p. 100, that ... the ; p. 200, On ... cask

Purple LI-like figured cloth. Spine titled in gilt.

DLC.

5Aa- THE | LIFE AND VOYAGES | OF | CHRISTOPHER COLUMBUS, |
  d. BY | WASHINGTON IRVING. | [rule] | ABRIDGED AND ARRANGED BY THE AUTHOR, EXPRESSLY FOR THE USE | OF SCHOOLS. | [rule] | *NEW-YORK*: | PUBLISHED BY N. AND J. WHITE, | 108 PEARL-STREET. | [rule] | 1834.

The school text.

(14.5 x 9.2): [1]^6 2-18^6 19^2. The last leaf is a blank. Not reckoned: four pages of preliminary advertisements for this work, beginning with a resolution by the New York state legislature, dated Albany, 30th May, 1833, recommending the book to schools; also preliminary illustration and three illustrations through the text.

[i]-[ii], title, the verso appears in four variant states; [iii]-iv, Introduction; [5]-200, text; 201-202, Appendix; [203]-218, Questions (i.e., for the student). The paragraphs are numbered in the text.

The verso of the title page appears in four variant states:

[A]. Copyright notice only: 1831.

[B]. Copyright notice: 1831. Printer's imprint, in one line: James Van Norden, Printer, 49 William-street.

[C]. Copyright notice: 1834. Printer's imprint, in one line: James Van Norden, Printer, 49 William-street.

[D]. Copyright notice: 1834. Printer's imprint, in two lines: James Van Norden, Printer, | 49 William-street.

The copyright notices give only the year of copyright. The two for the year 1831 presumably refer to the copyright taken out on the abridged text by the Carvills on 2 September 1831 (although here described as in the name of Washington Irving). The two for the year 1834 refer to the copyright taken out by Washington Irving on 16 August 1834, described on the copyright form, as in the title of the work, "abridged and arranged by the author expressly for the use of schools." The granting of copyright would have required the deposit of a title page on 16 August. A copy of the book was deposited later, on 19 September 1834.

Lineation: p. 100, roved ... his ; p. 200, directed ... posterity!

Noted or reported in blue-green paper boards with black leather shelfback, cover-title on front; or in publisher's full leather.

State [A]: CtY, TxU. State [B]: CtY. State [C]: ViU. State [D]: ViU.

e. *NEW YORK:* | PUBLISHED BY N. AND J. WHITE, | 108 PEARL-STREET. | [rule] | 1835.

Copyright 1834.

Blue-green paper boards with black leather shelfback. On front, cover-title within border of single frame lines with decorated corners. Below border: James Van Norden, Printer, 49 William-street. On back, advertisements.

ViU.

f. [New York: N. and J. White, 1836.]

Not seen. Copy reported in CtY.

g.   [New York: Collins, Keese & Co., 1838.]

      Not seen. Copies reported in CtY, CU.

h.   NEW-YORK: | *PUBLISHED BY COLLINS, KEESE & CO.* | NO. 254
      PEARL STREET. | 1839.

      Copyright 1834.

      MB.

i.   BATH, N. Y. | R. L. UNDERHILL & CO. | 1844.

      Copyright 1834.

      Full calf.

      ArU.

6Aa- THE | AMERICAN LIBRARY | OF | LITERATURE AND SCIENCE. |
  b. [rule] | VOL. I. | [rule] | INTRODUCTORY ESSAY TO THE | SCHOOL
      LIBRARY. | [rule] | IRVING'S LIFE AND VOYAGES OF |
      COLUMBUS, | WITH THE AUTHOR'S VISIT TO PALOS. | AND A
      PORTRAIT, MAP, AND OTHER ILLUSTRATIONS. | [rule] | BOSTON:
      | MARSH, CAPEN, LYON, AND WEBB. | 1839.

      A second title page appears following the "Introductory Essay": THE | LIFE
      AND VOYAGES | OF | CHRISTOPHER COLUMBUS. | BY |
      WASHINGTON IRVING. | (ABRIDGED BY THE SAME.) |
      INCLUDING THE AUTHOR'S | VISIT TO PALOS. | WITH | A
      PORTRAIT, MAP, AND OTHER ILLUSTRATIONS. | [cut of galley, as in
      the London editions] | BOSTON: | MARSH, CAPEN, LYON, AND
      WEBB. | 1839.

      Essentially the London text, with additional matter. On pp. v-vi (of the
      second numbering), a NOTE on the discovery of Vinland may well be by
      Irving. The "Glossary" and "Index" at the end certainly are not and were
      probably furnished by the anonymous editor, Joseph W. Ingraham.

      Copyright 1839 by March, Capen, Lyon, and Webb.

      (18.7 x 11.6): [i]-xlviii, [i]-xi[xii], [9]-325 [326]. Not reckoned: preliminary
      portrait by E. W. Bouvé, engraved series title, two illustrations, and twenty-
      two pages of terminal advertisements. Signed in 6's.

      At the end are bound sixteen pages of advertisements, headed THE
      SCHOOL ADVERTISER NO. II. | AUGUST, 1839, followed by six pages
      of specimen pages, including pp. 61 and 286 of this edition.

      Lineation: p. 100, small, ... and ; p. 200, already ... im-

Blue V cloth. Sides blank. On spine, in gilt, within boxes of frame lines, the title (without author) and series title: THE | AMERICAN | LIBRARY. | I

The edition also appeared in a variant impression:

THE | SCHOOL LIBRARY. | PUBLISHED UNDER THE SANCTION OF THE BOARD OF EDUCA- | TION OF THE STATE OF MASSACHUSETTS. | [rule] | VOL. I. | [rule] | INTRODUCTORY ESSAY TO THE | SCHOOL LIBRARY. | [rule] | IRVING'S LIFE AND VOYAGES OF | COLUMBUS, | WITH THE AUTHOR'S VISIT TO PALOS. | AND A PORTRAIT, MAP, AND OTHER ILLUSTRATIONS. | [rule] | BOSTON: | MARSH, CAPEN, LYON, AND WEBB. | 1839.

No advertisements noted in this impression.

Blue heavily-ribbed T cloth with black leather shelfback. Sides blank. Spine titled in gilt; with series title also: THE | SCHOOL | LIBRARY. | VOL. I. Brown endpapers.

Christian Examiner [Boston], January 1840, reviewed (with series title of "The School Library").

"The American Library": *BL*. "The School Library": TxU.

c. NEW YORK: | HARPER & BROTHERS, PUBLISHERS, | 82 CLIFF STREET. | 1847.

(18.7 x 11.5): [i]-xi [xii], [9]-325 [326]. Signed in 6's. Printed from the same setting, but with the "Introduction" omitted. Not reckoned: two pages of terminal advertisements.

Brown T cloth. Sides decorated in blind. Spine titled in gilt, within box of double frame lines: LIFE | OF | COLUMBUS ; at foot, NEW-YORK | HARPER & BROTHERS White endpapers.

NNU.

d. [New York: Harper & Brothers, 1851.]

Not seen. Copy reported in CtY.

e. [New York: Harper & Brothers, 1854.]

Not seen. Copy reported in OO.

f. NEW YORK: | HARPER & BROTHERS, PUBLISHERS | 329 & 331 PEARL STREET, | FRANKLIN SQUARE. | 1855.

MH.

g. NEW YORK: | HARPER & BROTHERS, PUBLISHERS | 329 & 331 PEARL STREET, | FRANKLIN SQUARE. | 1856.

MB.

h. NEW YORK: | HARPER & BROTHERS, PUBLISHERS | 329 & 331
PEARL STREET, | FRANKLIN SQUARE. | 1858.

Gray AR cloth. Sides decorated in blind. Spine titled in gilt. Cream
endpapers.

DLC.

i. NEW YORK: | HARPER & BROTHERS, PUBLISHERS | 329 & 331
PEARL STREET, | FRANKLIN SQUARE.

No date. 185-?

Z-like cloth embossed with small interconnected triangles. Sides elaborately
bordered in blind. Spine titled in gilt: LIFE AND VOYAGES | OF |
COLUMBUS. | [rule] | IRVING. | Harper & Brothers. White endpapers.

TxU.

1E. THE | LIFE AND VOYAGES | OF | CHRISTOPHER COLUMBUS. |
BY | WASHINGTON IRVING. | (ABRIDGED BY THE SAME.) | [cut of
galley] | LONDON: | JOHN MURRAY, ALBEMARLE-STREET. |
MDCCCXXX.

The London text.

(15.5 x 9.8): [a]^2 b^4 B-I^8 K-U^8 X-Z^8 AA^4. Not reckoned: preliminary
portrait of Columbus, four illustrations, maps, and two pages of terminal
advertisements for "The Family Library," dated January, 1830.

[i]-[ii], title, on verso quotation from Seneca, and printer; [iii]-vii, table of
contents; [viii], "Notice of the Plates"; [ix]-xi, Introduction; [xii], blank; [1]-
357, text; [358], printer.

Printer: Thomas Davison, Whitefriars.

Lineation: p. 100, leaving ... native ; p. 200, The ... ready

Light brown V cloth. On front, in black, within double frame lines: THE |
FAMILY LIBRARY. | No. XI. | [rule] | COLUMBUS. | [rule] |
LONDON: | JOHN MURRAY, ALBEMARLE STREET. | MDCCCXXX.
| *PRICE FIVE SHILLINGS.* On back, list of ten vols. of "The Family
Library" already published (not including this one). On spine: LIFE | OF |
COLUMBUS. | [rule] | 5s. | FAMILY | LIBRARY. | N° XI. White
endpapers.

In letters to his brother Peter, 29 October 1830 and 1 March 1831, Irving says
that 10,000 copies were printed.

Literary Gazette, 27 February 1830, reviewed. *Athenæum,* 6 March 1830, listed; 13 March 1830, reviewed. *English Catalogue of Books, 1801-1836* lists March 1830 as publication date.

CtY, TxU.

2E. THE | LIFE AND VOYAGES | OF | CHRISTOPHER COLUMBUS. | BY | WASHINGTON IRVING, | (ABRIDGED BY THE SAME.) | [cut of galley] | LONDON: | JOHN MURRAY, ALBEMARLE-STREET. | MDCCCXXXI.

The London text.

(15.2 x 9.7): [i]-xi [xii], [1]-357 [358]. Signed in 8's. Not reckoned: preliminary portrait of Columbus, four illustrations, and maps. P. [358] carries Murray advertisements for "New Books": six works by Irving. Preliminary catalogue of "The Family Library" and other works, undated, paged [1] 2-16; this work appears on p. 2; on p. 16 there is a brief quotation from Irving's review of *A Year in Spain* by A Young American.

In the same number of pages as the edition of 1830, and sometimes reproduced line for line, but reset.

Printer: W. Clowes, Stamford Street.

Lineation: p. 100, fidelity. ... na-; p. 200, The ... ready

The light brown V cloth binding (called "canvass" in the catalogue) is generally similar to the binding of the first London edition, except that on the back the list of works in "The Family Library" contains twenty titles, including this one.

In a letter to his brother Peter, 1 March 1831, Irving says that Murray "is putting another edition to press."

BL, ViU, Private hands.

3E. THE | LIFE AND VOYAGES | OF | CHRISTOPHER COLUMBUS. | BY | WASHINGTON IRVING, | (ABRIDGED BY THE SAME.) | [cut of galley] | SECOND EDITION. | LONDON: | PRINTED FOR THOMAS TEGG, | 73, CHEAPSIDE. | 1841.

The London text.

(14.8 x 9.6 rebound): [i]-vii [viii], [1]-356. Signed in 8's. A reprint of the Murray edition of 1831, sometimes reproduced line for line, but reset. Same illustrations.

Printer: J. Haddon, Castle Street, Finsbury.

Lineation: p. 100, river, ... na-; p. 200, The ... ready

BL.

1F.   THE | LIFE AND VOYAGES | OF | CHRISTOPHER COLUMBUS. | BY | WASHINGTON IRVING. | ABRIDGED BY THE SAME | FOR THE USE OF SCHOOLS. | [emblem: L. B within wreath] | PARIS: | BAUDRY, 9, RUE DU COQ SAINT-HONORÉ; | A. AND W. GALIGNANI, 18, RUE VIVIENNE; | BOBÉE AND HINGRAY, 14, RUE DE RICHELIEU. | 1830.

The London text.

(17.7 x 10.6 untrimmed): [i]-[iv], [1]-368. Signed in 12's.

Printer: Crapelet, Rue de Vaugirard, No. 9.

Lineation: p. 100, CHAPTER XIII. ... his ; p. 200, proper ... men.

Issued in paper wrappers. Seen only rebound, although untrimmed.

BL.

2F.   [Paris: Baudry, 1846.]

Pp. [i]-viii, [1]-414. 8vo.

Not seen. Copy reported in Bibliothèque Nationale.

1G.   THE | LIFE AND VOYAGES | OF | CHRISTOPHER COLUMBUS. | BY | WASHINGTON IRVING. | ABRIDGED BY THE SAME | FOR THE USE OF SCHOOLS. | [rule] | Mit grammatikalischen Erläuterungen | und | einem Wörterbuche. | *Zum Schul- und Privatgebrauche.* | [double rule] | Leipzig, | Baumgärtners Buchhandlung. | 1832.

Text in English; notes and vocabulary in German. The London text.

(17.9 x 10.4): [i]-x [xi]-[xii], [1]-304. Not reckoned: four pages of terminal advertisements, unpaged.

Lineation: p. 100, crusade ... sovereigns

Not examined. Description from Xerox of title page and other information supplied by ICU. Copy reported in Stadt- und Universitätsbibliothek Frankfurt.

2G.   THE | LIFE AND VOYAGES | OF | CHRISTOPHER COLUMBUS. | BY | WASHINGTON IRVING. | ABRIDGED BY THE SAME | FOR THE USE OF SCHOOLS. | [rule] | Mit grammatischen Erläuterungen | und | einem Wörterbuche. | *Zum Schul- und Privatgebrauche.* | ZWEITE | verbesserte Auflage. | [elaborated swelled rule] | Leipzig, | Baumgärtners Buchhandlung. | 1837.

Text in English; notes and vocabulary in German. The London text.

(17.9 x 10.6): [i]-xii, [1]-328. Signed in 12's.

Lineation: p. 100, member ... bay.

BL.

3G.   [Dritte verbesserte Auflage. Leipzig: Baumgärtners Buchhandlung, 1840.]

Not seen. Copy reported in Stadtbibliothek Braunschweig.

4G.   THE | LIFE AND VOYAGES | OF | CHRISTOPHER COLUMBUS. | BY | WASHINGTON IRVING. | ABRIDGED BY THE SAME | FOR THE USE OF SCHOOLS. | [rule] | Mit grammatischen Erläuterungen | und | einem Wörterbuche. | *Zum Schul- und Privatgebrauche.* | VIERTE | verbesserte, mit Stereotypen gedruckte Auflage. | [double rule] | Leipzig, | Baumgärtners Buchhandlung. | 1846.

Text in English; notes and vocabulary in German. The London text.

(17.6 x 11.2): [I]-XII, [1]-308. Signed in 8's.

Printer: Bernh. Tauchnitz jun.

Lineation: p. 100, lands ... [in footnote] haben.

BL, TxU.

5Ga. [Funfte, mit Stereotypen gedruckte Auflage. Leipzig: Baumgärtner, 1853.]

With two engravings.

Not seen. Copy reported in Staatsbibliothek Bamberg.

b[?]. [Sechste, mit Stereotypen gedruckte Auflage. Leipzig: Baumgärtner, 1857.]

With two engravings.

Not seen. Copy reported in Staats- und Stadtbibliothek Augsburg.

6G.   [*The Life and Voyages of Christopher Columbus.* By Washington Irving. Herausgegeben und mit einem ausführlichen Wörtebuche versehen von J. H. Lohmann. Quedlinburg: G. Basse.]

1830's.

Signed in 8's.

Not located. The edition is not listed in German libraries. Advertised and described under the heading SCHULSCHRIFTEN in the terminal advertisements in G. Basse's edition of *The Sketch Book*, [1838?].

7G.   THE | LIFE AND VOYAGES | OF | CHRISTOPHER COLUMBUS. |
      BY | WASHINGTON IRVING. | [rule] | WITH A COPIOUS
      VOCABULARY COMPILED | BY | Dr. E. AMTHOR. | [rule] |
      REVISED EDITION. | [elaborated swelled rule] | LEIPZIG, |
      PUBLISHED BY RENGER. | 1846.

      (14.7 x 10.4): [I]-VIII, [1]-326 [327]-[328]. Preliminary portrait of Columbus
      not reckoned. Signed in 8's.

      Printer: Alexander Wiede, Leipzig.

      Lineation: p. 100, CHAPTER XVI. ... holy ; p. 200, terms, ... Spanish

      NN. Copy reported in Stadtbibliothek Mainz.

1S.   THE | LIFE AND VOYAGES | OF | CHRISTOPHER COLUMBUS. |
      BY | WASHINGTON IRVING. | ABRIDGED BY THE SAME | *For the
      Use of Schools.* | [rule] | Med en Engelsk Grammatik | och |
      Pronunciations-Lära samt Ordbok. | [rule] | [double rule] | Läsebok i
      Engelska Språket för | Skolor och Sjelfundervisning. | [double rule] |
      [swelled rule] | Norrköping, [in fraktur] | hos Bokhandlaren A. Bohlin.
      [name in fraktur] | [rule] | 1834.

      Text in English; introduction to the English language, notes and vocabulary
      in Swedish. The London text.

      (19.3 x 10.8 trimmed): [6 pp. unpaged], [3]-45 [46], [I]-V [VI], [1]-258, [I]-
      LIII [LIV]-[LVI]. Signed in 4's.

      Lineation: p. 100, the ... ruins,; p. 200, he ... [in footnote] history.

      In copy examined, original tan paper wrappers bound in. On front, cover-
      title within decorative border. On back, statement by Abr. Bohlin within
      decorative border.

      DLC.

2S.   THE | LIFE AND VOYAGES | OF | CHRISTOPHER COLUMBUS, |
      BY | WASHINGTON IRVING. | ABRIDGED BY THE SAME | *For the
      Use of Schools.* | [rule] | MED UPPLYSANDE NOTER, EN KORT
      GRAMMATIK | OCH FULLSTÄNDIG ORDBOK. | [elaborated swelled
      rule] | *Andra Upplagan,* | Omarbetad | AF | C. N. Öhrlander. [in fraktur] |
      [swelled rule] | STOCKHOLM, [in fraktur] | ZACHARIAS
      HÆGGSTRÖM, | 1843.

      Text in English; introduction, notes and vocabulary in Swedish. The London
      text.

      (18.7 x 11.1): [6 pp. unpaged], [I]-XLIV, I-IV, [1]-342, [I]-LXXVIII. Signed
      in 4's.

Lineation: p. 100, driven 32) ... write.

BL.

TRANSLATIONS

Czech.

Život a cesty | KRISTOFA KOLUMBA. | [rule] | Z angličiny Washingtona Irvinga | přeložil | J. Malý. | [stylized swelled rule] | V PRAZE. [decorative hollow letters] | Tisk a náklad Jaroslava Pospísila. | 1853.

Preliminary series title: AMERIKA | od času svého odkrytí až na nejnovější | dobu. | *Sestavil J. Malý.*

(16.6 x 10.3): [12 pp. unpaged], [1]-348. Map before title not reckoned. Signed in 12's.

Lineation: p. 100, Hlava ... aby ; p. 200, tadem ... dítek.

CtY.

French.

[*Voyages et Aventures de Christophe Colomb.*   Traduit de l'anglais de Washington Irving par Paul Merruau. Paris: Lavigne, 1837.]

"Bibliothèque des Familles."

291 pp. Illustrations. Signed in 12's.

Printer: Dupuy, Paris.

Bibliographie de la France, 17 December 1836, # 6366, listed.

Not seen. Copy reported in Bibliothèque Nationale.

[2e édition. Paris: Lavigne, 1837.]

291 pp. 4 vignettes. Signed in 12's.

An edition is listed in *Bibliographie de la France,* 6 January 1838, #108; presumably it is this one.

Not seen. Copy reported in Bibliothèque Nationale.

[*Voyages et Aventures de Christophe Colomb.*   Traduit de l'anglais de Washington Irving par Paul Merruau. Tours: A. Mame, 1843.]

"Bibliothèque des Écoles Chrétiennes."

288 pp. Illustrated.

Not seen. Copy reported in Bibliothèque Nationale.

[Although not located, a second and a third impression or edition --
identified on the title pages as "Second Edition," "Third Edition" --
presumably were published.]

[4e édition. Tours: A. Mame, 1851.]

236 pp.

Not seen. Copy reported in Bibliothèque Nationale.

[5e édition. Tours: A. Mame, 1853.]

171 pp.

Not seen. Copy reported in Bibliothèque Nationale.

[6e édition. Tours: A. Mame, 1857.]

171 pp.

Not seen. Copy reported in Bibliothèque Nationale.

German.

Die Geschichte | des | Lebens und der Reisen | Christoph's Columbus | von
| Washington Irving. | [double rule] | Im Auszuge für die Jugend |
bearbeitet | von | Rudolph Friedner. | [swelled rule] | Mit einer Karte. |
[quadruple rule] | Neustadt a. d. Haardt bei Ph. Christmann. | 1829. [in
fraktur]

(17.6 x 10.7): [I]-VI [VII]-[VIII], [1]-312. Map inserted at end. Signed in 8's.

Printer: E. L. Rost, Zweibrücken.

Lineation: p. 100, günstigem ... Leuten ; p. 200, seine ... könne.

Not examined. Description from Xerox of title and other information
supplied by Universitätsbibliothek Giessen.

Christoph Columbus | Leben und Reisen. | Von | Washington Irving. |
[swelled rule] | Auszug von dem Verfasser. | [rule] | Aus dem Englischen

übersetzt. | [rule] | Stuttgart und Tübingen, | in der J. G. Cotta'schen Buchhandlung. | 1833. [in fraktur]

(11.4 x 19.4): [i]-x, [1]-366. Signed in 8's.

Printer: Buchdruckerei der J. G. Cotta'schen Buchhandlung.

Lineation: p. 100, forschen ... suchen ; p. 200, Zu ... folgte.

Not examined. Description from Xerox of title and other information supplied by Universitätsbibliothek Stuttgart.

Greek.

[Transliteration of title: O Christóphoros Kolómbos, íti istoría tís zoís ke ton thalassoporíon aftú kata tón O. Irving. Ek tú Gallikú ipó G. A. Aristídhu. En Athínes, 1858.]

"From the French" by G. A. Aristides. But what French edition? Perhaps one of the later impressions by A. Mame of Tours.

Not located. Listed by Williams and Edge, who had not seen a copy.]

Polish.

ŻYWOT I PÓDROŻE | KRZYSZTOFA KOLUMBA | PRZEZ | WASHINGTONA IRVINGA [in letters with outline about each character] | TŁUMACZYŁ Z ANGIELSKIEGO | Franciszek Chlewaski. [in semi-script] | [cut of sailing ship] | WARSZAWA [in hollow letters] | NAKLAD GUSTAWA LEONA GLÜCKSBERGA | KSIĘGARZA PRZY ULICY MIODOWEJ. | [elaborated short swelled rule] | 1843.

Franciszek Chlewaski, identified as the translator, is a pseudonym of Emanuel Glücksberg.

(21.7 x 13.3): [i]-[viii], [1?]-364. 8vo.

Printer: J. Wróblewskiego.

Not examined. Information based on copy in Biblioteka Narodowa, Warsaw.

Editions of Selections

A SHORT SKETCH | OF THE | FIRST VOYAGE ACROSS THE ATLANTIC OCEAN, | AND | LANDING OF CHRISTOPHER COLUMBUS | ON THE AMERICAN SHORE, IN 1492. | TAKEN FROM IRVING'S ABRIDGMENT OF HIS LIFE. | [cut of ship] | NEW-YORK: | PRINTED AND SOLD BY MAHLON DAY, | AT THE NEW JUVENILE BOOK-STORE, | No. 374, Pearl-street. | 1833.

(18.0 x 10.7): [1]^{10}. Paged [1]-23 [24]. Wrapper counted in pagination.

Lineation: p. 10, ence, ... the

Yellow paper wrapper. On front, title within ornate border. On back, advertisements for "Beautiful Colored Toy Books." First and last page of contents pasted to wrapper leaves.

CtY, NNHi.

THE CONQUEST OF GRANADA

On 31 August 1828, Irving wrote from Cadiz to Colonel Thomas Aspinwall, his agent in London, that he was sending a parcel of manuscript, "being part of a chronicle of the conquest of Granada," "founded on facts diligently gathered by my brother Peter & myself." He promised "upwards of nine hundred pages" and asked Aspinwall to find a publisher. He continued to send parcels of manuscript through 18 October, and by December 1828 Aspinwall had concluded arrangements for publication by John Murray. In the meantime, Irving sent to his brother Ebenezer on 16 October 1828 "the greater part (if not all) of the manuscript of my new work" and asked him to sell the publication rights to Carey, Lea & Carey of Philadelphia.

In December Irving heard from Aspinwall that Chapters 34 and 35 were missing from the London manuscript. (In fact, as we know now, they had been sent by mistake to America.) On 20 December, Washington wrote Ebenezer to send to Aspinwall a copy of the chapters from the American manuscript. But after finding his old notes, Washington sent to Aspinwall a rewritten version of the missing chapters. It was this rewritten version that was finally published in the London edition; the original chapters are now in the Berg Collection in the New York Public Library and were never employed by Irving for publication. To further complicate the differences between the original manuscript and the London version, on 18 September Irving sent to Aspinwall revised copy for the original Introduction and opening of Chapter One, but did not make the changes in his own manuscript destined for America.

It is of interest, although not of importance in the printing history itself, that Irving prepared a revised edition of the work, apparently in 1829-1830, that never found publication. Portions of the manuscript are now in the Barrett Library of The University of Virginia.

On 5 March 1829, Murray registered the new work at Stationers' Hall and made the required deposit of eleven copies. He had already begun advertising the book and continued to do so for some three months. But he witheld publication until late May, waiting for settlement of the Catholic question: the agitated question of the day that resulted in the Catholic Relief Act of 1829. Irving received a copy in Seville on 10 April, but the public had to wait. In the meantime, Carey, Lea & Carey brought out the American edition in the middle of April. Irving apparently brooded over his London copy for a month before writing Murray on 9 April a stiff objection to his

335

own name appearing on the title page rather than simply that of the purported author, Fray Antonio Agapida. Irving had read proof of neither edition and did not know of Murray's change in the title page until too late.

With separate manuscripts sent to London and to America -- the London version predominantly the work of Spanish copyists -- and with Irving's late revisions, voluntary and involuntary, for the London edition, and with two publishers' imposition of editorial changes as well as house styling brought to a careless manuscript, it is only to be expected that the two original printed versions differ noticeably from each other. Comparison reveals a number of small differences in word choice and a great number of differences in spelling, punctuation, and even paragraphing. The number and order of chapters remains the same, although a few chapters differ in title (spelling and punctuation of titles differ often): in Vol. I, for instance, Chapter XXVII of the American edition is titled, "Foray of Christian Knights into the territory of the Moors," but in the London edition, "Foray of Christian knights into the territories of the Moors"; in Vol. II, Chapter XXVII of the American edition is titled, "Siege of Baza. -- Embarrassments of the army," but in the London edition (there called Chapter LXXI, for the chapters are numbered consecutively through the work except for a repetition of the number XLV) it is titled, "Siege of Baza. Embarrassment of the army." The most dramatic of differences in text, however, appear in the chapters that Irving rewrote for the London edition.

The last sentence of Chapter XXXV will illustrate the difference in the two texts. The sentences are not as completely different as others that could be chosen, but they do illustrate Irving's reworking and expansion in his ironic style:

First American edition: "So it is, in the admirable order of sublunary affairs: every thing seeks its kind; the rich befriend the rich, the powerful stand by the powerful, the poor enjoy the patronage of the poor -- and thus a universal harmony prevails."

First London edition: "So it is in this wonderful system of sublunary affairs; the rich befriend the rich, the powerful stand by the powerful, while the poor enjoy the sterile assistance of their fellows: thus, each one seeking his kind, the admirable order of things is maintained, and a universal harmony prevails."

The London edition, oddly, has two chapters given the number XLV at the end of Vol. I. The second, titled "How Boabdil returned secretly to Granada...," is Chapter I of Vol. II in the American edition. The result is that the London edition appears at first to have ninety-nine chapters, as compared to the one hundred chapters of the American edition. In the London edition, the second or repeated chapter number is followed by an asterisk, both in the table of contents and in the text, but the meaning of the asterisk is not explained.

Irving revised the work for publication in the Author's Revised Edition, 1850, basing his text not on the London edition but on the American. In a "Note to the Revised Edition," dated Sunnyside, 1850, and added after the Introduction, Irving says that he has "brought [the] narrative more strictly within historical bounds" and has "corrected and enriched it in various parts with facts recently brought to light by the researches of Alcántara and others." That seems accurate. He also revised for stylistic purposes. The number of chapters remains one hundred, but titles and contents are often changed. In addition, Irving added two discussions to the Appendix: "Zoraya, the Star of the Morning," and "Fate of Aben Comixa."

Within two years of its first publication, the work was published in France by Baudry and Galignani, and was translated into Dutch, French, German (in two translations), Spanish and Swedish, all derived from the first London edition.

1Aa. *Small paper impression.*

A | CHRONICLE | OF THE | CONQUEST OF GRANADA. | [rule] | BY | FRAY ANTONIO AGAPIDA. | [rule] | IN TWO VOLUMES. | VOL. I. [II.] | [elaborated swelled rule] | Philadelphia: [fancy] | CAREY, LEA & CAREY -- CHESNUT-STREET. | [rule of 26 dots] | 1829.

(19.7 x 11.6 untrimmed): Vol. I. Signed and bound [A]^6 B-I^6 K-U^6 X-Z^6 Aa-Cc^6. Also signed [1]-[2]^4 3-39^4. Two leaves of terminal advertisements signed A^2. Vol. II. Signed and bound [A]^6 B-I^6 K-U^6 Aa-Cc^6 Dd^4. Also signed [1]^{4}2-28^4 30^4 30-35^4 33^4 37-40^4.

In Vol. I, the four pages of terminal advertisements are undated, unpaged. The first item on p. [1] is headed JUST PUBLISHED | BY | CAREY, LEA & CAREY, | IN AN ELEGANTLY ORNAMENTED CASE, | THE | ATLANTIC SOUVENIR, | ... | FOR 1829.

The terminal advertisements appear in two settings. The sequence is probable.

[A]. P. [2], lines 11-12: in the au-| tumn.

P. [4], lines 3-4 of the *Contents* of *Elia*. First Series: A | Quaker Meeting. -- The old and new Schoolmaster -- Valentine's

[B]. P. [2], line 11: in the autumn. |

P. [4], lines 3-4 of the *Contents* of *Elia*. First Series: A | Chapter on Ears. -- All Fools' Day. -- A Quaker Meeting. -- The

Vol. I. [i]-2, advertisements; [iii]-[iv], title, on verso copyright ("the sixth day of March, in the fifty-third year of the independence of the United States of America, A.D. 1829" by Washington Irving); [v]-viii, table of contents; [ix]-xii,

Introduction; [13]-311, text; [312], blank. Vol. II. [i]-[ii], title, on verso same copyright; [iii]-vi, table of contents; [7]-319, text; [320], blank.

In Vol. I, the advertisements on pp. [i]-2 (the second page is so numbered) are headed *The following works have been recently published by* | CAREY, LEA & CAREY. The first item on p. [i] is *The Sketch Book*; the last item on p. 2 is *Tokeah; or the White Rose*, a Novel.

Lineation: Vol. I. p. 100, enemy, ... through ; p. 200, gines ... [in note] Palacios. Vol. II. p. 100, way ... es-; p. 200, the ... God!"

Tan paper boards with red V cloth shelfback. Sides blank. White paper label on spines: [double rule] | IRVING'S | CONQUEST | OF | GRANADA, | IN 2 VOLS. | [rule] | VOL. I. [II.] | [double rule]. White endpapers. Flyleaf at beginning of Vol. I but not at end. Vol. II noted with flyleaf at beginning and at end, and also with two flyleaves at beginning but none at end.

A bookseller's catalogue, 1979, lists a copy in boards with green cloth shelfbacks, black leather label on spines. The measurements of the copy (20.7 cm., 8 1/8 x 5 3/8 in.) are said to differ from those of the small paper and large paper copies seen.

The Cost Book of Carey & Lea specifies 3000 copies of the small paper impression. It also names the printer: I. Ashmead.

Title page deposited 5 March 1829, despite the printed copyright notice for 6 March. *American Quarterly Review*, March 1829, reviewed. *National Gazette and Literary Register*, 18 April 1829, advertised. Irving to John Murray, 22 September 1850, "It appeared in New York 20th April 1829."

MH, TxU (4).

b.   *Large paper impression*.

Title page the same.

(23.2 x 14.6 untrimmed): Signed the same, in numbers and in letters, but bound in 8's. Printed from the same setting.

In Vol. I, the two pages of preliminary advertisements are the same. The terminal advertisements are undated, paged [1] 2-4. The first item on p. [1]: CAREY, LEA & CAREY | *Will Publish in March,* | MR. IRVING'S NEW WORK, | A CHRONICLE | OF | THE CONQUEST OF GRANADA. | In 2 vols. 12mo. | An edition will also be published in 2 vols. 8vo. to match with the 8vo. edi- | tions of his preceding works.

Copies are reported by Langfeld and Blackburn with no advertisements at the end of Vol. I, but four pages of advertisements, undated, unpaged, at the beginning of Vol. II.

The Cost Book of Carey & Lea specifies 500 copies of the large paper impression. The printer is the same: I. Ashmead.

Tan paper boards with tan cloth shelfback, and also with purple cloth shelfback. Sides blank. Same white paper labels on spines: [double rule] | IRVING'S | CONQUEST | OF | GRANADA, | IN 2 VOLS. | [rule] | VOL. I. [II.] | [double rule]. White endpapers. Flyleaves.

NN, TxU, Private hands.

c. Philadelphia: [fancy] | CAREY & LEA. -- CHESTNUT STREET. | [rule of 16 dots] | 1831.

TxU.

d. Philadelphia: [fancy] | CAREY & LEA -- CHESTNUT STREET. | [rule of 15 dots] | 1833.

NN.

e. A NEW EDITION. | [rule] | Philadelphia: [fancy] | CAREY, LEA, & BLANCHARD. | [rule of 21 dots] | 1835.

NN.

f. A NEW EDITION. | [rule] | Philadelphia: [fancy] | CAREY, LEA, & BLANCHARD. | [rule of 21 dots] | 1836.

Still copyright 1829.

CtY.

g. A NEW EDITION. | [rule] | Philadelphia: [fancy] | CAREY, LEA, & BLANCHARD. | [rule of 21 dots] | 1837.

Copyright 1836.

CtY.

h. A NEW EDITION. | [rule] | Philadelphia: [fancy] | CAREY, LEA, & BLANCHARD. | [rule of 21 dots] | 1838.

CtY, MB.

i. A NEW EDITION. | [rule] | PHILADELPHIA: | LEA & BLANCHARD, | [rule of 30 dots] | 1840.

Green V cloth. White paper label on spines.

AzU (Vol. I only).

j. [A New Edition. Philadelphia: Lea & Blanchard, 1841.]

Not seen. Copy reported in PP.

2Aa. CHRONICLE | OF THE | CONQUEST OF GRANADA. | FROM THE MSS. OF | FRAY ANTONIO AGAPIDA. | NEW-YORK: | GEORGE P. PUTNAM, 155 BROADWAY. | LONDON: JOHN MURRAY. | 1850.

"Author's Revised Edition," Vol. XIV.

(19.0 x 12.5): [-]^2 [1]^{12} 2-22^{12} 23^{10}. Page 21 mis-signed 2; p. 25 correctly signed 2.

[i]-[ii], Works title for Vol. XIV, dated 1850, verso blank; [iii]-[iv], title, on verso copyright (1950) and printer; [v]-xii, table of contents; [xiii]-xix, Introduction and Note to the Revised Edition, dated Sunnyside, 1850; [xx], blank; [17]-531, text; [532], blank; [533]-548, Appendix.

Printer: John F. Trow, Printer and Stereotyper, 49, 51, and 53 Ann-st., N. Y.

Lineation: p. 100, had ... [in footnote] Palacios.; p. 200, nada ... [in footnote] Aragon.

Blue-green TB cloth. On sides, in blind, publisher's initials within ornamental design; wide-rule border around. Spine decorated in blind, titled in gilt: IRVING'S | WORKS | [rule] | CONQUEST | OF GRANADA || PUTNAM Yellow-buff endpapers.

Other individual volumes of the Author's Revised Edition are advertised as available in cloth, cloth extra gilt, half-calf, calf extra, half-morocco, and morocco. Presumably this volume was also so available.

Deposited 2 August 1850. *Literary World*, 3 August 1850, noted for "this week"; 24 August 1850, listed. *Albion*, 3 August 1850, "Will publish on Saturday, August 3."

NN, TxU.

b. NEW-YORK: | GEORGE P. PUTNAM, 155 BROADWAY. | LONDON: JOHN MURRAY. | 1851.

Works title, dated 1851.

Same binding in green, but noted with beige-pink endpapers with publisher's advertisements.

TxU, ViU.

c. NEW-YORK: | G. P. PUTNAM & COMPANY, 10 PARK PLACE, | 1852.

Works title, dated 1852.

NN.

d. NEW-YORK: | G. P. PUTNAM & COMPANY, 10 PARK PLACE. | 1853.

Works title, dated 1853.

ViU.

e. NEW-YORK: | G. P. PUTNAM & COMPANY, 10 PARK PLACE. | 1854.

Works title, dated 1854.

DLC.

f. New York: [fancy] | G. P. PUTNAM & CO., 321 BROADWAY. | 1856.

Works title, dated 1856.

KU.

g. New York: [fancy] | G. P. PUTNAM & CO., 321 BROADWAY | 1857.

Works title, dated 1857.

Page 21 still mis-signed 2.

MH.

h. NEW YORK: | G. P. PUTNAM, 115 NASSAU STREET. | 1859.

Engraved portrait of Queen Isabella added before title, no artist or publisher given.

Page 21 unsigned.

Green BD cloth. Sides framed in blind. Spine titled in gilt, within gilt decoration on three sides: IRVING'S | WORKS | [rule] | GRANADA Green endpapers.

TxU.

i. NEW YORK: | G. P. PUTNAM (for the Proprietor) 506 BROADWAY. | 1859.

Engraving before title, published by Childs & Peterson, Philadelphia.

NjP.

1E. A | CHRONICLE | OF THE | CONQUEST OF GRANADA. | FROM THE MSS. OF FRAY ANTONIO AGAPIDA. | BY | WASHINGTON IRVING. | IN TWO VOLUMES. | VOL. I. [II.] | LONDON: | JOHN MURRAY, ALBEMARLE-STREET. | MDCCCXXIX.

(22.4 x 14.0 untrimmed): Vol. I. [A]^8 B-I^8 K-U^8 X-Z^8 AA-CC^8 DD^4. Vol. II. [A]^4 B-I^8 K-U^8 X-Z^8 AA-DD^8 EE^4. The last leaf contains advertisements.

Two pages of advertisements at the end of Vol. II, unpaged. The first page is headed LATELY PUBLISHED. The second page is dated *February*, 1829; the advertisements begin with 15 vols. of "The Family Library."

In some copies of Vol. II, the leaf of advertisements is followed by a four-page Murray catalogue, dated May, 1829, paged [1] 2-4.

Vol. I. [i]-[ii], half-title, on verso printer; [iii]-[iv], title, verso blank; [v]-ix, Introduction; [x], blank; [xi]-xv, table of contents; [xvi], blank; [1]-407, text; [408], printer. Vol. II. [i]-[ii], title, on verso printer; [iii]-viii, table of contents; [1]-421, text; [422], printer.

Printer: Thomas Davison, Whitefriars.

Lineation: Vol. I. p. 100, heights, ... De ; p. 200, the ... a Vol. II. p. 100, CHAPTER LIX. ... which ; p. 200, thing ... pursued.

Drab gray paper boards. Also, drab paper boards with purple or dark olive-green cloth shelfback. Sides blank. White paper label on spines: [rule] | A | CHRONICLE | OF THE | CONQUEST | OF | GRANADA. | BY | WASHINGTON IRVING. | [rule] | IN TWO VOLS. | VOL. I. [II.] | [rule] | 24s. | [rule].

Literary Gazette, 21 February - 21 March 1829, "in a few days"; 4-25 April 1829, "To be published in the course of the next six weeks"; 23 April 1829, reviewed; 30 May 1829, listed. *Athenæum*, 27 May 1829, "Published this day," listed. Deposited and registered in Stationers' Hall 5 March 1829. Irving to John Murray, 22 September 1850, "It appeared ... in London 23d May [1829]."

CtY, TxGeoS, TxU (2), ViU, Private hands.

2Ea.   HISTORY | OF THE | CONQUEST OF GRANADA. | FROM THE MSS. OF FRAY ANTONIO AGAPIDA. | BY | WASHINGTON IRVING. | [double rule] | LONDON: | GEORGE ROUTLEDGE AND CO., SOHO SQUARE. | 1850.

Routledge's "Popular Library."

The text is that of the first London edition.

(17.0 x 14.0): [i]-[ii], [1]-317 [318]. Signed in 8's.

Printer: Reynell & Weight, Little Pulteney St., Haymarket.

Lineation: p. 100, peared ... service.; p. 200, he ... albornoz,

Light blue paper boards. On front, cover-title, with identification of this as a volume of "The Popular Library." On back, advertisements for "The Railway Library." Advertisements on endpapers, including listings for Irving's *Mahomet, Sketch Book, Traveller, Bracebridge, Goldsmith*, all in "The Popular Library" series. The series is there advertised as available "In fancy boards or in cloth, full gilt."

Athenæum, 4 May 1850, listed, 1s.

TxU.

b. TALES OF THE ALHAMBRA: | LEGENDS OF THE CONQUEST | OF SPAIN, | AND THE | CONQUEST OF GRANADA. | BY | WASHINGTON IRVING. | [rule] | LONDON: | GEORGE ROUTLEDGE & CO., SOHO SQUARE. | 1851.

(16.9 x 10.5): [i]-iv, [1]-316; [i]-[ii], [1]-317 [318]. *The Conquest of Granada* occupies the last position, with separate pagination. No separate title page. Signed in 8's.

Printer: the same.

Blue L cloth. Sides decorated in blind with identification as "Popular Library." Spine titled in gilt: WASHINGTON | IRVING'S | WORKS. | ALHAMBRA | AND | CONQUEST OF GRANADA. Endpapers cream.

TxU.

3Ea. [London: Henry G. Bohn, 1850.]

Issued individually as "Bohn's Shilling Series"; printed with *Legends of the Conquest of Spain* as Vol. V of "Bohn's Library Edition."

The text is that of the first London edition.

Seen only in the Library Edition: A | CHRONICLE | OF THE | CONQUEST OF GRANADA. | FROM THE MSS. OF FRAY ANTONIO AGAPIDA. | TO WHICH IS ADDED | LEGENDS OF THE CONQUEST OF SPAIN. | BY | WASHINGTON IRVING. | IN TWO VOLUMES. | VOL. I. [II.] | LONDON: HENRY G. BOHN, YORK STREET, COVENT GARDEN. | 1850. 2 vols. in one.

(18.1 x 11.5): Two vols. in one, paged consecutively. Vol. I. [i]-viii, [1]-248. Vol. II. [a]-[b], [ix]-x, [249]-359 [360]; [i]-[vi], [361]-492. *Legends of the Conquest of Spain* is printed in the later part of Vol. II, without full title page. Signed in 8's.

Lineation: Vol. I. p. 100, for ... It ; p. 200, The ... [in footnote] 74. Vol. II. p. 300, tain ... and

Library Edition. Gray T cloth. Sides decorated in blind. Spine titled in gilt as Irving's Works, Vol. V, Bohn's Library Edition. Endpapers white with advertisements in blue. The Shilling Series was issued in boards.

Shilling Series. *Athenæum*, 18 May 1850, listed, 1*s*. 6*d*. Library Edition. *Athenæum* and *Literary Gazette*, 29 June 1850, listed, 3*s*. 6*d*. in cloth.

NN, Library Edition.

b.   LONDON: | HENRY G. BOHN, YORK STREET, COVENT GARDEN. |
     1854.

     Works title, dated 1854. Volume title missing in copy examined.

     "Bohn's Library Edition."

     MB. Copy reported in Staats- und Universitätsbibliothek Hamburg.

1Fa. A | CHRONICLE | OF THE | CONQUEST OF GRANADA. | FROM
      THE MSS. OF FRAY ANTONIO AGAPIDA. | BY | WASHINGTON
      IRVING. | IN TWO VOLUMES. | VOL. I. [II.] | [emblem: L.B. within
      wreath] | PARIS: | BAUDRY, AT THE FOREIGN LIBRARY, | N° 9,
      RUE DU COQ-SAINT-HONORÉ. | [rule] | 1829.

      (16.2 x 9.9): Vol. I. [i]-viii, [v]-viii, [1]-435 [436]. Vol. II. [i]-viii, [1]-454.
      Signed in 12's. Laid paper.

      Printer: Jules Didot, Senior, Rue du Pont-de-Lodi, N° 6.

      Lineation: Vol. I. p. 100, commander ... of ; p. 200, CHAPTER XXI. ... by
      Vol. II. p. 100, colour, ... prophet.; p. 200, CHAPTER LXXI. ... man

      Bibliographie de la France, 11 July 1829, # 4569: "Déjà annoncé sous le n.
      4262 [4 July 1829], mais avec l'omission grave du nom de M. Baudry, qui est
      le premier sur les frontispices dans les exemplaires du dépôt légal."

      BL. Copy reported in Bibliothèque Nationale.

b.   [emblem: D in star within wreath with pendant medal] | PARIS: |
      PUBLISHED BY A. AND W. GALIGNANI, | AT THE ENGLISH,
      FRENCH, ITALIAN, GERMAN, AND SPANISH | LIBRARY, N° 18,
      RUE VIVIENNE. | [rule] | 1829.

      Printer: Jules Didot, Senior.

      Bibliographie de la France, 4 July 1829, # 4262, listed.

      TxU.

2F.   [emblem: BEL intertwined] | PARIS, | BAUDRY'S EUROPEAN
      LIBRARY, | 3, QUAI MALAQUAIS, NEAR THE PONT DES ARTS, |
      AND STASSIN & XAVIER, RUE DU COQ, NEAR THE LOUVRE. |
      SOLD ALSO BY AMYOT, RUE DE LA PAIX; TRUCHY,
      BOULEVARD DES ITALIENS; | BROCKHAUS AND AVENARIUS,
      RUE RICHELIEU; LEOPARD MICHELSEN, LEIPZIC; | AND BY ALL
      THE PRINCIPAL BOOKSELLERS ON THE CONTINENT. | [rule] |
      1842.

(21.2 x 13.2): [i]-xii, [1]-301 [302]. Signed in 8's. Laid paper.

Lineation: p. 100, the ... less ; p. 200, CHAPTER LXVI. ... crowded.

NN.

1G.   A | CHRONICLE | OF THE | CONQUEST OF GRANADA. | BY | Washington Irving. | [rule] | Mit sprachwissenschaftlichen Noten | und | einem Wörterbuche. | [rule] | Leipzig, 1841. | Baumgärtners Buchhandlung.

Text in English, with notes and glossary in German.

(17.1 x 10.9): [i]-[ii], [1]-463 [464]. Signed in 12's.

Printer: J. B. Hirschfeld, Leipzig.

Lineation: p. 100, between ... 455. --; p. 200, there ... zeit. --

Noted in unprinted brown cloth embossed in diamond effect created by parallel rows of three wavy dashes. Publisher's cloth?

TxU. Copy reported in Universitätsbibliothek Giessen.

TRANSLATIONS

Dutch.

De | Verovering | VAN | GRANADA, | beschreven door | Washington Irving. | vaar het handschrift van Antonio Agapida. [in curved line] | *IN TWEE DEELEN.* | [rule] | uit het Engelsch. | EERSTE [TWEEDE] DEEL. | [ornament of helmet, shield, ax, sword] | Te Haarlem, by | de WED. A. LOOSJES PZ. | MDCCCXXX.

(23.1 x 13.4 untrimmed): Vol. I. [I]-XIV, [1]-547 [548]. Not reckoned: half-title, engraved title, one leaf of terminal advertisements, one leaf with extra paper labels for spines. Vol. II. [I]-VI, [1]-556. Not reckoned: half-title, engraved title. Signed in 8's. Laid paper.

Printer: Gebroeders Giunta d'Albani, 's Gravenhage.

Lineation: Vol. I. p. 100, aanvoerde, ... ne-; p. 200, door ... on- Vol. II. p. 100, verdeligde ... zoe-; p. 200, Toen ... [in footnote] *Palacios.*

NNC.

French.

HISTOIRE | DE LA CONQUÊTE | DE GRENADE, | TIRÉE DE LA CHRONIQUE MANUSCRITE DE FRAY ANTONIO AGAPIDA | PAR | WASHINGTON IRVING, | TRADUITE DE L'ANGLAIS | PAR | J. COHEN. | [rule] | TOME PREMIER. [SECOND.] | [rule] | PARIS, |

TIMOTHÉE DEHAY, LIBRAIRE, | RUE NEUVE-DES-BEAUX-ARTS, N°. 9. | [ornamental rule] | AOUT 1829.

(19.6 x 13.0): Vol. I. [a]-[b], [I]-III [IV], [1]-423 [424]. Vol. II. [I]-[IV], [1]-439 [440]. Signed in 8's. Laid paper.

Printer: Imprimerie de A. Belin, rue des Mathurins St.-J., No. 14.

Lineation: Vol. I. p. 100, CHAPITRE XI. ... per-; p. 200, leur ... le Vol. II. p. 100, ment ... [in footnote] Palacios.; p. 200, côté ... attaquer.

Bibliographie de la France, 5 September 1829, # 5342, listed.

NN. Copy reported in Bibliothèque Nationale.

HISTOIRE | DE LA CONQUÊTE | DE GRENADE, [hollow letters] | TIRÉE DE LA CHRONIQUE MANUSCRITE DE FRAY ANTONIO AGAPIDA | PAR | WASHINGTON IRVING, | TRADUITE DE L'ANGLAIS | PAR J. COHEN. | [rule] | TOME PREMIER. [SECOND.] | [rule] | [emblem: dolphin and fountain] | LOUVAIN, | CHEZ F. MICHEL, IMPRIMEUR-LIBRAIRE DE L'UNIVERSITÉ. | [rule] | 1830.

(19.6 x 12.5): Vol. I. [1]-254. Vol. II. [1]-256. Signed in 8's.

Lineation: Vol. I.   p. 100, cours ... leur ; p. 200, trouva ... très-distinguée. Vol. II.   p. 100, et ... fortes ; p. 200, S'étant ... en-

NN. Copy reported in Bibliothèque Nationale.

[*Conquête de Grenade,* par Adrien Lemercier, d'après Washington Irving. Tours: A. Mame, 1840.]

"Bibliothèque de la jeunesse chrétienne."

A simplified version for young people.

312 pp., with engraved title and illustrations. Signed in 12's.

Not seen. Copy reported in Bibliothèque Nationale.

Presumably a second impression was issued between 1840-42.

No copy located or reported.

[Troisième Édition. Tours: A. Mame, 1842.]

Not seen. Copy reported in Bibliothèque Nationale.

CONQUÊTE | DE | GRENADE | PAR | ADRIEN LEMERCIER | D'APRÈS WASHINGTON IRVING | Quartrième Édition | ORNÉE DE 4 GRAVURES SUR ACIER | [elaborate ornament of swords, turban, and crescent sceptres] | TOURS | A^d MAME ET Cie, IMPRIMEURS-LIBRAIRES | 1845. Copy examined has added imprint at foot: NEW-YORK | ROE LOCKWOOD & SON | 411 BROADWAY.

"Bibliothèque de la jeunesse chrétienne."

(17.2 x 10.5): [1]-312. Not reckoned: preliminary engraved illustration and title; four pages of advertisements before title. Signed in 12's.

Lineation: p. 100, La ... guerre ; p. 200, CHAPITRE XXVI. ... les

Black hard-pressed boards with elaborate decoration in green and gilt.

NjP. Copy reported in Bibliothèque Nationale.

CONQUÊTE | DE | GRENADE | PAR | ADRIEN LEMERCIER | D'APRÈS WASHINGTON IRVING | Cinquième Édition | [elaborated swelled rule] | TOURS | A^d MAME ET Cie, IMPRIMEURS-LIBRAIRES | [rule] | 1847.

"Bibliothèque de la jeunesse chrétienne."

(17.5 x 10.8): [i]-[iv], [1]-284. Not reckoned: engraved illustration and title. Signed in 12's.

Printer: Imp. Mame, Tours.

Lineation: p. 100, Cabra ... le ; p. 200, camp, ... à

Blue BD cloth. Sides decorated in gilt. Spine decorated and titled in gilt. Yellow endpapers.

KU, MH.

[Sixième Édition. Tours: A. Mame, 1852.]

Not seen. Copy reported in Bibliothèque Nationale.

[Septième Édition. Tours: A. Mame, 1856.]

Not seen. Copy reported in Bibliothèque Nationale.

[Huitième Édition. Tours: A. Mame, 1859.]

Not seen. Copy reported in Bibliothèque Nationale.

German.

Die | Eroberung Granada's, | aus den | Papieren Bruders Antonio Agapida, | von | Washington Irving. | [rule] | Aus dem Englischen übersetzt | von | K. Meurer. | [double rule] | Erstes bis drittes [Viertes bis sechstes] Bändchen. | [double rule] | Frankfurt am Main, 1829. | Gedruckt und verlegt bei Johann David Sauerländer. [in fraktur]

"Washington Irving's sämmtliche Werke," Bändchen 32-34, 35-37.

(14.5 x 10.5 untrimmed): Vol. I. [1]-338 [339]-[342]. Not reckoned: leaf of terminal advertisements, dated August 1, 1829. Vol. II. [1]-356 [357]-[360]. Signed in 8's.

Lineation: Vol. I. p. 100, meister ... der ; p. 200, rückzuziehen ... Weihge- Vol. II. p. 100, gebt ... Schanzen,; p. 200, nigin ... Heldenge-

In two vols., as issued. Heavy-weight drab gray paper wrappers. Sides blank. Backs missing in copy examined.

TxU. Copy reported in Stadtbibliothek München.

Die | Eroberung von Granada. | Von | Washington Irwing. | [rule] | Aus dem Englischen | von | Gustav Sellen. | [rule] | Erster [Zweiter, Dritter] Band. | [double rule] | Leipzig 1830, | bei A. Wienbrack. [in fraktur]

(15.5 x 10.2): Vol. I. [I]-X, [1]-227 [278]. Vol. II. [I]-VI,[1]-260. Vol. III. [I]-X, [1]-277 [278]. Signed in 8's. Laid paper.

Lineation: Vol. I. p. 100, leichte ... Streis- Vol. II. p. 100, her, ... Einflusse Vol. III. p. 100, um ... Palacios.

NN.

[Leipzig: A. Wienbrack, 1836.]

Apparently a later impression, described in Heinsius as "Wohlf[eil] Ausg[abe]," "Cheap edition."

Not located. Listed in Wilhelm Heinsius, *Algemeines Bücher-Lexicon, 1835-1841.*

Spanish.

CRÓNICA | DE LA CONQUISTA | DE GRANADA. [hollow letters] | ESCRITA EN INGLÉS | por Mr. Washington Irving. [fancy] |

TRADUCIDA AL CASTELLANO | POR DON JORGE W. MONTGOMERY, | Autor de las Tareas de un Solitario. | [double rule] | TOMO I. [II.] | [double rule] | MADRID: | Imprenta de I. SANCHA. | [rule] | ABRIL DE 1831. [Vol. II: JUNIO DE 1831.]

(15.7 x 11.1 untrimmed): Vol. I. [i]-[xiv] unpaged, [1]-272. Vol. II. [1]-263 [264]. Signed in 8's. Laid paper.

Lineation: Vol. I. p. 100, ferocidad ... rebato,; p. 200, CAPÍTULO XXVII. ... su Vol. II. p. 100, CAPÍTULO XVI. ... experimentar ; p. 200, CAPÍTULO XXXIV. ... salidas

Drab-gray unprinted heavy paper wrappers.

TxU (3).

[*Crónica de la conquista de Granada.* Sacada de los manuscritos de Fr. Antonio Agapido por Mr. Washington Irving, y traducida del inglés por Don Alfonso Escalante. Granada? 1844?]

Reported by Williams and Edge, unseen, as advertised in *El Abencerraje*, Granada, 1844. Not located.

Swedish.

Vol. I: KRÖNIKA | öfver | Granadas Eröfring, | *ur Munken Antonio Agapidas handskrifter.* | [rule] | AF | WASHINGTON IRWING. | [rule] | I Tvenne Delar. | [rule] | Första Delen. | [rule] | *Öfversättning* | *fran Engelska Originalet* | af | LARS ARNELL. | [swelled rule] | ÅBO. | Tryckt hos CHRIST. LUOV. HJELT. | [rule] | 1830.

Vol. II: KRÖNIKA | om | Granadas Eröfring, | utdragen | *ur Munken Antonio Agapidas handskrifter.* | [rule] | AF | WASHINGTON IRWING. | [rule] | I Tvenne Delar. | [rule] | Andra Delen. | [rule] | *Öfversättning* | *fran Engelska Originalet* | af | LARS ARNELL. | [swelled rule] | ÅBO. | Tryckt hos CHRIST. LUOV. HJELT. | [rule] | 1831.

(18.7 x 11.7): Vol. I. [i]-[iv], [I]-VI, [7]-249 [250]. Vol. II. [i]-[iv], [1]-247 [248]. Signed in 8's. Laid paper.

Printer: A. J. Wasenius.

Lineation: Vol. I. p. 100, tade ... cap. 31.; p. 200, CAP. XXXV. ... der- Vol. II. p. 100, Den ... budkaflar ; p. 200, de ... med

NN.

VOYAGES AND DISCOVERIES OF
THE COMPANIONS OF COLUMBUS

When Irving returned from Spain to England in the fall of 1829, he shipped to England a manuscript of some early form of *The Companions of Columbus*. Stanley T. Williams in the *Life*, in fact, says that he had a manuscript completed by 3 March 1829. On 3 August 1830 he reached agreement with John Murray for publication, and on the same day he wrote Murray, just before leaving for a short visit to France, "I take the earlier part of the MS with me to Paris, to make some trivial corrections & will send it ... through the ambassadors bag, as I get it ready." On 28 August, back in England, he wrote John Murray III that he was sending the manuscript except for some 110 pages of the introduction and earlier part that he was holding back for correction. Some of the manuscript may indeed have been submitted before then, since on 6 September he requested "a duplicate of the proof" to send that day to America. As was his custom, he apparently continued to revise on the proofs, until on 21 December 1830 he could write his brother Peter, "A few days since I sent the last page of the volume of Voyages to the printer...." On 31 December 1830 or 1 January 1831, the London edition was published in Murray's "Family Library" series.

The American edition, published by Carey and Lea in Philadelphia, did not appear until 7 March 1831. It was apparently set from the proofs of the London edition that Irving had requested in September. But between those early proofs and the final text of the London edition, Irving had done a good bit of "dressing" of the text, as he sometimes liked to term it. Then too, Carey and Lea would have imposed their own house style on the text. The result was an American text that differed noticeably in details -- although not in larger content -- from the London text. A selection of substantive variants in the "Introduction" will illustrate:

First London edition		*First American edition*	
[iii].12	visited; to	[3].11	visited, and to
iv.14	No paragraph break between "death." and "The expeditions here...."	4.7-8	Paragraph break. The second paragraph begins, "The expeditions herein...."

v.17	empire over the	5.1	empire in the
vi.7f	equip the heroes of these remoter adventures;	5.7f	equip the discoverers,
viii.8	civalric romance	6.7f	civalric tale
viii.8f	wherein that author has	7.4	wherein he has

Although a number of continental editions and translations were derived from the London edition, the text remained unrevised by Irving until the Author's Revised Edition in 1849, when *The Companions of Columbus* was added at the end of *The Life of Columbus* to form the third volume of the combined work. But even there, Irving's revisions were minor. The text was derived from that of the first London edition and follows it in large part. The "Introduction," for instance, follows the London text closely except for spelling and punctuation, and the six readings given in the table above for the London edition all appear in the Author's Revised Edition. The text of the body of the work is also only lightly revised, although some substantive changes do appear. The last sentence of Chapter II of the section on Alonzo de Ojeda, for instance, ended in the London edition (p. 9), "a treatment, adds Amerigo Vespucci, by which we saw many cured." In the Author's Revised Edition (p. 25) it ends, "a treatment, by which Amerigo Vespucci declares he saw many cured."

1E.   VOYAGES AND DISCOVERIES | OF THE | COMPANIONS OF COLUMBUS. | [rule] | BY | WASHINGTON IRVING. | [armorial shield with plumed helmet above] | LONDON: | JOHN MURRAY, ALBEMARLE STREET. | MDCCCXXXI.

(15.6 x 9.7 untrimmed): $[A]^8$ C^1 $B\text{-}I^8$ $K\text{-}U^8$ $X\text{-}Y^8$ $[Z]^1$.   Not reckoned: illustration of The Convent of La Rabida, before title; Palos, before Appendix; map, tipped to inside back endpaper.

Publisher's catalogue bound at front: "The Family Library Advertiser. December, MDCCCXXX."   12 pp.   At the foot of p. 5 appears an advertisement by Robert Wiss for his "Patent Portable Water Closet," and also for one of new design.

In most copies, perhaps originally in all, a slip is tipped to the front free endpaper: "This Day is Published, price Two Shillings, | India proofs Four Shillings, | TWELVE SKETCHES | ILLUSTRATIVE OF | SIR WALTER SCOTT'S LETTERS ON | DEMONOLOGY AND WITCHCRAFT, | Designed and Etched | BY GEORGE CRUIKSHANK. | [rule] | Published for the Artist, by James Robins and Co. Ivy Lane, | Paternoster Row; and Sold by all Book and Printsellers."

[i]-[ii], title, on verso quotation from P. Martyr, and printer; [iii]-ix, Introduction; [x], blank; [xi]-xviii, table of contents; [1]-305, text; [306], blank; [307]-337, Appendix; [338], list of ten "Entertaining Voyages and Travels."

A curious phenomenon appears in this book. The section on Vasco Nuñez de Balboa has a running head with the name in upper-case on the rectos of pp. 139-259. From p. 191 to p. 259, a tilde correctly appears above the second N in NUÑEZ -- with the exception of p. 233, where none appears -- in all copies examined. But from p. 139 to p. 189, the tilde appears completely irregularly. Of the eight copies examined after the irregularity was noted, not one duplicates another. On any given page, the presence or absence of the tilde seems completely random. No copy has all that should be there; no copy lacks them all; and no one page has the tilde or lacks it in all eight of the copies. A ready explanation is not apparent.

P. [xi], the beginning of the table of contents, appears in two states, with an incorrect and a corrected reading of lines 4-5:

1. ACCOMPA- | PANIED

2. ACCOMPA- | NIED

On p. 20, the first line of the footnote appears in two states: without (incorrectly) or with (correctly) the tilde over N. There is no correlation with the two states of p. [xi].

Printer: C. Roworth, Bell Yard, Temple Bar, London.

Lineation: p. 100, cheerfully ... voice ; p. 200, immortal ... striking

The standard, or common, binding noted in two states, sequence undetermined:

[A]. Tan V cloth printed in black. On front, within double frame lines: THE | FAMILY LIBRARY. | No. XVIII. | VOYAGES | OF THE | COMPANIONS OF COLUMBUS. | [rule] | LONDON: | JOHN MURRAY, ALBEMARLE STREET. | MDCCCXXXI. | *PRICE FIVE SHILLINGS.* On back, list of 12 works in 17 vols. in "The Family Library," headed NEW EDITIONS within square brackets, and 1 work in 2 vols., headed *DRAMATIC SERIES.* On spine, seven decorative horizontal double rules; titled, VOYAGES | OF THE | COMPANIONS | OF | COLUMBUS. | [rule] | 5*s.*; at foot, FAMILY | LIBRARY. | No. XVIII. White endpapers.

[B]. The same, except that on the back the heading NEW EDITIONS within square brackets is omitted and minor variations appear in the listing of the twelve works. The first work, *Life of Buonaparte*, for instance, is described at the end of its line as "(2 vols.) Vol. I.-II." rather than as "Two Vols."

Also noted in a variant, uncommon binding that does not identify this as "The Family Library." Brown T cloth. Sides decorated in blind with filigree within double frame lines. Spine titled in gilt. Yellow endpapers.

The Murray records show that 15,000 copies were printed, of which only 10,000 were first bound. When sales proved slow, the unsold copies, almost 8,000, were remaindered to Thomas Tegg. The history of at least two apparent times of binding, combined with later bulk sale, would seem to account for the variants.

Monthly Review, December 1830, "in the press." *Athenæum*, 1 January 1831, "This day is published"; 1, 22 January 1831, reviewed. *Literary Gazette*, 1 January 1831, advertised for 1 January. Irving to John Murray, 22 September 1850, "published in London 31st Decr 1830."

CtY, MH, NN, TxU (5), Private hands.

2E.   Issued as Vol. III of *The Life and Voyages of Christopher Columbus; Together With the Voyages of His Companions*, 3 vols., London: John Murray, 1849.

Printed from duplicate plates of the Author's Revised Edition, New York. For a description, see the account under *Columbus*.

3E.   [London: George Routledge, 1850]

"Routledge's Popular Library."

Not located. Listed in *Athenæum*, 25 May 1850, at 1s. in boards.

4E.   THE | VOYAGES AND DISCOVERIES | OF THE | COMPANIONS OF COLUMBUS. | BY | WASHINGTON IRVING. | [cut of galley] | Galley, from the tomb of Fernando Columbus, at Seville. | [the Latin quotation from the title page of *Columbus*] | SENECA: *Medea.* | AUTHOR'S REVISED EDITION. | WITH | AN APPENDIX OF HISTORICAL DOCUMENTS. | LONDON: | HENRY G. BOHN, YORK STREET, COVENT GARDEN. | 1850.

(17.6 x 11.1): [i]-x, [609]-926. Four pages of terminal advertisements in blue. Signed in 8's.

Issued individually as "Bohn's Shilling Series," Vol. XIV; bound with *Columbus* in two vols. as "Bohn's Library Edition," Vols. VI, VII. In the "Library Edition," *The Life of Columbus* (originally issued individually in two vols.) extends into the second vol., and the added Appendix swells the paging of *The Companions of Columbus* to [i]-x, [609]-962. If the "Shilling Series" state was issued with the paging of the text beginning with p. [1], it has not been so seen.

The "Library Edition" has an added common title page of the two works. For a description of the "Library Edition," see the account under *Columbus*.

Printer: Harrison and Son, St. Martin's Lane, London.

Lineation: p. 700, which ... [in footnote] companions.; p. 800, The ... [in footnote] MS.

Athenæum and *Literary Gazette*, 29 June 1850, in "List of New Books."

BL.

1Aa.   VOYAGES | AND | DISCOVERIES | OF | THE COMPANIONS OF COLUMBUS. | [rule] | BY | WASHINGTON IRVING. | [rule] | To declare my opinion herein, whatsoever hath heretofore been discovered by the famous tra- | vayles of Saturnus and Hercules, with such other whom the Antiquitie for their heroical | acts honoured as gods, seemeth but little and obscure, if it be compared to the victorious | labours of the Spanyards. *P. Martyr, Decad. III. c. 4. Lock's translation.* | [rule] | Philadelphia: [fancy] | CAREY AND LEA -- CHESNUT STREET. | 1831.

(23.2 x 14.5 untrimmed): $[1]^4 2\text{-}44^4$.

The last integral leaf is comprised of two pages of advertisements. The first is headed CABINET OF HISTORY. The last page ends with seventeen works headed PREPARING FOR PUBLICATION. Some copies, but not all, have bound before the title four pages of advertisements, paged [1] 2-4, of smaller size (approximately 19.1 x 10.9), for the *Encyclopaedia Americana*. The insert is dated Philadelphia, February, 1830.

[1]-[2], title, on verso copyright (December 31, 1830, the fifty-fifth year of the Independence, by Washington Irving) and printer; [3]-7, Introduction; [8], blank; [9]-322, text; [323]-[324], fly-title for Appendix, verso blank; 325-350, Appendix.

Printer: I. Ashmead & Co.

Lineation: p. 100, he ... with ; p. 200, The ... piloted.

Drab tan boards with red cloth shelfback. Sides blank. On spine, white paper label: [double rule] | VOYAGES | AND | DISCOVERIES | OF THE | COMPANIONS | OF | Columbus. [fancy] | [rule] | BY | *W. Irving.* | [double rule].

The Carey & Lea Cost Book specifies 3000 copies @ $1.75, "finished" February 1831.

Title page deposited 31 December 1830. *American Quarterly Review*, March 1831, reviewed. *National Gazette and Literary Register*, 9 March 1831, advertised. Irving to John Murray, 22 September 1850, "published ... New York [sic] March 7th 1831."

CtY, NNC, TxGeoS, TxU (2), ViU.

b.   CAREY, LEA & BLANCHARD -- CHESTNUT STREET. | 1835.

TxU.

2A.   Issued as Vol. III of *The Life and Voyages of Christopher Columbus; To Which Are Added Those of His Companions*, Author's Revised Edition, 3 Vols., New York: George P. Putnam, 1848-49. For a description of the various impressions of that edition, see the account under *Columbus*.

1F.   VOYAGES | OF THE | COMPANIONS OF COLUMBUS. | BY | WASHINGTON IRVING. | [rule] | [emblem: D in star within wreath with pendant medal] | PARIS: | PUBLISHED BY A. AND W. GALIGNANI, | AT THE ENGLISH, FRENCH, ITALIAN, GERMAN, AND SPANISH LIBRARY, | N° 18, RUE VIVIENNE. | [rule] | 1831.

(17.7 x 10.8): [i]-xvi, [1]-360. Inserted map. Signed in 12's. Laid paper.

Printer: Jules Didot, Senior, Rue du Pont de Lodi, No. 6.

Lineation: p. 100, corroding ... [in footnote] sup.; p. 200, they ... [in footnote] MS.

Bibliographie de la France, 26 February 1831, # 976, listed.

DLC.

2F.   VOYAGES | AND DISCOVERIES | OF THE | COMPANIONS OF COLUMBUS, | BY | WASHINGTON IRVING. | [emblem: L. B. within wreath] | PARIS, | BAUDRY, BOOKSELLER IN FOREIGN LANGUAGES, | 9, RUE DU COQ-SAINT-HONORÉ; | [wavy rule] | 1831.

(16.5 x 10.0): [i]-xij, [1]-354. Signed in 12's. Laid paper.

Printer: Crapelet, Rue de Vaugirard, No. 9.

Lineation: p. 100, THE ... was ; p. 200, enraged ... [in footnote] c. 2.

Bibliographie de la France, 26 March 1831, # 1441, listed.

TxU.

1G.   [*Voyages and Discoveries of the Companions of Columbus*. Mit Noten zur Erklärung des Textes und zur Erleichterung der Aussprache, nebst einem Wörterbuche. Leipzig: Baumgärtner, 1835.]

Signed in 8's. With a map.

Not located. Listed in C. G. Kayser, *Vollständiges Bücher-Lexicon 1833-1840*, and W. Heinsius, *Allgemeines Bücher-Lexicon 1835-1841*.

2G.   [2e Auflage. Leipzig: Baumgärtner, 1837.]

Not located. Listed in C. G. Kayser, *Vollständiges Bücher-Lexicon 1833-1840*.

3G. [*Voyages and Discoveries of the Companions of Columbus*. 3e verbesserte Auflage. Leipzig: Baumgärtner, 1840.]

Not located. Listed in C. G. Kayser, *Vollständiges Bücher-Lexicon 1833-1840*.

4G. [*Voyages and Discoveries of the Companions of Columbus*. With a complete vocabulary compiled by Dr. E[duard] Amthor. Leipzig: Renger, 1840.]

Not located. Listed by Williams and Edge as seen.

5G. VOYAGES AND DISCOVERIES | OF THE | COMPANIONS OF COLUMBUS, | BY | WASHINGTON IRVING. | [rule] | WITH A COMPLETE VOCABULARY | COMPILED | BY | Dr. E. AMTHOR | [rule] | REVISED EDITION. | [rule] | LEIPZIG, | PUBLISHED BY RENGER. | 1846.

(14.7 x 10.7): [I]-VIII, [1]-343 [344]. Preliminary woodcut of Irving not reckoned. Signed in 8's.

Printer: Breitkopf and Haertel.

Lineation: p. 100, the ... ornaments.; p. 200, For ... In

NN, TxU.

1S. [Engraved title, in a variety of styles]. VOYAGES AND DISCOVERIES | of the [surrounded by pen-stroke decoration] | Companions of Columbus [fancy] | [stylized swelled rule] | BY | WASHINGTON IRVING. [shaded letters] | [armorial shield with plumed helmet above] | [in curved line beneath shield:] Arms of the Pinzon Family. | Edited with Áccents, and | 1000 NOTES. | [rule] | *Intended for University Classes, and the* | *Private Student*. [the two lines in semi-script] | [rule] | STOCKHOLM. | *Printed by H. G. Nordström*. [in semi-script] | MDCCCXXXVI. An extra I at the end of the date, changing the date to 1837, is added by hand.

Engraved title, but no conventional printed title.

The editor's preliminary "Notice" is signed G. S., Stockholm, Feb. 1837. The initials are those of George Stephens.

(14.3 x 9.1): [I]-XXIV, [1]-504. Not reckoned: title, and lithograph of The Convent of La Rabida before title. Signed in 18's.

Lineation: p. 100, tion ... *soldat*.; p. 200, become ... little

Tan V cloth. On front, cover-title with imprint: STOCKHOLM. | PRINTED BY F. A. NORSTEDT & SONS. | MDCCCXXXVII. On back, advertisement for Shakespeare's *The Tempest*.

NN.

TRANSLATIONS

Czech.

Cesty a objevy | Soudruhů Kolumbových. | [rule] | Z angličiny Washingtona Irvinga | přeložil a vysvetleními opatřil | J. Malý. | [stylized, elaborated swelled rule] | V PRAZE. [elaborated hollow letters] | Tisk a n klad Jaroslova Pospíšila. | 1853.

Preliminary series title: AMERIKA | od času svého odkrytí az na nejnovější | dobu. | *Sestavil J. Malý.*

(16.6 x 10.2): [i]-[vi], [7]-342 [343]-[346]. Two pages of terminal advertisements. Fold-out map before title not reckoned. Signed in 12's.

Lineation: p. 100, jako ... svědectví ; p. 200, a ... ra-

CtY.

Dutch.

ONTDEKKINGSREIZEN | VAN EENIGE DER VROEGERE | TOGTGENOOTEN | VAN | *COLUMBUS.* | NAAR HET ENGELSCH VAN | *Washington Irving.* | IN EEN DEEL, MIT EENE KAART. | ZIJNDE EEN | AANHANGSEL | OP DESZELFS | *LEVEN EN REIZEN VAN* CHR. COLUMBUS. | [swelled rule] | TE HAARLEM, BIJ | DE WED. A. LOOSJES, PZ. | MDCCCXXXIV.

(20.0 x 11.7): [I]-VIII, [1]-390. Map at end not reckoned. Signed in 8's. Laid paper.

Lineation: p. 100, kers ... met ; p. 200, hoofde ... ge-

NN.

French.

HISTOIRE | DES VOYAGES ET DÉCOUVERTES | DES COMPAGNONS | DE | CHRISTOPHE COLOMB, | Par M. Washington Irving, [fancy] | SUIVIE DE | L'HISTOIRE DE FERNANDO CORTEZ | ET DE LA CONQUÊTE DU MEXIQUE, | ET DE | L'HISTOIRE DE PIZARRE ET DE LA CONQUÊTE DU PÉROU, | OUVRAGES TRADUITS DE L'ANGLAIS | PAR A.-J.-B. ET C.-A. DEFAUCONPRET, | TRADUCTEURS DES OEUVRES DE SIR WALTER SCOTT ET DE L'HISTOIRE | DE CHRISTOPHE COLOMB. | [stylized swelled rule] | TOME PREMIER. [DEUXIÈME., TROISIÈME.] | [stylized swelled rule] | PARIS, | LIBRAIRIE DE CHARLES GOSSELIN, | RUE SAINT-GERMAIN-DES-PRÉS, Nº 9.

1833.

The Companions of Columbus is complete in the first volume.

(20.3 x 13.0): Vol. I. [i]-[iv], 1-403 [404]. Vol. II. [i]-[iv], 1-389 [390]. Vol. III. [i]-[iv], 1-348. Signed in 8's. Laid paper.

Printer: Imprimerie de H. Fournier, Rue de Seine, N. 14.

Lineation: Vol. I. p. 100, Ayant ... gué-; p. 200, vous ... mar-

Bibliographie de la France, 23 November 1833, # 6291, listed.

NN.

VOYAGES ET DÉCOUVERTES | DES | COMPAGNONS DE COLOMB, | TRADUIT DE L'ANGLAIS | DE WASHINGTON IRVING, | Par Henri Lebrun. [fancy] | [cut of Spaniard and Indian] | Tours, [fancy] | CHEZ A.^{D} MAME ET CIE, IMPRIMEURS-LIBRAIRES. | 1839.

"Bibliothèque de la jeunesse chrétienne" series.

A translation of a somewhat abbreviated version of the full work.

(17.2 x 10.3): [1]-288. Not reckoned: preliminary engraved title and illustration; also engravings in text. Signed in 12's.

Printer: Imprimerie de Mame.

Lineation: p. 100, parvenir ... l'oubli ; p. 200, qui ... mais

TxU (2).

Deuxième Edition. | [cut] | TOURS, | A^d MAME ET Cie, IMPRIMEURS-LIBRAIRES. | 1841.

DLC.

TROISIÈME ÉDITION. [hollow letters] | [cut] | TOURS | A^D MAME ET CIE, IMPRIMEURS-LIBRAIRES. | 1843

CtY.

[Fourth Edition. Tours: A. Mame, 1846?.]

Not located. In Antonio Palau y Dulcet, *Manual del Librero Hispano-americano*, 2nd ed. the work is listed for 1846.

5ᵉ ÉDITION | [ornament with AM in center] | TOURS | Aᴰ MAME ET Cᴵᴱ, IMPRIMEURS-LIBRAIRES | [rule] | 1851.

Black hard-finished impressed leather. Sides decorated in blind and gilt. Spine titled in gilt. Endpapers marbled. All edges marbled.

NN.

6ᵉ EDITION | [ornament] | TOURS | Aᵈ MAME ET Cⁱᵉ, IMPRIMEURS-LIBRAIRES | [rule] | 1854

Elaborate flowered boards with sculpted bas-relief effect, in gold, pink, white, and other colors. AEG.

DLC.

[Seventh Edition. Tours: A. Mame, 1858.]

Not seen. Copy reported in Bibliothèque Nationale.

German.

Reisen | der | Gefährten des Columbus. | Von | Washington Irving. | [rule] | Uebersetzt | von | Ph. A. G. v. Meyer. | [double rule] | Erstes bis drittes Bändchen. | [quintuple rule] | Frankfurt am Main, 1831. | Gedruckt und verlegt bei Johann David Sauerländer. [in fraktur]

"Washington Irving's sämmtliche Werke," Bändchen 41-43.

It should be noted that the text of *The Companions of Columbus* in translation had earlier been added by Sauerländer, in 1829, to his translation of *The Life and Voyages of Columbus*, where it was then counted as the last three parts of Bändchen 20-31. See the entry for *Columbus*.

(13.2 x 9.6): [1]-410 [411]-[416]. Signed in 8's.

Lineation: p. 100, Geschrei ... seines ; p. 300, und ... und

ViU. Copy reported in Universitätsbibliothek Giessen.

Italian.

VIAGGI E SCOPERTE | DEI | COMPAGNI DI COLOMBO | DI | WASHINGTON IRVING | *PRIMA TRADUZIONE DALL' ORIGINALE INGLESE* | DI L. T. | MILANO | DALLA TIPOGRAFIA DI PAOLO ANDREA MOLINA | Contrada dell' Agnello, N.° 963. | [rule] | 1842.

The translation lacks the Appendices.

(18.7 x 12.1): [1]-318. Fold-out map bound at end. Signed in 8's.

Lineation: p. 100, mingo, ... abbattuto ; p. 200, l'oro ... ai

NN.

RACCOLTA | DI VIAGGI | DALLA SCOPERTA | DEL NUOVO
CONTINENTE | FINO A' DI NOSTRI | COMPILATA [hollow letters] |
DA F. C. MARMOCCHI | TOM. V. | [cut of recording angel on globe] |
PRATO | FRATELLI GIACHETTI [elaborated hollow letters] | 1842

Contains a translation by Dott. Bartolommeo Poli of the greatest part of
Companions of Columbus, although it lacks the Appendices. The sections
are presented in a different order than Irving's:

> "Viaggi di Alonso di Ojeda," XLIX.

> "Viaggio di Diego de Nicuesa," CXXXI.

> "Viaggi di Juan Ponce de Leon," CLXVII.

> "Viaggio di Vasco Nunez di Balboa," CXCI.

> "Avventure di Valdivia e dei suoi compagni, e destino dell' astrologo
> Micer Codro," CCXV.

This Vol. V of a multi-volume work also contains other material not by
Irving.

(Approx. 22.9 x 14.9 rebound): Paged in Roman numerals, but[1]-123 in
Arabic numerals at the end. Text of each page within single frame lines.

Lineation: p. XLVIII, perchè ... VIAGGIO ; p. CCXIV, Stava ... compagni
[in caption of illustration]

CU-B (examined in selected Xeroxes).

Spanish.

BIBLIOTECA ILUSTRADA DE GASPAR Y ROIG. | Bajo la direccion de
los mismos editores. [fancy] | [rule]| VIAJES Y DESCUBRIMIENTOS |
DE LOS | COMPAÑEROS DE COLON, | POR | WASHINGTON
IRVING. | [woodcut of ship, by Pizaro and Capuz] | MADRID. |
IMPRENTA DE GASPAR Y ROIG, EDITORES, | calle del Principe núm.
4. | [rule] | 1854.

(27.8 x 18.8 untrimmed): [1]-79 [80]. In double columns. Signed in 8's.

Lineation: p. 50, column 1, como ... MS.; column 2, escuadra ... reina.

Pink paper wrapper. On front, cover-title, and woodcut from p. 12. On back, advertisements, including one for Irving's *Vida y Viajes de Cristobal Colon*.

TxU (3).

Swedish.

[Engraved title, in a variety of styles]. COLUMBI FÖLJESLAGARE, [elaborated hollow letters] | DERAS RESOR OCH UPPTÄCKTER. [hollow letters] | af | Wash. Irwing. [fancy] | [rule] | *Från Original Språket.* | [rule] | [engraving of Nuñez and men] | *Vasco Nuñez upptäcker Stilla Hafvet.* | STOCKHOLM. [hollow letters] | [rule] | Wiborg & C° Förlag.

Two copies examined have the engraved title page but no conventional one. H. Linnström, *Svenskt Boklexikon 1830-1865* describes the work with a double title: *Columbi följeslagares upptäckter.* Perhaps that appears in a cover-title. A similar construction does appear on the half-title.

The printer's imprint, on the verso of the half-title, is dated 1832.

(16.2 x 10.2): [i]-[viii], [1]-387 [388]. Engraved title not reckoned. Signed in 12's.

Printer: Johan Hörberg, Stockholm.

Lineation: p. 100, ögon ... tviflande ; p. 200, åt ... öf-

CtY, NN.

THE ALHAMBRA

On 20 March 1832, Colonel Thomas Aspinwall, Irving's agent in London, reached agreement with Colburn and Bentley to publish *The Alhambra*, promising delivery of the completed manuscript by 5 April. Surviving portions of that manuscript, now in the University of Illinois library, show that it was a copy by a Spanish scribe with corrections in Irving's hand. He apparently continued to make corrections in it until the last minute -- a familiar pattern in Irving's preparation of a work for the press -- for in an undated letter, written at the end of March, he asked the publishers for "The Legend of the Arabian Astrologer," "as I have not looked over it since it was copied." The printed text, however, differs in many ways from the extant manuscript. Just who is responsible for those final changes is not clear. In his letter requesting the chapter to be "looked over," Irving says, "I leave town next Monday Morning for the Continent; but trust that Mr. William Wesley will do all that is needful in correcting the proofsheets." Irving himself apparently did not read the proof, or at least very much of it; on 2 April he left London for France, and on 12 April sailed for America, arriving on 21 May. The two volumes were officially published in early May, although they were available in some form for a review in *The Literary Gazette* published in the issue of 28 April. Presumably, house styling by the publishers and changes in proof by Mr. Wesley or someone else account for many details of the final text.

While preparations were going on for the London edition, and even before, Irving was busy on an American edition. On 6 February 1832 he wrote Pierre Paris Irving that he had sent Pierre's father, Ebenezer, a portion of the complete work; Ebenezer was to make arrangements for American publication. On 6 March he wrote Peter Irving that the first volume had been sent on the first of March for publication on the first of May. "The second volume is nearly ready; but I am not determined as to whether I shall bring it out at the same time...." On 28 March, according to Pierre M. Irving, he sent the dedication. The American edition, quite apparently printed from a separate manuscript that has not survived, was not to appear until the middle of June. When it did, it differed noticeably from the London edition.

For Carey, Lea and Blanchard's edition of the collected Works in 1836, Irving revised the American text to bring it more nearly in line with the text of the London edition. In general, he seems to have worked harder on Volume I than on Volume II, particularly on "The Journey," "The Author's

Chamber," and "The Balcony." That text was to remain the standard one until the appearance of the Author's Revised Edition in 1851. It would appear that even the late British and Continental editions used it.

The Author's Revised Edition brought major changes. As Irving says in the Preface, "I have revised and re-arranged the whole work, enlarged some parts, and added others, including the papers originally omitted...." It has been estimated that Irving added some 30,000 words, increasing the length by about one-third. He made it, with some exaggeration, almost a new work.

In all, then, during the course of its publishing history *The Alhambra* appeared in four distinct texts for which Irving was responsible. The nature of the differences in the three major ones may be defined by a table comparing the order and the titles of chapters, with a simplified statement of the derivation of each chapter in the last text, the Author's Revised Edition. For consistency, the chapter titles given are those in the three tables of contents, although in a few instances they may differ somewhat from the titles in the body of the text.

First English Edition	First American Edition	Author's Revised Edition
Vol. I	Vol. I.	
[Dedication to Wilkie]	[Dedication to Wilkie]	[Preface to the Revised Edition]
THE JOURNEY	The Journey	THE JOURNEY [Revised, with final paragraphs omitted]
GOVERNMENT OF THE ALHAMBRA	Government of the Alhambra	PALACE OF THE ALHAMBRA [Combines and rearranges "Government of the Alhambra" and "Interior of the Alhambra"; adds "Note on Morisco Architecture"]
INTERIOR OF THE ALHAMBRA	Interior	IMPORTANT NEGOTIATIONS.--THE AUTHOR SUCCEEDS TO THE THRONE OF BOABDIL [combines the end of "The Journey" with all of "The Household"]
THE TOWER OF COMARES	The Tower of Comares	INHABITANTS OF THE ALHAMBRA [common to all texts]

REFLECTIONS ON THE MOSLEM DOMINATION IN SPAIN	Reflections on the Moslem Domination in Spain	THE HALL OF AMBASSADORS [Combines "Reflections" with a passage from "Interior of the Alhambra"]
THE HOUSEHOLD	The Household	THE JESUITS' LIBRARY [Made up of the opening paragraphs of "Muhamed Abou Alahmar"]
THE TRUANT	The Truant	ALHAMAR, THE FOUNDER IF THE ALHAMBRA [Made up of the remaining parts, revised, of "Muhamed Abou Alahmar"]
THE AUTHOR'S CHAMBER	The Author's Chamber	YUSEF ABUL HAGIG, THE FINISHER OF THE ALHAMBRA [A revision of Jusef Abul Hagiag"]
THE ALHAMBRA BY MOONLIGHT	The Alhambra by Moonlight	THE MYSTERIOUS CHAMBERS [Combines revised versions of "The Author's Chamber" and "The Alhambra by Moonlight"]
INHABITANTS OF THE ALHAMBRA	Inhabitants of the Alhambra	PANORAMA FROM THE TOWER OF COMARES [A Revised version of "The Tower of Comares"]
THE COURT OF LIONS	The Balcony	THE TRUANT [Common to all texts]
BOABDIL EL CHICO	The Adventure of the Mason [In the text, under the running-head, "The Balcony"]	THE BALCONY [Common to all texts]
MEMENTOS OF BOABDIL	A Ramble Among the Hills	THE ADVENTURE OF THE MASON [Common to all texts]

THE BALCONY	The Court of Lions	THE COURT OF LIONS [Common to all texts; here also including material from "Interior of the Alhambra" and the first pages of Boabdil El Chico]
THE ADVEN-TURE OF THE MASON	Boabdil El Chico	THE ABENCERRAGES [Two pages taken from "Boabdil El Chico," but essentially new material in the text.
A RAMBLE AMONG THE HILLS	Mementos of Boabdil	MEMENTOS OF BOABDIL [A revised version of "Mementos of Boabdil," with added material from "Boabdil El Chico"]
LOCAL TRADITIONS	The Tower of Las Infantas	PUBLIC FETES OF GRANADA [An extensive revision of material that appeared in *The Knickerbocker*, July 1840, under the title "Letter from Granada"]
THE HOUSE OF THE WEATHER-COCK	The House of the Weathercock	LOCAL TRADITIONS [Common to all texts]
LEGEND OF THE ARABIAN ASTROLOGER	The Legend of the Arabian Astrologer	THE HOUSE OF THE WEATHERCOCK [Common to all texts; here new historical material is added]
THE TOWER OF LAS INFANTAS	Legend of the Three Beautiful Princesses	LEGEND OF THE ARABIAN ASTROLOGER [Common to all texts]

LEGEND OF THE THREE BEAUTIFUL PRINCESSES		VISITORS TO THE ALHAMBRA [Common to all texts; here some material is omitted, to be used as the basis of "A Fete in the Alhambra"]
Vol II.	*Vol. II.*	
VISITORS TO THE ALHAMBRA	Local Traditions	RELICS AND GENEOLOGIES [New]
LEGEND OF PRINCE AHMED AL KAMEL; OR, THE PILGRIM OF LOVE	Legend of the Moor's Legacy	THE GENERALIFE [New]
LEGEND OF THE MOOR'S LEGACY	Visitors to the Alhambra	LEGEND OF PRINCE AHMED AL KAMEL; OR THE PILGRIM OF LOVE [Common to all texts]
LEGEND OF THE ROSE OF THE ALHAMBRA; OR, THE PAGE AND THE GER-FALCON	Prince Ahmed al Kamel, or the Pilgrom of Love	A RAMBLE AMONG THE HILLS [Common to all texts; here a link to the following legend is added]
THE VETERAN	Legend of the Rose of the Alhambra	LEGEND OF THE MOOR'S LEGACY [Common to all texts]
LEGEND OF THE GOVERNOR AND THE NOTARY	The Veteran	THE TOWER OF LAS INFANTAS [Common to all texts]
LEGEND OF THE GOVERNOR AND THE SOLDIER	The Governor and the Notary	LEGEND OF THE THREE BEAUTIFUL PRINCESSES [Common to all texts; here a link to the following legend is added]
LEGEND OF THE TWO DISCREET STATUES	Governor Manco and the Soldier	LEGEND OF THE ROSE OF THE ALHAMBRA [Common to all texts]
MUHAMED ABOU ALAHMAR	Legend of the Two Discreet Statues	THE VETERAN [Common to all texts]

JUSEF ABUL HAGIAG	Mahamad Aben Alahmar, the Founder of the Alhambra	THE GOVERNOR AND THE NOTARY [Common to all texts]
	Jusef Abul Hagias, the Finisher of the Alhambra	GOVERNOR MANCO AND THE SOLDIER [Common to all texts]
		A FETE IN THE ALHAMBRA [A revised and expanded section from "Visitors to the Alhambra"]
		LEGEND OF THE TWO DISCREET STATUES [Common to all texts]
		THE CRUSADE OF THE GRAND MASTER OF ALCANTARA [New]
		SPANISH ROMANCE [Material first published in *The Knickerbocker*, September 1839, under the same title, used there too as a preface to "Legend of Don Munio de Hinojosa"]
		LEGEND OF DON MUNIO SANCHO DE HINOJOSA [Material first published in *The Knickerbocker*, September 1839, under the same title]
		POETS AND POETRY OF MOSLEM AUDALUS [New]
		AN EXPEDITION IN QUEST OF A DIPLOMA [New]

THE LEGEND OF THE
ENCHANTED SOLDIER
[New]

THE AUTHOR'S
FAREWELL TO
GRANADA [New]

1Ea- THE | ALHAMBRA. | BY GEOFFREY CRAYON, | AUTHOR OF
b.   "THE SKETCH BOOK," "BRACEBRIDGE HALL," | "TALES OF A
      TRAVELLER," &c. | IN TWO VOLUMES. | VOL. I. [II.] | LONDON: |
      HENRY   COLBURN   AND   RICHARD   BENTLEY, | NEW
      BURLINGTON STREET. | 1832.

(22.5 x 14.3 untrimmed): Vol. I. [A]^4 B-I^8 K-U^8 X-Y^8. Vol. II. [A]^4 B-I^8 K-
U^8. Laid paper; also occurs on mixed laid and wove papers.

In Vol. II, the first integral leaf, probably counted as pp. [i]-[ii], carries an
advertisement on the recto for five "Interesting Works of Fiction, Preparing
for Immediate Publication." The verso is blank. The last two integral leaves,
not counted in the pagination, carry four pages of advertisements, unpaged,
undated. The first two pages are given to fourteen "New Works of Fiction
Just Published," beginning with *The Contrast*; the second two pages are given
to fifteen "Standard Novels and Romances."

Vol. I. [i]-[ii], half-title, on verso printer; [iii]-[iv], title, verso blank; [v]-vi,
dedication to David Wilkie, dated May, 1832; [vii]-viii, table of contents; [1]-
[2], divisional fly-title, verso blank; [3]-333, text, printer at foot of last page;
[334], blank. Vol. II. [i]-[ii], advertisement, verso blank; [iii]-[iv], half-title,
on verso printer; [v]-[vi], title, verso blank; [vii]-[viii], table of contents, verso
blank; [1]-[2], divisional fly-title, verso blank; [3]-299, text; [300], printer.

Printer: Vol. I. Ibotson and Palmer, Savoy Street, London. Vol. II. Samuel
Bentley, Dorset-street, Fleet-street.

Lineation: Vol. I. p. 100, scarce ... believers.: p. 200, "The ... heir. Vol. II. p.
100, most ... of ; p. 200, ear, ... "I

Published in two impressions.

In the second impression of Vol. I, minor adjustments to type appear
occasionally through the volume. In the second impression of Vol II. in
addition to minor adjustments, Signature D is completely reset, Signature E
is reset in eight pages, and Signature S is reset in seven pages. Both title
pages are reset in part, but the differences are so minute that they defy clear
description.

Although a number of small changes of text appear on the reset pages, they do not bear the mark of authorial revision. Some are corrections of demonstrable errors; some are "improvements" in spelling, punctuation, sentence structure, or (in one instance) diction. It is interesting that the second edition by the same publishers prints the text of the first impression of Vol. II.

The following table will distinguish between the two impressions. In the examples chosen, emphasis is placed on representative textual changes appearing on the reset pages of Vol. II.

Page & line	First impression	Second impression
	VOL. I.	
[vii].2f	One dot between title and page number	Two dots between title and page number
115.foot	The I of I2 under the gs of paintings	The I under the ob of obliterated
[193].foot	The V of VOL. I under H of "Hark	The V under first quotation mark
289.foot	The V of VOL. I well to left of A in As above; the O under the A.	The V under the A
	VOL. II	
36.7	rapture?"	raptures?"
37.6f	earth!	earth.
38.5f	Heaven	heaven
39.8-7f	he: | "fly	he. | Fly
41.8	encouragement. Vain	encouragement: vain
46.4f	old mysterious [incorrect]	old, mysterious
48.8	grave talk	grave, talk
49.5	window; you	window. You
53.8	prince	Prince
56.11	parrot	Parrot
258.10f	Heaven	hcaven

259.5	digging. [incorrect]	digging,
262.10-11	sub- | teranean	the | subterranean
270.5f	traveller; though	tra- | veller. Though

Drab brown paper boards. Sides blank. Paper label on spines. (See the description below of variant labels.) One copy noted in rust brown paper boards with green flower-figured cloth shelfbacks with leather label. Cloth shelfbacks original?

The label on the spines occurs in two states:

[A]. [double rule] | THE | ALHAMBRA. | BY | GEOFFREY CRAYON. | [rule] | IN TWO VOLS. | VOL. I. [II.] | [double rule].

[B]. [double rule] | THE | ALHAMBRA. | BY | GEOFFREY CRAYON | [rule] | VOL. I. [II.] | [double rule].

The two states of the label may have been interchangeable. State [A] has been noted both on the first impression and on the second. State [B] has been noted only on the second impression but may well occur also on the first.

Athenæum, 14 April 1832, advertised for 1 May; 5 May 1832, listed and reviewed. *Literary Gazette*, 28 April 1832, reviewed; 5 May 1832, "just published." *The English Catalogue of Books, 1801-1836* lists April 1832 as the publication date.

Discussion based on copies in CtY, DLC, TxU.

2E.   THE | ALHAMBRA. | BY GEOFFREY CRAYON, | AUTHOR OF "THE SKETCH BOOK," "BRACEBRIDGE HALL," | "TALES OF A TRAVELLER," &c. | IN TWO VOLUMES. | VOL. I. [II.] | LONDON: | HENRY COLBURN AND RICHARD BENTLEY, | NEW BURLINGTON STREET. [comma in Vol. II] | 1832.

The similarity of the title page to that of the first edition should not mislead. This is a second edition, completely reset, described in advertisements as a "new and cheaper" edition. The text is that of the first impression of the first English edition with small changes in spelling and punctuation that are certainly the work of the publisher. Some correct errors, some introduce new errors, some are attempts to "improve" the punctuation.

(20.0 x 12.2 untrimmed): Vol. I. [A]^4 B-I^{12} K-O^{12}. Vol. II. [A]^2 B-I^{12} K-N^{12} O^6.

At end of Vol. II, four integral pages of advertisements, unpaged, undated. Although superficially alike, they differ from the terminal advertisements in the first edition. The first two pages are given to "New Works of Fiction," beginning with *Henry Masterton*; the second two are given to seventeen (rather than fifteen) "Standard Novels and Romances."

Vol. I. [i]-[ii], half-title, on verso printer; [iii]-[iv], title, verso blank; [v]-vi, dedication; [vii]-viii, table of contents; [1]-312, text, printer at foot of last page. Vol. II. [i]-[ii], title, on verso printer; [iii]-[iv], table of contents, verso blank; [1]-295, text, printer at foot of last page; [296], blank.

Printer: Vol. I. Samuel Bentley, Dorset-street, Fleet-street. Vol. II. Ibotson and Palmcr, Savoy Street, Strand.

Lineation: Vol. I. p. 100, entered ... as ; p. 200, insurrection, ... a Vol. II. p. 100, persist ... appeared ; p. 200, The ... just

Athenæum, 28 July 1832, listed and advertised.

CtY, NNC, Private hands.

3Ea. TALES | OF THE | ALHAMBRA. | BY | WASHINGTON IRVING, ESQ. | AUTHOR OF | "THE SKETCH-BOOK." | REVISED AND CORRECTED BY THE AUTHOR. | LONDON: | RICHARD BENTLEY, 8. NEW BURLINGTON STREET | (SUCCESSOR TO HENRY COLBURN): | BELL AND BRADFUTE, EDINBURGH; | CUMMING, DUBLIN. | 1835.

"Standard Novels," No. XLIX.

The text is revised by Irving in a relatively minor fashion, based primarily on the text of the first English edition. The first volume is revised somewhat more heavily than the second. The text is the same as that in the American edition of 1836, published in Philadelphia by Carey, Lea and Blanchard near the end of 1835, and is probably taken from that source.

(16.3 x 10.3): [i]-viii, [i]-395 [396]. Not reckoned: illustration and engraved title. Signed in 8's.

The engraved vignette title omits CUMMING, DUBLIN as publisher and substitutes GALIGNANI, PARIS.

The complete volume prints three separate works. Irving's *Alhambra* occupies pp. [iii]-viii, [1]-239 [240]. The remaining pages contain *The Last of the Abencerrages* by the Viscount de Chateaubriand (sic), and *The Involuntary Prophet* by Horace Smith.

Printer: A. Spottiswoode, New-Street-Square.

Lineation: p. 100, Mohamed ... a ; p. 200, not ... the

Athenæum, 5 December 1835, "Published this day ... price 6*s*."

BL.

b.   LONDON: | RICHARD BENTLEY, NEW BURLINGTON STREET: | AND BELL & BRADFUTE, EDINBURGH. | 1850.

The copy examined, rebound, lacks the series title and the engraved title.

Printer: Spottiswoodes and Shaw, New-street-Square.

DLC.

4E.   [London: George Routledge, 1850.]

"Popular Library" Series.

This 1850 first impression, in individual form, is almost certainly in the same setting as the following 1851 impression in the Works form of the "Popular Library." If so, it also includes at the end an edition of *Legends of the Conquest of Spain*, without a separate title page.

Other volumes in the series noted in boards printed in colors, or in brown AR cloth, sides decorated in blind with series name at center, spine titled in gilt.

Not located. Listed in *Athenæum*, 6 July 1850, at 1*s*.

5E.   [London: George Routledge, 1851.]

"Popular Library" series.

Issued individually in 1850 and probably also in 1851, although not located in that form. Seen only in the Works form, dated 1851, combined with other Irving works. There, the individual title page is omitted and replaced with a common title: TALES OF THE ALHAMBRA: | LEGENDS OF THE CONQUEST OF SPAIN, | AND THE | CONQUEST OF GRANADA. | BY | WASHINGTON IRVING. | [rule] | LONDON: | GEORGE ROUTLEDGE & CO., SOHO SQUARE. | 1851.

(16.9 x 10.5): [i]-iv, [1]-316. In the Works form, *The Alhambra* and *The Conquest of Spain* are paged and signed together, with *The Conquest of Spain* beginning on p. [197]. Almost certainly so issued as an individual volume. *Granada* is paged [i]-[ii], [1]-317 [318] and signed separately at the end, with a different printer credited for the work.

The text is not that of the Author's Revised Edition.

Printer of *The Alhambra* and *The Conquest of Spain*: J. & H. Cox (Brothers), 74 & 75 Great Queen Street, Lincoln's-Inn Fields.

Lineation: p. 100, The ... In ; p. 200, episcopal ... was

Royal blue L cloth. On sides, elaborate border and decoration in blind with POPULAR LIBRARY in circle at center. Spine decorated in blind, titled in gilt: WASHINGTON | IRVING'S | WORKS. | ALHAMBRA | AND | CONQUEST OF GRANADA. Light yellow endpapers.

TxU.

6Ea. THE | ALHAMBRA. | BY | WASHINGTON IRVING. | [rule] | NEW EDITION, | With an Historical Appendix. [fancy] | [rule] | LONDON: | HENRY G. BOHN, YORK STREET, COVENT GARDEN. | 1850.

(18.1 x 11.5): [i]-[iv], [1]-260. The text ends on p. 216. Pp. [217]-260, Appendix by Rev. Hartwell Horne. Signed in 8's.

Issued individually as "Bohn's Shilling Series"; bound with *Tales of a Traveller* as Vol. IV of "Bohn's Library Edition."

Lineation: p. 100, sung ... of ; p. 200, the ... wall

Seen only in "Bohn's Library Edition." Gray T cloth. Sides decorated in blind. Spine titled in gilt: IRVING'S | WORKS | [rule] | VOL. IV. | [rule] | ALHAMBRA | TALES OF A TRAV^R. | BOHN'S | LIBRARY | EDITION. White endpapers with advertisements in blue. Illustration at beginning of volume. (No works title in volume.)

Shilling Series. *Athenæum*, 13 July 1850, in "List of New Books," 1*s*.6*d*. Library Edition. *Athenæum* and *Literary Gazette*, 2 November 1850, the set of 10 vols. at 35*s* listed.

NN, in Library Edition.

b. LONDON: | HENRY G. BOHN, YORK STREET, COVENT GARDEN. | 1853.

"Bohn's Shilling Series."

Printer: R. Clay, Bread Street Hill, London.

TxU.

c. [London: Henry G. Bohn, 1854.]

"Bohn's Library Edition." With frontispiece.

Not seen. Copy reported in Staats- und Universitätsbibliothek Hamburg.

1A. THE | ALHAMBRA: | A SERIES | OF | TALES AND SKETCHES [hollow letters] | OF | THE MOORS AND SPANIARDS. | [rule] | BY THE AUTHOR | OF | THE SKETCH BOOK. | [rule] | IN TWO VOLUMES. | VOL. I. [II.] | [double rule] | Philadelphia: [fancy] [misprinted Philadelphla in Vol. II] | CAREY & LEA. | [rule] | 1832.

(19.7 x 11.5 untrimmed): Vol. I. [1]^2 2-19^6 20-21^2. Vol. II. [1]^2 2-21^6. See the discussion below of Sig. 21.

In Vol. II, Sig. 21 appears in two binding states:

[A]. Leaves 21_{3-4} present as blanks.

Leaf 21_5 used as a pasted-down endpaper.

Leaf 21_6 excised or in some instances perhaps pasted under leaf 21_5.

[B]. Leaves 21_{3-4} excised.

Leaves 21_{5-6} present as blanks.

Conventional flyleaf and endpapers at back.

The Cost Book of Carey and Lea specifies 5000 copies @ \$1.40 and 500 copies @ \$1.00. The nature of the difference is not known but may be relevant to the two binding states of Sig. 21 of Vol. II. Do those 500 copies represent binding State [B], which does appear to be scarcer than State [A]? But whether so or not, why would they be cheaper? Perhaps they might if they were an extension of the originally planned run of the press, or if they were held in sheets for later binding but were entered in the Cost Book at the time of printing. Or perhaps more likely, were 500 copies issued by the publishers unbound in sheets? The various possibilities are, or course, merely conjectures.

Some copies, but not all, have a catalogue bound at the end of Vol. I: 36 pp., three unsigned gatherings of six, unpaged, undated, with frame lines around each page. The leaves, 16.6 x 9.6, are considerably smaller than the volume itself. On p. [2], *The Alhambra* is listed among the books "just published." P. [2] is given to six works by Irving, not including this one.

Vol. I. [i]-[ii], title; on verso copyright (1832 by Washington Irving); [iii]-iv, dedication to David Wilkie; [13]-234, text; [1 leaf unpaged], table of contents, verso blank. Vol. II. [i]-[ii], title, verso blank; [iii]-[iv], table of contents, verso blank; [5]-236, text; [2 blank leaves].

Identification of the printer does not appear in the volumes. The Cost Book of Carey and Lea specifies "Griggs, Sherman."

Lineation: Vol. I. p. 100, Sometimes ... below ; p. 200, hard ... to Vol. II. p. 100, country ... mys-; p. 200, you ... not

Tan paper boards with purple cloth shelfbacks. Sides blank. On spines, white paper label: [double rule] | THE | ALHAMBRA. | BY THE AUTHOR | of the | SKETCH BOOK. | [rule] | *In Two Volumes.* | VOL. I. [II.] | [double rule]. White endpapers. Flyleaves in Vol. I. In Vol. II, flyleaves in State [B] but only at front in State [A].

Although the printed copyright notice in Vol. I gives only the year 1832, a title page was deposited for copyright on 16 May 1832. A copy of the work was deposited 25 June 1832.

National Gazette and Literary Register [Philadelphia], 5 June 1832, "about to be issued"; 16 June 1832, "This day is published." *New-York American*, 9 June 1832, "Published this day." Irving to John Murray, 22 September 1850, gives 11 June 1832 as publication date.

NN, States [A],[B]. NNU, rebound. TxU, 3 in State [A], 1 with catalogue. Private hands, State [A], with catalogue.

2Aa.   THE | ALHAMBRA: | A SERIES | OF | TALES AND SKETCHES | OF THE | MOORS AND SPANIARDS. | [rule] | BY | THE AUTHOR OF "THE SKETCH BOOK." | [rule] | IN TWO VOLUMES. | VOL. I. [II.] | A NEW EDITION. | *PHILADELPHIA:* | CAREY, LEA AND BLANCHARD. | 1836.

The text is revised by Irving in a relatively minor fashion, based primarily on the text of the first English edition. The first volume is revised somewhat more heavily than the second.

(17.6 x 10.6): Vol. I. [A]^6 B-I^6 K-S^6. Vol. II. [A]^6 B-I^6 K-S^6.

Printer: Stereotyped by L. Johnson, Philadelphia.

Lineation: Vol. I. p. 100, Christians. ... attend-; p. 200, was ... be Vol. II. p. 100, soared ... fountain.; p. 200, cities ... country.

Vol. I. [1]-[2], title, on verso copyright (1832, by Washington Irving) and printer; 3-4, table of contents; 5-6, dedication; 7-216, text. Vol. II. [1]-[2], title, on verso copyright and printer; 3-[4], table of contents, verso blank; 5-215, text; [216], blank.

The Cost Book of Carey and Lea specifies 2000 copies "finished" November 1835.

MH, TxU.

b.   A NEW EDITION. | PHILADELPHIA: | LEA & BLANCHARD, | SUCCESSORS TO CAREY & CO. | [rule of 27 dots] | 1839.

Drab tan boards with white paper label on spines. White endpapers.

CtY.

c.   [Philadelphia: Lea & Blanchard, 1840. 2 vols.]

Not seen. Copy reported in CtY.

d.   A NEW EDITION. | PHILADELPHIA: | LEA & BLANCHARD. | 1842.

MB, Vol. II only.

3Aa-b. THE ALHAMBRA. | BY | WASHINGTON IRVING. | AUTHOR'S REVISED EDITION. | NEW YORK: | GEORGE P. PUTNAM, 155 BROADWAY. | M.DCCC.LI.

The text is extensively revised, re-ordered, expanded by Irving.

(18.6 x 15.8): [1]^{10} 2-16^{12} [7]-[8]^{12} 9-17^{12} 18^{10}. The first leaf and the last leaf are blanks.

[i]-[ii], Works title (Vol. XV), verso blank; [iii]-[iv], title, on verso copyright (1851) and printer; [v]-vi, table of contents; [13]-425, text; [426], blank.

In two states:

A. Contents as described, without "Preface to the Revised Edition."

B. With "Preface to the Revised Edition," dated Sunnyside, 1851, added as pp. [9]-10.

Printer: John F. Trow, Printer & Stereotyper, 49 Ann-Street.

Lineation: p. 100, Even ... mere ; p. 200, THE GENERALIFE. ... inhabitant.

Green TB cloth. Sides decorated in blind with publisher's initials at center. Spine decorated in blind, titled in gilt: IRVING'S | WORKS | [rule] | THE | ALHAMBRA Light cream endpapers.

A contemporary Putnam catalogue offers the Works in Cloth, Sheep, Half Calf, Half Calf extra, Half Calf antique, Calf extra, Calf antique, Morocco extra with gilt edges.

Literary World, 5 April 1851, "Will be published immediately"; 26 April 1851, "G. P. Putnam publishes this week"; 3 May 1851, listed.

TxU, both states.

c. [Illustrated form]. THE ALHAMBRA. | BY | WASHINGTON IRVING. | AUTHOR'S REVISED EDITION. | With Illustrations [fancy] | BY FELIX O. C. DARLEY, | ENGRAVED BY THE MOST EMINENT ARTISTS. | NEW-YORK: | GEORGE P. PUTNAM, 155 BROADWAY. | M.DCCC.LI. All within single frame lines.

The text is from the same plates as the Works form, with single frame lines added around each page. In the preliminary matter, the Works title is omitted, and a table of illustrations is added, as well as the Preface to the Revised Edition that appears in State B of the Works form.

(21.5 x 15.0): Signed in 12's, as in the Works form, but bound [1]-[26]^{8} [27]^{4} [28]^{1} [29]^{2}. The first two leaves are blank. Sig. [29] is blank. Eight pages of plates not reckoned.

[i]-[ii], title, on verso copyright (1851) and printer; [9]-10, Preface to the Revised Edition; [v]-vi, table of contents; [1 leaf unpaged], table of illustrations, verso blank; [13]-425, text; [426], blank.

The table of illustrations lists fifteen engravings: a frontispiece, a half-title, and thirteen other illustrations through the text. Of the illustrations in the text, six are full-page insertions with tissue guard, and seven are smaller ones pasted down in appropriate blank spaces in the text. The Illustrated forms of other works by Irving have been noted occasionally with extra illustrations pasted down. No such copies of *The Alhambra* have been identified, but they may exist.

Printer: John F. Trow, Printer & Stereotyper, 49 Ann-Street.

Noted in blue T cloth. On sides, gilt illustration of the Alhambra: gate, fountain, tower; bordered in blind. Spine decorated and titled in gilt: Alhambra | [rule] | Illustrated [All in elaborated lettering]. AEG. Cream endpapers.

Advertised in *Literary World*, 16 August 1851, as available in "Dark cloth, extra gilt, $3 50; extra blue, gilt edges, $4; morocco extra, very elegant richly gilt edges, $6."

Literary World, 16 August 1851, advertised "for the Coming Season"; 27 September 1851, listed; 18 October 1851, reviewed.

TxU.

d. [Works form].   NEW-YORK: | GEORGE P. PUTNAM, 155 BROADWAY. | M.DCCC.LII.

Works title, dated 1852.

Private hands.

e. [Illustrated form]. NEW-YORK: | G. P. PUTNAM & COMPANY, 10 PARK PLACE, | 1852.

Noted in brown V cloth. On front, gilt illustration of the Alhambra: gate, fountain, tower; bordered in blind. Back the same except all in blind. Spine decorated and titled in gilt. Edges not gilt. White endpapers.

CtY.

f. [Works form]. NEW-YORK: | G. P. PUTNAM & COMPANY, 10 PARK PLACE. | 1853.

Works title, dated 1853.

Engraved title and illustration added at front.

DLC.

g.   [Works form].   New York: [fancy] | G. P. PUTNAM & CO., 321
     BROADWAY. | 1857.

Works title, dated 1857.

Copyright 1848.

DLC.

h.   NEW YORK: | G. P. PUTNAM (for the Proprietor), 506 BROADWAY |
     1859.

Works title, dated 1859.

Two preliminary engravings, published by CHILDS & PETERSON,
PHILAD^A.

Green BD cloth.   On sides, frame in blind.   Spine titled in gilt, with gilt
decoration around title.   Green endpapers.

TxU.

1F. THE | ALHAMBRA, | OR | THE NEW SKETCH BOOK, | BY
     GEOFFREY CRAYON, GENT. | AUTHOR OF THE SKETCH BOOK,
     TALES OF A TRAVELLER, | CONQUEST OF GRANADA, LIFE AND
     VOYAGES OF CHRISTOPHER | COLUMBUS, ETC. | [rule] | IN TWO
     VOLUMES. | VOL. I. [II.] | [emblem: L. B. within wreath] | PARIS, |
     BAUDRY'S FOREIGN LIBRARY, | RUE DU COQ-SAINT-HONORÉ. |
     SOLD ALSO BY THEOPH.   BARROIS, JUN., RUE RICHELIEU;
     TRUCHY, BOULEVARD | DES ITALIENS; AMYOT, RUE DE LA
     PAIX; LIBRAIRIE DES ÉTRANGERS, | RUE NEUVE SAINT-
     AUGUSTIN; AND FRENCH AND ENGLISH LIBRARY, | RUE
     VIVIENNE. | [rule] | 1832.

The text is that of the first English edition.

(16.7 x 10.5): Vol. I. [i]-x [xi]-[xii], [1]-294. Vol. II. [1]-264. Signed in 12's.
Laid paper.

Printer: J. Smith, 16, Rue Montmorency.

Lineation: Vol. I. p. 100, tower ... ancient Vol. II. p. 100, hands ... could

Copy in boards with paper label on spines reported in dealer's catalogue,
Rare Books I, Randall & Windle, San Francisco, 1977.

Bibliographie de la France, 26 May 1832, # 2574, listed.

NN.

2F.   THE | ALHAMBRA; | OR THE | NEW SKETCH BOOK. | BY | WASHINGTON IRVING. | [rule] | IN ONE VOLUME. | [emblem: D in star within wreath with pendant medal] | PARIS: | PUBLISHED BY A. AND W. GALIGNANI, | AT THE ENGLISH, FRENCH, ITALIAN, GERMAN, AND SPANISH LIBRARY, | N° 18, RUE VIVIENNE. | [rule] | 1832.

(11.3 x 9.1): [i]-viii, [1]-338, Laid paper.

Printer: Jules Didot, Paris.

Lineation: p. 100, entered, ... pave-; p. 200, on ... un-

Bibliographie de la France, 26 May 1832, # 2575, listed, with added note: "Cette édition fait suite aux Oeuvres complètes de cet auteur, publiée par les mêmes éditeurs, dans le format in-12."

MH.

3F.   [Paris: Baudry's Foreign Library, 1832.]

[i]-viii, [1]-356. Bound in 12's.

Printer: J. Smith, Paris.

Bibliographie de la France, 2 June 1832, # 2723, listed.

Not seen. Copies reported in CU, Bibliothèque Nationale.

4Fa. THE | ALHAMBRA; | OR THE | NEW SKETCH BOOK. | BY | WASHINGTON IRVING. | [ornament: six-petal simple flower] | *VOLUME I. [II.]* | [ornament: the same] | B. CORMON AND BLANC, | BOOKSELLERS. | [in two parallel columns:] PARIS. | 70, MAZARINE STREET. || LYONS. | 1, ROGER STREET. || 1834.

(14.0 x 8.5): Vol. I. [1]-136. Pp. [134]-136 are advertisements. Vol. II. [i]-[iv], [1]-124. Signed in 6's.

Printer: L. Perrin, 6, Amboise street.

Lineation: Vol. I. p. 100, At ... sorceres- Vol. II. p. 100, The ... enchant-

Examined only in Vol. II.

TxU, Vol. II. CtW, both vols. reported.

b.   B. CORMON AND BLANC, | BOOKSELLERS. | [in two parallel columns:] | PARIS. | 70, MAZARINE STREET. || LYONS. | 1, ROGER STREET. || 1835.

BL. TxU, Vol. I. Copy reported in ViU.

5F. TALES | OF THE | ALHAMBRA; | TO WHICH ARE ADDED |
LEGENDS | OF THE | CONQUEST OF SPAIN, | BY | WASHINGTON
IRVING, | AUTHOR OF THE SKETCH BOOK, CHRONICLE OF THE
CONQUEST OF GRANADA, LIFE AND | VOYAGES OF
CHRISTOPHER COLUMBUS, ETC., ETC. | [emblem: intertwined letters
BEL] | PARIS: | BAUDRY'S EUROPEAN LIBRARY, | 3, QUAI
MALAQUAIS, NEAR THE PONT DES ARTS, | AND STASSIN AND
XAVIER, 9, RUE DU COQ, NEAR THE LOUVRE. | SOLD ALSO BY
AMYOT, RUE DE LA PAIX; TRUCHY, BOULEVARD DES ITALIENS;
GIRARD FRÈRES, | RUE RICHELIEU; LEOPOLD MICHELSEN,
LEIPZIG; AND BY ALL THE PRINCIPAL | BOOKSELLERS ON THE
CONTINENT. | [rule] | 1840.

"Collection of Ancient and Modern British Authors," Vol. LXVIII.

The Alhambra is complete in this edition.

(21.3 x 13.3): [I]-VIII, [1]-208; [209]-346. Signed in 8's. Laid paper.

Printer: Fain and Thunot, 28, Rue Racine.

Lineation: p. 100, exclamations, ... lament,; p. 200, brief ... same ; p. 300,
Having ... [in footnote] renowned.

TxU.

6F. [*Tales of the Alhambra*. Paris: Baudry, 1840.]

[I]-IV, [1]-379 [380]. Signed in 16's.

Not seen. Copy reported in Bibliothèque Nationale.

1G. [*The Alhambra*. Vollständig akzentuirt und erlautert, zum Schul- und
Privatgebrauche vom Sprachlehrer Joh. Christ. Nossek. Znaim: Fournier,
1842.]

Paged x, 337. Bound in 12's.

Not seen. Listed W. Heinsius, *Allgemeines Bücher-Lexicon, 1842-1846*, and
C. G. Kayser, *Vollständiges Bücher-Lexicon, 1841-1846*. Copy reported in
Stadtbibliothek Nürnberg.

2Ga. [*Tales of the Alhambra*. Accentuirt und mit einem vollständigen
grammatikalischen Commentar und phraseologischen Noten zum Schul- und
Privatgebrauche hrsg. von Franz Bauer. Celle: E. H. C. Schulze, 1845.]

For a detailed description, see the following impression.

Not seen. Copy reported in Landesbibliothek Hannover.

b. TALES | OF | THE ALHAMBRA | by | Washington Irving, Esq. | [rule] | Accentuirt | und | mit einem vollständigen grammatischen Commentar | und phraseologischen Noten | zum | Schul- und Privatgebrauch | von | Franz Bauer, | Lehrer der englischen, französischen und italienischen Sprache. | [rule] | Mit einem Wörterbuche. [in fraktur] | [swelled rule] | Celle. | Druck und Verlag von E. H. C. Schulze. | [rule] 1847.

The text is in English; the foreword, notes, and vocabulary in German.

(14.5 x 10.3): [I]-VII [VIII], [1]-463 [464]. Signed in 8's.

Lineation: p. 100, there, ... [in footnote] 59*.; p. 200, and ... [in footnote] sweep.

.Purple V cloth. Front decorated in gilt. Back decorated in blind. Spine decorated and titled in gilt. Yellow endpapers. All edges marbled.

TxU. Copy reported in Stadtbibliothek Braunschweig.

3G. [*Tales of the Alhambra.* With a copious vocabulary compiled by E[duard] Amthor. Revised edition. Leipzig: Renger, 1846.]

The earlier edition, if one existed, has not been located nor identified.

Not seen. Copy reported in Universitätsbibliothek Mannheim.

4Ga. [Revised edition. Leipzig: Renger, 1851.]

Paged iv, 260. Bound in 8's.

Not seen. Listed W. Heinsius, *Allgemeines Bücher-Lexicon, 1847-1851*, and C. G. Kayser, *Vollständiges Bücher-Lexicon, 1847-1852*.

b. [Revised edition. Berlin: Renger, 1851.]

Not seen. Copy reported in Universitätsbibliothek Erlangen.

5G. [*Tales of the Alhambra.* Akkumuliert und mit einem Kommentar. Hrsg. von Franz Bauer. 2 vols. Celle, 1847.]

Publisher not listed.

Not seen. Copy reported in Niedersächsischer Staats- und Universitätsbibliothek Göttingen.

6G. [*Tales of the Alhambra.* Accentuirt mit einem vollständigen grammatikalischen Commentar und phraseologischen Noten, unter steter Hinweisung auf Wagner's "Neue englische Sprachlehre" und einem gedränkten Wörtebuche zum Schul-und Privatgebrauche, hrsg. von Franz Bauer. 2., revidirte Auflage. Celle: Schulze, 1853.]

Paged ix, 374. Engraved portrait not reckoned.

Not seen. Copy reported in Landesbibliothek Kassel.

TRANSLATIONS

Danish.

Alhambra. | [swelled rule] | Af | Washington Irving. | [swelled rule] | Oversat | af | Frederik Schaldemose. | [elaborate emblem of harp and wreath] | Første [Anden] Deel. | [double rule] | Kjøbenhavn. | Forlagt af H. G. Brill. Trikt i det Martinske Officin. [Vol. II: Trikt og forlagt af H. G. Brill.] | 1833. [Vol. II dated 1834.] [in fraktur]

(17.5 x 10.4): Vol. I. [i]-[iv], [1]-180. Vol. II. [1]-172. Signed in 8's.

Lineation: Vol. I. p. 50, Det ... forsvandt.; p. 100, Skuepladsen. ... hørde Vol. II. p. 50, ført ... Prind-; p. 100, Men ... Paganini.

DLC.

Dutch.

DE | ALHAMBRA, | OF | *NIEUWE* | SCHETSEN EN PORTRETTEN. | [stylized swelled rule] | Naar het Engelsch | VAN | WASHINGTON IRVING | DOOR | *H. FRIJLINK.* | EERSTE [TWEEDE] DEEL. | [engraved illustration. Below it, in curved line: Ik ben een zoon van de Alhambra. I. D. Bl. 40.] | Te AMSTERDAM, bij | HENDRIK FRIJLINK. | MDCCCXXXIII. Engraved title page in a variety of lettering styles.

(21.4 x 12.5): Vol. I. [I]-IV, [1]-250. Vol. II. [I]-IV, [1]-233 [234]. Engraved titles not reckoned. Signed in 8's. Laid paper.

Lineation: Vol. I. p.. 100, klein, ... te ; p. 200, is ... wil Vol. II. p. 100, *calde* ... be-; p. 200, man ... welgemeste,

NNC

French.

LES CONTES | DE | L'ALHAMBRA, [hollow letters] | PRÉCÉDÉS D'UN VOYAGE | DANS LA PROVINCE DE GRENADE; | TRADUITS | DE WASHINGTON IRVING, | PAR Mlle A. SOBRY, | TRADUCTEUR DE LADY MORGAN, LE COIN DU FEU D'UN | HOLLANDAIS, ETC. | [rule] | TOME PREMIER. [SECOND.] | [elaborated swelled rule] | PARIS, | H.. FOURNIER JEUNE, LIBRAIRE, | RUE DE SEINE, N° 29. | [rule] | 1832.

(21.8 x 14.0 untrimmed): Vol. I. [i]-[iv], [1]-312. Vol. II. [i]-[iv], [1]-327 [328]. Signed in 8's. Laid paper.

Lineation: Vol. I. p. 100, sur ... si ; p. 200, garde, ... laissé   Vol. II. p. 100, Limousins, ... des ; p. 200, il ... la-

Pink paper wrappers. On front, title (dated 1833) within decorative border. On back, advertisements. On spine, decoration, title, price (12 fr.), date (1833).

Bibliographie de la France, 9 June 1832, # 2752, listed.

CtY, *BL*.

[*L'Alhambra, chroniques du pays de Grenade*. Traduit par P. Christian. Paris: Lavigne, 1843.]

Not located. Listed in *Catalogue Général de la Librairie Française*, Vol. 3, 1869. Also listed by Williams and Edge as seen.

[*Nouveaux contes de l'Alhambra*. Bruxelles: Kiessling, Schnée et cie., 1855.]

Traduits de l'anglais par O. Squarr [Charles Flor].

Not located. Listed by Williams and Edge as seen.

[Bruxelles: A. Cadot, 1855.]

Not located . Listed by Williams and Edge as seen.

German.

Die | Alhambra, | oder | das neue Skizzenbuch. | Von | Washington Irving. | [rule] | Aus dem Englischen. | [heavy rule of multiple lines] | Frankfurt am Main, 1832. | Gedruckt und verlegt bei Johann David Sauerländer. [in fraktur]

"Washington Irving's sämmtliche Werke," Bändchen 44-47.

(13.5 x 10.1): [I]-VI, [7]-370 [371]-[372]. Signed in 8's.

Lineation: p. 100, der ... bleibt.; p. 200, des ... mitzu-

Issued in paper wrappers. Seen only rebound.

CtY. Copy reported in Bayerischer Staatsbibliothek, München.

[*Das Alhambra*. 2 vols. Berlin: Duncker und Humblot, 1832.]

Translated by Theodor Hell.

Bound in 12's.

Not seen. Copy reported in Universitätsbibliothek Tübingen.

[*Die Alhambra*. Aus dem Englischen von Johann Sporschil.   2 vols. Braunschweig: Vieweg, 1832.]

Bound in 8's.

Not seen. Copy reported in Stadtbibliothek Braunschweig.

[*Die Alhambra*, oder das neue Skizzenbuch. Halle a. d. S.: Hendel, (n.d.).]

229 pp. Bound in 8's.

Not seen. Copy reported in Landesbibliothek Kassel.

[*Alhambra*, oder das neue Skizzenbuch. *Abbotsford* und *Newstead-Abtei*. *Eine Reise auf den Prairien*. 2., sorgfältig verbesserte Auflage. Frankfurt am Main: Johann David Sauerländer, 1847.]

"Ausgewählte Schriften," No. 4.

With two engravings.

Not seen. Copy reported in Stadtbibliothek Braunschweig.

Italian.

[*L'Alhambra*. Edited by Giacomo Mosconi. 3 vols. Milano: Stella, 1834.]

Not located. Listed by Williams and Edge, although not seen.

[*L'Alhambra*; ossiano, Nuovi abbozzi di Goffredo Crayon. 2 vols. Torino: Tipografia dei fratelli Favole, 1841.]

Translated by Pietro Unia.

Not located. Listed by Williams and Edge, although not seen.

Spanish.

An edition of eight tales in Spanish translation by D. Luis Lamarca appears under a number of different imprints. No sequence has been determined. Three imprints are listed here; others may exist.

CUENTOS | DE | LA ALHAMBRA [hollow, shaded type] | DE | Washington Irving [fancy] | Traducidos | POR *D. L. L.* | [ornament with BS on shield] | PARIS, | LIBRERÍA HISPANO-AMERICANA, | CALLE DE RICHELIEU No. 60. | [rule] | 1833.

An engraved title specifies in a variety of lettering: Valencia | Libreria de | MALLEN Y BERARD | 1833 | Teodoro Blasco lo g.

(11.2 x 7.5): [i]-[viii], [1]-248. Preliminary illustration and engraved title not reckoned. Signed in 8's. Laid paper.

Printer: Imp. de J. Ferrer de Orga, Valencia, 1833.

Lineation: p. 100, canso, ... prisioneros.; p. 200, testó ... estaban

BL

Libreria [fancy] | DE MALLÉN Y BERARD, | frente á San Martin.

The engraved title again specifies Valencia.

Printer: Impr. de J. Ferrer de Orga, Valencia.

CtY. Copy reported in NNH.

[Paris: Salva, 1833.]

The engraved title again specifies Valencia.

Not seen. Listed A. Palau y Dulcet, *Manual del Librero Hispanoamericano*, 2nd ed.

[Los Cuentos de la Alhambra, precedidos de un viaje a la provincia de Granada, traducidos del francés por D. Manuel M. de Santa Ana. Madrid: Casa de la Unión Comercial, 1844.]

Translated from the French translation by Mlle. A. Sobry.

160 pp. in double columns. Bound in 4's. Illustrated.

Not located. Listed by Williams and Edge, as seen. Listed A. Palau y Dulcet, *Manual del Librero Hispanoamericano*, 2nd ed.

[Barcelona: Imprenta del Diario, 1856.]

Not located. Listed A. Palau y Dulcet, *Manual del Librero Hispanoamericano*, 2nd ed.

[*Las cinco perlas de la Alhambra*. Cuentos originales.... Escritos en inglés por Washington Irving, y traducidos del francés por D. Manuel M. de Santa Ana. Madrid, 1844.]

Five tales selected from the previous edition: "Historia de tres príncesas," "Una visita a la Alhambra," "Historia del príncipe Ahmed al Kamel," "La herencia del Moro," "La rosa de la Alhambra."

Not located. Listed by Williams and Edge, as seen.

CUENTOS | DE | LA ALHAMBRA, | DE | Washinglon (sic) Irving. | [ornament] | GRANADA. | Imprenta de Zamora. | 1859.

Contains 10 tales from the full work.

Bound in 16's.

Not examined. Information from copy in NNH, and from listing by Williams and Edge.

Swedish.

ALHAMBRA, | ELLER | NYA UTKAST | AF | *GEOFFREY CRAYON*, | FÖRFATTARE TILL UTKASTEN, BERÄTTELSER AF EN | RESANDE, GRANADAS ERÖFRING, CHRISTOFER | COLUMBI LEFNAD OCH RESOR M. M. | [swelled rule] | Komplett i en Volum. | [swelled rule] | STOCKHOLM, HOS L. J. HJERTA, 1833.

Series title: LÄSE-BIBLIOTHEK AF DEN NYASTE UTLÄNDSKA LITTERATUREN I SVENSK ÖFVERSÄTTNING. I.

(14.2 x 9.0): [1]-306. Signed in 12's . Laid paper.

Lineation: p. 100, *te!* ... bergstrakten.; p. 200, förän ... Alhambra.

TxU.

[Stockholm: L. J. Hjerta, 1834.]

Not located. Listed in Hjalmar Linnström, *Svenskt Boklexikon, 1830-1865*, and *Svensk Bokhandels-Katalog, År 1845*.

THE CRAYON MISCELLANY

In 1835 Irving included under the series title of *The Crayon Miscellany* three separate volumes, published at intervals, numbered as parts of the series: No. 1, *A Tour on the Prairies*; No. 2, *Abbotsford* and *Newstead Abbey*; No. 3, *Legends of the Conquest of Spain*. Number 2, *Abbotsford* and *Newstead Abbey*, consisted of two separate long pieces published together in one volume. Number 1, *A Tour on the Prairies*, and Number 3, *Legends of the Conquest of Spain*, was each an integral, self-contained work unrelated in subject to the other volumes. In this bibliography, in the following entries, each volume is described separately under its individual title.

In 1849 Irving and George P. Putnam used the title of *The Crayon Miscellany* again, this time for Volume IX of the Author's Revised Edition, although they included in the volume only *A Tour on the Prairies*, *Abbotsford*, and *Newstead Abbey*. That single volume of 1849 is described here under its given volume-title, following the descriptions of the three original component volumes of the series. For a discussion of its text, see the individual description of *A Tour on the Prairies* and of *Abbotsford* and *Newstead Abbey*.

The Crayon Miscellany, Volume 1: A Tour on the Prairies

When Irving completed a manuscript of *A Tour on the Prairies*, probably in December 1834, he engaged several copyists to transcribe it for English publication; he wanted to insure simultaneous publication on both sides of the Atlantic. As he revised his American manuscript, he entered the changes on the English copy. In early January 1835, he sent the English manuscript to his London literary agent, Colonel Thomas Aspinwall. In February, John Murray of London agreed to publish the work. In the meantime, Irving continued to revise the American manuscript, until his brother Ebenezer, at some time later in January, arranged for it to be stereotyped by Adoniram Chandler for publication by Carey, Lea & Blanchard of Philadelphia. (On 2 February 1835, Irving sent some proof sheets to Col. Aspinwall as a source of further corrections for the proposed English edition.) Despite Irving's plans for simultaneous publication, Murray brought out the book in early March, but Carey, Lea & Blanchard not until the middle of April.

In addition to the later revisions by Irving that appear in the American text, Irving added to the American edition a brief "Advertisement" to declare his intention for *The Crayon Miscellany*, and an "Introduction" to explain his long absence from America, his Rip-Van-Winkle-like return, and his pleasure at his warm reception upon his return to home. He also added to the Introduction a few words about the writing of this book. Neither the Advertisement nor the Introduction appears in the London edition, although Irving added there two brief paragraphs of "Preface" to characterize the work and to suggest the possibility of "further sketches of American scenes in some future numbers."

The English and the American texts may be distinguished by the differences in the synoptic headings for a number of chapters. (Since the American edition has no table of contents, the headings must be taken from those appearing before each chapter.) The first three chapters provide convenient examples.

Chapter	Item in heading	American text	English text
I	first	The Pawnee Hunting Grounds	THE PRAIRIE HUNTING-GROUNDS
II	first	Anticipations disappointed	ANTICIPATION DISAPPOINTED
III	second	Riflemen	RIFLEMAN

The work was quickly reprinted in Paris by Galignani and by Baudry, and translated into Dutch, French, German, Italian and Russian, all based upon the London text. A French translation continued to appear through Irving's lifetime.

Irving revised the text for the Author's Revised Edition, published by G. P. Putnam in 1849. Putnam combined the new revision of the work with a new revision of *Abbotsford* and *Newstead Abbey* and issued them together in a single volume carrying the original series title, *The Crayon Miscellany*. (For description of that volume, see *The Crayon Miscellany* at the end of this description of the series.) The revision was a light one, based on the Philadelphia edition of 1835, and made only a limited number of corrections and stylistic alterations in the body of the text. The Advertisement was omitted, and only the last four paragraphs of the Introduction retained.

1-2E.   The first and second London editions are so nearly alike in title page and in general appearance that they are more conveniently described, and the distinctions between them defined, in one entry than in two.

The relationship between the two editions is complicated by the fact that the disguised second edition is not reset in its entirety, and those signatures that are retained in their original setting are often redressed (that is, they demonstrate minor shifts within the forme and occasionally a change of position of running head or of signature mark) and in some instances show textual changes or the resetting of a line or two. As a rule, any resetting is a line-for-line reproduction of the first edition.

Specific representative text changes are detailed in a table below.   The general pattern of resetting in the second edition, however, is this:

Sig. [A]. The series title and the volume title are reset and substituted in the signature as cancels. The remaining leaves are in the original setting, although one page number is lost in the table of contents. In a second state of the series title of the second edition, an extraneous THE is removed from the identification of the author.

Sig. a. This singleton remains unchanged.

Sigs. B-F. Reset throughout.

Sig. G. Reset except for one page.

Sig. H. Two pages are entirely reset; seven pages reset in two lines or more; fifteen pages redressed, with several showing textual changes.

Sig I. One page is reset; the remainder redressed, with several showing textual changes.

Sigs. K-L. Occasionally redressed or lines reset, with a very few textual changes.

Sigs. M-P. Generally unchanged except for a few pages redressed.

The pattern of complete resetting in the early signatures of the text itself, through partial resetting and redressing in the middle signatures, to almost no change in the late signatures suggests the hypothesis that when Spottiswoode discovered that more copies would be required than originally planned, he reset and "corrected" the signatures whose type had already been distributed; saved, redressed, and occasionally corrected the middle signatures which had been used for printing but whose type had not yet been distributed; and simply printed or reprinted the last signature. Sig. [A] may have been earlier set aside or may have been first printed late in the process. The hypothesis would at least explain the general pattern. Ledger C in the Murray archives records that Spottiswoode printed for Murray two thousand copies first and then an additional one thousand. The addition was almost certainly the second edition.

The sequence of the two text states is clear. Thirty textual variants discovered in Sigs. B-H (not including such matters as page numbers and running heads) were compared with the readings in the setting manuscript for the first edition. Of the thirty changes between the two text states, six differ from the manuscript in both editions, indicating that in the process of house styling the text was changed immediately and then later changed again to remove it still further from the manuscript. But of the twenty-four remaining variants, the first edition follows the manuscript in twenty-one instances. Presumably the three instances in which the second edition follows the manuscript but the first edition does not are examples of house styling "corrections" made in the first edition and later, ironically enough, changed back to the manuscript readings, probably without awareness of the correspondence. All of the changes are in spelling or punctuation only, and none suggests authorial revision.

A | TOUR | ON | THE PRAIRIES. | BY | THE AUTHOR OF "THE SKETCH-BOOK." | [rule] | LONDON: | JOHN MURRAY, ALBEMARLE STREET. | MDCCCXXXV.

Series title: MISCELLANIES. | BY | THE AUTHOR OF THE "THE SKETCH-BOOK." | N° I. | CONTAINING | A TOUR ON THE PRAIRIES. | [rule] | LONDON: | JOHN MURRAY, ALBEMARLE STREET. | MDCCCXXXV. A second state of the series title of the second edition omits the superfluous THE in the third line.

First Edition. (20.2 x 12.3): [A]^6 a^1 B-I^{12} K-P^{12}. In some copies the stub of the singleton protrudes between Sigs. B-C, pp. 24-25. Laid paper.

Second Edition. (20.2 x 12.3): [A]^6([A]$_{1-2}$) a^1 B-I^{12} K-P^{12}. A copy in TxU in original binding but loose in the boards allows certainty about Sig. [A]: the first two leaves (the two titles) are cancels made before binding. Sig. a is pasted to the verso of [A]$_6$. Laid paper.

[i]-[ii], series title, on verso printer; [iii]-[iv], title, verso blank; [v]-vi, Preface; [vii]-xiii, table of contents; [xiv], blank; [1]-335, text; [336], printer. In one copy of the second edition examined, the two titles are reversed: the volume title precedes the series title.

Printer: A. Spottiswoode, New-Street-Square, London

Lineation: p. 100, The ... one ; p. 200, "Well, ... Pawnees?"

The common binding is gray-brown unprinted paper boards. White endpapers. White paper label on spine. The label appears in two states; no sequence apparent. Both states appear on both editions.

[A]. [double rule] | TOUR | ON THE | PRAIRIES. | BY | THE AUTHOR | OF THE | SKETCH BOOK. | [double rule]. Approx. 6.1 cm. tall.

[B]. With hyphen in SKETCH-BOOK. Approx. 5.1 cm. tall.

Also noted or reported bound in gray-brown boards with brown T cloth shelfback; and in various unprinted full cloths: blue-black H cloth, green P cloth, purple T cloth. All with paper label on spine in one of the two states. The cloth bindings are more common on second edition copies.

Representative variants in the first and second editions:

Sig.	Page & Line	First edition	Second edition
[A]	Series		
	title	Vertical extent of type, from top of A to baseline of date: 12.35 cm.	Vertical extent of type: 11.3 cm. Second state: same, except extra THE omitted in line 3.
	Title	Vertical extent of type: 11.1 cm.	Vertical extent of type: 11.5 cm.
B	5.4f	fire, and	fire; and
	13.9f	hunter's	hunters'
C	29.2f	boned old	boned, old
	41.6	blind!"	blind?"
D	51.7f	half breeds	half-breeds
	65.12	whisp	wisp
E	79.5	POLE-CAT	POLECAT
	89.14	debût	début
F	97.page no.	97	91
	103.12	"Ah Captain!	"Ah, Captain!
G	135.11	checquered	chequered
	141.10f	banterings	banterings,
H	146.6f	burthens	burdens
	153.10	us. An	us: -- an

	166.13	paralyzes	paralyses
I	172.5	far West	"far West"
	174.8	all	all,
L	222	[Sig. mark L3]	[no Sig. mark]
	235.6f	neck or nothing	neck-or-nothing

Athenæum, 21, 28 February 1835, advertised for 2 March; 7 March 1835, advertised "This day," and reviewed; 21 March 1835, listed. *Literary Gazette*, 7 March 1835, advertised "This day," listed, reviewed. *The English Catalogue of Books, 1801-1836* lists February 1835 as publication date. Deposited and registered by Murray in Stationers' Hall 2 March 1835.

Discussion based on copies in NN, TxDaM, TxGeoS, TxU (4), *BL*, private hands.

3Ea. A | TOUR ON THE PRAIRIES. | BY | WASHINGTON IRVING. | [rule] | LONDON: | HENRY G. BOHN, YORK STREET, COVENT GARDEN. | [rule] | 1850.

(18.2 x 11.5): [i]-v [vi], [1]-137 [138]. Signed in 8's.

Issued individually as "Bohn's Shilling Series"; bound with *Astoria* as Vol. VIII of "Bohn's Library Edition."

Printer: G. Barclay, Castle St. Leicester Sq.

Lineation: p. 50, to ... wound.; p. 100, he ... endea-

Seen only in "Bohn's Library Edition." Gray T cloth. Sides decorated in blind. Spine titled in gilt as Irving's Works, Vol. VIII, Bohn's Library Edition. White endpapers with advertisements in blue. Preliminary engraving added: portrait of Irving in one copy, "A Scene on the Prairies" in another. No Works title.

Shilling Series. *Athenæum*, 18 May 1850, listed. Library Edition. *Athenæum* and *Literary Gazette*, 2 November 1850, the set of 10 vols. at 35*s*. listed.

TxU, Private hands.

b. HENRY G. BOHN, YORK STREET, COVENT GARDEN. | [rule] | 1851.

Seen only in the Library Edition, bound with *Astoria*, 1850. Gray T cloth. Sides decorated in blind. Spine titled in gilt as Irving's Works, Vol. VIII, Bohn's Library Edition. White endpapers with advertisements in blue. No Works title.

NN.

c. HENRY G. BOHN, YORK STREET, COVENT GARDEN. | [rule] | 1854.

Seen only in the Library Edition, with Works title.

MB.

4E.   [London: George Routledge, 1850.]

"Routledge's Popular Library." Printed in a single volume with *Abbotsford* and *Newstead Abbey*.

Seen only in an incomplete copy, missing the title page and the text of *Abbotsford* and *Newstead Abbey*.

(16.6 x 10.5): [i]-viii, [1]-23-? *A Tour on the Prairies* occupies the first position in the volume, to p. 124.

Lineation: p. 50, passing ... short ; p. 100, while ... picture

Athenæum and *Literary Gazette*, 18 May 1850, listed, 1*s*. in boards.

TxU, incomplete.

1Aa-   The first American edition exists in two definable text states and a minimum
  c.   of two impressions. It is almost certain that the edition went through at least three impressions and possibly more, but the evidence is ambiguous and, at best, does not lead to chronological ordering of later impressions. The first and second text states may be defined with certainty; the number and sequence of impressions must be left to interpretation of the available evidence.

Letters in the Carey & Lea manuscript letter books, now in the Historical Society of Pennsylvania, reveal that the original print order was for 5000 copies, and the Cost Book of Carey & Lea records 5000 copies, "finished" on 10 April 1835. But Pierre M. Irving reports in the *Life* (III.68) that by 10 November 1835 the publisher had paid Irving for 8000 copies. That addition of 3000 copies, plus any more that may have been printed, would account for the later impressions but would not help in determining the exact number.

A | TOUR ON THE PRAIRIES. | [rule] | BY THE AUTHOR OF THE SKETCH BOOK. | [rule] | Philadelphia: [fancy] | CAREY, LEA, & BLANCHARD. | [rule of 21 dots] | 1835.

Series title: THE | CRAYON MISCELLANY. | [double rule] | BY THE AUTHOR OF THE SKETCH BOOK. | [double rule] | No. 1. | CONTAINING | A Tour on the Prairies. [fancy] | [double rule] | Philadelphia: [fancy] | CAREY, LEA, & BLANCHARD. | [rule of 15 dots] | 1835.

(17.8 x 11.1): $[1]^6$ 2-23^6. 23_6 is a blank. Catalogue in 12, 24, or 36 pp. bound at end. [See the discussion below.]

The publishers' catalogue bound at the end has been noted in six different states. No sequence to the six states is apparent. Although not all states of the catalogue have been seen present with both states of the text (or combined with both states of the label on the spine), no pattern emerges from those seen, and the suspicion is strong that if only enough copies could be examined, almost every combination would eventually appear.

All six states are undated and unpaged, and all begin on p. [1] with DR. BIRD'S NEW NOVEL -- CALAVAR.

[A1].   12 pp. P. [3] begins with THE | WONDROUS TALE OF ALROY.

[A2].   12 pp. P. [3] begins with THE MAGDALEN AND OTHER TALES.

[B1].   24 pp. P. [3] begins with THE | WONDROUS TALE OF ALROY.

[B2].   24 pp. P. [3] begins with Cooper's New Novel | THE HEADSMAN.

[C1].   36 pp. P. [36] is devoted to NATIONAL SCHOOL MANUAL.

[C2].   36 pp. P [25] is devoted to NATIONAL SCHOOL MANUAL.

[i]-[ii], series title, on verso copyright (1835 by Washington Irving) and printer; [iii]-[iv], Advertisement, verso blank; [v]-[vi], title, on verso same copyright and printer; [vii]-xv, Introduction; [xvi], blank; [17]-274, text.

Printer: Stereotyped by A. Chandler. The Cost Book of Carey & Lea reveals that the printer was C. Sherman & Co., Philadelphia.

Lineation: p. 100, winding ... year.; p. 200, when ... the

Blue-green, and green, V cloth. Sides blank. White paper label on spine. The label appears in two states; no sequence apparent. Both states appear on both text states.

[A]   [double rules] | THE | CRAYON | MISCELLANY. | [rule] | A | TOUR | ON THE | PRAIRIES. | BY THE AUTHOR OF | THE | Sketch Book. | [double rule].

[B]   [rule] | THE | CRAYON MISCELLANY | *No. 1.* | [rule] | A | TOUR | ON THE | PRAIRIES. | BY THE AUTHOR OF | THE | Sketch Book. | [rule].

Eight textual variants define the two text states:

Page & line	First text state	Second text state
18.2	regions	region
26.17-18	in | in	out | in
92.15	casewith	case with

119.1	wit	with
155.4f	Tonish,	Tonish
214.1	missed	missed.
247.6	binger	harbinger
270.1f	view, It	view. It

In a copy in the second text state, the printer's imprint on the verso of the series title has been noted in a variant state: the rules above and below the imprint are 3.35 cm. long, extending well past the printing, rather than 3.0 cm. long, approximately coterminous with the printing. (The same rules on the verso of the volume title have been seen only in the longer state.)

Copies in the second text state have been noted on two papers; sequence undetermined:

[A]. The sheets, exclusive of the publishers' catalogue, bulk 1.4 cm.

[B]. The sheets, exclusive of the publishers' catalogue, bulk 1.8 cm.

The Cost Book of Carey & Lea records 5000 copies "done up in cloth," "finished" on 10 April 1835. A letter to Irving from the Carey office, dated 10 April 1835, promises publication the following day with copies "forwarded to the New York booksellers at every part of the country."

Copyrighted and title page deposited 26 February 1835; complete copy deposited 7 May 1835. *Knickerbocker*, April 1835, extracted, "Will be published early in the present month." *New-York Mirror*, 25 April 1835, noticed as published "about a fortnight since." *Atkinson's Casket* [Philadelphia], May 1835 (the month is correct), extracted, "Will be issued ... early in April. We have been permitted to peruse a portion of the book in sheets." Irving to John Murray, 22 September 1850, gives 14 April as the publication date.

Discussion based on copies in MB (2), MH, TxDaM (2), TxGeoS, TxU (9), ViU.

1F. A TOUR | ON | THE PRAIRIES. | BY WASHINGTON IRVING, | AUTHOR OF "THE SKETCH BOOK," "THE ALHAMBRA," &c. &c. | [emblem: BEL intertwined] | PARIS. | BAUDRY'S EUROPEAN LIBRARY, | RUE DU COQ, NEAR THE LOUVRE; | SOLD ALSO BY AMYOT, RUE DE LA PAIX; TRUCHY, BOULEVARD DES | ITALIENS; THEOPH. BARROIS, JUN. RUE RICHELIEU; LIBRAIRIE DES | ÉTRANGERS, RUE NEUVE SAINT-AUGUSTIN; AND FRENCH | AND ENGLISH LIBRARY, RUE VIVIENNE. | [rule] | 1835.

(17.2 x 10.6): [i]-x, [1]-270. Signed in 12's.

Printer: J. Smith, Rue Montmorency.

Lineation: p. 100, CHAPTER XV. ... beautiful ; p. 200, that ... company."

Bibliographie de la France, 21 March 1835, # 1614, listed.

TxU. Copy reported in Bibliothèque Nationale.

2F.   [A *Tour on the Prairies*. Paris: Baudry; also Amyot, Truchy, Barrois, 1835.]

Paged [i]-x, [1]-242.

Bibliographie de la France, 28 March 1835, # 1751, listed.

Not seen. Copy reported in Bibliothèque Nationale.

3F.   A | TOUR | ON | THE PRAIRIES, | BY | WASHINGTON IRVING. |
[elaborated swelled rule] | PARIS: | PUBLISHED BY A. AND W.
GALIGNANI AND C°, | RUE VIVIENNE, N° 18. | [rule] | 1835.

(17.7 x 10.4): [i]-x, [1]-199 [200]. Signed in 12's. Low quality laid paper.

Printer: Bourgogne and Martinet, Rue du Colombier, 30.

Lineation: p. 100, was ... warfare,; p. 150, Neosho: ... the

Bibliographie de la France, 28 March 1835, # 1752, listed.

CtY.

4F.   [*A Tour on the Prairies, Over the Hunting Grounds of the Osage and Pawnee
Indians, in the Far West, on the Borders of Mexico*. Second Edition. Paris: A.
and W. Galignani, 1835.]

Not located. Listed by Williams and Edge as seen.

TRANSLATIONS

Dutch.

[Engraved title, in a variety of lettering styles] TOGT | DOOR DE |
PRAIRIËN [elaborated decorative letters] | VAN | NOORD-AMERIKA. |
[swelled rule] | *NAAR HET ENGELSCH* | VAN | WASHINGTON
IRVING. | [engraving of gathering on the prairie, identified in curved line
below: Men vroeg hem, of hij nu ean bordje uilensoep lustic. Bl. 61.] | Te
AMSTERDAM, bij | HENDRIK FRIJLINK. | MDCCCXXXV.

(22.3 x 13.0): [I]-XII, [1]-260. The engraved title is reckoned, but not a
preliminary engraved portrait of Irving, nor two pages of preliminary
advertisements. Signed in 8's. Laid paper.

Lineation: p. 100, berg ... die-; p. 200, het ... waarvan

The copy examined is rebound but preserves, bound at the front, an extra white paper label for the spine.

DLC.

French.

VOYAGE | DANS LES PRAIRIES | A L'OUEST | DES ÉTATS-UNIS, | PAR | WASHINGTON IRVING. | TRADUIT | PAR MADEMOISELLE A. SOBRY, | TRADUCTEUR DES *CONTES DE L'ALHAMBRA*. | [elaborated swelled rule] | PARIS. | LIBRAIRIE DE FOURNIER JEUNE, | RUE DE SEINE, N° 14. | 1835.

"Mélanges. Tome Premier."

(20.5 x 12.5): [i]-[iv], [1]-306 [307]-[308]. Signed in 8's. Laid paper.

Pp. [307]-[308], an integral leaf, has advertisements on the recto, including *Les contes de l'Alhambra*, tr. A. Sobry; *Histoire ... compagnons de C. Colomb*, tr. Defauconpret; *Histoire de New-York*. Verso blank.

Printer: De l'imprimerie de Crapelet, Rue de Vaugirard, No. 9.

Lineation: p. 100, chait. ... sur ; p. 200, une ... exige

NN reports a copy " In original yellow paper covers."

Bibliographie de la France, 18 April 1835, # 2158, listed.

ViU. Copy reported in Bibliothèque Nationale.

[UN TOUR DANS LES PRAIRIES A L'OUEST DES ÉTATS-UNIS, TRADUIT DE L'ANGLAIS DE WASHINGTON IRWING PAR ERNEST W***. Tours: R. Pornin, 1843.]

With additional imprint of Roe Lockwood, New York.

12mo. Plates. 320 pp.

For what is apparently a parallel in a separate edition of 296 pp., see the description below of Pornin's edition of 1845.

Not seen. Listed in a bookseller's catalogue, 1980. NN lists an edition of that date.

UN TOUR | DAN LES | PRAIRIES | A L'OUEST DES ÉTATS-UNIS, | TRADUIT DE L'ANGLAIS DE WASHINGTON IRWING | PAR ERNEST W***. | [elaborated swelled rule] | TOURS, | R. PORNIN ET Cᴵᵉ, IMP. -- LIBRAIRES-ÉDITEURS. | 1845.

"Gymnase moral d'éducation."

(17.2 x 10.4):   [i]-[iv], [1]-296.   Not reckoned: preliminary engraving, engraved title, and 2 engravings in the text. Signed in 12's.

Printer: Imprimerie de R. Pornin et Cie., Tours.

Lineation: p. 100, ruisseau ... lunette,; p. 200, en ... [in footnote] (couper).

Variant state noted with additional imprint at foot of title page, clearly added after original printing: NEW-YORK | ROE LOCKWOOD & SON | AMERICAN AND FOREIGN BOOKS. 411 BROADWAY

Original state noted in lime-green paper boards heavily impressed with gilt quasi-floral designs.   Sides unprinted.   Spine titled in gilt with a different publisher named at foot: A. MAME & Cie., Éditeurs, TOURS.   White endpapers.

TxU (2).

TOURS, | R. PORNIN ET Cie, IMPRIMEURS-L BRAIRES-EDITEURS. | 1846.

Noted in contemporary binding that may be publisher's: black hot-pressed leather with decoration in blind and gilt.

CtY.

[*Un tour dans les prairies*. Tours: A. Mame, 1850.]

See description below for impression of 1854.

Not seen. Copy reported in Bibliothèque Nationale.

[Tours: A. Mame, 1851.]

Not seen. Copy reported in Bibliothèque Nationale.

UN TOUR | DANS LES PRAIRIES | A L'OUEST DES ÉTATS-UNIS [special letters with circles in the verticals] | TRADUIT DE L'ANGLAIS | DE WASHINGTON IRWING | PAR ERNEST W*** | [rule] | NOUVELLE ÉDITION | [emblem: AM within elaborate frame] | TOURS | A^d MAME ET Cie, IMPRIMEURS-LIBRAIRES | [rule] | 1854.

(17.3 x 10.3):   [i]-[iv], [1]-235 [236].   Preliminary illustration and engraved title not reckoned.

Printer: Imp. Mame, Tours.

Lineation: p. 100, de ... les ; p. 200, prairie; ... eût

Dark green TZ cloth. Sides heavily decorated in gilt. Spine decorated and titled in gilt. Bright yellow endpapers.

ViU.

[Tours: A. Mame, 1858.]

"Bibliothèque des écoles chrétiennes. Première série."

Not seen. Copy reported in Bibliothèque Nationale.

German.

Eine | Reise auf den Prairien. | [rule] | Von | Washington Irving. | [double rule] | Aus dem Englischen. | Mit dem Bildniss des Verfassers. | [double rule] | Frankfurt am Main, 1835. | Druck und Verlag von J. D. Sauerländer. [in fraktur]

"Washington Irving's sämmtliche Werke," Bändchen 48-56.

(13.7 x 10.3): [I]-VI, [7]-256. Signed in 8's.

Lineation: p. 100, geschickt ... wen-; p. 200, augenscheinlich ... dachte

CtY, TxU.

Ausflug | auf die Prairien | zwischen | dem Arkansas und Red-river, | von | Washington Irving. | [elaborated swelled rule] | Stuttgart und Tubingen, | in der J. G. Cotta'schen Buchhandlung. | [rule] | 1835. [in fraktur]

"Reisen und Landerbeschreibungen der älteren und neuesten Zeit," Vierte Lieferung. Herausgegeben von Dr. Eduard Widenmann und Dr. Hermann Hauff.

(21.7 x 12.9): [i]-[iv], [1]-136. Signed in 8's.

Printer: in der Buchdruckerci der J. G. Cotta'schen Buchhandlung, Augsburg.

Lineation: p. 50, olches ... Male ; p. 100, im ... aber

Blue paper wrappers. On front, title and series titlc. On back, printer. Inside both covers, advertisements.

DLC. Copy reported in Stadtbibliothek Braunschweig.

Reise durch die Prairieen | von | Washington Irving. | [rule] | Aus dem Englischen. | [triple rule] | Berlin, | Verlag von Veit und Comp., 1835. [in fraktur]

"Washington Irvings Wanderbuch," Erster Theil.

(16.7 x 10.4): [i]-[iv], [I]-VIII, [1]-363 [364]. Signed in 8's.

Printer: A. W. Hayn, Berlin.

Lineation: p. 100, zwölftes ... durch-; p. 200, Einundzwanzigstes ... hatte,

CtY.

[Eine Wanderung in die Prairien. Übers. v. H. Roberts. Braunschweig: Vieweg, 1835.]

"Miscellaneen," Band 1.

Not seen. Copy reported in Stadtbibliothek Braunschweig.

[*Alhambra. Abbotsford* und *Newstead-Abtei. Eine Reise auf den Prairien.* 2., sorgfältig verbesserte Auflage.   Frankfurt am Main: Johann David Sauerländer, 1847.]

"Ausgewählte Schriften," No. 4.

With two engravings.

Not seen. Copy reported in Stadtbibliothek Braunschweig.

Italian.

VIAGGIO | PER | LE PRATERIE [in decorative hollow letters] | OCCIDENTALI | DE | STATI UNITI | DI | WASHINGTON IRVING. | *Prima versione italiana.* | *VOL. I. [II ED ULT.]* | MILANO | TIPOGRAFIA E LIBRERIA PIROTTA E C. | Contrada di S.ª Radegunda, N.º 964. | [rule] | 1837.

"Amenità dei Viaggi."

(12.8 x 8.3 untrimmed): Vol. I. [i]-[iv], [1]-216. Vol. II. [1]-282. Unreckoned in both vols.: preliminary engraved series title. Signed in 8's.

Lineation: Vol. I. p. 100, sciato ... quan-; p. 200, Incoraggito ... crol- Vol. II. p. 100, tempo ... hanno ; p. 200, cavalla ... verno

Light tan paper wrappers. On front, title within ornamental frame and background. On back, advertisements for the series. On spine, within ornamental border and dividing rules: AMENITÀ | DEI | VIAGGI | TERZA SERIE | IN 12 VOLUMI | 11 [12 | *ED ULTIMO.*] VIAGGIO | PER | LE PRATERIE | OCCIDENTALI | *VOLUME* I. [II. | *ED ULTIMO*:] | MILANO | 1837.

TxU.

Russian.

[Translated title:]   A Journey | in | the Meadowland Steppes. | by | Washington Irving. | [decorative cut of urn and flowers] | Moscow. | Nicolai Stepanov Press, | 1837. [in Cyrillic]

(15.1 x 10.6): [1]-340. Signed in 12's.

Lineation: p. 100, na ... zharkeem.

TxU.

The Crayon Miscellany, Volume 2:
Abbotsford and Newstead Abbey

Irving completed the manuscripts for *Abbotsford* and *Newstead Abbey* in early 1835, engaged copyists to transcribe them for English publication (as he had for *A Tour on the Prairies*), and sent the transcriptions on 8 March to his agent in London, Colonel Thomas Aspinwall, for publication by John Murray. After sending the English manuscript, he continued making small changes in the American manuscript until it was delivered to Adoniram Chandler for stereotyping for publication by Carey, Lea & Blanchard. By 11 April Irving had some American proof sheets, for he sent sheets to Aspinwall, asking that, if not too late, some changes in the "Annesley Hall" section of *Newstead Abbey* be substituted in the London edition. (It is not clear that they were.) Murray published the volume in early May; Carey, Lea & Blanchard, in early June.

The result of all the changes between the manuscript and published versions, including the house styling by each publisher, is that the first two editions of the text vary in a number of minor ways. The two texts of *Abbotsford* may be distinguished conveniently by the last sentence in the work:

English text: "I consider it one of the few unmingled gratifications that I have derived...."

American text: "I consider it one of the greatest advantages that I have derived...."

The two texts of *Newstead Abbey* may be distinguished by the first sentence of the last paragraph:

English text: "It seems, that on arriving in town, and dismounting from the cart, the farmer's wife had parted with her to go on an errand, and the Little White Lady continued on...."

American text: "It seems that on arriving in town and dismounting from the cart, the farmer's wife had parted with her to go on an errand, and the White Lady continued on...." Note particularly the ommission of "Little."

The two works were quickly reprinted in Paris by Baudry and by Galignani, and translated into French and German, all based upon the London text. After 1835, the works seem not to have appeared again on the continent during Irving's lifetime.

Irving revised the texts for the Author's Revised Edition, published by G. P. Putnam in 1849. Putnam combined the new revision of the works with a new revision of *A Tour on the Prairies* and issued them together in a single volume carrying the original series title, *The Crayon Miscellany*. (For a description of that volume, see *The Crayon Miscellany* at the end of this description of the series.) The revision was a light one, based on the Philadelphia edition of 1835, and made only a limited number of corrections and stylistic alterations.

1E. ABBOTSFORD, | AND | NEWSTEAD ABBEY. | BY | THE AUTHOR OF "THE SKETCH-BOOK." | [rule] | LONDON: | JOHN MURRAY, ALBEMARLE STREET. | MDCCCXXXV.

Series title: MISCELLANIES. | BY | THE AUTHOR OF "THE SKETCH-BOOK." | N° II. | CONTAINING | ABBOTSFORD, AND NEWSTEAD ABBEY. | [rule] | LONDON: | JOHN MURRAY, ALBEMARLE STREET. | MDCCCXXXV.

(19.7 x 12.3 untrimmed): [A]^4 B-I^{12} K-N^{12} O^2. Mixed papers, laid and wove.

[i]-[ii], half-title, on verso printer; [iii]-[iv], series title, verso blank; [v]-[vi], title, verso blank; [vii]-[viii], table of contents, verso blank; [1]-[2], fly-title for *Abbotsford*, verso blank; [3]-119, text; [120], blank; [121]-[122], fly-title for *Newstead Abbey*, verso blank; [123]-290, text, printer at foot of last page; [291], in two states (see description below); [292], blank.

Page [291] appears in two states, sequence undetermined.

[A]. Blank.

[B]. Imprinted: *Lately was published*, IN A SIMILAR VOLUME, | A | TOUR ON THE PRAIRIES, | BY THE | AUTHOR OF "THE SKETCH-BOOK," | FORMING NO. I. OF | MISCELLANIES, | BY | WASHINGTON IRVING.

One copy noted with four leaves of preliminary advertisements, undated, paged [1] 2-8, printer's imprint of J. Rider, Little Britain, London at foot of p. 8.

Printer: A. Spottiswoode, New-Street-Square, London.

Lineation: p. 100, however ... scenes ; p. 200, might ... she

Noted or reported in a number of different unprinted paper boards, sequence undetermined, if any exists.

[a]. Drab brown boards.

[b]. Drab brown boards with decorated cloth shelfback.

[c]. Drab brown boards with green T cloth shelfback.

[d]. Blue-green boards.

All have printed white paper label on spine: [double rule] | ABBOTSFORD | AND | NEWSTEAD | ABBEY. | BY | THE AUTHOR | OF THE | SKETCH-BOOK. | [double rule].

Irving in a letter to his brother Peter, 25 May 1835, states, "the first edition to consist of three thousand copies." The figure originated in a letter of John Murray to Col. Aspinwall, 9 April 1835.

Literary Gazette, 9 May 1835, listed, reviewed, advertised as "this day." *Athenæum*, 9 May 1835, reviewed. Deposited and registered by Murray at Stationers' Hall 4 May 1835.

DLC, ICN, NjP, TxU (2), *BL*.

2E. [London: George Routledge, 1850.]

"Routledge's Popular Library." Printed in a single volume with *A Tour on the Prairies*.

Seen only in an incomplete copy, missing the title page and the text of *Abbotsford* and *Newstead Abbey*.

Since the text of *A Tour on the Prairies* is that of the English edition of 1835, presumably the texts of *Abbotsford* and *Newstead Abbey* are similarly derived.

(16.6 x 10.5): [i]-viii, [1]-23-? *Abbotsford* begins on p. 125; *Newstead Abbey* on p. 172.

Lineation: p. 100, while ... picture

Athenæum and *Literary Gazette*, 18 May 1850, listed, ls. in boards.

TxU, incomplete.

3Ea. ABBOTSFORD, | AND | NEWSTEAD ABBEY. | BY | WASHINGTON IRVING. | With an Appendix, [fancy] | PECULIAR TO THE PRESENT EDITION. | LONDON: | HENRY G. BOHN, YORK STREET, COVENT GARDEN. | [rule] | 1850.

The anonymous Appendix is not by Irving.

(18.1 x 11.5): [i]-iv, [1]-131; Appendix, 131 (sic)-138. Signed in 8's.

Issued individually as "Bohn's Shilling Series"; bound with *Bracebridge Hall* as Vol. III of "Bohn's Library Edition." Seen only in Library Edition.

Printer: G. Barclay, Castle St. Leicester Sq.

Lineation: p. 50, found ... and ; p. 100, the ... up

Library Edition. Gray T cloth. Sides decorated in blind. Spine titled in gilt as Irving's Works, Vol. III, Bohn's Library Edition. White endpapers with advertisements in blue. Portrait of Scott before title. No works title.

Shilling Series. *Athenæum* and *Literary Gazette*, 3 August 1850, listed, 1*s*. Library Edition. *Athenæum* and *Literary Gazette*, 2 November 1850, the set of 10 vols at 35*s*. listed.

NN, Library Edition.

b. LONDON: | HENRY G. BOHN, YORK STREET, COVENT GARDEN. | [rule] | 1853.

In Library Edition, with Works title dated 1854.

MB.

1Aa- ABBOTSFORD | AND | NEWSTEAD ABBEY. | [rule] | BY THE
c. AUTHOR OF THE SKETCH BOOK. | [rule] | PHILADELPHIA: | CAREY, LEA & BLANCHARD. | [rule] | 1835.

Series title: THE | CRAYON MISCELLANY. | [double rule] | BY THE AUTHOR OF THE SKETCH BOOK. | [double rule] | No. 2. | CONTAINING | Abbotsford [fancy] | AND | Newstead Abbey. [fancy] | [double rule] | PHILADELPHIA: | CAREY, LEA, AND BLANCHARD. | [rule of 19 dots] | 1835.

(17.8 x 11.0): $[1]^6 2\text{-}19^6\ 20^2$. 20_2 is a blank (but see the discussion below).

In two collation states, sequence undetermined.

[A]. As described. The last gathering is 20^2. 20_2 is a blank, followed by a terminal catalogue in the various forms described below.

[B]. The last gathering is 20^6. The last five leaves of the signature are integral advertisements, followed by a gathering in 6 of advertisements, making twenty-two pages of advertisements in all.

The catalogue inserted at the end of Collation State [A] appears in three forms; the sequence is undetermined, if any exists. All are unpaged, and from p. [9] to the end all have frame lines around the page. On p. [4] appears an advertisement for: IRVING'S NEW WORK. | THE CRAYON MISCELLANY, Part 1, containing a | Tour on the Prairies....

[a]. 32 pp. $1^4\ [2]\text{-}[3]^6$.

[b]. 36 pp. $1^4\ [2]\text{-}[3]^6\ [4]^2$.

[c]. 36 pp. $1^4\ [2]^2\ [3]\text{-}[4]^6$.

[1]-[2], series title, on verso copyright (1835 by Washington Irving) and printer; [3]-[4], title, on verso copyright (1835) and printer; [5]-94, text of *Abbotsford*; [95]-[96], fly-title for *Newstead Abbey*, verso blank; 97-230, text of *Newstead Abbey*; [231]-[232], blank in State [A]. No fly-title for *Abbotsford*. See the discussion below for variants in the first two leaves.

In three states of the title leaves, sequence undetermined.

[A]. With copyright notice and printer's imprint on the verso of both title leaves, pp. [2] and [4].

[B]. With copyright notice and printer's imprint on verso of the series title only, p. [2]. The verso of the volume title, p. [4], is blank.

[C]. With copyright notice and printer's imprint on verso of the volume title only, p. [4]. The verso of the series title, p. [2], is blank.

Pages 70 and 151 appear in two states.

A. Without a period at the end of the Latin quotation on 70.10 and the end of the sentence on 151.6.

B. With a period on 70.10 and 151.6.

With three sets of significant variables in the edition, plus variant forms of the advertisements and the binding, definable patterns should exist. Perhaps extensive investigation would produce them. But for now, no clear patterns emerge. The two states of the text, for instance -- admittedly minor corrections -- have been noted in random combination with the various states of the title leaves. The two text states are probably in chronological sequence, unless -- and it is very possible -- they represent the detected differences in duplicate stereotype plates. But duplicate plates alone would not appear to explain the random combinations.

Printer: Stereotyped by A. Chandler.

Lineation: p. 50, mute ... young ; p. 150, black ... with

Blue-green, and green, V cloth. Sides blank. White paper label on spine, in two states:

[A]. [double rule] | THE | CRAYON | MISCELLANY. | No. 2. | [rule] | ABBOTSFORD | AND | NEWSTEAD | ABBEY. | BY THE AUTHOR OF | THE | Sketch Book. | [double rule].

[B]. *Sketch Book* in italics.

The [B] state is quite scarce.

The Cost Book of Carey & Lea records 5000 copies "done up in cloth," "finished" 30 May 1835.

Copyrighted and complete copy deposited 11 June 1835. *Knickerbocker*, June 1835, noticed. *New-England Magazine*, July 1835, reviewed. Irving to John Murray, 22 September 1850, gives 1 June 1835 as the publication date.

Discussion based on copies in CtY (2), MB (2), MH (2), TxGeoS, TxU (9).

1F. ABBOTSFORD | AND | NEWSTEAD ABBEY. | BY | WASHINGTON IRVING. | [stylized swelled rule] | PARIS, | PUBLISHED BY A. AND W. GALIGNANI AND C°, | RUE VIVIENNE, N° 18. | [rule] | 1835.

Series title: MISCELLANIES, | [rule] | N° II. | CONTAINING | ABBOTSFORD AND NEWSTEAD ABBEY.

(17.0 x 10.5): [i]-[iv], [1]-175 [176]. Signed in 12's.

Printer: Bourgogne and Martinet, Rue du Columbier, 30.

Lineation: p. 100, sixty ... it ; p. 150, "Then ... place;

Bibliographie de la France, 23 May 1835, # 2856, listed.

TxGeoS, *BL*.

2F. [Paris: Baudry, 1835. Sold also by Amyot, Truchy, Barrois, etc.]

Paged [i]-[viii], [1]-219 [220].

Printer: Smith, Paris.

Bibliographie de la France, 23 May 1835, # 2857, listed.

Not seen. Copy reported in CtY.

3F. ABBOTSFORD, | AND | NEWSTEAD ABBEY. | BY WASHINGTON IRVING, | AUTHOR OF "THE SKETCH BOOK," "THE ALHAMBRA," | "A TOUR ON THE PRAIRIES," &c. &c. | [emblem: BEL intertwined] | PARIS. | BAUDRY'S EUROPEAN LIBRARY, | RUE DU COQ, NEAR THE LOUVRE; | SOLD ALSO BY AMYOT, RUE DE LA PAIX; TRUCHY, BOULEVARD DES | ITALIENS; THEOPH. BARROIS, JUN. RUE RICHELIEU; LIBRAIRIE DES | ÉTRANGERS, RUE NEUVE SAINT-AUGUSTIN; AND FRENCH | AND ENGLISH LIBRARY, RUE VIVIENNE. | [rule] | 1835.

(17.1 x 10.5): [i]-[viii], [9]-249 [250]. Half-title missing in copy examined. Crude laid paper.

Lineation: p. 100, I ... ex-; p. 200, for ... green,

MB.

TRANSLATIONS

French.

[*Walter Scott et Lord Byron, ou Voyages à Abbotsford et à Newstead.* Traduit par Mlle. A. Sobry. Paris: Fournier jeune, 1835.]

"Mélanges," Vol. II.

Paged iv, 294. Bound in 8's.

Bibliographie de la France, 27 June 1835, # 3491, listed.

Not seen. Copy reported in Bibliothèque Nationale.

German.

Abbotsford | und | Newstead-Abtei. | [rule] | Von | Washington Irving. | [swelled rule] | Aus dem Englischen. | [double rule] | Frankfurt am Main, 1835. | Druck und Verlag von J. D. Sauerländer. [in fraktur]

"Washington Irving's sämmtliche Werke," Bändchen 51-53.

(13.2 x 9.8): [1]-246 [247]-[248]. Signed in 8's.

Lineation: p. 100, sich; ... so ; p. 200, Die ... wahr,

CtY. Copy reported in Bayerischer Staatsbibliothek, München.

Abbotsford und Newstead | oder | Walter Scott und Byron | von | Washington Irving. | [rule] | Aus dem Englischen. | [swelled rule] | Berlin, | Verlag von Veit und Comp. | 1835. [in fraktur]

"Washington Irvings Wanderbuch," Zweiter Theil.

(16.7 x 10.5): [i]-[iv], [1]-310. Signed in 12's.

Printer: A. W. Hayn, Berlin.

Lineation: p. 100, aufzerte ... Scott ; p. 200, gehört ... sehen.

CtY.

[*Abbotsford und Newstead-Abbey*. Übers. von H. Roberts. Braunschweig: Vieweg, 1835.]

"Miscellaneen," Band 2.

Not seen. Copy reported in Stadtbibliothek Braunschweig.

[*Alhambra*, oder das neue Skizzenbuch. *Abbotsford* und *Newstead-Abtei*. *Eine Reise auf den Prairien*. 2., sorgfältig verbesserte Auflage. Frankfurt am Main: Johann David Sauerländer, 1847.]

"Ausgewählte Schriften," No. 4.

With two engravings.

Not seen. Copy reported in Stadtbibliothek Braunschweig.

The Crayon Miscellany, Volume 3:
Legends of the Conquest of Spain

Irving completed the manuscript for *Legends of the Conquest of Spain* in June 1835, working in part with material first written in Spain. The manuscript was stereotyped by Adoniram Chandler of Philadelphia and proof sheets were sent on 15 July to Irving's agent in London, Colonel Thomas Aspinwall, for publication by John Murray. Irving hoped for simultaneous publication in Philadelphia and in London, but Carey, Lea & Blanchard brought out the work in October, while John Murray was delayed until December.

Before the proof sheets were sent to London, Irving made changes in proof for both editions. (In one apparent moment of forgetfulness, he added a footnote to the English edition but not to the American.) And then after the corrected sheets were sent to London, he continued to make minor changes on the American sheets before publication. When Murray reset the sheets, he in turn imposed his house styling on the text. The result of all the changes between manuscript and published version is that the two first editions of the text vary in a number of minor ways, particularly in spelling and punctuation. The two texts may be distinguished by the first sentence of the Preface. In the second half, following the semicolon, the American text reads, "yet ... the motives, and characters, and actions...." The English text reads, "yet ... the motives, characters, and actions...."

Unlike the other two volumes of *The Crayon Miscellany*, *Legends of the Conquest of Spain* did not appear in the Author's Revised Edition. In fact, the work was not reprinted in America in any form until its appearance in *Spanish Papers*, edited by Pierre M. Irving in 1866. In England, the London text was reprinted in the 1850's by Bohn and by Routledge for their series. On the continent, the work was quickly reprinted in Paris and translated into German, the texts derived from the original London edition, but does not seem to have been reprinted after 1840, at least in Irving's lifetime.

1Aa-　LEGENDS | OF THE | CONQUEST OF SPAIN. | [rule] | BY THE
c.　AUTHOR OF THE SKETCH BOOK. | [rule] | PHILADELPHIA: | CAREY, LEA & BLANCHARD. | 1835.

Series title: THE | CRAYON MISCELLANY. | [double rule] | BY THE AUTHOR OF THE SKETCH BOOK. | [double rule] | No. 3. | CONTAINING | LEGENDS | Of the Conquest of Spain. [fancy] | [double rule] | PHILADELPHIA: | CAREY, LEA & BLANCHARD. | 1835.

(17.8-18.0 x 10.9): [-]^2 [1]^6 2-23^6. Not reckoned: four leaves of terminal advertisements.

Eight pages of advertisements at end, undated, paged [1] 2-8. On p. 5 there is an advertisement for "IRVING'S NEW WORK, THE CRAYON MISCELLANY, Parts 1, 2."

[a]-[d], unpaged, see description of variant states below; [i]-[ii], series title, on verso copyright (1835 by Washington Irving) and printer; [iii]-[iv], title, on verso the same copyright and printer; [v]-ix, Preface; [x], blank; [11]-276, text.

The two preliminary unpaged leaves [a-d] contain a two-paragraph notice, headed BEAUTIES OF WASHINGTON IRVING, signed CAREY, LEA & BLANCHARD, explaining that the selection of a volume of "Beauties," first published in England, was not made by Irving; that when an American edition was about to appear, Irving purchased the plates to destroy them; that he gave permission to Carey, Lea & Blanchard to issue an edition for their own benefit; and that Irving is due this explanation to avoid any charge of "indelicacy."

The notice appears in two setting, sequence undetermined:

[A]. The last line of the first paragraph begins, "advertised".

[B]. The last line of the first paragraph begins, "vertised".

The notice appears either [a] on the verso of the first leaf, with the second leaf blank; or [b] on the verso of the second leaf (facing the series title), with the first leaf blank. The sequence is undetermined. Setting [A] has been noted on both the first and the second leaf, with appearance on the first leaf noticeably the more common. Setting [B] has been noted only on the second leaf.

Printer: Stereotyped by A. Chandler.

Lineation: p. 100, bandry; ... their ; p. 200, cadonozer. ... [in footnote] c. 13

Green V cloth. Sides blank. White paper label on spine: [double rule] | THE | CRAYON | MISCELLANY. | No. 3. | [rule] | LEGENDS | OF THE | CONQUEST | OF | SPAIN. | BY THE AUTHOR OF | THE | Sketch Book. | [double rule]. White endpapers. Langfeld and Blackburn report the binding as blue with the same label on the spine. No copy located.

The Cost Book of Carey & Lea records 5000 copies "done up in cloth," "finished" 30 September 1835.

Copyrighted and title page deposited 4 September 1835; complete copy deposited 12 October 1835. *Albion*, 10 October 1835, extracted. *New-York Mirror*, 24 October 1835, noticed, "has just been published." Irving to John Murray, 22 September 1850, gives 10 October 1835 as publication date.

Discussion based on copies in CtY, MB, TxGeoS, TxU (2), ViU, Private hands (2).

1Ea. LEGENDS | OF THE | CONQUEST OF SPAIN. | BY | THE AUTHOR OF "THE SKETCH-BOOK." | [rule] | LONDON: | JOHN MURRAY, ALBEMARLE STREET. | MDCCCXXXV.

In copies seen, the closing quotation mark after SKETCH-BOOK on the title is faulty: the two single marks that make up the double mark are out of horizontal alignment; the second mark is lower than the first.

Series title: MISCELLANIES. | BY | THE AUTHOR OF "THE SKETCH-BOOK." | N°. III. | CONTAINING | LEGENDS OF THE CONQUEST OF SPAIN. | [rule] | LONDON: | JOHN MURRAY, ALBEMARLE STREET. | MDCCCXXXV.

(19.7 x 12.4 untrimmed): [A]^{10} B-I^{12} K-P^{12} Q^2.

[i]-[ii], series title, on verso printer; [iii]-[iv], title, verso blank; [v]-xi, Preface; [xii], blank; [xiii]-xviii, table of contents; [xix]-[xx], fly-title for "The Legend of Don Roderick," verso blank; [1]-340, text, printer at foot of last page.

Printer: A. Spottiswoode, New-Street-Square, London.

Lineation: p. 100, riors ... "was ; p. 200, shall ... them,

Gray paper boards with maroon cloth shelfback. Sides blank. White paper label on spine: [double rule] | LEGENDS | OF THE | CONQUEST | OF SPAIN. | BY | THE AUTHOR | OF THE | SKETCH BOOK. | [double rule].

Deposited and registered at Stationers' Hall by John Murray, 15 December 1835. *Athenæum*, 12 December 1835, reviewed. *Literary Gazette*, 19 December 1835, listed.

NN, TxGeoS, TxU, *BL*.

b. LONDON: | JOHN MURRAY, ALBEMARLE STREET.| MDCCCXXXVI.

Examiner, 26 June 1836, "Just published." Presumably the advertisement is for this second impression.

TxU.

2Ea. [London: Henry G. Bohn, 1850.]

Issued individually as "Bohn's Shilling Series"; printed with *The Conquest of Granada* as Vol. V of "Bohn's Library Edition."

Seen only in the Library Edition. Common title page: A | CHRONICLE | OF THE | CONQUEST OF GRANADA. | FROM THE MSS. OF FRAY ANTONIO AGAPIDA. | TO WHICH IS ADDED | LEGENDS OF THE CONQUEST OF SPAIN. | BY | WASHINGTON IRVING. | IN TWO

VOLUMES. | VOL. I. [II.] | LONDON: | HENRY G. BOHN, YORK STREET, COVENT GARDEN. | 1850. Despite the form of two vols., the works were issued as two vols. in one.

(18.1 x 11.5): *Legends of the Conquest of Spain* is printed in the later part of "Vol. II," after the conclusion of *The Conquest of Granada*. Consecutively paged [i]-[vi], [361]-492. No separate title page. Signed in 8's.

Lineation: p. 400, Arabia ... Ten

Library Edition. Gray T cloth. Sides decorated in blind. Spine titled in gilt as Irving's Works, Vol. V, Bohn's Library Edition. Endpapers white with advertisements in blue. The Shilling Series was issued in boards.

Shilling Series. *Athenæum*, 18 May 1850, listed, 1*s*. 6*d*. Library Edition. *Athenæum* and *Literary Gazette*, 29 June 1850, listed, 3*s*. 6*d*. in cloth.

NN, Library Edition.

b.   LONDON: | HENRY G. BOHN, YORK STREET, COVENT GARDEN. | 1854.

"Bohn's Library Edition."

MB.

3E.   [London: George Routledge, 1850.]

Routledge's "Popular Library."

Not located. Presumably this single-title issue corresponds to the impression printed with *Tales of the Alhambra* and bound with *The Conquest of Granada* in 1851. See the description below.

Athenæum, 6 July 1850, listed, 1*s*.

4E.   TALES OF THE ALHAMBRA: | LEGENDS OF THE CONQUEST | OF SPAIN, | AND THE | CONQUEST OF GRANADA. | BY | WASHINGTON IRVING. | [rule] | LONDON: | GEORGE ROUTLEDGE & CO., SOHO SQUARE. | 1851.

(16.9 x 10.5): [i]-iv, [1]-316; [i]-[ii], [1]-317 [318]. *Legends of the Conquest of Spain* occupies the middle position, paged [197]-316. No separate title page. Signed in 8's.

Printer: J. & H. Cox (Brothers), 74 & 75, Great Queen Street, Lincoln's-Inn Fields. (*Granada* is printed by Reynell and Wright.)

Lineation: p. 200, episcopal ... was

Blue L cloth. Sides decorated in blind with identification as "Popular Library." Spine titled in gilt: WASHINGTON | IRVING'S | WORKS. | ALHAMBRA | AND | CONQUEST OF GRANADA. Endpapers cream.

TxU.

1Fa. LEGENDS | OF THE | CONQUEST OF SPAIN | BY WASHINGTON IRVING. | [rule] | PARIS; | PUBLISHED BY A. AND W. GALIGNANI AND C°, | RUE VIVIENNE, N° 18. | [rule] | 1836.

(17.2 x 10.9): [a]-[d], [i]-viii , [1]-206. Signed in 12's.

Printer: Bourgogne and Martinet, Rue du Colombier, no. 30, Paris.

Lineation: p. 100, and ... but ; p. 200, the ... her

Bibliographie de la France, 23 January 1836, # 444, listed.

BL. Copy reported in Bibliothèque Nationale.

b. LEGENDS | OF THE | CONQUEST OF SPAIN. | BY WASHINGTON IRVING. | AUTHOR OF "THE SKETCH BOOK," "A TOUR ON THE PRAIRIES," | "ABBOTSFORD AND NEWSTEAD ABBEY," ETC. ETC. | [emblem: BEL intertwined] | PARIS; | BAUDRY'S EUROPEAN LIBRARY, | RUE DU COQ, NEAR THE LOUVRE; | SOLD ALSO BY AMYOT, RUE DE LA PAIX; TRUCHY, BOULEVARD DES ITALIENS; | THEOPH. BARROIS. JUN. RUE RICHELIEU; LIBRAIRIE DES ÉTRANGERS, | RUE NEUVE SAINT-AUGUSTIN; AND HEIDELOFF AND CAMPE, | RUE VIVIENNE. | [rule] | 1836.

(16.9 x 10.0): a variant impression produced by the same printer.

Bibliographie de la France, 23 January 1836, # 445, listed.

TxU. Copy reported in Bibliothèque Nationale.

2F. TALES | OF THE | ALHAMBRA; | TO WHICH ARE ADDED | LEGENDS | OF THE | CONQUEST OF SPAIN, | BY | WASHINGTON IRVING, | AUTHOR OF THE SKETCH BOOK, CHRONICLE OF THE CONQUEST OF GRANADA, LIFE AND | VOYAGES OF CHRISTOPHER COLUMBUS, ETC. ETC. | [emblem: BEL intertwined] | PARIS: | BAUDRY'S EUROPEAN LIBRARY, | 3, QUAI MALAQUAIS, NEAR THE PONT DES ARTS, | AND STASSIN AND XAVIER, 9, RUE DU COQ, NEAR THE LOUVRE. | SOLD ALSO BY AMYOT, RUE DE LA PAIX; TRUCHY, BOULEVARD DES ITALIENS; GIRARD FRÈRES, | RUE RICHELIEU; LEOPOLD MICHELSEN, LEIPZIG; AND BY ALL THE PRINCIPAL | BOOKSELLERS ON THE CONTINENT. | [rule] | 1840.

"Collection of Ancient and Modern British Authors," Vol. LXVIII.

(21.3 x 13.3): [I]-VIII, [1]-208; [209]-346. *Legends of the Conquest of Spain* begins on p. [209]. No separate title page. Signed in 8's. Laid paper.

Printer: Fain and Thunot, 28, Rue Racine.

Lineation: p. 100, exclamations, ... lament,; p. 300, Having ... [in footnote] renowned.

TxU. Copy reported in Bibliothèque Nationale.

TRANSLATIONS

German.

Erzählungen | von der | Eroberung Spaniens. | [rule] | Von | Washington Irving. | [rule] | Aus dem Englischen. | [double rule] | Frankfurt am Main, 1836. | Druck und Verlag von J. D. Sauerländer. [in fraktur]

"Washington Irving's sämmtliche Werke," Bändchen 54-56.

(14.3 x 10.3 untrimmed): [1]-286 [287]-[288]. Signed in 8's. Laid paper.

Lineation: p. 100, das ... seinen ; p. 200, und ... Reichthum.

Blue-gray laid paper wrapper. Sides blank. White paper label on spine: Irving's | Werke | 54-56 | [rule] | Eroberung | Spaniens

TxU. Copy reported in Universitätsbibliothek Giessen.

Sagen | von der | Eroberung und Unterjochung | Spaniens. | [rule] | Aus dem Englischen | des | Washington Irving, | übersetzt von | Lenardo. | [swelled rule] | [triple rule] | Aachen, | Druck und Verlag von J. Hensen und Comp. | 1839.

(17.0 x 10.4): [a]-[d], [I]-V [VI], [1]-250. Signed in 12's.

Lineation: p. 100, weiss ... im ; p. 200, sig ... belohnen.

TxU. Copy reported in Stadt- und Universitätsbibliothek Göttingen.

The Crayon Miscellany, Combined Volume:
A Tour on the Prairies, Abbotsford, Newstead Abbey

1Aa.   THE | CRAYON MISCELLANY. | BY | WASHINGTON IRVING. | AUTHOR'S REVISED EDITION. | COMPLETE IN ONE VOLUME. | NEW-YORK: | GEORGE P. PUTNAM, 155 BROADWAY, | And 142 Strand, London. | 1849.

(18.9 x 12.9): [1]-[2]^{12} 3-6^{12} [7]^{12} 8-16^{12}. The first leaf is a blank. The last two leaves carry publisher's advertisements.

The four pages of terminal advertisements are integral, undated, paged 6, 8, 7, 9. At the foot of p. 6 appear advertisements for Irving's New Works, including "The Life of Mohammed" (sic) "(In January)."

[i]-[ii], blank; [iii]-[iv], Works title, Vol. IX, 1849, verso blank; [v]-[vi], title, on verso copyright (1849) and printer; [vii]-xii, table of contents; [xiii]-xiv, Introduction; [15]-[16], fly-title for *A Tour on the Prairies*, verso blank; [17]-198, text; [199]-[200], fly-title for *Abbotsford* (the title is incorrectly printed on the verso, leaving the recto blank); [201]-269, text; [270], blank; [271]-[272], fly-title for *Newstead Abbey*, verso blank; [273]-379, text; [380], blank.

Printer: John F. Trow, Printer and Stereotyper, 49 Ann-street, N.Y.

Lineation: p. 100, CHAPTER XVIII. ... and ; p. 200, [fly-title for *Abbotsford*]; p. 300, could ... Squire."

Blue-green TB cloth.   On sides, in blind, publisher's initials within ornamental design. Spine decorated in blind, titled in gilt: IRVING'S | WORKS | [rule] | CRAYON MISCELLANY || PUTNAM . Cream endpapers.

Although no specific advertisement has been noted for other bindings on this first edition, other individual volumes of the Author's Revised Edition are advertised as available in cloth, cloth extra gilt, half-calf, calf extra, half-morocco, and morocco.

Literary World, 5 May 1849, advertised in "List of New Publications"; 12 May 1849, listed, advertised under "The New Books of last week." *Albion*, 12 May 1849, noticed.

DLC, TxU (2), ViU.

b.   NEW-YORK: | GEORGE P. PUTNAM, 155 BROADWAY, | And 142 Strand, London. | 1850.

Works title, dated 1850.

In this impression the fly-title for *Abbotsford* is correctly on p. [199].

CtY.

c. NEW-YORK: | GEORGE P. PUTNAM, 155 BROADWAY, | And 142 Strand, London. | 1851.

Works title, dated 1851.

Noted in green TB cloth in same design as the first impression, but cream endpapers imprinted with publisher's advertisements.

TxU, ViU.

d. [New York: George P. Putnam, 1852.]

Not seen. Copy reported in PPGi.

e. NEW-YORK: | G. P. PUTNAM & COMPANY, 10 PARK PLACE. | 1853.

Works title, dated 1853.

Private hands. MH, missing volume title.

f. NEW-YORK: | G. P. PUTNAM & COMPANY, 10 PARK PLACE. | 1854.

Works title, dated 1854.

Purple T cloth. On sides, in blind, publisher's initials within ornamental design. Spine titled in gilt with leaf ornaments in panels. Yellow endpapers.

CtY.

g. New York: [fancy] | G. P. PUTNAM & CO., 321 BROADWAY. | 1856.

Works title, dated 1856.

ViU.

h. New York: [fancy] | G. P. PUTNAM & CO., 321 BROADWAY. | 1857.

Works title, dated 1857.

MH.

i. NEW YORK: | G. P. PUTNAM, 115 NASSAU STREET. | 1859.

Works title, dated 1859.

Two engravings added before title.

Brown HC-like cloth with round raised dots. On sides, in blind, square frame around decoration. Spine titled in gilt within gilt decoration at top and sides: IRVING'S | WORKS | [rule] | CRAYON || G. P. Putnam Green endpapers.

TxU.

j. NEW YORK: | G. P. PUTNAM (for the Proprietor), 506 BROADWAY. | 1859.

Works title, dated 1859.

In one copy examined, there are two engravings before title, published by Childs & Peterson, Philadelphia, but no Works title.

NjP, TxU.

ASTORIA

In the spring of 1836 Irving sent the first chapters of the manuscript of *Astoria* to Henry W. Rees, stereotyper. By 4 August, according to a letter of Irving to Carey, Lea & Blanchard, the first volume was complete in stereotype plates and a third of the second volume was in type. As usual with Irving, he apparently continued to "re-dress" the text in manuscript and in proof until the last moment.

In the meantime, Irving reached agreement on 5 September, through his agent, Colonel Thomas Aspinwall, for Richard Bentley to publish *Astoria* in London. The Bentley text was taken from proof sheets of the American edition, and appeared about 19 October 1836, preceding by eight or nine days the publication in America, even though it was derived from the American edition. It was immediately reprinted in Paris, and within three years was translated into Dutch, French, German, and Swedish, all with text from the London edition.

The London text imposed British conventions of spelling and punctuation -- calling for many small changes in accidentals -- and also introduced a number of minor substantive errors or changes. The text may be immediately recognized by the first sentence of the first chapter (Vol. I, p. [1], line 3 of the London edition, line 2 of the American): the London text reads "history of the Americans"; the American reads "history of the Americas." But the most obvious change was in the sub-title, from "Anecdotes of an Enterprise Beyond the Rocky Mountains" in the American edition to "Enterprise Beyond the Rocky Mountains" in the London.

In 1849, George P. Putnam published a revised edition as Vol. VIII of the Author's Revised Edition. Irving's revisions were, however, minor, consisting for the most part of the addition of a short paragraph at the end of the text proper to point out that since the 1836 edition "the question of dominion over the vast territory beyond the Rocky Mountains, which for a time threatened to disturb the peaceful relations with our transatlantic kindred, has been finally settled in a spirit of mutual concession...."

1Ea.   ASTORIA; | OR, | ENTERPRISE BEYOND | THE ROCKY MOUNTAINS. | BY WASHINGTON IRVING. | AUTHOR OF "THE SKETCH BOOK," "THE ALHAMBRA," &c. | IN THREE VOLUMES. | VOL. I. [II., III.] | LONDON: | RICHARD BENTLEY, | NEW BURLINGTON STREET. | [rule] | 1836.

(19.3 x 12.1): Vol. I. [a]^2 b^4 c^2 B-I^8 K-U^8 X^8. The final two integral leaves carry advertisements. Vol. II. [a]^1 b^4 B-I^8 K-U^8 X^8. Vol. III. [a]^1 b^2 c^1 B-I^8 K-T^8 U^2 X^1.

The advertisements at the end of Vol. I, undated, unpaged, are headed NEW NOVELS AND ROMANCES, | BY DISTINGUISHED AUTHORS, | They advertise 12 titles, beginning with *Vandeleur* and ending with *Tales of the Peerage*, Second Edition.

Vol. I. [a]-[b], half-title, verso blank; [i]-[ii], title, on verso printer; [iii]-viii, Introduction, dated *Sept.* 1836; [xi]-xvi, table of contents; [1]-317, text, printer at foot of last page; [318], blank. Vol. II. [i]-[ii], title, on verso printer; [iii]-ix, table of contents; [x], blank; [1]-320, text, printer at foot of last page. Vol. III. [i]-[ii], title, on verso printer; [iii]-vii, table of contents; [viii], blank; [1]-263, text; [264], blank; [265]-[266], fly-title for Appendix, verso blank; [267]-294, Appendix, printer at foot of last page.

Vol. I, p. 96 noted in two states: incorrectly paged 86, or correctly paged 96. Presumably that is the result of a stop-press correction.

In all copies, Vol. II, p. 143, line 5, "steril" is so spelled, with the missing final "e."

Printer: Whiting, Beaufort House, Strand.

Lineation: Vol. I. p. 100, coverer ... seas ; p. 200, swell ... to Vol. II. p. 100, and ... that ; p. 200, ing ... they Vol. III. p. 100, their ... Narrows."; p. 200, reward ... the

Drab brown paper boards, and drab gray paper boards with maroon cloth shelfback. Sides blank. On spines, white paper label of extra width that extends over the hinges and five or six mm. onto the sides: [double rule] | ASTORIA. | BY | WASHINGTON IRVING. | Author of | "The Sketch Book," | "The Alhambra," &c. &c. | [rule] | IN THREE VOLS. | VOL. I. [II., III.] | [double rule]. White endpapers. No flyleaves.

Athenæum, 8 October 1836, "preparing for immediate Publication"; 15 October 1836, "just ready"; 22 October 1836, "Is now ready," reviewed, listed, at 31*s*. 6*d*. in boards. *Literary Gazette*, 22 October 1836, "Is now ready," reviewed, listed. The Bentley Papers in *BL* are reported to list 19 October 1836 as the publication date.

NN, TxU (4).

b. In *The Athenæum*, 4 February 1837, appears an advertisement for "MR. WASHINGTON IRVING'S NEW WORK. SECOND EDITION. In 3 vols. post 8vo." In *The Literary Gazette* on the same day, 4 February 1837, appears an advertisement, under the heading "NEW WORKS Just published," "2d edition, in 3 vols. post 8vo." Does this represent a second impression? No copy dated 1837 has been located.

2E. ASTORIA; | OR, | ENTERPRISE BEYOND | THE ROCKY MOUNTAINS. | BY WASHINGTON IRVING, | AUTHOR OF "THE SKETCH BOOK," "THE ALHAMBRA," &c. | LONDON: RICHARD BENTLEY, NEW BURLINGTON STREET, | Publisher in Ordinary to her Majesty. [fancy] | [rule] | 1839.

"Bentley's Standard Library of Popular Modern Literature."

(16.3 x 10.3): [i]-viii, [1]-440. Not reckoned: engraved portrait of Irving before the title, "From the original painting by Newton. Engraved by permission of John Murray, Esq." Signed in 8's.

The volume is paged continuously, but chapter numbers follow those of the original 3-vol. edition, and the original volume divisions are noted.

Printer: Whiting, Beaufort House, Strand.

Lineation: p. 100, the ... them ; p. 200, goat, ... of

Literary Gazette, 15 December 1838, advertised: "Will form the Second Volume of BENTLEY'S 'STANDARD LIBRARY,' (Embellished with a Portrait of the Author), price Six Shillings. It will be published with the Magazines, on the 31st instant"; 29 December 1838, advertised for January 1, with the Magazines. *Athenæum*, 22 December 1838, "On Jan. 1, with the Magazines."

TxU, *BL*.

3E. In *The Athenæum*, 28 October 1848, under the heading, "CHEAP NEW POPULAR WORKS, In neat Pocket Volumes, bound in cloth, price Half-a-crown each," is an advertisement by Bentley for "WASHINGTON IRVING'S ASTORIA; or, Adventures beyond the Rocky Mountains." (Note the new sub-title, if the advertisement is correct.) Not located.

4Ea. [London: George Routledge, 1850.]

Routledge's "Popular Library."

For a description in a state bound with *Captain Bonneville*, see the next entry.

Athenæum, 13 July 1850, listed, 1*s*. boards, 1*s*. 6*d*. cloth.

Not located.

b.   ASTORIA, | AND | CAPTAIN BONNEVILLE'S | ADVENTURES. | BY
     | WASHINGTON IRVING. | [rule] | LONDON: | GEORGE
     ROUTLEDGE & CO., SOHO SQUARE. | 1851.

Routledge's "Popular Library."

The two individual volumes issued bound together; no separate title pages;
original individual pagination and collation retained.

(16.7 x 10.5): (Vol. I.) [1]-291 [292]. (Vol. II.) [1]-271 [272]. Signed in 8's.

Printer: (Vol. I.)   Saville & Edwards, 4, Chandos-street, Covent-garden.
(Vol. II.) Reynell and Weight, Little Pulteney Street, Haymarket.

Lineation: (Vol. I.) p. 100, He ... him ; p. 200, now ... leaped (Vol. II.) p.
100, day ... lava; --; p. 200, The ... his

Blue L cloth. Sides decorated in blind with POPULAR LIBRARY in
circular design at center. Spine missing in copy examined.

NN.

5Ea. ASTORIA; | OR, | ANECDOTES OF AN ENTERPRISE | BEYOND
       THE | ROCKY MOUNTAINS. | BY | WASHINGTON IRVING. |
       AUTHOR'S REVISED EDITION. | COMPLETE IN ONE VOLUME. |
       LONDON: | HENRY G. BOHN, YORK STREET, COVENT GARDEN. |
       1850.

(18.2 x 11.5): [i]-xii, [1]-340. Signed in 8's.

Issued individually in "Bohn's Shilling Series"; bound with *A Tour on the
Prairies* as Vol. VIII of "Bohn's Library Edition."

Printer: McCorquodale and Co., Printers, London -- Works, Newton.

Lineation: p. 100, to ... the ; p. 200, man, ... river,

Seen only in "Bohn's Library Edition," two copies bound with an 1850
impression of *A Tour on the Prairies*, one with an 1851 impression.
Preliminary engraving added: portrait of Irving in two copies, "A Scene on
the Prairies" in one. No works title.

Seen in original binding only in the Library Edition. Gray T cloth. Sides
decorated in blind. Spine titled in gilt as Irving's Works, Vol. VIII, Bohn's
Library Edition. White endpapers with advertisements in blue.

Shilling Series. *Athenæum*, 7 September 1850, listed, 2*s*. in boards. Library
Edition. *Athenæum* and *Literary Gazette*, 2 November 1850, the set of 10
vols. at 35*s*. listed.

TxU and Private hands, with 1850 *A Tour on the Prairies*. NN, with 1851
Tour.

b.   LONDON: | HENRY G. BOHN, YORK STREET, COVENT GARDEN. | 1854.

Seen only in the Library Edition, with Works title.

MB.

1Aa-   ASTORIA, | OR | ANECDOTES OF AN ENTERPRISE | BEYOND
b.   THE | ROCKY MOUNTAINS. | BY WASHINGTON IRVING. | IN
TWO VOLUMES. | VOL. I. [II.] | PHILADELPHIA: | CAREY, LEA, &
BLANCHARD. | 1836.

(21.8 x 13.7); some copies 21.9 x 13.8): Vol. I. $[1]^6$ 2-24^6. Last leaf blank.
Vol. II. $[1]^6$ 2-23^6 24^2. Followed by terminal advertisements, in a gathering
of 4, signed 1. Page 101 incorrectly signed 9 rather than 9*.

Fold-out engraved chart, "Sketch of the Routes of Hunt & Stuart," without
identification of cartographer, engraver or publisher, inserted before title;
noted predominantly in Vol. II but occasionally in Vol. I.

The advertisements at the end of Vol. II are headed BOOKS | PUBLISHED
| BY CAREY, LEA & BLANCHARD. Undated, paged [1] 2-6 [7] 8.
Unlike the later state, there are no frame lines around the advertisements.
On p. 4, there is an advertisement for *The Crayon Miscellany*: "To be pub- |
lished at intervals. Now ready -- | [The 3 parts named]. On p. 6, fourth item
from the foot, appears a listing for *Astoria*.

Vol. I. [1]-[2], title, on verso copyright (1836) and printer (but see the
discussion of the second state below); [3]-6, Introduction; [vii]-xii, table of
contents; [13]-285, text; [286], blank. Vol. II. [i]-[ii], title, on verso copyright
and printer; [iii]-viii, table of contents; [9]-262, text; [263]-[264], fly-title for
Appendix, verso blank; [265]-279, Appendix; [280], blank.

Volume I in two states.

    1.   Verso of title, copyright notice and printer's imprint, as
                  described.

                  P. 5, no signature at foot.

                  P. 217, signed 19.

    2.   Verso of title blank.

                  p. 5, signed 1*.

                  p. 217, signed 1.

Volume II in three states.

    1.   P. v, no signature at foot.

P. 148, line 4, "jirked."

P. 239, garbled footnote: *Bra6.db ury. P. 6 |
*Breckenridge.

Advertisements not boxed, headed NEW WORKS in caps.

2.   P. v, signed 1*.

P. 148, line 4, "jirked."

P. 239, no footnote.

[Advertisements not seen. Boxed?]

3.   P. v, signed 1*.

P. 50, page number missing.

P. 148, line 4, "jerked."

P. 239, no footnote.

Advertisements boxed, headed New Works in caps and
lower case.

The first state of Vol. I has been noted paired in a set with the second state
of Vol. II. The second state of Vol. I has been noted paired only with the
third state of Vol. II.

Whether the second state of Vol. I and the third state of Vol. II represent a
separate impression of the work is not certain. The Cost Book of Carey &
Lea offers no clear evidence, although the entry for the 1836 edition is
suggestive: "4000 printed. Author paid for 5000. Paper & printing for an
Ed. of 1000 would be 10% over the above cost." Did Carey, Lea & Blanchard
print some extra copies in a second impression (perhaps less than 1000,
judging from the scarcity now of the last states) to make up for some of that
extra payment to Irving? The accuracy of the payment for 5000 copies is
attested by a letter of Irving to Carey, Lea & Blanchard, 4 August 1836, in
which Irving asks for "$4000 for the right of printing 5000 copies."

Printer: Henry W. Rees, Stereotyper, 45 Gold Street, New-York.

Lineation: Vol. I. p. 100, the ... sequel.; p. 200, boats ... carbines, Vol. II. p.
100, the ... been ; p. 200, command ... horses,

Noted or reported in a wide variety of cloths, listed below. Others may well
exist. No sequence is known or implied. Sides blank. Spine title in gilt:
ASTORIA [in curved line] | BY | W. IRVING | [swelled rule] | VOL. | 1.
[2.]. (No publisher at foot.) White endpapers. Most copies have one flyleaf
at the front and the back of both volumes (plus the integral blank leaf at the

back of Vol. I). One copy noted with the flyleaf missing at the back of Vol. I. One copy noted with two flyleaves at the front of Vol. I.

Cloth A: Rose-purple V cloth embossed with wriggling lines.

Cloth B: V cloth embossed with regular large raised dots. Noted in blue, in green, in purple, in brown.

Cloth C: T cloth embossed in large stylized vine, leaf and blossom pattern. Noted in blue-green, and in brown.

Cloth D: S-like cloth damasked with a small branch and leaf pattern. Noted in blue, in purple, in tan, in brown.

Cloth E: CM-like cloth; the "squiggles" are large and irregular. Noted in bright blue, in light blue, and in slate.

Cloth F: Purple T cloth, heavily ribbed.

Cloth G: Blue-green V cloth embossed with cross-like stars.

Cloth H: Light blue P-like cloth embossed with a branch pattern.

Cloth I: Brown C-like cloth embossed with stars, dots, and ornaments composed of elongated tulip-like patterns.

Cloth J: Purple V cloth embossed with dots and hollow diamonds.

Cloth K: Brown cloth with horizontal ribbing varied in such a way as to give a "watered" effect.

Cloth L: Brown irregularly bumpy cloth embossed with a pattern of stars and four-leaved ornaments with cross in center.

Cloth M: Blue V cloth demasked with small branch and leaf pattern.

Cloth N: Purple V cloth impressed with diagonal alternating bands, one composed of two lines of small squares and diamonds, the other of two lines of facing short curves with rays on outer side (suggesting small symbols of rising sun).

Cloth O: S-like cloth. Noted in purple, and in blue. (Reported only on last states of the volumes.)

Copyrighted and title page deposited 20 September 1836; complete copy deposited 19 October 1836. The dates given in the Cost Book of Carey & Lea are: printed 18 October 1836; published 28 October 1836. *New-York Mirror*, 22 October 1836, extracted "previous to its publication." *Albion*, 12 November 1836, noticed. Irving to John Murray, 22 September 1850, gives 26 October 1836 as the publication date.

A Prospectus for the work was published by Carey, Lea & Blanchard, presumably in 1836: 8 pp., undated, approximately 23 x 12 cm., on canary-yellow paper. Contents: one page of advertisements for works by Washington Irving, John T. Irving, Jr., and Theodore Irving, unpaged; one page of advertisements for *Astoria* ("Lately Published," "Handsomely Bound -- in Two Vols. Embossed Cloth") with laudatory quotations, unpaged; the complete Introduction from Vol. I, paged [3] 4-6; one page from the table of contents of Vol. II, paged vii; and one page from the table of contents of Vol. I, paged xi. The Introduction and the two pages from the tables of contents are printed from the plates of the full volumes. The signature 1* at the foot of this reprinting of I, 5, however, indicates that the Introduction was taken from the second state of the plates.

Discussion based on copies in CtY (5), MH, NN, OrAst, TxDaM (2), TxU (9), ViU, the Columbia River Maritime Museum (Astoria, Or.), and Private hands.

Prospectus: NNC.

c.   [PHILADELPHIA: | LEA & BLANCHARD. | 1841.]

The text is that of State 2 of Vol. I and State 3 of Vol. II.

Printer: T. K. & P. G. Collins, Philadelphia.

Not examined. Information supplied by PPFr from its copy.

2Aa.   ASTORIA | OR, | ANECDOTES OF AN ENTERPRISE | BEYOND THE | ROCKY MOUNTAINS. | BY | WASHINGTON IRVING. | AUTHOR'S REVISED EDITION. | COMPLETE IN ONE VOLUME. | NEW-YORK: | GEORGE P. PUTNAM, 155 BROADWAY. | And 142 Strand, London | 1849.

(18.9 x 12.8): [-]^4 1-21^{12} 22^8. Fold-out map of the Oregon Territory, dated 1849, engraved by Edwd. Yeager, inserted before title.

[i]-[ii], Works title, Vol. VIII, 1849, verso blank; [iii]-[iv], title, on verso copyright (1849) and printer; [v]-viii, Introduction (undated); [1]-12, table of contents; [13]-501, text; [502], blank; [503]-[504], fly-title for Appendix, verso blank; [505]-519, Appendix; [520], blank.

Printer: Leavitt, Trow & Co., Printers and Stereotypers, 49 Ann-street, N.Y.

Lineation: p. 100, is ... [in footnote] syllable.; p. 200, form ... [in footnote] 110.

Dark green TB cloth. On sides, in blind, publisher's initials within ornamental design. Spine decorated in blind, titled in gilt: IRVING'S | WORKS | [rule] | ASTORIA   Light yellow endpapers. A copy in DLC, inscribed "Executive Mansion 1850," has endpapers imprinted with publisher's advertisements.

Within the next few years advertisements for the Works offer them in cloth, cloth extra, sheep extra, half calf, half calf extra, half morocco, calf extra, calf antique, morocco extra. Presumably *Astoria* was also available in some or all of these.

Literary World, 14 April 1849, advertised as "New Volume"; 21 April 1849, advertised as published "Wednesday, April 18," at $1.50; 28 April 1849, listed; 12 May 1849, advertised as "New book of last week."

DLC, MH, TxU.

b. NEW-YORK: | GEORGE P. PUTNAM, 155 BROADWAY. | And 142 Strand, London | 1850.

Works title, dated 1850.

ICN, NNC.

c. NEW-YORK: | GEORGE P. PUTNAM, 155 BROADWAY. | And 142 Strand, London | 1851.

Works title, dated 1851.

MH, TxU.

d. [New York: George P. Putnam, 1852.]

Works title, dated 1852.

Not seen. Copy reported in NcU.

e. [New York: George P. Putnam, 1853.]

Title missing in copy examined. Works title: NEW-YORK: | GEORGE P. PUTNAM. | 1853.

MH.

f. NEW-YORK: | G. P. PUTNAM & COMPANY, 10 PARK PLACE. | 1854.

Works title, dated 1854.

TxU.

g. NEW-YORK: | G. P. PUTNAM & COMPANY, 10 PARK PLACE. | 1855.

Works title, dated 1855.

The fold-out map of the Oregon Territory is still that engraved by Edwd. Yeager, dated 1849.

DLC.

h. New York: [fancy] | G. P. PUTNAM & CO., 321 BROADWAY | 1857.

Works title, dated 1857.

TxU.

i. NEW YORK: | G. P. PUTNAM, 115 NASSAU STREET. | 1859.

Works title, dated 1859.

Several minor text changes appear in this impression, including: on p. 370, lines 1-2, "Wood | vile" in place of "Wood | pile", and on p. 509, line 15, "relict" in place of "relics".

No map, but engraved illustration before title, printed by Childs & Peterson, Philadelphia.

Green BD cloth. Sides bordered in blind. On spine, extra decoration in gilt around title. Brown endpapers.

TxU.

j. NEW YORK: | G. P. PUTNAM (For the Proprietor), 506 BROADWAY. | 1859.

Works title, dated 1859.

TxU.

1Fa. ASTORIA; | OR, | ENTERPRISE BEYOND | THE ROCKY MOUNTAINS. | BY WASHINGTON IRVING, | AUTHOR OF "THE SKETCH BOOK," "THE ALHAMBRA," &c. | [emblem: BEL intertwined] | PARIS, | BAUDRY'S EUROPEAN LIBRARY, | RUE DU COQ, NEAR THE LOUVRE | SOLD ALSO BY AMYOT, RUE DE LA PAIX; TRUCHY, BOULEVARD DES ITALIENS; | THEOPHILE BARROIS, JUN., RUE RICHELIEU; HEIDELOFF AND CAMPE, | RUE VIVIENNE; AND BY ALL THE PRINCIPAL BOOKSELLERS ON | THE CONTINENT. | [rule] | 1836.

"Collection of Ancient and Modern British Authors," Vol. CXLVI.

(22.0 x 14.0 untrimmed): [i]-xvi, [1]-336. Signed in 8's. Laid paper.

Printer: J. Smith, 16, Rue Montmorency.

Lineation: p. 100, they ... His ; p. 200, need ... in-

Bibliographie de la France, 26 November 1836, # 5987, listed.

TxGeoS, TxU. Copy reported in Bibliothèque Nationale.

b. [ornamental rule] | PARIS, | PUBLISHED BY A. AND W. GALIGNANI AND Co., | RUE VIVIENNE, N° 18. | [rule] | 1836.

Apparently published simultaneously with the Baudry impression.

(22.0 x 13.7 untrimmed).

Printer: the same.

Tan paper wrapper. On front, cover-title within wide ornamental border. On back, within same border, two columns of NEW WORKS by Galignani. On spine, title, author, and small decorative printer's devices.

Bibliographie de la France, 26 November 1836, # 5988, listed.

BL. Description of wrapper from copy in NNS.

TRANSLATIONS

Dutch.

[Engraved title only, in a variety of styles, with penstroke and flowered decoration throughout upper two-thirds of page] ASTORIA | of | Avontuurlyke Reize | naar en over het | Klipgebergte van Noord-America, | ondernomen in het belang der door den Heer | J. J. ASTOR | opgerigte peltery compagnie, | en beschreven | DOOR | Washington Irving. | 1^e [2^e] Deel. | [rule] | naar het Engelsch. | [rule] | [decorative swelled rule] | Te HAARLEM by | De Wed. A. Loosjes, Pz. | MDCCCXXXVII.

(23.0 x 13.1 untrimmed): Vol. I. [I]-XII, [1]-338. 2 pp. of unpaged integral terminal advertisements. Vol. II. [I]-VI, V-X, [1]-339 [340]. Engraved titles not reckoned. Signed in 8's. Laid paper.

Printer: Ter Boekdrukkerij van J. C. La Lau, Leyden.

Lineation: Vol. I. p. 100, woners ... van ; p. 200, heid ... leven Vol. II. p. 100, indringende, ... maken.; p. 200, hut ... mede,

Red speckled paper boards. Sides blank. White paper label on spines. An extra paper label for each volume is attached to p. [I] of Vol. I.

TxU (2).

French.

VOYAGES | DANS LES CONTRÉES DÉSERTES | DE L'AMÉRIQUE DU NORD, | ENTREPRIS | POUR LA FONDATION DU COMPTOIR D'ASTORIA | SUR LA CÔTE NORD-OUEST. | PAR WASHINGTON IRVING, | AUTEUR DE LA VIE DE CHRISTOPHE COLOMB, ETC. ETC. | TRADUIT DE L'ANGLAIS PAR P. N. GROLIER. | TOME PREMIER. [SECOND.] | [elaborated swelled rule] | A PARIS, | CHEZ P. DUFART, LIBRAIRE, | RUE DES SAINTS-PÈRES, N° 1. | 1839.

(21.4 x 13.3): Vol. I. [i]-[iv], [1]-391 [392]. Vol. II. [i]-[iv], [1]-382. Signed in 8's.

Printer: de l'Imprimerie de Crapelet, Rue de Vaugirard, No. 9.

Lineation: Vol. I. p. 100, première ... raison.; p. 200, l'amour ... partir Vol. II. p. 100, lentement ... affamés ; p. 200, un. ... radeaux

Bibliographie de la France, 22 June 1839, # 3077, listed.

DLC, TxU.

ASTORIA | [rule] | VOYAGES | AU DELA | DES MONTAGNES ROCHEUSES | PAR WASHINGTON IRVING | TRADUIT DE L'ANGLAIS PAR P. N. GROLIER | TOME PREMIER [SECOND] | DEUXIÈME ÉDITION | [ornament] | A PARIS | CHEZ A. ALLOUARD, LIBRAIRE | SUCCESSEUR DE P. DUFART ET DE G^{et} WARÉE | QUAI VOLTAIRE, N. 21 | 1843

Printer: the same.

CtY. Copy reported in Bibliothèque Nationale.

German.

Astoria | [rule] | Von | Washington Irving. | [rule] | Aus dem Englischen. | [rule] | Erster [Zweiter, Dritter] Theil. | [double rule] | Frankfurt am Main, 1837. | Druck und Verlag von J. D. Sauerländer. [in fraktur]

"Washington Irving's sämmtliche Werke," Bändchen 57-65.

(13.0 x 9.4): Vol. I. [I]-X, [11]-288. Vol. II. [I]-[IV], [5]-274. Vol. III. [I]-[IV], [5]-272. Signed in 8's. Laid paper.

Lineation: Vol. I. p. 100, geordnetem ... belegen ; p. 200, unternehmen ... Einwanderer Vol. II. p. 100, Haide ... fernen ; p. 200, Pierre ... denn Vol. III. p. 100, Fall, ... zweiten ; p. 200, Neunundfünfzigstes ... Seelen --

TxU. Copy reported in Bayerischer Staatsbibliothek, München.

Astoria, | oder | die Unternehmung jenseit | des Felsengebirges. | [rule] | Von | Washington Irving, | Verfasser des Skizzenbuchs, Alhambra's &c. | Aus dem Englischen | von | A. von Treskow. | Erster [Zweiter] Band. | [stylized swelled rule] | Quedlinburg und Leipzig. | Druck und Verlag von Gottfr. Basse. | 1837. [in fraktur]

"Nachricht" by the translator dated Berlin, den 16. Januar 1837.

(18.3 x 11.1): Vol. I. [I]-VIII, [1]-280. Vol. II. [1]-275 [276]-[278]. The last three pages are given to advertisements. Signed in 8's.

Lineation: Vol. I. p. 100, Mündung. ... des ; p. 200, metschers ... er Vol. II. p. 100, Dreizehntes ... Hrn.; p. 200, Vierundzwanzigstes ... [in footnote] Nasen.

Yellow paper wrappers. On front, short title within triple border. On back, publisher. Spine missing on copy examined.

NN. Copy reported in Stadtbibliothek Braunschweig.

[Astoria, oder, Abenteuer in den Gebirgen und Wäldern von Canada. Aus dem Englischen von Dr. E. Brinckmeier. 3 Vols. Braunschweig: G. C. E. Meyer, Sen., 1837.]

Not seen. Copies reported in Stadtbibliothek Braunschweig and Stadtbibliothek Hannover.

Astoria | oder | Geschichte einer Handelsexpedition | jenseits | der Rocky Mountains. | [rule] | Aus dem Englischen | des | Washington Irving. | [stylized swelled rule] | Stuttgart und Tubingen, | Verlag der J. G. Cotta'schen Buchhandlung. | [rule] | 1838. [in fraktur]

"Reisen und Länderbeschreibungen der älteren und neuesten Zeit. Vierzehnte Lieferung. Herausgegeben von Dr. Eduard Widenmann und Dr. Hermann Hauff."

(22.5 x 14.2 untrimmed): [I]-XVIII, [1]-390. Signed in 8's.

Lineation: p. 100, die ... Chor ; p. 200, rend ... warteten.

Tan paper wrapper. On front, series title. On back, publisher.

TxU. Copy reported in Stadtbibliothek Braunschweig.

Russian.

[Translated title:] Astoria | Life, Travels, Discoveries | and | Adventures | in | the New World. | [swelled rule] | by | Washington Irving. | [stylized swelled rule] | Translation | by Dmitri Paskevitch. | [wavy rule] | Part I. [II.] | [wavy rule] | [stylized swelled rule] | Saint Petersburg. | At the Bookseller Vasili Polyakov. [in Cyrillic]

On verso of title, affidavit by Committee of Censorship that required copies were deposited July 9, 1839. On the same page, the printer is identified as the printshop of the staff of the Division of Internal Security, and the volume is dated 1839.

(21.4 x 12.5): Vol. I. [a]-[b], [I]-II, [1]-151 [152]. Vol. II. [a]-[b], [I]-II, [1]-215 [216]. Signed in 8's. Laid paper.

Lineation: Vol. I. p. 100, i ... sa- Vol. II. p. 100, on ... [in footnote] c. 10.

DLC.

Swedish.

ASTORIA, | ELLER | KOLONIEN BORTOM KLIPPBERGEN. | AF | WASHINGTON IRVING, | FÖRFATTARE TILL "ALHAMBRA," M. FL. | [rule] | ÖFVERSÄTTNING. | [rule] | FÖRRA [SEDNARE] DELEN. | [rule] | STOCKHOLM, HOS L. J. HJERTA, 1837.

Translated by A. F. Dalim.

Originally issued in 7 parts.

(14.3 x 9.5): Vol. I. [1]-310. Vol. II. [1]-302. Signed in 8's.

Lineation: Vol. I.   p. 100, Ändtligen ... [in footnote] nytta.; p. 200, SEXTONDE ... molnen, Vol. II. p. 100, som ... [in footnote] Lin.; p. 200, Stuart ... ha-

TxU.

THE ADVENTURES OF
CAPTAIN BONNEVILLE

Irving apparently completed the manuscript of *The Rocky Mountains* -- based upon a manuscript of Captain Benjamin Louis E. de Bonneville of the United States Army -- late in 1836 or early in 1837. On 10 January 1837 he asked his brother Ebenezer, "Let me hear, by mail, about the maps," and on 9 February 1837 he wrote his London literary agent, Colonel Thomas Aspinwall, to arrange for British publication of the new work, adding that "the Stereotype plates are cast." On 8 March he sent Col. Aspinwall proof sheets of the first volume, and on 16 March of part of the second volume (in addition to a duplicate set of proofs of the first volume). On 29 March he sent the last of the proof sheets. Aspinwall soon reached agreement with Richard Bentley for publication, although the formal statement was not signed until 16 May 1837.

For the American edition, Irving seems to have followed the pattern of his four previous books, from *A Tour on the Prairies* to *Astoria*: he had them stereotyped by Henry W. Rees of New York, and then published by Carey, Lea & Blanchard of Philadelphia. It is likely also that he followed his previous pattern of correcting and perfecting the proofs until the last moment, although we have no direct evidence, since both the manuscript and the proof sheets have disappeared.

The London edition was published first, in May 1837, although derived from the proofs of the American edition, which was not published until June. Bentley changed the title from *The Rocky Mountains* to *The Adventures of Captain Bonneville*. (On 20 June 1837 Irving wrote Col. Aspinwall that he was "pacified by the reasons [Bentley] gives for changing the title, though it is a great liberty to take with an author." Irving later used the title himself in the Author's Revised Edition.) Not only was the title changed, but the text itself was subject to a number of small changes, in part to bring it into conformity with British conventions, and in part to attempt to "correct" or "improve" it. In Vol. II, for example, on p. 177, line 6, "apt" is substituted for "prone," on p. 178, line 3f, "middle" for "midst." In Vol. III, on p. 186, line 6f, "catch these fish" is substituted for "take these fish." More obviously, Bentley added some footnotes and, from other sources, a fifteen-page Appendix on "The Buffalo" in Vol. I, and a twenty-four page Appendix on "The Flatheads and the Blackfeet" in Vol. III.

Within a few months of its London publication, the work was reprinted in Paris by Galignani and Baudry, and by 1838 had been translated into Dutch, French and German, the last in three separate translations. All of the continental texts are derived from Bentley's London edition.

In 1849, Irving revised the text moderately for the Author's Revised Edition, published in New York by George P. Putnam. The majority of his substantive changes were intended to smooth and better the style, although he took the opportunity also to correct a few errors. On p. 69, for instance, he added a footnote to correct his mistaken use, in the early editions, of the title of "Captain" for Nathaniel J. Wyeth.

1Ea.   ADVENTURES | OF | CAPTAIN BONNEVILLE, | OR | SCENES | BEYOND THE | ROCKY MOUNTAINS OF | THE FAR WEST. | [rule] | BY WASHINGTON IRVING. | AUTHOR OF | " THE SKETCH-BOOK," "THE ALHAMBRA," "ASTORIA," &C. | IN THREE VOLUMES. | VOL. I. [II., III.] | LONDON: | RICHARD BENTLEY, | NEW BURLINGTON STREET. | [rule] | 1837. In Vols. II, III, "SKETCH-BOOK" is not hyphenated. In Vol. III, in all copies examined, the letters in AUTHOR are not evenly aligned on the baseline.

(19.6 x 12.1 in boards; 20.2 x 12.5 in cloth): Vol. I. $[a]^2$ b^2 B-I^8 K-T^8 U^4 X^2. Vol. II. $[a]^2$ b^2 B-I^8 K-T^8. Vol. III. $[a]^2$ b^2 B-I^8 K-T^8 U^4 X^1.

Vol. I. [i]-[ii], half-title, verso blank; [iii]-[iv], title, on verso printer; [1]-4, table of contents; [5]-[19], Introductory Notice; [20], blank; [21]-288, text; 289-303, Appendix, printer at foot of last page; [304], blank. Vol. II. [i]-[ii], half-title, verso blank; [iii]-[iv], title, on verso printer; [1]-4, table of contents; [5]-292, text, printer at foot of last page. Vol. III. [i]-[ii], half-title, verso blank; [iii]-[iv], title, on verso printer; [1]-4, table of contents; [5]-266, text; [267]-302, Appendix, printer at foot of last page.

Printer: Whiting, Beaufort House, Strand.

Lineation: Vol. I. p. 100, of ... on ; p. 200, them. ... stout,   Vol. II. p. 100, them ... cups,; p. 200, river. ... plains; Vol. III. p. 100, nance, ... which ; p. 200, that ... hearts."

Gray-brown drab paper boards. Also, less commonly, old rose cloth irregularly diagonally-ribbed to give "watered" effect. Sides blank. White paper label on spines: [double rule] | ADVENTURES | OF | CAPTAIN | BONNEVILLE. | BY | WASHINGTON IRVING. | AUTHOR OF | "The Sketch Book," &c. | IN THREE VOLUMES. | VOL. I. [II., III.] | [double rule]. Off-white endpapers. Also reported, but not seen, in paper boards with cloth shelfbacks, paper label on spines.

Athenæum, and *Literary Gazette*, 6 May 1837, "Will immediately publish"; 13 May 1837, "Just published," reviewed, listed, 31*s*. 6*d*. in boards.

CtY (2), TxU (2).

b. CAPTAIN BONNEVILLE, | OR | ENTERPRISE | BEYOND THE | ROCKY MOUNTAINS. | A SEQUEL TO "ASTORIA." | BY WASHINGTON IRVING. | AUTHOR OF | "THE SKETCH BOOK," "THE ALHAMBRA," &C. | SECOND EDITION. | IN THREE VOLUMES. | VOL. I. [II., III.] | LONDON: RICHARD BENTLEY, NEW BURLINGTON STREET. | 1837.

Despite the new title and the claim of "Second Edition," this is simply a second impression from the same setting.

(20.0 x 12.2 untrimmed).

In some copies of Vol. I, but not all, there are eight pages of terminal advertisements, of a smaller size than the volume leaves, dated *March*, 1837, paged [1]-8. The first page is headed, *New Publications and Standard Works in Theology* | *and Miscellaneous Literature*, | PUBLISHED BY | JAMES DUNCAN, | 37 PATERNOSTER ROW.

Printer: Samuel Bentley, Dorset Street, Fleet Street. But at the foot of the last page, in the three volumes, the printer's imprint of Whiting, Beaufort House, Strand is continued from the first edition. Presumably, Samuel Bentley forgot to substitute his own imprint.

Gray-brown drab paper boards. Sides blank. White paper label on spines: [double rule] | CAPTAIN | BONNEVILLE. | A SEQUEL TO "ASTORIA." | BY | WASHINGTON IRVING. | [rule] | SECOND EDITION. | [rule] | IN THREE VOLUMES. | VOL. I. [II., III.] | [double rule]. White endpapers.

Athenæum, 15 July 1837, "Will immediately publish"; 29 July 1837, "SECOND SERIES OF 'ASTORIA.' The second Edition ... of MR. WASHINGTON IRVING'S NEW WORK, CAPTAIN BONNEVILLE ... IS NOW READY"; 5 August 1837, "Just published." *Literary Gazette*, 29 July 1837, "Is now ready."

TxGeoS (with advertisements), TxU. Both copies in original boards.

c. ADVENTURES | OF | CAPTAIN BONNEVILLE; | OR | SCENES | BEYOND THE | ROCKY MOUNTAINS OF THE FAR WEST. | BY WASHINGTON IRVING, | AUTHOR OF "THE SKETCH-BOOK," "THE ALHAMBRA," "ASTORIA," ETC. | THREE VOLUMES IN ONE. | LONDON: | RICHARD BENTLEY, NEW BURLINGTON STREET.

1840's. The copy examined is a prize book, Honiton Academy, 1847.

(19.9 x 12.4): the same setting of the three volumes, now bound in one volume. Individual titles are omitted, but the separate volume pagination is retained. Inserted before the title: Robert Cruikshank illustration of "A General in the Bush."

Red T cloth. Sides decorated in blind, with ornament at center, elaborated border with ornaments in corners. Spine decorated in gilt, titled ADVENTURES | OF | CAPTAIN | BONNEVILLE | BY | WASHINGTON IRVING. Yellow endpapers.

TxU.

2Ea.   [London: George Routledge, 1850.]

Routledge's "Popular Library."

For a description in a state bound with *Astoria*, see the next entry.

Athenæum, 29 June 1850, listed, 1*s*. boards, 1*s*. 6*d*. cloth.

Not located.

b.   ASTORIA, | AND | CAPTAIN BONNEVILLE'S | ADVENTURES. | BY | WASHINGTON IRVING. | [rule] | LONDON: | GEORGE ROUTLEDGE & CO., SOHO SQUARE. | 1851.

Routledge's "Popular Library."

The two individual volumes issued bound together; no separate title pages; original individual pagination and collation retained.

(16.7 x 10.5): (Vol. I.) [1]-291 [292]. (Vol. II.) [1]-271 [272]. Signed in 8's.

Printer: (Vol. I.) Saville & Edwards, 4, Chandos-street, Covent-garden. (Vol. II.) Reynell and Weight, Little Pulteney Street, Haymarket.

Lineation: (Vol. I.) p. 100, He ... him ; p. 200, now ... leaped   (Vol. II.) p. 100, day ... lava; --; p. 200, The ... his

Blue L cloth. Sides decorated in blind with POPULAR LIBRARY in circular design at center. Spine missing in copy examined.

NN.

c.   [London: George Routledge, 1855.]

In *Publishers' Circular*, 1 June 1855, a "new edition" is listed. Presumably this represents a new impression.

Not located.

3Ea. THE | ADVENTURES | OF | CAPTAIN BONNEVILLE, U. S. A., | IN THE | ROCKY MOUNTAINS AND THE FAR WEST. | DIGESTED FROM HIS JOURNAL AND ILLUSTRATED | FROM VARIOUS OTHER SOURCES. | BY | WASHINGTON IRVING. | AUTHOR'S REVISED EDITION. | COMPLETE IN ONE VOLUME. | LONDON: | HENRY G. BOHN, YORK STREET, COVENT GARDEN. | [rule] | 1850.

(18.1 x 11.4): [i]-x, [1]-280. Signed in 8's.

Issued individually in "Bohn's Shilling Series"; bound with Theodore Irving's *The Conquest of Florida* as Vol. X of "Bohn's Library Edition."

Printer: G. Woodfall and Son, Angel Court, Skinner Street, London.

Lineation: p. 100, lowance ... A ; p. 200, faction, ... presented.

Seen only in "Bohn's Library Edition." Preliminary illustration for "The Backwoods." Noted in original binding only in the Library Edition, with an 1850 impression of *The Conquest of Florida*. Gray T cloth. Sides decorated in blind. Spine titled in gilt as Irving's Works, Vol. X, Bohn's Library Edition. White endpapers with advertisements in blue. (No Works title in volume.)

Shilling Series. *Athenæum*, 29 June 1850, listed, 1*s*. 6*d*. boards. Library Edition. *Athenæum*, and *Literary Gazette*, 2 November 1850, the set of 10 vols. at 35*s*. listed.

NN, TxU.

b. LONDON: | HENRY G. BOHN, YORK STREET, COVENT GARDEN. | [rule] | 1854.

"Bohn's Library Edition," with Works title and frontispiece. Bound with *The Conquest of Florida*, 1850.

Printer: Woodfall and Kinder, Angel Court, Skinner Street, London.

MB.

c. [London: Henry G. Bohn, 1859.]

Not seen. Copy reported in CaBViPA.

1Aa- THE | ROCKY MOUNTAINS: | OR, | SCENES, INCIDENTS, AND
b. ADVENTURES | IN THE FAR WEST; | DIGESTED FROM THE JOURNAL OF CAPTAIN B. L. E. BONNEVILLE, | OF THE ARMY OF THE UNITED STATES, AND ILLUSTRATED | FROM VARIOUS OTHER SOURCES, | BY WASHINGTON IRVING. | IN TWO VOLUMES. | VOL. I. [II.] | PHILADELPHIA. | CAREY, LEA, & BLANCHARD. | 1837.

(19.2 x 11.5): Vol. I. [1]^{6}2-20^6 21^4. Fold-out map inserted before title. In some copies, twelve pages of terminal advertisements, not reckoned (see variant states below). Vol. II. [1]^6 2-20^6 21^4. In some copies, Sig. 3 signed 2. Fold-out map inserted before title.

Fold-out engraved map in Vol. I: "A Map of the Sources of the Colorado & Big Salt Lake, Platte, Yellow-Stone, Muscle-Shell, Missouri; & Salmon & Snake Rivers, branches of the Columbia River." Undated. Engraved by S. Stiles, New-York. In Vol. II: "Map of the Territory West of the Rocky Mountains." Undated. Engraved by S. Stiles.

Vol. II, p. 25 appears in two states of the signature mark at the foot:

1. Incorrectly signed 2.

2. Correctly signed 3.

Vol. II, p. 113 appears in two states of the signature mark at the foot:

1. Without signature mark.

2. Signed 10*.

The sequence is almost certainly correct. Not only do the signature marks change from incorrect (or missing) to correct, but the late impression of 1843 is in State 2 on both pages.

The two states of the two pages seem to appear indiscriminately within any copy of Vol. II. In twelve copies examined, three are in States 1-1, three in States 1-2, four in States 2-1, and two in States 2-2. Although the possibility of duplicate plates must be considered, since this edition was stereotyped, it does not seem likely; sheets printed from two sets of plates would need to have been thoroughly mixed in binding. Machine collation reveals no other differences between copies of Vol. II.

The terminal advertisements in Vol. I, if present, have been noted in two forms, and so produce three states of the advertisements. A sequence, if any exists, is only conjectural.

[A]. 12 pp. Undated. Paged: [2 pp.. unpaged], 4-6, vii, xi, [1] 2 [3] 4. The first eight pages are derived from the Prospectus for *Astoria*, reprinting in seven pages the Introduction and a page from each of the two tables of contents of the 1836 edition.

[B]. 12 pp.. Undated. Paged: [1] 2-6 [7] 8, [4 pp. unpaged]. In contrast to the alternate form, here *Astoria* is given only a two-line listing, on p. 2. On p. 4, the three vols. of *The Crayon Miscellany* ("To be published at intervals") are listed as "Now ready --."

[C]. Issued with no advertisements.

Vol. I. [1]-[2], title, on verso copyright (1837 by Washington Irving) and printer; [3]-9, Introductory Notice; [10], blank; [xi]-xvi, table of contents; [17]-248, text. Vol. II. [i]-[ii], title, on verso copyright and printer; [iii]-vii, table of contents; [viii], blank; [9]-239, text; 240-248, Appendix.

Printer: Stereotyped by Henry W. Rees, 45 Gold Street, New-York.

Lineation: Vol. I.   p. 100, Bridger, ... scattered ; p. 200, them ... misadventures. Vol. II. p. 100, in ... him,; p.200, winter ... unless

Blue V cloth. Sides blank. On spines, white paper label in two states (see below). White endpapers. Noted with, and without, flyleaves.

The paper labels appear in two states. No sequence determined.

[A]. [double rule] | THE | ROCKY | MOUNTAINS; | OR, ADVENTURES IN THE | FAR WEST. | [rule] | BY | WASHINGTON IRVING. |*In Two Vols.* | VOL. I. [II.] | [rule] | WITH MAPS. | [double rule].

[B]. [double rule] | THE | ROCKY | MOUNTAINS: | OR, | ADVENTURES | IN THE | FAR WEST. | [rule] | BY | WASHINGTON | IRVING. | *In Two Vols.* | VOL. I. [II.] | [rule] | WITH MAPS | [double rule].

The accounting for "Rocky Mountains" in The Cost Book of Carey & Lea is ambiguous about the number of copies printed. The printing costs for supplies and labor do not clearly define the number, and the publisher reckoned the total costs and profit in two columns, one for 5000 copies and one for 4000 copies. The accounting does specify that Irving was paid $3000 for 5000 copies. It would seem probable, then, that the situation was analogous to that of *Astoria* in the preceding year: Irving was paid, by agreement, for 5000 copies but only 4000 copies were first printed, with an extra 1000 copies produced as needed. Even if that interpretation were right, however, it would not explain the common mixed printing states of the first volume.

Copyrighted and title page deposited 30 March 1837; complete copy deposited 6 July 1837. *National Gazette and Literary Register*, 15 June 1837, extracted, and mentioned in editorial column, "Will shortly be issued"; 24 June 1837, advertised. *Gentleman's Magazine* [Philadelphia], July 1837, reviewed. *New-York Mirror*, 29 July 1837, extracted. Irving to John Murray, 22 September 1850, gives 20 June 1837 as the publication date.

Discussion based on copies in CtY (3), TxU (7), ViU (2).

c. PHILADELPHIA: | LEA & BLANCHARD. | 1843.

The Introductory Notice, although unchanged in text, is dated New-York, 1843. That is certainly the work of the publisher, and probably unauthorized.

In Vol. I, no advertisements. In Vol. II, p. 25 and p. 113 are in State 2.

Printer: T. K. & P. G. Collins, Philadelphia.

Green V cloth. Sides blank. On spines, paper label in State [B].

CtY.

2Aa.   THE | ADVENTURES | OF | CAPTAIN BONNEVILLE, U. S. A., | IN THE | ROCKY MOUNTAINS AND THE FAR WEST. | DIGESTED FROM HIS JOURNAL AND ILLUSTRATED | FROM VARIOUS OTHER SOURCES. | BY | WASHINGTON IRVING. | AUTHOR'S REVISED EDITION. | COMPLETE IN ONE VOLUME. | NEW-YORK: | GEORGE P. PUTNAM, 155 BROADWAY, | And 142 Strand, London. | 1849.

(18.6 x 12.8): [-]^2 1-17^{12} 18^{10}. Fold-out map inserted before title.

The fold-out map is titled, in a variety of engraved styles of lettering, MAP | *TO ILLUSTRATE* | CAP^T. BONNEVILLE'S ADVENTURES | *among the* | Rocky Mountains. | Compiled by J. H. Colton, | *N°. 86, Cedar Street,* | [rule] | NEW YORK. | GEO. P. PUTNAM. | 1849.

[a]-[b], Works title, Vol. X, dated 1849, verso blank; [c]-[d], title, on verso copyright (1849) and printer; [i]-xii, table of contents; [xiii]-xviii, Introductory Notice, dated New-York, 1843; [19]-422, text; [423]-428, Appendix.

Printer: John F. Trow, Printer and Stereotyper, 40 Ann-street, N. Y.

Lineation: p. 100, ing-party. ... they ; p. 200, it ... On

Blue-green TB cloth. On sides, publisher's initials within decorative design in blind. Spine decorated in blind, titled in gilt: IRVING'S | WORKS | [rule] | BONNEVILLE'S | ADVENTURES. | PUTNAM   Endpapers cream-white. Flyleaves.

Within the next few years advertisements for the Works offer them in cloth, cloth extra, sheep extra, half calf, half calf extra, half morocco, calf extra, calf antique, morocco extra. Presumably *Capt. Bonneville* was also available in some or all of these.

Literary World, 2 June 1849, "on the 4th of June"; 16 June 1849, reviewed; 23 June 1849, listed.

CtY, TxU (2).

b.   NEW-YORK: | GEORGE P. PUTNAM, 155 BROADWAY. | And 142 Strand, London. | 1850.

Works title, dated 1850.

The map is dated 1850 and is revised. GREAT SALT LAKE, for example, is so named, rather than L. BONNEVILLE OR GREAT SALT LAKE. In California, the name of the town is changed from "New Helvetia" to "Sacramento City."

TxU.

c.   NEW-YORK: | GEORGE P. PUTNAM, 155 BROADWAY. | And 142 Strand, London. | 1851.

Works title, dated 1851.

The map is dated 1851 and is revised again. The name of NEW MEXICO, for example, appears horizontally rather than vertically. The two separate names of CALIFORNIA and UTAH now replace the former single designation of UPPER OR NEW CALIFORNIA.

Green TB cloth in same design.

TxU.

d.   NEW-YORK: | GEORGE P. PUTNAM, 155 BROADWAY. | And 142 Strand, London. | 1852.

Works title, dated 1852.

The map is dated 1852 but is not revised from the map of 1851.

Noted in blue TB cloth in same design.

TxU.

e.   NEW-YORK: | G. P. PUTNAM & COMPANY, 10 PARK PLACE, | 1852.

Works title, dated 1852.

The map is the same, dated 1852.

Private hands.

f.   [New York: George P. Putnam, 1853.]

Not seen. Copy reported in PMA.

g.   NEW-YORK: | G. P. PUTNAM & COMPANY, 10 PARK PLACE, | 1854.

Works title, dated 1854.

The map is dated 1854. Revised?

Purple T cloth. On sides, publisher's initials within decorative design in blind. On spine, gilt leaf ornaments within blind panels; titled in gilt. Yellow endpapers.

CtY. TxDaM, map missing.

h. [New York: George P. Putnam, 1856.]

Not located, but copy said to exist. The map noted in an 1857 impression, dated 1856, would strengthen the belief.

i. New York: [fancy] | G. P. PUTNAM & CO., 321 BROADWAY. | 1857.

Works title, dated 1857.

The map in copy examined is dated 1856 and is revised from the map of 1851, 1852. One portion of Nebraska, for example, is marked "Indian Enchanted Ground | Petrefactions of every description | abound here".

Purple V cloth. On sides, publisher's intials within decorative design in blind. Spine titled in gilt. Cream endpapers.

TxU.

j. NEW YORK: | G. P. PUTNAM, 115 NASSAU STREET. | 1859.

Works title, dated 1859.

A number of the plates are repaired and reworked. Page 146, line 1 now reads "house" rather than "home."

The fold-out map is omitted. Two engraved illustrations, published by Childs & Peterson, Philadelphia, are added before the title.

Green BD cloth. Sides framed in blind. Spine titled in gilt, with extra gilt decoration around the title. Green endpapers.

TxU.

k. NEW YORK: | G. P. PUTNAM (for the Proprietor), 506 BROADWAY. | 1859

Works title, dated 1859.

Two engraved illustrations, published by Childs & Peterson, Philadelphia, before the title.

NjP. TxU, regular title missing.

1Fa. ADVENTURES | Of | CAPTAIN BONNEVILLE, | OR | SCENES | BEYOND THE | ROCKY MOUNTAINS OF THE FAR WEST; | BY WASHINGTON IRVING, | AUTHOR OF | "THE SKETCH-BOOK," "THE ALHAMBRA," "ASTORIA," ETC. | [ornamental rule] | PARIS, | PUBLISHED BY A. AND W. GALIGNANI AND C°., | RUE VIVIENNE, N° 18. | 1837.

(20.8 x 13.3): [i]-[iv], [1]-303 [304]. Signed in 8's.

Printer: Crapelet, 9, Rue de Vaugirard.

Lineation: p. 100, ing ... Flatheads,; p. 200, various ... their

Bibliographie de la France, 26 August 1837, # 4427, listed.

BL. Copy reported in Bibliothèque Nationale.

b. [emblem: BEL intertwined] | PARIS, | BAUDRY'S EUROPEAN LIBRARY, | RUE DU COQ, NEAR THE LOUVRE. | SOLD ALSO BY AMYOT, RUE DE LA PAIX; TRUCHY, BOULEVARD DES ITALIENS; | THÉOPHILE BARROIS, JUN., RUE RICHELIEU; HEIDELOFF AND CAMPE, | RUE VIVIENNE; AND BY ALL THE PRINCIPAL BOOKSELLERS | ON THE CONTINENT. | [rule] | 1837.

"Collection of Ancient and Modern British Authors," Vol. CXCIII.

(21.2 x 12.9): a variant impression from the same setting. Laid paper.

Printer: the same.

Bibliographie de la France, 9 September 1837, # 4666, listed.

NN, OrP.

TRANSLATIONS

Dutch.

[Engraved titles, in a variety of lettering styles] LOTGEVALLEN | EN | ONTMOETINGEN | VAN | Kapitein Bonneville, | OP ZIJNE AVONTHURLIJKE TOGTEN AAN GENE ZIJDE | VAN HET | KLIPGEBERGTE VAN NOORD-AMERIKA; | BESCHREVEN DOOR | Washington Irving. | EERSTE [TWEEDE EN LAATSTE] DEEL. | [rule] | Naar het Engelsch. | [rule] | [elaborated swelled rule] | Te HAARLEM, bij | De WED. A. LOOSJES, PZ. | MDCCCXXXVIII.

(22.2 x 12.8 rebound): Vol. I. [I]-IV, [III]-VIII, [I]-261 [262]. Vol. II. [I]-VIII, [1]-226. Engraved titles not counted. Signed in 8's. Laid paper.

Printed on a leaf at the end of Vol. II are two labels for the spine of Vol. II. Presumably, similar labels also appeared originally in Vol. I.

Lineation: Vol. I. p. 100, landstreek, ... beide ; p. 200, hij ... neder- Vol. II. p. 100, stier ... hadden.; p. 200, inderdaad ... aan-

NN.

French.

VOYAGES ET AVENTURES | DU | CAPITAINE BONNEVILLE | A L'OUEST DES ÉTATS-UNIS D'AMÉRIQUE, | AU DELA DES MONTAGNES ROCHEUSES; | PAR WASHINGTON IRWING, | Auteur du Sketck-Book [sic], de l'Alhambra, etc.: | TRADUITS DE L'ANGLAIS | PAR BENJAMIN LAROCHE, | Traducteur des OEuvres de Byron et de Cooper. | I. [II.] | PARIS, | CHARPENTIER, LIBRAIRE-ÉDITEUR, | 6, RUE DES BEAUX-ARTS. | [rule] | 1837.

(20.7 x 12.5): Vol. I. [i]-[iv], I-XI [XII], [1]-328. Vol. II. [i]-[iv], [1]-348. Signed in 8's. Laid paper.

Printer: Imprimerie de Mme. Huzard (Née Vallat la Chapelle), Rue de l'Eperon, No. 7.

Lineation: Vol. I. p. 100, profita ... dans ; p. 200, trappeurs; ... quitta Vol. II. p. 100, bonne ... ses ; p. 200, CHAPITRE XLIV. ... murailles.

Bibliographie de la France, 16 September 1837, # 4785, listed.

CtY, NN.

German.

Abentheuer | des | Capitäns Bonneville | oder | Scenen | jenseits der | Felsgebirge des fernen Westens. | Von | Washington Irving. | [rule] | Aus dem Englischen | von F. L. Rhode. | [rule] | Erster [Zweiter, Dritter] Theil. | [double rule] | Frankfurt am Main, 1837. | Verlag von J. D. Sauerländer. [in fraktur]

"Washington Irving's sämmtliche Werke," Bändchen 66-74.

(13.0 x 9.6): Vol. I. [I]-XIV, [15]-229 [230]. Not reckoned: ten pages of terminal advertisements, undated, unpaged. Vol. II. [1]-234. Vol. III. [1]-216. Not reckoned: eight pages of terminal advertisements, undated, unpaged. Signed in 8's.

Lineation: Vol. I. p. 100, seid, ... Schwarzfüsse ; p. 200, schossen ... kamen. Vol. II. p. 100, tergesunkene ... Ebene ; p. 200, bringen ... so Vol. III. p. 100, überwinden, ... Schnur ; p. 200, so ... er

CtY, TxU.

Abenteuer | des | Capitan Bonneville, | oder | Scenen jenseit des Felsengebirges | im fernen Westen. | [rule] | Von | Washington Irving. | [rule] | Aus dem Englischen | von | A. v. Treskow. | Erster [Zweiter] Band.

| [elaborated swelled rule] | Quedlinburg und Leipzig. | Druck und Verlag von Gottfr. Basse. | 1837. [in fraktur]

(16.7 x 10.9): Vol. I. [I]-XIV [XV]-[XVI], [1]-256. Vol. II. [1]-256. The last six pages are given to advertisements. Signed in 8's.

Lineation: Vol. I. p. 100, und ... gab.; p. 200, Zweiundzwanzigstes ... und Vol. II. p . 100, dieses ... ur-; p. 200, Charakter, ... Land

CtY.

[Abenteuer des Capitain Bonneville, oder Scenen im Felsengebirge Nordamerikas. Übertragen von Dr. Eduard Freisleben. Bändchen 1-3. Leipzig: B. Tauchnitz jun., 1837.]

Not seen. Copy reported in Stadtbibliothek Braunschweig.

BIOGRAPHY AND POETICAL REMAINS OF
MARGARET MILLER DAVIDSON

By 14 March 1841 Irving had completed the manuscript of his Memoirs of the unfortunate Margaret M. Davidson -- apparently undertaken at the request of her mother, and completed with the assistance of memoranda from Mrs. Miller -- and by 16 April was writing Lea and Blanchard to send more proof. The volume was published in the first half of June, and by November had reached a second edition. Before then, Irving had given the copyright proceeds to Mrs. Miller, reserving merely the right to republish. The original manuscript appears not to have survived.

The subsequent textual history of the work in America is one of early minor revision. The second edition contains some twenty-three substantive variations and more than four hundred variations in accidentals, some possibly the work of Irving. For the third edition, 1842, Irving provided an additional paragraph and a new poem by Margaret, as well perhaps as some minor touching up. After that, the occasional small changes would seem to be those of the publisher. The work was not included in the Author's Revised Edition.

The first English edition, dated 1843 but published in October of 1842, was derived from the third American edition, the expanded text with the new poem and new paragraph added to Irving's "Life," as it is called here. (An added explanatory footnote to the poem is omitted.) Minor editorial changes appear, but they are probably the work of the publisher. In the "Remains," the prose piece titled "A Tale, Written at the Age of Fifteen" is omitted, as well as fourteen of the poems; also, three poems are given shorter titles. Desultory British reprinting in the following years was derived from that first English edition. A German translation of the British text appeared promptly, in 1843, although it translated only the "Life" and not the "Poetical Remains."

1A. BIOGRAPHY | AND | POETICAL REMAINS | OF THE LATE | MARGARET MILLER DAVIDSON. | BY WASHINGTON IRVING. | [rule] | Thou wert unfit to dwell with clay, | For sin too pure, for earth too bright! | And death, who call'd thee hence away, | Placed on his brow a gem of light! | MARGARET TO HER SISTER. | [rule] | PHILADELPHIA: | LEA AND BLANCHARD. | 1841.

(19.2 x 11.9): [1]⁴ 2-10⁸ [11]⁸ 12-23⁸. Not reckoned: eight pages of terminal advertisements.

The advertisements, undated, unpaged, are in a single gathering of 4. The first page is given to Works of Washington Irving: *The Rocky Mountains, Astoria, Christopher Columbus, The Crayon Miscellany, The Beauties of Washington Irving.*

[i]-[ii], half-title, verso blank; [iii]-[iv], title, on verso copyright (1841, by Washington Irving) and printer; [v]-vii, table of contents; [viii], blank; [9]-152, "Biography of Miss Margaret Davidson"; [153]-359, text of the "Remains"; [360], blank.

Printer: C. Sherman & Co.

Lineation: p. 100, wrote. ... decay'd.; p. 200, From ... brave.

Black T cloth. On sides, urn and flowers in gilt within decorative design in blind. Spine titled in gilt: MEMOIR | OF | MARGARET | DAVIDSON | BY | W. IRVING ; with horizontal bars in blind. Yellow endpapers. Copies examined are now a dark black-brown, apparently the result of fading. Three flyleaves at beginning and at end.

Deposited 10 June 1841. *New-Yorker* and *New World*, 5 June 1841, reviewed. *Knickerbocker*, July 1841, reviewed.

TxU (2), ViU.

2A. BIOGRAPHY | AND | POETICAL REMAINS | OF THE LATE | MARGARET MILLER DAVIDSON. | BY WASHINGTON IRVING. | [rule] | [4-line quotation, and identification] | [rule] | Second Edition. [fancy] | PHILADELPHIA: | LEA AND BLANCHARD. | 1841.

Collation, advertisements, pagination, printer, lineation the same.

Although for the most part a line-for-line resetting of the first edition, there are a number of minor revisions in the text: some 23 in substantives and over 400 in accidentals.

Binding the same.

Christian Examiner [Boston], November 1841, reviewed.

CtY, DLC, NN.

3A. BIOGRAPHY | AND | POETICAL REMAINS | OF THE LATE | MARGARET MILLER DAVIDSON. | BY WASHINGTON IRVING. | [rule] | [4-line quotation, and identification] | [rule] | Third Edition. [fancy] | PHILADELPHIA: | LEA AND BLANCHARD. | 1842.

Collation, pagination, printer, lineation the same.   Eight pages of advertisements bound at end, but the advertisements for Irving are on p. [2] rather than on p. [1].

Although for the most part a line-for-line resetting of the second edition, there are a number of minor authorial revisions in the text. There are also two major additions: on p. 136, a new paragraph beginning, "We here interrupt..."; and a new poem by Margaret Davidson, "To My Soldier Brother in the Far West." A footnote to the poem explains, "This copy of verses has come to hand since the publication of the first edition of this memoir."

In copies examined, the page number for p. 359 is missing.

Binding the same.

CtY, TxU, *BL*.

4Aa.   BIOGRAPHY | AND | POETICAL REMAINS | OF THE LATE | MARGARET MILLER DAVIDSON. | BY WASHINGTON IRVING | [rule] | [4-line quotation, and identification] | [rule] | A New Edition, revised. [fancy] | PHILADELPHIA: | LEA AND BLANCHARD. | 1843.

(19.5 x 12.3): 9-13, xiv-xvi, 17-248. Twelve pages of advertisements bound at end. Signed in 6's.

Printer: J. Fagan, Stereotyper; T.K. and P.G. Collins, Printers.

Lineation: p. 100, let ... my ; p. 200, These ... light,

A new edition that corrects some errors of the previous edition and introduces some new variations. For example, p. 16, line 15 of the first edition reads "ecstasy"; the third edition reads "ecstacy"; this edition (22.10) returns to "ecstasy." P. 58, line 2 of the first edition reads "angel"; the third edition reads "angels"; this edition (50.17f) reads "angels'."

In two bindings:

[A].   Black T cloth, as earlier editions.

[B].   Lemon-yellow paper wrapper. On front, cover-title within wavy rules; at head: *Price Fifty Cents*.   On back, within straight rules, advertisements for THE LADY'S CABINET SERIES, of which this is listed as the third volume, with others to follow.   At foot, advertisements for three other titles, not in the series, nearly ready. Spine missing in copy examined, but a later impression has the spine titled vertically MARGARET MILLER DAVIDSON, and horizontally at the head LADIES' | CABINET | SERIES (note the variant title). The wrapper now appears tan, but the advertisement on the back describes the series as "handsomely done up in lemon-coloured glazed paper."

Seen in original binding only in paper wrapper. But the 1845 impression has been noted in cloth, and the 1846 impression both in cloth and in paper wrapper (although the wrapper is dated 1845). It is probable that the three impressions, and possibly some later ones, were issued in both forms.

TxU (2).

b. A New Edition, revised. [fancy] | PHILADELPHIA: | LEA AND BLANCHARD. | 1845.

Noted with a terminal catalogue of twenty-four pages, undated, unpaged, and also without a catalogue.

Printer: J. Fagan, Stereotyper. [Printer omitted].

Seen only in black T cloth. On sides, urn and flowers in gilt within decorative design and border in blind. Spine titled in gilt: MEMOIR | AND | POEMS | OF | MARGARET | DAVIDSON White endpapers.

TxU (2).

c. A New Edition, revised. [fancy] | PHILADELPHIA: | LEA AND BLANCHARD. | 1846.

The cloth-bound issue noted with a terminal catalogue of twenty-four pages.

In two bindings:

[A]. Black T cloth.

[B]. Lemon-yellow paper wrapper. On front, cover-title within wavy rules, dated 1845. On back, within straight rules, advertisements for six titles in THE LADY'S CABINET SERIES (of which this is listed as the third volume), two "to match the above," followed by twelve miscellaneous titles, some of them collected works. Spine titled vertically MARGARET MILLER DAVIDSON and horizontally at the head LADIES' | CABINET | SERIES.

TxU (2).

d. A New Edition, revised. [fancy] | PHILADELPHIA: | LEA AND BLANCHARD. | 1847.

Printer: Stereotyped by J. Fagan; printed by T. K. and P. G. Collins, Philadelphia.

Noted only in black T cloth.

TxU.

e. A New Edition, revised. [fancy] | PHILADELPHIA: | LEA AND BLANCHARD. | 1848.

TxU.

f. A New Edition, revised. [fancy] | NEW YORK: | PUBLISHED BY
    CLARK, AUSTIN & CO., | 205 BROADWAY. | 1850.

Despite the change in publisher, this impression is printed from the same
plates. The printer is not given.

Paged [4 pp. unpaged], 13, xiv-xvi, 17-248.

Red A cloth. On front, gilt urn within ornate border in blind. On back, the
border in blind. Spine titled in gilt. Buff endpapers.

CtY.

g. A new Edition, revised. [fancy] | NEW YORK: | PUBLISHED BY CLARK,
    AUSTIN & CO., | 205 BROADWAY. | 1851.

Red A cloth. Sides decorated in blind. Spine titled in gilt: MARGARET M.
| DAVIDSON'S | POEMS | [swelled rule] | SEDGWICK White endpapers
with blue decorations. The confusion of the title on the spine suggests that
this impression may have been intended to be bound, as several later
impressions were, with *Poetical Remains of the Late Lucretia Maria Davidson,
Collected and Arranged by Her Mother; With a Biography by Miss Sedgwick.*
Or, it may simply be an error.

TxU.

h. A New Edition, revised. [fancy] | NEW YORK: | PUBLISHED BY
    CLARK, AUSTIN & CO., | 205 BROADWAY. | 1852.

DLC, rebound.

i. A New Edition, revised. [fancy] | NEW YORK: | PUBLISHED BY
    CLARK, AUSTIN & CO., | 205 BROADWAY. | 1854.

Bound with *Poetical Remains of the Late Lucretia Maria Davidson,...With a
Biography by Miss Sedgwick*, Clark, Austin & Co. Noted bound with an
impression of 1854, and also with an impression of 1852.

Noted in two bindings:

[A]. Bright blue AR cloth. Sides decorated in gilt with flower and leaf
      designs within triple border. Spine decorated in gilt; titled, POETICAL
      | WORKS | OF THE | DAVIDSON | SISTERS | [swelled rule] |
      IRVING & SEDGWICK Gold-flowered endpapers. AEG.

[B]. Bright blue A cloth. On sides, decorative border in blind. Spine titled
      in gilt the same. Manilla endpapers. (Bound with 1852 impression of
      Lucretia Maria Davidson.)

CtY, TxU.

j. A New Edition, revised. [fancy] | BOSTON: | PHILLIPS, SAMPSON, AND COMPANY. | 1854.

Despite the change in publisher, this impression is printed from the same plates. The printer is not given.

Bound with *Poetical Remains of the Late Lucretia Maria Davidson, ... With a Biography by Miss Sedgwick.*

Brown T cloth. On front, gilt lyre, with decoration in blind. Back all in blind. Spine titled in gilt the same. Light yellow endpapers.

NcD.

k. A New Edition, revised. [fancy] | BOSTON: | PHILLIPS, SAMPSON, AND COMPANY. | NEW YORK: J. C. DERBY. | 1855.

Bound with *Poetical Remains of the Late Lucretia Maria Davidson, ... With a Biography by Miss Sedgwick*, Phillips, Sampson and Co., 1855.

Black T cloth. On sides, ornate gilt decoration. Spine decorated in gilt and titled, THE | POETICAL | WORKS | OF THE | DAVIDSON | SISTERS. Cream endpapers. AEG.

MH, TxU.

1. A New Edition, revised. [fancy] | BOSTON: | PHILLIPS SAMPSON, AND COMPANY. | 1857.

Bound with *Poetical Remains of the Late Lucretia Maria Davidson, ... With a Biography by Miss Sedgwick*, Phillips, Sampson and Co., 1857.

Red A cloth. Noted with sides decorated in gilt, and also with sides decorated in blind. Spine titled in gilt the same.

CtY, ViU.

m. A New Edition, revised. [fancy] | BOSTON: | PHILLIPS SAMPSON, AND COMPANY. | 1859.

Bound with *Poetical Remains of the Late Lucretia Maria Davidson, ... With a Biography by Miss Sedgwick*, Phillips, Sampson and Co., 1859.

MB.

1Ea. LIFE | AND | POETICAL REMAINS | OF | MARGARET M. DAVIDSON. | BY WASHINGTON IRVING. | Thou wert unfit to dwell with clay, | For sin too pure, for earth too bright! | And Death, who call'd thee hence away, | Placed on his brow a gem of light! | MARGARET TO HER SISTER. | LONDON: | TILT AND BOGUE, FLEET STREET. | MDCCCXLIII.

(17.4 x 10.6): [A]^4 B-I^8 K-U^8 X-Y^8 Z^4. The last leaf is one of advertisements. Not reckoned: illustration before title; sixteen-page catalogue at end.

The illustration, MARGARET AND HER MOTHER, is in "Griffith's Chromo-Graphic process," with tissue guard. In the lower right corner: "Page 148".

Page [351], the recto of the final leaf, is given to an advertisement for *Lucretia Davidson's Poetical Remains*, UNIFORM WITH THE PRESENT VOLUME.

The catalogue, undated, paged [1] 2-16, is on a slightly smaller leaf, bound in a single gathering of 8. On p. 11 is an advertisement for "Tilt's Miniature Classics," including "Irving's Essays and Sketches."

[i]-[ii], half-title, verso blank; [iii]-[iv], title, on verso printer; [v]-viii, table of contents; [9]-171, Irving's "Memoir"; [172], blank; [173]-[174], fly-title, verso blank; [175]-350, text of the "Remains," printer at foot of 350; [351]-[352], advertisements.

Printer: B. Clarke, Silver Street, Falcon Square, London.

Lineation: p. 100, often ... setting ; p. 200, ON ... streaming.

Purple V cloth. Sides decorated in blind. Spine titled in gilt: LIFE AND | REMAINS | OF | MARGARET | DAVIDSON || WASHINGTON | IRVING

Publishers' Circular, 1 October 1842, listed. *Athenæum*, 8 October 1842, listed, 5s. in cloth. *Literary Gazette*, 8 October 1842, listed; 29 October 1842, advertised as "now ready." *Mirror* [London], 29 October 1842, excerpted and reviewed.

Note: Some misunderstanding about a first English edition has arisen from an advertisement in *The Athenæum*, 14 May 1842, p. 438, for the "3rd edition." But the advertisement is by "Wiley & Putnam, Importers of American Books" and includes works not published in England. The reference is almost certainly to imported copies of the American third edition. No edition by Wiley & Putnam has been located.

BL (2).

b.   LONDON: | DAVID BOGUE, FLEET STREET, | LATE TILT AND BOGUE. | MDCCCXLIII.

The illustration before the title appears in two states:
    A. With "Page 148" in lower right corner.
    B. Without page number in corner.

The sixteen-page terminal catalogue appears in two states:
- A.   Catalogue of Tilt and Bogue, dated MDCCCXLI, paged [1] 2-16.
- B.   Catalogue of David Bogue, late Tilt and Bogue, undated, paged [1] 2-16.

Black T cloth. On sides, in blind, decoration within elaborated border. Spine titled the same in gilt. Copies examined are now a dark black-brown, apparently the result of fading.

OrP, TxU.

c.   In *The Athenæum*, 14 December 1850, appears an advertisement by David Bogue for "Books Specially Adapted for Presents": "MARGARET DAVIDSON'S LIFE AND POETICAL REMAINS. By WASHINGTON IRVING,.... Fcap, 8vo. 5*s*. cloth." Presumably that represents a later impression, about 1850. Not located.

2Ea.   BIOGRAPHY | AND | POETICAL REMAINS | OF THE LATE | MARGARET MILLER DAVIDSON. | BY WASHINGTON IRVING. | [4-line quotation, and identification] | LONDON: | T. ALLMAN, 42, HOLBORN HILL. | [rule] | 1846.

(11.9 x 7.3): [i]-viii, [1]-344. Illustration before title reckoned. Signed in 8's.

The illustration is an engraving of a girl leaning on elbow, hand on skull, gazing soulfully up; two cherubs above.

Printer: Knight and Son, Upper Holloway.

Lineation: p. 100, Though ... residence.; p. 200, "Then ... grief.

The complete text, with "A Tale, Written at the Age of Fifteen" restored, at the end.

Purple V cloth with decoration in blind and gilt. AEG.

BL.

b.   LIFE AND RECOLLECTIONS | OF | MARGARET DAVIDSON, | AND HER POETICAL REMAINS. | BY WASHINGTON IRVING. | WITH A | Biography of Lucretia Davidson, [fancy] | BY MISS SEDGWICK. | [4-line quotation, and identification] | LONDON: | W. TEGG AND CO.; AYLOTT AND JONES; | THOMAS NELSON; PARTRIDGE AND OAKEY. | GLASGOW: W. COLLINS; GRIFFIN AND CO. All within double frame lines.

1848.

(13.0 x 8.6): [i]-viii, [1]-376. Chromo illustration and preliminary title reckoned. Signed in 8's.

The illustration is one of a boat in a moonlit scene. The chromo-lithographed preliminary title, almost obscured by rubbing and by offset from the facing illustration in the copy examined, is for MARGARET AND LUCRETIA DAVIDSON | WITH POETICAL REMAINS. | BY[?] | WASHINGTON IRVING & MISS SEDGWICK. It is on a green panel within single frame lines with flowered corners.

Printer: Knight and Son, Upper Holloway.

The text is from the same setting, except for preliminaries, to p. 316. Then "A Tale, Written at the Age of Fifteen" is omitted and two items are added: Miss Sedgwick's "Biography of Lucretia Davidson," and Lucretia Davidson's poem "Amir Khan."

Red V cloth with decoration in blind and gilt. On front, identified as "The London Domestic Library."

Literary Gazette, 28 October 1848, advertised, 2*s*. cloth, 2*s*. 6*d*. "gilt elegant."

BL.

c. BIOGRAPHY | AND | POETICAL REMAINS | OF | MARGARET DAVIDSON. | BY WASHINGTON IRVING. | [4-line quotation, and identification] | LONDON: PUBLISHED BY KNIGHT AND SON, | 11, CLERKENWELL CLOSE. All within double frame lines.

1854.

(15.1 x 9.7): [i]-viii, [1]-344. Not reckoned: preliminary title, and two engraved illustrations. All pages within double frame lines. Signed in 8's.

The decorative preliminary title has type in gold, within elaborate flowered frame in green, red and gold, all within double frame lines with boxed corners, in gold.

The text, except for preliminaries, is from the same setting throughout as the London edition of 1846 by T. Allman; that is, the Lucretia Davidson material of the 1848 impression is omitted, and "A Tale, Written at the Age of Fifteen" is restored.

Brown figured cloth: vertical lines composed of parallel horizontal short wavy lines. Sides decorated in blind. Spine titled in gilt.

Athenæum, 14 October 1854, listing for "Davidson's Biography and Poetical Remains, royal 16mo. 2*s*. 6*d*. cl." No publisher named. That is probably this impression, since the *English Catalogue of Books 1835-1863* lists the Knight printing for 1854.

BL.

TRANSLATIONS

German.

Biographie | der | jungen amerikanischen Dichterin | Margarethe M. Davidson. | [rule] | Aus dem Englischen | des | Washington Irving. | [rule] | Du wurdest früh dem Staub entrückt, | Der Erde Du zu schön und rein! | Der Tod, Dich rufend, hat geschmückt, | Sich mit dem schönsten Edelstein. | Margarethe an ihre Schwester. | [swelled rule] | Leipzig: | F. A. Brockhaus. | [rule] | 1843. [in fraktur]

(16.0 x 10.2): [i]-iv?, [1]-160. Signed in 12's.

Lineation: p. 55, ihrer ... in

NjR. Copy reported in Universitätsbibliothek Heidelberg.

A BOOK OF THE HUDSON

A Book of the Hudson is a collection of selected short pieces by Irving that have a common concern with life on the Hudson River. It was probably assembled at the suggestion of George P. Putnam, who would have been eager for a new Irving title after going into the publishing business on his own. The collection consists for the most part of reprinted material, although the Introduction and the first piece, "Communipaw," do show some new work on the part of Irving:

"Introduction." The first paragraph is reprinted from "To the Editor of the Knickerbocker," *The Knickerbocker*, March 1839; the remaining portion is original.

"Communipaw." Reprinted from *The Knickerbocker*, September 1839, but extensively revised.

"Guests from Gibbet Island." Reprinted from *The Knickerbocker*, October 1839.

"Peter Stuyvesant's Voyage Up the Hudson." Reprinted from *A History of New York.*

"The Chronicle of Bearn Island." Reprinted from *A History of New York*.

"The Legend of Sleepy Hollow." Reprinted from *The Sketch Book.*

"Dolph Heyliger." Reprinted from *Bracebridge Hall.*

"Rip Van Winkle." Reprinted from *The Sketch Book.*

"Wolfert Webber." Reprinted from *Tales of a Traveller.*

The second edition, issued in the same year, is lightly revised. The revisions noted are probably the work of the publisher rather than the author, since most are matters of spelling or occasional punctuation. The infrequent variants in word choice appear to be unintentional or perhaps the casual changes of a compositor.

The text variations in the two-page Introduction are representative:

Page & line of First edition	First edition	Second edition
[vii], first paragraph	No quotation marks at beginning and end	Quotation marks at beginning and end
[vii], 10f	Hudson river	Hudson River
[vii], 7f	this river	the river
viii, 1	handbook	hand-book

The wide variety of publisher's bindings on the second edition suggest that it continued to be issued, perhaps in later impressions, for a good many years. One copy has been noted with a presentation inscription (not by Irving) dated 1858.

Unlike Irving's other titles, this one was not published on the other side of the Atlantic.

1A.   A | BOOK OF THE HUDSON. | COLLECTED FROM THE VARIOUS WORKS OF | Diedrich Knickerbocker.   [fancy] | EDITED BY GEOFFREY CRAYON. | NEW YORK: | G. P. PUTNAM, 155 BROADWAY. | 1849.

(15.6 x 10.6): Signed [1]-[2]^{12} 3-7^{12} [8]^{12} 9^{12}, but bound [1]-[13]^8 [14]^4. In some copies examined, some gatherings are on a different wove paper that has yellowed more with time, showing clearly the original printing in 8's. The first integral leaf is a blank. Sixteen-page terminal catalogue added.

The terminal catalogue is paged [1] 2-15 [16]. The first page, headed G. P. PUTNAM'S | NEW PUBLICATIONS, is dated *March*, 1849. The last page, distinct in subject from the catalogue, is dated *November*, 1848. On p. 7, the Works in thirteen volumes are advertised, with *History of New York, The Sketch Book*, and *Columbus* already published. On p. 8: "MR. IRVING'S NEW WORKS | Now nearly ready for the press: including | The Life of Mohammed; The Life of Washington; new | volumes of Miscellanies, Biographies, &c."

[i]-[ii], half-title, verso blank; [iii]-[iv], title, on verso copyright notice (1849) and printer; [v]-[vi], table of contents, verso blank; [vii]-viii, Introduction; [11]-215, text; [216], blank.

Printer: R. Craighead, Printer and Stereotyper, 112 Fulton Street.

Lineation: p. 100, light ... the ; p. 200, chains ... money-digging;

Green TB cloth (with the grain of the cloth either vertical or horizontal). On sides, in blind, vignette of Rip Van Winkle sleeping, his gun under his hip, his dog sitting behind him, a tall cloud in the background, all within an oval frame; the whole surrounded by triple rules with ornaments within the corners; the lower ornaments carry the name of the binder: Colton and Jenkins, Binder, New York. Spine decorated in blind and titled in gilt: Book | of the | Hudson | [rule] | Irving [all in fancy type] | PUTNAM Manila endpapers. Flyleaves (in addition to integral blank at front).

Langfeld and Blackburn report copies seen in one of the second edition bindings (see description below). That is very possible, although no such copy has been located.

A variant binding, probably representing a later issue, appears with gray paper wrappers. On front, cover-title within a frame resembling columns: Price 25 cents. | [rule] | A | BOOK OF THE HUDSON. | COLLECTED FROM THE VARIOUS WORKS OF | Diedrich Knickerbocker. [fancy] | EDITED BY GEOFFREY CRAYON. | [rule] | NEW YORK: | PUBLISHED, BY ARRANGEMENT WITH THE PROPRIETORS, | BY S. COLMAN, 55 WILLIAM ST. | Wholesale Agent and Publisher. | [rule] | 1849. On back, advertisements by G. P. Putnam for Irving's Works; Vols. XI-XV are marked "not yet ready, June, 1849" and Vol. XV is identified only as "[A new volume.]." On spine: Book | of the | Hudson [fancy]. The regular title and the contents are the same, but the terminal catalogue is omitted.

Literary World, 17 March 1849, "Nearly ready"; 14 April 1849, "Just published," in cloth at 63 cents (the advertisement reprints the conclusion of the Introduction); 21 April 1849, "Published on Saturday, April 14," reviewed.

NN, TxU (3), ViU, *BL*. In paper wrapper, ViU.

2A.   A | BOOK OF THE HUDSON. | COLLECTED FROM THE VARIOUS WORKS OF | Diedrich Knickerbocker. [fancy] | EDITED BY | GEOFFREY CRAYON | NEW-YORK: | G. P. PUTNAM, 155 BROADWAY. | 1849.

(14.6 x 10.3): [1]^8 2-17^8 18^6. Not reckoned: lithographed vignette title and three lithographed illustrations.

[i]-[ii], half-title, verso blank; [iii]-[iv], title, on verso copyright (1849) and printer; [v]-[vi], table of contents, verso blank; [vii]-viii, Introduction; [9]-283, text; [284], blank.

Printer: John F. Trow, Printer & Stereotyper, 49 Ann-street.

Lineation: p. 100, hard ... in ; p. 200, handbills, ... bystanders --

The second edition has been seen or reported in a bewildering variety of cloths, colors, and design elements. A new vignette stamping appears on the edition: Rip Van Winkle sleeping, his gun under his hip (but with the trigger toward his feet rather than toward his head), his dog lying with his head on Rip (rather than sitting), no tall cloud in the background, and the vignette not within an oval frame. Some states of the binding also add, in blind, branches, flowers, and a V-shaped tulip-like flower above and below the vignette, all within triple frame lines in blind. Some states have only the triple frame. The vignette itself, on front and back, appears both in gilt and in blind or in a combination of the two. On the spine, some copies retain the original title, *Book of the Hudson*, some change it to *Tales of the Hudson*, the latter noted in two different type styles. Copies have also been reported in the design of the first edition. The various cloths include T cloth in blue, purple, slate, brown; TB cloth in green; and A cloth in green, blue, slate, brown. Edges may be gilt or plain. With so many variables -- and probably others yet to be discovered -- there seems little point in describing the many combinations known to exist.

DLC, MB, NN (2), TxU (2), ViU.

MAHOMET AND HIS SUCCESSORS

As early as November 1827, while in Spain, Irving began work on a "Legend of Mahomet," a short version of what was to be the Life of Mahomet. In the fall of 1832 he offered a book-length version to John Murray, his English publisher. On 4 October 1832, believing that he had a verbal agreement with Murray to publish the work, he wrote Murray that Col. Aspinwall would deliver the first twenty-one chapters. And on 22 October he wrote Aspinwall, "The Mahomet is entirely ready...." Apparently he did deliver a complete manuscript, "in the rough," but Murray was hardly carried away by enthusiasm and acknowledged no agreement to publish. On 29 October Irving wrote, in some irritation, that he would "postpone for a time the publication of Mahomet." In fact, the work was not to be published for another seventeen years.

By October 1848, Irving was at work revising the manuscript for publication in the Author's Revised Edition being published by George P. Putnam in New York; he seems also to have worked on it earlier, in 1845-46. For the first volume of *Mahomet and His Successors*, he expanded the manuscript to nearly twice its earlier length, adding new material from the scholarly work on the life of Mahomet that had appeared during the century. (The manuscript of 1832 has survived in large part,, although only a small fragment of the manuscript of 1849.) The second volume, *The Successors of Mahomet*, Irving seems to have written hurriedly in later 1849 and early 1850, although drawing on earlier notes and information and interests. Typically, he seems to have continued revising and correcting on the proofs until the last minute.

Once published in 1849-1850, the textual history of *Mahomet and His Successors* is a simple one. After the work's first appearance in America, the text remained unchanged, except for a few minor emendations, for the rest of its history. Murray's London edition of 1850 -- he did after all finally publish it, but only as second publisher -- was printed from corrected American plates. And the partially reset Putnam edition-impression of 1857 shows no signs of authorial revision. The complications arise in recording the printing history. For the two volumes are separate works separately published -- each with its distinct character -- and yet also are two related parts of a two-volume work. To list them individually obscures the relationship between the pair as parts of an extended work; to list them together as a pair obscures the chronology of printing and the critical differences between the volumes.

After the first impressions, called Volume I and Volume II but published at different times, Putnam clearly considered the two volumes as a single work, as his title implies, and published them together. (Although it should be pointed out that mixed sets, with different dates on the two volumes, are common in the first years.) In England, John Murray issued only the one separate impression of each volume as the plates became available, but he used the common title for the set and separate titles for each volume. Henry G. Bohn, on the other hand, treated each volume as a separate work, avoiding a common title and the designation as Volume I or Volume II, and reprinted them as needed for his "Shilling Series"; yet he also bound them together as a pair in his "Library Edition." Here the two volumes are listed chronologically by publisher, the order following the date of publication of the first volume. The method of listing, as one work or two, follows the distinction chosen by the publisher. The rationale may seem a little obscure, but the listing itself is, I hope, clear enough.

1Aa-　MAHOMET | AND | HIS SUCCESSORS. | BY | WASHINGTON
b.　IRVING. | IN TWO VOLUMES. | VOL. I. [II.] | NEW-YORK: | GEORGE P. PUTNAM, 155 BROADWAY. | M.DCCC.L.

(18.8 x 12.9): Vol. I. $[-]^2$ $[1]^{12}$ $2\text{-}15^{12}$ 16^{10}. See the discussion below of variants in Sig. 16. Not reckoned: terminal catalogue in various forms. Vol. II. $[-]^2$ $1\text{-}20^{12}$ 21^{10}.

Vol. I. [a]-[b], Works title for Vol. XII (see the discussion below), verso blank; [c]-[d], title, on verso copyright (1849) and printer; [i]-vii, table of contents; [viii], blank; [ix]-xi, Preface, dated 1849; [xii], blank; [13]-373, text; [374], blank. See the discussion below of advertisements and terminal catalogue. Vol. II. [a]-[b], Works title for Vol. XIII, verso blank; [c]-[d], title, on verso copyright (1850) and printer; [i]-viii, table of contents; [ix]-xii, Preface, dated 1850; [13]-500, text.

Printer: John F. Trow, Printer and Stereotyper, 49 and 51 Ann-st., New-York.

Lineation: Vol. I. p. 100, rebuked ... circuits ; p. 200, and, ... in Vol. II. p. 100, Feeling ... the ; p. 200, and ... and

Volume I appears in a number of variant states of different sorts: states of the text, of collation, of advertisements, of works title, and of terminal publisher's catalogue. For distinctions between the first and later impressions, see the conclusion of the discussion of Vol. I. No variants have been noted in Vol. II.

Volume I

Nine pages appear in two text states:

Page & Line	Signature	First state	Second state
37.10	2	Ararat	*Arafat*
175.5	8	Jaffar	*Jaafar*
182.1	8	Kaled	*Khaled*
209.1	9	Hoyai	*Hoya*
212.12-13	9	of the / [blank]	*of the / Sword*
225.13-14	10	eyes Ma- / homet	*eyes of Ma- / homet*
265.10	12	Amir	*Musa*
333 & 335. running head	14	IMPORTANCE	*IMPOSTURE*

The distinction between states should be made in terms of individual pages rather than of the complete volume, since whole volumes are more often than not in mixed states. And the distinction should be made in terms of pages rather than of whole signatures, if only because of the complications exhibited in Signature 9. In that signature, copies have been seen in four different combinations of first and second state readings. If the two changes within the signature were made progessively, only three combinations would be possible. It is conceivable that one change was returned again to its original reading -- for instance, the dropped word "Sword" that constitutes the whole of line 13 of page 212 might somehow have been dropped again -- but it does not seem very probable. A more satisfactory explanation might at first seem offered by duplicate plates. (It is known that one set of duplicate plates was made for the London edition.) But it is difficult to see how individual pages from duplicate plates would be mixed in binding the same signature. I can only point out that four combinations of readings do exist.

Of the thirteen copies examined in detail, none exhibited all first state readings and only two all second state. But if the vexing variant on p. 212 is ignored, four copies were all in first state, four copies all in second state, and five copies in mixed states.

Signature 16 appears in two Collation states: a gathering of 10 leaves or a gathering of 8 leaves. (The two collations may be distinguished easily by noting whether the binding strings appear between pp. 370-371 or pp. 368-369.) Publisher's advertisements follow in various forms, some integral and some not; some copies lack advertisements altogether. The two states of Signature 16 and the various forms of the advertisements create six combinations in the copies examined; no sequence is clear, and the order here is for convenience only:

[A]. 16^{10}. The last three integral leaves of the signature bear advertisements variously paged:

[a]. 17A, 18-22.

[b]. 16, 15, 19, 20, 22, 7.

[c]. 34-39.

[B]. 16^{10}, with the last three leaves of the signature excised.   No advertisements.

[C]. 16^8. The last integral leaf of the signature bears advertisements paged 7, 8.

[D]. 16^8. The last integral leaf of the signature bears advertisements paged 7, 8; followed by another leaf of advertisements, not integral, paged 1,2.

Other combinations may exist.

The preliminary Works title appears in two states:

1. MAHOMET AND HIS SUCCESSORS. / VOL. XII.

2. VOL. XII. / MAHOMET AND HIS SUCCESSORS.

The sequence is clear when the two works titles are compared with the prevailing text states.

A publisher's catalogue bound at the end of the volume appears in three forms:

A.   Dated July 1849; paged 1-36. On p. 15 is a list of 15 vols. of Irving's Works, Author's Revised Edition; No. XV is "A new volume"; Nos. XI-XV are marked "not yet ready, June, 1849."

B.   Undated; paged 1-17, 17A, 18-23, 23-43, [44]-[45], [46] blank. On p. 19 is a list of 16 vols. of Irving's Works; No. XVI is "A NEW VOLUME" and Nos. XIV-XVI are "not yet ready."

C.   Undated; paged 1-13, 13A, 14-17, 17A, 18-[45], [46] blank; else the same as State B.

Some copies have no catalogue.

State A is clearly the earliest version, and all copies seen in the predominately first Text states have contained that version or no catalogue at all. States B and C are later, but their sequence in relation to each other, if any sequence exists, is not known. It is likely, as always, that catalogues were chosen at random from those available at the time of binding.

When all of the combinations of all of the variables of Volume I are considered, some general conclusions can be reached. A copy in the first Text states, with Works title 1 and Catalogue A, is almost certainly a first impression copy. A copy in the second Text states, with Works title 2 and Catalogue B or C, is almost certainly a second or later impression. The various collation states of Signature 16, and the various forms of the advertisements, may appear in either an earlier or a later copy. There were certainly two impressions dated 1850 on the title. Whether there were other impressions dated 1850 remains open to question.

Two external facts may be revealing when considering the question of later impressions. First, an advertisement for the first edition of Vol. I in *The Albion*, 8 December 1849, states, "The second edition cannot be ready before January." That would seem to point to what we would call a second impression early in 1850. Second, no copy of an impression of Vol. I dated 1851 on the title page has been located, despite an extensive search. (Vol. II dated 1851 is often paired with a Vol. I dated 1850 to make a complete set of the two volumes.) It is a reasonable conjecture that Putnam thought that he would need extra copies of Vol. I to pair with Vol. II when it appeared. He then optimistically reprinted in relatively large numbers, only to find later that he had enough copies on hand to satisfy the demand for Vol. I through 1851. That would be particularly likely if the work did not sell as well as expected.

Both Volumes

Blue-green, or occasionally green, TB cloth. On sides, in blind, publisher's initials in decorative design within border. Spines decorated in blind, titled in gilt. Vol. I: IRVING'S | WORKS | [rule] | MAHOMET   Vol. II: IRVING'S | WORKS | [rule] | MAHOMET'S SUCCESSORS   Cream-yellow or cream-buff endpapers. Some copies noted with publisher's advertisements on white endpapers; this probably is a later binding.

Vol. I. *Literary World*, 15 December 1849, "this week"; 22 December 1849, reviewed. *Albion*, 8 December 1849, extracted, "to be published next week"; 15 December 1849, "will be ready on Saturday, Dec. 15th." Vol. II. *Literary World*, 9 March 1850, "will be ready on April 1"; 6 April 1850, "this week."

Discussion based on copies in CtY (2), DLC, ICN, MH (3), MWA, NN, TxU (2), ViU (2), and private hands. Early impression: MH, TxU. Late impression: CtY, ViU.

c.   NEW-YORK: | GEORGE   P.   PUTNAM,   155   BROADWAY. |
     M.DCCC.LI.

Seen only in Vol. II, paired with a Vol. I dated M.DCCC.L. See the discussion above of the first two impressions. A copy of Vol. I dated 1851 may yet be found, of course.

Works title for Vol. II, dated 1851: VOL. XIII. | MAHOMET AND HIS SUCCESSORS.

TxU.

d. NEW-YORK: | GEORGE P. PUTNAM, 155 BROADWAY. | M.DCCC.LII.

Works titles, dated 1852.

Vol. I seen in private hands. Complete copy reported in PPGi.

e. NEW-YORK: | G. P. PUTNAM & COMPANY, 10 PARK PLACE. | 1853.

Works titles, dated 1853.

ViU.

f. NEW-YORK: | G. P. PUTNAM & COMPANY, 10 PARK PLACE. | 1854.

Works titles, dated 1854.

TxU.

g. NEW-YORK: | G. P. PUTNAM & COMPANY, 10 PARK PLACE. | 1855.

Works titles, dated 1855.

DLC.

h. New York: [fancy] | G. P. PUTNAM & CO., 321 BROADWAY. | 1857.

Works titles, dated 1857.

Partially reset and replated: 229 pages of Vol. I, and 8 pages of Vol. II. Minor changes appear in the reset pages, almost certainly the work of the publisher. The resetting caused an occasional shift in lineation: Vol. I. p. 100, rebuked ... circuits (the same lineation as that of the first impression, although the page is reset); p. 200, friends ... too (new lineation in this new setting). Vol. II. p. 100 and p. 200 are not reset.

MH.

i. NEW YORK: | G. P. PUTNAM, 115 NASSAU STREET. | 1859.

Works titles, dated 1859.

In the new partial resetting.

Two engraved illustrations added before the title of Vol. I, published by Childs & Peterson, Philadelphia. One added before the title of Vol. II, no publisher named.

Green BD cloth. On sides, frame in blind. On spine, extra decoration in gilt around title. Green endpapers.

TxU.

j. NEW YORK: | G. P. PUTNAM (for the Proprietor), 506 BROADWAY. | 1859.

Rebound copy seen lacks works title. Probably so issued.

In the new partial resetting.

TxU.

1E. LIVES OF MAHOMET | AND | HIS SUCCESSORS. | BY WASHINGTON IRVING. | IN TWO VOLUMES. -- VOL. I. [II.] | LONDON: | JOHN MURRAY, ALBEMARLE STREET. | 1850. All within single frame lines.

Each volume also has an individual title page:

LIFE | OF | MAHOMET. | BY WASHINGTON IRVING. | LONDON: | JOHN MURRAY, ALBEMARLE STREET. | 1850. All within single frame lines.

LIVES | OF THE | SUCCESSORS OF MAHOMET. | BY WASHINGTON IRVING. | LONDON: | JOHN MURRAY, ALBEMARLE STREET. | 1850. All within single frame lines.

Printed from duplicate plates of Putnam's first American edition, with preliminary matter reset and rearranged, and signatures signed in 8's rather than 12's. The publisher -- or perhaps publishers -- also made minor emendations in the plates.

Each of the nine readings listed in the discussion of the textual variants in the first American edition appears here in its first Text state, with the exception of the name "Mount Arafat" (37.10) which appears in its second Text state.

(22.2 x 14.2): Vol. I. [A]^8 B-I^8 K-U^8 X-Z^8 AA^4 [BB]^2. The last leaf carries advertisements. Not reckoned: eight leaves of terminal catalogue. Vol. II. [-]^8 A-I^8 K-U^8 X-Z^8 2A-2H^8 21^2. Not reckoned: eight leaves of terminal catalogue.

Vol. I. [i]-[ii], common title, verso blank; [iii]-[iv], individual volume title, on verso printer; [v]-vii, Preface; [viii], blank; [ix]-xv, table of contents; [xvi], blank; [13]-373, text, printer at foot of last page; [374], notice: TO BE FOLLOWED IMMEDIATELY BY | THE SUCCESSORS OF

MAHOMET.; [375]-[376], advertisements. Vol. II. [i]-[ii], individual volume title, verso blank; [iii]-[iv], common title, on verso printer; [v]-viii, Preface; [ix]-xvi, table of contents; [13]-500, text, printer at foot of last page. Single frame lines around all pages of both volumes.

In Vol. I, the advertisements on p. [375] list 11 titles by Irving, including LIFE OF GENERAL WASHINGTON and A NEW SERIES OF THE SKETCH BOOK described as "In the Press"; Knickerbocker's History, Granada, Crayon Miscellany described as "Nearly Ready." Also in Vol. I, the terminal Murray catalogue, dated January 1850, paged [1]-16, lists on p. 12, Life of Mahomet, "Now Ready"; Successors of Mahomet, "in March."

In Vol. II, the terminal Murray catalogue, dated January 1850, paged [1]-16, is apparently an earlier state of the catalogue. On p. 12, Life of Mahomet is listed as "in January"; Successors of Mahomet as "in March." Langfeld and Blackburn also report a copy of the catalogue dated July 1850 and mention one dated October 1849.

Printer: Bradbury and Evans, Whitefriars.

Lineation: Vol. I. p. 100, rebuked ... circuits ; p. 200, and, ... in Vol. II. p. 100, Feeling ... the ; p. 200, and ... and

Green S cloth. Sides decorated in blind. Spines decorated in blind and titled in gilt: MAHOMET | AND HIS | SUCCESSORS | [rule] | I. [II.] | WASHINGTON IRVING || LONDON | JOHN MURRAY Manilla or yellow endpapers.

The records of the Murray firm list a single printing of 1000 copies of each volume.

Vol. I. In the Register Book of the Stationers' Company, John Murray gives 26 January 1850 as the publication date. Athenæum, 19 January 1850, "Vol. I next week"; 26 January 1850, advertised in "Mr. Murray's List." Examiner, 26 January 1850, "This day is published." Literary Gazette, 26 January 1850, reviewed.

Vol. II. In the Register Book of the Stationers' Company, John Murray gives 28 March 1850 as the publication date. Athenæum, 9 March 1850, "Vol. II next week"; 16 March 1850, "On the 20th"; 23 March 1850, advertised. Examiner, 30 March 1850, "This day." Literary Gazette, 6 April 1850, listed; 13 April 1850, reviewed.

TxU (2), Private hands.

2E.   LIFE | OF | MAHOMET. | BY | WASHINGTON IRVING. | [rule] | LONDON: | HENRY G. BOHN, YORK STREET, COVENT GARDEN. | 1850.

See the description below of another edition by Bohn with the same title page. Both editions were issued individually, almost certainly as No. II of "Bohn's Shilling Series," and both almost certainly were issued bound with *The Successors of Mahomet* as Vol. IX of "Bohn's Library Edition." (The hesitancy to assign them absolutely to the two series arises only from my inability to find the four forms in original binding.) The edition described below, with 216 pages of text rather than 224 pages, is surely the second edition, since the impressions of 1852 and 1855 are in that setting.

Why Bohn should have issued two editions of a title that, for John Murray at least, earned only moderate sales is not known. The explanation may lie in the suit for infringement of copyright that Murray brought against Bohn at about this time.

On p. [iii], an "Advertisement" addresses the lack of international copyright. Speaking of this work, it says, "As it was published at New York in December last, imported and sold here in January, ... no one can reasonably complain of a competition...."

(17.8 x 11.1): [i]-viii, [1]-224. Not reckoned: preliminary engraved portrait of Mohammed (sic) by Duflos and Hinchcliff. Signed in 8's.

Printer: C. Whiting, Beaufort House, Strand.

Lineation: p. 100, been ... while ; p. 200, CHAPTER XXXIX. ... so

Noted in original binding in "Bohn's Library Edition." Red AR cloth. This is a variant binding; normally the series seems to have been issued in gray T cloth. No series title. Sides decorated in blind. Spine titled in gilt as Irving's Works, Vol. IX, Bohn's Library Edition. White endpapers with advertisements in blue.

Shilling Series. *Athenæum*, 23 February 1850, in "List of New Books," 1*s*. 6*d*. in boards. Library Edition. *Publishers' Circular*, 15 May 1850, listed. Which of the two editions is represented by the listings cannot be known but presumably is the first.

Shilling Series: TxU. Library Edition: Private hands.

3Ea. LIFE | OF | MAHOMET. | BY | WASHINGTON IRVING. | [rule] | LONDON: | HENRY G. BOHN, YORK STREET, COVENT GARDEN. | 1850.

(16.4 x 10.9): [i]-viii, [1]-216. Not reckoned: preliminary engraved portrait of Mohammed (sic) by Duflos and Hinchcliff. Signed in 8's.

See the discussion above of the first Bohn edition. This edition also contains the publisher's "Advertisement" about copyright.

Printer: C. Whiting, Beaufort House, Strand.

Lineation: p. 100, been ... while ; p. 200, in ... prophet.

Seen in original binding only in "Bohn's Library Edition," bound with *Lives of the Successors of Mahomet*. Gray T cloth. Sides decorated in blind. Spine titled in gilt as Irving's Works, Vol. IX, Bohn's Library Edition. White endpapers with advertisements in blue.

DLC as single volume, not original binding. Private hands, Library Edition.

b. LONDON: | HENRY G. BOHN, YORK STREET, COVENT GARDEN. | 1852.

Four pages of advertisements in blue bound at end.

BL.

c. LONDON: | HENRY G. BOHN, YORK STREET, COVENT GARDEN. | 1855.

Seen both in the individual volume of the "Shilling Series" and in the "Library Edition," bound with *The Successors of Mahomet*, Bohn, 1850. Series title, dated 1854: IN TEN VOLUMES. | VOL. IX. | MAHOMET AND HIS SUCCESSORS.

Shilling Series: *BL*. Library Edition: MB.

2E. LIVES | OF THE | SUCCESSORS OF MAHOMET. | BY | WASHINGTON IRVING. | [rule] | LONDON: | HENRY G. BOHN, YORK STREET, COVENT GARDEN. | 1850.

(17.8 x 11.1): [i]-viii, [1]-268. Signed in 8's.

Issued individually as Vol. V of "Bohn's Shilling Series"; bound with *Life of Mahomet* as Vol. IX of "Bohn's Library Edition."

Printer: C. Whiting, Beaufort House, Strand.

Lineation: p. 100, which ... he ; p. 200, deserts, ... the

Noted in original bindings only in "Bohn's Library Edition." Gray T cloth. Sides decorated in blind. Spine titled in gilt as Irving's Works, Vol. IX, Bohn's Library Edition. White endpapers with advertisements in blue. Also in red AR cloth, a variant cloth, with the same design.

Shilling Series. *Athenæum*, 20 April 1850, in "List of New Books," 1*s*. 6*d*. in boards. Library Series. *Publishers' Circular*, 15 May 1850, listed.

Shilling Series: *BL*, MB, TxU. Library Series: MB (with 1855 *Life*), NN, Private hands.

4Ea. THE | LIFE OF MAHOMET. | BY | WASHINGTON IRVING. | [rule] | LONDON | GEORGE ROUTLEDGE & CO., SOHO SQUARE. | 1850.

Seen only bound with *The Successors of Mahomet*, "Third Edition," 1850. The edition was, however, first issued as a single volume in Routledge's "Popular Library." Some copies of the combined volumes have a common title page: LIVES OF MAHOMET | AND | HIS SUCCESSORS.| BY WASHINGTON IRVING. | [rule] | LONDON: | GEORGE ROUTLEDGE & CO., SOHO SQUARE. | 1850. In such copies, or at least in the one examined, the first volume, the *Life*, has no separate title page.

(16.2 x 10.2 rebound): [i]-x, [1]-214. Signed in 8's.

Printer: Savill & Edwards, 4, Chandos Street.

Lineation: p. 100, for ... in ; p. 200, cepts ... and

Seen only rebound. Other single volumes in the series noted in paper boards printed in colors, or in brown AR cloth, sides decorated in darker brown with series name at center, spine titled in gilt.

Athenæum, 23 March 1850, "New volume," 1*s*.; in cloth gilt, 1*s*. 6*d*.

NN, TxU.

b.   LONDON | GEORGE ROUTLEDGE & CO., SOHO SQUARE. | 1851.

Routledge's "Popular Library." Seen as a single volume, and also bound with *The Successors of Mahomet*, "Third Edition," 1850.

One page of advertisements bound before title page.

BL (single volume), TxU (bound with *Successors*).

3Ea. LIVES | OF | THE SUCCESSORS | OF | MAHOMET. | BY WASHINGTON IRVING | [rule] | LONDON: | GEORGE ROUTLEDGE & CO., SOHO SQUARE. | 1850.

Issued as a single volume in Routledge's "Popular Library." Presumably also issued bound with *The Life of Mahomet* as a combined volume, although not seen in that form.

(16.6 x 10.5): [i]-viii, [1]-263 [264]. Page iv mispaged vi. Signed in 8's.

Printer: Savill and Edwards, Chandos Street, Covent Garden.

Lineation: p. 100, progenitor, ... Ab-; p. 200, not ... and

Red paper boards. On front, cover-title with elaborate wreath design woven through it; identified as "The Popular Library," priced at One shilling. On back, advertisement for "The Railway Library." Spine titled in black. Advertisements on endpapers.

Also advertised in cloth, gilt, at 1*s*. 6*d*.

Athenæum, 13 April 1850, "New volume."

CtY (in boards), *BL*.

b. *THIRD EDITION.* | LONDON: | GEORGE ROUTLEDGE & CO., SOHO SQUARE. | 1850.

In the same setting as the first impression. Page iv is still mispaged vi.

Seen only bound with *The Life of Mahomet*, 1850 or 1851.

If this is the third Routledge impression, a second impression must exist, although none has been located. Perhaps it is not identified on the title page.

NN, TxU.

1F. LIVES | OF | MAHOMET | AND | HIS SUCCESSORS. | BY | WASHINGTON IRVING. | [emblem: BEL intertwined] | PARIS, | [in parallel columns, with vertical rule between; in first column:] BAUDRY'S EUROPEAN LIBRARY, | 3, QUAI MALAQUAIS, AU 1er ÉTAGE. || [in second column:] A. AND W. GALIGNANI AND Co., | 18, RUE VIVIENNE. || [rule] | 1850.

"Collection of Ancient and Modern British Authors," Vol. CCCCXLIX.

(21.4 x 13.3): [-]^6 1-24^8.

[I]-[II], half-title, on verso printer; [III]-[IV], title, verso blank; [V]-VI, Preface; [VII]-XI, table of contents; [XII], blank; [1]-159, text of *The Life of Mahomet*; [160], blank; [161]-384, divisional title and text of *The Successors of Mahomet*.

Printer: E. Thunot and Co. Rue Racine, 26, near the Odéon.

Lineation: p. 100, through ... Greeks.; p. 200, Allah!" ... piteous

NN, TxU.

1G. THE | LIFE OF MAHOMET. | BY | WASHINGTON IRVING. | *Published for the Continent of Europe by contract with the Author.* | LEIPZIG | BERNHARD TAUCHNITZ | 1850.

"Collection of British Authors," Vol. CXCI.

The title page described, that of the copies seen, is not the title page of the first impression. An earlier state is represented by a copy reported in the Bibliothèque Nationale in which the publisher is given as BERNH. TAUCHNITZ JUN. On verso of the series title of the copies seen, a list of Tauchnitz editions of Irving includes *Wolfert's Roost* and *Life of Washington* in 5 vols., defining the state described as one of 1859 or later.

(15.5 x 11.1): [I]-X, [1]-302. Signed in 8's.

Lineation: p. 100, the ... Koreishites ; p. 200, occasion, ... house

White paper wrapper. On front, cover-title. On back and on inside of wrapper leaves, advertisements. In the wrapper seen, the advertisements for Irving's works also include *Wolfert's Roost* and *Life of Washington* in 5 vols.

BL (with wrapper bound in), NN, TxU, Private hands.

1G.   LIVES | OF THE | SUCCESSORS OF MAHOMET. | BY | WASHINGTON IRVING. | *Published for the Continent of Europe by contract with the Author.* | LEIPZIG | BERNH. TAUCHNITZ JUN. | 1850.

"Collection of British Authors," Vol. CXCII.

(16.2 x 11.2): [I]-XIV, [1]-404. Signed in 8's.

Lineation: p. 100, well ... replied ; p. 200, palace ... built

Issued in white paper wrapper with cover-title on front. Seen only rebound.

In a later state seen, the publisher's name on the title page is given as BERNHARD TAUCHNITZ, and on the verso of the series title a list of Tauchnitz editions of Irving includes *Wolfert's Roost* and *Life of Washington* in 5 vols., defining the state as one of 1859 or later.

Early state, Private hands. Later state, ViU.

TRANSLATIONS

Danish.

Mahomeds Levnet. | Af | WASHINGTON IRVING. | Oversat fra Engelsk | af | L. Moltke. | [stylized rule] | [stylized swelled rule] | Kjøbenhavn. | Forlagt af K. Schønberg. | Cohens Bogtrikkeri. | 1858. [in fraktur]

(17.1 x 11.0): [i]-[iv] unpaged, [1]-306. Signed in 8's.

Lineation: p. 100, Awsiterne, ... ved ; p. 200, han, ... djoevelsk

Noted in bright blue A cloth. Sides bordered in blind. Spine titled in gilt. Buff endpapers. Publisher's binding?

NN.

German.

[Das Leben Mohammed's, von Washington Irving. Leipzig: Carl B. Lorck, 1850.]

"Historische Hausbibliothek," Bd. 16.

Translated by Prof. Dr. Friedrich Bülau.

254 pp. Preliminary engraving of Mohammed. Signed in 8's.

Text apparently abridged.

Not seen. Listed in W. Heinsius, *Algemeines Bücher-Lexicon, 1847-1851* and in C. G. Kayser, *Vollständiges Bücher-Lexicon, 1847-1852.* Copy reported in Bibliothèque Nationale, and in Stadtbibliothek München.

Cover-title: Geschichte | der | Kalifen | von | Washington Irving. | [illustration of armed Arab on horseback] | [elaborated swelled rule] | Leipzig 1854. | Expedition der Hausbibliothek | Carl B. Lorck. All within border of double frame lines with decorative corners. [in fraktur]

"Historische Hausbibliothek," Bd. 33.

Translated by Prof. Dr. Friedrich Bülau.

Inner title missing in copy examined. There the book's title is given as "Geschichte der Kalifen, vom Tode Mohammed's bis zum Einfall in Spanien."

(20.3 x 12.7 untrimmed): [I]-VIII, [1]-333 [334]. 2 pp. of terminal advertisements. Signed in 8's.

Text abridged to 12 chapters.

Printer: Fr. Ries, Leipzig.

Lineation: p. 100, einer ... beherrschte ; p. 200, Ommiah ... ferngewesen,

Light gray paper wrapper. On front, the cover-title described. On back, illustration of a writer in classical robes with an angel behind blowing a trumpet, all within the same border. Spine titled within rectangles formed by ornate borders.

TxU. Copy reported in Stadtbibliothek München.

Italian.

[*Vita di Maometto*. Versione di Giuseppe de Tivoli. Milano: Guglielmini, 1854.]

Not located. Listed by Williams and Edge, but not seen by them.

Polish.

KORAN | (AL-KORAN) [elaborated decorative letters] | Z ARABSKIEGO PRZEKŁAD POLSKI | JANA MURZY TARAK BUCZACKIEGO, | TATARA Z PODLASIA. | WZBOGACONY OBJASNIENIAMI WŁADYSŁAWA KOSCIUSKI. | POPRZEDZONY | ZYCIORYSEM MAHOMETA | Z WASHINGTONA IRVINGA. |

POMNOŻONY | POGLADEM NA STOSUNKI POLSKI Z TURCJA, I TATARAMI, NA DZIEJE TATARÓW | W POLSCE OSIADLYCH, NA PRZYWILEJE TU IM NADANE, JAKO TEŻ | WSPOMNIENIAMI O ZNAKOMITYCH TATARACH POLSKICH | JULIANA BARTOSZEWICZA. | [8 lines of description of contents of the work] | TOM I. | WARSZAWA. | NAKŁADEM ALEKSANDRA NOWOLECKIEGO, KSIĘGARZA. | PRZY ROGU ULIC KRAKOWSKIE-PRZEDMIESCIE I SENATORSKIEJ | WPROST KOLUMNY ZYGMUNTA N. 457. | [rule] | 1858.

Irving's Life of Mahomet appears in Vol. I of the larger work.

(21.1 x 13.9): [4 pp. unpaged], [pages numbered to VIII], [1?]-142, [2 pp. unpaged]. 8vo.

Not examined. Information based on copy in Biblioteka Narodowa, Warsaw.

Russian.

[Translated title:] Life of Mahomet. | [rule] | by | Washington Irving. | [rule] | Translated from the English | by Peter Kirieski. | [elaborated swelled rule] | Moscow. | The University Press. | 1857. [in Cyrillic]

(22.8 x 15.2): [i]-[iv], [1]-290 [291]-[292]. Signed in 8's.

Lineation: p. 200, serdia, ... Pesianina.

DLC.

Spanish.

HISTORIA | DE MAHOMA. | ESCRITA EN INGLES | Por Washington Irving. [fancy] | Traducida al español | POR J. S. FACIO. | [rule] | Edicion del "Diario de Avisos." | [rule] | MEXICO. | IMPRENTA DE VINCENTE SEGURA, | *calle de S. Andrés N.* 14. | [rule] | 1857.

(16.1 x 11.1): [I]-V [VI], [7]-338. Signed in 8's.

Lineation: p. 100, poco ... Corán.; p. 200, CAPITULO XXII. ... Ibn-Obba.

TxU.

WOLFERT'S ROOST

When George P. Putnam brought out this collection of reprinted material, the book was probably the result of Putnam's own desire for a new Irving title. Irving no doubt needed the income it would bring, but he was immersed then in writing the *Life of Washington* and probably had no desire to take on a new work. As Putnam himself said in *Harper's*, May 1871, he had to "entice" the papers from Irving's drawer, since "I doubt whether he would have collected them himself." Irving, as always, was conscientious enough; he revised four old sketches with some care and touched up others. But in general he seems to have given the preparation of the volume no great time or attention: most of the pieces are all but untouched, and the volume shows little evidence of careful proofreading (although a few verbal changes seem to have been made in the proof). And once issued in 1855, the plates remained unchanged through the rest of Irving's lifetime. The volume was, after all, simply a collection of writing from Irving's past.

The contents, and the first publication of each piece:

WOLFERT'S ROOST. (*The Knickerbocker*, April 1839). Thoroughly revised.

THE BIRDS OF SPRING. (*The Knickerbocker*, May 1839). Thoroughly revised.

THE CREOLE VILLAGE. (*The Magnolia* for 1837).

MOUNTJOY. (*The Knickerbocker*, November-December 1839).

THE BERMUDAS,

The Three Kings of Bermuda. (*The Knickerbocker*, January 1840).

THE WIDOW'S ORDEAL. (*The Magnolia* for 1837).

THE KNIGHT OF MALTA,

The Grand Prior of Minorca. (*The Knickerbocker*, February 1840).

A TIME OF UNEXAMPLED PROSPERITY,

The Great Mississippi Bubble. (*The Rough-Hewer*, Albany, N. Y., 20 February 1840, and *The Knickerbocker*, April 1840).

SKETCHES IN PARIS IN 1825,

The Parisian Hotel

My French Neighbor

The Englishman at Paris

English and French Character

The Tuilleries and Windsor Castle

The Field of Waterloo

Paris at the Restoration. (*The Knickerbocker*, November-December 1840).

A CONTENTED MAN. (*The Literary Souvenir* for 1827, London, and The *New-York American*, 22 December 1826, as "The Contented Man").

BROEK: OR THE DUTCH PARADISE. (*The Knickerbocker*, January 1841).

GUESTS FROM GIBBET-ISLAND. (*The Knickerbocker*, October 1839).

THE EARLY EXPERIENCES OF RALPH RINGWOOD. (*The Knickerbocker*, August-September 1840).

THE SEMINOLES,

Origin of the White, the Red, and the Black Men

The Conspiracy of Neamathla. (*The Knickerbocker*, October 1840).

THE COUNT VAN HORN. (*The Knickerbocker*, March 1840).

DON JUAN: A SPECTRAL RESEARCH. (*The Knickerbocker*, March 1841).

LEGEND OF THE ENGULPHED CONVENT. (*The Knickerbocker*, March 1840).

THE PHANTOM ISLAND,

The Adalantado of the Seven Cities. (*The Knickerbocker*, July 1839, as "The Enchanted Island"). Thoroughly revised.

RECOLLECTIONS OF THE ALHAMBRA,

The Abencerrage. (*The Knickerbocker*, June 1839). Thoroughly revised.

In January 1855, nearly a month before Putnam's edition in February, Thomas Constable brought out the work in Edinburgh. The immediate source of the text is not certain. Irving's practice in earlier works had been to provide a duplicate manuscript for the publisher on the other side of the

Atlantic, and he probably followed the practice here again. The small differences in the two texts would then be explained by his continuing to touch up the American text after he had sent off the British copy, and by any small changes he made in the American proof. (There is no evidence that he read proof on the Edinburgh edition.) The theory is strengthened by the fact that when small substantive differences appear, particularly in pieces not thoroughly revised, the Edinburgh text is likely to be that of the original periodical publication. In "The Tuileries and Windsor Castle," for instance, the American edition on p. 205, line 17 reads "jingling spurs," but the Edinburgh edition on p. 185, line 29 reads "jingling spears," the error which also appears in *The Knickerbocker.* Constable also imposed British house styling: "My French Neighbor," for instance, appears as "My French Neighbour." That is, in fact, the most convenient way to distinguish between the two texts. In the first sentence of the text, the American edition names "New-Amsterdam," "New-York," and "New-Netherlands"; the Edinburgh edition hyphenates none of the names.

The work seems not to have been particularly popular on the continent, being republished only in Germany, where Tauchnitz promptly brought out an edition in English in 1855, and Wigand a selection in English of six pieces, published the same year. The six selections were also translated into German in 1855. All are derived from the Edinburgh edition.

1Ea.   CHRONICLES OF WOLFERT'S ROOST | AND OTHER PAPERS. | BY WASHINGTON IRVING. | AUTHOR'S EDITION. | EDINBURGH: THOMAS CONSTABLE AND CO. | S. LOW, SON, & CO.; HAMILTON, ADAMS, & CO., LONDON. | JAMES M'GLASHAN, DUBLIN. | MDCCCLV.

"Constable's Miscellany of Foreign Literature," Vol. IV.

(17.8 x 12.5):   [-]^6 A-I^8 K-U^8 X-Y^8.   The first three leaves carry advertisements. Unreckoned: two leaves of terminal advertisements.

The first three integral leaves (not reckoned in the pagination) consist of five pages of advertisements for "Constable's Miscellany of Foreign Literature"; the last page is blank. On the fifth page appears: "In the Press, 3s. 6d. cloth, Volume V. of | MISCELLANY OF FOREIGN LITERATURE. | [rule] | SKETCHES OF BRITTANY AND LA VENDÉE."

[i]-[ii], series title, verso blank; [iii]-[iv], title, on verso printer; [v]-vi, table of contents; [1]-351, text; [352], printer.

For distinctions from the second and third impressions, with the same title page, see the discussion of the later impressions.

Printer: Thomas Constable, Printer to Her Majesty.

Lineation: p. 100, THE ... these ; p. 200, noble ... or-

Tan T cloth. On front, in gilt, globe with wreath, all within border in blind. On back, the same except all in blind. Spine titled in gilt: WOLFERT'S ROOST | AND | OTHER PAPERS | [rule] | WASHINGTON IRVING | | [rule] | CONSTABLE'S | MISCELLANY. | IV | [rule]. Light yellow endpapers.

Athenæum, 13 January 1855, advertised for 15 January; 20 January 1855, listed. *Literary Gazette*, 20 January 1855, listed, and advertised as "New Work ... simultaneously with the American Edition," "Just published," price 3*s*. 6*d*.; 27 January 1855, reviewed.

CtY, TxU, *BL*.

b.   The second impression, with the same title page, may be distinguished by the collation and the advertisements.

Collation: $[-]^4$A-I^8 K-U^8 X-Y^8.

There is only one integral leaf of advertisements (not reckoned in the pagination) at the beginning of the volume. The advertisement on the recto is for "Volume VII. of | MISCELLANY OF FOREIGN LITERATURE." There are no advertisements at the end of the volume.

"Constable's Miscellany of Foreign Literature," Vol. IV.

Printer the same.

Binding the same.

Publishers' Circular, 15 March 1855, listed.

CtY.

c.   The third impression, with the same title page, may be distinguished by the collation, the advertisements, and the lack of identification as a volume in the "Miscellany of Foreign Literature" series.

Collation: $[-]^2$ A-I^8 K-U^8 X-Y^8. In the copy examined, the binding is too tight to determine whether the first signature of two leaves is formed by excision of leaves from a larger gathering.

No advertisements at the beginning of the volume.   Two leaves of advertisements at the end.

No series title; the pagination begins with the title, p. [iii].

Tan A cloth. The design is the same, except that at the foot of the spine the identification of series is omitted and "Constable & Co." is substituted.

With the omission of the preliminary advertisements, the series title, and the identification of "Constable's Miscellany" on the spine, it is apparent that this impression was intended to be independent of the "Miscellany of Foreign

Literature" series. Its sequence in relation to the other two impressions is not determined. In *The Literary Gazette*, 31 March 1855, the "Summary" column says, "a cheap edition is published by Messrs. Constable and Co., under an arrangement with the author," but the "cheap edition" may be simply the series edition.

TxU (Bret Harte's copy).

2E.   WOLFERT'S ROOST | AND OTHER TALES. | NOW FIRST COLLECTED. | BY | WASHINGTON IRVING. | LONDON: | HENRY G. BOHN, YORK STREET, COVENT GARDEN. | 1855.

Issued individually in "Bohn's Cheap Series." At some time after publication the edition appears to have been bound with *Captain Bonneville* to form Vol. X of Bohn's "Library Edition" of the works of Irving. It would then have substituted for Theodore Irving's *Conquest of Florida* in the combined volume.

Printer: Harrison and Sons, London Gazette Office, St. Martin's Lane.

Lineation: p. 100, my ... carried ; p. 200, dainty- ... a

Seen only rebound. Michael Sadleir's *XIX Century Fiction* describes a copy in boards: bright green glazed boards printed in black; publisher's advertisements in blue on endpapers. The edition was also advertised in "a fine edition," presumably in cloth.

One copy noted bound with an 1881 George Bell & Sons edition of *Captain Bonneville*; the combination has an added volume title page for "The Works of Washington Irving. Vol. X."

Athenæum, 10 March 1855, listed and advertised. *Publishers' Circular*, 15 March 1855, listed and advertised.

TxU, ViU.

3E.   WOLFERT'S ROOST: | AND | OTHER SKETCHES. | BY WASHINGTON IRVING. | LONDON | GEO. ROUTLEDGE & CO., FARRINGDON STREET. | 1855.

Seen only in an impression marked *Twelfth Thousand*.

(16.4 x 9.9): [i]-iv, [1]-251 [252]. Signed in 8's.

Printer: Savill and Edwards, Chandos-Street, London.

Lineation: p. 100, For ... that ; p. 200, previous ... revolt.

In the rebound copy seen, the original paper wrappers are bound in: on front and back, title and gaudy colored picture of castle-like roost in moonlight. No series identification. Price one shilling. Spine not present. Michael

Sadleir's *XIX Century Fiction* describes a copy in boards: cream pictorial boards, printed in blue, brown and black. Front cover design repeated on back. Lettered on spine.

Publishers' Circular, 15 March 1855, listed.

BL ("Twelfth Thousand").

1Aa.   WOLFERT'S ROOST | AND | OTHER PAPERS, NOW FIRST COLLECTED. | BY | WASHINGTON IRVING. | NEW YORK: | G. P. PUTNAM & CO., 12 PARK PLACE. | 1855.

(18.5 x 12.6): $[1]^{12}$ $2\text{-}16^{12}$. The first leaf is a blank. The second leaf is excised. Preliminary engraved title and illustration (on single cut sheet folded to make two leaves) not reckoned; pasted to stub of excised leaf $[1]_2$. Also not reckoned: terminal catalogue of twelve pages, in a gathering of six leaves.

The terminal catalogue of 12 pages is paged [1] 2-12. Dated at head: 10 PARK PLACE, Feb'y., 1855. Note the address of 10 Park Place, rather than 12 Park Place. 10 Park Place is a later address of George P. Putnam, and the one that appears on the title page of the third and later impressions of *Wolfert's Roost*. Page 2 of the catalogue is given to Washington Irving, beginning with COLLECTED WRITINGS in 15 vols. and ending with: PORTRAIT OF WASHINGTON IRVING, on steel, from original | by MARTIN, price 50 cents; India proofs, with Autograph, price | $1 50. *Chronicles of Wolfert's Roost* is listed as *New Volume*.

For distinctions from the second impression, with the same title page, see the discussion of the second impression.

First preliminary matter unpaged: 1 blank leaf; 2 leaves with illustration and vignette engraved title; 1 leaf with title, on verso copyright (1854) and printer. [7]-8, table of contents; [9]-383, text; [384], blank.

Printer: John F. Trow, Printer and Stereotyper, 49 Ann Street.

Lineation: p. 100, THE BERMUDAS. ... died ; p. 200, fellow, ... every

Slate-green TZ cloth. On front, at center, gilt vignette of Wolfert's Roost, with elaborated frame in blind around edges. On back, the frame in blind. Spine decorated in blind and titled in gilt: WOLFERT'S | ROOST | [swelled rule] | IRVING Buff-yellow endpapers. Fly leaves. Other bindings, listed below in the description of the third and later impressions, may also appear but have not been seen.

Deposited 6 February 1855. *New-York Tribune*, 3 February 1855, "will publish on February 7." *New-York Daily Times,* 5 February 1855, "will publish on

February 10"; 10 February 1855, "now ready." *United States Review*, March 1855, reviewed.

TxU (6), ViU, Private hands.

b. The second impression, with the same title page, may be distinguished by the collation: $[1]^{10}$ 2-16^{12}. For easy identification of the collation, note the presence of the binding strings between pp. 14-15 (rather than between pp. 12-13, as in the first impression).

The illustration and engraved title are inserted (rather than pasted to a stub, as in the first impression). In the table of contents, p. [7], line 8$_p$ there are two dots, rather than the five of the first impression, between the title ("My French Neighbor") and the page number.

The terminal catalogue is the same.

The binding is the same.

New-York Tribune, 15 February 1855, "will publish on Friday, Feb. 16, the second edition (10th thousand) "; 17 February 1855, "have now ready."

TxU (5).

c-f. In the third and later impressions of 1855, the publisher's address in the title imprint is changed to 10 PARK PLACE.

Although the sequence of these later impressions (or in some instances, perhaps, merely states) is not certain, the variants in collation and printing suggest the following order:

Third impression: collation $[1]^{10}$ 2-16^{12} (with binding strings between pp. 14-15).

Fourth impression: collation $[1]^{12}$ 2-16^{12} (with binding strings between pp. 12-13).

Fifth impression: collation $[1]^{12}$ 2-16^{12}. On p. 205, lines 1-2$_p$ the first letter is missing in each line.

Sixth impression: collation $[1]^{12}$ 2-16^{12}. On p. 205, lines 1-2$_p$ the first letters have been crudely and unmistakably replaced.

Although the possibility of duplicate plates must be entertained, an examination of type batter and wear reinforces the probability of the sequence. Notice, for a clear example, the increasing degeneration of "Act of Congress" in the first line of the copyright notice.

Although a sequence of four impressions may be reasonably adduced, there is at least the possibility of other hidden impressions, or impressions from duplicate plates, that should not be overlooked. The so-called "Sixth

Impression," for instance, has been noted in three different bindings: [A], [B], [G] in the list of bindings below.

A complication that needs further study is provided by the frontispiece illustration for "The Contented Man," appearing in all impressions. There the illustration title has been noted with and without a period at the end, and the engraving itself in at least three states. The differences in the engraving are minor matters of shading lines, examined easily only on a mechanical collator. Note, for instance, the small differences in the rear leg and cross-piece in the back of the chair. Various combinations of the characteristics have been noted, and no clear sequential pattern appears.

The later impressions of 1855 have been noted or reported in a variety of bindings. No sequence has been established, beyond the common binding of the first two impressions.

[A]. Slate-green TZ cloth. On front, at center, gilt vignette of Wolfert's Roost, among trees, overlooking the river, within elaborated frame in blind. On back, the frame in blind. Spine decorated in blind and titled in gilt: WOLFERT'S | ROOST | [swelled rule] | IRVING Buff-yellow endpapers. [The common binding of the first two impressions, it appears on later impressions as well.]

[B]. Slate-green TZ cloth. The gilt vignette of Wolfert's Roost, within frame in blind, appears on both front and back. Spine titled in gilt: IRVING'S | WORKS | [swelled rule] | WOLFERT'S | ROOST

[C]. Slate-green, and black, TZ cloth. On front, gilt vignette of Wolfert's Roost, within an oval frame in blind, on a field of rectangular ornaments in blind with rules around edges. On back, the field of rectangular ornaments but no vignette. Spine titled in gilt the same as [A].

[D]. Black TZ cloth. Front and back the same as [C]. Spine titled in gilt, IRVING'S WORKS.

[E]. Slate-green TZ cloth. On front and back, publisher's monogram in blind at center, within wide-rule border in blind. Spine titled in gilt the same as [A].

[F]. Slate-green TZ cloth. Front and back the same as [E]. Spine titled in gilt, IRVING'S WORKS.

[G]. Red A cloth. Sides decorated in gilt with frame lines and vine-like border; no vignette or monogram. Spine decorated and titled in gilt. AEG. [This is probably the binding advertised on p. 2 of the catalogue in the earlier impressions -- there described as "Choice Volumes for Presents, gilt extra" -- although it has not been noted on the first two impressions. Such copies may, however, exist.]

Discussion based on copies in DLC (2), MH, TxGeoS, TxU (7), ViU (2), Private hands.

g. NEW YORK: | G. P. PUTNAM & CO., 321 BROADWAY. | 1856.

[Not examined in detail.]

DLC.

h. NEW YORK: | G. P. PUTNAM (for the Proprietor), 506 BROADWAY. | 1859.

Works title, Vol. XVI, added.

Green BD cloth. Sides framed in blind. Spine titled in gilt with decorative border around title. Green endpapers.

TxU.

1G. CHRONICLES OF WOLFERT'S ROOST | AND | OTHER PAPERS. | BY | WASHINGTON IRVING. | *AUTHOR'S EDITION.* | LEIPZIG | BERNHARD TAUCHNITZ | 1855.

"Collection of British Authors," Vol. CCCXXIV.

(15.6 x 10.9): [i]-vi, [1]-386. Signed in 8's.

Printer: Bernhard Tauchnitz.

Lineation: p. 100, tunately, ... year:; p. 200, Sometimes ... game,

In the rebound copy seen, the original tan-brown paper wrappers are bound in: on front, cover-title; at foot, THE CORRECTIONS OF THE PRESS BY D^R. FLÜGEL. On back, advertisements for Irving's *Sketch Book, Life of Mahomet, Successors of Mahomet, Life of Goldsmith, Wolfert's Roost.* Spine not present.

BL. Copy reported in Bayerischer Staatsbibliothek, München.

2G. WOLFERT'S ROOST. | [rule] | TRANSATLANTIC SKETCHES | BY | WASHINGTON IRVING. | WITH PORTRAIT OF THE AUTHOR. | [rule] | GOETTINGEN: | GEORGE H. WIGAND. | 1855.

"Wigand's Pocket Miscellany," Vol. IV.

A publisher's Preface points out that this is a selection from the complete volume, "guided by the wish to present such descriptions of American life and manners as ... would be acceptable to the German reader." The selections: "Wolfert's Roost," "Guests from Gibbet-Island," "The Early Experiences of Ralph Ringwood," "The Seminoles," "The Creole Village," "The Phantom Island."

(14.9 x 10.8): [I]-VI [VII]-[VIII], [1]-168. Not reckoned: engraved portrait before title. Signed in 8's.

Printer: J. S. Wassermann, Leipzig.

Lineation: p. 50, the ... house-; p. 100, but ... said

Noted in contemporary black and white marbled boards with gray cloth shelfback. So issued? Probably issued in paper wrapper.

TxU. Copy reported in Stadtbibliothek Lübeck.

TRANSLATIONS

German.

Wolfert's Rust. | Transatlantische Skizzen | von | Washington Irving. | Aus dem Englischen von W. E. Drugulin. | [elaborated swelled rule] | Leipzig | Verlag von Carl B. Lorck. | 1855. [in fraktur]

"Conversations- und Reisebibliothek," Bd. XI.

(16.5 x 11.0): [I]-VI, [1]-130. Signed in 8's.

This is a selection from the complete work: a translation of the same six selections included in the Wigand edition, a German edition in the English language, except that the final selection uses for a title the secondary title, "The Adalantado of the Seven Cities."

Printer: Fr. Ries, Leipzig.

Lineation: p. 50, sich ... wagte ; p. 100, getroffen ... Eichhörnchenau-

TxU. Copy reported in Bayerischer Staatsbibliothek, München.

LIFE OF WASHINGTON

Upon the publication of Irving's last book, the *Life of Washington*, appearing volume by volume over a period of five years from 1855 to 1859, George P. Putnam exploited the work to his full ability, trying nearly every publishing form then thought of: a handsome edition of five octavo volumes (apparently sold at first by subscription and subsequently in the conventional ways), a cheaper popular edition of duodecimo volumes, publication in parts over a number of years, an octavo illustrated set, and a large-paper "limited edition" illustrated set. He even sold separate collections of the illustrations, bound in volumes, boxed, or individually. Most of the forms were available in a wide variety of bindings, from cheaper cloth to the most expensive full Turkey morocco extra gilt. Some were also offered unbound in sheets.

The American forms appeared in this order:

The Octavo Edition, 5 vols. May 1855 to May 1859.

The Large-Paper Limited Edition, 5 vols. February (?) 1856 to May (?) 1859.

The Duodecimo Edition, 5 vols. August 1856 to May 1859.

The Illustrated Edition in Parts, 68 parts. September 1856 to 1859.

The Illustrated Edition, 5 vols. August (?) 1857 to July or August 1859.

Then in 1859, after first publication was completed in the five forms, Putnam reprinted the Duodecimo Edition and the Octavo Edition, both with illustrations, as "The Sunnyside Edition" and "The Mount Vernon Edition."

Despite the many forms over a long period, the textual history is clear. The Octavo Edition appeared first, was the edition for which Irving and his nephew Pierre read proof, and was the textual basis for all other forms; its setting in various impressions, in fact, provided the sheets for the other American forms except for the Duodecimo Edition which was printed from a different setting but derived its text from that of the Octavo Edition. (Despite the fact that its last two volumes were published more or less simultaneously with the last two volumes of the Octavo Edition, it is clearly a second edition, derivative in text, while all the other forms are variant or later impressions of the first Octavo Edition.) Irving apparently made no revisions for the Duodecimo Edition, although minor publisher's emendations do appear. As new impressions of the Octavo Edition were produced over the years, Irving and Pierre provided small corrections and emendations, but the basic text remained unchanged.

In Britain, Irving's usual publisher, John Murray, did not choose to publish the *Life of Washington* but sold the rights to Henry G. Bohn who added the volumes to his "Bohn's Cheap Series." Bohn set his edition from advance sheets of Putnam's Octavo Edition and, as customary, issued the volumes more or less simultaneously with the American edition. British spelling is substituted in the text and a few minor "corrections" appear, certainly the work of the publisher, but the text in general follows that of the Octavo Edition. Irving never saw proof sheets; in fact, he apparently did not even know of the edition until shortly before the appearance of the first volume. On the continent, the Tauchnitz edition in Germany and the translations into German and Swedish were derived from the Bohn edition.

To make the publishing history clear, each American form is here described separately in an individual section. That defines the variety of the forms and the chronology of the impressions of each form, but unfortunately obscures -- at least in the listing itself -- the detailed chronology of the myriad impressions of the five volumes of the work as a whole in all its various forms. I hope that the general introduction and the individual introductions to the separate forms will offer the additional clarity.

The Octavo Edition

1A.   The Octavo Edition, sometimes called by the publisher "The Subscribers' Edition," or "The Subscribers' Library Edition," or "The Library Edition," was printed from the author's manuscript and supervised by Washington Irving or Pierre M. Irving. All other editions of the work are derived from this one. It is textually the first edition and chronologically either the first published or published simultaneously with others.

Since each volume, in the year in which it was individually published, presents a number of textual or bibliographical variants, the five-volume work must be discussed volume by volume. The first volume, as would be expected in a work coming out over a period of years, with demand for the earlier volumes increasing as later ones appear, occurs in the greatest number of variants. New buyers of later volumes would want to complete their sets. And yet it is almost impossible now to define distinct impressions of entire volumes. The plates of individual sheets were corrected, changed or repaired when the need arose (in a few sheets of Vol. I as many as four times); ones that apparently needed no change would simply be reprinted in subsequent impressions. Then too, it is very probable that the bulk of the supply of old sheets would be used up before new ones were substituted, so that mixed sheets are the rule rather than the exception. It should be recognized, then, that in the definition of chronological textual states of the gatherings discussed in each volume below, each state may well appear in more than one of the impressions to which the volume--or, for that matter, the individual gathering--was subjected. Still, the order of changes in the plates does point toward the order of impressions even though it does not define the number of impressions, which remain unknown.

Volume I.

LIFE | OF | GEORGE WASHINGTON. | BY | WASHINGTON IRVING. | IN THREE VOLS. | VOL. I. | NEW YORK: | G. P. PUTNAM & CO., 10 PARK PLACE. | 1855.

(23.6 x 15.3): $[-]^8$ $[1]^8$ $2\text{-}31^8$ 32^4. Not reckoned in collation or pagination: portrait of Washington by A. Wertmüller (engraved by H. B. Hall; on single leaf pasted to inner edge of title) before title; two maps (on single sheet folded to make two leaves) inserted between pp. 168-169; map (on single sheet folded to make two leaves) pasted to stub inserted between pp. 466-467.

[i]-[ii], title, on verso copyright (1855 by G. P. Putnam & Co.) and printer; [iii]-v, Preface, dated Sunnyside, 1855; [vi], blank; [vii]-xvi, table of contents, with table of illustrations at the end; [1]-498, text; [499]-504, "Appendix [Publishers' Notice]".

Printers:

A. John F. Trow, Printer and Stereotyper, 49 Ann St., New York.

B. R. Craighead, Printer, 53 Vesey Street, New York.

C. No printer's imprint.

D. John F. Trow, Printer and Stereotyper, 377 & 379 Broadway, cor. White St., New York.

The sequence of the printers' imprints is probably correct. The A imprint has been seen only in copies containing A and B text states; the B imprint in copies containing A, B, and C text states; the C lack of imprint in copies containing B and C text states; the D imprint in copies containing B, C, and D text states.

Lineation: p. 100, CHAPTER X. ... with ; p. 300, CHAPTER XXXIII. ... to

Bindings: See the discussion at the end of the entry for the entire set of five volumes.

Signature states: variant readings in the gatherings of impressions dated 1855.

When more than one example has been discovered in a single gathering, it is by good fortune possible to assign variants of each example to a relatively specific (A, B, C, or D) state of the sheets. For instance, in Signature 3, on p. 44, line 26, "dormar" is changed to "dormer," but on p. 45, line 19, "lord" appears with both "dormar" and "dormer," while "Lord" appears only with "dormer." "Lord," therefore, must represent a C state of the gathering. When only one variant has been found in a signature, it can only be listed in a simpler sequence, based upon the change itself, the bibliographical context, and the reading of later impressions. (The imprint provides a special problem, discussed under "Printers.")

Sig	Page &line	A state	B state	C state	D state
[-]	Imprint	Trow, 49 Ann St.	Craighead	[no imprint]	Trow, 377 & 379 Broadway
2	7.22	O.S.), in	O.S.), 1732, in		
	32.10	induce		induces	
3	44.26	dormar	dormer		
	45.19	lord		Lord	
5	68.22	climate;	climate,		
	72.8	Shurtee's		Chartier's	
6	82.15	November.	December.		
	86.3	pallisades		palisades	
7	101.25	constructon	construction		
	101.ftnte	1751.		1754.	
9	136.ftnte.2	*fan faron*	*fanfaron*		
	137.3$_f$	Stobo,		Muse,	
10	154.22	Annapolis		Alexandria	
	155.15	whom	who		
11	165.16	huts,	hut,		
	174.17	war; "		war;"	
12	183.10	was	were		
	191.4	six pounders		six-pounders	
16	242.RH	1756.]	[1756.		
	242.14	laid		lay	

19	294.8	thouand		thousand	
	300.ftnte	Robinson	Robison		
21	327.4	Duke de Choiseul		Count de Vergennes	
	328.1$_f$	monarchial	monarchical		
25	385-386, &388-396.RH	[1773.		[1774.	
	393.ftnte.	Washington	Washington's		
26	409.3	of Mount	in Mount		
	414.20	western			northern
	414.22	Santislaus		Stanislaus	
27	425.RH	1774.]			1775.]
	428.22	councils		counsels	
	430.19	Pitcairne	Pitcairn		

Signatures containing only one example:

Sig.	Page & line	First state	Second state	Third state
[1]	8.23	Carlvarock	Carlaverock	
4	50.20	was	were	
8	115.2$_f$	thir	their	
13	193.2	six pounders	six-pounders	
14	212.29	Davis,	Davies,	
17	260.RH	[1757	[1757.	
18	273.24	favored	favorite	
20	308.15	*off her*	*for her*	*off* all
22	341.14	were	was	
23	[356].4	PROMISES	PREMIER	
24	376.RH	[1773	[1773.	
28	445.10	quarters. They were	quarter. It was	

29	[459].2$_f$	leaguring	leaguering
30	[471].18	Read	Reed
31	481.6	of	off
32	498.2	beleaguring	beleaguering

Deposited 16 August 1855. *Norton's Literary Gazette*, 15 March 1855, "in press," "ready in May"; 1 June 1855, reviewed; 15 June 1855, listed. *Knickerbocker*, and *United States Review*, July 1855, reviewed. On 30 May 1855, George Bancroft wrote Irving, "I gained a copy last night."

In 1856 (dated 1857) Volume I was published separately with the title of *Washington's Earlier Years* under the imprint of G. P. Putnam in New York and Sampson Low in London. An advertisement in *American Publishers' Circular*, 15 November 1856, promises, *"in a few days, the Historical Presentation Book*, WASHINGTON'S EARLIER YEARS, Being the first volume of Washington's Life. By WASHINGTON IRVING, Illustrated with 21 beautiful Engravings on steel, ... and several maps and wood-cuts.... Price in extra cloth, bevelled gilt edges, $5 00; Turkey morocco, antique or gilt, $7 50."

Volume II.

LIFE | OF | GEORGE WASHINGTON. | BY | WASHINGTON IRVING. | IN THREE VOLS. | VOL. II. | NEW YORK: | G. P. PUTNAM & CO., 10 PARK PLACE. | 1855.

(23.4 x 14.7): [-]^6 1-32^8 33^4, or 33^2 [34]^2. Not reckoned in collation or pagination: portrait of Washington by C. W. Peale (engraved by Geo. Parker; on single leaf pasted to inner edge of title) before title; map (on single sheet folded to make two leaves) pasted to stub inserted variously between pp. 226-227, or 270-271, or 276-277; map (on single leaf) inserted between pp. 308-309; map (on single leaf) inserted variously between pp. 430-431, or 432-433. One copy seen with frontispiece portrait of Washington from the Illustrated Edition, engraved by J. B. Forrest; but the copy is rebound and the variant is probably the work of an owner.

In two collation states, no sequence established.

[A]. 33^4.

[B]. 33^2 [34]^2.

[i]-[ii], title, on verso copyright (1855 by G. P. Putnam & Co.) and printer; [iii]-xii, table of contents, with table of illustrations at end; [1]-518, text; [519]-[520], errata notice for Vol. I, "Error Corrected," verso blank.

Printer: John F. Trow, Printer and Stereotyper, 377 & 379 Broadway, cor. White-st., New York.

Lineation: p. 100, The ... unwil-; p. 300, Such ... most

Bindings: See the discussion at the end of the entry for the entire set of five volumes.

Signature states: variant readings in the gatherings of impressions dated 1855.

Sig.	Page & line	First state	Second state
[-]	xii.21	226	270
1	15.RH	1775.	1775.]
7	107.26	[line not present]	to ... and
10	160.5$_f$	Claiborne	Dearborn
18	273.sig	[not present]	VOL. II. - 18
20	307.RH	PHOEBE	PHOENIX
23	353.ftnte.1	Memoirs, p. 174.	Memoirs, Littell's ed., p. 174.
31	483.16	former,	latter,
33	518.RH	1777.	[1777.

Note: Despite the change of page number in the table of illustrations, on xii.21, the map of Westchester County continued to be variously inserted.

To emphasize the random combinations of signature states to be found, it is worth recording that one copy has been noted with an 1856 title page but with Sigs. 10, 20, 23, 31, 33 all in the first state.

Deposited 16 February 1856. *American Publishers' Circular*, 22 December 1855, "next week." *Christian Examiner*, March 1856, reviewed. Pierre M. Irving, *Life and Letters*, "issued in December, 1855."

Volume III.

LIFE | OF | GEORGE WASHINGTON. | BY | WASHINGTON IRVING. | VOL. III. | NEW YORK: | G. P. PUTNAM & CO., 321 BROADWAY. | 1856.

(23.4 x 14.9): [-]^8 1-3^8 3^8 5-32^8 33^6. [The missigned sig. number 4 has not been seen corrected earlier than in an 1857 impression.] Not reckoned in collation or pagination: portrait of Washington by G. Stuart (engraved by H.

B. Hall; on single leaf pasted to inner edge of title) before title; map (on single leaf) inserted between pp. 92-93; map (on single leaf) inserted between pp. 182-183; map (on single sheet folded to make two leaves) pasted to stub inserted between pp. 244-245; map (on single leaf) inserted between pp. [278]-279; engraving by Geo. Parker from Daguerreotype of statue of Washington by Houdon (on single leaf) inserted between pp. 518-519 (although the table of illustrations lists it on p. 524). Note: The maps on pp. 205, 286, and 429 are integral and paged.

[i]-[ii], title, on verso copyright (1855 by G. P. Putnam & Co.) and printer; [iii]-[iv], "Note to the Third Volume," verso blank; [v]-xiv, table of contents, with table of illustrations at end; [1]-523, text; [524], blank.
A publisher's notice, on a hand-cut sheet averaging 15.5 x 11.5, is inserted at the end of the volume.   It consists of two parts: PUBLISHERS' ADVERTISEMENT at the top, and TO CORRESPONDENTS below.

The PUBLISHERS' ADVERTISEMENT appears in two settings, sequence, if any, unknown:
[A]. Lines 5-6. com- | pletion
[B]. Lines 5-6. the | completion

TO CORRESPONDENTS appears in two states:
[A]. Author's initials at foot. W. I
[B]. Author's initials at foot. W. I.

The changes were made independently, and copies have been seen in three combinations: [A]-[A]; [A]-[B]; [B]-[B]. No correspondence of the various combinations with states of the collation or signatures is apparent.

Printer: John F. Trow, Printer and Stereotyper, 377 and 379 Broadway, Corner of White street.

Lineation: p.100, On ... a ; p. 300, at ... Morgan's

Bindings: See the discussion at the end of the entry for the entire set of five volumes.

Signature states: variant readings in the gatherings of impressions dated 1856.

Sig. 31, p. 496, line 24, the first state is "Northern", the second is "Eastern".
[The variant reported by BAL on p. 248, line 7_f has been discovered in no 1856 impression. It has been noted in one copy of an 1857 impression, although not in several others.]

Deposited 5 July 1856. *American Publishers' Circular*, 14 June 1856, "will be delivered ... between the 15th and 20th inst."; 21 June 1856, listed. *North American Revue*, and *United States Review*, July 1856, reviewed.

Volume IV.

LIFE | OF | GEORGE WASHINGTON. | BY | WASHINGTON IRVING. | VOL. IV. | NEW YORK: | G. P. PUTNAM & CO., 321 BROADWAY. | 1857.

In two states of collation, no sequence determined.

[A]. (23.4 x 14.8): $[\text{-}]^6$ 1-32^8 33^4. The first and last leaf are blanks. In some copies, the blank at the end is excised.

[B]. (23.2-23.6 x 14.7): $[\text{-}]^8$ 1-33^8. The first leaf is a blank. $[\text{-}]_{2\text{-}3}$ and 33$_{4\text{-}8}$ carry publisher's advertisements. In a variant of State [B], the advertisements are excised. The variant may easily be identified by the presence of the binder's strings between pp. [ii]-[iii], rather than between pp. iv-v as they are in State [A].

In Collation State [B] (with advertisements), the four pages of preliminary advertisements are undated, paged [1] 2-4. The ten pages of terminal advertisements are undated, paged [2 pp. unpaged], 30, 13, 14, 15, 21, 12, 20, 23. Langfeld and Blackburn report the terminal advertisements paged 1-6, 21, 12, [2 pp. unpaged]. Not seen in that pagination.

Not reckoned in collations or pagination: portrait of Mrs. Washington by J. Woolaston (engraved by J. Rogers; on single leaf pasted to inner edge of title) before title; map (on single leaf) inserted between pp. 108-109; map (on single leaf) inserted between pp. 356-357; silhouette of Washington (on single leaf) inserted between pp. 406-407.

[i]-[ii], title, on verso copyright (1857 by G. P. Putnam & Co.) and printer; [iii]-x, table of contents, with table of illustrations at end; [1]-518, text.

The caption of the silhouette between pp. 406-407 appears in two states of the lettering.

[A]. End of first line. N. J, 1783

[B]. End of first line. N. J., 1783.

Both states of the caption appear in both collation states of the volume.

Printer: John F. Trow, Printer, Stereotyper, and Electrotyper, 377 and 379 Broadway, Cor. White Street, New York.

Lineation: p. 100, All ... he ; p. 300, of ... the

Bindings: See the discussion at the end of the entry for the entire set of five volumes.

Signature states: variant readings in the gatherings of impressions dated 1857.

Sig.	Page & line	First state	Second state
30	473.ftnte	Geo.	Jos.
31	481.RH	1776.]	1786.]
32	498.4	mortals."	mortals.

Deposited 8 July 1857. *American Publishers' Circular*, 2 May 1857, "about the first week in May"; 9 May 1857 to 8 August 1857, "will issue, in a few days." Pierre M. Irving, *Life and Letters*, "published in May."

Volume V.

LIFE | OF | GEORGE WASHINGTON. | BY | WASHINGTON IRVING | VOL. V. | NEW YORK: | G. P. PUTNAM, 115 NASSAU STREET. | 1859.

(23.2 x 14.6): [-]^8 1-21^8 32^8 23-28^8 29^4. First leaf excised; the second leaf a blank. In a later state, Sig. 22 is correctly signed. Not reckoned in collation or pagination: portrait of Washington by R. Peale and view of tomb of Washington by Duthie (engraved by H. B. Hall and an unidentified engraver; apparently on two leaves pasted together, and in turn pasted to inner edge of title) before title; reproduction of letter of Washington (on single sheet folded to make two leaves) pasted to stub inserted between pp. xii-[1].

[i]-[ii], title, on verso copyright (1859 by Washington Irving) and printer; [iii]-iv, Preface, dated Sunnyside, April, 1859; [v]-xii, table of contents (with no table of illustrations); [1]-321, text; [322], blank; [323]-398, Appendix; [399]-456, Index.

Printer: John F. Trow, Printer, Stereotyper, and Electrotyper, 377 and 379 Broadway, Cor. White Street, New York.

Lineation: p. 100, veyance ... [in footnote] 1791.; p. 300, CHAPTER XXXIII. ... to

Bindings: See the discussion at the end of the entry for the entire set of five volumes.

Signature states: variant readings in the gatherings of impressions dated 1859.

Sig.	Page & line	First state	Second state
[-]	vi.1$_f$	4 dots before p. no.	2 dots before p. no.
5	65.6	ase h	as he
13	207.ftnte.1	Lears,	Lear,

14	213.4	expedition; "The	expedition. The
22	337.sig.	32	22

Pierre M. Irving in his private journal, 12 April 1859, gives 500 copies as the initial printing.

Deposited 9 August 1859. *American Publishers' Circular*, 23 and 30 April 1859, "unavoidably delayed, in the press, ... publication is deferred until the 10th May"; 14 May 1859, listed; 21 May 1859, "the first large edition was exhausted ... before the second was through the press. A full supply is expected next week." *New-York Times*, 6 and 7 May 1859, "Will be published on Monday, May 9, Price $2. Agents and Canvassers supplied with 8vo Edition on Saturday, May 7."

Bindings for the five volumes.

As might be expected for a work published in the mid-nineteenth century in multiple volumes and in multiple impressions over a period of five years, a number of different bindings have been seen, reported, or seen advertised. The standard binding is in T cloth, in some shade of purple, blue-black, or slate. On the sides, in blind, are two outer frame lines; within them is a double frame, each element made up of three single frame lines, with a rosette in the corners; at the center, a wreath. The spines are titled in gilt: LIFE| OF | WASHINGTON. | [rule] | IRVING. | VOL. I. [II. - V.] | Putnam. The endpapers are yellow, yellow-buff, or white. But minor variants also appear among the other combinations. The dies, particularly of the purples and blue-blacks, were volatile, and most surviving copies are faded, sometimes to a brown, making color distinctions difficult if not impossible. Volume I in its many impressions also shows variants in the titling on the spine: the volume number appears both as a roman and as an arabic 1; the period after WASHINGTON may be present or absent. No sequence has been determined. In Volume V the period after the publisher is omitted. No other variants in the standard bindings have been noted, although they may exist.

Publisher's advertisements list other bindings also available. The terminal advertisements in some copies of Vol. IV of the Octavo Edition list the first four volumes as available in cloth at $8; half calf, extra at $13; full calf, extra at $16; morocco extra, gilt edge at $20. The terminal advertisements in some copies of Vol. V of the Duodecimo Edition list the five volumes in cloth at $10; sheep at $12.50; half calf, extra at $16; half calf, antique at $16; full calf at $20. In the same advertisement, THE 5TH AND OTHER SEPARATE VOLS. OF "WASHINGTON," TO COMPLETE SETS are offered in cloth at $2; and "folded, for binding" at $1.75. The last is particularly interesting in its evidence that the volumes at some point were also issued in sheets, unbound.

Note: The "Publishers' Advertisement" at the end of Vol. III points out the intention of the author to extend the work beyond the three volumes originally planned, and promises, "New title-pages, with the number of volumes correctly stated, will be furnished with the concluding volume." If the promise was carried out -- and no such set of separate new titles has been located -- rebound copies of the first three volumes may appear with the substitute title pages.

Discussion based on copies examined in CtY, MH (3), NN, TxDaM, TxU (8), ViU (5), and private hands.

As the later volumes of the original five-volume work were published, G. P. Putnam continued to print new impressions of the earlier volumes in their standard octavo form as well as in later forms. The individual volumes were available from the publisher in sets of the volumes already published, apparently made up of various available impressions chosen at random, or the buyer of a new volume could obtain at almost any time single earlier volumes to complete or to bring up to date his own set. In the advertisement at the end of some copies of Vol. V of the Duodecimo Edition (1859), the publisher advertises, "THE 5TH AND OTHER SEPARATE VOLS. ... TO COMPLETE SETS. For the present any Vol. will be supplied to match the original binding in cloth." The result is that it is not feasible to try to define a standard "set" of the work for any one time or to define later impressions of the work as a whole. Coupled with the ambiguity of the number of impressions of each volume, particularly in the first year of its publication, the entire question of later impressions is one that demands more investigation and may never be fully answered. Impressions of individual volumes carrying on the title page a date later than the first year of publication have been noted as follows. Others may exist.

Vol. I (1855):   1856, 1857 (two impressions at least), 1859 (with two imprints), 1860 and later.

Vol. II (1855):   1856, 1857, 1859, 1860 and later.

Vol. III (1856):   1857, 1858, 1859, 1860 and later.

Vol. IV (1857):   1858, 1859, 1860 and later.

Vol. V (1859):   1860 and later.

Errors continued to be corrected down through the years, and pages occasionally reset when necessary: twenty pages in Vol. I in 1857, for instance. By 1859, and perhaps earlier, the printer was using duplicate plates, certainly for Vol. I (as George P. Putnam admitted in a letter to the

Historical Magazine, November 1860) and possibly for other volumes. The correction of the duplicate plates for Vol. I was haphazard; some of the original errors that had been earlier corrected on the first plates were corrected on the second, but some were not.

The Duodecimo Edition

2A.   The Duodecimo Edition, called by the publisher "The Popular Edition," was produced by Putnam as a cheaper edition that would complement, and eventually join, the Author's Revised Edition of the other works of Irving. The text is taken from that of the Octavo Edition, with occasional changes by the printer, and there is no evidence that Irving ever read the proof sheets. Although Vols. IV and V were issued simultaneously with the Octavo volumes in July 1857 and May 1859, Vols. I, II, III were issued in 1856 after the publication of the first three Octavo volumes. The edition is a derivative, second edition, and one with little textual significance.

Despite its lack of primacy or textual authority, the Duodecimo Edition is certainly the "popular" edition and the one that presumably was more likely to be bought by the ordinary reader (even if it is today less common in library collections). It therefore deserves more nearly complete description than a second edition with a reprinted text would normally be given.

Volume I.

LIFE | OF | GEORGE WASHINGTON. | BY | WASHINGTON IRVING. | VOL. I. | NEW YORK: | G.P. PUTNAM & CO., 321 BROADWAY. | NEARLY OPPOSITE PEARL STREET. | 1856.

(18.8 x 12.4): $[A]^8$ $1-19^{12}$ $[20]^2$. Not reckoned in collation or pagination: engraving of Washington before title; map, between pp. 154-155; map, between pp. 160-161.

[i]-[ii], half-title, verso blank; [iii]-[iv], title, on verso copyright (1855, by G.P. Putnam & Co.) and printer; [v]-vii, Preface; [viii], blank; [ix]-xvi, table of contents; [1]-454, text; [455]-459, "Appendix [Publishers' Notice]"; [460], blank.

Printer: John F. Trow, Printer, Stereotyper, and Electrotyper, 377 and 379 Broadway, Cor. White Street, New York.

Lineation: p. 100, absent ... tant.; p. 300, had ... polity.

American Publishers' Circular, 9 August 1856, "will be ready August 1, for the Trade," listed as "Popular Edition." *Christian Examiner*, September 1856, "The duodecimo edition ... presents now its first volume."

Volume II.

LIFE | OF | GEORGE WASHINGTON. | BY | WASHINGTON IRVING. | VOL. II. | NEW YORK: | G.P. PUTNAM & CO., 321 BROADWAY. | M.DCCC.LVI.

(18.7 x 12.4): [-]^6 1-20^{12} 21^4. The last leaf is a blank. Not reckoned: engraving of Gen. Schuyler before title.

[i]-[ii], half-title, verso blank; [iii]-[iv], title, on verso copyright (1855) and printer; [v]-xii, table of contents; [1]-486, text.

Note: in copies seen, p. 349, line 1$_f$ reads "take" for "taken."

Printer: John F. Trow, Printer, Stereotyper, and Electrotyper, 377 Broadway, cor. White St., New York.

Lineation: p. 100, CHAPTER X. ... the ; p. 300, Cornwallis ... of

American Publishers' Circular, 16 August 1856, "will publish a Duodecimo Edition ... on the 1st September"; 6 September 1856, listed; 20 September 1856, "now ready."

Volume III.

LIFE | OF | GEORGE WASHINGTON. | BY | WASHINGTON IRVING. | VOL. III. | NEW YORK: | G.P. PUTNAM & CO., 321 BROADWAY. | NEARLY OPPOSITE PEARL STREET. | 1856.

(18.7 x 12.4): [-]^8 1-20^{12} 21^2. Not reckoned: engraving of Gen. Putnam before title.

[i]-[ii], half-title, verso blank; [iii]-[iv], title, on verso copyright (1855) and printer; [v]-[vi], Note to the Third Volume, verso blank; [vii]-xiv, table of contents; [1]-483, text; [484], blank.

Printer: John F. Trow, Printer, Stereotyper, and Electrotyper, 377 and 379 Broadway, Cor. White Street, New York.

Lineation: p. 100, CHAPTER X. ... preceding ; p. 300, of ... [in footnote] 122.

American Publishers' Circular, 16 August 1856, "will publish a Duodecimo Edition ... on the 1st October"; 20 September 1856, "now ready"; 4 October 1856, listed.

Volume IV.

LIFE | OF | GEORGE WASHINGTON. | BY | WASHINGTON IRVING. | IN FOUR VOLS. | VOL. IV. | NEW YORK: | G.P. PUTNAM & CO., 321 BROADWAY. | 1857.

The title leaf appears in five states:

A. As described, with the statement IN FOUR VOLS. on the title page. On verso, the last two lines of the copyright notice read, " ... the | Southern..." Trow's imprint is in four lines.

B. As described, with the statement IN FOUR VOLS. on the title page. On verso, the last two lines of the copyright notice read, "... the | Southern..." Trow's imprint is in three lines.

C. The statement IN FOUR VOLS. is omitted from the title page. The date is in Arabic numerals, 1857. On verso, the last two lines of the copyright notice read, "... the | Southern...." Trow's imprint is in four lines.

D. The statement IN FOUR VOLS. is omitted from the title page. The date is in Arabic numerals, 1857. On verso. the last two lines of the copyright notice read, "... the Southern | District...." Trow's imprint is in four lines.

E. The statement IN FOUR VOLS. is omitted from the title page. The date is in Roman numerals, M.DCCC.LVII. On verso, the last two lines of the copyright notice read, "... the Southern | District..." Trow's imprint is in three lines.

In the copies examined, none of the title leaves is obviously a cancel. It is difficult to be certain, particularly with tightly bound copies, but the leaf in each instance appears to be either integral or inserted singly or, perhaps, cancelled before binding.

Commonsense says that the three states that omit IN FOUR VOLS. are later ones. But some caution should be exercised in arguing from the sequence of title leaves to a sequence of the volumes in which the leaves appear. A copy at TxU with the title leaf in State B shows noticeably more batter and type wear in the body of the text than a copy with the title leaf in State E. New titles may have been added indiscriminately to existing sheets, and the possibility of duplicate plates always exists.

(18.6 x 12.5): [-]^6 ([-]$_2$a cancel?) 1-20^{12}. Not reckoned: engraving of Gen. Greene before title.

[i]-[ii], half-title, verso blank; [iii]-[iv], title, on verso copyright (1857) and printer; [v]-xi, table of contents; [xii], blank; [1]-479, text; [480], blank.

Printer: John F. Trow, Printer, Stereotyper, and Electrotyper, 377 and 379 Broadway, Cor. White Street, New York.

Lineation: p. 100, in ... [in footnote] Redman.; p. 300, above, ... too

American Publishers' Circular, 2 May 1857, "about the first week in May"; 9 May to 8 August 1857, "will issue, in a few days."

Volume V.

LIFE | OF | GEORGE WASHINGTON. | BY | WASHINGTON IRVING. | VOL. V. | NEW YORK: | G.P. PUTNAM, 115 NASSAU STREET. | M.DCCC.LIX.

(18.3 x 12.3): $[-]^6$ $1\text{-}17^{12}$ 12^{12} 19^1. Not reckoned: engraved portrait of Washington and view of tomb of Washington, on two leaves, before title; eight pages of terminal advertisements in some copies.

In a second state, signature 18 is correctly signed.

In some copies, perhaps most copies, there are eight pages of terminal advertisements, undated, paged [1] 2-8. The first page is headed, "List of the Works [fancy] | OF | Washington Irving, Bayard Taylor, | and others,". Page 3 and most of page 4 are given to the various forms of the *Life of Washington*; page 7 lists 96 illustrations for the *Life*, each for sale separately.

[i]-[ii], half-title, verso blank; [iii]-[iv], title, on verso copyright (1859) and printer; [v]-vi, Preface; [vii]-xii, table of contents; [1]-302, text; [303]-370, Appendix; [371]-434, Index.

Printer: John F. Trow, Printer, Stereotyper, and Electrotyper, 377 and 379 Broadway, Cor. White Street, New York.

Lineation: p. 100, At ... hundred ; p. 300, presidential. ... [in footnote] 412.

Pierre M. Irving in his private journal, 12 April 1859, gives 5000 copies as the initial printing.

American Publishers' Circular, 12 March 1859, "will publish early in April"; 7 May 1859, "will publish, May 10th"; 14 May 1859, listed. *New-York Times,* 6 and 7 May 1859, "Will be published on Wednesday, May 11, Price $1.50."

Bindings noted for the five volumes.

No sequence has been determined, although Binding [C] is similar to later bindings on other Irving volumes.

[A]. Gray-green or blue-green TB cloth. On sides, wide rule border in blind. On front, in gilt, reverse and obverse of Washington medal. On back, in blind, publisher's initials within ornament. Spine decorated in blind, titled in gilt: IRVING'S | LIFE | OF | WASHINGTON | [rule] | VOL. I. [II. - V.] | Putnam. & C°. Yellow endpapers.

[B]. Gray-green, blue-green, or green TB cloth. On sides, in blind, wide rule border with publisher's initials within ornament at center. Spine decorated in blind, titled in gilt: IRVING'S | LIFE | OF | WASHINGTON | [rule] | VOL. I. [II. - V.] | Putnam. Yellow endpapers.

[C]. Green TB cloth, or Gray-green BD cloth. On sides, in blind, an elaborated border of a zig-zag within rules; within, a box of double rules; center blank. Spine titled in gilt: IRVING'S | LIFE | OF | WASHINGTON | VOL. 1 [2-5] | G.P. Putnam. Ornate gilt border around sides and top of the title. Yellow-buff endpapers.

Publisher's advertisements list other bindings also available. The advertisement present in some copies of Vol. V of the Duodecimo Edition lists the five volumes as available in cloth at $7; sheep at $8.50; half calf, extra at $12.50; and half calf, antique at $12.50. It also advertises Irving's collected works, including the *Life of Washington*, uniformly bound in 21 vols.: in cloth; sheep; half roan; half calf, neat; half calf, extra; half calf, antique; half morocco, extra; full calf, extra; full calf, antique; full morocco, extra. Finally, it advertises THE 5TH AND OTHER SEPARATE VOLS. OF "WASHINGTON," TO COMPLETE SETS in green cloth at $1.50, and "folded, for binding" at $1.25.

Later impressions of the Duodecimo Edition have been noted with two imprints (the same imprint in all five volumes):

NEW-YORK: | G. P. PUTNAM, 115 NASSAU STREET. | M.DCCC.LIX.

NEW-YORK: | G. P. PUTNAM (for the Proprietor), 506 BROADWAY. | 1859.

Intervening impressions may exist also.

Discussion based on copies in CtY (3), MH, TxFTC, TxGeoS, TxU (3), ViU.

The Illustrated Edition in Parts

Sheets of the Octavo Edition, generally in later states of the text, with added single frame lines around each page, were issued from 1856 to 1859 or 1860 in a series of sixty-eight semi-monthly parts, some in single parts, some in double. Each part was issued bound in a printed paper wrapper, without an inner part-title. With each part was bound two or more engravings, woodcuts or maps. By the end of the series, the purchaser would own the complete Illustrated Edition (see the discussion of that form). Judging from the volume-title pages included in some parts, and from contemporary advertisements, the first issue of at least the first part of each volume preceded the publication of the Illustrated Edition in conventional bound volumes. An advertisement on the back of the wrapper of some of the early parts promises that the series in parts "will commence on the 1st of September [1856]." But an advertisement of the Illustrated Edition in *American Publisher's Circular*, 8 August 1857, says "now publishing for subscribers," although that is not very specific and may possibly refer to either form of publication. Whatever the exact sequence of the first issues of the two forms, however, it is apparent that the parts continued to be produced and sold well after the first issue of the bound volumes. Commonsense would require that conclusion, even without direct evidence: purchasers who began acquiring the parts late in the series would want the earlier parts too -- necessitating frequent reprinting -- and some purchasers would want to buy the complete set in small, relatively inexpensive installments, even after the complete volumes were available.

No two sets located are alike, varying widely in the alternation of single and double parts, in the volume-title pages included (or not included), and in the wrappers on the parts. Any set that has passed through the hands of a book dealer, and presumably most that can be located have done so, must also be viewed with some caution: are the parts all from an original set, or is the set made up of available parts from several sets? No set with an original owner's signature on each part has been seen. But even if one were found, who knows how the owner compiled his set over the years? A part that includes a printed title for one of the volumes offers a certain amount of acceptable internal evidence, but it can offer only limited evidence about the other accompanying parts for that volume, parts that generally show no internal means of dating or of establishing a chronological sequence.

Even two of the same parts that contain the same volume-title can differ in other components of the part. Part 1 in the New York Public Library's Arents Collection and Part 1 in the University of Virginia library, for instance, contain each a printed title for 1857 and an engraved title for 1857, yet the two parts have different wrappers, front and back.

In view of the complexities and ambiguities, no attempt is made here to define first impressions or a positive sequence in the individual parts. Even so, a general accounting is possible, and even some hesitant suggestion of sequence. The information is drawn primarily from four sets examined in detail.

Title Pages Bound in the Parts for Volumes of the Complete Work

These are the title pages noted or reported. In a given set of parts, the printed title and the engraved title included for each volume may not match.

Vol. I.	Printed titles dated 1856, 1857.
	Engraved titles dated 1856, 1857.
Vol. II.	Printed title dated 1857.
	Engraved titles dated 1856, 1857.

Vol. III.	Printed title dated 1858.
	Engraved title dated 1859.
Vol. IV.	Printed titles dated 1858, 1860.
	Engraved titles dated 1859, 1860.
Vol. V.	Printed titles dated 1859, 1860.
	Engraved title dated 1859 (Seen only in a set with an 1860 printed title; apparently not included in earlier sets).

THE WRAPPERS

The wrappers are of lightweight green wove paper varying randomly through a spectrum from light yellow-green to a darker bluish green. In size, generally matching that of the leaves within, they average about 27.4 x 18.5, although individual parts may vary noticeably.

The wrappers are classified here by the outer fronts and backs. The inside of the wrapper leaves carry various advertisements. The spines read vertically, IRVING'S LIFE OF WASHINGTON -- Part 1. [2., 3., etc.], with minor variations in type.

Front of Wrappers

Type A. Title for the work, with reverse and obverse of Washington medal at center, within frame of triple rules. Inside the frame itself, on the four sides, appear statements by the publisher such as, "Early subscribers will secure the best impressions of the Plates. -- India Proof Impressions, large size, 50 cents each." Or, at foot, "Original Copyright Edition -- Sold to Subscribers only." Above the frame appears the identification of the part: "Part 2. Illustrated Edition of Irving's Washington. 25 Cts." Below the frame: "Payable on delivery only. -- No carrier allowed to give credit, or to receive money in advance." Imprint: NEW YORK: | G. P. PUTNAM & CO., 321 BROADWAY. | C. T. EVANS, General Agent for Canvassers.

A later variant of the imprint of Type A adds a line between the original second and third lines: C. B. RUSSELL & BROS., 12 TREMONT STREET, BOSTON. Noted occasionally from Part 9 on.

Type B. The same except for the imprint: NEW YORK: | G. P. PUTNAM & CO., 321 BROADWAY. | CHARLES T. EVANS, GENERAL AGENT. | BOSTON: C. B. RUSSELL & CO. -- PHILADELPHIA: J. F. WILLETS, | AND E. THOMAS. -- BALTIMORE: JOHN WALLACE. -- | ST. LOUIS: A. R. THOMPSON. -- CHICAGO: | CARNES & WILSON. -- DETROIT: | LYMAN BRIGGS.

Type C.   Generally similar, although in some copies the publisher's statements at the top and sides are omitted from the frame. The identification at the top reads, typically, "Nos. 43-44.   IRVING'S WASHINGTON ILLUSTRATED. 50 Cts". Imprint: NEW YORK; | CHARLES T. EVANS, 305 BROADWAY, | BOSTON: C. B. RUSSELL & CO.   In a later variant, the address of Evans is 321 BROADWAY.

An occasional Type C wrapper has no printed part number at the head but leaves a blank after "No" at the left for adding the number by pen; at the right, "Cts." may or may not appear after the blank space provided for writing in the price.   The spine also lacks a part number.   Occasionally a wrapper with printed part number has the number scratched out by pen and a different number written in; sometimes that requires changing the price also. The part number is generally changed on the spine as well, although sometimes the penman was forgetful.

Back of Wrappers

Type A.   Advertisement and Terms of Publication for the Illustrated Edition in parts.   At foot, a long quotation from the *Philadelphia Evening Bulletin*.   First line: THE ILLUSTRATED EDITION

Type B.   Advertisement for Irving's *Life of Washington* and for Capt. Charles Wilkes' *Narrative of the United States Exploring Expedition Around the World*.   First line: TO INTELLIGENT AGENTS.

Type C.   Advertisement for various works by Bayard Taylor published by Putnam, beginning with *Travels in Various Parts of the World*, 5 vols., and ending with *A Visit to India, China, and Japan*.   First line: G. P. PUTNAM & CO.'S PUBLICATIONS.

Type D.   Advertisement for Irving's Works.   The *Life of Washington* is listed as 4 vols., and *Wolfert's Roost* as "now ready."   At foot, comments from eight periodicals.   First line: WASHINGTON IRVING'S WORKS.

Type E.   Advertisement, within double frame lines, for Irving's *Life of Washington* in parts, "COMPLETING THE | HISTORY OF THE REVOLUTION."   At foot: "A COMPANION VOLUME, | THE PRESIDENTIAL LIFE. | Is in preparation, and will be published uniform."   First line, above frame: TO BE COMPLETED IN 56 NUMBERS.   The specification of 56 numbers is retained as late as Parts 65, 66.

Type F.   Advertisement for various works published by Evans & Fitzpatrick, New York, beginning with *Berlin and Its Pleasures* and ending with

Frederick the Great, After the Battle of Collin. First line: NOW
PUBLISHED IN PARTS AT 25 CTS. EACH,

THE INDIVIDUAL PARTS

In this table, the four examined sets are described, as representative of the
variety of all surviving sets. It should be pointed out that although the parts
are listed here under the volume to which each finally belongs in the
Illustrated Edition, that is simply for convenience and clarity. The wrappers
themselves do not give the volume number, nor does it appear inside the
part.

The description of Part 1, not only the first part but also the part that
contains both the printed and the engraved title for Vol. I of the Illustrated
Edition, is presented in an order of observed copies that represents a possible
sequence, however tentative and hesitant the conclusion may be. That
sequence of the individual copies of Part 1, in turn, determines the order in
which the characteristics are presented of all the individual examined sets of
the parts that constitute Vol. I; that is, Parts 1-14. If Part 1 of an examined
set is listed second, for instance, Parts 2-14 of that set will also be listed
second. Similarly, the order of information about the observed copies of
double parts 27, 28, which contain the printed title for Vol. II, determines the
order of presentation of the four examined sets of Parts 15-28. A similar
sequence within each remaining volume is determined by double Parts 41, 42,
which contain the printed title for Vol. III; by double Parts 55, 56, which
contain the printed title for Vol. IV; and by double Parts 67, 68, which
contain the printed title for Vol. V. The order of presentation of any one of
the examined sets of the complete work, then, may vary here from volume to
volume. The intent is to describe the parts in manageable discrete units,
volume by volume (letting the title page and any other information about the
part in which it appears determine the place of that set in the order), and to
avoid possibly misleading implications about any existing set of the complete
work. Present knowledge simply does not allow precise definition of the
sequence of states or impressions of each of the parts, and certainly not of
complete sets of the parts.

Volume I

Part 1. Pp. [i]-xvi, [1]-32.

    Printed title dated 1856; engraved title 1856. Wrapper types A-A.

    Printed title dated 1857; engraved title 1856. Wrapper types A-B.

    Printed title dated 1857; engraved title 1857. Wrapper types [blank]-B.

    Printed title dated 1857; engraved title 1857. Wrapper types C-E.

Part 2. Pp. 33-80. Wrapper types A-B; A-D; A-B; A-A.

Part 3. Pp. 81-[112]. Wrapper types A-B; A-C; A-C; C-E.

Part 4. Pp. 113-160. Wrapper types A-C; A-C; A-A; C-E.

Part 5. Pp. 161-192. Wrapper types A-C; A-B; A-D; C-E (no printed part number; 5 entered by pen).

Part 6. Pp. 193-240. Wrapper types A-C; A-C; A-C; C-E.

Part 7. Pp. 241-272. Wrapper types A-A; A-A; A-D; printed Part 36 (A-A) changed by pen to part 7.

Part 8. Pp. 273-304. Wrapper types A-C; A-C; A-A; A-A.

Part 9. Pp. 305-[336]. Wrapper types A-D; A-D; A-D; A-A.

Part 10. Pp. 337-368. Wrapper types A-B; A-B; A-B; printed part 22 (A-A) changed by pen to Part 10.

Part 11. Pp. 369-400. Wrapper types A-B; A-B; A-A; A-D.

Part 12. Pp. 401-432. Wrapper types A-D; A-D; A-C; printed Part 14 (A-A) changed by pen to Part 12.

Part 13. Pp. 433-464. Wrapper types A-B; A-B; A-B; B-A.

Part 14. Pp. 465-504, plus table of illustrations: [v]-vii [viii]. One copy has no table of illustrations. Wrapper types A-D; A-D; A-D; B-A (no table of illustrations).

Volume II

Part 15. Pp. [1]-48. Wrapper types A-C; A-C; A-C; [in double Parts 15, 16, described below].

Parts 15, 16. Pp. [1]-80. Wrapper types A-A.

Part 16. Pp. 49-80. Wrapper types A-D; A-D; A-D; [in double Parts 15, 16, described above].

Part 17. Pp. 81-112. Wrapper types A-D; A-D; A-D; [in double Parts 17, 18, described below].

Parts 17, 18. Pp. 81-133. Wrapper types C-E.

Part 18. Pp. 113-144. Some copies have a green paper slip inserted inside the back wrapper, offering cloth covers and various bindings for the parts. Wrapper types A-D; A-D; A-D; [in double Parts 17, 18, described above].

Part 19. Pp. 145-192. Wrapper types A-C; A-C; A-C; [in double Parts 19, 20, described below].

Parts 19, 20. Pp. 145-224. Wrapper types A-A.

Part 20. Pp. 193-224. Wrapper types A-C; A-C; A-C; [in double Parts 19, 20, described above].

Part 21. Pp. 225-256. Wrapper types A-A; A-A; A-A; [in double Parts 21, 22, described below].

Parts 21, 22. Pp. 225-304. Wrapper types A-A.

Part 22. Pp. 257-304. Wrapper types A-A; A-A; A-A; [in double Parts 21, 22, described above].

Parts 23, 24. Pp. 305-384. Wrapper types A-A for all four copies.

Parts 25, 26. Pp. 385-464. Wrapper types A-A; A-A; A-A; C-E.

Parts 27, 28. Pp. 465-518, plus [i]-xii of Vol. II. Some copies have a small notice inserted inside the front wrapper, saying that the publishers are not able to give a list of illustrations at present but that the last number will contain a complete list. Printed title dated 1857 in all four copies. Wrapper types A-A; A-A; A-A; printed Part 36 (A-A) changed by pen to Parts 27, 28, and "each" written after printed "25 cts".

Volume III

Parts 29, 30. Pp. [1]-80. Wrapper types A-A for all four copies.

Parts 31, 32. Pp. 81-160. Wrapper types B-A for all four copies.

Parts 33, 34. Pp. 161-240. Wrapper types A-A; A-A; A-A; C-E (no printed part number: "33.34" entered by pen, and 50 before printed "Cts").

Parts 35, 36. Pp. 241-320. Wrapper types A-A ("Part 35" is printed, "&36" added by pen, and price changed by pen to 50 cts); same; same; C-E.

Parts 37, 38. Pp. [321]-400. Wrapper types A-A; A-A; C-F (no printed part number: "37-8" entered by pen, and 50 in the blank space in the right corner); C-E.

Parts 39, 40. Pp. 401-480. Wrapper types A-A; A-A; C-F (no printed part number: "39-40" entered by pen, and 50 before printed "Cts"); C-E.

Parts 41, 42. Pp. [481]-523, plus [i]-xiv of Vol. III, and [1]-16 of Vol. IV.

Printed title dated 1858. Wrapper types A-A.

Printed title dated 1858. Wrapper types probably A-A (the imprint is torn off).

No title included. Wrapper types: printed Parts 47, 48 (C-F) changed by pen to "41.2".

Printed title dated 1858. Wrapper types C-E.

Volume IV

Parts 43,44. Pp. 17-96. Wrapper types C-E; A-E; printed Parts 35, 36 (C-E) changed by pen to "43, 44"; printed Parts 39, 40 (C-E) changed by pen to "43.44".

Parts 45, 46. Pp. 97-160. Wrapper types C-E; C-E; C-E; C-F.

Parts 47, 48. Pp. 161-240. Wrapper types C-E; C-E; C-E; C-F.

Parts 49, 50. Pp. 241-[320]. Wrapper types C-E; C-E; printed parts 43, 44 (C-E) changed by pen to "49-50"; C-E.

Parts 51, 52. Pp. 321-400. Some copies include an engraved title for one or more volumes; some include a table of illustrations for various volumes. Wrapper types C-E (engraved title for Vol. II dated 1856); C-E; C-E (engraved title for Vol. II dated 1857, and Vol. III dated 1859, and Vol. IV dated 1859); C-E.

Parts 53, 54. Pp. 401-480. Wrapper types C-E; C-E; C-E; C-F.

Parts 55, 56. Pp. 481-518, plus [i]-x of Vol. IV. At least one copy includes an engraved title for various volumes; some include a table of illustrations for various volumes. One copy has a large yellow slip lightly tipped onto the front of the wrapper, headed, "COMPLETION OF | IRVING'S LIFE OF WASHINGTON, | Notice to Subscriber." The notice gives prices and arrangements for binding. Subscribers are asked to apply to the publishers, named here as Evans & Fitzpatrick, 305 Broadway, cor. Duane Street. Other copies may easily have lost the slip.

Printed title dated 1858. Engraved title for Vol. III dated 1859, for Vol. IV 1859. Wrapper types C-E (with yellow slip tipped to front).

Printed title dated 1858. Wrapper types C-E.

Printed title unnoted. Wrapper types C-E (no printed part number: 55, 56 entered by pen after "No", and 50 entered before "Cts.").

Printed title dated 1860. Wrapper types C-E.

Volume V

(Discussion based on three sets of parts)

Parts 57, 58. Pp. [1]-80. Wrapper types C-F for all three copies.

Parts 59, 60. Pp. 81-160. Wrapper types C-F; C-F; C-E.

Parts 61, 62. Pp. 161-240. Wrapper types C-F; C-F; C-E.

Parts 63, 64. Pp. 241-320. Wrapper types C-F; C-F; C-E.

Parts 65, 66. Pp. 321-398 [399]-[400]. Wrapper types: printed Parts 65-68 (C-F) changed by pen to "65 & 66" and "$1" changed to "50 cts"; [in quadruple Parts 65-68, described below]; [in quadruple Parts 65-68].

Parts 65-68. Pp. 321-456, plus [i]-xii of Vol. V, plus unpaged table of illustrations.

[in two double Parts 65, 66 and 67, 68, described above and below].

Printed title dated 1859. No engraved title included. Wrapper types C-F.

Printed title dated 1860. Engraved title 1859. Wrapper types C-[blank].

Parts 67, 68. Pp. [401]-456, plus [i]-xii of Vol. V, plus unpaged table of illustrations. The one copy seen has tipped onto the front of the wrapper the same yellow slip described in Parts 55, 56, except that the address of Evans & Fitzpatrick, 305 Broadway, is scratched out and "26 Walker --" is added by pen at the foot. Inserted at the front is a light blue sheet carrying an advertisement for *Italy, or Struggles for Freedom* published by Evans & Fitzpatrick.

Printed title dated 1859. No engraved title included. Wrapper types: printed Parts 65-68 (C-F) changed by pen to "67-68" and "$1" changed to "50 cts".

[in quadruple Parts 65-68, described above].

[in quadruple Parts 65-68, described above].

Discussion based on copies in NN (2), NNC (Vols. I-IV), ViU.

The Illustrated Edition

The Illustrated Edition in parts was also issued in bound volumes. The earlier states of each volume may have been made up of sheets of the parts, the later states from sheets newly printed. But the distinction is unimportant, since all sheets were simply reimpressions of the Octavo Edition with frame lines and an occasional illustration added. They are generally in a later signature state. The engravings produced for the purpose are again inserted, and a few woodcuts are printed in appropriate blank spaces at chapter endings, title breaks and the like. Bound copies of the Illustrated Edition in parts, if not in the publishers' standard bindings, could easily pass for the Illustrated Edition. (That was, of course, Putnam's intention, and a selling point for the parts; the two forms were supposed to be one.) It should be remembered also that in three of the original parts the publishers offered to provide binding. Those special bindings may have matched the standard ones.

Volume I.

LIFE | OF | GEORGE WASHINGTON. | BY | WASHINGTON IRVING. | ILLUSTRATED EDITION. | VOL. I. | NEW YORK: | G. P. PUTNAM & CO., 321 BROADWAY. | NEARLY OPPOSITE PEARL STREET. | 1857. All within single frame lines.

One state of the Illustrated Edition in parts includes a printed title page for Vol. I dated 1856, but that title page has not been seen in the Illustrated Edition in volumes. It may, however, exist.

(26.0 x 17.3 in cloth; 25.2 x 16.9 in leather).

Engraved title noted in two states: dated 1856; dated 1857.

No printer's imprint present.

Later impressions noted:

NEW YORK: | G. P. PUTNAM 321 BROADWAY. | NEARLY OPPOSITE PEARL STREET. | 1858. Engraved title dated 1857.

NEW YORK: | G. P. PUTNAM & CO., BROADWAY. | 1859. Engraved title dated 1857.

Volume II.

NEW YORK: | G. P. PUTNAM & CO., 321 BROADWAY. | 1857.

Engraved title dated 1856.

Printer: John F. Trow.

Volume III.

NEW YORK: | G. P. PUTNAM 321 BROADWAY. | NEARLY OPPOSITE PEARL STREET. | 1858

Punctuation is missing after the publisher and the date in the copies seen. One copy noted with the period also missing after BROADWAY.

Engraved title dated 1859.

Printer: John F. Trow.

Another, probably later, impression noted:

NEW YORK: | G. P. PUTNAM BROADWAY | 1858. Engraved title dated 1859.

No printer's imprint present.

Volume IV.

NEW YORK: | G. P. PUTNAM & CO., BROADWAY. | 1858.

Engraved title dated 1859.

Printer: John F. Trow.

Later impression noted:

NEW YORK: | CHARLES T. EVANS, 305 BROADWAY. | G. P. PUTNAM, NASSAU STREET. | 1859. Engraved title dated 1859.

Volume V.

NEW YORK: | CHARLES T. EVANS, 305 BROADWAY. | G.P. PUTNAM, NASSAU STREET. | 1859.

Engraved title dated 1859.

Printer: John F. Trow.

Bindings noted for the five volumes:

Bright blue L cloth. On front, in gilt, ornamental border with four inset illustrations; title and author within the border. On back, the ornamental border with inset illustrations; center blank. Spine titled in gilt and decorated in gilt with portrait in oval at center. Yellow endpapers. AEG.

Gray TZ cloth with black morocco shelfback and corners. Sides blank. Spine decorated and titled in gilt. Marbled endpapers. All edges marbled.

Brown morocco. On sides, gilt frame line around edges; within frame, in blind, double frame line with ornamental corners. Spine titled in gilt. Marbled endpapers. All edges marbled.

The advertisement sometimes found in Vol. V of the Duodecimo Edition (1859) offers the Illustrated Edition in cloth; in half morocco, extra; in half calf, antique; and in full morocco, extra. The bindings seen appear to correspond to those listed in the advertisement.

American Publishers' Circular, 8 August 1857, "Now Publishing for Subscribers. ILLUSTRATED EDITION. With nearly 100 superior engravings on steel and 50 wood cuts ... to be completed in 5 vols."; 11 December 1858, "Now Complete. With Eighty-seven engravings on steel and

Forty-seven Woodcuts. Elegantly printed in Four vols."; 21 May 1859, "The ILLUSTRATED EDITION of the Fifth Volume will not be ready until July"; 27 August 1859, "The ILLUSTRATED EDITION, with 102 plates on steel, and 50 woodcuts. Complete in 5 volumes, Royal 8vo, $20, and in various extra bindings."

DLC, MH (2), TxFTC, TxU.

A copy of a salesman's sample survives. It may have been produced for use in obtaining subscriptions for the Illustrated Edition in parts, or for the Illustrated Edition itself, or perhaps simply for the illustrations. It has no printed title. Engraved title: LIFE | OF | WASHINGTON [each line of title curved] | [vignette of Mount Vernon] | BY | WASHINGTON IRVING. | Vol. 2. [all to here in hollow letters] | NEW YORK. G.P. PUTNAM & C^O. 321 BROADWAY. | 1856. | LONDON. SAMPSON, LOW & CO. The contents consist only of thirteen engraved illustrations, with no printed text. Leaf size 26.2 x 17.8.

The publisher's binding is of green TZ-like cloth. On front, in gilt, LIFE OF WASHINGTON | [stylized swelled rule] | IRVING || SPECIMEN, NOT FOR SALE. All within elaborate decorative border that contains an illustration on each of the four sides. On back, the border in blind. Spine blank. Yellow endpapers.

TxU.

The Large-Paper Limited Edition

The Large-Paper Limited Edition, called by the publisher the "Quarto Edition," is simply an impression of the Octavo Edition on large paper with extra illustrations. (The extra illustrations, beyond those in the later Illustrated Edition, are not listed in the tables of illustrations.) For the most part, signatures in each volume are in one of the later states. Pages are all within single frame lines. The leaf size is 31.2 x 24.3 untrimmed.

Vol. I carries on the copyright page a limitation notice within a box of single frame lines: *No. _____ | of the edition in quarto, One hundred and ten copies only are | printed.* R CRAIGHEAD, *Printer.* In Vol. II, the limitation notice substitutes JOHN F. TROW as printer, and drops his name to a lower line. In Vols. III and IV, JOHN F. TROW is again raised to the same line with the word *printed.* In Vol. V, the limitation notice is omitted.

Vol. I. LIFE | OF | GEORGE WASHINGTON. | BY | WASHINGTON IRVING. | IN THREE VOLS. | VOL. I. | NEW YORK: | G. P. PUTNAM & CO., 10 PARK PLACE. | 1855.

Vol. II. IN THREE VOLS. | VOL. II. | G. P. PUTNAM & CO., 10 PARK PLACE. | 1856.

Vol. III. NEW YORK: | G.P. PUTNAM & CO., 321 BROADWAY. | 1856.

Vol. IV. NEW YORK: | G. P. PUTNAM & CO., 321 BROADWAY. | 1857.

Vol. V. NEW YORK: | CHARLES T. EVANS, 305 BROADWAY. | G. P. PUTNAM, NASSAU STREET. | 1859.

Noted in brown L cloth. On sides, in blind, double frame around edges, each frame composed of three frame lines; center blank. On spine, in gilt: LIFE | OF | WASHINGTON. | [rule] | IRVING. | VOL. I. [II., III., IV., V.] | Putnam. On Vol. IV there is no period after WASHINGTON or IRVING, and the name of the publisher at the foot of the spine is expanded to Putnam & C°. White endpapers.

A catalogue found at the end of some copies of Vol. V of the Duodecimo Edition (1859) lists the Quarto Edition as available "folded and collated" at $50 the set, and in "turkey mor[occo], extra" at $85 the set.

Vol. I in NjP is a presentation copy from George P. Putnam to Pierre M. Irving and so presumably is an early copy; the presentation is dated February 1856. *American Publishers' Circular,* 11 December 1858, Putnam advertises: "*A few copies of the Magnificent Quarto Edition,* beautifully printed on superfine paper, with *Proof Impressions* of the plates on *India Paper,* superbly bound in Turkey morocco extra. Price, $80." That would be the first four volumes only. Presumably the fifth volume was issued at about the same time as the fifth volume of the Octavo and Duodecimo Editions, May 1859.

MB (2), NjP.

The Illustrations

Although not the work of Washington Irving nor an integral part of the first publication of the *Life of Washington* in the Octavo or the Duodecimo Editions, the illustrations for the *Life* have a bibliographical relationship to the later forms. First produced for use in the Illustrated Edition, in parts or in bound volumes, the illustrations were also made available to the public for insertion by owners in the Octavo Edition or for collection as a group.

In the advertisement sometimes found at the end of Vol. V of the Duodecimo Edition (1859), the illustrations are offered in a number of forms: proofs in quarto (at $20.00, container or binding unspecified); octavo size in box ($5.00), in cloth ($5.00), in half calf ($6.50), and in morocco extra ($8.00). Ninety-six prints could also be purchased individually (in octavo, 15 cts.; proofs on India paper, quarto, 50 cts.; proofs in passe-partout frames, $1.50).

Bound form in octavo size.

The bound volume of illustrations has been noted in two states -- one including the illustrations for the first four volumes only, the other for all five volumes -- with the same title page.

ILLUSTRATIONS | TO | IRVING'S | LIFE OF WASHINGTON. | TO HIS INAUGURATION AS PRESIDENT. | COMPRISING | 87 ENGRAVINGS ON STEEL, | AND 45 WOOD-CUTS. | NEW YORK: | G. P. PUTNAM, (FOR THE PROPRIETOR,) | 506 BROADWAY. | 1859.

(23.3 x 14.8): sewn. The only letterpress is in the tables of illustrations for the individual volumes of the *Life*.

First state: Illustrations for Vols. I to IV only. Despite the claim on the title, the volume contains 88 engravings and 42 woodcuts. No maps are included, although maps are listed in the tables of illustrations. Each entry in the tables is given, at the left, a roman numeral.

Second state: Illustrations for Vols. I to V. The volume contains 97 engravings, 1 reproduction of a letter, and 53 woodcuts, although the title remains unchanged. No maps are included, although maps are listed in the tables of illustrations. Entries in the tables do not have an identifying roman numeral.

The cloth bindings are designed to be compatible with the binding of the Octavo Edition. On front, bust of Washington in gilt within blind frame lines. On back, in blind, wreath within frame lines. On spine, in gilt: LIFE | OF | WASHINGTON. | [rule] | IRVING. | ILLUSTRATIONS | Putnam Brown endpapers. The first state noted in bright blue BD cloth, AEG; the second state in purple T cloth. It is likely that the first state was also issued in purple, to match the Octavo Edition. Advertised, but not seen, in half calf, in half morocco extra, and in morocco extra.

American Publishers' Circular, 11 December 1858, the first state advertised as "now ready": "To match the Subscribers' Edition. In 8vo. Neatly put up in a box, ready to be inserted in their places, ... $5 00. THE SAME in cloth, gilt edges, to match the sets, ... 5 00. THE SAME, half calf, extra. THE SAME, half morocco, extra."

ViU, first state. TxU, ViU, second state.

Other Forms.

In NN there is a collection of the advertised "proofs in quarto" on India paper, unbound in five portfolios.

In MB there is a collection of some illustrations in a private binding catalogued as a "portfolio." The illustrations do not appear to represent the advertised "octavo edition in box." The leaf size, 29.9 x 23.9, is noticeably larger than that of the bound volumes. Two puzzling title pages at the beginning of the portfolio are similar to others scattered through the collection: LIFE | OF | GEORGE WASHINGTON. [in red] | BY | WASHINGTON IRVING. [in red] | ILLUSTRATED. | [elaborated swelled rule] | NEW YORK. [in red]. Just what this collection *is* is not determined; perhaps it was designed for a later printing of the *Life of Washington.*

The Sunnyside Edition
and
The Mount Vernon Edition

After the completion in 1859 of the first editions in all their various forms, Putnam apparently reprinted the Duodecimo Edition as part of a complete collected works of twenty-one volumes, calling the collection "The Sunnyside Edition." I have not examined a set identified as such, but an advertisement in *American Publishers' Circular*, 27 August 1859, is specific enough: "This new and beautiful edition is now ready. It is handsomely printed on superfine tinted paper, several volumes being newly stereotyped. Each volume has one, and most of them have two, fine Steel Plates." The *Life of Washington*, available separately, is given its own section in the advertisement:

SUNNYSIDE EDITION OF WASHINGTON, WITH FORTY-EIGHT PLATES,

5 volumes.	12mo.	Cloth	$8 00
"	"	Half calf	$13 00
"	"	Half calf, antique	$13 00
"	"	Half morocco, gilt edges	$14 00
"	"	Full calf, extra	$16 00
"	"	Full morocco, extra	$18 00

In the same long advertisement, but distinct from that for "The Sunnyside Edition," appears:

THE "MOUNT VERNON" EDITION OF WASHINGTON,

In OCTAVO, with 95 beautiful engravings on steel, and 50 woodcuts. 5 volumes, 8vo. Half morocco, or half calf, gilt edges, $22. The same, full calf, ... $24.

Not seen with such an identification. Presumably, this was simply a reprint of the Octavo Edition with illustrations. It was not the Illustrated Edition as such, for that form is described separately in the same advertisement: "With 102 plates on steel, and 50 woodcuts. Complete in 5 volumes, Royal 8vo, $20, and in various extra bindings."

1Ea-   Henry G. Bohn published the only contemporary British edition of the *Life of*
b.   *Washington*. It derives its text from advance sheets of each volume of Putnam's Octavo Edition, although British spelling conventions are substituted for American, and a few "corrections" appear, certainly the work of the publisher. Irving never saw the proof sheets.

Volume I.

LIFE | OF | GEORGE WASHINGTON. | BY | WASHINGTON IRVING. | IN THREE VOLUMES. | VOL. I. | COMPRISING HIS EARLY LIFE, EXPEDITIONS, AND CAMPAIGNS. | LONDON: | HENRY G. BOHN, | YORK STREET, COVENT GARDEN. | 1855.

(18.1 x 11.2): $[A]^8$ B-I^8 K-U^8 X-Z^8. The last two leaves are blank. Not reckoned: preliminary engraved portrait of Washington by G. Stuart; one leaf of preliminary advertisements and two leaves of terminal advertisements, printed in blue.

[i]-[ii], half-title, verso blank; [iii]-[iv], title, on verso printer; [v]-vii, Preface; [viii], blank; [ix]-xvi, table of contents; [1]-348, text, printer at foot of last page.

Printer: W. Clowes and Sons, Stamford Street and Charing Cross.

Lineation: p. 100, triumph, ... [in footnote] 329.

Later impression noted: IN THREE VOLUMES omitted from the title page.

Athenæum, 2 June 1855, listed. *Literary Gazette*, 2 June 1855, listed; 23 June 1855, reviewed.

Volume II.

LIFE | OF | GEORGE WASHINGTON. | BY | WASHINGTON IRVING. | IN THREE VOLUMES. | VOL. II. | THE AMERICAN WAR, INVASION OF CANADA, &c. | LONDON: | HENRY G. BOHN, YORK STREET, COVENT GARDEN. | 1856.

(18.1 x 11.2): [-]^6 2A-2I^8 2K-2U^8 2X-2Z^8· Not reckoned: two leaves of preliminary advertisements and two leaves of terminal advertisements, printed in blue.

[i]-[ii], half-title, verso blank; [iii]-[iv], title, on verso printer; [v]-xii, table of contents; 349-715, text; [716], printer.

Printer: W. Clowes and Sons, Stamford Street and Charing Cross.

Lineation: p. 500, Carleton's ... [in footnote] 17.; p. 700, had ... them.

Analogy with Vol. I would suggest a later impression with IN THREE VOLUMES omitted from the title page. Not seen.

Athenæum, 2 February 1856, listed. *Literary Gazette*, 2 February 1856, listed; 23 February 1856, reviewed.

Volume III.

LIFE | OF | GEORGE WASHINGTON. | BY | WASHINGTON IRVING. | VOL. III. | THE AMERICAN WAR | DURING THE YEARS 1777, 1778, AND 1779. | LONDON: | HENRY G. BOHN, YORK STREET, COVENT GARDEN. | 1856.

(18.1 x 11.2): [-]^8 3A-3I^8 3K-3U^8 3X-3Z^8. On recto of first leaf, advertisements for Irving's Works, and NOTICE concerning English copyright on them. Not reckoned: two leaves of preliminary advertisements and two leaves of terminal advertisements, printed in blue.

[unpaged leaf], half-title, verso blank; [i]-[ii], title, on verso printer; [iii]-[iv], "Note to the Third Volume," verso blank; [v]-xii, table of contents; [715]-1080, text; [unpaged leaf], printer, verso blank.

Printer: W Clowes and Sons, Stamford Street.

Lineation: p. 800, could ... to ; p. 1000, mont, ... some-

Athenæum, 2 August 1856, listed. *Literary Gazette*, 2 August 1856, listed; 9 August 1856, reviewed.

Volume IV.

LIFE | OF | GEORGE WASHINGTON. | BY | WASHINGTON IRVING. | VOL. IV. | CONCLUSION OF THE AMERICAN WAR, ETC.

| LONDON: | HENRY G. BOHN, YORK STREET, COVENT GARDEN. | 1857.

(18.1 x 11.2): $[a]^2 b^4$ 4A-4I^8 4K-4U^8 4X-4Y^8 4Z^6. Not reckoned: two leaves of preliminary advertisements and two leaves of terminal advertisements, printed in blue.

[i]-[ii], half-title, verso blank; [iii]-[iv], title, on verso printer; [v]-xi, table of contents; [xii], blank; 1081-1444, text, printer at foot of last page.

Printer: W. Clowes and Sons, Stamford Street and Charing Cross.

Lineation: p. 1200, warmest ... dis-; p. 1400, him, ... to

Athenæum, 1 August 1857, listed. *Literary Gazette,* 1 August 1857, listed; 22 August 1857, reviewed.

Volume V.

LIFE | OF | GEORGE WASHINGTON. | BY | WASHINGTON IRVING. | VOL. V. | CONCLUSION, WITH GENERAL INDEX. | LONDON: | HENRY G. BOHN, YORK STREET, COVENT GARDEN. | 1859.

(18.1 x 11.2): $[-]^6$ 5A-5I^8 5K-5T^8 5U^2. Not reckoned: preliminary engraving of tomb of Washington by Duthie; two leaves of preliminary advertisements and two leaves of terminal advertisements, printed in blue.

[i]-[ii], title, on verso printer; [iii]-iv, Preface; v-xii, table of contents; 1445-1669, text; [1670], blank; [1671]-1706, Appendix; 1707-1752, Index, printer at foot of last page.

Printer: William [on p. 1752, simply W.] Clowes and Sons, Stamford Street and Charing Cross.

Lineation: p. 1600, Knox ... by ; p. 1700, these ... [in footnote] Washington.

Athenæum, and *Literary Gazette,* 2 July 1859, listed.

Binding for the five volumes:

Light green paper boards. On front, within decorative border, AUTHORIZED EDITION, PRICE 2s. 6d. | [double rule] | LIFE | OF | GEORGE WASHINGTON. | BY WASHINGTON IRVING. | [wavy rule] | EARLY LIFE, | EXPEDITIONS INTO THE WILDERNESS, | AND | CAMPAIGNS ON THE BORDER. [Later volumes, unlike Vol. I, repeat verbatim the description from the title page] | [wavy rule] | London: | Henry G. Bohn, York Street, Covent Gardens. | 1855. [1856., 1856., 1857., 1859.]. On back, advertisement for *Wolfert's Roost* and the Complete Works of

Irving, dated June 1, 1855. On spine, title, volume, abbreviated description, price. Endpapers printed in blue with publisher's advertisements.

NN, ViU (Vol. I in later impression).

c.   [In four vols.] LONDON: | HENRY G. BOHN, YORK STREET, COVENT GARDEN. | 1859.

This later impression, followed by a number of others through the next two decades, is bound in four rather than five volumes. The text, still printed from the original plates, is divided by volumes as follows: Vol. I, pp. [1]-436; Vol. II, pp. 437-908; Vol. III, pp. 909-1304; Vol. IV, pp. 1305-1752. The table of contents for all four volumes is in Vol. I. The four-volume edition was designed to be "Uniform with the Standard Library" and to take its place at the end of Bohn's edition of the Complete Works.

The 1859 impression in four volumes seen only in Vol. IV. Presumably Vols. I-III exist in 1859 impressions also, although they have been seen only with later dates under the imprint of George Bell and Sons, or Bell & Daldy, York Street, Covent Garden.

TxU, Vol. IV and later impressions of Vols. I-III.

1G.   The text of the Tauchnitz edition is derived from Bohn's London edition of 1855-1859.

Volume I.

LIFE | OF | GEORGE WASHINGTON. | *AUTHOR'S EDITION.* | IN THREE VOLUMES. | VOL. I. | LEIPZIG | BERNHARD TAUCHNITZ | 1856.

"Collection of British Authors," Vol. CCCXLII.

(15.6 x 11.2): [I]-XIV, [1]-426. Signed in 8's.

Printer: Bernhard Tauchnitz.

Lineation: p. 100, that ... mira-; p. 200, CHAPTER XX. ... fine

Volume II.

IN THREE VOLUMES. | VOL. II. | LEIPZIG | BERNHARD TAUCHNITZ | 1856.

"Collection of British Authors," Vol. CCCXLIX.

(15.6 x 11.2): [I]-XII, [1]-452. Signed in 8's.

Lineation: p. 100, will ... [in footnote] Phila-; p. 200, still ... [in footnote] May.

Volume III.

[number of volumes omitted] | VOL. III. | LEIPZIG | BERNHARD TAUCHNITZ | 1856.

"Collection of British Authors," Vol. CCCLXVIII.

(15.6 x 11.2): [I]-XVI, [1]-454. Signed in 8's.

Lineation: p. 100, surrounded, ... Americans ; p. 200, on ... [in footnote] Papers.

A later impression adds IN FIVE VOLUMES to the title page. In the copy of the later impression examined, pp. [XVII]-[XVIII] are added to the preliminary matter.

Volume IV.

[number of volumes omitted] | VOL. IV. | LEIPZIG | BERNHARD TAUCHNITZ | 1857.

"Collection of British Authors," Vol. CCCCVI.

(15.6 x 11.2): [I]-X, [1]-454. Signed in 8's.

Lineation: p. 100, from ... among ; p. 200, give ... difference.

A later impression adds IN FIVE VOLUMES to the title page.

Volume V.

IN FIVE VOLUMES. | VOL. V. | LEIPZIG | BERNHARD TAUCHNITZ | 1859.

"Collection of British Authors," Vol. CCCCLXXXIV.

(15.6 x 11.2): [I]-XII, [1]-424. Signed in 8's.

Lineation: p. 100, tion, ... [in footnote] 102.; p. 200, had ... Philadelphia.

Bindings for the five volumes.

Drab-white paper wrappers. On front, cover-title. On back, publisher's advertisements.

The details of the cover-titles vary in different impressions or issues of the individual volumes and do not always correspond with the inner titles. One copy examined in mixed states provides an example:

Vol.	*Cover-title*	*Inner title*
I	IN THREE VOLUMES	IN THREE VOLUMES

II	IN FIVE VOLUMES	IN THREE VOLUMES
III	IN FIVE VOLUMES	IN FIVE VOLUMES
IV		IN FIVE VOLUMES
V	IN FIVE VOLUMES	IN FIVE VOLUMES

In that same copy, in mixed states, the advertisement for the *Life of Washington* on the back cover varies from volume to volume in the number of volumes listed for the work: Vol. I, as one volume; Vol. II, as five volumes; Vol. III, as five volumes; Vol. IV, as four volumes; Vol. V, as five volumes. Presumably the advertisement differs for different impressions or issues of each of the first four volumes.

The wrapper for Vol. V, at least in the copy examined in wrappers, has at the foot of the front: *New and correct title-pages to vol. 1-4 are added to this volume.* The four corrected title pages inserted in the volume all state IN FIVE VOLUMES, but bear the original dates. Also included with the extra title pages are four corrected half-titles, stating IN FIVE VOLUMES and giving the Tauchnitz volume numbers. Readers should be alert to the possibility of the substitution of these corrected titles and half-titles in rebound copies. The original pages are integral rather than inserted.

DLC: first states, rebound. BL: mixed states, with wrappers bound in, and the extra titles and half-titles bound in Vol. V. Complete copy, in unknown states, reported in Universitätsbibliothek Kiel.

TRANSLATIONS

German.

Das Leben | George Washingtons | von | Washington Irving. | [rule] | Aus dem Englischen von W. C. Drugulin. | [rule] | Zweiter Band. | [elaborated swelled rule] | Leipzig | Verlagsbuchhandlung von Carl B. Lorck. | 1856. [in fraktur]. Vol. I in an 1858 impression substitutes for line 6: Herausgegeben von Prof. Dr. Friedr. Bülau. The complete edition, in 5 vols., seen only in Vol. II and a later impression of Vol. I.

Vol. I, 1855. Presumably as described, with correct volume and date.

A later impression is dated 1858.

Vol. II, 1856. As described.

Vol.III, 1856. Paged [I]-XII, [1]-404.

A later impression is dated 1857.

Vol. IV, 1858. Paged [I]-XI [XII], [1]-393 [394].

Vol. V, 1860. Paged [I]-XIII [XIV], [1]-280.

"Moderne Geschichtsschreiber," No. 5-7, 12-13.

(19.1 x 12.0): Vol. I. [I]-XII, [1]-388. Vol. II. [I]-XIV, [1]-410. Three leaves of terminal advertisements not reckoned. Signed in 8's.

Printer: Ries'schen Buchdrukerei, Leipzig.

Lineation: Vol. I. p. 100, William ... habe Vol. II. p. 100, Da ... die

NN: Vol. I (1858), Vol. II. Vols. III-V listed in Wilhelm Heinsius, *Allgemeines Bücher-Lexicon, 1852-1856*, and *1857-1861.* Complete copy (1855-1860) reported in Universitätsbibliothek Düsseldorf. Vol. II for 1856 is reported in Universitätsbibliothek Erlangen, for 1857 in Hessischer Landes- und Hochschulbibliothek, Darmstadt.

Lebensgeschichte | Georg Washington's. | Von | Washington Irving. | [rule] | Aus dem Englischen | von dem | Uebersetzer der Werke Prescott's. | [rule] | Erster [Zweiter ... Fünfter] Band. | [swelled rule] | Leipzig: | F. A. Brockhaus. | [rule] | 1856. The second vol. is dated 1856; the third vol., 1857; the fourth vol., 1858; the fifth vol., 1859. [in fraktur]

Vol. I translated by J. H. Eberty; Vols. II-V by F. M. Kirbach.

(17.4 x 10.9): Vol. I. [I]-XVI, [1]-423 [424]. Vol. II. [I]-XVI, [1]-484. Vol. III. [I]-XVI, [1]-471 [472]. Vol. IV. [I]-XIII [XIV], [1]-470 [471]-[472]. Vol. V. [I]-XV [XVI], [1]-336. Signed in 8's.

Printer: F. A. Brockhaus, Leipzig.

Lineation: Vol. I. p. 100, den ... Ge- Vol. II. p. 100, putation ... sind." Vol. III. p. 100, Baum ... beob- Vol. IV. p. 100, am ... darauf Vol. V. p. 100, sammtbevölkerung ... Am

TxU. Complete copy reported in Bayerischer Staatsbibliothek, München.

Swedish.

GEORGE WASHINGTONS | LEFNAD. | AF | WASHINGTON IRVING. | [rule] | ÖFVERSÄTTNING. | [rule] | FÖRSTA DELEN. | [stylized swelled rule] | STOCKHOLM, | PÅ E. T. BERGEGRENS FÖRLAG.

Issued in three separately-bound parts with individual cover-titles but with a conventional inner title only for the first part. The three parts, dated 1857, 1858, 1859 on the cover-titles, are paged continuously.

Translated by O. V. Ålund.

(22.4 x 14.4 untrimmed): Part 1. [1]-144. Part 2. 145-255 [256]. Part 3. 255 (a reprint of p. 255 of Part 2) - 337 [338]. Signed in 8's.

Printer: J. & A. Riis, Stockholm.

Lineation: p. 100, männen. ... Con-; p. 200, nas ... sedan ; p. 300, minutmän ... (grants)

Paper wrappers: Part 1, pink; Part 2, yellow; Part 3, beige. Cover-titles.

ViU.

CONTRIBUTIONS
TO
OTHER BOOKS

THIS SECTION OF "Contributions to Other Books," divided into Original Contributions and Reprint Contributions, is given to books that contain work by Irving but are not books by Irving himself. Of the reprint contributions, not much needs to be said. The list should be of value in demonstrating the wide popularity of Irving in his lifetime and, by listing the particular writing that someone chose to reprint, in defining the literary tastes of the time. My aim has been to identify the first edition of each book clearly, and to describe its title, form, and function -- anthology, school reader, gift book, annual, or whatever -- but to condense and to limit the description in a reasonable fashion. Lines omitted from the transcription of title pages are indicated by three dots. The pagination is given rather than a full collation. Impressions or editions after the first are only suggested; I have mentioned only those that I have happened to notice. I have scanned a great many library shelves of nineteenth-century schoolbooks and annuals or gift books, but it is inevitable that I have missed some titles. Early schoolbooks in particular tend to be scarce and generally uncollected or unpreserved, despite the intellectual impact they must have had on growing generations. And, unfortunately, a copy of each book must be examined in some detail to determine whether it contains anything by Irving.

The list of original contributions needs a little more discussion, particularly of the question of exactly what constitutes an "original contribution." That traditional term might seem to suggest that Irving of his own volition contributed something to someone else's book. But that is not necessarily so. He would indeed have volunteered when a piece found its first publication in, say, an annual. Or clearly, in the instance of his work on the translation of Depons' *Voyage*, he knew that he was taking part in that effort, even if he did not want his name to appear in the book. Presumably the same argument would apply to his editorial efforts, such as those with Alexander Slidell's *A Year in Spain*. But in other books, particularly ones that simply print a letter or a polite commendation, it is probable that Irving never knew that he was writing something for that particular publication. In a sense, the printing of a letter might hardly seem to merit a place in the list, but where is one to draw the line? A more questionable definition is made implicitly by the inclusion of writing that had indeed been published before, but only in periodical form. The analogy can be drawn to such original books by Irving as *The Letters of Jonathan Oldstyle* or the first London edition of *The Sketch Book* or *Wolfert's Roost*, books that drew on writing previously published in periodicals. This is a list of any first appearance in a book, as long as the book was not one of Irving's own.

The phrase "not Irving's own," however, raises other questions. When Irving, either in his own name or under a pseudonym, is listed on the title page of a book as author or editor, there is no question about the classification of that work as an "original book." But what of collaborative efforts? *Salmagundi*, of which Irving was only one of at least three authors, has traditionally been classified under "original book," and that seems to me valid. But such works as the plays of John Howard Payne in which Irving certainly had a hand call for more careful distinctions, even though the parallel of *Salmagundi* still holds. If I have determined that Irving was the major author, or at least took a large and significant part in the composition-- as in *Charles II* -- I have classified the book as "original"; if I believe that Irving took a lesser part, perhaps some revision or editorial aid or the authorship of a small portion -- as in *'Twas I* -- I have classified the work as a "contribution." Such decisions are always open to question, as any definition based on a sliding scale is, but they do seem useful in distinguishing between works in which Irving was a major author, even if not the major author, and works in which he was simply a lesser contributor.

*Original Contributions
to Other Books*

A Voyage to the Eastern Part of Terra Firma

1Aa-
b.
A Voyage [fancy] | TO THE | EASTERN PART OF TERRA FIRMA, | OR THE | *SPANISH MAIN*, | IN | SOUTH-AMERICA, | DURING THE YEARS 1801, 1802, 1803, AND 1804. | CONTAINING | A description of the Territory, under the jurisdiction of the Captain - Ge- | neral of Caraccas, composed of the Provinces of Venezuela, Maracaibo, | Varinas, | Spanish Guiana, Cumana, and the Island of Margaretta; and | embracing every thing relative to the Discovery, Conquest, Topography, | Legislation, Commerce, Finance, Inhabitants and Productions of the | Provinces, together with a view of the manners and customs of the Spa- | niards, and the savage as well as civilized Indians. | [double rule] | BY *F. DEPONS*, | LATE AGENT OF THE FRENCH GOVERNMENT OF CARACCAS. | [double rule] | IN THREE VOLUMES. | VOL. I. [II., III.] | WITH A LARGE MAP OF THE COUNTRY, &C. | [elaborated swelled rule], | TRANSLATED BY AN AMERICAN GENTLEMAN. | [elaborated swelled rule, in a different style] | *NEW-YORK*: | PRINTED BY AND FOR I RILEY AND CO. [Period present after I in Vols. II, III and in some copies of Vol. I] | NO. I, CITY-HOTEL, BROADWAY. | [swelled rule] | 1806. The title of Vol. II varies in lineation and in the style of the second swelled rule.

An account of the work by Luther S. Livingston (see discussion below) reproduces a title page of Vol. I in which the period is present after the I in the publisher's name and, uniquely, a period replaces the comma after AMERICA in line 7. The copy is not identified. If the reproduction is indeed accurate, no such copy has been located.

(21.0 x 12.9): Vol. I. [A]^4 B-I^4 K-U^4 X-Z^4 Aa-Ii^4 Kk-Nn^4. Folded map inserted. Vol. II. [A]^4 B-I^4 K-U^4 X-Z^4 Aa-Ii^4 Kk-Uu^4 XX-ZZ^4 [-]^1. Vol. III. [A]^4 B-I^4 K-U^4 X-Z^4 Aa-Ii^4 Kk-Nn^4 OO$^{4.}$

Vol. I. [i]-[ii], title, on verso copyright (the twenty-second day of September, in the thirty-first year of the Independence); [iii]-[iv], letter of Sam. L. Mitchill to the publisher, verso blank; [v]-xxxii, Introduction; [1]-248, text; [249], printer; [250], blank; [251]-[256], table of contents, unpaged. Vol. II.

[i]-[ii], title, on verso same copyright; [iii]-[iv], blank; [5]-362, text; [363]-[370], table of contents, unpaged. Vol. III. [i]-[ii], title, on verso same copyright notice; [iii]-[iv], blank; [5]-288, text; [289]-[293], table of contents, unpaged; [294], blank; [295], blank; [296], advertisement for *The Picture of New-York*, "In the press, and speedily will be published."

A translation by Washington Irving, Peter Irving, and George Caines, a New York lawyer and author, of François de Pons, *Voyage à la partie orientale de la Terre-Ferme....* 3 vols. Paris: Colnet, Fain, Debray, Mongie, F. Buisson, 1806. The division of the work among the translators is not known. A confused and partly-erroneous account, in which the title is not identified, appears in the Pierre M. Irving *Life*. A fuller account, with an identification of the title, appears in Luther S. Livingston, "The First Books of Some American Authors: III.--Irving, Poe and Whitman," *The Bookman* [New York], 8 (November 1898), 230-231.

Printer: I. Riley and Co.

Lineation: Vol. I. p. 100, thirty ... ad-; p. 200, in ... de- Vol. II. p. 100, *Mission* ... and ; p. 200, *Cane* ... the   Vol. III. p. 100, a ... and ; p. 200, and, ... souls.

In contemporary binding, seen only in leather. The prospectus (see description below) promises the volumes "in handsome extra boards," and the work was listed in boards. The Luther S. Livingston article reports that "Roos's copy, in the original boards, uncut, was sold in 1897 for $15.75."

In Vol. I, signature B occurs in two settings. The following representative textual changes, chosen from a number that appear, will distinguish the two:

Page & line	Setting A	Setting B
x.18	5 millions	five millions
xii.19	head waters	head-waters
xiii.9	seventy five-years	seventy-five years
xiv.1	dictionary	Dictionary
xiv.9$_F$	merchandize	merchandise
xv.2	says also that	says, also, that
xvi.23-24	the / "Hollanders	the / "latter

It is probable that setting A is the earlier. The text changes from setting A to setting B tend toward contemporary "correctness," and the heavier use of the comma--the most frequent change appearing--seems in keeping with contemporary taste. The shift of the hyphen in xiii.9 is the only correction of a clear error. The Prospectus is in setting A.

Sufficient evidence is lacking to establish a correlation with the variants of the title page.

In Vol. II, page 361 occurs in two states: mispaged 359, or correctly paged 361. There is no correlation with the two settings of signature B of Vol. I: setting A of Vol. I has been seen paired with both states of the page.

Title deposited 22 September 1806. *Monthly Anthology, and Boston Review*, September 1806, "in press"; April 1807, listed. The Prospectus (see below) promises the work on 10 December 1806. *Monthly Register, Magazine, and Review* [New York], May 1807, listed, with publisher named as Brisban & Brannan, "Price in boards, Six Dollars Fifty Cents"; December 1807, reviewed.

TxU (4).

A Prospectus, consisting of the first four gatherings of Vol. I, was issued by the publisher before the appearance of the full work. The title is the same as that of Vol. I (with no period after the I in the publisher's name) and signature B is in setting A.

(23.2 x 14.6 untrimmed): [i]-xxxii.

Light tan paper wrapper. On front, a partial title and a prospectus:

...printed on an entire new type and | superfine medium paper, and embellished with a hand- | some frontispiece and a large map of the country, vig- | nettes, &c. and delivered to subscribers at two dollars | and a half per volume, in handsome extra boards. To | non-subscribers, the price will be three dollars per vo- | lume in extra boards.

The three volumes are now translating by three gen- | tlemen well skilled in the French and English lan- | guages, and fully competent to the task....

This publication will be ready for delivery on the | 10th of December next.

On back, a notice that subscriptions will be received by I. Riley & Co. and the principal booksellers in New-York, followed by a list of 71 booksellers outside of New York city (the number 71 has a small margin of error because of the ambiguity of multiple names listed for the larger publishing centers). At the end, all subscription lists are requested "by the first of December next."

Note: the "handsome frontispiece" promised in the prospectus apparently was not in fact furnished. No copy with one has been located.

MH: bound with wrapper, pp. xxvii-xxxii and back of wrapper mutilated. ViU: disbound, trimmed, without wrapper.

1E. TRAVELS | IN | SOUTH AMERICA, | DURING | THE YEARS 1801, 1802, 1803, AND 1804; | CONTAINING | A DESCRIPTION OF THE CAPTAIN-GENERALSHIP OF CARACCAS, | AND AN ACCOUNT OF THE DISCOVERY, CONQUEST, TOPO- | GRAPHY, LEGISLATURE, COMMERCE, FINANCE, AND NA- | TURAL PRODUCTIONS OF THE COUNTRY; | WITH A | VIEW OF THE MANNERS AND CUSTOMS | OF THE | *SPANIARDS AND THE NATIVE INDIANS.* | [double rule] | BY F. DEPONS, | LATE AGENT TO THE FRENCH GOVERNMENT AT CARACCAS. | IN TWO VOLUMES. | VOL. I. [II.] | TRANSLATED FROM THE FRENCH. | [double rule] | LONDON: | PRINTED FOR LONGMAN, HURST, REES, AND ORME, | PATERNOSTER-ROW. | 1807.

(21.1 x 12.8): Vol. I. $[A]^8$ $B-I^8$ $K-U^8$ $X-Z^8$ $Aa-Ii^8$ KK^4. Folded map inserted before title page. Vol. II. $[A]^6$ $B-I^8$ $K-U^8$ $X-Z^8$ $AA-BB^8$.

Vol. I. [i]-[ii], half-title, verso not seen; [iii]-[iv], title, verso blank; [v]-[xv], table of contents; [xvi], blank; [xvii]-lii, Introduction; [1]-503, text; [504], blank. Vol. II. [i]-[ii], half-title, verso not seen; [iii]-[iv], title, verso blank; [v]-[xi], table of contents; [xii], blank; [1]-384, text.

Printer: H. Bryer, Bridge-Street, Blackfriars.

Lineation: Vol. I. p. 100, Channel ... Oronoko,; p. 200, in ... de- Vol. II. p. 100, sion ... that ; p. 200, *Merchants.* ... Juan)

The text of the London edition is a slightly revised version of the American translation: an occasional word or phrase is changed, but relatively few, averaging perhaps one every page. A few corrections of misprints also appear. The British text is clearly set from the American edition, often in a line-for-line reproduction. A few representative changes chosen from the first pages of Vol I. will identify the two texts:

Page & line of London Edition	American ed.	London ed.
4.19	when that becomes	when it becomes
5.4	upon an analysis of	upon the detail of
6.16	interrupt the communications	interrupt communications
7.5	It was	This was
$7.4-3_f$	frequent / with him.	frequent / in his work.

In contrast to the slightly revised body of the text, the Introduction in Vol. I is so heavily revised as almost certainly to represent a new translation. The opening sentence will identify the two translations:

American edition: "The work which I offer to the public has no other foundation than truth, nor any ornament but that which is derived from correctness."

London edition: "The Work which I here lay before the public has no foundation but truth, nor any ornament besides its accuracy."

It is not known who is responsible for the text revision or the new translation of the Introduction. No evidence now points to Washington Irving.

Bent's Monthly Literary Advertiser [London], June 1807, "In the press"; July 1807, "Now first published."

TxU, and also a facsimile.

The New-York Review

1A.   THE | NEW-YORK REVIEW; | OR, | CRITICAL JOURNAL. | TO BE CONTINUED AS OCCASION REQUIRES. | March 1809. | CONTAINING | *Strictures on a Pamphlet entitled "Fragments of the Journal* | *of a Sentimental Philosopher.*" | [elaborated swelled rule] | [9 lines of Greek, including one line of joined dashes to indicate omission; identified as Iliad II.211 and Iliad II.275] | [elaborated wavy rule] | *NEW-YORK:* | PUBLISHED BY INSKEEP & BRADFORD, | No. 128, Broadway.

(21.0 x 12.5): [A]^4 B-C^4. The first and last leaves provide a self-wrapper.

[i]-[ii], title, verso blank; 103-119, text; [120], blank.

Although the work purports to be an issue of a periodical, even paging the text from 103 to 119, it is not. It appears only in this single issue.

Stanley T. Williams in the *Life* ascribes the work to a joint effort of Washington Irving, his brother William, and James K. Paulding, assisted perhaps by others. Wayne Kime in the *Miscellaneous Writings* presents evidence that Gulian C. Verplanck in 1829 claimed authorship of one description in the work, attributing it to "an anonymous jeu d'esprit of my own, written when I was very young."

Lineation: p. 105, and ... belief.; p. 110, insidious ... world

Self-wrapper. On front, *THE* | NEW-YORK REVIEW; | &c. | March 1809. Verso of front leaf blank. The back leaf is blank.

New York *American Citizen*, 29 March 1809, "This day is published." (The advertisement by Inskeep & Bradford is dated March 28.)

NHi (2).

Sketches of American Naval Officers

In 1813-1814 Irving published in *The Analectic Magazine* a series of four biographical sketches of American naval officers: "Biography of Captain James Lawrence" (August 1813, with an additional note September 1813); "Biographical Notice of the Late Lieutenant Burrows" (November 1813); "Biographical Memoir of Commodore Perry" (December 1813); and "Biographical Memoir of Captain David Porter" (September 1814). The biography of Capt. Lawrence proved the most popular and was picked up by at least six books within the decade. In two of them the biographical sketches of Burrows and Perry appear also. The memoir of Commodore Porter appears by itself in one book.

Biographical memoirs of these naval heroes by other authors were current at the time, and care must be taken to distinguish Irving's from the others.

Although four of the seven books should be listed among the reprint contributions, there seems some value in listing them all together so that the early printing history is clear.

A.   AN | ACCOUNT | OF THE FUNERAL HONOURS BESTOWED | ON THE REMAINS OF | CAPT. LAWRENCE AND LIEUT. LUDLOW, | WITH | THE EULOGY | PRONOUNCED AT SALEM, ON THE OCCASION, BY | HON. JOSEPH STORY. | To which is prefixed, | AN ACCOUNT OF THE ENGAGEMENT BETWEEN THE CHESAPEAKE | AND SHANNON, WITH DOCUMENTS RELATIVE TO THE SAME, | AND BIOGRAPHICAL AND POETICAL NOTICES. | "A nation's tears bedew the hero's grave." | [double rule] | *BOSTON*: | PRINTED BY JOSHUA BELCHER. | [rule] | 1813.

(23.6 x 14.4): [1]^4 2-8^4. Laid paper.

[1]-[2], title, on verso "Advertisement" and copyright (August 28, thirty-eighth year of independence); [3]-64, text.

"Biography of Captain James Lawrence," 17-32 [credited to Mr. Irvine]. Footnotes added by an unknown hand.

Page 40 in two states:

      [A].   Letter by Crowninshield addressed to committee of three.

      [B].   Letter addressed to committee of seven.

Page 64 in two states:

      [A].   Without tailpiece.

      [B].   With tailpiece: FINIS on gravestone before bare tree and setting sun.

It is probable that the two states of the two pages were intended to correspond, but mixed states have been noted.

Lineation: p. 20, ris ... sailed.; p. 50, fect; ... on

Self-cover

Boston Daily Advertiser, 3 September 1813, repeated 6 September, "This day at 12 o'clock." *Salem* [Mass.] *Gazette*, 7 September 1813, advertised for sale by J. Dabney at his Salem Bookstore.

DLC (2): both pages State A; both pages state B. MB: both pages State B. MH (2): both pages State A; p. 40 State A, p. 64 State B.

B. BIOGRAPHY [hollow letters] | OF | JAMES LAWRENCE, ESQ. | LATE A CAPTAIN IN THE NAVY OF THE | UNITED STATES: | together with | A COLLECTION OF THE MOST | INTERESTING PAPERS, | RELATIVE TO | The Action between the Chesapeake and Shannon, | and the Death of | *CAPTAIN LAWRENCE,* | &c. &c. | [double rule] | EMBELLISHED WITH A LIKENESS. | [double rule] | *NEW-BRUNSWICK:* | PRINTED AND PUBLISHED BY L. DEARE, | AT WASHINGTON'S HEAD. | [swelled rule] | 1813.

(15.5 x 9.8 in boards; 13.5 x 8.4 in leather): $[A]^4$ $B\text{-}I^8$ $K\text{-}P^8$ Q^4 R^2. Portrait of Lawrence before title not reckoned.

[1]-[2], title, on verso copyright (twenty-eighth day of September, in the thirty-eighth year of the Independence, by Lewis Deare); [3]-[4], table of contents, verso blank; [5]-8, Preface; [9]-244, text.

"Biography of Captain James Lawrence," [9]-55. "Notes," 56-60, credited to "Editor"; this does not reprint Irving's note on Lawrence from the September *Analectic*. Footnotes on pp. 32, 50 by Irving; other footnotes by editor.

On p. [241] appears a notice, "After the foregoing work was printed, and the binding in considerable forwardness, we received ... permission to copy the two following poetical pieces:--the publication of the book has therefore been delayed a short time ...."

Lineation: p. 20, vessel ... at ; p. 100, It ... war.

Noted only in leather, and apparently so issued. P.C. Blackburn in *Bulletin of The New York Public Library*, 36 (November 1932), 742-743, describes a copy (in private hands) in boards. Dark gray-green paper boards. On front, title within elaborated border. On back, ad for Lewis Deare. Spine titled: [two double rules] | BIOGRAPHY | OF | CAPT. LAWRENCE. | [double rule] | [swelled rule] | [double rule] | DEAR'8 [sic] | EDITION. | [double rule]. Illustration on loose sheet laid in before title. Flyleaves.

New-York Evening Post, 25 October 1813, "Eastburn Kirk & Co. have just received and for sale"; advertisement dated at foot, Oct. 25.

TxU (2).

C.   A | COMPILATION | OF | BIOGRAPHICAL SKETCHES | OF | DISTINGUISHED OFFICERS | IN | THE AMERICAN NAVY, | WITH OTHER | *INTERESTING MATTER*. | "Fresh leaves of martial laurel shall shade the heroes grave, | "Who dies with arm uplifted his country's rights to save." | [wavy rule] | BY BENJAMIN FOLSOM. | [wavy rule] | NEWBURYPORT: | PUBLISHED BY THE COMPILER, | And for sale at Newburyport-Bookstore, No. 13 Cornhill, and by various other | Booksellers in the United States. | [rule of small type ornaments] | Horatio G. Allen, *Printer*. | 1814.

(21.8 x 12.6 rebound): $[A]^4$ B-I^4 K-U^4 W-Y^4 Z^2. Not reckoned: preliminary folded wood block of "Constitution and Guerriere."

[1]-[2], title, verso blank; [3]-[4], Preface; [5]-187, text; [188], blank.

"Captain James Lawrence," [67]-89 [abbreviated; first 2 paragraphs and other matter omitted]; "Lieut. William Burrows," 123-132; "Com. Oliver Hazard Perry," 132-147 [abbreviated; the first several pages and other matter omitted].

Lineation: p. 80, Shannon's ... possession.; p. 135, So ... Commo-

Boards?

NN.

D.   NAVAL BIOGRAPHY, | CONSISTING OF | MEMOIRS | OF THE MOST DISTINGUISHED OFFICERS | OF THE AMERICAN NAVY; | TO WHICH IS | ANNEXED THE LIFE OF | GENERAL PIKE. | [elaborated swelled rule] | *CINCINNATI*: | PRINTED AND PUBLISHED BY | MORGAN, WILLIAMS, & CO. | JUNE 1815.

(Approx. 17.6 x 10.0 trimmed): $[A]^4$ B-I^6 K-U^6 W-Z^6 Aa^6 Bb^4.

[i]-[ii], title, verso blank; [iii]-vi, Preface; [vii]-[viii], table of contents, verso blank; [1]-296, text.

"Biographical Memoir of Captain David Porter," 249-274.

Lineation: p. 100, gallantry ... [in note] Virginia.; p. 250, ran's ... in

Boards?

MWA.

E.   NAVAL BIOGRAPHY; | OR | LIVES | OF THE | *MOST DISTINGUISHED* | AMERICAN NAVAL HEROES | OF THE | PRESENT DAY, | ... | PITTSBURGH: | *PUBLISHED BY R. PATTERSON.* | S. ENGLES, PRINTER. | [rule of 11 dots] | 1815.

(Approx. 14.6 x 8.5 trimmed): [1]-144. Signed in 6's.

"James Lawrence, Esq.," 44-70; "Commodore O.H. Perry," 70-95; "Lieutenant Burrows," [134]-144 [abbreviated; first 3 paragraphs and other matter omitted].

Lineation: p. 50, satisfied ... St.; p. 100, he ... testimo-

MWA.

F.   AMERICAN | NAVAL BIOGRAPHY. | COMPILED | BY ISAAC BAILEY. | ... | *PROVIDENCE, (R.I.)* | PUBLISHED BY ISAAC BAILEY, | NEAR THE TURK'S HEAD. | [two rules of 14 dots] | *H. Mann & Co. Printers.* -- 1815.

(17.6 x 10.7 rebound): [i]-iv, [5]-257 [258]. Signed in 6's.

"Biography of Captain James Lawrence," [104]-125.

Lineation: p. 120, membrance-- ... honoured,; p. 200, the ... commodore,

NN.

G.   THE LIFE | OF | OLIVER HAZARD PERRY. | WITH AN | APPENDIX, | COMPRISING BIOGRAPHICAL SKETCHES OF THE LATE | GENERAL PIKE AND CAPTAIN LAWRENCE, AND A | VIEW OF THE PRESENT CONDITION AND FUTURE | PROSPECTS OF THE NAVY OF THE UNITED STATES. | ... | BY JOHN M. NILES, ESQ. | [double rule] | HARTFORD: | PUBLISHED BY WILLIAM S. MARSH. | R. Storrs....Printer. | 1820.

(18.0 x 10.5 rebound): [i]-xii, [13]-376.

"Biography of Captain James Lawrence," [338]-359.

Lineation: p. 100, to ... called ; p. 350, guns, ... Budd,

NN.

On the Death of the Princess Charlotte

1E.   A Poem [fancy] | ON THE | DEATH OF HER ROYAL HIGHNESS | THE | PRINCESS CHARLOTTE OF WALES | AND SAXE COBOURG. | BY | THE REV. R. KENNEDY, A.M. | LATE OF ST. JOHN'S COLLEGE, CAMBRIDGE, AND NOW | MINISTER OF ST. PAUL'S CHAPEL, IN BIRMINGHAM. | [elaborated swelled rule] | [3-line quotation from Shakespeare's *King John*] | [elaborated swelled rule] | THIRD EDITION. | [elaborated swelled rule] | LONDON: PRINTED FOR THE AUTHOR, | By A. J. Valpy, Tooke's Court, Chancery Lane. | SOLD BY J. HATCHARD, PICCADILLY; AND BALDWIN, CRADOCK, | AND JOY, PATERNOSTER-ROW, LONDON; A. CONSTABLE | AND CO., EDINBURGH; AND BY BEILBY | AND KNOTTS, BIRMINGHAM.

[n.d.; 1817 or later]

(20.7×13.4):$[A]^8$ B^8 C^4 D^2. It is probable that D_2 is a cancel--probably a substitute for an original blank leaf--but tight binding prohibits certainty.

[1]-[2], half-title, verso blank; [3]-[4], title, verso blank; [5]-[6], prefatory note, verso blank; [7]-[8], preliminary quotation from *Æneid*, verso blank; [9]-38, text; [39]-42, notes, printer's colophon at foot of last page; [43]-[44], laudatory letter to author from Irving, with introductory note, verso blank.

Original contribution: Letter to Rann Kennedy, dated Springfield, December 29, 1817, p. [43]. The later part of the full letter omitted.

Printer: A. J. Valpy, Tooke's Court, Chancery Lane.

Lineation: p. 20, And ... die.

Copy examined bound with R. Kennedy's *A Tribute in Verse, to the Late Right Honourable George Canning*, London, 1827. A presentation copy from the author in what appears to be a presentation binding: purple cloth figured with small vertical diamonds; sides and spine blank.

The prefatory note to the Irving letter says, "Some of Mr. Kennedy's friends, to whom copies of the Poem were presented, admiring this brief review of it, ... requested that it should be printed at the end of the Copies they received; and this circumstance has occasioned it to be continued in other Copies." Noted, however, only in the third edition.

TxU.

Peter Smink

On 2 October 1825 Irving wrote from Bordeaux to John Howard Payne in Paris, "I forwarded yesterday by coach a parcel containing the Plays you gave me to correct -- viz -- Red Riding Hood -- Mazeppa -- Peter Smink -- Twas I. -- & the Maid of Erin. I have made such corrections as were in my power considering the little time I have in travelling." *Peter Smink* had originally been produced at the Royal Surrey Theatre in 1822 under the title of *The Armistice* but was revived at the Haymarket Theatre 26 September 1826, apparently in a revised version for which Irving made "corrections." The printed text is based on the "corrected" version, since the actors who played the various parts in the 1826 London performance are specified on p. [2]. It should be noted that Lacy's editions of Payne's plays routinely omitted any songs in the plays.

1E. PETER SMINK; | OR, | THE ARMISTICE. | A comic Drama, [fancy] | *IN ONE ACT.* | *Adapted from the French.* | BY | JOHN HOWARD PAYNE. | AUTHOR OF | CHARLES THE SECOND, CLARI, ALI PACHA, THE LANCERS, LOVE IN | HUMBLE LIFE, TWO GALLEY SLAVES, THERESE, BRUTUS, | ACCUSATION, RICHELIEU, ADELINE, FALL OF ALGIERS. | ETC., ETC. | THOMAS HAILES LACY | 89, STRAND, LONDON.

(17.3 x 10.8): [-]^8.

[1]-[2], title, on verso production information, including the statement, *First Performed at the Royal Surrey Theatre, July* 1822.; [3]-16, text.

Lineation: p. 5, NINETTE. ... petter.; p. 10, betray ... brothers.

Lacy's Acting Editions were issued in volumes in the 1850's. Individual editions were probably published earlier.

TxU (in Vol. 75 of Acting Editions).

The Literary Souvenir for 1827

1Ea. THE | LITERARY SOUVENIR; | OR, | CABINET OF POETRY AND ROMANCE. | EDITED BY | ALARIC A. WATTS. | [four-line quotation from Sir Walter Scott] | [rule] | LONDON: | LONGMAN, REES, ORME, BROWN, & GREEN; | AND JOHN ANDREWS. | 1827.

(13.4 x 8.7): [a]^6 b^6 B-I^6 K-U^6 X-Z^6 AA-II^6 KK-LL^6 MM^4. Some copies MM^6, with advertisements on the last two leaves. Not reckoned: preliminary illustration and engraved title, and ten other engravings through the volume.

[i]-[ii], title, on verso printer; [iii]-[iv], dedication to the Marchioness of Stafford, verso blank; [v]-xvi, Preface; [xvii]-xxii, table of contents; [xxiii]-xxiv, list of the plates; [1]-402, text, printer at foot of last page.

Original contribution: "A Contented Man" by Geoffrey Crayon, Gent., [1]-9.

Printer: T. and J. B. Flindell, 67, St. Martin's-Lane, London.

Lineation: p. 100, afterwards ... nance.; p. 200, The ... rose."

Noted in black leather impressed to resemble A cloth. On sides, ornate border in gilt and blind. Spine titled in gilt and decorated in gilt and blind. Marbled endpapers. AEG.

For date of publication, see the account of the large-paper impression below.

MH, without advertisements. MiU, with advertisements.

b.   Also issued in a large-paper impression with proofs of the engravings on India paper. The setting is the same but the collation differs.

(18.9 x 12.6): $[a]^8$ b^4 B-I^8 K-U^8 X-Z^8 AA-CC^8 DD^1. In the rebound copy examined, it is probable that a blank leaf is missing at the end. High grade wove paper.

[The publication information given in the periodicals applies to both the common and the large-paper impression.] *Literary Gazette*, 14 October 1826, "Early in November will be published," price for common impression 12s.; 4 November 1826, "Reached us too late for a review this week"; 11 November 1826, "This day is published," "A limited number of copies, on a larger size, with proofs of the plates on India paper, has been struck off, as also a few separate sets of the engravings...."

MH.

The Atlantic Souvenir for 1827

1A.   THE | ATLANTIC SOUVENIR; | A | CHRISTMAS AND NEW YEAR'S | OFFERING. | [rule] | 1827. | [rule] | PHILADELPHIA: | H. C. CAREY & I. LEA.

(14.1 x 9.0): $[-]^6$ 1-30^6. Not reckoned: preliminary embossed presentation plate in white on blue, preliminary engraved illustration of "Imagination," and eight other illustrations through the volume. (Note: the "embellishment" listed for p. 240 is apparently missing.)

[i]-[ii], half-title, verso blank; [iii]-[iv], title, on verso copyright (19 September 1826); [v]-vi, Preface, dated Philadelphia, 1st October, 1826; [vii]-ix, table of

contents; [x], blank; [xi]-[xii], List of Embellishments, verso blank; [1]-360, text.

Original contribution: "On Passaic Falls, Written in the Year 1806," 146-148. (An engraved illustration of Passaic Falls by T. Doughty is inserted between pp. 146-147.)

Lineation: p. 100, THE ... tian.; p. 147, Oh! ... flood.

Light green paper boards. On front, embellished title, with shell design, American eagle and "E Pluribus Unum." On back, classical figures of two women with musical instruments. On spine, vertical decoration but no title. Pink endpapers. AEG. Pink ribbon for page marking attached to top of inside back cover. Issued in tan paper board slipcase with pasted-on green paper sides matching the binding of the volume.

The Cost Book of Carey & Lea specifies 4500 copies, in cases, at $2.50.

United States Literary Gazette, November 1826, reviewed. *Albion*, 11 November 1826, "On Passaic Falls" extracted.

TxU.

'Twas I

On 2 October 1825 Irving wrote from Bordeaux to John Howard Payne in Paris, "I forwarded yesterday by coach a parcel containing the Plays you gave me to correct -- viz -- Red Riding Hood -- Mazeppa -- Peter Smink -- Twas I. -- & the Maid of Erin. I have made such corrections as were in my power considering the little time I have in travelling." *'Twas I* was produced at the Theatre Royal Covent Garden, 3 December 1825.

The American edition and the English edition of the play differ markedly in text. The gross differences are immediately apparent. The American, for instance, is divided into two acts, each with two scenes; the English has only one act. Act I Scene 1 of the American text is omitted entirely from the English. (It is set in The Town Hall, and opens with a song from the Chorus: "Attend! attend! | While public choice selects a fair | The crown of innocence to wear! | Attend! attend!") All of the songs are omitted from the English edition. But the differences are greater than might be accounted for by a simple attempt to shorten the play and reduce the playing time. Individual parts in the English text are not only shorter and less developed, they also differ in word choice, in expression, and in such details as the attempt to convey dialect. The two editions are clearly derived from two distinctly different sources, whatever those sources may have been.

The different endings of the two versions provide ready identification. The English text ends on these curtain lines:

MAR. Huzza! our virtue has gained the day! And if ever my Georgette is made unhappy, she sha'n't have cause to say "'Twas I!"

The American text moves a variant of those lines back to a slightly earlier position:

Mar. Huzza! huzza! huzza! my wife that almost is, has got the crown of virtue; the parson always said the virtuous woman brought a crown to her husband.

They are followed by a speech by *Delorme*, another by *Marcel*, and a song by *Georgette* that ends, "You give me your leave to repeat | 'TWAS I.!"

1A.   'TWAS I, | OR | THE TRUTH A LIE. | A FARCE, IN TWO ACTS, | AS PERFORMED | AT THE THEATRE ROYAL, COVENT GARDEN, LONDON, | AND | *AT THE PARK THEATRE, NEW-YORK.* | [rule] | *BY JOHN HOWARD PAYNE,* | Author of Adeline, Brutus, Therese, Richelieu, Charles | the Second, Accusation, &c. &c. | [rule] | NEW-YORK: | Published by E. M. Murden, Circulating Library and | Dramatic Repository, 4 Chambers-st. | [rule of 11 dots] | 1827. [in copy examined, "Circulating" smudged and type damaged]

(15.0 x 9.5 approx.): $[1]^6 2^6 3^4$.

[1]-[2], title, on verso Dramatis Personæ; [3]-31, text; [32], advertisement for printed operas and dramas available.

Lineation: p. 10, hand, ... the ; p. 20, for ... nought!

PU, examined in microprint reproduction.

1Ea.   'TWAS I! | A FARCE, | IN ONE ACT. | BY | JOHN HOWARD PAYNE. | THOMAS HAILES LACY, | WELLINGTON STREET, STRAND, | LONDON.

(18.6 x 10.8): $[-]^8$.

[1]-[2], title, on verso production information, including the statement, *First Performed at the Theatre Royal Covent Garden,* | *Saturday, December 3rd,* 1825.; [3]-15, text; [16], blank.

Lineation: p. 5, DEL. ... virtue.; p. 10, so ... how?

Lacy's Acting Editions were issued in volumes in the 1850's. Individual editions were probably published earlier.

TxU (individual edition, and in Vol. 9 of Acting Editions).

b.   THOMAS HAILES LACY, | THEATRICAL PUBLISHER, | LONDON.

NN.

The Atlantic Souvenir for 1828

1A. THE | ATLANTIC SOUVENIR; | A | CHRISTMAS AND NEW YEAR'S | OFFERING. | [rule] | 1828. | [rule] | PHILADELPHIA: | CAREY, LEA & CAREY.

Also issued in another state, sequence undetermined, with SOLD IN BOSTON BY | HILLIARD, GRAY, & Co. added below the imprint on the title page.

(14.0 x 8.7): [A]^6 1-32^6. Not reckoned: preliminary embossed presentation plate in pink, preliminary engraved illustration by G. S. Newton for "The Dull Lecture," and twelve other leaves of illustrations through the volume.

[i]-[ii], half-title, verso blank; [iii]-[iv], title, on verso copyright (27 August 1827) and printer; [v]-vi, Preface, dated October 1, 1827; [vii]-x, table of contents; [xi]-xii, List of Embellishments; [1]-384, text.

Original contribution: "The Dull Lecture" [poem], 294.

Printer: Skerrett, Ninth street, Philadelphia.

Lineation: p. 100, Was ... man.; p. 294, 'Tis ... IRVING.

Green paper boards. On front, embellished cover-title. On back, engraving of angel playing a harp. Cream-yellow endpapers. AEG. Dark green ribbon for page marking attached to top of inside back cover. Issued in pink paper board slipcase with pasted-on green paper sides matching the binding of the volume.

A bookseller's catalogue, 1980, lists a copy in "Original full red morocco, gilt extra, AEG." Not seen.

The Cost Book of Carey & Lea specifies 7000 copies. It also records "150 proofs; 150 proofs 4°; 150 proofs 8vo; Cases for Proofs"; the illustrations must have been also sold separately.

Philadelphia Monthly Magazine, November 1827, "Just published." *Boston Recorder and Telegraph,* 21 December 1827, bookseller's advertisement, "Just received."

Without added imprint: TxU (3). With added imprint: NN.

A Year in Spain

In Spain in 1826, Irving became acquainted with Alexander Slidell, a young American naval officer who later took the name Alexander Slidell Mackenzie. In 1829 Slidell published in America *A Year in Spain,* "by a Young American." In 1830, when a second edition appeared, Slidell sent a copy to Irving, by then in London, asking him for help in finding an English publisher. At Irving's request, John Murray agreed to publish the book; Irving agreed to revise the work for the English market and to write an article on it for Murray's *Quarterly Review*. In editing the book, he made numerous excisions, rewrote a few passages, made some corrections and word changes, and added a few sentences. It is probable too that Irving had a hand in selecting the twelve line drawings that illustrate the Murray edition. When Slidell brought out a new American edition of his own in 1836, he retained many of Irving's revisions and additions, although he put back in much of what Irving had called the "heavy gazeteer material," swelling the work to three volumes. In the prefatory "Advertisement" to that third American edition, Slidell asserts that he himself had struck out material from the earlier editions and is now restoring it. It is interesting that neither Slidell nor Irving received any payment from Murray for the English edition, and Slidell gave Irving no public credit or thanks for the help, neither in the Murray edition nor in the later American editions.

1E.   A | YEAR IN SPAIN. | BY | A YOUNG AMERICAN. | Bien se lo que son tentaciones del demonio, y que una de las mayores es | ponerle a un hombre en el entendimiento que puede componer y imprimir un | libro, con que gane tanta fama como dineros, y tantos dineros cuanta fama. | CERVANTES. | IN TWO VOLUMES. | VOL. I. [II.] | LONDON: | JOHN MURRAY, ALBEMARLE-STREET. | [rule] | 1831.

(19.1 x 11.9 rebound): Vol. I. [A]^6 B-I^8 K-U^8 X-Z^8 AA-DD^8. Last leaf a blank?; not seen. Vol. II. [A]^4 B-I^8 K-U^8 X-Z^8 AA^8 BB^4 CC. CC seen only as a single leaf; so issued?

Vol. I. [i]-[ii], title, on verso printer; [iii]-[iv], dedication to Alexander H. Everett, verso blank; [v]-vii, Preface; [viii], blank; [ix]-xi, table of contents; [xii], blank; [1]-413, text, printer at foot of last page; [414], advertisements headed "Mr. Murray's List." Vol. II. [i]-[ii], half-title, on verso printer; [iii]-[iv], title, verso blank; [v]-vii, table of contents; [viii], blank; [1]-377, text; [378], advertisement for *The Journal of a Naturalist, Third Edition*, printer at foot.

Printer: T. Davison, Whitefriars.

Lineation: Vol. I. p. 100, snug ... and ; p. 200, thousand ... [in note] Antillon. Vol. II. p. 100, though ... cup ; p. 200, have ... fre-

Athenæum, 26 February 1831, "This day is published," advertised at 16*s*.

TxU (2).

ETT ÅR I SPANIEN. | AF | EN UNG AMERIKANARE. | [swelled rule] | ÖFVERSÄTTNING FRÅN ENGELSKAN | I TVÅ VOLYMER. |

FÖRSTA [ANDRA] DELEN. | [swelled rule] | STOCKHOLM, | HOS L. J. HJERTA, 1832.

A Swedish translation of the Murray edition of 1831.

(18.0 x 11.3): Vol. I. [i]-[ii], [1]-424. Vol. II. [i]-[ii], [1]-368. Signed in 8's.

Lineation: Vol. I. p. 100, framkasta ... blif- ; p. 200, först ... sådana Vol. II. p. 100, att ... [in note] Cordova.; p. 200, CAPITLET ... ut-

TxU.

Poems by William Cullen Bryant

1E. POEMS | BY | WILLIAM CULLEN BRYANT, | AN AMERICAN. | EDITED BY | WASHINGTON IRVING. | [rule] | LONDON: | J. ANDREWS, 167, NEW BOND STREET. | [rule] | M.DCCC.XXXII.

(19.5 to 19.9 x 12.1 to 12.3 untrimmed): $[-]^4$ $[A]^2$ $B-I^8$ $K-P^8$ Q^2 R^4. Some copies R^6 with two integral leaves of terminal advertisements.

[i]-[ii], title, on verso printer; [iii]-vi, Dedication to Samuel Rogers, dated *London, March* 1832; [vii]-viii, Author's Preface, dated *New York, January* 1832; [ix]-xii, table of contents; [1]-235, text, printer at foot of last page; [236], blank.

Printer: J. Moyes, Castle Street, Leicester Square, London.

Lineation: p. 100, THE SIESTA. [Note: The A is in too large a font and extends above the line.] ... below.; p. 200, ODE. ... nations.

Noted in three binding states, sequence, if any, undetermined.

[A]. Drab gray paper boards with red cloth shelfback. Paper label on spine: [double rule] | BRYANT'S | POEMS. | EDITED | BY | WASHINGTON IRVING [period?] | [double rule]. White endpapers. No advertisements at end of text. Leaf size 19.5 x 12.1.

[B]. Cream-yellow paper boards impressed in small cross-hatch design. Sides blank. Paper label on spine: the same. White endpapers. No advertisements at end of text. Leaf size 19.7 x 12.3.

[C]. Blue-gray paper boards with drab gray paper shelfback. Paper label on spine [not readable in copy examined]. White endpapers. At end of text, four pages of advertisements for works published by W. Simpkin and R. Marshall, London, undated. Leaf size 19.9 x 12.3.

Literary Gazette, 3 March 1832, reviewed; 10 March 1832, listed. *Athenæum*, 10 March 1832, listed at 9*s.*, also advertised, "This day is published."

MH, NN, TxU.

The Young Orator

1Aa. THE | YOUNG ORATOR; | CONSISTING OF | PROSE, POETRY, AND DIALOGUES. | FOR | Declamation in Schools; [fancy] | SELECTED FROM THE BEST AUTHORS. | [rule] | BY REV. J.L. BLAKE, A.M. | Author of 'First Book in Astronomy,' 'First Book in Natural Philosophy,' | and the 'American Universal Geography.' | [rule] | BOSTON: | LILLY, WAIT, COLMAN AND HOLDEN. | [rule] | 1833.

(16.1 x 9.9): [1]^{6}2-21^6. The signature mark 21 is defective: the "1" is something like an opening parenthesis mark.

[i] - [ii], title, on verso copyright (1833) and printer; [iii] - [iv], Preface, verso blank; [v] - viii, table of contents; [9]-252, text.

Original contribution: "Irving in New York," 83-85, Irving's acceptance speech at the public dinner in New York, May 30, 1832. The text differs from that of the newspaper accounts: punctuation is changed, Irving's remarks on his fear that he had been thought "alienated in heart from my country" are omitted from the first paragraph, and the toast, "*Our City*--May God continue to prosper it," is omitted at the end. Previously published in *The New-York Mirror,* June 9, 1832 and in newspapers of the day.

Printer: Stereotyped by Lyman Thurston & Co., Boston.

Lineation: p. 84, native ... [in footnote] *Brooklyn.; p. 200, exist? ... and

Deposited in Massachusetts District Clerk's Office 23 December 1833.

DLC.

b. THE | YOUNG ORATOR; | AND | NEW-YORK CLASS BOOK; | ESPECIALLY DESIGNED TO PREVENT | DULLNESS AND MONOTONY | IN THE | READING AND DECLAMATION OF SCHOOLS. | BY THE REV. J. L. BLAKE, D.D. | ... | SECOND EDITION. | ... | *NEW-YORK:* | PUBLISHED BY ROBINSON AND FRANKLIN, AND A.V. BLAKE. | [rule] | 1839.

A new Preface, dated 1839, is substituted, and the work is copyrighted 1839, but the text is in the same setting as the 1833 impression.

OO.

c.   There are a number of subsequent impressions, published in New York and Philadelphia. The last reported is the so-called "Fifteenth Edition," Philadelphia, 1846. By the "Twelfth Edition," New York, 1844, new material is added at the end of the volume to increase the number of pages to 288.

12th: TxU.

History of the Arts of Design
in the United States

1A.   HISTORY | OF THE | RISE AND PROGRESS | OF THE | ARTS OF DESIGN | IN THE UNITED STATES. | [rule] | BY WILLIAM DUNLAP, | Vice President of the National Academy of Design, Author of the History of the | American Theatre, -- Biography of G. F. Cooke, -- &c. | [rule] | IN TWO VOLUMES. | VOL. I. [II.] | [double rule] | NEW-YORK: | GEORGE P. SCOTT AND CO. PRINTERS, 33 ANN STREET. | 1834.

(23.5 x 14.5): Vol. I. [1]^4 2-54^4 55^2. Not reckoned: facsimile of bill by J. S. Copley, inserted between pp. 106-107. Vol. II. [-]^4 1-60^4.

Vol. I. [i]-[ii], title, on verso copyright (1834); [iii]-iv, Preface; [v]-viii, table of contents; [9]-435, text; [436], blank. Vol. II. [i]-[ii], title, on verso copyright (1834); [iii]-viii, table of contents; [1]-466, text; [467]-477, Appendix; [478]-480, index.

Original contribution: Letter to Dunlap on Gilbert Stuart Newton, dated New-York, March 9th, 1834, in Vol. II, pp. 302-304. The degree of Irving's total contribution is not known with certainty, but there was more than the single printed letter.   In the discussion of Newton, the author says, "Washington Irving, in conversation has represented Newton to me as ..." (II, 304). In the discussion of Washington Allston, the author says, "Washington Irving tells me that he first met Allston ..." (II, 188). In the discussion of Charles Robert Leslie, the author says, "Washington Irving, Esq., has told me ..." (II, 250). It is known that in the composition of the work William Dunlap gathered as much information as he could by letter and by word of mouth from friends and acquaintances. Whether he quoted literally or not is not known.

Lineation: Vol. I. p. 100, in ... lasting.; p. 200, Stuart, ... devoted Vol. II. p. 100, Steam ... life.; p. 200, the ... became

Noted in two bindings:

[A].   Green paper boards with dark blue-green coarse H cloth shelfback. Sides blank. Spines titled in gilt: DUNLAP'S | HISTORY | OF THE | ARTS OF DESIGN | [rule] | I [II]. White endpapers.

[B]. Tan paper boards with light green coarse H cloth shelfback. Sides blank. Spines titled the same. White endpapers.

The copy in TxU has Vol. I in Binding [A], Vol. II in Binding [B]. Other copies so issued?

New-York Mirror, 20 September 1834, "Is now in a state of forwardness, and will be ready for publication in the course of a few weeks," Vol. I excerpted; 1 November 1834, Vol I. reviewed. *New-England Magazine,* and *American Quarterly Review,* March 1835, both vols. reviewed.

TxU.

The Conquest of Florida

1A. THE | CONQUEST OF FLORIDA, | BY | HERNANDO DE SOTO | [rule] | BY THEODORE IRVING. | [rule] | Son quattromila, e bene armati e bene | Instrutti, usi al disagio e tolleranti. | Buona è la gente, e non può da più dotta | O da più forte guida esser condotta. -- TASSO. | [rule] | IN TWO VOLUMES. | VOL. I. [II.] | [rule] | *PHILADELPHIA*: | CAREY, LEA & BLANCHARD. | [rule of 12 dots] | 1835.

(18.3 x 11.2): Vol. I. $[1]^6$ 2-24^6 $[25]^1$. $[1]_2$ missigned 2. Vol. II. $[1]^6$ 2-25^6 26^1. The first leaf is a blank.

Vol. I.   [i]-[ii], title, on verso copyright (1835); [iii]-iv, dedication to Washington Irving, dated March 1835; [v]-viii, Preface; [9]-284, text; [285]-290, table of contents. Vol. II.   [i]-[ii], blank; [iii]-[iv], title, on verso copyright; 5-280, text; 281-294, Appendix; 295-302, table of contents.

Irving's editorial contribution is suggested by the first paragraph of the dedication: "MY DEAR UNCLE, I know of no person to whom I can with more propriety dedicate the following pages than to yourself, since they were written at your suggestion, and the materials of which they are composed were moulded into their present form and feature under your affectionate and judicious advice." A publisher's advertisement for the work, bound in Washington Irving's *Legends of the Conquest of Spain,* 1835, praises the author's style, "very much resembling the attractive and captivating narration of his uncle, from whom he derived important assistance in his labours."

Lineation: Vol. I. p. 100, land, ... safety.; p. 200, any ... them Vol. II. p. 100, them ... sur-; p. 200, that ... barbar-

Blue-green LG-type cloth. Sides blank. Spine titled in gilt: IRVING'S [in curved line] | CONQUEST | OF | FLORIDA | 1 [2]. White endpapers. Flyleaves.

The Cost Book of Carey & Lea records 1500 copies in cloth.

Knickerbocker, June 1835, reviewed. *North American Review*, July 1835, in "Quarterly List of New Publications." Irving to Peter Irving, 17 April 1835, Theodore's work is in the press at Philadelphia, and will soon be published."

CtY, NN, TxU.

2Aa. THE | CONQUEST OF FLORIDA, | BY | HERNANDO DE SOTO. | BY | THEODORE IRVING, M.A. | Son ... bene | Instrutti, ... tolleranti. | Buona ... dotta | O ... condotta. -- TASSO. | COMPLETE IN ONE VOLUME. | NEW-YORK: | GEORGE P. PUTNAM, 155 BROADWAY. | 1851.

(18.7 x 12.8): [iii]- xxii, [23]-457 [458]. Fold-out map inserted before title, with imprint of George P. Putnam, 1851. Either the map or the blank leaf that precedes it is apparently counted as the first two pages. Signed in 12's.

"Preface to the Revised Edition," [xi]-xiii. The revised Preface contains no further reference to Washington Irving.

Printer: John F. Trow, Printer & Stereotyper, 49 Ann-Street.

Lineation: p. 100, A ... pieces.; p. 200, Cofa ... [in footnote] c. 13.

Green TB cloth. On sides, publisher's initials in blind. Spine titled in gilt: CONQUEST | OF | FLORIDA | [rule, slightly swelled] | THEO. IRVING | PUTNAM The binding matches that of Washington Irving's ARE Putnam bindings.

TxU.

b. NEW YORK: | G. P. PUTNAM & CO., 321 BROADWAY. | NEARLY OPPOSITE PEARL STREET. | 1857.

NN, ViU.

1E. THE | CONQUEST OF FLORIDA, | UNDER | HERNANDO DE SOTO. | BY THEODORE IRVING. | Son ... bene | Instrutti, ... tolleranti. | Buona ... dotta | O ... condotta. -- *Tasso*. | IN TWO VOLUMES. | VOL. I. [II.] | LONDON: | EDWARD CHURTON, LIBRARY, HOLLES STREET, | 1835.

(18.4 x 11.7 rebound): Vol. I. [A]^6 B-I^{12} K-N^{12} O^4. Vol. II. [A]^2 B-I^{12} K-O^{12} P^2.

Vol. I. [i]-[ii], half-title, verso blank; [iii]-[iv], title, on verso printer; [v]-vi, Dedication to Washington Irving; [vii]-xii, Preface; [1]-296, text, printer at foot of last page. Vol. II. [i]-[ii], half-title, verso blank; [iii]-[iv], title, printer on verso ; [1]-302, text; [303]-315, Appendix; [316], printer.

Printer: Schulze and Co., Poland Street, London.

Lineation: Vol. I. p. 100, of ... [in footnote] 14.; p. 200, two ... dis- Vol II. p. 100, by ... and ; p. 200, CHAPTER XXV. ... of

Athenæum, 19 September 1835, listed; 26 September 1835, noticed.

ICN.

2E. THE | CONQUEST OF FLORIDA, | UNDER | HERNANDO DE SOTO. | [rule] | BY THEODORE IRVING. | [rule] | "Son ... bene | Instrutti, ... tolleranti. | Buona ... dotta | O ... condotta." -- *Tasso.* | [rule] | LONDON: | HENRY G. BOHN, YORK STREET, COVENT GARDEN. | 1850.

(18.1 x 11.4): [i]-viii, [1]-280. Signed in 8's.

Contains the original, unrevised Preface.

Issued individually as "Bohn's Shilling Series"; bound with Washington Irving's *Capt. Bonneville* as Vol. X of "Bohn's Library Edition."

Printer: Joseph Rickerby, Printer, Sherbourn Lane, London.

Lineation: p. 100, train ... mus-; p. 200, These ... [in note] 257.

Noted in original binding only in "Bohn's Library Edition." Gray T cloth. Sides decorated in blind. Spine titled in gilt as Irving's Works, Vol. X, Bohn's Library Edition. Illustration at beginning of volume. No works title in copies bound with Bohn's 1850 edition of *Capt. Bonneville*; works title in copy seen bound with 1854 edition.

Shilling Series. *Athenæum*, 13 July 1850, in "List of New Books," 1*s*.6*d*. Library Edition. *Athenæum* and *Literary Gazette*, 2 November 1850, the set of 10 vols. at 35*s*. listed.

MB, with 1854 *Bonneville*, rebound. NN, with 1850 *Bonneville*, original cloth. TxU, with 1850 *Bonneville*, rebound.

Die | Eroberung Florida's | unter | Hernando de Soto, | von | Theodor Irving. | [rule] | Aus dem Englischen übersetzt. | [rule] | Erster [Zweiter] Band. | [double rule] | Berlin, 1836. | Verlag von Duncker und Humblot. [In fraktur]

(16.3 x 10.2): Vol. I. [i]-[ii], [1]-275 [276]. Vol. II. [i]-[ii], [1]-308. Signed in 12's.

Printer: Vol. I. Vetsch, Berlin. Vol. II. C. Feister.

Lineation: Vol. I. p. 100, neigt ... auch Vol. II. p. 100, der ... sie

NN.

The Gift for 1836

1A. THE GIFT: | A CHRISTMAS AND NEW | YEAR'S PRESENT FOR | 1836. | EDITED BY MISS LESLIE. | [rule] | PHILADELPHIA: | E. L. CAREY & A. HART. All except rule in hollow letters.

(15.4 x 9.6): [1]^6 2-18^8 19^2. Not reckoned: engraving before the title and 8 other illustrations through the volume.

[i]-[ii], presentation leaf?; [iii]-[iv], title, on verso printer; [v]-vii, Preface, dated October 1835; [viii], blank; [ix]-x, table of contents; [xi]-[xii], table of illustrations, verso blank; [17]-292, text.

Original contribution: "An Unwritten Drama of Lord Byron," 166-171.

Printer: C. Sherman & Co.

Lineation: p. 100, not ... father,; p. 170, foregoing ... kind,

Red, and also dark green, hot-pressed boards. On sides, in blind, American eagle within oval at center, with elaborate border around (the eagle is oriented vertically rather than horizontally). Spine decorated in blind, titled in gilt: The [in script] | GIFT. | | Phila. [in script] | 1836. White endpapers with small leaf designs in gold. AEG.

Knickerbocker, August 1835, excerpted, "forthcoming," "to be published ere long." *North American Review*, January 1836, listed in quarterly list.

MH, TxGeoS, TxU.

Heath's Book of Beauty for 1836

1E. HEATH'S | BOOK OF BEAUTY. | 1836. | WITH | NINETEEN BEAUTIFULLY FINISHED ENGRAVINGS, | FROM | DRAWINGS BY THE FIRST ARTISTS. | EDITED BY | THE COUNTESS OF BLESSINGTON. | [rule] | LONDON: | LONGMAN, REES, ORME, BROWN, GREEN, AND LONGMAN, | PATERNOSTER ROW; | RITTNER & GOUPIL, PARIS; AND A. ASHER, BERLIN.

(19.5 x 12.4): [A]^4 B-I^6 K-U^6 X-Z^6 AA^6 BB^2. Not reckoned: engraved title, preliminary engraving, and 17 other engravings through the volume.

[i]-[ii], half-title, on verso printer; [iii]-[iv], title, verso blank; [v]-vi, table of contents; [vii]-[viii], list of plates, verso blank; [1]-280, text.

Original contribution: "The Haunted Ship: A True Story -- As Far as It Goes," [253]-257. Attributed to "The Author of 'The Sketch-Book.'"

Printer: J. Moyes, Castle Street, Leicester Square.

Lineation: p. 100, "I ... un-; p. 250, believed ... story.

Noted in two bindings: [A]. Blue paper boards impressed to resemble pebbled cloth. On sides, gilt decorations in the corners. Spine titled in gilt. Yellow endpapers. AEG. [B]. Full black morocco. On sides, border in blind with gilt decorations in the corners. Spine replaced in copy examined. AEG.

Athenæum, 5 December 1835, reviewed. *Examiner*, 6 December 1835, reviewed, and advertised as, "Just published, in 8vo. elegantly bound, 1*l*. 1s.; royal 8vo. India Proofs, 2*l*. 12s. 6d."

CtY, TxU.

The Magnolia for 1837

1A.   THE MAGNOLIA | FOR | 1837. [hollow letters] | EDITED BY | HENRY WILLIAM HERBERT. | NEW-YORK: | BANCROFT & HOLLEY, | 8, Astor House, Broadway. | COLLINS, KEESE & CO., PEARL-STREET. OTIS, BROADERS & CO., BOSTON. | CHARLES H. BANCROFT, NEW-ORLEANS.

(18.9 x 12.0):   [1]^6 2-28^6.   Not reckoned: engraved title, preliminary engraving, and 11 other engravings through the volume.

[1]-[2], title, on verso copyright (1836) and printer; [3]-4, Advertisement; [5]-vi, table of contents; [7]-[8], list of embellishments, verso blank; [9]-352, text.

Original contributions:

"The Widow's Ordeal, or a Judicial Trial by Combat," [257]-274. Attributed to "The Author of the 'Sketch Book.'"

"The Creole Village.   A Sketch from a Steamboat," [315]-326. Attributed to "The Author of the 'Sketch Book.'"

Reprint contribution:

"The Wrath of Peter Stuyvesant," [254].   Identified as taken from *Knickerbocker's History of New-York*, Vol. II, p. 81.

Printer: G. F. Hopkins & Son, Printers.

Lineation: p. 260, "is ... over ; p. 320, venture ... the

Noted in full black morocco. On sides, center decoration of gilt magnolia leaves and flower, with MAGNOLIA inscribed on flower; leafy border and straight frame line around in blind; within top line: B^D BY H & R

GRIFFIN; within bottom line: BANCROFT BROADWAY . Spine titled and decorated in gilt. Light yellow endpapers. AEG.

Knickerbocker, October 1836, extracted, "will be published in the course of the ensuing month." *New-York Mirror,* 29 October 1836, extracted, "just published."

TxU (2).

The Romancist, and Novelist's Library

1E. THE | ROMANCIST, | AND | NOVELIST'S LIBRARY: | THE BEST WORKS OF THE BEST AUTHORS. | [rule] | VOLUME I. [II., III., IV.] | [rule] | LONDON: PRINTED BY C. REYNELL, LITTLE PULTENEY STREET. | J. CLEMENTS, Nos. 21 and 22 LITTLE PULTENEY STREET, REGENT STREET. | [rule] | MDCCCXXXIX. Vols. III and IV: dated MDCCCXL; also added, before volume number, EDITED BY WILLIAM HAZLITT. All within double frame lines with circular ornaments in the corners.

(32.2 x 23.7): unsigned; bound in 8's. The four volumes have the same pagination: [i]-[iv], [1]-412. Text in triple columns.

Bound volumes of twopenny weekly numbers.

Original contributions:

"The Enchanted Island; or, The Adelantado of the Seven Cities," II, [346]-348. First published in *The Knickerbocker,* July 1839 .

"The Abencerrage; or, Recollections of the Alhambra," III, [223]-224. First published in *The Knickerbocker,* June 1839 .

Reprint contributions:

"The Young Robber," II, [142]. From *Tales of a Traveller* .

"Rip Van Winkle," III, [78]-80. From *The Sketch Book* .

Printer: Charles Reynell, 16, Little Pulteney street, Haymarket.

Lineation: Vol. II. p. [142], second column, and ... earth ; p. 347, second column, parted, ... Cities." Vol. III. p. 79, second column, liquor, ... Instead ; p. 224, second column, proscribed ... the

Michael Sadleir in *XIX Century Fiction,* Vol. II, describes the work in book form as bound in navy blue fine-ribbed cloth; embossed front, back, and spine; gold lettered on front and spine; light green glazed endpapers.

TxU.

Tales of the Grotesque and Arabesque

1A.   TALES | OF THE | GROTESQUE AND ARABESQUE. | [rule] | BY EDGAR A. POE | [rule] | Seltsamen tochter Jovis | Seinem schosskinde | Der *Phantasie*. | GOETHE. | [rule] | IN TWO VOLUMES. | VOL. I. [II.] | [rule] | PHILADELPHIA: | LEA AND BLANCHARD. | 1840.

(19.1 x 11.1): Vol. I. [1]^4 2-20^6 21^4. Vol. II. [-]^2 [1]^2 2^2 3-20^6 21^2.

Vol. I. [1]-[2], title, on verso copyright (1839) and printer; [3]-[4], dedication, verso blank; [5]-6, Preface; [7]-[8], table of contents, verso blank; [9]-243, text; [244], blank. Vol. II. [i]-iv, advertisements; [1]-[2], title, on verso copyright and printer; [3]-[4], table of contents, verso blank; [5]-222, text; 223-228, Appendix.

Original contribution: Two statements (edited by Poe?) used as testimonials, one on "The Fall of the House of Usher" and one on "William Wilson," Vol. II, p. [i].

Vol. II, p. 213 in two states; sequence uncertain: [A] paged 213; [B] paged 231.

Printer: Haswell, Barrington, and Haswell.

Lineation: Vol. I. p. 100, taken ... undis- Vol. II. p. [i], TALES ... *a Bridge*.; p. 100, as ... idolator

Dark purple V cloth. Sides blank. Paper label on spines: [double rule] | TALES | OF THE | GROTESQUE | AND | ARABESQUE. | BY | E. A. POE. | [rule] | *In Two Vols.* | Vol. I. [II.] | [double rule]. In some copies, the period after ARABESQUE has been lost in trimming. White endpapers. Flyleaves.

The bibliographies of Poe specify 750 copies printed.

Deposited 27 November 1839. *New-York Mirror*, 21 December 1839, noticed; 28 December 1839, reviewed.

TxU (5).

[Rufus W. Griswold quotes the letters in part in a preliminary "Memoir of the Author" in Poe's posthumous work, THE LITERATI: | SOME HONEST OPINIONS ABOUT | AUTORIAL MERITS AND DEMERITS, | ... | NEW-YORK: | J. S. REDFIELD, CLINTON HALL, NASSAU-STREET. | BOSTON: B. B. MUSSEY & CO. | 1850. The letters appear on p. xxxv. Copy in TxU.]

The American Lycoeum in Paris

1F.　Cover-title: THE | AMERICAN LYCOEUM [hollow, shaded letters] | IN | PARIS. [hollow letters] [stylized swelled rule] | Paris, | PRINTED BY E. BRIÈRE, 55, RUE SAINTE-ANNE. | [rule] | 1840.

(16.3 x 9.8): single unsigned gathering of 12 leaves.

[First leaf], fly-title, verso blank; [second leaf], blank; [3]-22, text and testimonials, title at head of p. [3], address for correspondence at foot of p. 22.

Letter of recommendation by Washington Irving for the Rev. Mr. Warner and the school, dated New-York, September 2, 1839, pp. 20-21.

Lineation: P. 21, to ... abundant

In paper wrapper. On front, cover-title as described. Back blank.

CtY.

The Moorish Drum

1A.　Caption title: *The Moorish Drum* | *Sung by* | MISS SHERIFF. [hollow letters] | In the Musical Romance of | The Moorish Captive. | *Written by* | *Washington Irving Esq.* | COMPOSED BY | *GEORGE PERRY.* [hollow letters] | [slightly swelled rule] | NEW YORK published by HEWITT & JAQUES 239 Broadway. Engraved in a variety of lettering styles.

1840.

(32.0 x 21.0 approx.): one leaf folded.

[1], caption title and beginning of score for Voice and Piano Forte; 2-3, score and words of song; [4], blank.

At foot of p. 3, "G. W. Quidor Eng^{vr}."

Nothing is known of the origin or the circumstances of composition of this song. Neither the song nor *The Moorish Captive* seems to be listed in the standard reference works, and I have been unable to discover a mention of either in the periodicals of the time. The song itself also appears in *The Casket, and Philadelphia Monthly Magazine,* June 1840. There the score is reduced to two pages, the name of Miss Shirreff is spelled correctly, reference to *The Moorish Captive* is omitted, the publisher is given as Geo. W. Hewitt & Co. No. 184 Chesnut Street, Philadelphia, and no engraver is named. Unfortunately, no further information is offered about the history of the song.

Irving's Journal of the mid-twenties reveals that he not only worked with John H. Payne and Barham Livius on plays, operas and musical productions but during that period began work on at least one other play of his own, called *The Cavalier*. He specifically mentions in letters to Payne writing songs for their plays. It is clear that he was active in composition for the theater, although he always carefully preserved his anonymity in the work.

Note the ambiguity of the title caption for this song; is authorship by Irving attributed to *The Moorish Captive* or only to the song?

George Frederick Perry (1793-1862) was an English composer and musician, and was the director of the music at London's Haymarket Theatre for a number of years after 1822. Jane Shirreff [the correct spelling of her name] (1811?-1883) was an English soprano signer. She was associated primarily with London's Covent Garden Theatre from 1831 to 1837, and in 1838 came to America for two years, where she was associated with New York's National Theater until its burning in 1840. In 1840 -- having become "a universal favourite" -- she also gave several concerts of songs in New York. In 1840 she returned to England, married, and retired. Extant playbills of the Haymarket Theatre and the Covent Garden Theatre do not list *The Moorish Captive*.

Lineation: p. 2, See ... bound--ing.

DLC. A copy in the collection of William R. Langfeld was sold at auction in 1942.

The Family Visitor

1A.   THE | FAMILY VISITOR. | [rule] | BY | JOHN HAYWARD, | AUTHOR OF THE NEW ENGLAND GAZETTEER, | &c. &c. | [rule] | BOSTON: | WEEKS, JORDAN, AND COMPANY. | NEW YORK: TANNER AND DISTURNELL. | PHILADELPHIA: WILLIAM MARSHALL AND COMPANY. | BALTIMORE: CUSHING AND BROTHERS. | [rule] | 1840.

(18.5 x 11.7): [-]^2 [1]^6 2-18^6 19^4. The first leaf is a blank. Not reckoned: four pages of terminal advertisements.

[i]-[ii], title, on verso notice of index with printed pointing hand, copyright (1840), printer; [1]-[2], Preface, dated February 1840, on verso notice of delay of publication of *The Northern Register* until July; [3]-220, text; [221]-224, index.

Original contribution: "The Birds of Spring," 110-114. First published in *The Knickerbocker*, May 1839.

Reprint contribution: "Female Influence and Energy," 94.

Printer: Stereotyped at the Boston Type and Stereotype Foundry.

Lineation: p. 112, approaches ... leaves.; p. 200, Ridgway, ... *democrats*.

Bright green wide-ribbed T cloth. On sides, leaves and flowers in gilt surrounded by decorative frame in blind. Spine titled in gilt: [double rule] | FAMILY | VISITOR | 1840. | [double rule]. Brown endpapers.

OU.

Scenes of the Primitive Forest of America

1A.   HARVEY'S SCENES | OF THE | PRIMITIVE FOREST | OF | AMERICA, | AT THE | FOUR PERIODS OF THE YEAR, | SPRING, SUMMER, AUTUMN & WINTER, | ENGRAVED FROM HIS ORIGINAL PAINTINGS, | Accompanied with Descriptive Letter-Press. [fancy] | [wavy rule] | ENTERED ACCORDING TO ACT OF CONGRESS, IN THE YEAR 1841, BY G. HARVEY, IN THE CLERK'S OFFICE OF THE DISTRICT COURT | OF THE SOUTHERN DISTRICT OF NEW YORK. | [wavy rule] | New-York: [fancy] | PUBLISHED BY GEORGE HARVEY, OFFICE 8, FULTON STREET, | PRINTED BY CHARLES VINTEN, 63, VESEY STREET, NEAR GREENWICH. | [rule] | 1841.

(49.1 x 40.0): unsigned, 7 leaves of letterpress, plus blank leaf at beginning and end, plus 4 leaves of heavier stock with single plate on rectos. Tissue guards inserted before engravings.

Contents: unpaged. [1]-[2], title, verso blank; [3]-[4], Dedication to Queen, verso blank; [5]-[6], Preface, verso blank; [7]-[8], blank, on verso text for "Spring"; [plate of "Spring"]; [9]-[10], blank, on verso text for "Summer"; [plate of "Summer"]; [11]-[12], blank, on verso text for "Autumn"; [plate of "Autumn"]; [13]-[14], blank, on verso text for "Winter"; [plate of "Winter"].

Statement in the Preface: "Being ... less practiced with the pen than with the pencil, I have obtained the promise of my friend, Washington Irving, Esq. to revise my manuscript." A Prospectus [see below] promises the work "edited by Washington Irving, Esq."

Lineation: p. [8], SPRING. ... landscape.

Dark blue paper boards with black leather shelfback. On front, cover title in gilt with imprint "London: [fancy] | PUBLISHED BY GEORGE HARVEY, 16, FOLEY PLACE, GREAT PORTLAND STREET. | AND | MESSRS. ACKERMAN & Co. STRAND. | 1841. | Johnson & Co. Printers,

10, Brooke Street, Holborn."; all surrounded by ornate "Moorish" frame. On back, in gilt, surrounded by same frame, proposal for a series of "Atmospheric or Dioramic Effects" to be published by subscription if the present work should awaken sufficient interest. Spine blank. Tan endpapers.

BAL reports the same cover-title imprint with the place of publication New York rather than London. Not located.

A Prospectus, 4 pp., 2 leaves, headed COLORED ENGRAVINGS OF AMERICAN SCENERY. [hollow letters], proposes the publication of 40 views: "The Work will be comprised in 8 numbers, to be issued every three months; each number to consist of 5 Views, and accompanied with a sheet of Letter-press, descriptive of the scene and effect, edited by WASHINGTON IRVING, ESQ." Apparently only this first number was issued, with four views.

Deposited 8 March 1842. The copy in DLC, rebound and first blank leaf missing, has "English Printed" written in pencil on the title. A deposit copy? *Boston Miscellany*, June 1842, reviewed.

The Prospectus for the series, and a version of the first part itself, are noticed in the "Editors' Table" of *The Knickerbocker*, March 1841: "Mr. George Harvey, A. N. A., has issued proposals.... We have seen the first number [in Mr. Harvey's rooms].... They are four wood scenes ... and an emblematic title-page. ... Each part is afforded at the low price of ten dollars."

DLC, rebound. ViU. Prospectus, ViU.

1E.   The London impression: same except for the title imprint. London: [fancy] | PUBLISHED BY GEORGE HARVEY, 16, FOLEY PLACE, GREAT PORTLAND STREET, & Messrs. ACKERMANN & Co. STRAND. | PRINTED BY JOHNSON & Co., 10, BROOKE STREET, HOLBORN. | [rule] | 1841.

NN, rebound.

International Copy-Right Law

1A.   Printed folded sheet headed: INTERNATIONAL COPY-RIGHT LAW. | [stylized swelled rule] | TO THE HONOURABLE THE SENATE AND HOUSE OF REPRESENTATIVES | IN CONGRESS ASSEMBLED. Dated at foot, *February*, 1842.

A petition, printed in one paragraph, for an international copyright law. Signed by pen by 24 American authors, headed by Washington Irving.

United States National Archives. The document is reproduced in facsimile in the *Emerson Society Quarterly*, # 51, Part III (II Quarter 1968), 108-110.

The Knickerbocker Sketch-Book

1A.   THE | Knickerbocker [fancy] | SKETCH-BOOK: | A LIBRARY OF | SELECT LITERATURE. | [rule] | EDITED BY | LEWIS GAYLORD CLARK, | EDITOR OF THE KNICKERBOCKER. | [rule] | NEW-YORK: | BURGESS, STRINGER AND COMPANY. | [rule] | 1845.

(18.9 x 11.4): collation uncertain. Pagination: [i]-vi, 4 pp. unpaged, [13]-46, 2 pp. unpaged, [41]-243 [244].

[i]-[ii], title, on verso copyright (1845); [iii]-vi, Preface; [one leaf unpaged], table of contents, verso blank; [one leaf unpaged], divisional fly-title, verso blank; [13]-46, first part of text; [one leaf unpaged], divisional fly-title, verso blank; [41]-243, remainder of text; [244], blank.

Original contributions:

> Quotations from a note to the Editor, incorporated in the Editor's Preface, iv.

> "The First Locomotive Again," [27]-29. First published in *The Knickerbocker*, May 1839.

> "The Early Experiences of Ralph Ringwood," [41] (the *second* p. 41)-83. First published in *The Knickerbocker*, August and September 1840.

> "Guests from Gibbet-Island. A legend of Communipaw," [117]-132. First published in *The Knickerbocker*, October 1839.

> "The Iron Footstep," [153]-162. First published in *The Knickerbocker*, April 1840. (See the discussion of Irving's contribution to this story.)

> "Mountjoy: or, Some Passages Out of the Life of a Castle-Builder," [165]-218. First published in *The Knickerbocker*, November and December 1839.

Printer: [Identified on paper wrapper only]. William Osborn's Power Press, 88 William-Street, [N.Y].

Lineation: p. 120, Some ... a ; p. 200, deavored ... it

Green paper wrapper. On front, title, price (fifty cents), and printer. Inside front cover, blurb for the volume and promise of a series under the title. On back, list of "Works in Preparation." Inside back cover, blank.

Broadway Journal, 31 May 1845, listed; 7 June 1845, reviewed. *Knickerbocker*, June 1845, in "Editor's Table," "Messrs. Burger, Stringer and Company have published ... under the supervision of the Editor of this magazine.... It is retailed at *fifty cents* a copy."

NN (2).

Friendship's Offering for 1849

1A. FRIENDSHIP'S OFFERING: | A | CHRISTMAS, NEW YEAR | AND | BIRTHDAY PRESENT, | FOR | MDCCCXLIX. | [stylized swelled rule] | BOSTON: | PUBLISHED BY PHILLIPS & SAMPSON. | 1849.

(18.5 x 11.9): [1]4 2-266 272 . Not reckoned: lithographed title, preliminary illustration, and 7 other illustrations through the volume.

[i]-[ii], title, on verso copyright (1848); [iii]-[iv], Advertisement, verso blank; [v]-vi, table of contents; [vii]-[viii], list of illustrations, verso blank; [13]-330, text, printer at foot of last page. The illustrations within the text are counted in the pagination.

Original contribution: "The Haunted Ship. A True Story--As Far as It Goes," [326]-330. First published in England in *Heath's Book of Beauty*, 1836; in America in the *New-York Mirror*, 9 January 1836.

Printer: King & Baird, No. 9 George Street, Philadelphia.

Lineation: p. 100, FAITH ... units ; p. 328, some ... on

Red-brown leather heavily impressed and varnished. On sides, decorations in blind, signed A C MORIN PHILA at foot. Spine titled in gilt and decorated in blind. Manila endpapers. AEG.

TxU.

Memorandum

1A. STRICTLY CONFIDENTIAL. | [rule] | MEMORANDUM: | The following are selected from letters placed before the State Department, recommending the subject | of them [John Howard Payne] to office under the present administration;....

N.p., N.d., probably Washington, D.C., 1850.

(29.0 x 18.2): cut sheet folded to four pages.

[1]-3, text; [4], blank. No formal title.

Original contribution: Letter to Secretary J. M. Clayton, dated New York, April 4th, 1849, recommending John Howard Payne, p. 3.

Lineation: p. 3, self ... *Washington, D.C.*

Unbound.

MH.

Life and Letters of Thomas Campbell

1Aa. LIFE AND LETTERS | OF | THOMAS CAMPBELL. | EDITED BY | WILLIAM BEATTIE, M. D., | ONE OF HIS EXECUTORS. | IN TWO VOLUMES. | VOL. I. [II.] | NEW YORK: | HARPER & BROTHERS, PUBLISHERS, | 82 CLIFF STREET. | 1850.

(19.6 x 12.5): Vol. I. $[1]^{12}$ $2\text{-}23^{12}$ 24^2. The first leaf is a blank. Not reckoned: engraved portrait before title. Vol. II. $[1]^{12}$ $2\text{-}21^{12}$ 22^{10}. The last leaf is a blank.

Vol. I. [i]-[ii], title, verso blank; [iii]-iv, letter from Beattie to Samuel Rogers; [v]-x, Preface; xi-xvi, letter from publisher to Irving and Irving's letter in return; [xvii]-xxii, table of contents; [25]-556, text. Vol. II. [i]-[ii], title, verso blank; [iii]-[vii], table of contents; [viii], blank; [9]-521, text; [522], blank.

Original contribution: Letter in reply to letter from Harper & Brothers, commenting on Thomas Campbell, I, xi-xvi.

Lineation: Vol. I. p. xv, poet ... con-; p. 100, In ... regarded Vol. II. p. 100, ceive! ... 1825.; p. 200, *Nov. 18th.* ... kind.

Red cloth figured in small interlocking lozenges. Sides bordered in blind. Spine titled in gilt. Top edges stained green. Yellow endpapers.

Literary World, 2 December 1848, "BEATTIE, in his forthcoming memoirs of Campbell, purchased from the London publishers by Harpers..."; 27 July 1850, "Will publish on Friday, July 26th," at $2.50; 24 August 1850, reviewed.

TxU.

b. NEW YORK: | HARPER & BROTHERS, PUBLISHERS, | FRANKLIN SQUARE. | 1855.

ViU.

Bertie

1A.   BERTIE: | OR, | LIFE IN THE OLD FIELD. | A HUMOROUS NOVEL.
| BY | CAPT. GREGORY SEAWORTHY. | AUTHOR OF "NAG'S
HEAD." | "Leves, non praecter solitum." -- HORACE. | "Faith, thin! it's a
pairt o' me systim, sir!" -- THE IRISH TUTOR. | WITH A LETTER TO
THE AUTHOR FROM | WASHINGTON IRVING. | PHILADELPHIA:
| A. HART, LATE CAREY AND HART. | 126 CHESTNUT STREET. |
1851.

(17.4 x 11.3): $[1]^4$ $2\text{-}20^6$ 21^2. The last leaf is a blank.

[i]-[ii], title, on verso copyright (1851) and printer; [iii]-[iv], dedication to A.
Harte, dated December 15, 1850, verso blank; [v]-vi, "Prolegomena" in verse;
[vii]-viii, "Introductory Word to the Reader"; [13]-242, text.

Original contribution: Letter to the author (George H. Throop), dated
Sunnyside, September 17, 1850, pp. [vii]-viii.

Printer: T. K. and P. G. Collins, Philadelphia.

Lineation: p. 100, "Precisely. ...me,; p. 200, strict ... butt!"

Paper cover in blue, gold and black. On front, cover-title; at top, in curved
line of special lettering, "LIBRARY OF HUMOROUS AMERICAN
WORKS, | with Illustrations by Darley"; Darley drawings and elaborate
frame; at foot, "T. Sinclair's, Lith. Phil[a]." On back, list of eight works in the
"Library of Humorous American Works" (each at 50¢) within blue and gold
frame. On spine, in blue and black, title only.

Southern Literary Messenger, September 1851, reviewed.

NN (2).

Dictionary Pamphlets

In the early 1850's a "war of the dictionaries" was waged between the
publishers of Webster's and Worcester's Dictionaries. The heavy weapons
were pamphlets written by supporters of one dictionary or the other, and the
lighter weapons were the advertisements that appeared in the periodicals or
other publications of the day and often in the dictionary pamphlets
themselves.   The publishers solicited many of the best-known writers,
educators, and public figures of the time for testimonials, and then published
the testimonials -- generally in a carefully edited excerpt -- in the
advertisements. One of the first major battles, following the beginning of a
long running skirmish in Massachusetts, would seem to have been fought
over the selection by the New York legislature of a dictionary to be used in

the state's schools. Webster's won that one in 1851, gaining the recommendation of a special "Committee on Literature." But the spoils were great and the war continued.

Washington Irving, through bad luck or bad judgment, and a little unscrupulous exploitation by publishers, provided ammunition for both sides. Three letter can be identified in the advertisements and the surrounding discussions, and one line from what appears to be a fourth letter. The broad outline of his role emerges from a study of the letters and the circumstances in which they appeared. When Webster's brought out a new edition in 1848, they sent a copy to Irving. He then wrote G. and C. Merriam a letter praising it, although adding some qualifications and saying that he did not take part in the dictionary controversy. The nearest to a full contemporary publication of that letter -- with a date for it of February 1849 offered by the Merriams in an introduction to the letter -- appeared in an advertisement in *The Literary World*, 13 September 1851. The Merriams used parts of the letter in advertisements. Irving was annoyed, and on 25 June 1851 wrote James W. Beekman, Chairman of the New York State Senate Committee on Literature, to complain that edited portions of his letter were being used in "puffs and advertisements." The letter appeared in the Minority Report of the Committee, published in *The Literary World*, 26 July 1851, and then in a pamphlet published by Jenks, Hickling and Swan (later Hickling, Swan and Brown, or Swan, Brewer and Tileston) of Boston. On 3 October 1855, after receiving a complimentary copy of Worcester's new edition, Irving wrote a letter of thanks and praise to the publishers, who promptly used it in their advertisements. The nearest to a full contemporary publication of that letter appeared in a pamphlet by Hickling, Swan and Brown of Boston as well as in other advertisements, such as those in *The (Old) Farmer's Almanac* for 1857 and 1858. Finally, in a late advertisement for Worcester's Dictionary there appeared a commendation by William Cullen Bryant followed by a statement of concurrence by Irving. The source of Irving's statement is unknown.

The dictionary pamphlets in which the various Irving statements appear are listed here together. Even though inconsistent in organization with the other entries in this section of Original Contributions, in which each publication is listed separately, it seems more revealing to list them together, in the order of composition of the original letters by Irving. It is possible that other pamphlets exist, and that the ones that have been discovered exist in other printing states, but these are the representatives located. It is also possible that the testimonials were published separately in advertising leaflets, but none has been found.

I. Excerpt from letter of February 1849, undated, to G. and C. Merriam: "I consider this Lexicon, in many respects, the best in our language, and find it an invaluable *vade mecum*; I must frankly tell you, however, I do not make it my standard for orthography in the publication of my works. My reason simply is, that it differs occasionally from the orthography in use among the best London Publishers." (A further part of the letter, "I do not pretend to take any part in the controversy...," appears only in an advertisement in *The Literary World*, 13 September 1851.)

A. No formal title page. Heading on first page: SKETCH OF REMARKS | ADDRESSED TO "THE COMMITTEE ON EDUCATION," IN BOSTON, FEB- | RUARY, 2D AND 4TH, 1850, ON THE RESOLUTION REFERRED TO THEM, | BY THE GENERAL COURT OF MASSACHUSETTS, TO INTRODUCE AN | ENGLISH DICTIONARY INTO EACH OF THE PUBLIC SCHOOLS OF | THE COMMONWEALTH. | BY PROF. PORTER, OF YALE COLLEGE, CONN.

No publisher. No date. New Haven, Conn. (?), 185-. The author is Professor Noah Porter.

(22.0 x 13.9): [1]-14; plus testimonials and advertisements for Webster's Dictionary, [1]-8, [1]-4. In 4's, unsigned.

On p. 7 of the advertisements appears one line from the Irving letter: "I find it an invaluable *vade mecum*," followed by a facsimile signature. The page has an ornate border of printer's ornaments.

Lineation: p. 10, and ... every

Unbound, sewn.

CtY.

Ba. THE DICTIONARY | IN | THE SCHOOL-ROOM: | CONTAINING | HINTS UPON THE IMPORTANCE OF ITS USE AS A TEXT-BOOK, | And the Manner of Using it; [fancy] | ALSO | FACTS WHICH MAY AID IN THE SELECTION | OF | THE BEST WORK. | [wavy rule] | SPRINGFIELD, MASS.: | GEO. & CHAS. MERRIAM. | 1854.

(21.5 x 13.3): [1]-16; plus Appendix, [17]-20; plus testimonials and advertisements: paged at top, 23-24, 9-11, 22, [-], 4-8, [-], 16-22, 25-32; also paged at foot, 21, [-], 33-35, [-], 27-32, 39-46, 49-56. Irregular gatherings, unsigned.

On p. 19 (top), p. 43 (foot) appears the longer excerpt from Irving's letter, followed by a facsimile signature.

Lineation: p. 10, teacher ... tongue."

Unbound, sewn.

TxU.

Bb. 1855.

The same, except the testimonials and advertisements are paged at top, 23-24, 27, 4-11, 22, [-], 16-22, 25-32; also paged at foot, 21, [-], [-], 28-35, [-], 39-46, 49-56.

CtY.

C. WEBSTER'S | DICTIONARIES. | [rule] | FROM THE MARIETTA (OHIO) INTELLIGENCER, | APRIL 1-8, 1856. | [rule] | BY I. W. ANDREWS, A.M., | PRESIDENT OF MARIETTA COLLEGE. | [stylized swelled rule] | SPRINGFIELD, MASS.: | GEO. AND CHAS. MERRIAM. | 1856.

(23.0 x 15.0): [1]-11; plus testimonials and advertisements, 18-22, [-], [-], [-], [-], 13-14, 9-11, [-], [-], 17, [-], 18, 3, 20; the last thirteen pages are also paged at the foot, 36-38, 33-35, 39, [-], 41, [-], [-], [-], [-]. Irregular gatherings, only one signed.

On p. 19 (top), p. 43 (foot) appears the longer excerpt from Irving's letter, followed by a facsimile signature.

Lineation: p. 10, as ... cor-

Unbound, sewn.

CtY.

II. Letter of 25 June 1851 to James W. Beekman. The letter begins, "Several months since, I received from Messrs. G. and C. Merriam a copy of ... Webster's Dictionary.   In acknowledging the receipt of it, I expressly informed them that I did not make it my standard of orthography, and I gave them my reasons for not doing so.... At the same time I observed the work had so much merit in many respects *that I made it quite a vade mecum.* [Paragraph division] They had the disingenuousness to extract merely the part of my opinion which I have underlined, and to insert it among their puffs and advertisements...."

Aa. A | REPLY | TO | MESSRS. G. AND C. MERRIAM'S ATTACK | UPON THE | CHARACTER OF DR. WORCESTER | AND | HIS DICTIONARIES. | [stylized swelled rule] | BOSTON: | JENKS, HICKLING AND SWAN. | 1854.

(23.7 x 14.5): [1]^6 2-4^6. Paged [1]-44; plus catalogue of school books published by Jenks, Hickling and Swan, 45-48.

On p. 30 appears Irving's entire letter.

Printer: Stereotyped by Hobart & Robbins, New England Type and Stereotype Foundery, Boston.

Lineation: p. 30, spelling ... Webster! --

Unbound, sewn.

CtY, DLC, NN.

Ab. BOSTON: | HICKLING, SWAN AND BROWN. | 1854.

The same, except that the catalogue is for school books published by Hickling, Swan and Brown.

DLC.

III. Letter of 3 October 1855 to the publishers of Worcester's Dictionary. The letter begins, "Accept my thanks for the copy of your Pronouncing, Explanatory, and Synonymous Dictionary which you have had the kindness to send me. As far as I have had time to examine it, it gives me great satisfaction...."

A. RECOMMENDATIONS | OF | Worcester's Dictionaries; | TO WHICH IS PREFIXED | A REVIEW OF | WEBSTER'S SYSTEM OF ORTHOGRAPHY, | FROM THE | UNITED STATES DEMOCRATIC REVIEW, | FOR MARCH, 1856. | [stylized swelled rule] | BOSTON: | HICKLING, SWAN AND BROWN. | 1856.

(23.3 x 14.8): $[1]^4 2^4$, plus in some copies 3^4. Paged [1]-15; plus testimonials and advertisements, [16]-[24] unpaged. Another copy adds two pages, unpaged, of advertisements, and an article, DICTIONARIES IN BOSTON, taken from the *Mercantile Library Reporter* for March 1855, paged 3-8.

On p. [20] appears Irving's entire available letter.

Lineation: p. 10, 4. ... to

Unbound, sewn.

One copy noted bound with *The Critic Criticized: A Reply to a Review of Webster's System in The Democratic Review for March, 1856,* by Epes Sargent. Springfield, Mass.: Geo. and Chas. Merriam, 1856. Certainly that is the work of some previous owner, since the two pamplets belong to opposite camps. There is no statement by Irving in the Sargent pamphlet.

CtY, shorter state. TxU, longer state.

IV. Following a commendatory statement for Worcester's Dictionary by William Cullen Bryant, undated, appears the statement, "I concur with the opinion of Mr. Bryant. -- WASHINGTON IRVING." The source of Irving's statement is unknown.

A. THE CRITIC CRITICIZED, | AND | WORCESTER VINDICATED; | CONSISTING OF A | REVIEW OF AN ARTICLE IN THE "CONGEGATIONALIST," | UPON THE COMPARATIVE MERITS OF | WORCESTER'S AND WEBSTER'S | QUARTO DICTIONARIES. | TOGETHER WITH | A REPLY TO THE ATTACKS OF MESSRS. G. & C. MERRIAM, | UPON THE CHARACTER OF DR. WORCESTER | AND HIS DICTIONARIES. | BY WILLIAM D. SWAN. | BOSTON: | SWAN, BREWER AND TILESTON | MARCH, 1860.

(22.4 x 14.2): [1]^8 2-4^8 5^6. In some states, 5^8. Paged [1] 2-67; plus testimonials and advertisements, 68-76, or in some states, 68-80.

On p. 70 appears Irving's statement.

Lineation: p. 10, too ... [in footnote] defective.

Unbound, sewn.

Noted in three states, sequence undetermined.

[A]. As described.

[B]. With variant imprint: BOSTON: | SWAN, BREWER & TILESTON. | CLEVELAND: INGHAM & BRAGG. | 1860. In brown wrapper carrying the title.

[C]. With the variant imprint of State [B] but with the author's name omitted from the title.

State [A], TxU. State [B], CtY. State [C], DLC.

The Home Book of the Picturesque

1Aa. THE HOME BOOK | OF THE | PICTURESQUE: | OR | AMERICAN SCENERY, ART, AND LITERATURE. | COMPRISING | A SERIES OF ESSAYS BY WASHINGTON IRVING, W. C. BRYANT, FENIMORE COOPER, | MISS COOPER, N.P. WILLIS, BAYARD TAYLOR, H.T. TUCKERMAN, | E.L. MAGOON, DR. BETHUNE, A.B. STREET, MISS FIELD, ETC. | WITH THIRTEEN ENGRAVINGS ON STEEL, | FROM PICTURES BY EMINENT ARTISTS, | ENGRAVED EXPRESSLY FOR THIS WORK. | NEW-YORK: | G. P. PUTNAM, 155 BROADWAY. | MDCCCLII.

(23.4 x 20.5): [a]^4 [b]^2 1-23^4 24^2. Not reckoned: preliminary engraving, engraved titled, and eleven other engravings through the volume.

Contents: [1]-[2], half-title, verso blank; [3]-[4], title, on verso copyright (1851) and printer; [5]-[6], dedication to A.B. Durand, verso blank; [7]-8, publisher's notice; [9]-[10], table of contents, verso blank; [11]-[12], list of illustrations, verso blank; [1]-188, text.

Original contribution: "The Catskill Mountains," [71]-78. Illustrated by "Cattskill Mountain Scenery" by J.F. Kensett [spelled "Catskill" in table of illustrations].

Printer: John F. Trow, 49 Ann-street. Engravings printed by Coats & Cosine.

Lineation: p. 75, phenomena ... attracted ; p. 100, these ... bewil-

According to *The Literary World*, 8 November 1851, the volume was issued in cloth at $7, in morocco at $10, and with India proofs at $16. Noted in two cloths: [A]. Royal blue L cloth. On front, title in gilt with decorative border and triple frame lines. Spine titled in gilt. AEG. Endpapers light yellow. [B]. Red pebbled cloth. On front, title in gilt and decoration in blind; on back, decoration in blind. Spine titled in gilt. All edges stained red. Endpapers marbled.

Literary World, 1 November 1851, excerpted; 8 November 1851, "Now Ready"; 15 November 1851, reviewed.

MH, *BL*.

b. HOME AUTHORS | AND | HOME ARTISTS; | OR, | AMERICAN SCENERY, ART, AND LITERATURE. | ... | NEW YORK: | LEAVITT AND ALLEN, 27 DEY STREET.

[1852]. Copyright notice omitted.

The new title leaf, a cancel, is printed on a whiter and coarser stock than the remainder of the volume. The engraved title is the original one; in some copies at least, the date is erased.

Blue coarse AR cloth. On sides, in gilt, HOME AUTHORS | AND | HOME ARTISTS, with upper and lower lines curved to form an oval, all within leafy border surrounded by three straight rules. Spine titled in gilt and decorated with vine and leaf design. AEG.

New-York Daily Times, 23 December 1852, "*A new issue*. 4to cloth extra gilt (reduced to) $5; morocco extra, $8; India proofs, $10."

CtY (in cloth), MB, NN.

The Autobiography of William Jerdan

1E. THE | AUTOBIOGRAPHY | OF | WILLIAM JERDAN, | M. R. S. L., CORRESPONDING MEMBER OF THE REAL ACADEMIA DE LA HISTORIA | OF SPAIN, &c. &c. | WITH HIS | Literary, Political, and Social Reminiscences and Correspondence [fancy] | DURING THE LAST FIFTY YEARS. | VOL. I. [II. - IV.] | LONDON: | ARTHUR HALL, VIRTUE, & Co., 25, PATERNOSTER ROW. | 1852. Vols. III, IV dated 1853 .

(17.4 x 11.1 trimmed): Vol I. $[A]^4$ B-I^8 K-T^8 U^4. Vol. II. $[A]^4$ B-I^8 K-U^8 X-Z^8 AA^8 BB^4. The last leaf is a blank. Vol. III. $[A]^4$ B-I^8 K-U^8 X-Z^8 AA^8. Vol. IV. $[A]^4$ B-I^8 K-U^8 X-Z^8 AA-DD^8 EE^2. In all volumes, not reckoned: preliminary engraving and engraved vignette title page.

A different vignette appears on the engraved title page for each volume; the engraved titles for Vols. I-III are dated 1852, Vol. IV, 1853.

Vol. I. [i]-viii, [1]-294 [295]-[296]. Vol. II. [i]-[ii], half-title, on verso note on the illustration; [iii]-[iv], title, on verso printer; [v]-[vi], dedication to George Canning, verso blank; [vii]-viii, table of contents; [1]-374, text, printer at foot of last page. Vol. III. [i]-viii, [1]-368. Vol. IV [i]-viii, [1]-386 [387]-420.

Original contribution: Letter to William Jerdan, undated (probably 1819), Vol. II, p. 290.

Printer: Bradbury and Evans, Whitefriars.

Lineation: Vol. II. p. 100, He ... more ; p. 200, locks. ... Bulwers,

Literary Gazette, 8 May 1852, "This day is published the First Volume, ... price 5s. cloth, gilt. It is proposed to complete the Work in Four or Six Volumes, to be published Quarterly"; 14 August 1852, "Second Volume is published this day"; 21 August 1852, Vol. II reviewed.

CtY, TxU.

Memorial of James Fenimore Cooper

1A. Memorial | of | James Fenimore Cooper | New York | G P Putnam | 1852 [all except the date is in fancy type]

(21.4 x 15.0): bound [1]-$[7]^8$, although signed in 12's. The first two leaves are blank. Not reckoned: preliminary portrait of Cooper.

[1]-[2], portrait of Cooper, verso blank; [3]-[4], title, on verso copyright (1852) and printer; [5]-[6], table of contents in the form of a listing of tributes on

three occasions in 1851-52, no page numbers given; [7]-106, text; [107]-[108], advertisements for works by the Coopers, verso blank.

Original contributions:

Letter to Rufus W. Griswold, dated Sunnyside, Thursday, 18 September 1851, p. [7].

Letter to Rufus W. Griswold, dated Sunnyside, 15 October 1851, p. 12.

Remarks upon introducing Daniel Webster to preside at commemorative meeting, p. 23.

Printer: Stereotyped by Billin & Brothers, No. 10 North William-St., New York; John F. Trow, Printer, 49 Ann-Street, New York.

Lineation: p. 23, The ... grateful ; p. 100, brought ... winds

Dark blue T cloth. On front, MEMORIAL | OF | COOPER in gilt, within floral frame in blind. On back, the frame in blind. On spine, COOPER in gilt, and four bands of decoration in blind. Light yellow endpapers.

Literary World, 8 May 1852, "Putnam Publishes This Week," "Large 8vo. elegantly printed"; 15 May 1852, listed.

NN.

Homes of American Authors

1Aa.   HOMES | OF | AMERICAN AUTHORS; | COMPRISING | Anecdotal, Personal, and Descriptive Sketches, [fancy] | BY | VARIOUS WRITERS. | ILLUSTRATED WITH VIEWS OF THEIR RESIDENCES FROM ORIGINAL DRAWINGS, | AND A FAC-SIMILE OF THE MANUSCRIPT OF EACH AUTHOR. | NEW-YORK: | G. P. PUTNAM AND CO., 10 PARK PLACE. | M.DCCC.LIII.

(20.9 x 14.9): [-]^4 [1]^8 2-23^8. The last leaf is a blank. Not reckoned: preliminary illustration and engraved title; eighteen other engravings and sixteen facsimiles through the volume. Fourteen colored woodcuts are pasted down in appropriate blank areas of the text; one, on p. 366, is uncolored and printed on the page.

[i]-[ii], title, on verso copyright (1852) and printer; [iii]-iv, Preface; [v]-viii, tables of contents, contributors, and illustrations; [1]-366, text.

Original contributions:

"To the Editor of the Knickerbocker," 53-61. First published in *The Knickerbocker*, March 1839.

One page of reproduced manuscript, between pp. 60-61. Identified as "Knickerbocker's New-York, revised ed., 1848."

Both contributions are included in an article on Irving, anonymous but the work of Henry T. Tuckerman.

Printer: John F. Trow, Printer and Stereotyper, 49 Ann-street.

Lineation: p. 60, ous ... the ; p. 200, member ... manfully,

Noted in black morocco. On sides, ornate gilt border. Spine decorated and titled in gilt. AEG. Marbled endpapers.

Literary World, 20 November 1852, reviewed; 27 November 1852, "will publish on Friday, the 26th inst., in one handsome volume, cloth, $5; gilt ext., $6; mor. ex., $8; proofs, $12." *New-York Daily Times*, 29 November 1852, "is this day published."

TxU.

b. NEW-YORK: | G. P. PUTNAM AND CO., 10 PARK PLACE. | LONDON: SAMPSON LOW, SON & Co. | M.DCCC.LIII.

(20.9 x 15.2): signed in 8's, just as the first impression, but bound irregularly, apparently the result of the requirements of printing the woodblocks on individual leaves.

The same setting, illustrations, printer, except that the colored wood blocks are printed rather than pasted down.

Noted in royal blue AR cloth. On sides, deeply impressed oval at center, with vignette in gilt of farm gate and trees within the oval; leafy gilt border around the outside of the oval. Spine decorated and titled in gilt. AEG. Yellow endpapers.

New-York Daily Times, 23 December 1852, "The second edition," "square 8vo cloth, gilt tops, $5; blue cloth, gilt extra, $6; Mor. Antiq., $8; India proofs, Russia and mor. super, gilt clasps, $14; vellum, gilt clasps, $16."

TxU.

c. ... DRAWINGS, | AND FAC-SIMILES OF THEIR MANUSCRIPTS. | NEW-YORK: | D. APPLETON & COMPANY, | 346 & 348 BROADWAY. | M.DCCC.LV.

The text is extended to p. 374, with a discussion of Fitz-Greene Halleck added at the end. Else, the same setting, illustrations, printer, except for an additional illustration and additions to the preliminary tables. Wood blocks printed. Engraved title, with Appleton imprint, dated 1854.

Noted in brown morocco. On sides, elaborated impressed border in brown. Spine decorated in blind and titled in gilt. AEG. Marbled endpapers.

TxU.

d.   New-York: | D. APPLETON & COMPANY, | 346 & 348 BROADWAY. | M.DCCC.LVII.

Same as the 1855 impression, except no printer's imprint.

Noted in blue A-like cloth. On front, border in blind, with title in gilt within shield at center. On back, the border in blind. Spine titled in gilt. TEG. Endpapers yellow.

TxU.

The Knickerbocker Gallery

1Aa.   THE | Knickerbocker Gallery: [hollow, fancy type] | A TESTIMONIAL | TO THE EDITOR OF THE | Knickerbocker Magazine [hollow, fancy type] | FROM ITS CONTRIBUTORS. | WITH FORTY-EIGHT PORTRAITS ON STEEL, FROM ORIGINAL PICTURES | ENGRAVED EXPRESSLY FOR THIS WORK. | NEW-YORK: | SAMUEL HUESTON, 348 BROADWAY. | [rule] | MDCCCLV.

(22.1 x 15.4): [1]^6 2-31^8 32^6. The first and last leaves are blanks. Not reckoned: engraved title and illustrations.

[i]-[ii], blank; [iii]-[iv], blank, on verso engraved portrait of L. Gaylord Clark; [v]-[vi], engraved title, verso blank; [vii]-[viii], title, on verso copyright (1854) and printer; [ix]-x, table of contents; [xi]-xii, list of engravings; [xiii]-xiv, Preface, dated November 7, 1854; [15]-505, text; [506], blank.

Original contribution: "Conversations with Talma; From Rough Notes in a Common-Place Book," [15]-22.

Printer: John A. Gray, Printer and Stereotyper, 95 & 97 Cliff, cor. Frankfort.

Lineation: p. 20, and... romantic ; p. 300, otherwise; ... been

Noted in two bindings:

[A]. Red TZ cloth. On sides, in gilt, house in center with decorations and border around. Spine decorated and titled in gilt. AEG. Flowered endpapers.

[B]. Black morocco. Sides decorated in gilt and blind. Spine decorated and titled in gilt. Yellow endpapers. AEG.

Deposited 8 December 1854. *Norton's Literary Gazette*, 15 August 1854, advertised for October; 15 January 1855, listed.

TxU (2).

b. The second impression may be identified by a few changes:

Title imprint. New-York in fancy type.

Copyright page. John A. Gray listed as stereotyper; C.A. Alvord, 29 Gold-street as printer.

P. [x], 6th entry. Karl corrected to Jarl.

P. xii, 5th entry. Curtis plate added.

P. [503], 4th line of poem. Final comma omitted.

Noted in two bindings:

[A]. Black imitation morocco. Sides decorated in blind with inset blue leather oval bearing title and decoration in gilt. Yellow endpapers. AEG.

[B]. Black morocco. On sides, gilt decorations. Spine decorated and titled in gilt. Marbled endpapers. AEG.

TxU (2).

The Literary Life and Correspondence of the Countess of Blessington

1E. THE | LITERARY LIFE AND CORRESPONDENCE | OF | THE COUNTESS OF BLESSINGTON. | BY | R. R. MADDEN, M. R. I. A. | AUTHOR OF | "TRAVELS IN THE EAST," "INFIRMITIES OF GENIUS," "THE MUSSULMAN," | "SHRINES AND SEPULCHRES," "THE LIFE OF SAVONAROLA," ETC. | "L'homme marche vers le tombeau, trainant apres lui, la chaine de ses esperances [in Vols. II, III, no "s" at end] | trompèes." | IN THREE VOLUMES. | VOL. I. [II., III.] | LONDON: | T. C. NEWBY PUBLISHER, 30, WELBECK STREET, | CAVENDISH SQUARE. | 1855. (The French quotation is incorrectly accented, as reproduced here, in all three vols.)

(22.0 x 14.0): Vol. I. $[A]^4$ $B-I^8$ $K-U^8$ $X-Z^8$ $AA-HH^8$ II^4 KK^2. Not reckoned: preliminary lithograph of a bust of the Countess of Blessington. Vol. II. $[-]^1$ $[A]^2$ $B-I^8$ $K-U^8$ $X-Z^8$ $AA-IIH^8$ II^2. Not reckoned: preliminary lithograph of Alfred d'Orsay; terminal catalogue. Vol. III. $[-]^1$ $[A]^2$ $B-I^8$ $K-U^8$ $X-Z^8$ $AA-II^8$ $KK-MM^8$ NN^4 $[OO]^2$. Not reckoned: preliminary lithograph of the tomb of the Countess of Blessington.

In Vol. II, the terminal catalogue of books published by Newby is paged [1]-32. On the first page, this work is listed in two vols. at 1*l*. 10*s*. in cloth.

Vol. I. [i]-viii, [1]-491 [492]. Vol. II. [i]-vi, [1]-484. Vol. III. [i]-[ii], title, on verso printer; [iii]-vi, table of contents; [1]-375, text; [376]-534, Appendix; [535]-555, Index; [556], Errata, printer at foot of page.

Original contribution: Letter to "My dear sir," dated Newhall, May 2d, 1835, accompanying "The Haunted Ship" for *Heath's Book of Beauty* for 1836, edited by the Countess of Blessington. Vol. III, pp. 309-310. ("Newhall" is probably a mistranscription of "New York.")

Printer: J. Billing, Printer and Stereotyper, Woking, Surrey.

Lineation: Vol. I. p. 100, the ... bird Vol. II. p. 100, tributed ... [in footnote] age. Vol. III. p. 100, "Covent ... eyes

Bright pink AA-like cloth. On fronts, in gilt, the initials MB in copperplate style with coronet above, within elaborated frame in blind. On backs, the frame only. On spines, in gilt: [elaborated horizontal bar] | MEMOIR | AND | CORRESPONDENCE | OF THE | COUNTESS OF | BLESSINGTON | [coronet] | MB [in copperplate style] | VOL. I. [II., III.] | [elaborated horizontal bar]. Yellow endpapers. No flyleaves.

Literary Gazette, 27 January 1855, listed, at 2*l*. 2*s*. in cloth; 17 March 1855, reviewed. *Athenæum*, 3 February 1855, reviewed.

TxU.

2E.   "L'homme marche vers le tombeau, trainant apres lui, la chaine de ses expèriences | trompèes." | SECOND EDITION. | VOL. I. [II., III.] | LONDON: | T. C. NEWBY, PUBLISHER, 30, WELBECK STREET, | CAVENDISH SQUARE. | 1855. (Note the substitution of "expèriences" for "esperances" in the quotation. The French is still incorrectly accented.)

(21.9 x 13.9): Vol. I. [-]^1 [A]^2 B-I^8 K-U^8 X-Z^8 AA-II^8 KK^8 LL^4 [MM]^1. Not reckoned: preliminary engraved portrait of the Countess of Blessington by A. E. Chalon, R. A. Vol. II. [-]^1 [A]^2 B-I^8 K-U^8 X-Z^8 AA-II^8 KK^8 LL^4. Not reckoned: preliminary lithograph of Alfred d'Orsay. Vol. III. [-]^1 [A]^2 B-I^8 K-U^8 X-Z^8 AA-II^8 KK^8 LL^4. Not reckoned: preliminary lithograph of the tomb of the Countess of Blessington.

Vol. I. [i]-v [vi], [1]-522. Vol. II. [a]-[b], [i]-iv, [1]-520. Vol. III. [i]-[ii], title, on verso printer; [iii]-vi, table of contents; [1]-345, text; [346]-490, Appendix; [491]-520, Index, Errata at foot of last page.

The second edition is revised and expanded. The two texts may be distinguished immediately by the opening of the first sentence of Vol. I.

First edition: "The task of biography is not comprised only in an attempt to make a word-picture, and likeness of a person...."

Second edition: "The task of biography is not comprised in a mere attempt to make a word-picture of a person...."

In Vol. I, the dedication to Dr. Frederick Quin is omitted, and an engraved portrait of the Countess is substituted for the lithograph of a bust.

Original contribution: Letter to "My dear Sir," dated Newhall, May 2, 1835. Vol. III, p. 277. The text of Irving's letter remains the same, although in the date "May 2" is substituted for "May 2d."

Printer: J. Billing, Woking, Surrey.

The binding is in the same cloth and same design as that of the first edition except for the titling of the spines: [elaborated horizontal bar] | MEMOIR | AND | CORRESPONDENCE | OF THE | COUNTESS OF | BLESSINGTON. | [elaborated rule] | SECOND EDITION | [coronet] | MB [in copperplate style] | VOL. I. [II., III.] | [elaborated horizontal bar].

Athenæum, 16 June 1855, noticed.

MoKU.

1Aa. THE | LITERARY LIFE AND CORRESPONDENCE | OF THE | COUNTESS OF BLESSINGTON. | BY | R. R. MADDEN, M. R. I. A., | AUTHOR OF | "TRAVELS IN THE EAST," "INFIRMITIES OF GENIUS," "THE MUSSULMAN," | "SHRINES AND SEPULCHRES," "THE LIFE OF SAVONAROLA," ETC. | "L'homme marche vers le tombeau, trainant après lui, la chaine de ses esperances trompées." | IN TWO VOLUMES. | VOL. I. [II.] | NEW YORK: | HARPER & BROTHERS, PUBLISHERS, | 329 & 331 PEARL STREET, | FRANKLIN SQUARE. | 1855.

(19.4 x 12.5): Vol. I. [-]^4 A-I^{12} K-U^{12} X-Z^{12}. The last two leaves are blanks. Not reckoned: preliminary lithograph of bust of the Countess of Blessington. Vol. II. [-]^2 A-I^{12} K-U^{12} X-Z^{12} AA-BB^{12}.

Vol. I. [i]-viii, [1]-547 [548]. Vol. II. [i]-[ii], title, verso blank; [iii]-vi, table of contents; [1]-428, text; [429]-584, Appendix; [585]-599, Index; [600], blank. Note: no copyright notice in either volume.

Original contribution: Letter, dated Newhall, May 2d, 1835, Vol. II, p. 382.

The text of the letter varies noticeably in punctuation and spelling from that in the first London edition. The first sentence of the London edition ends, "a few years since, by one of my sea-faring countrymen." The sentence in the American edition ends, "a few years since by one of my seafaring countrymen."

Lineation: Vol. I. p. 100, the ... [in footnote] 370. Vol. II. p. 100, los ... [in footnote] Time."

Noted in three cloths: Green TZ cloth, blue A cloth, blue T cloth. On sides, in blind, oval design at center within wide border composed of diamond shapes within straight rules (a square at each corner). On spines, in gilt: [decorative horizontal bar] | MEMOIRS | OF | THE COUNTESS | OF | BLESSINGTON. | [rule] | MADDEN. | [rule] | VOL. I. [II.] | | NEW-YORK. | HARPER & BROTHERS. | [decorative horizontal bar]. Yellow endpapers. Flyleaves. The copy examined in blue T cloth has double flyleaves.

Harper's Magazine, May 1855, reviewed. *Knickerbocker*, May 1855, reviewed.

TxU (3).

b.   NEW YORK: | HARPER & BROTHERS, PUBLISHERS, | 329 & 331 PEARL STREET, | FRANKLIN SQUARE. | 1860.

In the same setting as the first edition, with the same illustration. Still no copyright notice.

Noted in dark black-brown TB-like cloth. On sides, in blind, small oval design within elaborated border of broad intertwined lines with fleur de lys decorations in the corners. Spines titled in gilt: MEMOIRS | OF | THE COUNTESS | OF | BLESSINGTON. | [rule] | MADDEN. | [rule] | VOL. I. [II.] | | Harper & Brothers. Buff endpapers. Flyleaves.

TxBeaL.

Critical Dictionary of English Literature

A testimonial letter from Irving, dated Sunnyside, 23 August 1855, addressed to Childs & Peterson, the publishers of S. Austin Allibone's *Critical Dictionary of English Literature,* begins (in the printed version), "*Gentlemen*:-- Accept my thanks for the specimen you have sent me of Mr. Allibone's Critical Dictionary of English Literature. The undertaking does honour to that gentleman's enterprise; and the manner in which, from the specimen before me, (464 pages,) he appears to execute it, does honour to his intelligence, perspicuity, wide and accurate research, impartiality, and good taste."

A second testimonial letter, dated Sunnyside, 12 January 1859, addressed to S. Austin Allibone, begins, "*My dear Sir*: -- I have to thank you for a copy of the first volume of your Dictionary of Authors, which you have had the kindness to send me. It fully comes up to the high anticipations I had formed from the specimen submitted to my inspection in 1855."

Printed versions of the letters appear in [1] sheets of testimonials, [2] prospectuses, and [3] bound in the Dictionary itself. It is possible that other examples exist than those noted.

[1]. *Sheets of testimonials.*

A. Heading: TESTIMONIALS | TO | Allibone's Critical Dictionary | OF | ENGLISH LITERATURE, AND BRITISH AND AMERICAN AUTHORS.

No place, no publisher, no date. [Philadelphia, Childs & Peterson, 1855?]

(25.7 x 17.2): single cut sheet of light blue wove paper. Apparently printed on one side only. (The copy examined is pasted down.)

Contains the 1855 letter of Irving, with similar letters, all dated 1855, from Bryant, Sparks, Bancroft, Prescott, Everett, Lieber.

The same testimonials appear in an advertisement in *American Publishers' Circular,* 15 December 1855.

CtY.

B. [Heading: *Testimonials to Allibone's Critical Dictionary of English Literature....* Imprinted: *Published by Childs & Peterson, No. 124 Arch Street, Philadelphia.....*]

No date [1855?]

(25.5 x 16.9): single cut sheet. Printed on one side only.

Contains the 1855 letter of Irving, with similar letters from others.

Not located. The description is taken from *BAL,* which locates a copy in private hands, now missing. Is this the same as Form A?

[2]. *Prospectuses.*

A. [Heading: *A Critical Dictionary of English Literature, and British and American Authors.... By S. Austin Allibone....* Philadelphia: Childs & Peterson, 1856.]

16 pp., printed self-wrapper.

Contains the 1855 letter of Irving, with similar letters from others.

Not located. The description is taken from *BAL,* which locates a copy at MH, not found despite a search.

B. Heading: TO THE LITERATURE OF THE LANGUAGE WHAT A DICTIONARY OF WORDS IS TO THE LANGUAGE ITSELF. | Allibone's Dictionary of Authors, | .... At foot of page: Address CHILDS & PETERSON, | 602 *Arch Street, Philadelphia.*

No date. 1859?

In two states.

1. (25.8 x 17.8): paged [1]-[2] 3-15 [16]. Page [16] is blank.

Irving's letters of 1855 and 1859 appear on p. 5.

2. (25.8 x 17.8): paged [1]-[2] 3-13 [14]. Page [14] is blank.

Irving's letters of 1855 and 1859 appear on p. 4.

Both states contain common settings of some pages, including the one on which Irving's letters appear. The sequence given here is suggested by the presence of State 1 in the copies examined of the 1859 Dictionary, State 2 in a later impression.

State 1, CtY. State 2, NN.

[3]. *Bound in the Dictionary.*

A. The copy examined of the "specimen" of the Dictionary, to which Irving refers in his letters, does not contain a Prospectus or the Irving letter of 1855. It is possible, perhaps even probable, that some later copies did contain a Prospectus. The specimen copy examined carries the imprint PHILADELPHIA: | CHILDS & PETERSON, 124 ARCH ST. | 1855. It is paged [i]-xii, 13-464, and this first portion of the complete volume is in the same setting as the first edition of the full volume when it appeared in 1858 or 1859.

B. A | CRITICAL | DICTIONARY OF ENGLISH LITERATURE, | AND | BRITISH AND AMERICAN AUTHORS, | Living and Deceased, [fancy] | FROM THE EARLIEST ACCOUNTS | TO THE MIDDLE OF THE NINETEENTH CENTURY. | CONTAINING | THIRTY THOUSAND BIOGRAPHIES AND LITERARY NOTICES, | WITH FORTY INDEXES OF SUBJECTS. | BY | S. AUSTIN ALLIBONE. | [rule] | *"THE CHIEF GLORY OF EVERY PEOPLE ARISES FROM ITS AUTHORS."* -- DR.. JOHNSON. | [rule] | VOL. I. | PHILADELPHIA: | CHILDS & PETERSON, 602 ARCH STREET. | 1859.

(25.0 x 16.9): [-]^2 [1]^8 2-63^8. The last leaf is blank. Not reckoned: preliminary prospectus and engraved title.

[a]-[b], half-title, verso blank (?); [1]-[2], title, on verso copyright (1854, 1858) and printer; [c]-[d], dedication, dated 1 September 1858, verso blank; 3-1005, text; [1006], blank. Text in double columns.

Prospectus B, State 1 bound at the beginning.

Printer: Stereotyped by L. Johnson and Co., Philadelphia; printed by Deacon and Peterson.

Lineation: p. 100, Dr. ... cha-; p. 500, Dickens, ... force

Both states of the 1859 Prospectus advertise Vol. I: "$5.00 in muslin binding; $6.00 in fine sheep binding, or $7.50 in library style, half turkey morocco antique."

Vols. II, III were published subsequently, as well as later supplements. The Prospectus has been noted in none of them. An 1882 impression of Vol. I, enlarged, has been seen with State 2 of the Prospectus bound in.

Atlantic Monthly, March 1859, Vol. I listed; June 1859, reviewed. (In the heading of the review, 1858 is given as the year of publication.) *Harper's Magazine*, April 1859, reviewed.

In addition to the letters in the Prospectus, the text of the full Dictionary itself contains original extracts from Irving letters. Vol. I was first published in its full commercial version in 1859. Vol. II appears to have been published in 1870, although there are some grounds for questioning the date. On p. [2] of Child's & Peterson's Prospectus B, bound in the 1859 edition of Vol. I, appears the statement, "The second volume, which will complete the work, is now more than one-half stereotyped." And some late copies of Vol. II of the work print a copyright date of 1858 by George W. Childs as well as later dates. (1858 is the second copyright date for Vol. I.) But the earliest copy of Vol. II seen is dated 1870 on the title page, and copyright 1870 by J. B. Lippincott & Co., the publisher. In that edition, the dedication of Vol. II and Vol. III, printed in Vol. II, is dated 1870. It is likely that 1870 is correct.

Volume I, 1859.

In the entry on Washington Irving, a letter from Irving to Allibone, dated Sunnyside, Nov. 2, 1857, on the truth of *The Alhambra.* Vol. I, p. 943. [Note: The letter does not appear in the version of the entry that is printed as the Preface by Allibone to *Irving Vignettes,* 1858.]

Volume II, 1870.

In the entry on Charles Lanman, a letter from Irving to Lanman [23 January 1852]. Vol. II, p. 1058. [First published in Lanman's *Adventures in the Wilds of the United States*, 1856.] Also, a letter from Irving to Lanman, dated Sunnyside, March 2, 1857. Vol. II, p. 1058.

In the entry on Obadiah Rich, a letter from Irving to Allibone, dated Sunnyside, Sept. 17, 1857. Vol. II, p. 1788.

Vol. I: Specimen 1855, CtY; 1859, 1882, TxU. Vol. II: 1870, TxU.

Cyclopædia of American Literature

1Aa.   CYCLOPÆDIA | OF | AMERICAN LITERATURE; | EMBRACING | PERSONAL AND CRITICAL NOTICES OF AUTHORS, | AND SELECTIONS FROM THEIR WRITINGS. | FROM THE EARLIEST PERIOD TO THE PRESENT DAY; | WITH | PORTRAITS, AUTOGRAPHS, AND OTHER ILLUSTRATIONS. | BY | EVERT A. DUYCKINCK AND GEORGE L. DUYCKINCK. | IN TWO VOLUMES. | VOL. I. [II.] | NEW-YORK: | CHARLES SCRIBNER. | [rule] | 1855.

(25.1 x 17.6): Vol. I. [-]^8 1-42^8 43^2· Preliminary engraving not reckoned. Vol. II. [-]^8 1-49^8. First and last leaves are blanks; in some copies, last blank leaf apparently excised. Preliminary engraving not reckoned. Bound at end: nine page catalogue, dated 1 January 1856, paged [1]-9; p. [10] blank.

Vol. I. [i]-[ii], half-title, on verso quotation from Josiah Quincy, *History of Harvard University*; [iii]-[iv], title, on verso copyright (1855) and printers; [v]-x, Preface; [xi]-xv, table of contents; [xvi], list of illustrations; [1]-676, text. Text in double columns. Vol. II. [i]-[ii], half-title, verso blank [?]; [iii]-[iv], title, on verso copyright (1855) and printers; [v]-xii, table of contents; [xiii]-xiv, list of illustrations; [1]-742, text; [743]-781, index; [782], blank. Text in double columns.

Original contributions:

Letter to the authors, on Washington Allston, undated, II, 14-16.

The biographical sketch of Irving by the Duyckincks, II, 47-53, was edited by Irving in the proof; he made minor changes and rewrote one passage.

Reprint contributions:

"The Dull Lecture," II, 50. First published in *The Atlantic Souvenir,* 1828.

"The Stout Gentleman," II, 53-56. From *Bracebridge Hall.*

"The Broken Heart," II, 56-57. From *The Sketch Book.*

"Description of the Powerful Army Assembled at the City of New Amsterdam," II, 57-59. From *A History of New York.*

Printer: R. Craighead, Electrotyper & Stereotyper, 58 Vesey Street, N. Y.; C. A. Alvord, Printer, 29 Gold Street, N. Y.

Lineation: Vol. I. p. 100, in ... fit,; p. 200, He ... Intell. Vol. II. p. 15, and ... Artists.; p. 50, *Astoria*, ... lover; p. 200, and ... five;

Noted in dark brown L cloth. On sides, triple frame lines in blind. Spine titled in gilt. Black tie strings attached to center of front edges.

In catalogues at end of Vol. II, this work is described as "Sold only by Subscription, ...7 00."

American Publishers' Circular, 29 December 1855 (repeated until 26 January 1856), advertised: "It can be had in good English cloth, price $7 00; in half-calf, neat $10 00; half calf and morocco extra, $11; full calf and mor. ex., $16. SOLD ONLY BY SUBSCRIPTION." *North American Review*, January 1856, listed. *Knickerbocker*, February 1856, Vol. I reviewed.

CtY, TxU.

b. NEW YORK: | CHARLES SCRIBNER. | [rule] | 1856.

Bound at end of Vol. II: eleven pp. catalogue, paged [2 pp. unpaged] 6-12 [13] [14]. The catalogue begins on the verso of the last leaf of the text; that page is blank in the first impression.

American Publishers' Circular, 18 October 1856, "Sixth Edition, now ready and for sale by Booksellers and Agents. (*Heretofore sold only by subscription.*)" The advertisement includes a "puff" by Irving: "*From Washington Irving, Esq.*"; "I commend it most heartily to the reading public, for I consider it not merely a desideratum, but, in some sort, a necessity to every well-furnished American Library."

TxU (2).

An Appeal in Behalf of Lamartine

1A. [Caption-title]: AN APPEAL TO THE PEOPLE OF THE UNITED STATES | IN BEHALF OF LAMARTINE.

1856.

(25.5 x 20.6): single sheet folded to make two leaves.

Unpaged: [1]-[2], the Appeal to take part with Lamartine "in his struggle with the evil days on which he has fallen," signed by forty-two people, principally authors, senators and representatives, and also a letter by J. B. Desplace forwarding the appeal, dated July, 1856; [3]-[4], advertisement by D. Appleton & Co. for a proposed publication in twelve monthly numbers of Lamartine's *Familiar Course of Literature*, with blurbs from journals following.

Original contribution: The Appeal is signed first by Irving.

American Publishers' Circular, 19 July 1856, noted in column of "Literary Intelligence."

ViU.

Adventures in the Wilds of the United States

1A. ADVENTURES | IN THE | WILDS OF THE UNITED STATES | AND | British American Provinces. [fancy] | BY | CHARLES LANMAN, | AUTHOR OF "ESSAYS FOR SUMMER HOURS," "PRIVATE LIFE OF DANIEL WEBSTER," ETC., ETC. | ILLUSTRATED BY THE AUTHOR AND OSCAR BESSAU. | [rule] | "Without registering these things by the pen they will slide away unprofitably." -- OWEN FELLTHAM. | [rule] | IN TWO VOLUMES. | VOL. I. [II.] | [elaborated swelled rule] | PHILADELPHIA: | JOHN W. MOORE, No. 195 CHESTNUT STREET. | 1856.

Title page in two states:

1. As transcribed.

2. With an extra line added as line 13: WITH AN APPENDIX BY LIEUT. CAMPBELL HARDY.

(22.3 x 13.8): Vol. I. [-]^8 1-32^8 33^2. The last leaf is a blank. Not reckoned: preliminary illustration and five illustrations through the text. Vol. II. [A]^4 B-I^8 K-U^8 W-Z^8 A*-H*^{8}. Not reckoned: six illustrations through the text. Terminal catalogue of eight pages.

The terminal catalogue in Vol. II is paged [1] 2-8, signed I*. Page 2, the first page of listings, begins with CHAMBERS' PAPERS FOR THE PEOPLE.

Vol. I. [i]-[ii], title, on verso copyright (1856) and printer; [iii]-vii, Preface, dated Georgetown, D.C., Summer of 1856; [viii], blank; [ix]-xi, table of contents; [xii], blank; [xiii]-[xiv], table of illustrations, verso blank; [xv]-[xvi], fly-title for "A Summer in the Wilderness," verso blank; [1]-514, text. Vol. II. [i]-[ii], title, on verso copyright (1856) and printer; [iii]-iv (mispaged v), table of contents; [v]-[vi], table of illustrations, verso blank; [vii]-[viii], fly-title for "A Tour to the River Restigouche," verso blank; [9]-480, text; [481]-517, Appendix; [518], blank; [519]-[520], "A Parting Paragraph" of errata, verso blank.

The Appendix consists of quotations from Lt. Campbell Hardy, *Sporting Adventures in the New World.*

Original contributions:

Letter to Charles Lanman, undated [15 October 1847], headed SUNNY SIDE, Vol. I, p. iv.

Letter to Charles Lanman, undated [23 January 1852], headed SUNNY SIDE, Vol. I, p. v.

Printer: H. B. Ashmead, George Street above Eleventh.

Lineation: Vol. I. p. [100], LAKE ... been ; p. [200], LAKE ... on Vol. II. p. 100, interesting ... the ; p. 200, bited ... a

State 1: KyU. State 2: NmU.

1E.   ADVENTURES | IN THE | WILDS OF NORTH AMERICA. | BY | CHARLES LANMAN. | EDITED BY | CHARLES RICHARD WELD. | LONDON: | LONGMAN, BROWN, GREEN, AND LONGMANS. | 1854.

This London edition in one volume, published earlier than the New York edition in two volumes, might be considered a short preliminary of the full version of the work, or might be considered an earlier transatlantic trial. It lacks the author's Preface -- substituting a two-page Preface by an editor -- and prints many fewer selections from Lanman's works. It also lacks the Appendix and the illustrations.

(17.2 x 11.0 trimmed): [i]-[iii] iv-vi, [7]-300. Signed in 8's.

[i]-[ii], title, verso blank; [iii]-iv, table of contents; [v]-vi, Preface signed C. R. Weld; [7]-300, text.

The Preface prints the greater part of the same two letters of Irving, p. vi, but omits the salutations and polite closing remarks, omits the first sentence and part of the second sentence of the first letter, and changes the paragraphing of both letters.

Lineation: p. 9, while ... glided

Not examined. Information and reproductions provided by OkTU.

The (Old) Farmer's Almanack

1A.   THE | (OLD) | FARMER'S ALMANACK, | CALCULATED ON A NEW AND IMPROVED PLAN, | FOR THE YEAR OF OUR LORD | 1857; | ... | FITTED FOR BOSTON, BUT WILL ANSWER FOR ALL THE NEW ENGLAND STATES. | ... | BY ROBERT R. THOMAS. | [elaborate cut of winged Father Time] | ... | BOSTON: | PUBLISHED BY HICKLING, SWAN & BROWN. | Sold by the Booksellers and Traders throughout New England. | [copyright notice, 1856]. All surrounded by triple frame with NUMBER SIXTY-FIVE within the top.

(18.4 x 11.2): $[1]^{12} 2^{12}$.

Paged [1]-46 [47]-[48]. Double frame line around all pages. Not reckoned: terminal advertisements.

Original contribution: Testimonial for Worcester's Dictionary, dated Sunny Side, N. Y., October 3, 1855, on inner front wrapper. This is the letter which appears in the same year in a dictionary pamphlet, *Recommendations of Worcester's Dictionaries.*

Lineation: p. 40, WORK ... two."

Yellow paper wrapper. On front, simplified title with elaborate pictorial frame. On back and inner sides, advertisements.

The testimonial is repeated on the inner front of the orange paper wrapper of the Almanack for 1858.

MH.

Sartaroe

James Maitland's novel, *Sartaroe*, created a minor literary scandal among the publishing fraternity in its own day, and still raises some unanswered questions. It prints on its title page an adulatory -- and embarrassing -- letter from Washington Irving, date November 1, 1857. The letter is a forgery, apparently created by Maitland, although he blamed it on some party unknown. Upon weighing the various contemporary accusations and defenses, claims and counter-claims, the following explanation emerges.

W. P. Fetridge and Co. of New York was originally to publish the novel, complete with the purported letter from Irving furnished them by James Maitland. But before official date of publication, W. P. Fetridge ran into financial difficulties and T. B. Peterson and Brothers of Philadelphia took over the publication rights and issued the novel, about 20 March 1858. It was reviewed as early as February 1858 in *Peterson's Magazine*. On 15 March 1858, George P. Putnam, as Irving's publisher and friend, wrote Peterson declaring the letter spurious. On 17 March, Peterson answered, enclosing a copy of the "spurious" letter provided by W. P. Fetridge and a copy of a different letter from Irving to Maitland, politely congratulatory and apparently genuine (although at first also altered by Maitland), dated 12 December 1857. On 18 March, Maitland wrote a letter, addressed to "Gentlemen," admitting that the letter of 1 November was never written to him by Irving and had been published without Irving's knowledge or consent. On the same day, W. P. Fetridge wrote T. B. Peterson declaring innocence and saying that the letter had been accepted by him as genuine. By this time, the controversy was being carried on almost daily in a series of advertisements, "cards," and letters to the editor in the *New-York Times*, the *New-York Tribune*, and the *New York Evening Post.*

On 20 March, Putnam wrote the editor of the *Times*, claiming that Maitland had altered the "real" letter of 12 December. But by 23 March, the two publishers shifted the grounds of the immediate attack from the question of the genuineness of the letter of 1 November and the accuracy of the published versions of the letter of 12 December to the accusation by Peterson (declared in the *Tribune* and the *Evening Post* of 24 March) that Putnam had altered the "card" that was placed in the papers after both publishers had agreed on the statement -- and besides, Putnam had not given the papers the "real" letter. For several days both publishers, again in public print, gathered statements by witnesses and continued to accuse each other of acting in bad faith. The last published utterances that I have found are a final direct blast by Peterson and an answer by Putnam in the *Tribune* and the *Evening Post* for 29 March, and an indirect comment, again by Peterson, in an advertisement for the novel in the *Tribune* of 27 and 29 March in which he prints the "real" letter and says, "The ORIGINAL of the above LETTER, in Mr. Irving's own handwriting, can be seen by calling at our store."

Out of all the accusations and counter-accusations, a few conclusions seem valid. The letter of 1 November 1857 printed in the novel is a forgery. There was a much milder genuine letter of 12 December 1857 which eventually was published in an accurate copy. Peterson was probably innocent in his original acceptance of the spurious letter given him by Fetridge, although he continued for too long to let the letter appear in advertisements. Beyond those, the reader can draw his own conclusions. It should be added that throughout the controversy, Irving himself seems to have made no public statement. Perhaps he was embarrassed.

For two contemporary summaries of the affair, neither altogether accurate, complete, nor unbiased, see the long discussion (with a number of the relevant statements reproduced) in the "Literary Intelligence" column of *American Publishers' Circular*, 27 March 1858, 150-151, and the review of *Sartaroe* in *Graham's Illustrated Magazine*, May 1858, 471.

1Aa- SARTAROE: | A | TALE OF NORWAY. | BY JAMES A. MAITLAND. |
 b.   AUTHOR OF "THE WATCHMAN," "THE WANDERER," "THE
      LAWYER'S STORY," | "THE DIARY OF AN OLD DOCTOR," ETC.,
      ETC. | [wavy rule] | *Sunnyside, Irvington, Nov. 1st,* 1857. | MY DEAR
      FRIEND: | According to promise I have read "Sartaroe," and now will give
      you my | opinion of the book in a word. It is highly creditable to your genius
      -- it is excel- | lent; all in all, the best novel issued from the American press
      for some years past. | It *must certainly* meet with success. I will do my best
      for you. You ought to | clear, at least, $4,000 or $5,000 by it. I have written
      to Murray, of London, my | old publisher, as I told you I would, and I have
      advised him to reprint the book | there, and have assured him that he ought
      to send the author £ 200 sterling for the | privilege of printing the work in
      England. * * * * You | may use this when the book comes out. | With the
      greatest esteem, I am your friend, | WASHINGTON IRVING. [Irving's
      name is preceded on the line by the name of the recipient, JAMES A.
      MAITLAND, N. Y.] | [wavy rule] | Philadelphia: [fancy] | T. B.
      PETERSON & BROTHERS, | No. 306 CHESTNUT STREET.

Copyright 1857, 1858.

[i]-[ii], half-title, verso blank; [iii]-[iv], title, on verso copyright (1857 by W. P.
Fetridge, 1858 by T. B. Peterson); [v]-[vi], dedication to Washington Irving,
verso blank; [vii]-viii, Preface, dated 18 August 1857; [ix]-xii, table of
contents; [13]-448, text.

Lineation: p. 100, pleton ... apostrophizing,; p. 200, wharf, ... times

In two states. (See the discussion of sequence below.)

State A.

(18.5 x 12.4): [1]^8 2-28^8 29^2. The first and last leaves contain advertisements.

The purported testimonial letter of Irving that appears on the title page also
appears on the recto of the first leaf, unreckoned in the pagination of the
book. Although not reckoned, the leaf is paged (xvii) at the foot of the recto
and xviii at the top of the verso. The version of the letter on the advertising
leaf reads, "your genius. It is," and the four marks of omission are themselves
omitted.

The pagination of the advertising leaf suggests that the leaf was first
produced as part of a catalogue. This may have been the "circular" that W. P.
Fetridge is said to have distributed in 1857.

Noted in two cloths: red AR cloth, and brown T cloth. On sides, elaborated
border in blind. Spine titled in gilt, with no decoration. Endpapers blank
yellow.

Advertised as available in cloth or two volumes, paper cover.

State B.

(18.4 x 12.2): $[1]^{12}$ 2-19^{12}. The last four leaves of Sig. 19 are excised.

No advertisements.

The purported testimonial letter appears only on the title page.

Brown BD cloth. On sides, in blind, publisher's name in shield, within elaborated border. Spine titled in gilt, with decoration of branch and leaves at foot. Yellow endpapers with illustrated advertisements for four books by Q. K. Philander Doesticks, P. B. (pseud. for Mortimer Thomson).

A Note on the Sequence of the Two States.

The two states represent two separate impressions. The sequence of the two impressions is probably correct. If the advertising leaf in State A is indeed taken from Fetridge's "circular," that would seem to suggest production by Fetridge, and so an earlier state. The advertisements with comic illustrations on the endpapers of State B may be evidence of a later state. The titles of those works that can be dated appeared in 1858 or before, but published by other publishers. And the advertisements themselves were created by an earlier publisher, Livermore and Rudd of New York. Presumably, Peterson took over the publication rights, publishing the books and using the advertisements (with his own imprint substituted) at some later date. Finally, the appearance of T. B. Peterson's name as an integral part of the decoration of the binding of State B suggests that he alone was responsible for that binding.

Related Printed Items.

The letter from Peterson to Putnam, 17 March 1858, says that W. P. Fetridge "over four months ago" issued "circulars" for the novel and there printed the spurious letter by Irving. No such circulars have been located, although the presence of the letter on a preliminary mis-paged leaf in State A of the edition suggests that the leaf had been produced originally for a prospectus or a catalogue.

The letter from Putnam to Peterson, 24 March 1858, says, "I am informed by your New York agent that the spurious letter has been lithographed to accompany every copy of the book hereafter issued." No facsimile of the letter of November 1 has been discovered, but an accurate reproduction of the letter of December 12 is known. It is described in a three-line heading as *"a perfect fac simile"* of the letter *"Washington Irving did write to the author of | 'Sartaroe,'"* the same wording that appears in Peterson's heading to the genuine letter in the *New York Evening Post* 29 March 1848. The facsimile covers two pages, with no publisher or date of publication given. Copies are located in PHC and MdHi. It is likely that this is the facsimile to which Putnam referred, being mistaken only in identifying the wrong letter.

American Publishers' Circular, 26 September 1857, advertised by W. P. Fetridge for "about the first of October." *New-York Tribune*, 15-17 March 1858, advertised by T. B. Peterson for "SATURDAY, March 20," and prints the spurious letter; 20 March 1858, "PUBLISHED THIS DAY. Complete in one volume, neatly bound in cloth, for One Dollar and Twenty-five Cents; or in two volumes, paper cover, for One Dollar"; 27-28 March 1858, advertised, and prints the real letter. *New York Evening Post*, 22 March 1858, advertised by T. B. Peterson as "Published this day," and prints the real letter (described here as "the Simon Pure Letter from Washington Irving"). *Peterson's Magazine*, February 1858, reviewed, publisher named as W. P. Fetridge. *Graham's Illustrated Magazine* and *Southern Literary Messenger*, May 1858, reviewed, with comments on the controversy.

State A: CtY, TxU. State B: TxU.

Reprinted
Contributions

1810

TRAVELS | THROUGH | LOWER CANADA, | AND THE | UNITED STATES | OF | NORTH AMERICA, | IN THE YEARS | 1806, 1807, AND 1808. | TO WHICH ARE ADDED, | Biographical Notices and Anecdotes of some of the leading Cha- | racters in the United States; and of those who have, at va- | rious Periods, borne a conspicuous Part in | the Politics of that Country. | [swelled rule] | BY JOHN LAMBERT. | [swelled rule] | IN THREE VOLUMES. | *WITH ENGRAVINGS.* | VOL. I. [II., III.] | [double rule] | *LONDON*: | PRINTED FOR RICHARD PHILLIPS, | BRIDGE-STREET, BLACKFRIARS. | [rule] | 1810. | T. Gillet, Printer, Crown-court, Fleet-street.

(21.1 x 13.0): Vol. I. [i]-xxiv, [1]-496. Vol. II. [i]-ix [x], [1]-494. Vol. III. [a]-[b], [i]-iv, [1]-506. Eighteen maps and illustrations, through the 3 vols., not reckoned. Signed in 8's.

Extracts from *Salmagundi*, II, 234-349 [mispaged 394]. *Salmagundi* is described, II, 232-233, as "one of the most successful specimens of original composition that has hitherto been produced in the United States."

Lineation: Vol. I. p. 300, fond; ... the Vol. II. p. 300, *lets*, ... as Vol. III. p. 300, ROBERT ... the

Seen only in calf.

BAL reports a copy seen with "Printer" missing after "Gillet" on the title page of Vol. I.

The "second edition, corrected and improved," 2 vols., London: C. Cradock and W. Joy, 1814, contains only a brief 13-line quotation from *Salmagundi*, II, 112.

First ed., ViU. Second ed., TxU.

1822

[*The Bouquet of Popular Literature.* London: T. C. Hansard, 1822. Vol. 1 (the only vol. published).]

"Review [of *Bracebridge Hall*], with selected extracts," 11-26.

Not seen. Copy reported in NN.

1823

THE | AMERICAN FIRST CLASS BOOK; | OR, | EXERCISES | IN | READING AND RECITATION: | SELECTED PRINCIPALLY | FROM MODERN AUTHORS | OF | GREAT BRITAIN AND AMERICA; | AND DESIGNED FOR THE USE | OF | THE HIGHEST CLASS | IN PUBLICK AND PRIVATE SCHOOLS. | [elaborated swelled rule] | BY JOHN PIERPONT, | ... | BOSTON: | PUBLISHED BY WILLIAM B. FOWLE, | No. 45, Cornhill. | STEREOTYPED BY T. H. AND C. CARTER. | [double rule of 9 dots] | 1823.

(17.2 x 10.7): [1]-480. Signed in 6's.

"Feelings Excited by a Long Voyage -- Visit to a New Continent," 54-58 (from "The Voyage," *Sketch Book*); "The Widow and Her Son," 158-164 (from *Sketch Book*); "Diedrich Knickerbocker's New-England Farmer," 244-245 (from *History of New York*); "Midnight Musings," 199-201 (from "St. Mark's Eve," *Bracebridge Hall*); "Forest Trees," 295-297 (from *Bracebridge Hall*).

Lineation: p. 55, you ... completely ; p. 200, However ... endearments?

Full calf.

Noted in a number of later impressions by different publishers: 1825, 1826, 1830, 1831, 1836, 1839, 1840 [the last three marked "Twenty-fifth Edition"], and one undated marked "Thirty-Fifth Edition." The impression of 1825 says in the "Publisher's Advertisement," "But six thousand copies of this work had been printed when the stereotyped plates, which had been brought to an unusual degree of correctness, were destroyed by fire. The proprietor has been at the trouble and expense of re-stereotyping the whole, ... *October, 1824*."

TxU.

[*Romantische Denksteine; oder Schaustücke, Glanzmomente und Curiosa aus der Welt des Lebens und Wirkens....* Von A. F. Rittgräff. 2 vols. Wien: Tendler und v. Manstein, 1823.]

A. F. Rittgräff is a pseudonym for Franz Graffer.

"Das Haus des Shakespeare," I, 91-94. ("Stratford-on-Avon," *Sketch Book*).

Not seen. Copy reported in NIC, NN.

1824

[*Der Kranz; oder Erholungen für Geist und Herz.* Eine Unterhaltungsschrift für gebildete Leser. Herausg. von Karoline von Woltmann. Prag: 1824. Jahr. 1824.]

"Stratford am Avon" (from *Sketch Book*).

Not located. Listed in Wilhelm Heinsius, *Allgemeines Bücher-Lexicon, 1822-1827.*

1826

THE | CLASS BOOK | OF | AMERICAN LITERATURE: [hollow, shaded type] | CONSISTING PRINCIPALLY OF | SELECTIONS IN THE DEPARTMENTS OF HISTORY, BIOGRAPHY, | PROSE FICTION, TRAVELS, THE DRAMA, | POPULAR | ELOQUENCE, AND POETRY; | FROM THE BEST WRITERS OF OUR OWN COUNTRY. | Designed to be used as a Reading Book in American Schools. | [rule] | BY JOHN FROST. | [rule] | [double rule] | BOSTON: | PRINTED AND PUBLISHED BY J. H. A. FROST, | No. 39 Washington street. | [rule] | 1826.

(17.3 x 11.0): [i]-xii, [13]-312. Signed in 6's.

"The Golden Age of New York," 21-24 (from *History of New York*); "The Angler," 49-51 (from *Sketch Book*); "Doctor Knipperhausen," 63-65 (from "Dolph Heyliger," *Bracebridge Hall*); "The New Year," 151-153 (from *Salmagundi*); "Stage Coach Adventure of Mr. Geoffrey Crayon in England," 155-159 (from "The Stage Coach," *Sketch Book*); "The Schoolmaster," 267-270, and "The School," 271-273 (both from *Bracebridge Hall*).

Lineation: p. 50, rod ... forest.; p. 100, continual ... endlessly.

Full calf. Red leather label on spine.

TxU.

THE | CLASSICAL READER: | A | SELECTION OF LESSONS | IN | PROSE AND VERSE. | FROM THE MOST ESTEEMED | ENGLISH AND AMERICAN WRITERS. | INTENDED FOR THE USE OF THE HIGHER CLASSES | IN PUBLICK AND PRIVATE SEMINARIES. | [rule] | BY REV. F. W. P. GREENWOOD AND G. B. EMERSON, | OF BOSTON. | [rule] | Boston: [fancy] | PRINTED AND PUBLISHED BY LINCOLN & EDMANDS, | No. 59 Washington-Street, (Cornhill.) | 1826.

(17.4 x 10.5): [i]-viii, [9]-420. Signed in 6's.

"Description of Roscoe," 42-45 (from *Sketch Book*); "Visit to the Grave of Shakespeare," 45-48 (from "Stratford-On-Avon," *Sketch Book*).

Lineation: p. 45, not ... boy,; p. 200, must ... July.

Full calf.

A second edition, with the same selections from Irving, was published in 1828 by the same publisher; also noted in later impressions of 1829, 1833. An "Improved Stereotype Edition," published in Boston by Robert S. Davis, 1843, is in fact a still later impression; under that description it apparently appeared in a number of impressions: one advertisement noted for the "Tenth stereotype edition."

TxU.

LEGENDS OF TERROR [,?] | AND | TALES | OF THE | WONDERFUL AND THE WILD. | [rule] | *Original and Select*, | [rule] | IN PROSE AND VERSE. | *WITH HISTORICAL ILLUSTRATIONS.* | AND | Elegant engravings [fancy] | ON WOOD. [last 3 lines within cut of tree and forest] | . . . | London: [fancy] | PRINTED BY T. RICHARDSON, 98, HIGH HOLBORN. | PUBLISHED BY SHERWOOD, GILBERT, AND PIPER, PATERNOSTER ROW; | AND HUNTER, EDINBURGH. | [rule] | 1826

(20.0 x 12.3): [i]-[iv], 1-638. Text in double columns. Signed in 8's. Seen only in incomplete copy.

"Rip Van Winkle, An American Legend," 599-609 (from *Sketch Book*). The table of contents lists "The Spectre Bridegroom," p. 615; probably Irving's from *Sketch Book*, but the pages are missing in this copy.

Lineation: p. 100, Now . . . place ; p. 600, "The . . . even-

CtY.

[*Passatempi morali; ossia Scelta di novelle e storie piacevoli, da autori celebri inglesi e francesi tradotte ad uso delle giovani, studiose dell'italiana favelle.* Londra: N.Hailes, 1826.]

Dedication signed: A. M. D.

Described as paged [i]-xvi, [1]-224. 12⁰.

"La Sposa" (from "The Wife," *Sketch Book*); "La Vedova e suo figlio," (from "The Widow and Her Son," *Sketch Book*); "La Vittima del crepacuore," (from "The Broken Heart," *Sketch Book).*

Not seen; copy reported in *BL.*

1827

THE | NATIONAL READER; | A | SELECTION OF EXERCISES | IN | READING AND SPEAKING, | DESIGNED | TO FILL THE SAME PLACE | IN THE | SCHOOLS OF THE UNITED STATES, | THAT IS HELD IN | THOSE OF GREAT BRITAIN | BY THE COMPILATIONS OF | MURRAY, SCOTT, ENFIELD, MYLIUS, THOMPSON, | EWING, AND OTHERS. | [double rule] | BY JOHN PIERPONT, | . . . | Boston: [fancy] | PUBLISHED BY HILLIARD, GRAY, LITTLE, AND WILKINS, | AND RICHARDSON AND LORD. | [rule] | 1827.

(17.2 x 10.8): [i]-vii [viii], [9]-276. 30 pp. catalogue bound at end. Signed in 6's.

"The Little Man in Black," 75-82 (from *Salmagundi*).

Lineation: p. 80, The ... sun."; p. 200, ble ... no

Full calf.

An impression of 1828 noted by the same publisher. A number of later impressions noted by other publishers: 1829, 1831, 1833, 1834, 1835 [called "Twenty-Eighth Edition," as are subsequent impressions], 1836, 1839, 1842.

DLC.

1828

THE | AMERICAN | COMMON-PLACE BOOK | OF | PROSE, [hollow letters] | A COLLECTION OF | ELOQUENT AND INTERESTING EXTRACTS | FROM | THE WRITINGS OF AMERICAN AUTHORS. | [cut of singing cherubim, signed Hartwell] | BOSTON: | PUBLISHED BY S. G. GOODRICH. | [rule] | MDCCCXXVIII.

(15.9 x 9.8): [1]-468. Not reckoned: engraving before title. Signed in 6's.

"Extract from the Legend of Sleepy Hollow," 46-51 (from *Sketch Book*); "The Stout Gentleman. A Stage-Coach Romance," 153-161 (from *Bracebridge Hall*); "Christmas," 228-230 (from *Sketch Book*); "The Storm-Ship," 298-304 (from *Bracebridge Hall*); "Scenery in the Highlands on the River Hudson," 346-350 (from "Dolph Heyliger," *Bracebridge Hall*).

Lineation: p. 50, woody ... and ; p. 300, was ... however,

Tan paper boards with brown cloth shelfback; paper label on spine.

A later impression noted, published in Cooperstown, N.Y. by H. & E. Phinney, 1841.

TxU.

THE | AMERICAN READER: [hollow letters] | CONTAINING EXTRACTS SUITED TO EXCITE | A LOVE OF SCIENCE AND LITERATURE, | TO REFINE THE TASTE, | AND TO | IMPROVE THE MORAL CHARACTER. | DESIGNED FOR THE USE OF SCHOOLS. | [elaborated swelled rule] | Brookfield: [fancy] | E. & G. MERRIAM. | BOSTON: PEIRCE AND WILLIAMS. | [rule] | MDCCCXXVIII.

(18.2 x 10.9): [I]-VII [VIII], [9]-276. Four pages of advertisements bound at end. Signed in 6's.

"Reception of Columbus in Spain after His Discovery of America," 70-72 (from *Columbus*).

Lineation: p. 70, LESSON XXIV. ... were ; p. 200, of ... press,

Full calf.

Noted in another state with variant imprint: Boston: [fancy] | PEIRCE & WILLIAMS. | BROOKFIELD: E. AND G. MERRIAM. | [rule] | MDCCCXXVIII.

Noted in a later impression by the original publishers, 1829.

MH.

THE | CYPRESS WREATH, | OR | MOURNER'S FRIEND. | A SELECTION OF PIECES, | ADAPTED TO THE | *CONSOLATION OF THE AFFLICTED.* | . . . | GREENFIELD, MASS. | PRINTED AND PUBLISHED BY PHELPS & CLARK. | [double rule of 12 dots] | 1828.

The "Advertisement" signed T. Strong.

(14.7 x 8.5 trimmed): [1]-108. Signed in 6's.

"The Spirits of the Departed," 86-88 (from "St. Mark's Eve," *Bracebridge Hall*).

Lineation: p. 50, Follow ... soul,; p. 87, tinually ... set

NN.

PIERPONT'S INTRODUCTION. | [rule] | INTRODUCTION | TO THE | NATIONAL READER; | A SELECTION | OF | EASY LESSONS, | DESIGNED | TO FILL THE SAME PLACE | IN THE | COMMON SCHOOLS OF THE UNITED STATES, | THAT IS HELD BY | MURRAY'S INTRODUCTION, | AND THE | COMPILATIONS OF GUY, MYLIUS, AND PINNOCK, | IN THOSE OF GREAT BRITAIN. | [double rule] | BY JOHN PIERPONT, | . . . | BOSTON: [fancy] | RICHARDSON AND LORD, | No. 133, Washington Street. | [rule] | 1828.

(17.8 x 11.0): [i]-vii [viii], [9]-168. Four pages of advertisements bound at end. Signed in 6's.

"Ichabod Crane, --his School, and his Horse," 108-110 (from "The Legend of Sleepy Hollow," *Sketch Book*).

Lineation: p. 109, terror ... my ; p. 150, German, ... tears.

Light gray-brown boards with brown leather shelfback. Title on front, advertisements on back. Spine blank.

Four later impressions noted: 1832, published in Boston by Carter, Hendee & Co.; 1833, same; 1836, "Sixteenth Edition," published in Boston by Charles Bowen; 1841, published in Boston by David H. Williams.

TxU.

1829

THE | ELOCUTIONIST, | CONSISTING OF | DECLAMATIONS AND READINGS, | IN PROSE AND POETRY; | FOR THE USE OF COLLEGES AND SCHOOLS. | [double rule] | BY JONATHAN BARBER, | ... | NEW HAVEN: | PUBLISHED BY HEZEKIAH HOWE AND A. H. MALTBY. | [rule] | PRINTED BY HEZEKIAH HOWE. | 1829.

(17.6 x 10.8): [i]-xi [xii]. [1]-359 [360]. Signed in 6's.

"The Widow and Her Son," 180-187 (from *Sketch Book*).

Lineation: p. 181, of ... unthinking ; p. 300, But ... town?"

Full Calf.

TxU.

SPECIMENS | OF | AMERICAN POETRY, | WITH | CRITICAL AND BIOGRAPHICAL | NOTICES. | IN THREE VOLUMES. | [rule] | BY SAMUEL KETTELL. | [rule] | [rule] | VOL. I. [II., III.] | [rule] | BOSTON, -- | S. G. GOODRICH AND CO., | [rule] | MDCCCXXIX.

(17.8 x 10.9): Vol. I. [i]-xlviii, [1]-353 [354]. Vol. II. [i]-x, [1]-408. Vol. III. [i]-x, [1]-406. Signed in 6's.

"The Falls of the Passaic," II, 173-174 (from *The Atlantic Souvenir* for 1827, shortened to 8 stanzas).

Lineation: Vol. I. p. 173, to ... wave.; Vol. II. p. 300, THE ... lea,

Issued in boards with cloth shelfbacks and paper labels.

TxU. Copy in boards advertised in dealer's catalogue.

Tareas [fancy] | DE UN | SOLITARIO | Ó | NUEVA COLECCION DE NOVELAS. | [ornament] | CON LICENCIA: | MADRID: *IMPRENTA DE* ESPINOSA. | [double rule] | 1829.

(15.1 x 10.1): [a]-[b], [I]-IV, [1]-220, [221]-[222]. Signed in 8's. Laid paper.

"El Sueño," [1]-15.   (A composite sketch founded upon "The Art of Bookmaking" and "The Mutability of Literature" from *The Sketch Book*).

"El Serrano de las Alpujarras," 63-94. (An adaptation of "Rip Van Winkle" from *The Sketch Book*).

"El Cuadro Misterioso," 95-157. (A loose translation of "The Story of the Young Italian" from *Tales of a Traveller*).

This is apparently the first translation of Irving's writings into Spanish. The adaptations-translations are by George Washington Mongomery, a friend of Irving and a translator at the American Legation at Madrid. Irving saw the manuscript before publication, and undoubtedly the two men had earlier discussed Montgomery's work. Irving's letter of 14 February 1829 to Alexander H. Everett reveals that there was difficulty in winning approval by the censor for publication. Spanish censorship at the time may account in part for the adaptation, rather than translation, of "Rip Van Winkle," which could be read as political satire.

Lineation: p. 100, parecia ... fantasía.; p. 150, mi ... sangrienta

TxU.

1830

THE | ACADEMICAL SPEAKER: | A SELECTION | OF | EXTRACTS IN PROSE AND VERSE, | FROM | ANCIENT AND MODERN AUTHORS; | . . . | BY B. D. EMERSON. | [rule] | BOSTON: | RICHARDSON, LORD AND HOLBROOK, | 133 WASHINGTON STREET. | [rule] | 1830.

(18.1 x 11.5): [i]-xii, [13]-321 [322]. One leaf of advertisements in this copy, and perhaps more in some copies, bound at end. Signed in 6's.

"The Right of Discovery," 173-174, and "The Right of Cultivation," 174-176 (from *History of New York*); "Death of King Philip," 183-184 (from "Philip of Pokanoket," *Sketch Book*).

Lineation: p. 175, ground ... hav-; p. 300, of ... captain

Full calf.

A later impression noted by same publisher, 1831.

MH.

THE | CLASSICAL SPEAKER. | [rule] | BY | CHARLES K. DILLAWAY, A.M. | . . . | Boston: [fancy] | PUBLISHED BY LINCOLN & EDMANDS. | Sold also by Carter & Hendee, Boston; D. F. Robinson & Co. Hartford; Roe Lockwood, | New-York; Thomas T. Ash, Philadelphia; and Cushing & Sons, Baltimore. | 1830.

(18.3 x 11.2): [i]-viii, [5]-272. Signed in 6's.

"Extract from Knickerbocker's History of New-York," 186-188.

Lineation: p. 100, lassie, ... *Lubens.* ; p. 187, But ... thy

Full black leather. Spine titled in gilt.

TxU.

THE | NATIONAL CLASS BOOK; | A | SELECTION OF EXERCISES | IN | READING, [hollow, shaded type] | FOR THE USE OF THE | HIGHER CLASSES [hollow, shaded type] | IN | Common Schools. [fancy] | [rule] | BY THOMAS J. LEE, | ... | *HALLOWELL*: | PRINTED AND PUBLISHED BY GLAZIER, MASTERS & CO. | No. 1, Kennebec-Row. | 1830.

(17.6 x 11.1): [i]-vi, [7]-288. Signed in 6's.

"Christmas," 155-157 (from *Sketch Book*); "First Landing of Columbus in the New World," 231-234, and "Character of Columbus," 234-236 (both from *Columbus*); "A Thunderstorm," 286-287 (from "Dolph Heyliger," *Bracebridge Hall*).

Lineation: p. 156, social, ... childhood.; p. 235, jecture ... colours.

Full calf.

A second edition noted, by same publisher, 1833, with same selections from Irving.

DLC.

THE | ORATOR'S TEXT BOOK: | CONTAINING A VARIETY OF | PASSAGES IN PROSE AND VERSE, | SELECTED AS EXERCISES IN READING AND RECITATION: | BY DONALD MACLEOD, A.M. | ... | WASHINGTON CITY: | PUBLISHED BY PISHEY THOMPSON. | Rothwell & Ustick, Printers. | 1830.

(20.3 x 12.3): [i]-xi [xii], [1]-300. Signed in 6's.

"Character of Columbus," 26-29 (from *Columbus*); "The Broken Heart," 57-60 (from *Sketch Book*).

Lineation: p. 60, and ... nor ; p. 200, With ... flows,

Tan boards. On front, title with ornamental frame. Back blank.

MH.

1831

THE | AMERICAN MANUAL, | OR | NEW ENGLISH READER: | CONSISTING OF | EXERCISES IN READING AND SPEAKING, | BOTH IN | Prose and Poetry; [fancy] | SELECTED FROM THE BEST WRITERS. | ... | FOR THE USE OF SCHOOLS. | [rule] | BY MOSES SEVERANCE. | [rule] | Waterloo, N.Y. [fancy] | PUBLISHED BY M. SEVERANCE. | [rule] | STEREOTYPED BY JAMES CONNER, NEW-YORK. | [rule] | 1831.

(15.5 x 9.9): [1]-298. Signed in 8's.

"The Widow and her Son," 82-88 (from *Sketch Book*); "The incidents of a Voyage across the Atlantic," 139-143 (from "The Voyage," *Sketch Book*); "Description of a Thunder-Storm on the Highlands of the Hudson," 143-144 (from "Dolph Heyliger," *Bracebridge Hall*).

Lineation: p. 85, which ... [in footnote] weakness.; p. 144, mountains ... [in footnote] alternate.

Full calf with black leather label on spine.

A later impression noted, published in Geneva, N. Y. by R. Robbins & Co., 1832.

DLC.

THE | LONDON CARCANET. | CONTAINING | SELECT PASSAGES | FROM THE | MOST DISTINGUISHED WRITERS. | FROM THE SECOND LONDON EDITION. | [rule] | NEW-YORK: | CHARLES H. PEABODY, 129, BROADWAY. | [rule of 9 dots] | 1831.

(15.9 x 10.1): [i]-x, [11]-244. Not reckoned: preliminary illustration, engraved title, and four leaves of advertisements at end. Signed in 6's.

Four short untitled extracts: [On love of mother for a child], 139, and [On poverty], 187 (both from "The Widow and Her Son" *Sketch Book*); [On the role of the woman and the wife], 193, 215 (both apparently from "Wives," *Bracebridge Hall*).

Lineation: p. 100, Breathes . . . tears.

Green paper boards. On front, full cover-title. On back and spine, the title. White endpapers.

CtY.

NOVELAS ESPAÑOLAS. | EL SERRANO | DE LAS ALPUJARRAS; | Y | EL CUADRO MISTERIOSO. | [rule] | BRUNSWICK: | IMPRENTA DE GRIFFIN. | SE HALLA DE VENTA EN LA LIBRERIA | DE COLMAN -- PORTLAND | 1830.

(18.7 x 12.2): [1]-80. Signed in 6's.

Edited, with a dedication, p. [2], and a preface, p. [3], by Henry W. Longfellow.

The text of "El Serrano de las Alpujarras" and "El Cuadro Misterioso" are taken from the adaptation-translation by George W. Montgomery, first published in *Tareas de un Solitario*, Madrid, 1829. For a discussion, see the description of that volume.

Luther S. Livingstone in his bibliography of Longfellow, 1908, reports that in the earliest state, the leaf containing pp. 9-10 is integral, with seven words in the last line; in a later state, the leaf is a cancel, with two words in the last line. But no copy in that later state has been located. In the second edition,

1831, the leaf does have only two words (nueva edicion) in the last line, and copies in mixed sheets are known, such as one in MH.

Lineation: p. 50, un ... ya ; p. 75, vendido: ... saber

Issued in marbled paper boards, some with black T cloth shelfback, without label.

A second edition (Brunswick: Griffin, 1831) omits the dedication and makes some small changes in text as well as in lineation. In 1842, an edition prints the Spanish text and an English translation by Julio Soler on opposite pages (New York: Printed by R. Rafael). In 1845 the original volume was reprinted in a new edition with additional material (Brunswick: J. Griffin; Se hallara en las librerías de J. Munroe, Boston; y de Wiley y Putnam, N. York y Londres).

TxU, rebound.

THE | RHETORICAL READER | CONSISTING OF | INSTRUCTIONS FOR REGULATING THE VOICE, | WITH A | RHETORICAL NOTATION, | ... | AND A |COURSE OF RHETORICAL EXERCISES. | [Designed for the use of Academies and High-Schools.] | BY EBENEZER PORTER, D.D. | ... | ANDOVER: | PRINTED AND PUBLISHED BY FLAGG & GOULD. | NEW-YORK: | J. LEAVITT, No. 182, BROADWAY. | 1831.

(20.1 x 12.6): [i]-[xii], 13-304, Eight pages of advertisements bound at end. Signed in 6's.

"Character of Columbus," 136-137 (from *Columbus*).

Lineation: p. 137, of ... posterity!; p. 200, And ... appear)

Red V cloth.

A number of later impressions noted by other publishers: 1835, 1842 (marked "One Hundredth Edition"), undated (marked "Two Hundred and Twentieth Edition"). A "New and Enlarged Edition" of 1857 retains the same selection from Irving.

DLC.

SPECIMENS | OF THE | NOVELISTS AND ROMANCERS, [hollow type, except for comma] | WITH | CRITICAL AND BIOGRAPHICAL NOTICES | OF THE AUTHORS. | [rule] | BY RICHARD GRIFFIN. | [rule] | FIRST AMERICAN FROM THE SECOND EDINBURGH EDITION. | [rule] | IN TWO VOLUMES--VOL. I. [II.] | [rule] | *NEW--YORK*: | PUBLISHED BY J. LANGDON, 210 BROADWAY. | Sold by

Collins & Hannay, George Long, G. & C. & H. Carvill, White, Gallaher | & White, E. Bliss, A. Hawley, J. Doyle, and C. S. Francis.--*Albany*, O. Steele, | and Little and Cummings.--*Philadelphia*, John Grigg, Tower & Hogan, E. L. | Carey & A. Hart, T. Desilver, jr., and U. Hunt--*Boston*, Richardson, Lord & | Holbrook, Carter, Hendee & Babcock, and Hilliard, Gray & Co.-- *Baltimore*, [comma at end omitted in Vol. II] | W. & J. Neal, J. Jewett, and Cushing & Sons. | [rule] | 1831.

(19.3 x 11.5 untrimmed): Vol. I. [i]-vi [vii]-[viii], [9]-216. Vol. II. [i]-[vi], [5]-215 [216]. Signed in 6's.

"Von Poffenburgh," II, 208-215 (from *History of New York*).

Lineation: Vol. I. p. 100, all, ... I; Vol II. p. 100, JOHN ... [in footnote] Corunna.

Drab tan paper boards with brown muslin shelfback. Yellow paper label on spines.

MB.

THE | YOUNG LADIES' CLASS BOOK; | A SELECTION OF | LESSONS FOR READING, | IN | PROSE AND VERSE. | [rule] | BY EBENEZER BAILEY, | ... | BOSTON: | LINCOLN AND EDMANDS. | COLLINS AND HANNAY, NEW YORK; KEY AND MEILKE, PHILADEL- | PHIA; CUSHING AND SONS, BALTIMORE. | [rule] | 1831.

(18.5 x 11.4): [i]-[ii] [v]-vi v-iv [vii]-viii (sic), [9]-408. Signed in 6's.

"The Wife," 60-67 (from *Sketch Book*); "Diedrich Knickerbocker's Description of Tea-Parties in New York," 265-266 (from *History of New York*).

Lineation: p.65, "But," ... a ; p. 265, knows ... immense

Full calf.

Noted in four later impressions, called "Revised Stereotype Edition," in 1832, 1834, 1851, 1859.

TxU.

1832

COBB'S SEQUEL | TO THE JUVENILE READERS; | COMPRISING | A SELECTION OF LESSONS IN PROSE AND POETRY, | FROM

HIGHLY ESTEEMED | AMERICAN AND ENGLISH WRITERS. | DESIGNED FOR THE USE OF HIGHER CLASSES IN SCHOOLS AND ACADEMIES; | AND TO IMPRESS THE MINDS OF YOUTH WITH | SENTIMENTS OF VIRTUE AND RELIGION. | BY LYMAN COBB, | ... | STEREOTYPED BY REES, REDFIELD, AND RIPLEY ..... NEW-YORK. | [rule] | HAVANA, N.Y. | PRINTED AND PUBLISHED BY HENRY W. RITTER. | 1832.

(16.2 x 10.2): [i]-vi, [7]-210. Catalogue bound at end, paged [211]-215 [216]. Signed in 6's.

"The Broken-hearted Woman," 161-162 (from "The Broken Heart," *Sketch Book*).

Lineation: p. 100, revolutions, ... and ; p. 161, and ... conceal

Purple V cloth. Sides blank. Black leather label in gilt on spine.

A later impression noted, published in Philadelphia by James Kay, Jr. & Brother, 1835. A later edition, fairly heavily revised, noted: *Cobb's New Sequel to the Juvenile Readers, or, Fourth Reading Book.* Cincinnati: B. Davenport, 1850. It contains the same selection from Irving.

IU.

[*Contes Américains, Traduits de l'Anglais de M. Irving, Miss Sedgwick [Paulding et Flint].* Paris: A. Auffray, 1832.]

240 pp. In 16's.

Reported to contain "The Creole Village." According to the *Life*, II, 43, Irving found the idea for the sketch on his trip to the West and South in 1832. But no publication of it has been found before 4 November 1836 in the *New-York Mirror*, taken from *The Magnolia* for 1837. There may be some error or confusion at work here.

Bibliographie de la France, 18 February 1832, listed, #826.

Not seen. Copy reported in Bibliothèque Nationale.

THE | ECLECTIC READER, | DESIGNED FOR | SCHOOLS AND ACADEMIES. | [double rule] | BY B. B. EDWARDS, | ... | BOSTON: | PUBLISHED BY PERKINS & MARVIN. | PHILADELPHIA: FRENCH & PERKINS. | [rule] | 1832.

(18.3 x 11.4): [1]-324. Signed in 6's.

"Discovery of the New World," 243-247; "Reception of Columbus on His Return to Spain," 247-250; "Character of Columbus," 250-254 (all from *Columbus*).

Lineation: p. 100, ten ... to ; p. 250, ed ... benign

Full calf.

TxU.

THE | HIGH SCHOOL READER, | DESIGNED FOR | A FIRST CLASS BOOK. | CONSISTING OF | EXTRACTS IN PROSE AND POETRY. | [rule] | BY REV. J. L. BLAKE, A. M. | ... | BOSTON: | PUBLISHED BY WILLIAM HYDE & CO. | [rule] | 1832.

(17.9 x 11.1): [i]-viii, [9]-408. Signed in 6's.

"The Brokenhearted Woman," 150-151 (from "The Broken Heart," *Sketch Book*).

Printer: Stereotyped by Lyman Thurston & Co., Boston.

Lineation: p. 150, we ... down; p. 300, main ... from

Full calf.

A later impression noted, published in Boston by Allen & Ticknor, 1834.

DLC.

A | HISTORY | OF THE | AMERICAN THEATRE. | BY WILLIAM DUNLAP, | ... | NEW-YORK: | PRINTED AND PUBLISHED BY J. & J. HARPER, | No. 82 CLIFF-STREET, | SOLD BY THE PRINCIPAL BOOKSELLERS THROUGHOUT | THE UNITED STATES. | [rule] | 1832.

(22.4 x 13.5): [i]-viii, [1]-420. Four pages of advertisements bound at end, paged [1]-4. Signed in 12's. Errata slip pasted down on front endpaper in one copy; originally inserted?

Extensive extracts from *Oldstyle*, 299-309: all of Letter III and Letter V except the opening paragraph of each; all of the Andrew Quoz letter of Letter VI; a large part of Letter VII and a small part of Letter IV.

Lineation: p. 100, Lewis ... of ; p. 300, ments; ... ample

Purple V cloth. Sides blank. Paper label on spines. White endpapers.

New-York Mirror, 22 September 1832, extract "from the manuscript," and notice in literary column, "will be ready for the public in about three weeks"; 3 November 1832, noticed. *American Quarterly Review*, December 1832, reviewed.

TxU (3).

[London edition]. HISTORY | OF THE | AMERICAN THEATRE. | BY | WILLIAM DUNLAP, | ... | IN TWO VOLUMES. | VOL. I. [II.] | [rule] | LONDON: | RICHARD BENTLEY, NEW BURLINGTON STREET. | [rule] | 1833.

A reprint of the text of the American edition.

(21.0 x 13.4): Vol. I. [i]-xii, [1]-412. Vol. II. [i]-vi, [1]-387 [388]. Signed in 8's.

The extracts from *Oldstyle*, II, 173-183.

Printer: F. Shoberl, Jun., Long Acre, London listed on verso of both titles and on p. 412 of Vol. I; Ibotson and Palmer, Printers, Savoy Street, Strand listed on p. [388] of Vol. II.

Lineation: Vol. I. p. 100, Cumberland's ... did ; p. 200, the ... to Vol. II. p. 100, himself ... exer-; p. 200, CHAPTER XXIX. ... Wood

TxU.

THE | LADY'S | CABINET ALBUM. | ... | NEW-YORK: | PUBLISHED BY PEABODY AND CO. | [rule] | MDCCCXXXII.

(17.5 x 10.8 trimmed): [i]-[iv], 5, vi, 7, [viii], 9, x-xii, 1-348. Preliminary engraving and 20 others through volume not reckoned.

"The Dull Lecture," 291 (poem from *The Atlantic Souvenir* for 1828).

Printer: J. H. A. Frost, Boston.

Lineation: p. 100, emerging ... situation ; p. 291, FROM ... IRVING.]

Later impressions, all but one under a different title or published by another publisher, are numerous. The following have been noted or are reported in Frederick W. Faxon, *Literary Annuals and Gift Books*, 1973.

The Lady's Cabinet Album.

New York: Peabody and Co., 1834.

New York: E. Sands, 1835, 1837.

New York: Published for the Booksellers, n.d. [1840 on spine].

The Lady's Album.

New York: Nafis & Cornish, n.d. [1845], [1846], [1848].

New York: Cornish, Lamport & Co., [1851].

The Moss Rose.

New York: Nafis & Cornish, [1845].

New York: Lamport, Blakeman & Law, 1854.

TxU.

1833

AN | ESSAY ON ELOCUTION, | DESIGNED | FOR THE USE OF SCHOOLS | AND | PRIVATE LEARNERS. | [rule] | BY SAMUEL KIRKHAM, | ... | BALTIMORE: | JOHN W. WOODS, PRINTER, | No. 1, N. Calvert street. | 1833.

(18.4 x 10.5): [i]-xviii, [19]-324. Twelve pages of advertisements bound at end. Signed in 6's.

"Beautiful Metaphor," 155 (not identified); "Reflections on the Tomb of Shakespeare," 158 (from "Stratford-On-Avon," *Sketch Book*); "Affection for the Dead," 166-168 (from "Rural Funerals," *Sketch Book*); "Traits of Indian Character," 237-244, and "Reflections on Westminster Abbey," 269-271 (both from *Sketch Book*).

Lineation: p. 155, PART II. ... dear'?; p. 270, dust ... [in footnote] urge.

Full calf. Spine decorated in gilt.

A second edition by the same publisher, 1834, adds to the original selections from Irving the following: "Beautiful Simile," 160 (from "The Wife," *Sketch Book*); "The Broken Heart," 307-309 (from *Sketch Book*); "The Alhambra by Moonlight," 323-324 (from *Alhambra*) ; Reflections on the Moslem Domination in Spain," 324-327 (from *Granada*).

A second impression of the second edition, marked "Third Edition, Enlarged and Improved," was published in New York by Robinson, Pratt and Co., 63 Wall Street, 1843. A later impression noted, published in New York by Pratt, Woodford and Co., No. 4 Cortlandt Street, 1852.

First ed., TNJ. Second ed., NIC.

EXCURSIONS | DANS | L'AMÉRIQUE MÉRIDIONALE, | LE NORD-OUEST DES ÉTATS-UNIS ET LES ANTILLES, | Dans les Annés 1812,

1816, 1820, et 1824; [fancy] | AVEC DES INSTRUCTIONS TOTALEMENT NEUVES | SUR LA CONSERVATION DES OISEAUX; | PAR | CHARLES WATERTON, ESQ.; | SUIVIES D'UNE NOTICE | SUR LES SAUVAGES DE L'AMÉRIQUE SEPTENTRIONALE. | [rule] | Traduit de l'Anglais. [fancy] | [elaborated swelled rule] | PARIS, | LANCE, LIBRAIRE, RUE DU BOULOY, N° 7. | [rule] | ROUEN, NICÉTAS PERIAUX, IMPRIMEUR-ÉDITEUR. | 1833.

(21.1 x 12.9): [I]-XVI, [1]-470. Signed in 8's. Laid paper.

"Des Sauvages de l'Amérique Septentrionale," 445-470 (from "Traits of Indian Character," *Sketch Book*). On p. XI appears an editorial note: "*N.B.* La Notice sur les sauvages ... n'est pas de M. Waterton, elle est de M. Washington Irving...."

MB.

THE | FIRST-CLASS READER: | A SELECTION | FOR EXERCISES IN READING, | FROM | STANDARD BRITISH AND AMERICAN AUTHORS, | IN PROSE AND VERSE. | FOR THE USE OF SCHOOLS IN THE UNITED STATES. | BY B. D. EMERSON, | ... | BOSTON: | RUSSELL, ODIORNE, AND METCALF. | PHILADELPHIA, HOGAN & THOMPSON: NEW YORK, N. & J. WHITE: MOBILE, | SIDNEY SMITH. WINDSOR, VT., IDE & GODDARD. | [rule] | 1833.

(17.7 x 10.6): [i]-viii, [9]-276. Signed in 6's.

"Rural Life in England," 24-26, and "Christmas in England," 93-97 (both from *Sketch Book*); "Reception of Columbus on His Return to Spain," 127-130 (from *Columbus*); "Reflections on the Moslem Domination in Spain," 163-166 (from *Alhambra*); "Surrender of Granada by the Moors to Ferdinand and Isabella," 166-169 (from *Granada*); "The American in England," 176-177 (from "The Author," *Bracebridge Hall*); "A Scene Nearly Two Centuries Ago on the River Hudson," 244-246 (from *History of New York*).

Printer: Stereotyped by Lyman Thurston & Co., Boston.

Lineation: p. 25, ed with ... but ; p. 245, The ... beings.

Full calf. Red leather label on spine.

Later impressions noted: the same publisher, 1833; Claremont, N.H.: The Claremont Manufacturing Co., Simeon Ide, 1841.

DLC.

THE | PREMIUM; | A PRESENT FOR ALL SEASONS: | CONSISTING OF | ELEGANT EXTRACTS | FROM | BRITISH AND AMERICAN WRITERS | OF THE | NINETEENTH CENTURY. | [rule] |

PHILADELPHIA: | CAREY, LEA & BLANCHARD. | [rule of 9 dots] | 1833.

(12.3 x 7.9 trimmed): [i]-viii, [1]-310. Preliminary engraving and engraved title not reckoned. Signed in 8's.

"The Rainy Sunday," 58-61 (from "The Stout Gentleman," *Bracebridge Hall*); "Reception of Columbus on his Return to Spain," 192-195 (from *Columbus*); "The Adventure of the Mason," 257-261 (from *Alhambra*).

Lineation: p. 60, nothing ... world.; p. 260, The ... and

A later impression noted, by the same publisher, 1835. It is bound in wine-colored P-type cloth; sides blank, spine titled in gilt.

NN.

THE | SECOND-CLASS READER: | DESIGNED | FOR THE USE OF THE MIDDLE CLASS OF SCHOOLS | IN THE UNITED STATES. | BY B.D. EMERSON, | . . . | BOSTON: | RUSSELL, ODIORNE, & METCALF: | PHILADELPHIA, HOGAN & THOMPSON: WINDSOR, VT., IDE & GODDARD, | NEW-YORK, N. & J. WHITE: MOBILE, SIDNEY SMITH. | [rule] | 1833.

(17.8 x 11.2): [i]-[iii], 4, [v]vi-viii, [9]-168. Signed in 6's.

"Discovery of the Pacific Ocean," 39-41 (from *Companions of Columbus*); "Ingenious Stratagem of Columbus," 53-55 (from *Columbus*); "Adventures of the Popkins Family in Italy, as Narrated to a Traveller at the Inn in Terracina," 112-116 (from *Tales of a Traveller*).

Lineation: p. 40, folded ... pow-; p. 115, denly ... Hobbs.

Tan paper boards. Cover-title on front. On back, advertisements for Russell, Odiorne, and Metcalf. Spine not titled.

Later impressions noted: Windsor, Vt.: Ide & Goddard, 1834; Claremont, N.H.: Claremont Manufacturing Co., Simeon Ide, 1845.

DLC.

THE | SELECT READER, | OR | UNION No. 6. | DESIGNED FOR THE | HIGHER CLASSES IN ACADEMIES AND SCHOOLS: | . . . | BY OLIVER ANGELL, A. M. | . . . | PHILADELPHIA: | MARSHALL, CLARK AND CO. | PROVIDENCE: MARSHALL, BROWN AND CO.-- HARTFORD: | ANDRUS AND JUDD. | [rule] | 1833.

(18.2 x 11.1) : [1]-504. Signed in 6's.

"The Discovery of America," 13-19 (from *Columbus*); [Unititled: "The Graves of Those We Loved"], 166-167 (from "Rural Funerals," *Sketch Book*);

"Scenery in the Highlands," 277-281 (from "Dolph Heyliger," *Bracebridge Hall*); "Interior of the Alhambra," 457-463 (from "Palace of the Alhambra," *Alhambra*).

Printer: Stereotyped at the Boston Type and Stereotype Foundry.

Lineation: p. 100, tentous ... formed ; p. 280, came ... call-

MH.

THE | WESTERN READER; | A | SERIES OF USEFUL LESSONS, | ... | SELECTED AND ARRANGED BY | JAMES HALL. | CINCINNATI: | COREY AND FAIRBANK, | AND | HUBBARD AND EDMUNDS. | [rule | 1833.

(17.4 x 10.4 trimmed): [i]-viii, [9]-216. Signed in 6's.

"The Little Man in Black," 114-121 (from *Salmagundi*).

Printer: Stereotyped by J. A. James, No. 1, Baker Street.

Lineation: p. 120, it ... it,; p. 200, 3. Just ... Jesus."

Seen only rebound. An impression of 1834 by the same publisher noted in green-blue boards with title on front and advertisements on back.

NN.

1834

A | FOURTH BOOK | OF | LESSONS FOR READING; | WITH | RULES AND INSTRUCTIONS. | [rule] | BY SAMUEL WORCESTER, | ... | Stereotype Edition. [fancy] | [double rule] | BOSTON: | CARTER, HENDEE & CO. | [rule] | 1834.

(19.0 x 11.5): [1]-408. Signed in 6's.

"Columbus," 204-208 (from *Columbus*); "Scenery in the Highlands on the Hudson River," 325-329 (from "Dolph Heyliger," *Bracebridge Hall*).

Printer: Stereotyped at the Boston Type and Stereotype Foundry.

Lineation: p. 100, died ... poetry.; p. 325, nouncing ... of

Full calf with red leather label on spine.

Later impressions noted, all published in Boston: Carter, Hendee & Co., 1835; Charles J. Hendee, 1836; Charles J. Hendee, and, Jenks and Palmer, 1839; "Enlarged and Improved Edition" (reset, with same selections from Irving), Jenks, Palmer & Co., 1848; same, 1851.

DLC, MH.

THE | INTELLIGENT READER: | DESIGNED AS | A SEQUEL | TO | THE CHILD'S GUIDE. | ... | SPRINGFIELD: | PUBLISHED BY G. AND C. MERRIAM. | [rule of 19 dots] | 1834.

(15.6 x 10.1): [i]-xii, [13]-252. Signed in 6's.

"The Sage Decision of the Renowned Governor Van Twiller," 159-161 (from *History of New York*) [Attributed to Irving only in the table of contents].

Lineation: p. 160, 4. He ... commentator,; p. 200, their ... of

Green paper boards with calf shelfback. On front, pictorial title, dated 1834, with picture of children and schoolhouse, decorative frame around. On back, advertisements.

Noted in later impressions by the same publisher, 1835, 1837.

DLC.

SELECTIONS | FROM THE | AMERICAN POETS, | WITH | SOME INTRODUCTORY REMARKS. | DUBLIN: | WILLIAM FREDERICK WAKEMAN, | 9, D'OLIER-STREET. | LONDON: SIMPKIN AND MARSHALL, AND | RICHARD GROOMBRIDGE. | EDINBURGH: FRAZER AND COMPANY. | 1834.

(16.0 x 10.4): [i]-xxiii [xxiv], [1]-357 [358]. Signed in 8's.

"The Falls of the Passaic," 261-262 (from *The Atlantic Souvenir* for 1827).

Printer: John S. Folds, 5, Bachelor's Walk, Dublin.

Lineation: p. 100, But ... flourishing.; p. 262, With ... foam.

Seen only rebound, but with original AEG remaining.

DLC.

1835

THE | NORTH AMERICAN READER; | CONTAINING | A GREAT VARIETY OF PIECES IN PROSE AND POETRY, | FROM VERY HIGHLY ESTEEMED | AMERICAN AND ENGLISH WRITERS; | ... | DESIGNED FOR THE USE OF THE HIGHEST CLASSES IN SCHOOLS AND ACADEMIES. | BY LYMAN COBB, | ... | NEW YORK: | PUBLISHED BY HARPER & BROTHERS, | NO. 82 CLIFF-STREET, | AND SOLD BY THE PRINCIPAL BOOKSELLERS THROUGHOUT THE | UNITED STATES. | [rule] | 1835.

(18.1 x 10.7): [i]-xxi [xxii], [23]-498. Not reckoned: preliminary woodblock illustration, and catalogue bound at end, paged [499]-504. Signed in 12's.

"Traits of Indian Character," 49-52 (from *Sketch Book*); "Feelings Excited by a Long Voyage," 90-94 (from "The Voyage," *Sketch Book*); "Death of King Philip," 130-131 (from "Philip of Pokanoket," *Sketch Book);* " A Scene Nearly Two Centuries Ago on the River Hudson," 148-150 *(from "Dolph Heyliger," Bracebridge Hall)*; "Forest Trees," 198-201 (from *Bracebridge Hall*); "Reception of Columbus on His Return to Spain," 222-225 (from *Columbus*); "The Wife," 241-242, and "Roscoe," 267-270 (both from *Sketch Book*).

Lineation: p. 50, regarded ... repining ; p. 200, He ... deep

Full calf. Spine titled in gilt.

A later impression noted, published in Zanesville, Ohio by J. R. & A. Lippitt, 1836.

DLC.

1836

THE | AMERICAN CLASS-READER; | CONTAINING | A SERIES OF LESSONS | IN | READING; | WITH | INTRODUCTORY EXERCISES | IN | ARTICULATION, INFLECTION, EMPHASIS, | AND THE | OTHER ESSENTIAL ELEMENTS | OF | CORRECT NATURAL ELOCUTION; | DESIGNED FOR | ACADEMIES AND COMMON SCHOOLS. | [rule] | BY GEORGE WILLSON. | [rule] | CANANDAIGUA: | PUBLISHED AND SOLD, WHOLESALE AND RETAIL, BY | C. MORSE. | SOLD ALSO BY COLLINS, KEESE & CO., N. & J. WHITE, AND LEAVITT, | LORD & CO., NEW YORK; OLIVER STEELE, AND W. C. LITTLE, | ALBANY; AND BENNET & BRIGHT, UTICA. | [rule] | 1836.

(18.3 x 11.3): [1]-252. Signed in 6's.

"Sorrow for the Dead," 79-80 (from "Rural Funerals," *Sketch Book*); "Diedrich Knickerbocker's New-England Farmer," 213-214 (from *History of New York*).

Lineation: p. 80, 5 daily ... men, --; p. 200, one ... to

DLC.

THE | AMERICAN [hollow letters] | ORATOR'S OWN BOOK: | OR THE ART OF | EXTEMPORANEOUS PUBLIC SPEAKING, | ... | WRITTEN AND COMPILED FOR THE USE OF COLLEGES, | SCHOOLS, AND STUDENTS OF ORATORY. | [rule] |

PHILADELPHIA: | JAMES KAY, JUN. AND BROTHER, | 122 Chestnut Street--near Fourth. | PITTSBURGH: JOHN I. KAY & CO. | 1836.

(12.1 x 8.0): [i]-xvi, [1]-328. Not reckoned: Preliminary illustration and engraved title. Signed in 16's.

"Right of Discovery," 241-243, and "Right of Cultivation,"243-245 (from *History of New York*).

Lineation: p. 100, observe ... Testament.; p. 244, spontaneous ... Heaven.

A second edition, dated 1840, contains the same selections.

ViU.

THE | DESCRIPTIVE, | SENTIMENTAL, AND HUMOROUS | ALBUM: [in hollow letters] | CONSISTING OF CHOICE SELECTIONS FROM THE | WRITINGS OF | [21 authors in 3 columns, beginning with IRVING and ending with PAULDING] | [double rule] | BALTIMORE: | PUBLISHED BY N. HICKMAN, | No. 86, MARKET STREET. | [rule of 6 dots] | 1836.

(14.2 x 9.0): [i]-xi [xii], [9]-356. Signed in 6's.

"The Busybody," 50-55 (from "The Busy Man," *Bracebridge Hall*); "The Rookery," 141-148 (from *Bracebridge Hall*); "A Scene ... on the river Hudson," 211-214 (from *History of New York*.)

Lineation: p. 50, stantly ... mi-; p. 200, ken; ... of

CtY.

AN | INTRODUCTION | TO THE | GRAMMAR OF ELOCUTION. | DESIGNED FOR THE USE OF SCHOOLS. | [rule] | BY JONATHAN BARBER, | ... | SECOND EDITION REVISED AND IMPROVED. | BOSTON: | MARSH, CAPEN & LYON, | [rule] | 1836.

(18.7 x 11.5): [i]-vii [viii], [9]-174. Signed in 6's.

"Knickerbocker's Characteristics of the New-Englanders," 157-161 (from *History of New York*).

Lineation: p. 100, be ... is ; p. 158, nothing ... imme-

Drab brown paper boards with brown cloth shelfback.

The first edition, Boston: Marsh, Capen & Lyon, 1834, contains no Irving.

TxU.

THE | READER'S GUIDE, | ... | WITH | NUMEROUS EXAMPLES FOR ILLUSTRATION, | AND | LESSONS FOR PRACTICE. | [rule] |

BY JOHN HALL, | ... | HARTFORD: | PUBLISHED BY CANFIELD & ROBINS. | [rule] | 1836.

(18.8 x 11.2): [i]-xii, [13]-360. Signed in 6's.

"The Hunters of the Prairie," 169-170, and "A Republic of Prairie Dogs," 181-183 (both from *Tour on the Prairies*), "The Adventure of a Mason," 208-210, and "The Governor, and the Notary," 246-251 (both from *Alhambra*); "A Thunderstorm on the Prairies," 251-253, and "Deer Bleating. Magic Balls," 257-259, and "A Frontier Farm House," 260-261 (all from *Tour on the Prairies*).

Lineation: p. 100, verse; ... con- ; p. 210, that ... heir.

Full calf.

A later impression noted by same publisher, 1837.

MH.

THE | YOUNG LADY'S | GIFT, | A | Common-Place Book | OF | Prose and Poetry. | PROVIDENCE: | B. CRANSTON & CO. | 1836. Engraved title, in a variety of lettering styles.

(14.6 x 9.2): [i]-viii, [1]-316. Signed in 6's.

"The Wife," 218-225 (from *Sketch Book*).

Lineation: p. 100, "Oh, ... Reverses.; p. 225, I ... breast?

CtY, TxU.

1837

The McGuffey readers, now the most famous of the American nineteenth-century readers, provide a challenging problem in listing, since the series included seven different school readers, evolving through a complex process of revision, reissue, change of title, change of content and grade level, and addition of new readers. Many editions too were issued by several different publishers in a number of different impressions. The exact bibliographical sequence has yet to be defined satisfactorily and needs further study. For a general history of the series and some attempt at a bibliographical accounting, see *A History of the McGuffey Readers* by Henry H. Vail, Cleveland: Privately printed, 1910; and *William Homes McGuffey and His Readers* by Harvey C. Minnich, New York: American Book Company, [1936]. Both should be approached with a certain bibliographical skepticism. Minnich locates many copies; in addition to those listed there, the Library of Congress has a particularly large and fine collection.

Although out of keeping with the chronological order of this list of Irving's contributions to other books, the McGuffey readers, as a special series of special interest, are listed here together. But an overview of a generalized history of the series might help to put the individual volumes in context and show their relationship to the series as a whole.

1836. First and Second Readers published. (They contain nothing by Irving.)

1837. Third and Fourth Readers published.

1838. The Second, Third, and Fourth Readers "Revised and Improved" or "Enlarged and Improved."

1841. The First and Second Readers "Revised and Improved."

1844. A former "Rhetorical Guide" revised and added as the Fifth Reader. The earlier readers "Newly Revised" (the Third Reader in 1843): "Revised and Improved" or "Enlarged and Improved."

1848. Some readers, certainly including the First, Third, and Fourth, "Newly Improved" or "Newly Revised."

1853. The entire series "Newly Revised."

1857. The Sixth Reader and High School Reader added. The series thoroughly recast and revised. With the addition of the higher readers, the "New Third" and the "New Fourth Eclectic Reader" are now aimed at younger children and the Irving selections omitted; a new set of selections is made for the Fifth Reader.

THE | ECLECTIC THIRD READER; | CONTAINING | SELECTIONS IN PROSE AND POETRY, | FROM THE BEST | AMERICAN AND ENGLISH WRITERS. | WITH | PLAIN RULES FOR READING, | AND | DIRECTIONS FOR AVOIDING COMMON ERRORS. | [rule] | BY WILLIAM H. McGUFFEY, | ... | CINCINNATI: | PUBLISHED BY TRUMAN AND SMITH. | 1837.

Title noted in three states; no sequence established.

[A]. As described, with comma after READING in line 8, and McGUFFEY spelled with a "c" in line 12.

[B]. With comma after READING in line 8, and M'GUFFEY spelled with an apostrophe in line 12.

[C]. With no punctuation after READING in line 8, and M'GUFFEY spelled with an apostrophe in line 12.

Harvey C. Minnich, referring to the Maude Blair List of the collection at Detroit, suggests as many as five printings dated 1837.

(18.5 x 11.0): [1-11, unpaged], 12-165 [166]-[168]. Advertisements on last three pages. Signed in 6's.

"Description of Pompey's Pillar," 103-105 (source not identified; Pierpont's *American First Class Book* assigns the selection to "Irwin").

Lineation: p. 100, and ... accounts ; p. 150, LESSON LVIII. ... you

Henry H. Vail reports that the reader was issued in boards with a picture on the cover of Napoleon on his rearing charger. Not seen.

The revised editions of 1838, 1843, 1848, 1853 contain the same selection from Irving. The edition of 1857 contains no Irving. From 1843, the editions are published by two or more publishers.

State [A]: DLC. State [B]: OOxM. State [C]: OOxM.

THE | ECLECTIC FOURTH READER: | CONTAINING | ELEGANT EXTRACTS IN PROSE AND POETRY, | FROM THE BEST | AMERICAN AND ENGLISH WRITERS. | WITH | COPIOUS RULES FOR READING, | AND | DIRECTIONS FOR AVOIDING COMMON ERRORS. | [rule] | BY WILLIAM H. McGUFFEY, | ... | CINCINNATI: | PUBLISHED BY TRUMAN AND SMITH. | 1837.

(18.8 x 11.0):   [i]-x, [2 pp. unpaged], [13]-279 [280].   Eight pages of advertisements bound at end. Signed in 6's.

"The Wife," 172-173 (from *Sketch Book*); "Capturing the Wild Horse," 259-263 (from *Tour on the Prairies*).

Lineation: p. 100, phical ... canvass.; p. 200, LESSON LXXV. ... reproach.

The edition of 1838, noted only in an impression by Truman and Smith, described as "Enlarged and Improved, Stereotype Edition," adds to the original selections from Irving, "The Alhambra by Moonlight" (from *Alhambra*). The revised editions of 1844, 1848, 1853, by various publishers, retain the three selections. The edition of 1857 contains no Irving.

DLC.

ECLECTIC SERIES, NEWLY IMPROVED. | [rule] | McGUFFEY'S | RHETORICAL GUIDE: | OR, | FIFTH READER | ... | CONTAINING | ELEGANT EXTRACTS IN PROSE AND POETRY, | WITH | COPIOUS RULES AND RHETORICAL EXERCISES. | [wavy rule] | Compiled by A. M. McGuffey, A. M. [fancy] | [wavy rule] | PUBLISHER, | WINTHROP B. SMITH, CINCINNATI. | [rule of 13 dots].

Copyright 1844.

(18.3 x 11.3): [1]-480. Signed in 8's and 4's.

"The Voyage," 194-198 (from *Sketch Book*); "A Bee Hunt," 213-216 (from *Tour on The Prairies*); "The Grave," 246-247 (from "Rural Funerals," *Sketch Book*); "Character of Columbus," 247-249, and "Reception of Columbus, on

His Return to Spain," 250-252 (both from *Columbus*); "A Republic of Prairie Dogs," 417-418 (from *Tour on the Prairies*).

Printer: Stereotyped by J. A. James, Cincinnati.

Lineation: p. 215, One ... bears ; p. 418, while ... IRVING.

Two other later impressions noted: one adds "& CO." after SMITH in the imprint; the other, published in New York by Clark, Austin & Smith, calls itself "Stereotype Edition."

The 1853 edition, "Revised and Improved," published by three publishers, adds Irving's "The Broken Heart," 130-132 (from *Sketch Book)* to the other selections.

The 1857 edition, the "New Fifth Eclectic Reader," is in effect a new book and contains different selections from Irving: "The Alhambra by Moonlight," 141-143 (from *Alhambra*); "The Wife," 169-170 (from *Sketch Book*); "The Boblink," 310-313 (from "The Birds of Spring," *Wolfert's Roost*); "Capturing the Wild Horse," 315-319 (from *Tour on the Prairies*).

Two impressions of the 1857 edition noted:

Cincinnati: Winthrop B. Smith & Co.; New York: Clark, Austin, Maynard & Co.

Cincinnati: Sargent, Wilson & Hinkle; New York: Clark and Maynard. "Stereotype Edition."

Harvey C. Minnich reports others also.

TxU (1844, 1853, 1857)

ECLECTIC EDUCATIONAL SERIES. | [rule] | McGUFFEY'S | NEW | SIXTH ECLECTIC READER: | EXERCISES IN | RHETORICAL READING, | WITH | INTRODUCTORY RULES AND EXAMPLES. | [rule] | BY WM. H. McGUFFEY, LL. D. | [rule] | *STEREOTYPE EDITION*. | PUBLISHERS: | CINCINNATI, WINTHROP B. SMITH & CO. | NEW YORK, CLARK, AUSTIN, MAYNARD & CO. | [rule of 18 dots].

Copyright 1857.

(18.2 x 11.9): [1]-448. The first four pages contain advertisements. Bound at end, six pages of advertisements, unpaged. Signed in 8's and 4's.

"The Broken Heart," 140-142, and "The Voyage," 226-231 (both from *Sketch Book*); "The Grave," 408-410 (from "Rural Funerals," *Sketch Book*).

Lineation: p. 140, Have ... the ; p. 410, benefit ... unknown.

Brown BD cloth with black leather shelfback. Sides blank.

Another impression noted: published in Cincinnati by Sargent, Wilson & Hinkle; in New York by Clark & Maynard. Harvey C. Minnich reports others also.

TxU.

ECLECTIC EDUCATIONAL SERIES. | [rule] | McGUFFEY'S | NEW | HIGH SCHOOL READER; | FOR ADVANCED CLASSES. | EMBRACING ABOUT | Two Hundred Classic Exercises. [fancy] | [rule] | *STEREOTYPE EDITION.* | [rule] | CINCINNATI: | SARGENT, WILSON & HINKLE. | PHILADELPHIA: J. B. LIPPINCOTT & CO.

Copyright 1857.

"Ferdinand and Isabella," 42-43, and "Columbus in Spain," 49-52 (both from *Columbus*); "Shakespeare's Home and Tomb," 130-133 (from "Stratford-On-Avon," *Sketch Book*); "Book-Making," 140-144, and "Rural Life in England," 202-206 (both from *Sketch Book*); "The Bee Hunt," 338-341 (from *Tour on the Prairies*).

Lineation: p. 50, regions. ... some ; p. 340, tree, ... been

Brown BD cloth with black leather shelfback. On sides, series title in blind.

An earlier impression reported by Harvey C. Minnich: published in Cincinnati by Winthrop B. Smith & Co. A later impression noted: published in Cincinnati and in New York by Wilson, Hinkle & Co.

TxU.

THE | MOURNER'S GIFT. [hollow letters] | EDITED BY | MRS. M. A. PATRICK. | ... | NEW YORK: VAN NOSTRAND & DWIGHT. | MDCCCXXXVII.

(10.5 x 7.0): [1]-192. Not reckoned: preliminary engraved title and illustration.

"Strewing Flowers upon Graves," 190-192 (from "Rural Funerals," *Sketch Book*).

Printer: Stereotyped by F. F. Ripley, New York.

Lineation: p. 100, My ... good-night.; p. 191, from ... in

Noted in two bindings: [A]. Brown cloth with fleur de lys-like figuring. On sides, publisher and decoration in gilt. AEG. Cream endpapers. [B]. White cloth with raised gold diamond-shaped figuring. Sides decorated in blind. Spine titled in gilt. AEG. Yellow endpapers.

A later impression noted by the same publisher, 1841.

CtY, TxU.

THE | NEW-YORK BOOK | OF | POETRY. | ... | NEW-YORK: | GEORGE DEARBORN, PUBLISHER, | NO. 38 GOLD STREET. | [rule] | 1837.

(21.9 x 13.6 rebound): [i]-x, [1]-253 [254]. Preliminary engraved title not reckoned. Signed in 4's.

"The Falls of the Passaic," 105-106 (from *The Atlantic Souvenir* for 1827).

Printer: Scatcherd & Adams, No. 38 Gold Street.

Lineation: p. 100, Their ... race.; p. 200, To ... Europe.

NN.

1839

THE | FOURTH | READER | FOR THE USE | OF | SCHOOLS. | [rule] | BY S. G. GOODRICH. | [rule] | BOSTON: | OTIS, BROADERS, & COMPANY. | 1839. All within decorative frame: "Industry" above, "Farming" below, horse at lower left, alligator at lower right.

(18.2 x 11.2): [i]-vi, [7]-312. Signed in 6's.

"The Widow and Her Son," 46-48 (from *Sketch Book*); "Scenes on the Hudson River in Early Times," 225-227 [listed as p. 226 in table of contents] (from *History of New York*); "The Broken Heart," 230-231 (from *Sketch Book*).

Printer: Stereotyped by Folsom, Wells, and Thurston, Printers to the University, Cambridge.

Lineation: p. 50, fended, ... learned ; p. 225, And ... retreating,

Full calf.

A later impression noted, published in Louisville, Ky. by Morton and Griswold, undated.

DLC.

THE | MONITORIAL READER, | DESIGNED FOR THE USE OF | ACADEMIES AND SCHOOLS; | AND AS | A MONITOR TO YOUTH, | HOLDING UP TO THEIR VIEW MODELS WHEREBY TO FORM |

THEIR OWN CHARACTERS. | [rule] | BY DANIEL ADAMS, M. D. | ... | CONCORD, N. H. | BOYD AND WHITE. | 1839.

(18.6 x 11.1): [i]-vii [viii], [9]-288. Signed in 6's.

"Rural Life in England," 266-267 (from *Sketch Book*).

Printer: Stereotyped by William White, Concord, N.H.

Lineation: p. 100, gregate, ... parted.; p. 266, dull, ... pal-

Full calf.

A later impression noted, published in Concord, N. H. by Roby, Kimball & Merrill, 1841.

MH.

THE | READER'S MANUAL. | DESIGNED FOR THE USE OF COMMON SCHOOLS | IN THE UNITED STATES. | BY JOHN HALL, | ... | HARTFORD. | GURDON ROBINS, JR., 180 MAIN STREET. | 1839.

(18.6 x 11.2): [i]-x [xi]-[xiii], 1-300. Signed in 6's.

"The Stage Coach," 165-169 (from *Sketch Book*).

Lineation: p. 166, portance ... [in footnote] nosegay.; p. 250, seen ... [in footnote] *Guide*.

Full calf.

A later impression noted by the same publisher, 1840.

MH.

THE | SOUTHERN FIRST CLASS BOOK; | OR EXERCISES IN | READING AND DECLAMATION. | SELECTED PRINCIPALLY FROM | AMERICAN AUTHORS | AND DESIGNED FOR | THE USE OF SCHOOLS AND ACADEMIES | IN THE | SOUTHERN AND WESTERN STATES. | [rule] | BY M. M. MASON, A. B. | ... | MACON: | B. F. GRIFFIN AND JOHN M. COOPER. | AUGUSTA, J. W. & T. S. STOY, & T. H. PLANT. -- SAVANNAH, | T. PURSE & W. T. WILLIAMS. -- COLUMBUS, S. C., J. J. M'CARTER & CO. | [rule] | 1839.

(18.1 x 10.5): [i]-v [vi], [7]-336. Twelve pages of advertisements bound at front. Signed in 6's.

"The Character of Columbus," 137 (from *Columbus*).

Lineation: p. 100, A ... then ; p. 200, Behind ... strays

Brown marbled paper boards with black leather shelfback. Sides blank. Spine titled in gilt.

DLC.

1840

THE | AMERICAN MISCELLANY | OF | Popular Tales, Essays, Sketches of Character, [fancy] | POETRY, | AND | JEUX D'ESPRIT. | BY TRANSATLANTIC AUTHORS. | VOL. II. | [rule] | LONDON: | G. BERGER, HOLYWELL STREET, STRAND; | SIMPKIN, MARSHALL, & CO.; | AND ALL BOOKSELLERS. | [rule] | 1840.

(22.0 x 13.8) : [i]-[iv], [1]-316. In double columns. Signed in 8's.

"The Bermudas. A Shaksperian Research," 109-112, and "The Three Kings of Bermuda, and Their Treasure of Ambergris," 123-124 (both from *The Knickerbocker*, January 1840); "A Time of Unexampled Prosperity and The Great Mississippi Bubble," 135-139, 150-154, 168-172 (from *The Knickerbocker*, April 1840); "Pelayo and the Merchant's Daughter," 187-191 (from *The Knickerbocker*, January 1840); "Legend of the Engulphcd Convent," 215-217 (from *The Knickerbocker*, March 1840); "The Crayon Papers: The Taking of the Veil," 277-280, and "The Charming Letorieres," 280-282 (both from *The Knickerbocker*, June 1840).

Lineation: p. 150, herself ... December,; p. 200, vance ... impart;

An annual volume, apparently first issued in parts.

MH.

THE | AMERICAN READER: | CONTAINING SELECTIONS IN | PROSE, POETRY AND DIALOGUE. | DESIGNED | FOR THE USE OF ADVANCED CLASSES | IN | PUBLIC SCHOOLS, HIGH SCHOOLS AND ACADEMIES. | [rule] | BY P. H. SNOW. | [rule] | HARTFORD: | SPALDING AND STORRS. | BOSTON: GOULD, KENDALL AND LINCOLN. | NEW-YORK: | F. J. HUNTINGTON AND CO. | 1840.

(18.6 x 11.6): [i]-x, [11]-324. Signed in 6's.

"The Wife," 30-37 (from *Sketch Book*); "The Rocky Mountains," 79-82 (from *Capt. Bonneville*); "Reflections in Westminster Abbey," 103-106 (from

"Westminster Abbey," *Sketch Book*); "Park Scenery," 164-165, and "Rural Life," 165-166 (both from "Rural Life," *Sketch Book*).

Printer: L. Skinner, Hartford.

Lineation: p. 80, early ... are ; p. 165, bosom, ... harmony.

Full calf.

TxU.

[*Contes, morceaux et anecdotes tiré de W. Irving, Gally Knight, W. Scott, etc., suivies de quelques poésies.* Paris: Derache, 1840.]

vi, 88 pp. In 8's.

"Rip Van Winkle" and "The Spectre Bridegroom" (from *Sketch Book*).

Not seen. Copy reported in Bibliothèque Nationale.

THE | GEMS [in elaborate lettering designed to resemble gems and settings] | OF | AMERICAN POETRY, | BY | DISTINGUISHED AUTHORS. | [rule] | NEW YORK: | A. & C. B. EDWARDS. | [rule] | 1840.

(21.8 x 13.7): [?]-[vii]-x, [1]-253 [254]. (In copy examined, some preliminary leaves missing). Illustrations not reckoned. Signed in 4's.

"The Falls of the Passaic," 105-106 (from *The Atlantic Souvenir* for 1827).

Lineation: p. 105, How ... clear.; p. 200, To ... [in footnote] Europe.

Fine-crisscrossed H-like red cloth. On sides, triple-ruled border in blind, with gilt decoration at center. Spine titled and dated in gilt. AEG.

ViU.

NEW SERIES. | [rule] | LEGENDS OF TERROR, [shaded letters] | AND | TALES | OF THE | WONDERFUL AND THE WILD. | BEING A COMPLETE COLLECTION OF | LEGENDARY TALES, | National Romances, & Traditional Relics, [fancy] | OF EVERY COUNTRY, | AND OF THE MOST INTENSE INTEREST. | ... | [cut of death's head with snake and sceptre] | [double rule] | ORIGINAL AND SELECT. | [rule] | WITH ELEGANT ENGRAVINGS. | [rule] | London; [fancy] | Printed by T. Richardson, 98, High Holborn; | PUBLISHED by G. CREED, 71, CHANCERY LANE, HOLBORN, | And Sold by all Booksellers. Border of single frame line with floral corners.

No date. [1840?]

(23.0 x 14.3): [1]-479 [480]. Text in double columns. Signed in 8's.

"The Black Woodman; or, The Devil and Tom Walker," 97-104 (from *Tales of a Traveller*).

Lineation: p. 100 (first column), if ... as ; p. 300 (first column), space ... pre-

Brown V cloth. Sides blank. Paper label on spine.

ViU.

THE | POETS OF AMERICA: | ILLUSTRATED | BY ONE OF HER PAINTERS. | ... | EDITED BY JOHN KEESE. | NEW YORK: | PUBLISHED BY S. COLMAN, | VIII ASTOR HOUSE. | 1840.

(18.4 x 11.6): [1]-284. Preliminary engraved title not reckoned.

"The Falls of the Passaic," [194]-195 (from *The Atlantic Souvenir* for 1827).

Lineation: p. 100, That ... bright ; p. 195, With ... foam.

This popular anthology appeared in a bewildering variety of states. Further study is required to identify all the states and to establish a defensible sequence, but a general sequential outline can be offered tentatively:

First edition. No printer's imprint on copyright page. Imprint of H. Ludwig, 72, Vesey-st., N. Y. on verso of engraved title. Gatherings unsigned. On p. 15 of the table of contents, the third item is "Extract from Geraldine"; the tenth item is "The Bugle"; the fourteenth item is "The Parting -- A Picture." Pp. [207]-208 contain "The Bugle."

Second edition. The imprint of Alex. S. Gould, 144 Nassau-St., N. Y. on copyright page. Signed in letters. P. 15 of the table of contents is the same as in the first edition. Pp. [207]-208 contain "To Time."

Third and later editions. The imprint of Alex. S. Gould on copyright page. Signed in letters. [At least four different sequences of signatures known.] On p. 15, the third item is "Song of the Waves and the Air"; the tenth item is "To Time"; the fourteenth item is "The Bugle." Pp. [207]-208, as in the second edition, contain "To Time"; "The Bugle" appears on pp. [215]-216, on a cancel leaf in some copies, an integral leaf in others.

To illustrate a few of the many complexities of the volume, the varieties observed or reported in two of the engraved leaves follow. The order is arbitrary.

Pages [48]-[49]:

    a. Both pages in black.

b. Both pages in sepia.

c. Both pages in blue.

d. Decorations and author in sepia, text in black, both pages.

e. Decorations and author in blue, text in black, both pages.

Other combinations may well exist.

Pages 222-223;

a. Decorations in blue.

b. Decorations in sepia.

c. Decorations on p. 222 in sepia, on p. 223 in blue.

d. Decorations on p. 222 in blue, on p. 223 in sepia.

e. P. 222 all in black, p. 223 all in sepia.

Other combinations may well exist.

Similar examples of variant engraved leaves appear on p. 18, pp. [90]-[91], p. [269], and in the vignette title page.

Bindings appear in at least four designs. The order is arbitrary.

a. Black or brown-black calf or green morocco. Sides decorated in blind and gilt, with a gilt flowered ornament at the center that includes a lyre. Spine in gilt, decorated with an American shield and a female figure. AEG.

b. Brown-black leather. Sides decorated in blind and gilt, with a gilt pitcher within a scroll at center. Spine in gilt, decorated with a gilt pitcher. AEG.

c. Brown leather. Sides decorated in blind and gilt, forming a box of gilt lines with filigrees at the corners. The date MDCCCXL appears on the spine. AEG.

d. Tan paper boards with an elaborated semi-geometrical design on sides in multi-colors. Edges plain.

MH (2), TxU (3), private hands.

[London edition]. LONDON: | CHARLES TILT, FLEET STREET. | MDCCCXL.

Made up of sheets of the American first edition, with substituted title and added ADVERTISMENT (sic) TO THE ENGLISH EDITION, dated Fleet Street, November, 1839.

Pp. [48]-[49], State a. Pp. 222-223, State b.

Dark green H-like cloth formed of tiny diamond shapes. Sides decorated in blind. Spine titled in gilt: THE | POETS | OF | AMERICA. | ILLUSTRATED | BY ONE OF | HER PAINTERS No publisher given. Yellow endpapers.

Private hands.

1841

AMERICAN MELODIES: | CONTAINING | A SINGLE SELECTION | FROM THE PRODUCTIONS OF | TWO HUNDRED WRITERS. | COMPILED BY GEORGE P. MORRIS. | WITH ILLUSTRATIONS DESIGNED AND ENGRAVED | BY L. P. CLOVER, JR | NEW-YORK: | PUBLISHED BY LINEN AND FENNELL, | NO. 229 BROADWAY. | 1841.

(14.4 x 9.0): [i]-[ii], [1]-286. Not reckoned: preliminary engraving and engraved title, and two engravings in the text. Signed in 6's.

"The Falls of the Passaic," 48-49 (from *The Atlantic Souvenir* for 1827).

Printer: Stereotyped by Richard C. Valentine, 45 Gold-street.

Lineation: p. 49, He ... death!; p. 100, All ... save?

Noted in four leather bindings: [A]. Red leather, brown calf, black morocco. On sides, in gilt, three muses before a classical temple, with wreath around and American eagle above; decorative border in blind. Spine decorated and titled in gilt. AEG. Yellow endpapers. [B]. Black hard-finished leather. On sides, in blind, flower at center that sends out star-like rays, with oval border around; rectangular border around all. Spine titled in gilt. Signed on front, GASKILL PHILA.; on back, ACM. The leaves in this state are smaller: 13.9 x 8.9.

Another impression noted, published in Philadelphia by Henry F. Anners, [n.d.]. Another reported under a different title, *The Gift Book of American Melodies*, published by Anners, 1854.

CtY, MH, NN, TxU.

EVERY BODY'S BOOK: | OR | SOMETHING FOR ALL. | ... | FIRST
SERIES. | NEW-YORK: | WILEY AND PUTNAM, | 161 BROADWAY.
| [rule] | 1841.

(15.3 x 9.6): [i]-xi [xii], [13]-216. Signed in 6's.

"Birds of Spring," [13]-24 (from *The Knickerbocker*, May 1839, and *The
Family Visitor*, ed. John Hayward, Boston, 1840).

Printer: William Osborn, 88 William-street, N. Y.

Lineation: p.. 20, topmost ... up, p. 200, the ... days.

Brown wide-ribbed T cloth. Sides decorated in branch and leaf design in
blind. Spine titled in gilt with gilt arabesque above and below. Manila
endpapers.

ViU.

THE | POETRY AND HISTORY | OF | WYOMING: | CONTAINING |
CAMPBELL'S GERTRUDE, | WITH | A BIOGRAPHICAL SKETCH
OF THE AUTHOR, | BY WASHINGTON IRVING, | AND THE |
HISTORY OF WYOMING, | FROM ITS DISCOVERY TO THE
BEGINNING OF THE PRESENT CENTURY, | BY WILLIAM L.
STONE. | [rule] | NEW-YORK & LONDON: | WILEY AND PUTNAM.
| 1841.

(18.6 x 11.5): [i]-xxiv, [1]-324. Signed in 6's.

"A Biographical Sketch of Thomas Campbell," [ix]-xxiv (from the 1815 text,
with minor revisions, of *The Poetical Works of Thomas Campbell*).

Printer: Hopkins & Jennings, 111 Fulton-street.

Lineation: p. xx, skilful ... etiquette ; p. 100, of ... faith.

The "Second Edition, Enlarged," published in New York by Mark H.
Newman, 1844, also contains the Biographical Sketch.

First edition: NN. Second edition: TxU.

A SYSTEM | OF | ELOCUTION, | WITH | SPECIAL REFERENCE |
TO | GESTURE, | TO THE TREATMENT OF | STAMMERING, |
AND | DEFECTIVE ARTICULATION, | . . . | BY ANDREW
COMSTOCK, M.D., | . . . | PHILADELPHIA: | PUBLISHED BY THE
AUTHOR. | VOCAL GYMNASIUM, FOURTH STREET ABOVE
CHESTNUT -- | DWELLING HOUSE, No. 100 MULBERRY STREET. |
1841.

(18.0 x 10.1): [i]-x, 11-364. Bound at end: Appendix, [i]-iii; Questions, [iv]; advertisement for Vocal Gymnasium, with recommendations, [5]-32. Portrait of Comstock before title not reckoned. Signed in 6's.

"Reception of Columbus on His Return to Spain," 349-353 (from *Columbus*).

Printer: Stereotyped by J. Fagan; printed by J. Kay, Jun. and Brother.

Lineation: p. 100, for ... commenced.; p. 350, as ... [in footnote] woman.

A later impression noted, published in Philadelphia by Butler & Williams, 1844.

DLC.

1842

SANDER'S SERIES. | [rule] | THE | SCHOOL READER. | [rule] | FOURTH BOOK. | [rule] | CONTAINING | INSTRUCTIONS IN THE ELEMENTARY PRINCIPLES OF READING, | AND SELECTED LESSONS FROM THE MOST | ELEGANT WRITERS. | FOR THE USE OF ACADEMIES AND THE HIGHER CLASSES | IN COMMON AND SELECT SCHOOLS. | [wavy rule] | BY | CHARLES W. SANDERS, | ... | NEW YORK: | MARK H. NEWMAN & Co., 199 BROADWAY. | ROCHESTER: | SAGE & BROTHER.

Copyright 1842. This is probably a later impression.

(17.5 x 11.3): [i]-x, [11]-304. Pp. [i]-[ii], advertisements. Signed in 6's.

"Scenery of Snake River," 158-160, and "The Free Trapper's Indian Bride," 186-187 (both from *Capt. Bonneville); "Moslem Rule in Spain," 271-273 (from Alhambra).*

Printer: Stereotyped by T. B. Smith, 216 William-Street, N.Y.; J. D. Bedford Printer, 138 Fulton st., N. Y.

Lineation: p. 160, service ... shall; p. 272, 5. Laying ... of

Full calf.

Another impression noted:

New York: Mark H. Newman & Co.; Cincinnati: William H. Moore & Co.; Auburn: J. C. Ivison & Co.

A new edition published in New York by Ivison & Phinney, 1856, contains different selections: "Prairie Dogs," 47-48 (from *Tour on the Prairies*); "The Bobolink," 93-96 (from "The Birds of Spring," *Wolfert's Roost*).

TxU.

1843

AN | ESSAY | ON | ELOCUTION: | WITH | ELUCIDATORY PASSAGES FROM VARIOUS AUTHORS | TO WHICH ARE ADDED | REMARKS | ON | READING PROSE AND VERSE, | WITH | SUGGESTIONS TO INSTRUCTORS OF THE ART. | [wavy rule] | BY JOHN HANBURY DWYER, | ... | SIXTH EDITION, WITH ADDITIONS. | ALBANY: | WEARE C. LITTLE. | [wavy rule] | 1846.

Copyright 1843.

First edition, Cincinnati: Printed by Morgan and Lodge, 1824. 300 pp. Copies reported in OC, NcD.

(18.2 x 11.2): [I]-VI, [7]-300. Signed in 6's.

"The Widow and Her Son," 191-198 (from *Sketch Book*).

Printer: C. Van Benthuysen & Co.

Lineation: p. 100, his ... final ; p. 195, The ... and

Dark brown horizontally-ribbed T cloth. Sides decorated in blind. Spine titled in gilt. Buff endpapers.

Subsequent impressions reprinted in Albany by Little: 1847, 1849, 1850, 1855, 1856, 1857, 1860.

TxU.

THE | FAMILY CHRISTIAN ALMANAC | FOR THE UNITED STATES, | Calculated for the Horizons and Meridians of | BOSTON, NEW-YORK, BALTIMORE, AND CHARLESTON; | ADAPTED TO FOUR PARALLELS OF LATITUDE, | And for use in every part of the Country; | *For the Year of our Lord and Saviour Jesus Christ* | 1843: | ... | ASTRONOMICAL CALCULATIONS, IN EQUAL OR CLOCK TIME, | BY DAVID YOUNG, HANOVER, NEW JERSEY. | ... | Published by the American Tract Society; and sold, wholesale and retail, at 150 Nassau-street, | New-York; and by [17 named agents].

(18.6 x 11.5): [1]-[17] 18-35 [36]. The contents continue onto the recto of the back wrapper. Unsigned.

"The Bride," 25 (from "The Wedding," *Bracebridge Hall*).

Printer: [on front wrapper only] D. Fanshaw.

Lineation: p. 25, *The* ... too."

Blue paper wrapper. On front, title with cut of harvesting scene. Advertisements on verso of front and on back.

MH.

1844

THE | AMERICAN | COMMON-SCHOOL READER | AND | SPEAKER: | BEING A | SELECTION OF PIECES IN PROSE AND VERSE, | WITH | RULES FOR READING AND SPEAKING. | BY | JOHN GOLDSBURY, A.M., | ... | AND WILLIAM RUSSELL, | ... | BOSTON: | PUBLISHED BY CHARLES TAPPAN, | 114 WASHINGTON STREET. | 1844.

(18.7 x 11.3): [i]-xii, [13]-428. Not reckoned: twelve pages of "Recommendations" at beginning, and four pages of advertisements at end. Signed in 6's.

"Wouter Van Twiller," 149-151; "William Kieft," 159-161 [listed as p. 160 in the Table of Contents]; "Peter Stuyvesant," 169-171 (all from *History of New York*); "The Thunder Storm," 342-343 (from "Dolph Heyliger," *Bracebridge Hall*).

Printer: Stereotyped by George A. Curtis, New England Type and Stereotype Foundry.

Lineation: p. 150, little, ... mag-; p. 300, But ... depths,

Full calf.

TxU.

THE | CHRISTIAN | FAMILY ANNUAL, | 1844. [All but THE in hollow letters] | EDITED BY | REV. DANIEL NEWELL. | 132 Nassau-street. All surrounded by urn-shaped border, symbolic birds at sides, Bible and stylized dove at top, NEW-YORK at base, signed Lossing.

(22.0 x 13.5): [i]-[vi] (p. v mispaged vi), [5]-302. Not reckoned: preliminary engraving and illustrated poem. Signed irregularly.

"The Broken Heart," 117-120 (from *Sketch Book*).

Lineation: p. 119, some ... waste ; p. 200, flower, ... child

Noted in red leather. Sides and spine decorated in gilt. AEG. Endpapers buff-yellow. Probably issued in a number of different bindings.

A periodical bound as an annual.

TxU.

THE | COMMON SCHOOL SPEAKER; | A | NEW COLLECTION | OF | ORIGINAL AND SELECTED PIECES, | FOR | READING AND RECITATION. | [rule] | BY WILLIAM B. FOWLE, | ... | [rule] | PUBLISHED BY | S. BABCOCK, -- NEW HAVEN; AND | FOWLE & CAPEN, -- BOSTON. | [rule] | 1844.

(16.0 x 10.0): [i]-xi [xii], [13]-288. Signed in 6's.

"The Tea Party," 187-188 (from "Tea, a Poem," *Salmagundi* #XIX). The poem is attributed to Irving.

Lineation: p. 188, Did ... and ; p. 200, Then ... bright,

Brown cloth with embossed interlocked "squiggles." Sides blank. Spine missing on copy examined.

TxU.

... | COBB'S | NEW NORTH AMERICAN READER; | OR, | FIFTH READING BOOK; | CONTAINING A GREAT VARIETY OF | INTERESTING, HISTORICAL, MORAL, AND INSTRUCTIVE | READING LESSONS | IN PROSE AND POETRY, | FROM HIGHLY ESTEEMED | AMERICAN AND ENGLISH WRITERS; | . . . | DESIGNED FOR THE USE OF THE HIGHEST CLASSES IN SCHOOLS AND ACADEMIES; | And to impress the minds of youth with sentiments of Virtue and Religion. | ... | BY LYMAN COBB, A.M., | ... | NEW YORK: | CALEB BARTLETT, 225 PEARL-STREET. | [rule] | 1844.

(18.6 x 11.2): [i]-xviii, [19]-384. Not reckoned: preliminary woodblock illustration. Signed in 6's.

"The Wife," 110-111 (from *Sketch Book*); "Death of King Philip," 352-354 (from "Philip of Pokanoket," *Sketch Book*).

Printer: Stereotyped by T.B. Smith, 216 William-Street, N.Y.

Lineation: p. 111, than ... decayed.; p. 353, treachery ... his

DLC.

[Facing title pages, in English and in German]:

Selections | from | British Authors | in Prose and Poetry. | A Class-Book for the use | of Schools | by | Edward A. Moriarty | Lecturer on English Language and Literature | at the Commercial College of Berlin. | [elaborated short swelled rule] | Leipsic | Bernh. Tauchnitz jun. | 1844.

Chrestomathie | aus | Englischen Autoren | in Prosa und Poesie. | Zum | Schul- und Privatgebrauche | von | Edward A. Moriarty | Lector der Englischen Sprache und Literatur an der | öffentlichen Handelslehranstalt zu Berlin. | [elaborated short swelled rule] | Leipzig | Bernh. Tauchnitz jun. | 1844.

(15.2 x 10.8): [I]-X, [1]-414. Signed in 8's.

"The Spectre Bridegroom, a Traveller's Tale," 142-157 (from *Sketch Book*).

Except for the "Preface" or "Vorrede," [V]-VI, in parallel columns of English and German, the volume is in English.

Printer: Bernh. Tauchnitz jun.

Purple T-like cloth. Sides decorated in blind. Spine decorated in gilt, titled simply "Selections". All edges marbled. White endpapers.

Private hands.

EL [hollow letters] | MUSEO [elaborated, shaded letters] | MEXICANO, | Ó | MISCELANEA PINTORESCA DE AMENIDADES CURIOSAS | E INSTRUCTIVAS. [hollow letters] | [rule] | Miscuit utile dulci. -- *Horat.* | [rule] | TOMO CUARTO. | MEXICO. | [rule] | | LO IMPRIME Y PUBLICA IGNACIO CUMPLIDO, | Calle de los Rebeldes casa número 2. | [rule] | 1844.

(26.5 x 17.0): [1]-570 [571]-[572]. In double columns. Signed in 8's.

"Costumbres Inglesas: La Noche Buena," 522-523 (translation of "Christmas Eve" from *Sketch Book*).

Lineation: p. 522 (first column), anlogas ... paz,

TxU.

1845

THE | DISTRICT SCHOOL READER; | OR, | EXERCISES | IN | READING AND SPEAKING; | DESIGNED | FOR THE HIGHEST CLASS | IN | PUBLIC AND PRIVATE SCHOOLS. | [rule] | BY

WILLIAM D. SWAN, | ... | BOSTON: | CHARLES C. LITTLE AND JAMES BROWN. | [rule] | 1845.

(18.0 x 11.0 rebound): [1]-468. Signed in 6's.

"Voyage to Europe," 58-65 (from "The Voyage," *Sketch Book*); "Life on the Prairies," 131-135, and "A Bee Hunt," 184-187 (both from *Tour on the Prairies*); "Shakespeare's Tomb," 322-325 (from "Stratford-On-Avon," *Sketch Book*); "The Broken Heart," 442-445 (from *Sketch Book*).

Printer: Stereotyped at the Boston Type and Stereotype Foundery.

Lineation: p. 60, tell, ... communion;; p. 200, But ... knee

Later impressions noted: 1846, by same publishers; 1848, 1849, 1851, in Philadelphia by Thomas, Cowperthwait (the last called "Improved Edition").

NN.

ELOCUTION MADE EASY: | CONTAINING | Rules and Selections for Declamation and Reading, [fancy] | ... | BY R. CLAGGETT, A. M. | ... | NEW YORK: | PAINE & BURGESS, No. 62 JOHN STREET. | [rule] | 1845.

(17.8 x 11.5): [1]-144. Signed in 6's.

"Midnight Musings," 101-103 (from "St. Mark's Eve," *Bracebridge Hall*); "The Broken Heart," 114-116 (from *Sketch Book*).

Lineation: p. 50, was ... soldiers.; p. 115, had ... giddy

Green paper boards with leather shelfback. On front, title. On back, advertisements.

A later impression noted, called "Stereotype Edition," published in New York by Cady & Burgess, 1848.

TxU.

INTRODUCTION | TO THE | AMERICAN | COMMON-SCHOOL READER | AND SPEAKER; | COMPRISING | SELECTIONS IN PROSE AND VERSE: | ... | BY | WILLIAM RUSSELL AND JOHN GOLDSBURY, | AUTHORS OF THE ABOVE-MENTIONED READER. | [rule] | BOSTON: | PUBLISHED BY CHARLES TAPPAN, | 114 WASHINGTON STREET. | 1845.

(18.7 x 11.2): [1]-6 [7], viii, [9]-288. Signed in 6's.

"Obstinacy," 202-204, and "Reception of a Governor," 217-218 (both from *History of New York*).

Printer: Stereotyped by Dickinson & Co., Boston.

Lineation: p. 100, The ... ago!; p. 218, occasions; ... *effect*.

Brown boards with black leather shelfback.   On front, title.   On back, advertisements. On spine, gilt ornamentation but no title.

Two later impressions noted: 1846, marked "Seventeenth Thousand" and "Nineteenth Thousand."

DLC.

INTRODUCTION | TO THE | YOUNG LADIES' | ELOCUTIONARY READER: | CONTAINING | A SELECTION OF READING LESSONS: | TOGETHER WITH | THE RUDIMENTS OF ELOCUTION, | ADAPTED TO FEMALE READERS. | BY | WILLIAM AND ANNA U. RUSSELL, | . . . | BOSTON: | JAMES MUNROE AND COMPANY. | [rule] | 1845.

(18.5 x 11.4): [1]-252. Four pages of advertisements bound at end; this work listed as "Now Ready." Signed in 6's.

"Margaret Davidson," 98-99.

Printer: Stereotyped at the Boston Type and Stereotype Foundry.

Lineation: p. 98, And ... en-; p. 200, just; ... with

TxU.

THE | LITERARY EMPORIUM; | A | COMPENDIUM | OF | Religious, Literary, and Philosophical Knowledge. [fancy] | VOL. I & II. 1845 | ... | NEW YORK: [hollow type] | PUBLISHED BY J. K. WELLMAN, | No. 118 NASSAU STREET. | [zig-zag rule] | This book is published monthly, at $1 a year--6 months to a volume, | each volume complete in itself.

(21.9 x 14.1): [i]-[iv], [1]-378. Numerous illustrations not reckoned. Signed in 8's.

"Sorrow for the Dead," 28-29 (from "Rural Funerals," *Sketch Book*).

Printer: S. W. Benedict & Co., Stereotypers and Printers, No. 116 Spruce Street, N. Y.

Lineation: p. 29, fond ... of ; p. 200, Clos'd ... blood!

Dark green T cloth. Sides decorated in gilt. Spine decorated and titled in gilt. AEG. Light yellow endpapers with orange flower pattern.

Another, presumably later, state noted: on the title, the statement of monthly publication is omitted and the date 1846 is added after the publisher's address.

First state, Private hands. Second state, TxU.

ORTHOPHONY: | OR | VOCAL CULTURE IN ELOCUTION; | A MANUAL OF ELEMENTARY EXERCISES, | ... | BY JAMES E. MURDOCH, | ... | AND | WILLIAM RUSSELL, | ... | BOSTON: | WILLIAM D. TICKNOR AND CO. | [rule] | MDCCCXLV.

(19.2 x 12.1): [1]-336. Four leaves of illustrations not reckoned. Publisher's catalogue bound at end, paged 1-8, dated January 1, 1846. Signed in 6's.

"A Sea Voyage," 317-318 (from "The Voyage," *Sketch Book*).

Printer: Freeman and Bolles, Washington Street, Boston.

Lineation: p. 100, the ... [in footnote] Greeks.; p. 317, emotion, ... portions

Dark brown T cloth. Sides blank. Spine missing in copy examined. Manilla endpapers.

Two impressions of a later edition noted: one by the same publisher, 1848, "Improved Edition"; one published in Boston by Ticknor, Reed, and Fields, 1852, "Seventh Edition."

PU.

THE | PROSE AND POETRY | OF | EUROPE AND AMERICA: | CONSISTING OF | LITERARY GEMS AND CURIOSITIES, | AND CONTAINING | THE CHOICE AND BEAUTIFUL PRODUCTIONS | OF MANY OF | THE MOST POPULAR WRITERS OF THE PAST AND PRESENT AGE: | ... | COMPILED | BY G. P. MORRIS AND N. P. WILLIS. | ... | NEW YORK: | PUBLISHED BY LEAVITT & ALLEN, | No. 379 BROADWAY.

Copyright 1845.

(24.7 x 15.7): [1]-600. In double columns. Signed in 8's.

"The Wife," 47-48 (from *Sketch Book*).

Lineation: p. 48 (column 1), had ... herself;; p. 200 (column 1), THE ... Dazzles

The last impression noted is called "Fifth Edition," published in New York by Leavitt, Trow and Co., 191 Broadway, 1847.

NN.

SCENES AND INCIDENTS | OF | DOMESTIC | AND | FOREIGN TRAVEL. | WITH | Sketches in Natural History, [fancy] | AND | POETICAL SELECTIONS. | [elaborated swelled rule] | PHILADELPHIA: | THOMAS WARDLE, CHESNUT STREET.

1845?

(15.2 x 9.6): [i]-viii, [9]-338. (First pp. missing in copy examined.) Preliminary illustration and two illustrations in text not reckoned. Signed in 8's.

"Life of Christopher Columbus," [9]-29 (from the abridged version of *Columbus*); "Scenes in the Prairie," 300-313 (from *Tour on the Prairies*; ascribed here to *Tour in the Prairies*).

Printer: King and Baird, 9 George Street.

Lineation: p. 100, Child ... persons.; p. 300, SCENES ... we

DLC.

1846

THE | CHRISTIAN | FAMILY ANNUAL. | VOL. 3. [all but THE in hollow letters] | EDITED AND PUBLISHED BY | REV. DANIEL NEWELL. | NEW YORK: | No. 126 Nassau-street. All within urn-shaped border, with symbolic birds at sides, Bible and stylized dove at top, NEW-YORK at base, signed Lossing.

Not dated. 1846?

(22.0 x 13.5): [1]-432. Unsigned.

"The Feathered Songsters," 396-399 (from "The Birds of Spring," *The Family Visitor*, 1840).

Lineation: p. 200, joys ... vo-; p. 398, pronounced, ... song

A periodical bound as an annual.

TxU.

A | COURSE OF READING | FOR | COMMON SCHOOLS | AND THE | LOWER CLASSES OF ACADEMIES, | ... | BY H. MANDEVILLE, | ... | NEW YORK: | D. APPLETON & CO., 200 BROADWAY. | PHILADELPHIA: | G. S. APPLETON, 148 CHESNUT STREET. | MDCCCXLVI.

(19.1 x 11.6): [1]-377 [378]. Two sets of advertisements bound at end: 6 pp. and 12 pp. Signed in 6's.

"Sorrow for the Dead," 255-257 (from "Rural Funerals," *Sketch Book*); "The Fortitude of Women Under Reverses of Fortune," 319 (from "The Wife," *Sketch Book*).

Lineation: p. 100, That ... burden ; p. 256, 7 voice ... afflic-

Several later impressions noted. One of 1849 is called "Seventh Edition"; one of 1851 is called "New Edition, Revised and Corrected."

DLC.

... | THE | FOURTH | SCHOOL READER. | [rule] | BY S. G. GOODRICH, | ... | PUBLISHED BY | MORTON AND GRISWOLD, | LOUISVILLE, KY. | [rule]. All within wavy frame lines.

Copyright 1846.

(18.9 x 11.0): [1]-240. Wavy frame line around all pages. Signed in 6's.

"The Grisly Bear," 186-188 (from *Tour on the Prairies*); "The Discovery," 216-217, and "Character of Columbus," 219-220 (both from *Columbus*).

Lineation: p. 187, good ... it ; p. 220, from ... 236.

Bright brown paper boards with black leather shelfback. On front, the title elaborately framed. On back, advertisements for "The Comprehensive Readers." Spine untitled.

This work should not be confused with the same author's *Fourth Reader for the Use of Schools*, 1839. The undated "Preface to the Revised Edition" here states, "This volume was originally published as the *Third Reader*."

TxU.

THE | GEM OF THE SEASON: | WITH | TWENTY PLATES BY SARTAIN. | [wavy rule] | EDITED BY | JOHN HOLMES AGNEW. | [wavy rule] | NEW-YORK: | LEAVITT, TROW & COMPANY, 194 BROADWAY. | 1846. All within double frame lines.

(24.0 x 15.8): [i]-viii, [1]-60. Not reckoned: engraved title and plates. Double frame lines around all pages. Signed in 4's.

"Columbus," 55 (from *Columbus*).

Printer: John F. Trow & Co.

Lineation: p. 20, THE ... grass.; p. 40, Landseer! ... clime;

Brown leather. On sides, elaborate gilt decoration. Spine missing in copies seen. AEG.

CtY, MH.

THE | PARLOR [hollow letters] | ANNUAL | AND | CHRISTIAN FAMILY | CASKET. [hollow letters] | EDITED BY AN ASSOCIATION OF | CLERGYMEN. | PUBLISHED BY J. E. D. COMSTOCK, | 126 NASSAU-STREET. All within floral wreath with Bible and dove at top, N-YORK within lower portion.

1846.

(20.6 x 13.1): [i]-vi, [two leaves of illustrations], [9]-428. Unsigned.

"The Widow and Her Son," 192-195 (from *Sketch Book*); "The Grave," 216-217 (from "Rural Funerals," *Sketch Book*).

Lineation: p. 194, lonely ... of ; p. 217, the ... should

A periodical bound as an annual. An advertisement on p. 428 offers to exchange bound volumes for the individual numbers "by paying 37, 50, 62, or 75 cents, according to the value of the binding." Presumably, then, the annual was issued in four publisher's bindings. Two bindings seen: [A]. Brown H cloth with black leather shelfback. Sides blank. Spine titled in gilt. [B]. Brown V cloth. On sides, gilt urn and birds at center, within elaborated blind border. Spine decorated and titled in gilt, dated 1846.

MH, TxU.

1847

REVISED EDITION. | [rule] | THE | FOURTH READER, | OR | EXERCISES | IN | READING AND SPEAKING. | DESIGNED | FOR THE HIGHER CLASSES, | IN OUR | PUBLIC AND PRIVATE SCHOOLS. | [rule] | BY SALEM TOWN, A. M. | [rule] | SANBORN & CARTER, | PORTLAND, | MAINE.

Copyright 1847. The Preface calls this a revised edition of the former *Third Reader*, with additions and improvements.

(18.2 x 11.4): [i]-viii, [9]-408. Signed in 6's.

"Return and Reception of Columbus," 79-82 (from *Columbus*); "Rural Life in England," 175-178 (from *Sketch Book*); "Home," 179-180 (from "Christmas Eve," *Sketch Book*); "The Wife," 180-184 (from *Sketch Book*); "Sorrow for the Dead," 217-219 (from "Rural Funerals," *Sketch Book*).

Lineation: p. 80, were ... houses.; p. 180, waters ... islands.

Dark gray L cloth with black leather shelfback. Sides blank. Spine decorated in blind, titled in gilt.

Four later impressions noted:

1848, 1853. Portland: Sanborn & Carter.

Undated. Buffalo: Phinney & Co.; Portland: Sanborn & Carter.

1859. Buffalo: Phinney & Co.

DLC.

HALF HOURS | WITH THE | BEST AUTHORS | FIRST [SECOND, THIRD, FOURTH] QUARTER. | [rule] | CHARLES KNIGHT, FLEET STREET. The title itself is hand-drawn. At head of page, drawing of muse within a circle.

[No date. 1847-1848?]

(22.0 x 14.0): Vol. I. [i]-[iv], [1]-312. Vol. II. [i]-[iv], [1]-312. Vol. III. [i]-[iv], [1]-312. Vol. IV. [i]-[iv], [1]-316 (313-316, Index). Each vol. has a leaf of illustration before the title, not reckoned. Signed in 12's.

"Columbus," I, 235-237 (from *Columbus*); "Rural Life in England," II, 89-93 (from *Sketch Book*); "Columbus at Barcelona," III, 131-133 (from *Columbus*).

Lineation: Vol. I. p. 236, picked ... this Vol. II. p. 90, metropolis ... hare, Vol. III. p. 132, the ... ambition, Vol. IV. p. 100, giving ... beg."

Noted in two binding states:

[A]. In 4 vols. Brown coarse AR cloth. On sides, title and drawing of muse in blind. Spine titled in gilt. Yellow endpapers.

[B]. In 2 vols., with 2 "Quarters" to the vol. Brown TZ cloth. On sides, title and drawing of muse in blind. Spine titled in gilt. Yellow endpapers.

CtY, ViU.

[American edition]. HALF-HOURS | WITH | THE BEST AUTHORS. | SELECTED AND ARRANGED, | WITH SHORT BIOGRAPHICAL AND CRITICAL NOTICES, | BY CHARLES KNIGHT. | [wavy rule] | VOL. I. [II., III., IV.] | [wavy rule] | NEW YORK: | JOHN WILEY, 161 BROADWAY. | [OF THE LATE FIRM OF "WILEY AND PUTNAM."] | [rule] | 1848. Vol. IV substitutes for line 3f: AND 13 PATERNOSTER ROW, LONDON. It is dated 1849.

First impression not seen. See the comment below on other impressions.

(18.6 x 12.5): Vol. I. [i]-iv, [1]-610. Vol. II. [i]-iv, [1]-559 [560]. Vol. III. [4pp., the last paged vi], [1]-578. Six pages of advertisements bound at end. Vol. IV. [i]-v [vi], [1]-616. Signed in 12's.

"Columbus," I, 432-435; "Rural Life in England," II, 70-76; "Columbus at Barcelona," III, 275-279.

Lineation: Vol. I. p. 100, heaven ... in- Vol. II. p. 100, with ... wil- Vol. III. p. 100, 196. ... edge. Vol. IV. p. 100, useless ... [in footnote] history.

Noted in 3 bindings: [A]. Red CM-like cloth. On sides, in blind, JOHN WILEY'S LIBRARY OF CHOICE READING in a circle around a W, elaborate border around all. Spine titled in gilt, with LIBRARY OF CHOICE READING at head. Yellow endpapers. [B]. Brown T cloth. Sides decorated in blind. Spine titled in gilt. Yellow endpapers. [C]. Bright green TB-like cloth. Sides decorated in blind. Spine titled in gilt. Yellow endpapers.

Published in a number of impressions. An earlier one is reported, published by Wiley and Putnam, New York. Later impressions noted in scattered individual volumes, published by John Wiley, New York. An impression dated 1856 seen in 4 vols., published by Wiley and Halsted, New York. One later edition with no date noted in 6 vols., published by Porter and Coates, Philadelphia.

CtY, MB.

THE HEMANS YOUNG LADIES' READER. | [rule] | THE | HEMANS READER | FOR | FEMALE SCHOOLS: | CONTAINING | EXTRACTS IN PROSE AND POETRY, | SELECTED FROM THE WRITINGS OF MORE THAN | ONE HUNDRED AND THIRTY DIFFERENT AUTHORS. | [rule] | BY T. S. PINNEO, A.M., M.D. | [rule] | ECLECTIC SERIES. | [double rule] | PUBLISHERS: | PRATT, WOODFORD & CO., NEW YORK: | W. B. SMITH & CO., CINCINNATI. | 1847.

(18.1 x 11.3): [i]-xi [xii], [13]-480. Advertisements for Eclectic Series on pp. [i]-[ii]. Signed in 8's and 4's.

"The Wife," 117-123 (from *Sketch Book*); "Tea-Parties in New York," 286-287 (from *History of New York*); "The Widow and Her Son," 439-445, and "Westminster Abbey," 467-471 (both from *Sketch Book*).

Printer: James & Co., Stereotypers, Cincinnati; Morgan & Overend, Printers.

Lineation: p. 120, of ... IRVING.; p. 440, responses ... the

Full calf with black leather label.

A later impression noted: headed ECLECTIC EDUCATIONAL SERIES, published in New York by Clark, Austin, & Smith, and in Cincinnati by W. B. Smith & Co., undated.

DLC.

THE | PROSE WRITERS | OF | AMERICA. | WITH | A SURVEY OF THE HISTORY, CONDITION, AND PROSPECTS OF | AMERICAN LITERATURE. | BY | RUFUS WILMOT GRISWOLD. | ... | PHILADELPHIA: | CAREY AND HART. | 1847. All within double frame lines.

(23.4 x 15.0): [1]-552. Preliminary engraving of Irving (from painting by G. S. Newton), engraved title, and 7 other engraved portraits throughout the volume not reckoned. Text in double columns. Double frame lines around all pages. Signed in 6's.

"The Vision of Oloffe van Kortlandt," 206, "The Fatness of Aldermen," 206, "The Dismissal of General von Poffenburgh," 206, "Primitive Habits in New Amsterdam," 207, "Ladies of the Golden Age," 207-208, "Last Days of Peter Stuyvesant," 208-209, and "The Uses of History," 209-210 (all from *History of New York*); "Rip Van Winkle," 210-215, and "The Wife," 215-218 (both from *Sketch Book*); "The Love of a Mother," 218, and "Broken Hearts," 218-219 (both from "The Broken Heart," *Sketch Book*); "Historical Criticism," 219, and "Columbus at Barcelona," 219-220 (both from *Columbus*); "A Letter from Mustapha Rub-A-Dub Keli Khan, to Asem Hacchem," 220-222 (from *Salmagundi*).

Printer: Stereotyped by L. Johnson & Co.; T. K. & P. G. Collins, printers.

Lineation: p. 208, had ... turned ; p. 300, numbers ... arrows."

Maroon morocco. Sides decorated in gilt and blind; spine in gilt. AEG.

The anthology appeared in at least three subsequent "editions," with a new preface, but the body of the text is reprinted from the original plates. The last noted: Philadelphia: Parry & McMillan, Successors to A. Hart, Late Carey & Hart, 1855.

TxU.

THE | SCENERY [hollow letters] | OF THE | CATSKILL MOUNTAINS | AS DESCRIBED BY | IRVING, COOPER, BRYANT, | WILLIS GAYLORD CLARK, N. P. WILLIS, | MISS MARTINEAU, | TYRONE POWER, | PARK BENJAMIN, THOMAS COLE, | AND OTHER EMINENT WRITERS. | [stylized swelled rule] | NEW-YORK: | PUBLISHED BY D. FANSHAW, 575 BROADWAY, | Printing-office, 35 Ann, corner of Nassau-st. All within elaborate, decorative frame. Below frame at foot: PRICE 12 1/2 CENTS. The title appears as a cover-title on the wrapper only.

1847?

(22.9 x 14.6): [1]-39 [40]. In double columns. Not signed.

"Rip Van Winkle," 4-11 (from *Sketch Book*; here attributed to "Sketch Book, Vol. 1. p. 45.").

Lineation: p. 10, and [in first column] ... The [in second column]

Tan paper wrapper. On front, cover-title. On verso of front, advertisement for Catskill Mountain House, at The Pine Orchard. Back wrapper missing this copy, but the advertisement on the verso of the front says, "See page 3 of Cover." Later impressions show there a continuation of the advertisement, with the back blank.

A later impression, within Irving's lifetime, is reported with the imprint of D. Fanshaw, Publisher, and Book and Job Printer, Corner of Ann and Nassau-streets, [n.d.]. The "Notice" on p. [1] is in 10 lines rather than in 7 lines.

NNHi.

1848

THE | FAMILY [hollow letters] | CIRCLE, | AND | PARLOR ANNUAL, [hollow letters] | 1848. [hollow numbers] | EDITED AND PUBLISHED BY | REV. D. NEWELL. | NEW-YORK: | 126 NASSAU-STREET. All within wreath of flowers and ribbons; Bible and dove at top, N-York at base. At foot of page: STEREOTYPED BY VINCENT DILL, JR., 17 ANN ST, N. Y.

(20.8 x 13.3): [i]-vi, [one leaf of illustration], [9]-425 [426]. Two preliminary leaves of illustrations not reckoned. Unsigned.

"The Graves of Those We Love," 142-144 (from "Rural Funerals," *Sketch Book*).

Lineation: p. 100, Kate ... is.; p. 200, A ... epitaph.

A periodical bound as an annual.

Probably issued in a number of bindings, of which two have been seen: Red leather and black leather. On sides, gilt urn and birds at center, with elaborated blind border around. Spine decorated and titled in gilt. AEG.

CtY, DLC, MH.

THE | MARRIAGE OFFERING: | A | COMPILATION | OF | PROSE AND POETRY. | [swelled rule] | BOSTON: | WM. CROSBY AND H. P. NICHOLS, | 111 WASHINGTON STREET. | 1848. All within single frame lines.

Preface signed A. A. L. [Abiel Abbot Livermore].

(17.3 x 11.4): [i]-viii, [1]-207 [208]. Signed in 6's.

"A Testimony," 186 (from "The Wife," *Sketch Book*).

Printer: Stereotyped and printed by Metcalf and Co., Printers to the University, Cambridge.

Lineation: p. 100, Around ... HALE.; p. 200, WOMAN. ... each,

Brown fine-wavy-grain cloth. On front, gilt lyre design with elaborate frame in blind. On back, only the frame. Spine decorated and titled in gilt. No edges gilt. Apparently also issued in another binding: a copy noted rebound but with original AEG preserved.

Later impressions noted: "Third Edition," 1849; "Eighth Edition," 1852; "Tenth Edition."

CtY, DLC.

NORTH AMERICAN | FIRST CLASS READER; | THE | FIFTH BOOK | OF | TOWER'S SERIES FOR COMMON SCHOOLS; | IN WHICH | THE HIGHER PRINCIPLES OF ELOCUTION ARE EXPLAINED | AND ILLUSTRATED BY APPROPRIATE EXERCISES; | ... | BY | DAVID B. TOWER, A. M. | AND | CORNELIUS WALKER, A. M. | ... |

NEW YORK: | CADY AND BURGESS, 60 JOHN STREET, | BOSTON: | BENJAMIN B. MUSSEY & CO. | 1848.

(18.4 x 11.3): [1]-426. Six pages of advertisements bound at end. Signed in 6's.

"The Love of Fame," 196-198 (from # XVI, *Salmagundi*); "The Broken Heart," 334-338 (from *Sketch Book*).

Printer: Stereotyped at the Boston Type and Stereotype Foundry.

Lineation: p. 197, upon ... possession.; p. 335, ruin, ... early

Full calf.

Later impressions noted, published in New York by Daniel Burgess & Co.: 1853 ("Seventh Edition"); and 1854 ("Seventh Edition"), called TOWER'S SIXTH READER | ... | NORTH AMERICAN | FIRST CLASS READER; | THE | SIXTH BOOK.

MH.

1849

[*Colección de novelas*. Traducidas por Don Rafael García Tapia. Granada, 1849.]

"La Rosa de la Alhambra."

Not seen. Copy reported by Stanley T. Williams in the Biblioteca de la Universidad de Granada.

NORTH AMERICAN | SECOND CLASS READER; | THE | FOURTH BOOK | OF | TOWER'S SERIES FOR COMMON SCHOOLS; | ... | WITH | READING LESSONS, | ... | BY | DAVID B. TOWER, A. M. | AND | CORNELIUS WALKER, A. M. | ... | NEW YORK: | CADY AND BURGESS. | BOSTON: | BENJAMIN B. MUSSEY & CO. | 1849.

(18.3 x 11.5): [1]-276. Six pages of advertisements bound at end. Signed in 6's.

"Rural Life in England," 80-85 (from *Sketch Book*); "The Dutch Money-Digger," 119-125 (from "Wolfert Webber," *Tales of a Traveller*); "Sorrow for the Dead," 128-130 (from "Rural Funerals," *Sketch Book*); "My Mother's Grave," 210-215 (from "Grave Reflections of a Disappointed Man," *Tales of a Traveller*).

Printer: Stereotyped at the Boston Type and Stereotype Foundry.

Lineation: p. 120, never ... [in footnote] 340.; p. 210, Shows ... [in footnote] 155.

Dark gray H cloth with black leather shelfback. Sides blank. Spine in gilt and decorative blind stamping.

Several later impressions noted by same publisher: 1850 ("Second Edition"), 1852 ("Eighth Edition"); in 1854 the so-called "Twelfth Edition" changes the title to TOWER'S FIFTH READER ... THE FIFTH BOOK OF TOWER'S SERIES, published by Daniel Burgess & Co.

DLC.

1850

THE | LITERARY READER, | FOR | ACADEMIES AND HIGH SCHOOLS: | CONSISTING OF | SELECTIONS, IN PROSE AND VERSE, | FROM | AMERICAN, ENGLISH AND OTHER FOREIGN LITERATURE, | ... | BY MISS A. HALL, | ... | BOSTON: | PUBLISHED BY JOHN P. JEWETT & CO., | NOS. 17&19 CORNHILL. | 1850.

(18.8 x 11.4): [I]-XII, [13]-408. Signed in 6's.

"The Fatness of Aldermen," 294, and "Primitive Habits in New Amsterdam," 295-297 (both from *History of New York*).

Printer: Stereotyped by Hobart & Robbins, New England Type and Stereotype Foundery, Boston.

Lineation: p. 100, knew ... means,; p. 296, merely ... nor

Brown AR cloth with brown leather shelfback. Sides decorated in blind. Spine titled in gilt.

MH, TxU.

THE NORMAL SERIES. | [rule] | WEBB'S | NORMAL READER. | NO. 4. | DESIGNED | TO TEACH CORRECT READING, | TO | IMPROVE AND EXPAND THE MIND, | AND TO | PURIFY AND ELEVATE THE CHARACTER. | ... | BY J. RUSSELL WEBB. | NEW YORK: | HUNTINGTON & SAVAGE, AND MASON & LAW, | 216 PEARL-STREET. | CINCINNATI: -- H. W. DERBY & COMPANY. | AND FOR SALE BY BOOKSELLERS GENERALLY. | 1850. All within double frame lines.

(18.6 x 11.5): [1]-312. Double frame lines around all pages. Signed in 6's.

"The Wife," 292-297 (from *Sketch Book*).

Lineation: p. 100, 4. We ... genius.; p. 295, but ... the

Gray-black horizontal T cloth with black leather shelfback. Sides blank. Spine in blind and gilt.

DLC.

THE PRESENT, | OR A | GIFT FOR THE TIMES. | [rule] | EDITED BY F. A. MOORE. | ... | MANCHESTER, N. H. | ROBERT MOORE. | 1850.

(13.7 x 8.5): [i]-viii, [9]-192. Not reckoned: lithographed half-title and title. Signed in 8's.

"Woman and Marriage," 127-131 (not identified)

Printer: C. C. P. Moody, 52 Washington Street, Boston.

Lineation: p. 100, nothingness! ... BULWER.; p. 130, with ... then

Red AR cloth. On sides, in gilt, winged cherub holding flowers and ornament, within ornate border, all surrounded by triple frame lines. Spine decorated and titled in gilt. AEG. Yellow endpapers.

TxU.

[*The Student's Pastime*, Being a Selection of the Most Esteemed Works of Miss Edgeworth, W. Irving, Miss Mitford, T. Moore, to Which Are Added Numerous Anecdotes and Other Amusing Pieces, by Sidney Dawson. Paris: A. Derache, 1850.]

104 pp. Signed in 8's.

"Murad the Unlucky." (Not identified).

Not seen. Copy reported in Bibliothèque Nationale.

1851

AMERICAN MISCELLANY. | CONSISTING OF | CHOICE SELECTIONS | FROM THE WRITINGS OF | [List of 20 authors in 4 columns, beginning HEADLEY, COOPER, IRVING, ending with BRAINARD] | AND OTHER ENGLISH AUTHORS. | [elaborated swelled rule] | BATH, N. Y. | R. L. UNDERHILL & Co. | 1851.

(18.7 x 10.7): [1]-264. Signed in 12's.

"A Hunt for a lost Comrade," 18-21 (from ch. 31 of *Tour on the Prairies*); "The Widow and her Son," 82-88 (from *Sketch Book*); "The Incidents of a Voyage Across the Atlantic," 139-143 (from "The Voyage," *Sketch Book*); "Description of a Thunder Storm on the Highlands of the Hudson," 143-144 (from "Dolph Heyliger," *Bracebridge Hall*).

Lineation: p. 140, on ... into ; p. 200, Tell ... create,

Brown V Cloth. Sides decorated in blind. Spine titled in gilt.

CtY.

THE | CHRISTIAN DIADEM, | AND | FAMILY KEEPSAKE | A REPOSITORY OF | RELIGIOUS AND LITERARY GEMS. | [wavy rule] | EDITED BY | Z. PATEN HATCH. | [wavy rule] | VOLUME I. | NEW-YORK: | Z. P. HATCH, 128 NASSAU-STREET. | 1851.

(22.7 x 14.3): [i]-iv, [5]-308. Twelve illustrations not reckoned. Unsigned.

"The Graves of Those We Love," 249-250 (from "Rural Funerals," *Sketch Book*).

Lineation: p. 100, of ... word?; p. 250, From ... living.

Purple V cloth. Sides and spine elaborately decorated in gilt. AEG. Manila endpapers.

CtY.

THE | FIRST BOOK OF ORATORY: | A NEW COLLECTION OF EXTRACTS IN | PROSE, POETRY, AND DIALOGUE, | FROM DISTINGUISHED AMERICAN AND ENGLISH ORATORS, | DIVINES, AND POETS; | INCLUDING | SPECIMENS OF THE ELOQUENCE OF STATESMEN OF THE | PRESENT DAY. | FOR THE USE OF SCHOOLS | BY EDWARD C. MARSHALL, M. A. | ... | NEW YORK: | D. APPLETON & COMPANY, 200 BROADWAY. | MDCCCLI.

(18.8 x 11.7): [1]-237. The first four counted pages are made up of a publisher's catalogue; p. [1] is paged 8. Signed in 12's.

"Sorrow for the Dead," 27-29 (from "Rural Funerals," *Sketch Book*).

Lineation: p. 28, feels ... contrition!; p. 100, or ... all

Dark gray T cloth with black leather shelfback titled in gilt. Endpapers buff-yellow.

TxU.

THE | (OLD) | FARMER'S ALMANACK, | ... | FOR THE YEAR OF OUR LORD | 1852; | ... | NEW, USEFUL, AND ENTERTAINING MATTER. | ... | BY ROBERT B. THOMAS. | ... | BOSTON: | PUBLISHED BY JENKS, HICKLING & SWAN. | Sold by the Booksellers and Traders throughout New England. | [copyright notice, 1851]. All within ornate triple frame with NUMBER SIXTY in top portion.

(18.7 x 11.8): [1]-48. Advertisements on pp. 47-48. Signed in 6's.

"Ready-Money Jack and His Farm-House," 39 (from "'Ready-Money Jack," *Bracebridge Hall*).

Lineation: p. 39, POETRY, ... nigh.

MH.

PARKER'S FOURTH READER. | [rule] | NATIONAL SERIES | OF | SELECTIONS FOR READING; | ADAPTED TO THE STANDING OF THE PUPIL. | BY RICHARD G. PARKER, A. M. | ... | PART FOURTH. | DESIGNED FOR THE HIGHER CLASSES IN SCHOOLS, ACADEMIES, &C. | ... | NEW YORK: | PUBLISHED BY A. S. BARNES & CO. | CINCINNATI: H. W. DERBY & Co. ST. LOUIS: KEITH & WOODS. NEW | ORLEANS: J. B. STEEL & JOHN BALL. MOBILE: J. K. RANDALL & Co. | 1851.

(18.3 x 11.8): [I]-VIII, [9]-360. Preliminary illustration not reckoned. Signed in 6's.

"Birds of Spring," 12-15 (from *The Knickerbocker*, May 1839, and *The Family Visitor*, ed. John Hayward, 1840); "Rural Taste," 35-36 (from "Rural Life in England," *Sketch Book*, here attributed only uncertainly to Irving); "The Wife," 44-51 (from *Sketch Book*).

Lineation: p. 45, tender ... tale."; p. 200, only ... your

Gray H cloth. Sides blank. Black leather shelfback titled in gilt.

A later impression noted by the same publisher, 1855. A later edition, by Richard G. Parker and J. Madison Watson, published in New York by A. S. Barnes & Burr, 51 & 53 John Street, 1859 (copyright 1857), contains different selections: "Birds of Spring," 49-52; "Mt. Vernon in 1759," 196-198 (from *Washington*); "The Golden Age of New York," 254-258 (from *History of New*

York); "The Wife," 316-324; "Feelings Excited by a Long Voyage," 333-338 (from"The Voyage," *Sketch Book*); "Sorrow for the Dead," 374-376 (from "Rural Funerals," *Sketch Book*).

DLC.

THE | YOUNG LADIES' READER: | CONTAINING | ... | EXERCISES IN READING, | IN PROSE AND POETRY. | [rule] | BY WILLIAM D. SWAN, | ... | PHILADELPHIA: | THOMAS, COWPERTHWAIT, & CO. | 1851.

(18.0 x 11.0): [1]-428. Signed in 8's and 6's.

"The Wife," 123-131 (from *Sketch Book*); "Columbus at Barcelona," 425-428 (from *Columbus*).

Printer: Smith & Peters, Franklin Buildings, Sixth Street, below Arch, Philadelphia.

Lineation: p. 125, been ... together ; p. 300, into ... on

Red-brown T cloth with brown leather shelfback.

A later impression noted, published in Philadelphia by Cowperthwait, Desilver, & Butler, 1854.

DLC.

THE | YOUNG WOMAN'S GIFT, | OF | Literature, Science and Morality, [fancy] | EDITED BY | COTESWORTH PINCKNEY. | [rule] | BOSTON: | PUBLISHED BY J. BUFFUM, | 1851.

(13.4 x 8.5): [i]-viii, [9]-192. Preliminary illustration not reckoned. Signed in 8's.

"Female Influence and Energy," 57-59 (from "The Wife," *Sketch Book*).

Printer: C. C. P. Moody, 52 Washington St., Boston.

Lineation: p. 50, of ... her ; p. 100, Here's ... ottoman,

Red L cloth. Sides decorated in gilt with urn, dove, and elaborate border. Spine decorated and titled in gilt. AEG. Yellow endpapers.

CtY.

1852

Garden Walks with the Poets. | By Mrs. C. M. Kirkland. | New-York: | G. P. Putnam & Company, 10 Park Place. | 1852. All in fancy type. All surrounded by single frame line.

(18.3 x 12.3): [i]-xii, 9-340. Preliminary colored lithographed title not reckoned. Signed in 12's.

"The Falls of the Passaic," [242]-243 (from *The Atlantic Souvenir* for 1827).

Lineation: p. 100, But ... confute.; p. 243, With ... foam.

TxU.

THE | IRVING OFFERING. | A | Token of Affection, [fancy] | FOR 1852. | NEW-YORK: | LEAVITT AND COMPANY, | 12 VESEY-STREET. | 1852

(18.5 x 12.2): [1]-6, [2 leaves unpaged], [13]-312. Not reckoned: engraved title and six illustrations. Signed in 12's.

"The Stout Gentleman: A Stage-Coach Romance," [13]-26 (from *Bracebridge Hall*). No attribution of authorship. This is the only identified piece by Irving. The other material of the volume, says the Preface, "consists of pieces which might be submitted to the inspection of the accomplished author of the Sketch Book himself, with full confidence of his approval."

Printer: John F. Trow, 49 Ann-street.

Lineation: p. 25, gradually ... along ; p. 200, shook ... some

Seen only rebound, although with the gilt on all edges retained.

DLC.

THE | SCHOOLMATE, | A | MONTHLY READER | FOR | SCHOOL AND HOME INSTRUCTION | OF | YOUTH | EDITED BY | A. R. PHIPPEN. | WITH THE ASSISTANCE OF | EMINENT PRACTICAL TEACHERS. | VOLUME 1. | 1852. | GEORGE SAVAGE, | 58 FULTON STREET, | NEW YORK. An elaborate engraved title, in many styles of lettering, with drawings of children.

(24.2 x 15.9): [i]-[viii], [1]-288. In double columns. Signed in 4's.

"Rip Van Winkle," 146-148 ("this dialogue is taken, with slight alteration, from Irving's beautiful legend"; from *Sketch Book*).

Lineation: p. 100, Scanning ... despair.; p. 147, to ... know.

Dark brown fine-vertically-ribbed cloth. Sides decorated in blind. Spine in gilt and blind.

A periodical issued as an annual.

TxU.

THE STUDENTS' SERIES. | [rule] | FOURTH | READING BOOK, | CONTAINING | A VARIETY OF ORIGINAL AND WELL SELECTED LESSONS | IN PROSE AND POETRY. | DESIGNED | FOR ADVANCED CLASSES | IN | PUBLIC AND PRIVATE SCHOOLS. | [RULE] | BY J.S. DENMAN, | . . . | THIRD EDITION. | NEW-YORK: | PRATT, WOODFORD & CO. | NO. 4 CORTLANDT-STREET. | 1852.

Copyright 1852. First edition not located.

(17.8 x 11.3): [i]-x, [11]-336. Eight pages of advertisements bound at end. Signed in 12's.

"Sorrow for the Dead," 162-164 (from "Rural Funerals," *Sketch Book*).

Printer: J.P. Jones & Co., Stereotypers, Cor. of William and Spruce-Strs.

Lineation: p. 163, of . . . sure ; p. 300, again, . . . their

Dark blue L cloth with black leather shelfback. Sides blank. Spine titled in gilt.

MH.

1853

THE | AMERICAN ORATOR: | WITH | AN APPENDIX, | CONTAINING | THE DECLARATION OF INDEPENDENCE, WITH THE FAC-SIMILES OF | THE AUTOGRAPHS OF THE SIGNERS; THE CONSTITUTION OF THE | UNITED STATES; WASHINGTON'S FAREWELL ADDRESS; AND | FAC-SIMILES OF THE AUTOGRAPHS OF A LARGE NUM- | BER OF DISTINGUISHED INDIVIDUALS. | BY LEWIS C. MUNN. | [stylized swelled rule] | BOSTON: | PUBLISHED BY THE COMPILER, | 120 WASHINGTON STREET. | 1853.

(19.0 x 11.9): [I]-IV, [5]-448. Pp. [409]-448 contain facsimiles of autographs; Irving's on p. 423.

"Sorrow for the Dead," 24-26 (from "Rural Funerals," *Sketch Book*).

Printer: Stereotyped by Hobart & Robbins, Boston; printed by Stacy and Richardson, No. 11 Milk street.

Lineation: p. 25, Where ... existence;; p. 200, may ... sub-

Purple A cloth. Sides decorated in blind. Spine titled in gilt. Cream endpapers.

In copy seen, the owner's inscription is dated 5 February 1853.

Another impression noted, presumably the first commercial impression: BOSTON: | TAPPAN AND WHITTEMORE. | 1853. Fewer facsimiles reduce the pagination, pp. [409]-436.

CtY; commercial impression, TxU.

THE | HUMOROUS SPEAKER: | BEING | A Choice Collection of Amusing Pieces, [fancy] | BOTH IN PROSE AND VERSE, | ORIGINAL AND SELECTED; | CONSISTING OF | DIALOGUES, SOLILOQUIES, PARODIES, &C. | DESIGNED | FOR THE USE OF SCHOOLS, LITERARY SOCIETIES, DEBATING | CLUBS, SOCIAL CIRCLES AND DOMESTIC ENTERTAINMENT. | BY OLIVER OLDHAM. | ... | NEW YORK: NEWMAN & IVISON, 178 FULTON STREET. | CINCINNATI: MOORE, ANDERSON & CO. CHICAGO: S. C. GRIGGS & CO. | AUBURN: J. C. IVISON & CO. DETROIT: A. M'FARREN | 1853.

(18.4 x 11.0 rebound): [i]-x, [11]-408. 24 pp. catalogue bound at end. Signed in 12's.

"Knickerbocker's New-England Farmer," 290-291 (from *History of New York*).

Printer: Stereotyped by Thomas B. Smith, 216 William St., N.Y.; printed by J. D. Bedford, 59 Ann St.

Lineation: p. 100, days ... of ; p. 291, zeal ... wander.

NN.

RANDALL'S | FIFTH READER; | CONTAINING | SELECTIONS FROM A VARIETY OF STANDARD ENGLISH AND | AMERICAN AUTHORS, IN PROSE AND POETRY. | ADAPTED TO | FAMILY AND SCHOOL READING. | [wavy rule] | BY S. S. RANDALL, | ... | ALBANY: PUBLISHED BY E. H. BENDER, 75 STATE-STREET, | AND SOLD BY BOOKSELLERS GENERALLY. | [rule of 6 dots] | 1853.

(18.3 x 11.1): [i]-x, [1]-360. Two pages of advertisements bound at end. Signed in 6's.

"The Widow and Her Son," 108-111 (listed as p. 101 in table of contents) (from *Sketch Book*).

Lineation: p. 110, motion ... can ; p. 200, 5. Where ... futurity!

Gray L cloth with black leather shelfback. Sides blank. Spine in gilt and blind.

MH.

THE SOUTHERN SERIES. | [rule] | THE | RHETORICAL MANUAL, | OR | SOUTHERN FIFTH READER: | EMBRACING COPIOUS AND ELEGANT EXTRACTS BOTH IN | PROSE AND POETRY. | ... | BY D. BARTON ROSS, A. M., N. G. | ... | NEW ORLEANS, LA.: | PUBLISHED BY J. B. STEEL, 60 CAMP STREET. | NATCHEZ, MI.: JACKSON WARNER. -- FOR SALE BY BOOKSELLERS GENERALLY. | 1853. | [rule] | N. B. -- FOR ONE DOLLAR, postpaid to either of the above-named publishers, a copy of this | work will be mailed in a strong wrapper, to any address named.

(17.9 x 11.0 rebound): [1]-549 [550]. Signed in 6's.

"Columbus before the Council at Salamanca," 95-101, and "Columbus First Discovers Land in the New World," 101-103, and "First Landing of Columbus in the New World," 104-106 (all from *Columbus*); "Westminster Abbey," 170-180, and "Christmas," 181-182 (both from *Sketch Book*); "Death," 182-185 (from "Rural Funerals," *Sketch Book*); "Discovery of the Pacific Ocean," 200-202, and "Vasco Nunez on the Shores of the South Sea," 203-204, and "Execution of Vasco Nunez," 204-206 (all from *Companions of Columbus*); "The 'Parliament Oak': Sherwood Forest," 342-343 (from *Newstead Abbey*); "The Wife," 343-351 (from *Sketch Book*); "Love of Fame," 400-401 (from # XVI, *Salmagundi*); "Some Traits of Sir W. Scott's Character," 402-403 (from *Abbotsford*); "Character of Goldsmith," 403-404 (from *Goldsmith*); "Domestic Life of an Indian," 404-405 (from *Tour on the Prairies*); "Voyage up the Hudson," 428-432 (from *History of New York*); "The Character of Columbus," 432-435 (from *Columbus*); "A Thunderstorm on the Hudson," 435-437 (from "Dolph Heyliger," *Bracebridge Hall*); "The Broken Heart," 442-446 (from *Sketch Book*); "A Practical Philosopher," 451 (from *Tales of a Traveller*); "Filial Affection," 451-454 (from "Grave Reflections of a Disappointed Man," *Tales of a Traveller*); "Wives," 455-457 (from *Bracebridge Hall*); "Invisible Companions," 457-460 (from "St. Mark's Eve," *Bracebridge Hall*); "The Storm Ship," 460-466 (from *Bracebridge Hall*); "Pompey's Pillar," 488-490 (not identified; reprinted from McGuffey's Readers); "Traits of Indian Character,"

492-503 (from *Sketch Book*); "Thunderstorm on the Prairies," 522-524 (from *Tour on the Prairies*); "Lamentations of the Moors for the Battle of Lucena," 525-528 (from *Granada*).

Printer: Stereotyped at the Boston Stereotype Foundry.

Lineation: p. 200, No. 41. ... to ; p. 400, It ... breathes

TxU.

THE | Rural Wreath; [fancy] | OR | LIFE AMONG THE FLOWERS. | EDITED BY | LAURA GREENWOOD. | ... | BOSTON: | DAYTON AND WENTWORTH, | 86 WASHINGTON STREET. | 1853.

(17.6 x 11.9): [1]-272. Preliminary illustration not reckoned. Signed in 6's.

"The Broken Heart," 120-127 (from *Sketch Book*).

Printer: Stereotyped at the Boston Stereotype Foundry.

Lineation: p. 125, dwell ... wisely."; p. 200, ROSEBUD, ... JR.

Red A cloth. On sides, in gilt, flowers and pendant within ornate frame. Spine ornately decorated in gilt; titled: Life | Among the | Flowers [in ornate lettering] | 1854 [with the 4 turned backwards]. AEG. Yellow endpapers.

Noted in an impression of 1854 by the same publishers; bound in red V cloth, sides decorated with cherub in swing within ornate border, no date on spine. Also reported in an impression of 1855 by the same publishers; 247 pp. Noted in an impression of 1857, published in Boston by Wentworth & Co.; bound in light green A cloth, sides decorated with flowers within an ornate border in blind, in gilt on front, in blind on back, no date on spine; 247 pp. Also reported in an impression of 1856 by the same publisher.

NNC.

BOOK THIRD. | [wavy rule] | THE | SOUTHERN | READER AND SPEAKER; | CONTAINING | SELECTIONS IN PROSE AND POETRY, | FOR | EXERCISES IN READING AND SPEAKING, | IN THE | ACADEMIES AND SCHOOLS OF THE SOUTHERN STATES. | ... | CHARLESTON: | PUBLISHED BY WILLIAM R. BABCOCK. | RICHMOND: DRINKER & MORRIS. | MOBILE: J. K. RANDALL & CO. | [rule] | 1853

Copyright 1848. First impression not seen.

(18.8 x 11.5): [i]-viii, [9]-360. Signed in 6's.

"Rights of Discovery," 120-124 (from *History of New York*); "The Wife," 237-244 (from *Sketch Book*); "A Frontier Farm-House," 272-274 (from *Tour on the Prairies*).

Printer: Thomas B. Smith, Stereotyper, 216 William Street, N. Y.

Lineation: p. 120, dow, ... debating ; p. 273, turkeys, ... his

Green AR-like cloth with black leather shelfback. Sides blank. Spine titled in gilt.

A later impression noted by the same publisher, 1856.

CtY.

THE | WHEAT-SHEAF; | OR, | GLEANINGS FOR THE WAYSIDE | AND FIRESIDE. | ... | Philadelphia: [fancy] | WILLIS P. HAZARD, 178 CHESTNUT STREET. | 1853. All within double frame lines.

(20.6 x 13.0): [i]-xii, [13]-416. Double frame lines around all pages. Numerous illustrations not reckoned. Signed in 6's.

"War," 388-389 (from *History of New York*).

Printer: Stereotyped by S. Douglas Wyeth Agt., No. 7 Pear Street; printed by C. Sherman & Co.

Lineation: p. 100, THE ... old,; p. 200, And ... glides!

DLC.

1854

THE | AMERICAN CLASSICAL AUTHORS. | [rule] | SELECT SPECIMENS | OF THE | ANGLO-AMERICAN LITERATURE. | PRECEDED BY | AN INTRODUCTORY ESSAY | ON ITS ORIGIN AND PROGRESS | WITH | BIOGRAPHICAL AND CRITICAL SKETCHES | BY | L. HERRIG, PH.D. | ... | BRUNSWICK: | PRINTED AND PUBLISHED BY GEORGE WESTERMANN. | [rule] | 1854.

(23.5 x 15.3): [I]-XII, [1]-119 [120], [i]-[ii], [1]-434. The selections, pp. [1]-434, in double columns. Preliminary title, in German, not reckoned. Preliminary matter in German. Signed in 8's.

"Ferdinand and Isabella," 204-206, and "On the Character of Columbus," 206-208, and "Customs and Characteristics of the Indians," 208-210 (all from *Columbus*); "The Foray of the Spanish Cavalier Among the Mountains of

Malaga," 210-215 (from Ch. XII of *Granada*); "Rip Van Winkle," 297-305 (from *Sketch Book*); "Legend of the Rose of the Alhambra," 305-311 (from *Alhambra*); "A Letter from Mustapha Rub-A-Dub Keli Khan. . .," 311-314 (from IX, *Salmagundi*); "Rural Life in England," 314-317 (from *Sketch Book*); "The Busybody," 318-320 (from "The Busy Man," *Bracebridge Hall*); "Love for the Dead," 320-321 (from "Rural Funerals," *Sketch Book*).

Lineation: p. 200, coming ... institutions!; p. 300, some ... lack-

MH.

THE STANDARD SERIES. | [rule] | THE | FIRST-CLASS | STANDARD READER | FOR | PUBLIC AND PRIVATE SCHOOLS; | ... | BY | EPES SARGENT, | ... | FOURTH THOUSAND. | BOSTON: | PHILLIPS, SAMPSON AND COMPANY. | NEW-YORK: J. C. DERBY; PHILADELPHIA: LIPPINCOTT, GRAMBO & CO.; | CINCINATTI: H. W. DERBY; CHICAGO: D. B. COOK & CO.; | DETROIT: S. D. ELWOOD & CO.; BALTIMORE: | CUSHINGS & BAILEY. | 1854.

Copyright 1854. First impression not seen.

(19.0 x 12.0): [I]-XII, [13]-478. Two pages of advertisements bound at end. Signed in 6's.

"Climate of the Catskill Mountains," 111-112 (from "The Catskill Mountains," *Home Book of the Picturesque*); "Ferdinand and Isabella," 281-282 (from *Columbus*); "The North American Indians Among Themselves," 382-383 (from *Tour on the Prairies*).

Printer: Stereotyped by Hobart & Robbins, New England Type and Stereotype Foundry, Boston.

Purple L cloth with black leather shelfback. Sides blank. Spine in gilt and blind stamping.

Later impressions noted by the same publisher: 1855 ("Sixth Thousand"); 1856 ("Twenty-Fifth Thousand"), called THE STANDARD FIFTH READER.

MH.

HIGH-SCHOOL | LITERATURE: | A | SELECTION OF READINGS | FOR THE | HIGHER CLASSES OF SCHOOLS. | SELECTED AND ARRANGED BY | JOHN F. MONMONIER, M. D., | AND | JOHN N. McJILTON, A. M. | SECOND EDITION. | NEW YORK: | PUBLISHED

BY A. S. BARNES & CO. | BALTIMORE: J. W. BOND & CO. |
CINCINNATI H. W. DERBY & CO. | 1854.

Copyright 1852 in Maryland. First edition not seen. Nothing is said in the
Preface about revision; this probably represents the original text in a later
impression.

(19.5 x 12.3): [i]-xii, [13]-480. Signed in 6's.

"A Visit to Shakespeare's Birth-Place and Grave," 127-131 (from "Stratford-
On-Avon," *Sketch Book*); "Sorrow for the Dead," 156-158 (from "Rural
Funerals," *Sketch Book*).

Printer: Stereotyped at the Baltimore Type and Stereotype Foundry,
Fielding Lucas, Jr., Proprietor.

Lineation: p. 128, of ... simple,; p. 300, Up ... Lord!"

TxU.

THE NORMAL SERIES. | [rule] | WEBB'S | NORMAL READER. |
NO. 5 | ... | COMPRISING | INSTRUCTION IN ELOCUTION AND
READING, | COPIOUSLY ILLUSTRATED BY | *EXTRACTS FROM
THE BEST AUTHORS*. | FOR THE USE OF ACADEMIES, PUBLIC
AND PRIVATE SCHOOLS. | ... | BY J. RUSSELL WEBB. | NEW
YORK: | SHELDON, LAMPORT & BLAKEMAN, | 115 NASSAU-
STREET. | 1854.

Copyright 1853 by George Savage. Any earlier impression not seen.

(18.4 x 11.7): [i]-[ii], [1]-490. Signed in 6's.

"The Thunder-Storm. -- Scenery in the Highlands, on the River Hudson,"
244-245 (from "Dolph Heyliger," *Bracebridge Hall*); "The Graves of Those We
Love," 265-267 (from "Rural Funerals," *Sketch Book*); "Walter Van Twiller,"
284-287 (from *History of New York*).

Lineation: p. 245, reflecting ... in ; p. 285, clearly ... ex-

Purple L cloth with brown leather shelfback. Sides blank. Spine in blind and
gilt.

TxU.

OLDHAM'S AMUSING | AND | INSTRUCTIVE READER: | A
COURSE OF READING, | ORIGINAL AND SELECTED, | IN PROSE
AND POETRY, | WHEREIN | WIT, HUMOR, AND MIRTH | ARE
MADE THE MEANS OF AWAKENING INTEREST, AND IMPARTING
| INSTRUCTION. | FOR THE USE OF SCHOOLS AND ACADEMIES.

| BY OLIVER OLDHAM, | ... | NEW YORK: | IVISON & PHINNEY, 178 FULTON STREET; | (SUCCESSORS OF NEWMAN & IVISON, AND M. H. NEWMAN & CO.) | CHICAGO: S. C. GRIGGS & CO. | BUFFALO: PHINNEY & CO. | CINCINNATI: MOORE, ANDERSON & CO. | AUBURN: J. C. IVISON & CO. | [rule] | 1854.

(18.0 x 11.0): [i]-xvii [xviii], [19]-384. Signed in 12's.

"A Contrast," 241-245 (from "The Country Church," *Sketch Book*); "A Rainy Sunday at an Inn," 342-344 (from "The Stout Gentleman," *Bracebridge Hall*).

Printer: Stereotyped by Thomas B. Smith, 216 William Street, N. Y.; printed by J. D. Torrey, 18 Spruce Street.

Lineation: p. 242, hereditary ... style.; p. 343, his ... lurking-places

NN.

THE | WEDDING DRESS. | EDITED BY A LADY. | ... | BOSTON: | THOS. O. WALKER. | 1854. All within single frame lines.

(11.2 x 7.0): [1]-128. Preliminary engraving not reckoned. Signed in 8's.

"The Wife," 45-60 (from *Sketch Book*).

Printer: Stereotyped by Hobart & Robbins, Boston.

Lineation: p. 50, sickly ... madness!"; p. 100, the ... of

Red A cloth. Front decorated in blind and gilt; back in blind. Spine titled in gilt. AEG. Endpapers of textured paper in blue and gold.

TxU.

THE | WHITE VEIL: | A BRIDAL GIFT. | EDITED BY | MRS. SARAH JOSEPHA HALE, | ... | PHILADELPHIA: | PUBLISHED BY E. H. BUTLER & CO. | 1854. All within single frame lines.

(20.7 x 16.7): [i]-[ii], 3, iv, 5, [vi]-viii [ix]-[x], 17-324. Not reckoned: preliminary colored title and 10 engravings. A "Frontispiece" listed in contents but apparently not present. All pages within single frame line. Signed in 4's.

"Influence of the Wife," 197-199 (from "The Wife," *Sketch Book*).

Printer: E. B. Mears, Stereotyper; C. Sherman, Printer.

Lineation: p. 100, settled ... shoulder.; p. 198, As ... that

Parchment-colored calf. A handsome period binding: on sides, decorations in gilt; and within deeply impressed oval, gilt symbolic emblem of clasped hands, anvil, and cherub forging chains. Spine in gilt. AEG. Yellow endpapers.

TxU.

1855

SWAN'S COMPREHENSIVE SERIES. | [rule] | THE | AMERICAN COMPREHENSIVE | READER: | FOR | THE USE OF SCHOOLS. | CONTAINING | EXERCISES IN ENUNCIATION, AND NUMEROUS SELECTIONS | IN POETRY AND PROSE. | BY | WILLIAM D. SWAN, | ... | BOSTON: | HICKLING, SWAN AND BROWN. | 1855.

(19.5 x 12.2): [I]-X, [11]-312. The first two pp. are blank. Signed in 6's.

"Sorrow for the Dead," 296-297 (from "Rural Funerals," *Sketch Book*).

Printer: Stereotyped by Hobart & Robbins, New England Type and Stereotype Foundery, Boston.

Lineation: p. 100, on ... [in footnote] keeping ; p. 297, mute, ... [in footnote] works.

Green L cloth. Sides blank. Spine missing this copy; leather?

TxU.

THE | FIFTH | OR | ELOCUTIONARY READER, | IN WHICH THE | PRINCIPLES OF ELOCUTION | ARE | ILLUSTRATED BY READING EXERCISES IN CONNECTION | WITH THE RULES: | DESIGNED FOR THE USE OF | SCHOOLS AND ACADEMIES. | [rule] | BY SALEM TOWN, LL. D. | [rule] | BOSTON: | SANBORN, CARTER & BAZIN. | PORTLAND: | BLAKE & CARTER. | 1855.

(18.5 x 11.4): [i]-x, [11]-480. Signed in 12's.

"Description of a Thunder-Storm," 373-374 (from "Dolph Heyliger," *Bracebridge Hall*).

Printer: Stereotyped by Erastus F. Beadle, Buffalo.

Lineation: p. 100, which ... [in footnote] applies?; p. 374, brilliancy ... action.

Gray TB-like cloth with black leather shelfback. Sides blank. Spine in gilt and blind stamping.

A revised edition noted by the same publisher, copyright 1856, called *The Progressive Fifth, or Elocutionary Reader.*

DLC.

A | FIRST CLASS READER; | CONSISTING OF EXTRACTS IN PROSE AND VERSE, | ... | FOR THE USE OF ADVANCED CLASSES | IN PUBLIC AND PRIVATE SCHOOLS. | BY G. S. HILLARD. | BOSTON: | BREWER AND TILESTON. | CLEVELAND: | INGHAM & BRAGG. | PHILADELPHIA: MARTIN & RANDALL.

Copyright 1855.

(18.0 x 11.5): [1]-552. Signed in 6's.

"The Boblink," 16-19 (from "The Birds of Spring," *Wolfert's Roost*); "Washington at Mount Vernon," 367-371 (from *Washington*).

Printer: Stereotyped at the Boston Stereotype Foundry.

Lineation: p. 18, up, ... homely; p. 368, still ... England.

Dark gray BD cloth with black leather shelfback. Sides blank. Spine in gilt and decorative stamping in blind, with publisher's emblem at foot.

A later impression noted, published in Boston by Hickling, Swan, and Brown, 1856.

TxU.

LILIES AND VIOLETS; [special lettering to suggest woodgrain] | OR, | Thoughts in Prose and Verse, [fancy] | ON THE | TRUE GRACES OF MAIDENHOOD. | BY | ROSALIE BELL. [elaborated Victorian type] | ... | NEW YORK: | J.C. DERBY, 119 NASSAU STREET. | BOSTON: | PHILLIPS, SAMPSON & CO. | CINCINNATI: | H. W. DERBY. | [rule] | 1855.

(19.2 x 12.0) : [i]-xiv [15]-442. Not reckoned: engraved title. Signed in 12's.

"Broken Hearts," 169-171 (from *Sketch Book*).

Printer: W. H. Tinson, Stereotyper, 24 Beekman Street, N.Y.

Lineation: p. 100, blank; p. 150, LINES ... beam, ; p. 170, to ... the

Blue AR cloth, decorated in blind on front and back. Spine in gilt: Lilies and Violets | or | the | TRUE GRACES | of | MAIDENHOOD | Rosalie Bell [all in special lettering]; surrounded by floral wreath.

A later impression noted, 1855, called "Second Edition."

NN.

SANDERS' SERIES. | [double rule] | THE | SCHOOL READER. | [wavy rule] | FIFTH BOOK. [hollow type] | ... | FOR THE USE OF ACADEMIES | AND THE | HIGHEST CLASSES IN COMMON AND SELECT SCHOOLS. | [wavy rule] | BY CHARLES W. SANDERS, A.M. | AND | JOSHUA C. SANDERS, A.M. | [wavy rule] | NEW YORK: | IVISON & PHINNEY, 321 BROADWAY, | (SUCCESSORS OF MARK H. NEWMAN & CO.) | CHICAGO: S. C. GRIGGS & CO., 111 LAKE ST. | BUFFALO: PHINNEY & CO. | CINCINNATI: MOORE, WILSTACH, KEYS & CO. | ST. LOUIS: KEITH & WOODS. | AUBURN: SEYMOUR & ALWARD. DETROIT: MORSE & SELLECK.

Copyright 1855. The Preface describes this as "a revised and corrected edition." First edition not seen.

(18.0 x 11.6): [i]-xii, [13]-456. Signed in 12's.

"The Uses of History," 440-441 (from *History of New York*).

Printer: Stereotyped by Thomas B. Smith; Printed by J. D. Torrey.

Lineation: p. 100, "Art ... song.; p. 440, in ... [in footnote] war.

Full calf.

TxU.

SARGENT'S STANDARD SERIES. -- No. 3. | [rule] | THE | STANDARD | THIRD READER | FOR | PUBLIC AND PRIVATE SCHOOLS. | ... | BY | EPES SARGENT, | ... | BOSTON: | PHILLIPS, SAMPSON AND COMPANY. | 13 WINTER STREET. | 1859.

Copyright 1855. First impression not seen.

(18.8 x 12.0): [I]-VIII, [9]-216. Signed in 6's.

"Sir Walter Scott and His Dogs," 88-90 (from *Abbotsford*); "Early Habits of Washington," 188-189 (from *Washington*).

Printer: Stereotyped by Hobart & Robbins, New England Type and Stereotype Foundry, Boston; Printed by R. M. Edwards.

Lineation: p. 89, the ... him ; p. 188, and ... midshipman's

Tan boards with brown leather shelfback. Engraved title on front, with picture of family group reading. Advertisements on back. Spine in gilt and blind.

TxU.

SARGENT'S STANDARD SERIES. -- No. 4. | [rule] | THE | STANDARD | FOURTH READER | FOR | PUBLIC AND PRIVATE SCHOOLS; | ... | BY | EPES SARGENT, | ... | BOSTON: | PHILLIPS, SAMPSON AND COMPANY, | No. 13 WINTER STREET. | 1855.

Although copyright in 1855, the copy examined is a later impression.

(18.8 x 11.8): [I]-XII, [13]-332. Four pages of advertisements bound at end. Signed in 6's.

"Life at Sea," 185-187 (from "The Voyage," *Sketch Book*).

Printer: Stereotyped by Hobart & Robbins, New England Type and Stereotype Foundery, Boston.

Lineation: p. 186, deserted ... with ; p. 300, *Officer.* ... of.

Brown L cloth with brown leather shelfback. Sides blank. Spine decorated in blind, titled in gilt.

TxU.

1856

THE | CHRISTIAN READER. | [rule] | GLEANINGS FROM DIVERS FIELDS. | [rule] | A New Miscellany, [fancy] | INTENDED FOR A FIRST-CLASS BOOK IN SCHOOLS, | AND FOR | GENERAL DISTRIBUTION IN FAMILIES. | [rule] | BOSTON: | PRINTED BY JOHN WILSON AND SON, | 22, SCHOOL STREET. | 1856.

(19.1 x 12.0): [i]-xi [xii], [1]-363 [364]. Signed in 6's.

"The Love of Fame," 175-177 (from # XVI, *Salmagundi*).

Lineation: p. 100, the ... top ; p. 176, which ... immortality

Purple TZ cloth. Sides decorated in blind. Spine titled in gilt. Yellow endpapers.

TxU.

OSGOOD'S | Progressive Fourth Reader: [fancy] | CONTAINING LESSONS IN PROSE AND POETRY, FROM THE | BEST AUTHORS. | Designed for Grammar Schools. [fancy] | [rule] | BY LUCIUS OSGOOD. | [rule] | PITTSBURGH: | PUBLISHED BY A. H. ENGLISH & CO. | 98 FOURTH STREET.

Copyright 1856

(18.5 x 12.1): [1]-352. Signed in 8's.

"Birds of Spring," 108-112 (from *Wolfert's Roost*); "Sorrow for the Dead," 202-204 (from "Rural Funerals," *Sketch Book*); "The Wife," 208-216 (from *Sketch Book*).

Printer: Stereotyped by L. Johnson & Co., Philadelphia.

Lineation: p. 110, rivals ... lot ; p. 210, delicate ... harshest

Gray heavily-pebbled cloth with black leather shelfback. Sides decorated in blind. Spine in blind and gilt, publisher at foot.

TxU.

THE SOUTHERN SERIES. | [rule] | THE | SOUTHERN SPEAKER, | OR | SIXTH READER; | CONTAINING, IN GREAT VARIETY, | THE MASTERPIECES OF ORATORY | IN PROSE, POETRY, AND DIALOGUE. | ... | BY | D. BARTON ROSS, A. M., N. G., | ... | NEW ORLEANS, LA.: | PUBLISHED BY J. B. STEEL, 60 CAMP STREET. | Alexandria, La., E. Johnson. -- Vicksburg, Miss., M. Emanuel. -- Mobile, Ala., J. K. Randall & Co. | Montgomery, Ala., A. P. Pfister. -- Augusta, Ga., M. G. McKinne. -- Charleston, S. C., J. McCarthers. | Raleigh, N. C., H. D. Turner. -- Richmond, Va., Harrold & Murray. -- Washington City, Franck Taylor. -- Baltimore, Md., Armstrong & Berry. -- Louisville, Ky., C. Hagan. | St. Louis, Mo., Edwards & Bushnell. -- Memphis, Tenn., Cleaves & Guion. | Nashville, Tenn., F. Hagan. -- Indianola, Texas, H. B. Cleveland. | [rule] | 1856.

(20.4 x 12.6 rebound): [i]- xvi, 13-556. Preliminary engraving not reckoned. Signed in 8's.

"Knickerbocker's New England Farmer," 297-299 (from *History of New York*).

Lineation: p. 100, And ... impure ; p. 298, to ... scene

TxU.

THE | Young Lady's Own Book: [fancy] | AN OFFERING | OF | LOVE AND SYMPATHY. | BY | EMILY THORNWELL, | ... | NEW YORK: J. C. DERBY, 119 NASSAU STREET. | BOSTON: PHILLIPS, SAMPSON, & CO. | CINCINNATI: H. W. DERBY. | 1856.

(18.2 x 12.5): [i]-xiv, [15]-442. Engraved vignette title not reckoned. Signed in 12's.

"Broken Hearts," 168-171 (from "The Broken Heart," *Sketch Book*).

Lineation: p. 170, to ... the ; p. 300, Once ... them.

Brown V cloth. Sides decorated in blind. Spine titled in gilt.

CtY.

1857

THE | ANGEL VISITOR; | OR, | THE VOICES OF THE HEART. | EDITED BY | FRANCES E. PERCIVAL. | ... | BOSTON: | L. P. CROWN & COMPANY. | TORONTO: C. W. BOSTWICK & BARNARD. | PHILADELPHIA: J. W. BRADLEY. | PROVIDENCE: O. W. POTTER. | 1857.

(17.4 x 11.7): [1]-272. Lithograph before title not reckoned. Eight pages of advertisements bound at end. Signed in 8's.

"Remembrance of the Dead," 157-160 (from "Rural Funerals," *Sketch Book*).

Printer: Stereotyped at the Boston Stereotype Foundry.

Lineation: p. 100, Yet ... all!; p. 160, ing ... dear

Bright blue L cloth. On front, gilt rose in center with decoration in blind around. On back, the rose in blind also. Spine decorated and titled in gilt. Manila-yellow endpapers.

Two later impressions noted: one published in Boston by Crown & Emery, 1857; one by Crown & Company, 1858.

MH.

... | GOODRICH'S | FIFTH | SCHOOL READER, | EDITED BY | NOBLE BUTLER, A. M. | [swelled rule] | LOUISVILLE, KY. | JOHN P. MORTON & CO. All within wavy frame lines.

Copyright 1857.

(19.1 x 12.9): [I]-VII [VIII], [9]-384. Wavy frame line around all pages. Signed in 8's.

"Christmas in England," 213-214 [Credited to Irving but simplified for children] (from *Sketch Book*); "The Prairie-Dog," 296-298 ("Compiled from Irving and Kendall") (from *Tour on the Prairies*).

Lineation: p. 200, 7. after ... teeth.; p. 297, houses, ... hole.

Black C cloth with black leather shelfback. On sides, publisher's emblem in blind. Spine in gilt and blind stamping.

TxU.

... | GOODRICH'S | SIXTH | SCHOOL READER, | EDITED BY | NOBLE BUTLER, A. M. | [swelled rule] | LOUISVILLE, KY: | JOHN P. MORTON AND COMPANY, | PUBLISHERS. All within wavy frame lines.

Copyright 1857.

(18.8 x 12.3): [I]-X, [11]-551 [552]. Wavy frame line around all pages. Signed in 8's.

"The Boblink," 73-74 (from "The Birds of Spring," *Wolfert's Roost*); "The Widow and Her Son," 103-105 (from *Sketch Book*); "A Bee-Hunt," 122-124 (from *Tour on the Prairies*); "Rip Van Winkle's Awakening," 152-157 (from "Rip Van Winkle," *Sketch Book*); "Primitive Habits in New-Amsterdam," 187-188 (from *History of New York*); "A Rainy Day at a Country Inn," 189-190 (from "The Stout Gentleman," *Bracebridge Hall*); "Robert Emmett" and "The Broken Heart," (from *Sketch Book*); "Scenes on the Hudson in Early Times," 208-210 (from "Dolph Heyliger," *Bracebridge Hall*).

Lineation: p. 105, tottering ... dust!"; p. 210, 12. Now ... streams,

Lightly-pebbled black cloth with black leather shelfback. On sides, publisher's emblem in blind. Spine in gilt and blind stamping.

TxU.

THE | NEW YORK SPEAKER. | A SELECTION OF PIECES | DESIGNED | FOR ACADEMIC EXERCISES IN ELOCUTION. | BY | WARREN P. EDGARTON, | ... | WITH | INTRODUCTORY REMARKS ON DECLAMATION, | BY | WILLIAM RUSSELL, | ... | REVISED EDITION. | [rule] | NEW YORK: | SHELDON & CO., No. 677 BROADWAY | AND 214 & 216 MERCER STREET, | UNDER GRAND CENTRAL HOTEL.

Copyright 1857. The unrevised edition, if one existed, not located.

(19.7 x 12.6): [I]-XIX [XX], [21]-502. Signed in 24's.

"The Grave of the Beloved," 155-156 (from "Rural Funerals," *Sketch Book*); "Spiritual Visitations," 362-364 (from "St. Mark's Eve," *Bracebridge Hall*).

Lineation: p. 156, watchful ... cataract.; p. 300, As ... Stump?"

A later impression noted, published in New York by Mason Brothers, 1859.

MB.

Wigand's [in fraktur] | POCKET MISCELLANY. [in special lettering] | [rule] | VOLUME I. | [emblem] | SECOND EDITION. [fancy] | [rule] | GOETTINGEN: | GEORGE H. WIGAND. | 1857.

First edition not located.

(15.1 x 10.9): [i]-xii, [1]-180. Not reckoned: preliminary engraving of Irving. Signed in 8's.

"The Catskill Mountains," 170-180 (from *Home Book of the Picturesque*).

Lineation: p. 175, treasury ... then

Drab paper wrapper. On front, title. On back, advertisements.

BL.

A | SECOND CLASS READER; | CONSISTING OF EXTRACTS, | IN PROSE AND VERSE. | FOR THE USE OF THE | SECOND CLASSES IN PUBLIC AND PRIVATE SCHOOLS. | ... | BY G. S. HILLARD. | BOSTON: | HICKLING, SWAN AND BROWN. | 1857.

(19.2 x 11.9): [i-ii, blank] [iii]-lviii, [1]-278. Signed in 6's.

"A Visit to the Village of Broek," 42-46 (from *Wolfert's Roost*); "Boyhood of Washington," 219-222 (From *Washington*).

Printer: Electrotyped at the Boston Stereotype Foundry.

Lineation: p. 45, and ... [in footnote] York.; p. 220, a ... and

Gray L cloth with black leather shelfback. Sides blank. Spine in gilt and decorative stamping in blind, with publisher's emblem at foot.

Noted in a number of later impressions published in Boston: Hickling, Swan and Brewer, 1859 and 1860; Swan, Brewer and Tileston, 1861 and undated.

TxU.

1858

A | COMPENDIUM | OF | AMERICAN LITERATURE; | ... | BY | CHARLES D. CLEVELAND. | PHILADELPHIA: | E. C. & J. BIDDLE, No. 508 MINOR STREET. | (*Between Market and Chestnut, and Fifth and Sixth Sts.*) | *Boston*: PHILLIPS, SAMPSON & Co.; SHEPARD, CLARK & BROWN. | *New York*:   A. O. MOORE ......*Cincinnati*:   RICKEY, MALLORY & Co. | *Chicago*: W. G. KEEN; D. B. COOKE & Co. | 1858.

(19.2 x 12.2): [i]-xx, [25]-740.

"Columbus First Discovers Land in the New World," 398-399 (from *Columbus*); "Filial Affection," 399-401 (from "Grave Reflections of a Disappointed Man," *Tales of a Traveller*); "Christmas," 401-402 (from *Sketch Book*); "The Alhambra by Moonlight," (from *Alhambra*); "The Grave," 404-405 (from "Rural Funerals," *Sketch Book*); "English Scenery," 405-406 (from "Rural Life in England," *Sketch Book*); "Portrait of a Dutchman," 406-407 (from *History of New York*).

Printer: Collins, Philadelphia.

Lineation: p. 100, himself ... country.; p. 400, been ... from

Bright blue TZ-like cloth. On sides, border in blind. Spine titled in gilt. Endpapers brown.

A second edition, by the same publisher, called "Stereotype Edition," 1859, drops "Christmas" and "English Scenery." A third edition, published in Philadelphia by J. A. Bancroft & Co., and in New York by J. W. Schermerhorn & Co., n.d. [copyright 1859], retains the second edition selections. Noted: an illustrated impression of the third edition, published in Philadelphia by Parry & McMillan, and others, 1859.

MH.

... | THE | NATIONAL | FIFTH READER: | CONTAINING | A TREATISE ON ELOCUTION; | EXERCISES IN | READING AND DECLAMATION; | WITH | BIOGRAPHICAL SKETCHES, AND COPIOUS NOTES. | ADAPTED TO THE USE OF STUDENTS IN | ENGLISH AND AMERICAN LITERATURE. | BY | RICHARD G. PARKER, A.M., | AND | J. MADISON WATSON. | [emblem] | NEW YORK: | A.S. BARNES & BURR, | 51 & 53 JOHN STREET. | SOLD BY

BOOKSELLERS, GENERALLY, THROUGHOUT THE UNITED STATES. | 1860.

Copyright 1858. First edition not seen.

(19.5 x 12.3): [1]-600. Signed in 12's.

"Broken Hearts," 109-114 (from "The Broken Heart," *Sketch Book*); "The Uses of History," 143-145 (from *History of New York*); "The Widow and Her Son," 253-259, and "Westminster Abbey," 267-272 (both from *Sketch Book*); "Forest Trees," 427-430 (from *Bracebridge Hall*); "The Stolen Rifle," 498-499 (from *Astoria*).

Printer: R. C. Valentine, Stereotyper & Electrotyper, 81, 83, & 85 Centre-street, N.Y.; Geo. W. Wood, Printer, No. 2 Dutch-street, N.Y.

Gray BD cloth with black leather shelfback. Series title in blind on sides.

TxU.

OSGOOD'S | Progressive Fifth Reader: [fancy] | EMBRACING | A SYSTEM OF INSTRUCTION IN THE PRINCIPLES OF | ELOCUTION, | AND | SELECTIONS FOR READING AND SPEAKING FROM THE BEST | ENGLISH AND AMERICAN AUTHORS. | DESIGNED FOR THE | Use of Academies and the highest Classes in Public and Private | Schools. [both lines fancy] | [rule] | BY LUCIUS OSGOOD. | [rule] | PITTSBURGH: | PUBLISHED BY A. H. ENGLISH & CO. | 98 FOURTH STREET.

Copyright 1858.

Variant impression noted: publisher's address, No. 79 WOOD STREET.

(18.6 x 11.9): [1]-480. Signed in 8's.

"The Broken Heart," 121-124 (from *Sketch Book*); "Manners in New York in Early Times," 161-163 (from *History of New York*); "The Widow and Her Son," 270-276, and "The Voyage," 462-464 (both from *Sketch Book*).

Printer: Stereotyped by L. Johnson & Co., Philadelphia; R. Singerly & Co., Printers and Binders, Harrisburg, Pa.

Lineation: p. 122, 2. The ... His ; p. 463, rather ... end.

Gray fine-pebbled cloth. On sides, decoration and publisher's initials in blind.

TxU.

THE | PROGRESSIVE SPEAKER | AND | COMMON SCHOOL READER; | COMPRISING CHOICE SELECTIONS FOR | READING, | RECITATION, AND DECLAMATION. | ... | BY AN EMINENT PRACTICAL TEACHER, | AUTHOR OF "PROGRESSIVE PRIMER," AND SEVERAL OTHER POPULAR SCHOOL BOOKS. | [rule] | BOSTON: | SANBORN, BAZIN AND ELLSWORTH. | 1858.

(19.0 x 12.1): [1]-528. Signed in 6's.

"Primitive Habits in New Amsterdam," 102-104, and "Ladies of the Golden Age," 194-197 (both from *A History of New York*); four selections from "The Widow's Son," 213-215 (from "The Widow and Her Son," *Sketch Book*); "Westminster Abbey," 243-248 (from *Sketch Book*); "The Unknown Wreck," 321-323 (from "The Voyage," *Sketch Book*); "Boblink, Reed-Bird, or Rice-Bird," 385-388 (from "The Birds of Spring," *Wolfert's Roost*).

Printer: Stereotyped at the Boston Stereotype Foundry; Printed by George C. Rand & Avery.

Lineation: p. 244, will ... whole ; p. 350, Assuredly ... bones."

Brown-gray V cloth with black leather shelfback. Sides decorated in blind. Spine in gilt and blind stamping. All edges stained yellow.

TxU.

1859

THE | ATLANTIC SOUVENIR, | FOR 1859. | ... | NEW YORK: | DERBY & JACKSON, 119 NASSAU STREET. | 1859.

(23.7 x 17.0): [i]-[x], [11]-288. Not reckoned: preliminary engraving of bust of Irving, and eleven other illustrations through the volume. Signed in 8's.

The portrait of Irving (from a bust by Ball Hughes) is listed in the list of engravings as facing p. 33, but in fact appears before the title.

"Conversations with Talma; from Rough Notes in a Common-Place Book," [33]-40 (from *The Knickerbocker Gallery*).

Printer: W. H. Tinson, Stereotyper, Rear of 43 & 45 Centre St.; George H. Russell & Co., Printers, 61 Beekman Street.

Lineation: p. 35, He ... if ; p. 200, our ... con-

Noted in three bindings: [A]. Blue AA cloth. On sides, title and heavy decoration in gilt. Spine decorated in gilt, titled: THE | ATLANTIC | SOUVENIR in special lettering. Blue endpapers. AEG. [B]. Bright blue TZ cloth. Same design. White endpapers with design of small stars in gold.

AEG. [C]. Brown morocco-like leather. On sides, in gilt, title within ornate oval, all within elaborate border in blind. Spine decorated in blind, titled in gilt the same. Brown endpapers in one copy, manilla in another. AEG.

The Irving contribution and others are reprinted from the plates of the second impression of *The Knickerbocker Gallery*.

CtY, TxGeoS (2), TxU.

ILLUMINATED QUADRUPLE SHEET. | The Constellation. | New York, 1859. George Roberts, Editor & Publisher. Price Fifty Cents. [In a variety of lettering styles, designed to represent a newspaper heading. In background, drawing to represent transportation, the arts, farming, etc.]

A special eight-page publishing curiosity, described in the first column of p. 8 as "The great wonder of the age!"; "The largest sheet of paper ever made and printed?"; "Being one sheet 70 x 100 inches!"; "A limited edition of only 28,000 copies." Dated July 4, 1859.

(124.7 x 87.0): [1]-8. In newspaper format.

"A Haunted Ship," 8, columns 3-4 (from *Heath's Book of Beauty*, 1836, and *Friendship's Offering* for 1849); "My Mother's Grave," 8, column 4 (from "Grave Reflections of a Disappointed Man," *Tales of a Traveller*).

Lineation: p. 8, column 3, causing ... the

Issued unbound.

TxU.

*Writings in
Periodicals*

WASHINGTON IRVING began writing early for the periodicals of his day. His first work of any length, *Letters of Jonathan Oldstyle, Gent.*, appeared in a series of pseudonymous letters in his brother Peter's newspaper, the *Morning Chronicle*, among many other squibs and satires and jokes that are probably his. In 1813-1814 he even edited a periodical, *The Analectic Magazine*, and published a number of his own pieces there. The form of *Salmagundi*, too, was somewhere between periodical and book form. In contrast, as he began to make a broad public reputation with *The Sketch Book* in 1819-1820, he turned increasingly to publication in book form, even though later in life he did consent to an agreement with another magazine, *The Knickerbocker*, to which he contributed regularly from 1839 to 1841. Beyond an occasional letter to the editor, he was not to write again for the periodicals, although they reprinted his other writing widely and often.

The impression of Irving in his early career as a writer for the periodicals would be strengthened -- and our knowledge of Irving's literary beginnings greatly enlarged -- if only there were some way to identify all of the writing that he must have done. Occasional public hints do appear: on 19 November 1819, for instance, he wrote to Walter Scott to refuse the editorship of an anti-Jacobin magazine; it is difficult to believe that the offer would have been made to an American if Irving had not been known in Great Britain as a writer for the magazines. (Near the end of the letter, Irving offered "the wares I have at present on hand" to Archibald Constable, the publisher of *The Edinburgh Magazine*. It is sometimes assumed that Irving was referring to *The Sketch Book*, but why should that be assumed?) Or -- particularly revealing -- on 1 September 1831 Irving in writing to John G. Lockhart referred casually to "the Tory Review in which I occasionally write." For an example of external evidence, the anonymous "X.Y.Z." in an article on "American Writers. No. II" in *Blackwood's Edinburgh Magazine*, October 1824, says that "Mr. I[rving] ... wrote a paper or two ... for the NEW MONTHLY." For other evidence, in part circumstantial, see the discussion, in this section, of the New York *Morning Chronicle* and *The Analectic Magazine*, particularly the introduction at the end of the *Analectic* entry to Irving's probable but unproven contributions to the magazine.

The problem is that Irving was very secretive about his early writing. Few of his early letters have survived -- apparently in part because he wanted them to be destroyed -- and in those that we do have, as well as in the very few surviving journals and notebooks for the more important years, Irving talks only sparingly and indirectly about his writing. Explanations are not difficult to find. Irving began writing in a tradition of anonymity, a convention that he followed faithfully even when, in later years, it fooled no one. Try to find hard evidence from his contemporary letters or journals, for instance, that he was in fact the author of *The Letters of Jonathan Oldstyle*. And, except for one letter to James K. Paulding that somehow survived, it would be difficult to prove his hand in *Salmagundi*. He did not talk about his writing, and neither did his friends.

A more compelling explanation, however, is difficult to prove directly. Irving seems to have been ambitious to make a literary reputation for himself, and he ruthlessly suppressed public acknowledgment of his authorship of anything that he considered second-rate, evanescent, a mere pot boiler. (See, for instance, his correspondence with John Howard Payne, one of the few rich exchanges of letters to survive. Irving repeats over and over that he does not want his name connected in any public way with those plays on which he worked. He even insists that one play be withdrawn from consideration since his hand had been detected.) That prickly consciousness of reputation would have been particularly true during his early period in England; Irving wanted to return to America in triumph, an esteemed American author. He was not going to be known as a writer of tripe and triviality. As he wrote to Moses Thomas the publisher, 3 March 1818, "Whatever my literary reputation may be worth, it is very dear to me, and I cannot bring myself to risk it by making up books for mere profit." Or at least he would not risk it if he thought he would be caught.

The result of his carefully maintained secrecy -- and that seems the only fitting word -- is that we simply do not have reliable identification of what I assume to be a considerable body of early periodical writing. Once the scholarly world becomes conscious of the strong possibility of such a body of writing, however, perhaps more of it will be identified than we know of now. Irving wrote rapidly and easily, and he characteristically turned to his pen when in want. He must have turned to it often in those years from, roughly, 1810 to 1825, but he is not going to tell us about it directly.

A listing of Irving's periodical appearances poses other problems than identification, particularly if it lists reprints of his writing. Irving was very popular in his day, and particularly after his return to America in 1832, was hailed as one of the great representatives of American letters. The result is that periodicals reprinted his work often, generally without permission. One favorite and quasi-legal method was the so-called review. A number of the more serious literary periodicals did indeed print reviews that attempted to judge and to comment on Irving's books. But many more, particularly in the United States, used the pretext of the review simply to print lengthy extracts from the book. (The intent is not always clear; sometimes the editor or reviewer may have been hurried, or incompetent, or simply thought that was what a review should be.)   When a review consists for the most part of extracts, I list it here as an extract, although I also identify it as a review. Obviously, that quickly becomes a matter of subjective decision. For a while I tried to devise a usable formula -- some percentage of lines of extracts to lines of comment, for instance -- but soon gave up the attempt. The decision is mine, and the reader may not always agree. A clearer case is presented, I would think, when a genuine review prints a longer, nearly complete piece for illustration.

Equally common was the open reprinting of Irving's writing, sometimes not even giving him credit as author. But whether disguised as a review or openly pirated, there is much of Irving's reprinted writing to be found in the contemporary periodicals. Reprint or original, it will probably never all be found. Periodicals appeared and disappeared in short order, and many are now extremely scarce. Periodicals in reproduction, such as the American Periodical Series, have made it easier for the scholar, but many of the lesser periodicals have yet to be reproduced. And even when a periodical can be examined, there is no surety. Some lack indexes altogether, others commonly index only by title -- and the editor was likely to assign a new title to a reprinted piece. Short of going through each periodical page by page, one is likely to miss whatever Irving is there, even assuming that it would be recognized if found. If magazines constitute a major problem, newspapers constitute a disaster. Small newspapers abounded, surviving long runs are scarce, and there were no indexes at all.

The easiest solution to the problems is not to list periodical reprint material at all, and I have done that with continental periodicals as well as with those printed in languages other than English. But to fail to suggest, however imperfectly, the richness of the reprints is to prohibit the use of the bibliography for many scholarly purposes. The reprints are tangible evidence of Irving's popularity and reputation, and the information on what pieces were being reprinted is evidence that can be very useful for studying the literary tastes of the age. Further, it should be remembered that many readers outside of the conventional literature-reading class knew Irving's writing only through his periodical appearances, or at least first met it there.

Here then is an account of all of Irving's writings in periodicals that I have identified with any confidence and that I have located. Although the account of the major periodicals in which he published or which showed a particular partiality for his work is largely complete, the account of lesser periodicals should be considered no more than representative, and the account of newspapers only an occasional sounding.

Of the various possible ways of listing the periodical pieces found, there is something to be said for each. The most revealing might be to list each periodical chronologically. But how is one to define the chronology in any useful manner when Irving may have appeared in a periodical over a number of years? I have, finally, fallen back on the alphabetical, by title of the periodical. There are some difficulties there too; magazines sometimes changed title during their publishing life; and it is often difficult to be certain whether the place of publication is a part of the formal title of a newspaper or not. But those are minor challenges: magazines are listed under the title they bore when Irving appeared in them, and newspapers are simply alphabetized under the name of the place of origin, whether a part of the formal title or not. Within the individual listing for each periodical, Irving's contributions are entered chronologically, with the source of reprinted pieces identified. *Original writing which had not previously appeared elsewhere is identified by an asterisk in the margin*. If the original piece later appeared in book form (and not all did), the book is named.

A

Albany Argus [Albany, N.Y.].

"Dinner to Washington Irving." (4 and 5 June 1832), [2]. First published in the New York *Morning Courier* and other New York newspapers, 2 June 1832.

Letter to Charles Dickens, dated New-York, 24th January 1842, greeting him on arrival in America and proposing a public dinner. Signed by forty-one eminent New Yorkers, including Irving. (10 February 1842), [2]. The letter had appeared 9 February in the *New-York Tribune*.

* Account of the public dinner for Charles Dickens chaired by Irving. (23 February 1842), [2]. Unlike the account in the *New-York Tribune*, 19 and 21 February, this account quotes Irving's remarks.

Albany Journal [Albany, N. Y.}.

"The Poor Lawyer." 12 (3 November 1841), [2]. From "The Early Experiences of Ralph Ringwood," in *The Knickerbocker*, August-September 1840.

The Albion; or British, Colonial, and Foreign Weekly Gazette [New York].

"On Passaic Falls. Written in the Year 1806." 5 (11 November 1826), 174. From *The Atlantic Souvenir* for 1827.

Extracts from *Companions of Columbus*. 9 (5 March 1831), 307-308. In review of the London edition.

* [Lines Written in the Album at Stratford-on-Avon]. N.S.1 (2 March 1833), 72. In an anonymous account of a visit to Stratford, entitled "Washington Irving at Stratford-On-Avon," headed "For the Albion." The poem had been published earlier, in what may be a separate transcription, in *The Port Folio*, Philadelphia, 1825.

Selections from *A Tour on the Prairies*: [on Pierre Beattte], "Night Piece," "The Stoics of the Woods, the Men Without a Tear," "A Hint for Crossing a River." N.S.3 (11 April 1835), 120.

"Legend of Count Julian and His Family." N.S.3 (10 October 1835), 326-327. From *Legends of the Conquest of Spain*.

Account of the Booksellers' Dinner, with a summary of Irving's toast to Samuel Rogers. N.S.5 (8 April 1837), 111.

"The Bermudas: A Shakespearean Research." 2nd N.S.2 (25 January 1840), 29-30. From *The Knickerbocker*, January 1840.

Letter to Charles Dickens, dated New York, 24th January, 1842, proposing a public dinner. Signed by 41 eminent New Yorkers, including Irving. N.S.1 (12 February 1842), 79. The letter had previously appeared in the *New-York Tribune* and other papers of the day.

Account of the public dinner for Charles Dickens chaired by Irving. N.S.1 (26 February 1842), 99. This account merely describes Irving's remarks, although it quotes his "sentiment" to Dickens. The account had previously appeared in the *New-York Tribune* and other papers of the day.

Extract from "Guests from Gibbet-Island." N.S.4 (14 June 1845), 286-287. In review of *The Knickerbocker Sketch Book*.

"Walter Scott and Washington Irving." N.S.7 (21 October 1848), [505]. From the Preface to the Author's Revised Edition of *The Sketch Book*.

"Gold Hunting." N.S.7 (30 December 1848), 629. Extract from *Columbus*, "happily quoted by the *Literary World*."

Introduction to *A Book of the Hudson*. N.S.8 (21 April 1849), 189. In "Notices of New Works."

Selections from *Mahomet and His Successors*: "Marriage of Mahomet with Ayesha," "The Sword Announced as the Instrument of Faith," "General View of His Life and Character." N.S.8 (8 December 1849), [577]-578. "From the proof-sheets, to be published next week."

Letter on Thomas Campbell, from *Life and Letters of Thomas Campbell* by William Beattie. N.S.9 (3 August 1850), 369. In review.

The Album [London].

"The Stout Gentleman," "Forest Trees," "Annette Delarbre," and shorter extracts from *Bracebridge Hall*. 1 (July 1822), 400-428. In review.

The American Magazine, and Repository of Useful Literature [Albany, N. Y.].

"Neamathla, the Head Chief of the Creek Indian Nation." Anonymous. 1 (October 1841), 105-107. From *The Knickerbocker*, October 1840.

"The Bride." 1 (December 1841), 180. From "The Wedding," *Bracebridge Hall*.

The American Monthly Magazine [Boston].

"The Gift Horse," "French and American Trappers," "The Delaware Hunter," "Death of a Bold Partisan," "Anecdote of a Young Mexican and an Indian Girl." N.S.4 (August 1837), 186-190. In a "Critical Notice" of *The Rocky Mountains*.

American Publishers' Circular [New York].

*   Letter to Childs & Peterson, publishers, dated Sunnyside, August 23, 1855, in advertisement headed "Testimonials to Allibone's Critical Dictionary." 1 (15 December 1855), 244. (So paged individually).

*   Statement in commendation of the Duyckincks' *Cyclopaedia of American Literature*. In advertisement. 2 (18 October 1856), 641.

"The Siege of Yorktown." 3 (23 May 1857), [321]-322. From *Life of Washington*, Vol. IV.

The American Quarterly Review [Philadelphia].

Extracts from *Columbus*. 3 (March 1828), 173-190. In review of New York edition, 1828 (given here as published by Elliot & Palmer).

Letter on Gilbert S. Newton, dated March 9th, 1834. 17 (March 1835), 169-170. From Dunlap's *History of the Rise and Progress of the Arts of Design in the United States*.

The American Review [New York].

Letter "To the Editor of the Knickerbocker" on international copyright. 10 (October 1849), 421. From *The Knickerbocker*, January 1840.

The Analectic Magazine [Philadelphia].

Late in 1812, Moses Thomas, a Philadelphia publisher, bought an established magazine called *Select Reviews, and Spirit of Foreign Magazines* and employed Washington Irving as its editor. In January 1813 the two gave the periodical a new title: *The Analectic Magazine, Containing Selections from Foreign Reviews and Magazines, of Such Articles as Are Most Valuable, Curious, or Entertaining.* An advertisement inserted in *The Bridal of Triermain, or The Vale of St. John,* Philadelphia: Bradford and Inskeep, 1813 announced the new title and the new editor, promised "Portraits (accompanied with Biographical Sketches) of our most distinguished NAVAL OFFICERS," and offered a free copy to anyone who would procure eight subscribers and be responsible for the payment.

During his two years as editor, until January 1815, Irving must have written or had a hand in writing much that cannot now be identified. But eleven anonymous full pieces (twelve if a note to one is counted separately) are known to be his; all except those on Paulding and Byron were reprinted by Pierre M. Irving in *Spanish Papers,* 2 vols., 1866, and the two omitted were identified by Stanley T. Williams in the *Life.* In addition, Wayne R. Kime in the *Miscellanies* has identified an editorial note on the "Defence of Fort M'Henry."

The title page varies slightly from year to year in the long list of secondary publishers printed after Moses Thomas of Philadelphia. The monthly numbers of the magazine were also issued in two bound illustrated volumes for each year, with an engraved vignette title as well as a conventional title page for each volume. An advertisement on the inside wrapper of the monthly issue for December 1814 offers the two yearly volumes bound: "boards, $6.50"; "half bound, morocco backs, $7.25"; "full bound in sheep, $7.25"; "half bound, calf gilt backs, $8.00."

* "The Works, in Verse and Prose, of the Late Robert Treat Paine, Jun." [review]. Anonymous. 1 (March 1813), [249]-266. Reprinted in *Spanish Papers*.

* Biography of Captain James Lawrence." Anonymous. 2 (August 1813), [122]-139. Reprinted in *An Account of the Funeral Honours Bestowed on the Remains of Capt. Lawrence and Lieut. Ludlow,* 1813, in five other collections, and in *Spanish Papers.*

* "Captain Lawrence." [an additional note to the Biography]. Anonymous. 2 (September 1813), 222-223. Reprinted in *Spanish Papers* as an untitled addendum to the Biography.

* "The Lay of the Scottish Fiddle: A Tale of Havre de Grace." [an introduction to and selections from James K. Paulding's poem; the poem not ascribed here to Paulding but described as "A little work, 'supposed to be written by Walter Scott, Esq.'"]. Anonymous. 2 (September 1813), 223-230.

* "Biographical Notice of the Late Lieutenant Burrows." Anonymous. 2 (November 1813), [396]-403. Reprinted in *A Compilation of Biographical Sketches of Distinguished Officers in the American Navy* by Benjamin Folsom, 1814, in one other collection, and in *Spanish Papers*.

* "Biographical Memoir of Commodore Perry." Anonymous. 2 (December 1813), 494-510. Reprinted, abbreviated, in *A Compilation of Biographical Sketches of Distinguished Officers in the American Navy* by Benjamin Folsom, 1814, in one other collection, and in *Spanish Papers*.

* "Traits of Indian Character." Anonymous. 3 (February 1814), 145-156. Reprinted, revised, in the fourth American edition of *The Sketch Book*, the first English edition, and all subsequent editions.

* *"Odes, Naval Songs, and Other Occasional Poems*, by Edwin C. Holland, Esq. Charleston." [review]. Anonymous. 3 (March 1814), 242-252. Reprinted in *Spanish Papers*.

* "Philip of Pokanoket: An Indian Memoir." Anonymous. 3 (June 1814), 502-515. Reprinted, revised, in the fourth American edition of *The Sketch Book*, the first English edition, and all subsequent editions.

* "Lord Byron." [a biographical and critical introduction]. Anonymous. 4 (July 1814), 68-72.

* "Biographical Memoir of Captain David Porter." Anonymous. 4 (September 1814), [225]-243. Reprinted in *Naval Biography; or Lives of the Most Distinguished American Naval Heroes*, 1815, and in *Spanish Papers*.

* "Defence of Fort M'Henry." [an editor's introduction, within square brackets, to the anonymous poem later to be known as "The Star Spangled Banner". Anonymous. 4 (December 1814), 433-434.

* "A Biographical Sketch of Thomas Campbell." Anonymous. 5 (March 1815), 234-250. First published in *The Poetical Works of Thomas Campbell*, 1810. "It has now been revised, corrected, and materially altered by the author."

There is a strong presumption, based upon Irving's surviving letters as well as his known character, that when Irving left the editorship and began his long stay in Europe he continued, after an interval, to write for *The Analectic*. It is known that he procured periodicals and scouted out books for republication by Moses Thomas. That can be proved from the letters. But his own writing for Thomas cannot be proved by external evidence; characteristically, he seems to have covered his tracks too thoroughly. But even so, the letters do support the assumption. A few seem particularly revealing.

On 21 January 1815, Irving wrote to Gulian C. Verplanck, "I told him [Moses Thomas] that should he continue the magazine on his own account, I should cheerfully contribute to it gratuitously for the purpose of setting him a going again." But his contributions appear not to have been altogether gratuitous. Irving drew money from Thomas from time to time to pay for the purchase of periodicals and the like, but in a letter of 22 March 1818 to Henry Brevoort, after discussing such a draft, he continued, "I now inclose the second of a set of Exchg on M Thomas for five hundred Dollars which I will thank you to collect[.] I shall draw on you when I have occasion for money for my current expenses...." It is perhaps suggestive that he asks Brevoort not to put the note in circulation but to account privately to Thomas for it. Shortly after that, Irving drew another draft on Thomas for five hundred dollars, and wrote Brevoort on 7 July 1818 that he hoped the drafts had been honored, since "I depend upon them for my ways & means." And then on 29 January 1822, when Irving had made a literary name for himself abroad and had solved many of his financial problems, he wrote his brother Ebenezer about the publication of *Bracebridge Hall*, "*I wish, expressly, Moses Thomas to have the preference over every other publisher*. I impress this upon you.... Whatever may have been his embarrassments and consequent want of punctuality, he is one who shewed a disposition to serve me, and who did serve me in the time of my necessity, and I should despise myself could I for a moment forget it."

During the year of 1817, the affairs of the firm of P. and E. Irving, with which Washington Irving worked occasionally at Liverpool, grew worse and worse. Bankruptcy proceedings were begun; in January of 1818, Washington and Peter appeared before the Commissioners on Bankruptcy, and in March the proceedings were complete, leaving Irving without any income from the company. This period, presumably, was "the time of my necessity." It would appear that Irving then, as he was to do later, turned to his pen in times of want. On 11 July 1817 he wrote to Henry Brevoort, "I have a plan which, with very little trouble, will yield me for the present a scanty but sufficient means of support.... I cannot at present explain to you what it is -- you would probably consider it precarious, & inadequate to my subsistence...." And on 24 April 1818 he wrote to his brother Ebenezer, "I feel confidant that I shall be able to rub along with my present means of support...." Just what "the plan" and the "means" were, we do not know (the future *Sketch Book*, of course, could not have offered present income). But it is reasonable to assume that Irving was writing for the periodicals, both English and American.

Even if the presumption is accepted that Irving was writing for *The Analectic*, identification of specific pieces must remain speculative, a matter of "possible" -- at best, "probable" -- rather than "certain." And yet, in conscience, the attempt must be made. After considerable study, the conclusion is defensible that one major likelihood of Irving's authorship lies in the reviews in *The Analectic* of current books and periodicals published in England during Irving's stay. That would be in keeping with his inclinations and opportunities, and would also be in keeping with his activity in collecting periodicals for Thomas. Reviews openly reprinted from British periodicals must be omitted, even though the possibility should be entertained that some may still be by Irving.

One recurring identification deserves particular mention. In July 1817, *The Analectic* began a monthly feature called "Notaria; or Miscellaneous Articles of Philosophy, Literature, and Politics." The first installment, in July, describes the intent: "We design ... to present our readers, every month, with a compendious view of the most interesting philosophical, literary, and political news, from both sides of the Atlantic. For this purpose we have chosen the title -- *Notaria* -- which, as our readers know, was the name given to the periodical dispatches received at Rome from the various quarters of her Empire. Such dispatches we should be grateful to receive from our countrymen, in the various parts of the United States." It is probable that Irving was supplying the British material each month. The editor, it will be noted, asks for no additional British news; and one month, March 1818, the British material obviously failed to arrive, suggesting a single source. But even if Irving were supplying the copy, it is possible to make a distinction between reprint material supplied and original writing for the feature. The following list contains only those columns that may well contain, in however small an amount, some original writing.

Possible Contributions by Irving

Review of *Memoirs of the Life and Writings of the Late John Coakley Lettsom* by Thomas Joseph Pettigrew. 10 (August 1817), [89]-99.

"Notaria." 10 (August 1817), 156-176.

"Analytical Notice of the Quarterly Review, No. XXXII. for April, 1817." 10 (September 1817), 220-233.

"Analysis of the Papers contained in the Edinburgh Review for March, 1817. No. 55." 10 (October 1817), [265]-298.

"Mr. Grenfell's Speech." [Introduction to a review from the *Monthly Magazine*]. 10 (November 1817), 404-405.

"Notaria." 10 (November 1817), 423-440.

"Notaria." 10 (December 1817), 510-519.

Review of *Travels in the Interior of America, in the Years 1809, 1810, and 1811* by John Bradbury. 11 (January 1818), 10-21.

"Tribute to departed Genius. Notice of the late right honourable R. B. Sheridan." 11 (January 1818), 27-34.

Review of *Rob Roy* by the author of *Waverley, Guy Mannering*, etc. 11 (April 1818), [273]-311.

Review of *Memoirs of the Life and Writings of Benjamin Franklin*, now first published from the original MSS. 11 (June 1818), [449]-484.

"Notaria." 11 (June 1818), 524-532.

"Life and Writings of James Hogg." 11 (May 1818), 414-421. Although not attributed in *The Analectic*, this life and evaluation was in fact first printed in *The Edinburgh Magazine* for January 1818.

Review of three works of travels in Italy: by "an American," by Joseph Forsyth, and by the Count de Stendhall. 12 (July 1818), [1]-36.

"Notaria," 12 (July 1818), 74-88.

"Madame de Stael." 12 (August 1818), [89]-106.

Review of *Views of England* by Maj. Gen. Pillet, and *The Truth Respecting England*, or An Impartial Examination of the Work of Mr. Pillet, by J. A. Vievard. 12 (September 1818), [177]-201.

Review of three works by William Hazlitt: *A View of the English Stage, Characters of Shakespeare's Plays,* and *Lectures on the English Poets.* 12 (September 1818), 201-219.

"Notaria." 12 (September 1818), 251-264.

Review of *Travels in Canada and the United States in 1816 and 1817* by Lt. Francis Hall. 12 (November 1818), 363-377.

Review of *Select, Political, Philosophical, and Miscellaneous Writings of Benjamin Franklin*, published from the Originals. 12 (December 1818), 462-482.

"Notaria." 13 (January 1819), 73-88.

"On the Edinburgh and Quarterly Reviews." 13 (February 1819), 116-127.

Review of *Florence Macarthy* by Lady Morgan. 13 (February 1819), 127-129.

"Notaria." 13 (February 1819), 169-176.

"Notaria." 13 (March 1819), 259-264.

Arcturus [New York].

"Mr. Mathews' Speech on the International Copyright." 3 (March 1842), 312-318. Begins by quoting a version of Irving's "sentiment" to International Copyright given at the public dinner for Charles Dickens, 18 February 1842. See the earlier account in the *New-York Tribune,* 19 February 1842. This speech by Mathews is reprinted in *The Various Writings of Cornelius Mathews,* New York: Harper & Brothers, 1843 (misprinted 1863). For a corrected full version of Irving's toast, see *The New World,* 5 March 1842.

The Ariel: A Literary Gazette [Philadelphia].

"The Discovery of America." 1 (5 April 1828), [192]-193. From *Columbus.*

"Sketches of Isabella of Spain." 2 (3 May 1828), 7. From *Columbus.*

Arkansas Gazette [Little Rock].

Letter to unnamed correspondent [Peter Irving], dated Washington City, 18 December 1832. (26 June 1833). The letter had appeared earlier in *The Athenæum,* 2 March 1833, and in other newspapers.

The Athenæum [London].

"Character of Columbus" and "Note" from the abridged *Columbus.* (13 March 1830), 148-149. In review of the Murray edition.

Extracts from *A Year in Spain* by a Young American. (26 February 1831), 135-136; continued (5 March 1831), 146-147. In review.

Irving's dedication to Samuel Rogers from *Poems,* by William Cullen Bryant. (3 March 1832), 143-144. In review.

"Dinner to Washington Irving." (14 July 1832), 458. Almost all of Irving's acceptance speech at his public dinner in New York. The text is credited to the account in the New York *American.*

* "Extract of a Letter from Washington Irving." Recipient not given [Peter Irving]; dated Washington City, December 18, 1832. On Irving's western trip. (2 March 1833), 137-138.

Extracts from *A Tour on the Prairies.* (7 March 1835), [177]-180. In review.

Extracts from *Abbotsford* and *Newstead Abbey.* (9 May 1835), [345]-346. In review.

Extracts from Theodore Irving's *The Conquest of Florida.* (15 August 1835), [609]-611. In review of the American edition.

["Florinda"]. (12 December 1835), [921]-923. In review of *Legends of the Conquest of Spain.*

Extracts from *Astoria.* (22 October 1836), [741]-748; continued (29 October 1836), 762-765. In review.

Extracts from *Captain Bonneville.* (13 May 1837), 341-343. In review.

Extract from the Memoir of Thomas Campbell. (12 March 1842), 222-223. In review of *The Poetry and History of Wyoming;* the book here attributed to Irving.

[The story of Don Manuel de Manara, with introductory extract]. (From "Don Juan: A Spectral Research"). (17 February 1855), 192-193. In review of *Wolfert's Roost.*

Extracts from *Life of Washington,* Vols. I-III. (16 August 1856), 1013-1015. In review of Bohn editions.

Extracts from *Life of Washington,* Vol. IV. (15 August 1857), 1031-1033. In review of Bohn edition.

The Atlantic Magazine [New York].

Extract from "The Adventure of the German Student." 2 (November 1824), 72-74. In notice of the London 1824 edition of *Bracebridge Hall.*

B

The Balance [Hudson, N. Y.].

"Letter from Mustapha Rub-A-Dub Keli Kahn, to Asem Hacchem." 6 (5 May 1807), 140-142. From *Salmagundi* No. VII.

"Plans for Defending Our Harbour, by William Wizard." 6 (8 September 1807), 284-285. From *Salmagundi* No. XIII.

La Belle Assemblée; Being Bell's Court and Fashionable Magazine [London].

"The Wife." N.S.20 (November 1819), 211-215. Anonymous; but signed EDWIN. From *The Sketch Book.*

"The Widow and Her Son." N.S.23 (May 1821), 208-211. From *The Sketch Book.*

"The Stout Gentleman." N.S.26 (Supplement, 1822), 542-546. In review of *Bracebridge Hall.*

Extracts from the abridged *Columbus.* 11 (April 1830), 181-182. In review.

The Belles-Lettres Repository [New York].

"The Wife." 1 (July 1819), 226-230. In notice of *The Sketch Book.*

Bentley's Miscellany [London].

"Wolfert's Roost." 6 (1839), 24-32; continued 159-164. From *The Knickerbocker,* April 1839.

"Sleepy Hollow." 6 (1839), 164-171. From *The Knickerbocker,* May 1839.

"Recollections of The Alhambra; The Abencerrage." 6 (1839), 185-194. From *The Knickerbocker,* June 1839.

"The Enchanted Island; The Adalantado of the Seven Cities." 6 (1839), 274-286. From *The Knickerbocker,* July 1839.

Blackwood's Edinburgh Magazine.

"The Royal Poet" and "The Country Church." 6 (February 1820), 556-561. From *The Sketch Book,* "now in the course of publication at New York." In article, "On the Writings of Charles Brockden Brown and Washington Irving."

Extracts from *A History of New York.* 7 (July 1820), 360-369. In review-notice of the 1812 New York edition.

Bolster's Quarterly Magazine [Cork, Ireland].

"A Biographical Sketch of Thomas Campbell, Esq." 1 (February 1826), 28-39. Reprinted, but source unknown.

Boston Daily Advertiser & Patriot.

Account of the public dinner for Irving, with some of the speeches by others omitted. (5 June 1832), [1]. "From the New-York American."

The Boston Literary Magazine.

"The Alhambra" and "Reflections on the Moslem Domination in Spain." 1 (July 1832), 149-152. In "review" of *The Alhambra,* with one brief paragraph of comment.

The Boston Weekly Magazine.

"The Pride of the Village." 1 (16 March 1839), 218-219. From *The Sketch Book.*

"Legend of Don Munio Sancho de Hinojosa." 2 (7 December 1839), 109-110. From *The Knickerbocker,* September 1839.

"Female Influence." 2 (25 January 1840), 168. From "The Wife," *The Sketch Book.*

"Legend of the Engulphed Convent." 2 (2 May 1840), [257]-258. From *The Knickerbocker,* March 1840.

The Bouquet: Flowers of Polite Literature [Hartford, Conn.].

"Sorrow for the Dead." 1 (19 May 1832), 196. From "Rural Funerals," *The Sketch Book.*

The British Critic [London].

Extracts from *The Sketch Book,* particularly from "English Writers on America." N.S.13 (June 1820), 645-654. In review of London edition of Vol. I.

Extracts from *Bracebridge Hall.* N.S.18 (September 1822), 299-311. In review.

Burton's Gentleman's Magazine [Philadelphia].

Extracts from *The Rocky Mountains.* 1 (July 1837), 71-75. In review.

C

*The Casket; Flowers of Literature, Wit and Sentiment (*later called *Atkinson's Casket; or Gems of Literature, Wit and Sentiment;* later called *The Casket, and Philadelphia Monthly Magazine;* the forerunners of *Graham's Lady's and Gentleman's Magazine;* later called *Graham's Illustrated Magazine) [Philadelphia].*

"On Passaic Falls -- Written in the Year 1806." 2 (February 1827), 68-69. From *The Atlantic Souvenir* for 1827.

"The Contented Man." 2 (March 1827), 92-93. From *The Literary Souvenir* for 1827.

"The Discovery of America." 3 (May 1828), 203-205. From *Columbus.*

Extracts from *Columbus.* 4 (December 1829), [529]-531. To accompany a portrait of Columbus.

"An Account of a Literary Dinner." 5 (August 1830), 367-368. From *Tales of a Traveller.* Printed anonymously, without credit to Irving or the source.

"Interior of the Alhambra." 7 (June 1832), 272-275. From *The Alhambra,* called here *The New Sketch Book,* "will be published in a few days."

Extract from *A Tour on the Prairies*. 10 (May 1835), 298-299. "We have been permitted to peruse a portion of the book in sheets...."

Extracts from *A Tour on the Prairies*. 10 (August 1835), 437-438.

"Lord Byron and Mary Chaworth." 10 (October 1835), 563-564. From *Newstead Abbey*.

"Legend of Count Julian and His Family." 10 (December 1835), 699-701. From *Legends of the Conquest of Spain*.

"The Ruined One." 10 (December 1835), 703-705. This is "The Pride of the Village," from *The Sketch Book*.

"An Unwritten Drama of Lord Byron." 10 (December 1835), 708. From *The Gift* for 1836.

"Washington Irving's First Breakfast with Scott." 11 (April 1836), 180. From *Abbotsford*.

"The Falls of the Passaic." 11 (May 1836), 264. Here credited to the Montreal Gazette.

"A Delicious Picture." 11 (July 1836), 364-365. From *Legends of the Conquest of Spain*.

"Perilous Passage of the Great Morass." 12 (October 1837), 471-472. From Theodore Irving's *The Conquest of Florida*.

Extract from "The Wife." 12 (October 1837), 474. From *The Sketch Book*.

"Anecdote of a Young Mexican and an Indian Girl." 13 (February 1838), 71. From *Capt. Bonneville*.

"The Moorish Drum." 16 (June 1840), [282]-283. Probably from the printed sheet music.

The Christian Examiner [Boston].

Letter, dated Sunny Side, 3 October 1855, on Worcester's Dictionary. 60 (May 1856), advertising supplement, unpaged. The advertisement accompanies a printing of *Recommendations of Worcester's Dictionaries*, 1856.

The Corrector [New York].

This short-lived journal, published in ten numbers from 28 March to 26 April 1804, was established to support and defend Aaron Burr. It was apparently edited by Irving's brother Peter under the pseudonym of Toby Tickler (although Washington late in his life denied that Peter was the editor, and said that the periodical was simply "thrown together occasionally by different hands"). At any rate, Peter invited Washington to contribute. Washington later told Pierre M. Irving -- who wrote an account of the matter for the *Life and Letters* but on second thought witheld the account from that work -- "They would tell me what to write, and then I'd dash away." The trouble now is that there is no outside evidence to use in determining which particular pieces Washington Irving wrote. And even in those for which attribution by internal evidence seems convincing, there is no way to know whether others may have collaborated in the writing. For a discussion of the problem, a list of attributions of varying degrees of probability, and a reprinting of attributed pieces, the interested reader should see Martin Roth's *Washington Irving's Contributions to The Corrector* (Minneapolis: University of Minnesota Press, 1968) and the *Miscellanies* volume of the Twayne edition, edited by Wayne R. Kime. Further information also appears in Kime's article, "Pierre M. Irving's Account of Peter Irving, Washington Irving, and the Corrector," *American Literature,* 43 (March 1971), 108-14.

My conservative list of attributions to Irving includes only the fifteen accepted by Kime, all of which are also accepted by Roth. The reader should be aware, however, that there were almost certainly more pieces written by Irving. Roth prints forty-five in all, and Kime offers a list of thirty-five "possibles" beyond the fifteen that he accepts, thirty of which are printed by Roth. Kime summarizes the two lists in his *Miscellanies* volume, pointing out that the large area of agreement between the two may bring with it some degree of confidence, at least in the independent recognition of a style that is probably Irving's.

* "Beware of Impostors!!" No. 2 (31 March 1804), 6, cols. 2-3.

* "Billy Luscious." No. 2 (31 March 1804), 7, cols. 1-2.

* "Aristidean Gallery of Portraits." No. 3 (4 April 1804), 11, col. 3.

* "The Congressional Fracas, A True Story." No. 4 (7 April 1804), 15, cols. 1-3.

* "Ebenezer." No. 5 (11 April 1804), 18, cols. 2-3. Title preceded by FOR THE CORRECTOR.

* "To Toby Tickler, Esq." No. 5 (11 April 1804), 19, cols. 2-3. Title preceded by COMMUNICATION.

* "To Toby Tickler, Esq." No. 6 (14 April 1804), 22, cols. 1-3.

* "Characteristic Portraits, Lately Added to the Shakespeare Gallery. (Continued.)." No. 7 (18 April 1804), 26, col. 3 - 27, col. 1.

* "Isaac." No. 7 (18 April 1804), 27, col. 2.

* "Col. Blubber." No. 7 (18 April 1804), 27, cols. 2-3.

* "To Toby Tickler, Esq." No. 8 (21 April 1804), 30, col. 3 - 31, col. 1.

* "Original Pictures for the Pandemonian Gallery. (Continued.)." No. 8 (21 April 1804), 31, cols. 1-2.

* "To Toby Tickler, Esq." No. 9 (24 April 1804), 33, col. 2 - 34, col. 1.

* "To Toby Tickler, Esq." No. 9 (24 April 1804), 34, cols. 1-3.

* "Rare Fun!!!" No. 10 (26 April 1804), 39, cols. 1-2.

The Critic: A Weekly Review [New York].

Extracts from *The Conquest of Granada.* 1 (25 April 1829), 400-404. With a few introductory words of review.

The Critical Review [London].

Extracts from *Salmagundi.* Third Series, 23 (July 1811), 316-322. In review of Lambert's edition.

* *The Congressional Globe [Washington, D.C.].*

Petition to the Congress for a law of international copyright. Signed by many, including Irving. Vol. 24 - Part 3 (20 July 1852), 1832. Read to the Senate by Charles Sumner, 19 July 1852.

D

The Dollar Magazine: A Monthly Gazette [New York].

"Parisian Sketches in 1825." 1 (January 1841), 3-6. From *The Knickerbocker,* December 1840.

The Dublin Literary Gazette.

Extracts and summary from *Columbus.* 1 (13 March 1830), 162-163. In review.

Dublin University Magazine.

Extracts from *A Tour on the Prairies.* 5 (May 1835), 554-572. In review.

Extracts and summary from *Astoria.* 9 (February 1837), 167-176. In review.

E

The Eclectic Review [London].

"John Bull." N.S.14 (October 1820), 293-296. In review of London edition of *The Sketch Book*.

Extracts from *Bracebridge Hall*. N.S.19 (March 1823), 233-243. In review.

The Edinburgh Literary Gazette.

Extracts and summary from *The Conquest of Granada*. 1 (June 1829), 71-72. In review.

Edinburgh Literary Journal.

Chapter on discovery of the Pacific by Vasco Nuñez de Balboa. 5 (22 January 1831), 63. In review of *Companions of Columbus*.

The Edinburgh Magazine and Literary Miscellany.

"The Author's Account of Himself," "The Voyage," "Rural Life in England." N.S.5 (September 1819), 207-213. In article, "Specimens of American Literature." Text from American edition of *The Sketch Book*.

"English Writers on America," "Rip Van Winkle." N.S.5 (October 1819), 317-329. From American edition of *The Sketch Book*.

Extracts from *Bracebridge Hall*. N.S.11 (July 1822), 91-96. In review.

The Edinburgh Monthly Review (after 1821 called *The New Edinburgh Review*).

Extracts from *The Sketch Book*. 4 (September 1820), 303-334. In review.

Extracts from *A History of New York*. 5 (February 1821), 232-248. In review.

Extracts from *Bracebridge Hall*. 2 (July 1822). 151-177. In review.

The Edinburgh Review, or Critical Journal.

Extracts from "Rip Van Winkle," "English Writers on America," "The Country Church." 34 (August 1820), 160-176. In review of London edition of *The Sketch Book*.

Extracts from *Columbus*. 48 (September 1828), [1]-32. In review of London edition.

Emerson's United States Magazine [New York].

Extracts from *Life of Washington.* Monthly, from 5 (July 1857), [1]-13 to 6 (June 1858), [565]-575.

The English Journal [London].

"Don Juan: A Spectral Research." 1 (5 June 1841), 357-360. From *The Knickerbocker,* March 1841.

The European Review [London].

"The Bold Dragoon" and "The Story of the Young Robber." 5 (1824), 124-135. In review of *Tales of a Traveller.*

The Evergreen: A Monthly Magazine of New and Popular Tales and Poetry [New York].

"Pelayo and the Merchant's Daughter." 1 (February 1840), 100-102. From *The Knickerbocker,* January 1840.

"The Knight of Malta; The Grand Prior of Minorca." 1 (March 1840), 155-158. From *The Knickerbocker,* February 1840.

"The Conspiracy of Neamathla." 1 (October 1840), 583-584. From *The Knickerbocker,* October 1840.

F

The Family Favorite, and Temperance Journal [Adrian, Mich.].

"The Adventure of a Mason." 1 (July 1850), 155-156. From *The Alhambra.*

G

The Gentleman's Magazine [London].

"A Village Politician." 92 (July 1822), 55. In review of *Bracebridge Hall.*

The Gentleman's Magazine [Philadelphia].

Extracts from *The Rocky Mountains.* 1 (July 1837), 71-75. In review.

Gold's London Magazine, and Theatrical Inquisitor.

See *London Magazine and Monthly Critical and Dramatic Review.*

The Gridiron [Dayton, Ohio].

"The Stout Gentleman." 1 (6 February 1823), 132-135 to 1 (27 February 1823), 155-157. From *Bracebridge Hall.*

The Guardian: A Family Magazine [The Female Institute, Columbia, Tenn.].

"Siege and Capture of Jerusalem." 8 (January and February 1850), 161-162. From *Mahomet and His Successors.*

Letter to Jesse Merwin, dated Sunny Side, February 12, 1851. 11 (May and June 1851), 51-52. Credited to the *Kinderhook Sentinel.*

H

The Hive [Waltham, Mass.].

"A Bee Hunt." 1 (15 August 1835). From *A Tour on the Prairies.*

Hudson's Dollar Magazine [New York].

"The Author's Apology." 2 (October 1848), 628-629. In review of Author's Revised Edition of *History of New York.*

Extracts from *The Sketch Book.* 2 (December 1848), 755-756. In review of the illustrated edition.

"The Voyage." 3 (April 1849), 207-208. In article on Irving. From *The Sketch Book.*

Extract from introduction to *A Book of the Hudson.* 3 (June 1849), 373. In review.

Account of Goldsmith's visit to Miss Horneck. 4 (September 1849), 572. From the Author's Revised Edition of *Goldsmith,* in sheets.

The Huntingdon Literary Museum, and Monthly Miscellany [Huntingdon, Penn.].

"Witchcraft of New England." 1 (June 1810), 263-267. From *History of New York.*

I

The Imperial Magazine [London].

Extracts from *Tales of a Traveller.* 7 (January 1825), 82-86. In review.

The International Magazine of Literature, Science and Art [New York].

"Campbell and Washington Irving." 1 (19 August 1850), 230-231. From Irving's letter on Campbell in William Beattie's *Life and Letters of Thomas Campbell,* 1850. The piece is here attributed to *The Albion.*

Letter to Andrew Wilson, dated Madrid, Dec. 24th, 1827. 3 (April 1851), 35. The letter is attributed to the *Art Journal.*

* Two letters to Rufus Griswold, dated Sunnyside, Sept. 18, 1851 and October, 1851, on James F. Cooper and the memorial committee to honor him. 4 (November 1851), 457, 460.

K

The Kaleidoscope; or, Literary and Scientific Mirror [Liverpool].

In August of 1819, *The Kaleidoscope* introduced *The Sketch Book* to the British audience; over the next fourteen months it reprinted the entire work, piece by piece. In the ensuing years, the periodical increasingly prided itself on having been the first to discover *The Sketch Book* in print, ignoring the similar--and roughly equal--claims of *The Literary Gazette.* By the issue of 11 June 1822, the editor is writing, "We were among the first, we might justly say the very first, to introduce some of the works of this gentleman to the English reader." In the issue of 14 September 1824, the editor praises the magazine as "the first medium through which Mr. Washington Irving's popular Sketch Book was introduced to the British public." And in 12 February 1828, the magazine is bragging that it had introduced *The Sketch Book* "almost before it was heard of in London." More modest claims began even earlier: from the reprinting of "Christmas" on 21 March 1820, through the reprinting of "The Broken Heart" on 23 May 1820, each piece is labeled "Never before published in this country," apparently an accurate claim.

The periodical's problems in obtaining a text for the early pieces from *The Sketch Book* are apparent in the editorial comments. The first piece, 24 August 1819 (attributed to "that elegant scholar, George Washington Irving"), is "copied from one of the latest New York papers." For the next two, 5 October 1819, a friend commissioned to procure the work itself in America had not yet arrived in New York, and the text is taken from *The Literary Gazette.* The source of the fourth, 12 October 1819, is not given but presumably was again *The Literary Gazette.* But copy for the fifth, 28 December 1819, "has just been received from a friend, who procured it for us in America." (Years later, on 12 February 1828, the friend is revealed as "the late much lamented Dr. Robert Taylor.") On 26 September 1820, the editor writes, "It was with pleasure and surprise ... that we found upon a second examination of the latter part of the Sketch Book, recently published in London, that two or three of these masterly compositions had escaped us," and proceeds forthwith to reprint them, even if not the first to do so.

"The Wife." 2 (24 August 1819), [25]-26. From *The Sketch Book;* text from "one of the latest New York papers."

"The Author's Account of Himself" and "The Voyage." 2 (5 October 1819), [49]-50. From *The Sketch Book;* text from *The Literary Gazette.*

"Roscoe." 2 (12 October 1819), 56. From *The Sketch Book;* text from *The Literary Gazette.*

"Rip Van Winkle." 2 (28 December 1819), [97]-99. From *The Sketch Book;* text from the American 1819 edition.

"Rural Life in England." 2 (4 January 1820), [101]-102. From *The Sketch Book.*

"The Art of Book Making." 2 (11 January 1820), [105]-106. From *The Sketch Book.*

"A Royal Poet." 2 (18 January 1820), [109]-110. From *The Sketch Book.*

"The Country Church." 2 (25 January 1820), [113]. From *The Sketch Book.*

"The Inn Kitchen" and "The Spectre Bridegroom." 2 (1 February 1820), [117]-119. From *The Sketch Book.*

"The Mutability of Literature." 2 (8 February 1820), [121]-122. From *The Sketch Book.*

"Christmas." 2 (21 March 1820), [141]. From *The Sketch Book.*

"The Stage Coach." 2 (28 March 1820), [145]-146. From *The Sketch Book.*

"Christmas Eve." 2 (4 April 1820), [149]-150. From *The Sketch Book.*

"Christmas Day." 2 (11 April 1820), [153]-154; continued 2 (18 April 1820), [157]-158. From *The Sketch Book.*

"The Pride of the Village." 2 (25 April 1820), [161]-162. From *The Sketch Book.*

"The Legend of Sleepy Hollow." 2 (2 May 1820), [165]-166; continued 2 (9 May 1820), [169]-172. From *The Sketch Book.*

"John Bull." 2 (16 May 1820), [173]-174. From *The Sketch Book.*

"The Broken Heart." 2 (23 May 1820), [177]. From *The Sketch Book.*

"Rural Funerals." 2 (30 May 1820), [181]-182. From *The Sketch Book*. The statement "Never before published in this country" does not appear on this printing; text from the first London edition?

"The Widow and Her Son." 2 (13 June 1820), [189]-190. From *The Sketch Book*.

"The Boar's Head Tavern, Eastcheap." 2 (20 June 1820), [193]-194. From *The Sketch Book*.

"Little Britain." New Series 1 (26 September 1820), [97]-100. From *The Sketch Book;* text attributed to the first London edition.

"The Angler." N.S.1 (3 October 1820), [105]-107. From *The Sketch Book*.

"Stratford-On-Avon." N.S.1. (10 October 1820), [113]-116; continued N.S.1 (17 October 1820), [121]-123. From *The Sketch Book*.

"Westminster Abbey." N.S.1. (31 October 1820), [137]-140. From *The Sketch Book*.

"The Rookery." N.S.2 (11 June 1822), [385]-387. From *Bracebridge Hall*.

"The Stout Gentleman." N.S.2 (18 June 1822), [393]-395. From *Bracebridge Hall*.

"Popular Superstitions." N.S.3 (16 July 1822), [9]. From *Bracebridge Hall*.

"Letter of Jonathan Oldstyle, Gen." N.S.4 (18 May 1824), 386.

"The Adventure of a German Student." N.S.5 (14 September 1824), [85]-86. From *Tales of a Traveller*.

"The American Usurer." N.S.5 (21 September 1824), 94-95. From "The Devil and Tom Walker," *Tales of a Traveller*.

"The Bold Dragoon." N.S.5 (28 September 1824), 110-111. From *Tales of a Traveller*.

"A Literary Dinner." N.S.5 (5 October 1824), 115. From *Tales of a Traveller*.

"The Contented Man." N.S.7 (21 November 1826), 163. From *The Literary Souvenir* for 1827.

Extracts from *The Life and Voyages of Christopher Columbus*. N.S.8 (12 February 1828), 265; continued N.S.8 (26 February 1828), 285-286; continued N.S.8 (4 March 1828), 291.

The Knickerbocker, or New-York Monthly Magazine.

In the March issue of 1839 the editor, Louis (or Lewis) Gaylord Clark, announced ecstatically that Irving had agreed to contribute regularly to the magazine: "In the words, then, of a brief circular to our agents..., we may state, that 'WASHINGTON IRVING, Esq.... has associated himself with this Magazine, as a regular and permanent contributor; and that there will appear, in every subsequent number, original articles from the pen of this delightful author....' The programme of GEOFFREY CRAYON, in preceding pages [i.e., "To the Editor of The Knickerbocker" in that issue], will assure the reader that his *heart* is in the matter; and if a new and copious 'Sketch-Book,' with abundant 'Tales of a Traveller,' to say nothing of important additions to KNICKERBOCKER'S veracious History, and anonymous tributes to different departments of the work, be not introduced to our readers through the pages of the KNICKERBOCKER, then we are no seer." (p. 264) In fact, a variety of original pieces -- a few anonymous, most pseudonymous under familiar or unfamiliar pen names -- appeared regularly from March 1839 to January 1841, and then irregularly and less frequently until October 1841.

"The Grand Prairie" and "A Buffalo Hunt." 5 (April 1835), [352]-355. In notice of *A Tour on the Prairies*, to be published "early in the present month."

[The close of the journey]. 5 (May 1835), 458-459. From *A Tour on the Prairies*.

"An Unwritten Drama of Lord Byron." 6 (August 1835), 142-144. From *The Gift* for 1836, described as "the forthcoming annual."

"The Widow's Ordeal: or a Judicial Trial by Combat." 8 (October 1836), [480]-496. In notice of *The Magnolia* for 1837. Text from preliminary "plates."

"The Creole Village. A Sketch from a Steam-Boat." 8 (November 1836), 601-604. In review of *The Magnolia* for 1837.

Extract from *Astoria*. 9 (January 1837), 88-90. In review.

["Lines Written at Stratford"]. 19 (August 1837), 151. In an anonymous article, not by Irving, "Random Passages, from Rough Notes of a Visit to England, Scotland, France, Switzerland, and Germany. Number Four." The poem had appeared earlier in *The Port Folio* and *The Albion*.

* "To the Editor of *The Knickerbocker*." Signed Geoffrey Crayon. 13 (March 1839), 206-210. Reprinted in *Spanish Papers* under the title, "Letter to the Editor of 'The Knickerbocker,' on Commencing His Monthly Contributions"; the first paragraph was also used as the first paragraph of the Introduction to *A Book of the Hudson*.

* "A Chronicle of Wolfert's Roost. Found Among the Papers of the Late Diedrich Knickerbocker." With an introductory letter, "To the Editor of the Knickerbocker," signed Geoffrey Crayon. 13 (April 1839), 317-328. Reprinted, without letter, in *Wolfert's Roost* under the title, "Wolfert's Roost."

* "Sleepy Hollow." Signed Geoffrey Crayon. 13 (May 1839), 434-437. Reprinted in *Wolfert's Roost.*

* "The Birds of Spring." Signed Geoffrey Crayon. 13 (May 1839), 434-437. Reprinted in *Wolfert's Roost.*

* "To the Editor of The Knickerbocker." Signed Hiram Crackenthorpe, of Saint Louis. [On the first locomotive]. 13 (May 1839), 445-446. Reprinted under the title, "The First Locomotive Again," in *The Knickerbocker Sketch-Book,* 1845.

* "The Abencerrage: A Spanish Tale." With an introduction, titled "Recollections of the Alhambra," signed Geoffrey Crayon. 13 (June 1839), 487-494. Reprinted in *The Romancist, and Novelist's Library,* Vol. III, 1840, and in *Wolfert's Roost.*

* "The Enchanted Island." The greater part is under the subtitle, "The Adalantado of the Seven Cities: A Legend of St. Brandan." Credited to The Author of The Sketch Book. 14 (July 1839), 26-38. An errata notice on p. 98 corrects the spelling to "Adelantado." Reprinted in *The Romancist, and Novelist's Library,* Vol. II, 1839, and in *Wolfert's Roost.*

* "National Nomenclature." In the form of a letter, "To the Editor of The Knickerbocker," signed Geoffrey Crayon. 14 (August 1839), 158-162. Reprinted in *Spanish Papers.*

* "Desultory Thoughts on Criticism." Signed G. C. 14 (August 1839), 175-178. Reprinted in *Spanish Papers.*

* "Legend of Don Munio Sancho de Hinojosa." With introductory letter, "To the Editor of The Knickerbocker," signed Geoffrey Crayon; introduction also titled "Spanish Romance." 14 (September 1839), 225-231. Reprinted, with letter, in *Spanish Papers.*

* "Communipaw." In the form of a letter, "To the Editor of the Knickerbocker," signed Hermanus Vanderdonk. 14 (September 1839), 257-262. Reprinted entire in *Spanish Papers.* Portions appear in a different piece with the same title, "Communipaw," an introductory essay to "Guests from Gibbet Island" in *A Book of the Hudson.*

* "Conspiracy of the Cocked Hats." In the form of a letter, "To the Editor of The Knickerbocker," signed Roloff Van Ripper. 14 (October 1839), 305-309. Reprinted entire in *Spanish Papers.* Portions appear in "Communipaw," an introductory essay to "Guests from Gibbet Island" in *A Book of the Hudson.*

* "Guests from Gibbet-Island." Under head title, "A Legend of Communipaw." With introductory letter, "To the Editor of the Knickerbocker Magazine," signed Barent Van Schaick. 14 (October 1839), 342-350. Reprinted in *The Knickerbocker Sketch-Book*, 1845, and in *A Book of the Hudson* and *Wolfert's Roost* without the letter and its pen name.

* "Mountjoy: or Some Passages Out of the Life of a Castle-Builder." Credited to Geoffrey Crayon, Gent. 14 (November 1839), 402-412 and 14 (December 1839), 522-538. At the end of the second installment appears the statement, "To Be Continued," but no continuation appears under this title in *The Knickerbocker*; see, however, the Editor's statement on p. 280 of the issue for August 1840, quoted below. Reprinted in *The Knickerbocker Sketch-Book*, 1845, and in *Wolfert's Roost*.

* "The Bermudas: A Shakespearian Research." The second part of the piece is entitled "The Three Kings of Bermuda, and Their Treasure of Ambergris." Credited to The Author of The Sketch-Book. 15 (January 1840), 17-25. Reprinted in *Wolfert's Roost*.

* "Pelayo and the Merchant's Daughter." Credited to The Author of The Sketch-Book. 15 (January 1840), 65-70. Reprinted, with revision and great addition, in *Spanish Papers* under the title, "The Legend of Pelayo."

* "To the Editor of The Knickerbocker." [A letter on international copyright]. Signed Washington Irving. 15 (January 1840), 78-79.

* "The Grand Prior of Minorca: A Veritable Ghost Story." With introductory letter, "To the Editor of The Knickerbocker," signed Geoffrey Crayon; introduction also titled "The Knight of Malta." 15 (February 1840), 108-118. Reprinted in *Wolfert's Roost*, with both titles.

* [Anecdote of Admiral Harvey]. Anonymous. 15 (February 1840), 166-167.

* "Legend of the Engulfed Convent." Credited to Geoffrey Crayon, Gent. 15 (March 1840), 234-237. Reprinted in *Wolfert's Roost*.

* "The Count Van Horn." Anonymous. 15 (March 1840), 241-249. Reprinted in *Wolfert's Roost*.

* "The 'Empire of the West.'" [Essay-review of an essay-review titled "Discovery Beyond the Rocky Mountains" in the *North American Review* for January 1840]. Anonymous. 15 (March 1840), 260-261.

* "The Wooden-Legged Ghost," by John Waters (pseud. for Henry Cary). In the table of contents for the volume, and in the "Editor's Table" at the end of the issue, the story is titled "The Iron Footstep" or "The Iron Foot-step." 15 (April 1840), 280-284. Irving acted as intermediary between author and publisher for the manuscript and for the proofs, provided the title of "The Iron Footstep," and may possibly have made some minor editorial suggestions. Inadvertently, editor L. Gaylord Clark's suggestion for a title, "The Wooden-Legged Ghost," appeared above the story itself, although Irving's title is substituted in other references. See Clark's discussion in the issue of April 1860 (although he fails to mention there the slip in printing the wrong title).

* "'A Time of Unexampled Prosperity.'" The titled section acts as an introduction to the major part, titled "The Great Mississippi Bubble." Anonymous. 15 (April 1840), 303-324. The Editor's discussion at the end of the issue refers to the piece as "the '*Mississippi Bubble*,' by Mr. IRVING." Reprinted in *Wolfert's Roost*.

* [Anecdote of "a colony of Patlanders" beset by headless goblins in modern Sleepy Hollow]. The author is identified only as "an estimable friend and correspondent at Tarrytown." 15 (April 1840), 349-350. The entire letter from which the anecdote is drawn is printed in the issue of April 1860, after Irving's death. The two texts differ in accidentals and in substantives.

* [Anecdote of the French Revolution]. Anonymous. 15 (April 1840), 351.

* "Abderahman: Founder of the Dynasty of the Ommiades in Spain." With introductory letter, "To the Editor of The Knickerbocker," signed G. C. Credited to The Author of the Sketch-Book. 15 (May 1840), 427-440. Reprinted, revised and without letter, in *Spanish Papers*.

* "The Taking of the Veil" and "The Charming Letoriéres [sic]." With introductory letter to the two related sketches, "To the Editor of The Knickerbocker," signed Geoffrey Crayon. 15 (June 1840), 513-519 and 519-521. Neither sketch reprinted until *The Crayon Papers*, 1883.

* "Letter from Granada." With introductory letter, "To the Editor of The Knickerbocker," signed G. C. 16 (July 1840), 57-61. Reprinted, revised, in the Author's Revised Edition of *The Alhambra*, 1850, under the title, "Public Fêtes of Granada." Reprinted in original form, with letter, in *Spanish Papers*.

* "The Early Experiences of Ralph Ringwood, Noted Down from His Conversations." Credited to Geoffrey Crayon, Gent. 16 (August 1840), 152-165; continued 16 (September 1840), 258-266. On p. 280 of the August issue, the Editor speaks of the pieces as "the remaining numbers of this 'Mountjoy of the West.'" Reprinted in *The Knickerbocker Sketch-Book*, 1845, and in *Wolfert's Roost*.

*   "The Seminoles." Divisional subtitles: "Origin of the White, the Red, and the Black Men: A Seminole Tradition"; and "The Conspiracy of Neamathla: An Authentic Sketch." Unsigned, but with Editor's heading, "The Crayon Papers." 16 (October 1840), 339-347. Reprinted in *Wolfert's Roost*.

*   "Sketches in Paris in 1825, From the Travelling Note-Book of Geoffrey Crayon." Divisional subtitles: "A Parisian Hotel"; "My French Neighbor"; "The Englishman at Paris." 16 (November 1840), 425-430. Continued 16 (December 1840), 519-530. The continuation with introductory letter, "To the Editor of The Knickerbocker," signed Geoffrey Crayon. Divisional subtitles: "English and French Character"; "The Tuilleries and Windsor Castle"; "The Field of Waterloo"; "Paris at the Restoration." Reprinted, without letter, in *Wolfert's Roost*.

Selections from *The Life of Goldsmith*. 16 (November 1840), [442]-445. An editorial note attributes the selections to proof sheets of the two-volume Harper edition of 1840, "now passing through the press."

*   "Broek: or The Dutch Paradise." Credited to Geoffrey Crayon, Gent. 17 (January 1841), 55-58. Reprinted in *Wolfert's Roost*.

*   "Don Juan: A Spectral Research." Credited to Geoffrey Crayon, Gent. 17 (March 1841), 247-253. Reprinted in *Wolfert's Roost*.

*   "American Researches in Italy. Life of Tasso; Recovery of a Lost Portrait of Dante." In the form of a letter, "To the Editor of The Knickerbocker," signed G. C. 18 (October 1841), 319-322. Not reprinted until *The Crayon Papers*, 1883.

"The Legend of Don Roderick." Credited to The Author of The Sketch-Book. 23 (March 1844), 262-275; continued 23 (April 1844), 324-336; continued 23 (May 1844), 418-430. Reprinted from *Legends of the Conquest of Spain*. Curiously, the Editor in a comment in the March issue, p. 287, says that the text is taken from a recently-reported London edition by Murray, since the book "was never republished in this country" and "We have good reason to believe it has been encountered by few if any readers on this side of the Atlantic." The book was, of course, originally published in Philadelphia in 1835 as the third volume of *The Crayon Miscellany*.

"A Passage from a Legend of the Subjugation of Spain." Credited to The Author of The Sketch-Book. This extended reprinting, which taken in conjunction with earlier and later extracts in *The Knickerbocker* reproduces most of *Legends of the Conquest of Spain*, requires four installments: 23 (June 1844), 572-577; 24 (July 1844), 52-60; 24 (August 1844), 165-172; 24 (September 1844), 246-256. Presumably it is again taken from a London edition.

"Legend of Count Julian and His Family." Credited to The Author of The Sketch Book. 24 (October 1844), 350-357. From *Legends of the Conquest of Spain*.

* Brief comment on value to a man of the Hudson scenery. 32 (September 1848), 276. From "one of his communications to this magazine."

"Preface" to the Author's Revised Edition of *The Sketch Book*. 32 (October 1848), 377-379. From "early sheets of the volume."

Extract from "Wolfert Webber, or Golden Dreams." 33 (May 1849), 448-449. In review of *A Book of the Hudson*.

Extract from *A Tour on the Prairies*. 33 (June 1849), 537. In review of the Author's Revised Edition.

Extracts from *Oliver Goldsmith*. 34 (October 1849), [348]-351. In review of the Author's Revised Edition.

* Letter to L. Gaylord Clark, dated Sunnyside, October 6, 1851. On James F. Cooper. 38 (November 1851), 561-562. The letter is reprinted in the issue of February 1860.

Extracts from "Legend of Sleepy Hollow" and "The Widow and Her Son." 50 (August 1857), 194-196. From *The Sketch Book*.

The greater part of "To the Editor of The Knickerbocker," reprinted from the issue of March 1839. 54 (October 1859), 428-430.

Posthumous Original Writing

(Since *The Knickerbocker* was associated so closely with Irving, it seems fitting to list his letters published in the magazine immediately after his death.)

* Letter to George P. Putnam, dated Sunnyside, December 27, 1852. A three-page facsimile. 55 (January 1860), tipped in before the first page.

* Letter to L. Gaylord Clark, undated. In "Washington Irving upon the Late Fenimore Cooper," by Louis Gaylord Clark. 55 (January 1860), 94-95.

* Three letters to L. Gaylord Clark: Sunnyside Cottage, July 8, 1841; Sunnyside, July 28, 1847; New-York, April 27, 1849. In "Memorial of Washington Irving," by Louis Gaylord Clark. 55 (January 1860), 113-118.

* Letter to Abdiel S. Thurston, dated Sunnyside, December 11, 1855. Five letters to L. Gaylord Clark: Sunnyside, October 6, 1851; Sunnyside, April 10, 1852; Greenburgh, December 21, 1839; Sunnyside, June 14, 1855; Sunnyside, September 18, 1854. In "Reminiscences of the Late Washington Irving: Number Two," by Louis Gaylord Clark. 55 (February 1860), 222-233. The letter of 6 October 1851 was earlier published in the issue of November 1851.

* Letter to W. P. Van Ness, dated New-York, December 18, 1809. Letter to L. Gaylord Clark, dated Greenbush [Greenburgh], March 17, 1840. In "Reminiscences of the Late Washington Irving," by Louis Gaylord Clark. 55 (April 1860), 439-444. The letter to Clark contains the anecdote of "a colony of Patlanders" published in the issue of April 1840.

L

The Ladies Companion [New York].

"Catskill Mountains." (To accompany an engraving by A. B. Durand) 3 (May 1835), 1. From "Rip Van Winkle," *The Sketch Book.*

Extract from "The Wife." 4 (November 1835), 13. From *The Sketch Book.*

The Ladies' Garland [Harpers Ferry, Va.].

"Adventure of a German Student." 1 (22 January 1825), [197]-198. From *Tales of a Traveller.*

The Ladies' Literary Cabinet [New York].

"Philip of Pokanoket." N.S. 2 (26 August 1820), [121]-123; continued 2 (2 September 1820), [129]-131. From *The Sketch Book.*

The Ladies' Monthly Museum; or, Polite Repository of Amusement and Instruction [London].

"The Wife." (With engraved illustration by Charles Heath) Improved Series 24 (September 1826), [121]-124. From *The Sketch Book.*

Ladies Museum [Providence, R. I.].

"The Story of the Young Robber." 1 (20 May 1826). From *Tales of a Traveller.*

The Ladies' Pearl, and Literary Gleaner [Lowell, Mass.].

"Female Influence." 1 (June 1840), 10. From "The Wife," *The Sketch Book.*

"The Bride." 1 (July 1840), 42-43. From "The Wedding," *Bracebridge Hall*.

The Ladies' Repository [New York].

"Our Changing Sky and Climate." 12 (February 1852), 75. From "The Catskill Mountains" in *The Home Book of the Picturesque*, 1852.

The Lady's Book [Philadelphia].

"The Grave." 6 (February 1833), 80. From "Rural Funerals," *The Sketch Book*.

The Lady's Magazine; or Entertaining Companion for the Fair Sex [London].

["Little Britain" under the title, "Sketch Book"]. N.S.2 (May 1821), 248-256. From *The Sketch Book*.

Extracts from "The German Student" and "The Young Robber." N.S.5 (September 1824), 484-491. In review of *Tales of a Traveller*.

Democratic Press and Lansingburgh Advertiser [Lansingburgh, N. Y.].

"Adventures of a Mason." (23 February 1839). From *The Alhambra*.

The Leeds Correspondent.

Extracts from *Bracebridge Hall*. 4 (July 1822), 185-195. In review.

The Literary Chronicle and Weekly Review [London].

Extracts from "English Writers on America" and "The Broken Heart." 2 (18 March 1820), [177]-180. In review of the London 1820 edition of *The Sketch Book*, Vol. I.

Extracts from "The Wife" and "The Country Church." 2 (25 March 1820), 195-197. In continuation of review.

Extracts from "The Mutability of Literature." 2 (1 April 1820), 216-218. In continuation of review.

Extracts from "Little Britain." 2 (26 August 1820), 546-549. In review of the London 1820 edition of *The Sketch Book*, Vol. II.

Extracts from "The Stage Coach" and "The Pride of the Village." 2 (2 September 1820), 565-568. In continuation of review.

Extracts from *A History of New York*. 2 (7 October 1820), [641]-644; continued 2 (14 October 1820), 659-661; continued 2 (21 October 1820), 678-681. In review of the London edition of 1820.

Extracts from "The Author," "Family Reliques," and "Ready Money Jack." 4 (25 May 1822), [321]-324. In review of *Bracebridge Hall*, "published too late in the week for us to enter into a critical analysis."

Extracts from "Love Charms," "A Village Politician," and "Gipsies." 4 (1 June 1822), 344-347. From *Bracebridge Hall*. "We resume our extracts."

Extracts from "The Tabard Inn," "Travelling," and "The Author's Farewell." 4 (8 June 1822), 358-360. In continuation.

[Description of Aunt Charity Cockloft]. 5 (13 December 1823), 791-793. From *Salmagundi* No. IX. In review of the London edition of 1823.

Extracts from "A Literary Dinner," "Notoriety," and "Story of the Young Robber." 6 (28 August 1824), [545]-549. In review of *Tales of a Traveller*.

Extracts from "The Young Italian" and "Kidd the Pirate." 6 (4 September 1824), 563-567. In continuation of review.

Extracts from *Columbus*. 10 (23 February 1828), 118-120; continued 10 (22 March 1828), 184-185. In review.

The Literary Emporium; A Compendium [New York].

"Sorrow for the Dead." 5 (January 1847), 28-29. From "Rural Funerals," *The Sketch Book.*

The Literary Gazette, and Journal of the Belles Lettres [London].

Under the editorship of William Jerdan from 1817 to 1850, *The Literary Gazette* paid particular attention to Irving and took pride in claiming to have been the first to print extracts from *The Sketch Book* in England. As Jerdan said in his autobiography, "No doubt, without my aid, the beautiful American canoe would soon have been safely launched on the British waters; but as it was, I had the pleasure and honour to launch it at once, fill the sails, and send it on its prosperous voyage." (In fact, *The Kaleidoscope* of Liverpool beat the London periodical by about a month in the first publication of the first piece from *The Sketch Book*, but had to take its second and third installments from *The Literary Gazette*. Over the ensuing months the two periodicals stayed about even, although *The Kaleidoscope* eventually printed the entire work. In Scotland, to make a fine geographical distinction and further complicate the chronology, *The Edinburgh Magazine* published five pieces in September and October 1819.) After that auspicious beginning, *The Literary Gazette* continued to foster Irving: it said in a review of *A Tour on the Prairies* in the number for 7 March 1835, "As the fame of Irving grew, more than fulfilling all our prognostics, we felt as if we had more than a common interest in the success we had been the first to predict."

Issued under the title of *The Literary Gazette* on stamped paper and *The London Literary Gazette* on unstamped, the periodical was also available "collected and stitched up" in quarterly parts or annual volumes. Its "reviews" of Irving's works were, typically, little more than a few words of introduction to lengthy extracts. In this listing, therefore, they are considered primarily as extracts rather than reviews, although the fact of the ostensible review is noted.

"The Author's Account of Himself" and "The Voyage." No. 140 (25 September 1819), 617-620. From the American 1819 edition of *The Sketch Book*.

"Roscoe." No. 141 (2 October 1819), 634-635. From the American 1819 edition of *The Sketch Book*.

"The Wife." No. 142 (9 October 1819), 648-650. From the American 1819 edition of *The Sketch Book*.

"The Art of Book-Making." No. 168 (8 April 1820), 228-229. In review of the London 1820 edition of *The Sketch Book*.

"John Bull." No. 183 (22 July 1820), [465]-467. From the London 1820 edition of *The Sketch Book*.

Extracts from *A History of New York*. No. 196 (21 October 1820), 674-676; continued No. 197 (28 October 1820), 695-696; continued No. 198 (4 November 1820), 707-709. In review of the London 1820 edition.

"The Rookery." No. 280 (1 June 1822), 340-341. In review of *Bracebridge Hall*.

"The Adventure of a German Student." No. 397 (28 August 1824), 545-546. In review of *Tales of a Traveller*.

"The Young Robber." No. 398 (4 September 1824), 566-568. In continuation of the review of *Tales of a Traveller*.

"The Contented Man." No. 512 (11 November 1826), [705]-706. In review of *The Literary Souvenir* for 1827.

Extract from *The Life and Voyages of Columbus*. No. 576 (2 February 1828), [65]-67. In review of the London 1828 edition; "will appear in the course of the ensuing month."

Extract from *The Conquest of Granada*. No. 644 (23 May 1829), [329]-331. In review.

Extract from *The Companions of Columbus*. No. 731 (22 January 1831), 55-56. Ostensibly in continuation of the review.

Extract from *A Tour on the Prairies*. No. 946 (7 March 1835), 146-148. In review.

Extracts from *Abbotsford* and *Newstead Abbey*. No. 955 (9 May 1835), 292-294. In review.

Extracts from Theodore Irving's *The Conquest of Florida*. No. 975 (26 September 1835), 613-616; continued No. 976 (3 October 1835), 632-633. In review of the London 1835 edition.

"Story of the Marvellous and Portentous Tower." No. 986 (12 December 1835), 787-788. Ostensibly in continuation of the review of *Legends of the Conquest of Spain*.

Extract from "Count Julian and His Family." No. 988 (26 December 1835), 827-828. Ostensibly in continuation of the review of *Legends of the Conquest of Spain*.

Extracts from *Astoria*. No. 1031 (22 October 1836), 673-676; continued No. 1034 (12 November 1836), 728-729. In review.

Extracts from *Adventures of Capt. Bonneville*. No. 1060 (13 May 1837), 300-302. In review.

Extracts from *Wolfert's Roost*. No. 1984 (27 January 1855), 53-54. In review.

Extracts from *Life of Washington*, Vol. I. No. 2005 (23 June 1855), 387-389. In review of the London 1855 edition.

Extracts from *Life of Washington*, Vol. II. No. 2040 (23 February 1856), 115-116. In review of the London 1856 edition.

Extracts from *Life of Washington*, Vol. IV. No. 2118 (22 August 1857), 800-802. In review of the London 1857 edition.

The Literary Guardian [London].

["Legend of the Three Beautiful Princesses"]. 2 (5 May 1832), [65]-68. In notice of *The Alhambra*.

Literary Inquirer: Repertory of Literature, Science and General Intelligence [Buffalo, N. Y.].

"The Wife." 3 (3 September 1854), 54-55. From *The Sketch Book*.

The Literary Magnet [London].

"The Bold Dragoon." 2 (1824), 204-208. In notice of *Tales of a Traveller*.

"The Young Robber." 2 (1824), 243-247. From *Tales of a Traveller*.

"A Contented Man." N.S.2 (December 1826), 338-340. In notice of *The Literary Souvenir* for 1827.

The Literary Sketch-Book [London].

Extracts from *Salmagundi*. 1 (13 December 1823), 275-296. In review.

The Literary Tablet [New Haven, Conn.].

"The Pride of the Village." 2 (12 October 1833), [105]-107. From *The Sketch Book*.

The Literary World [New York].

This was an influential literary journal of its time, edited by Evert Duyckinck from February 1847 to April 1847, by Charles Fenno Hoffman from May 1847 to September 1848, and by Evert Duyckinck and his younger brother George from October 1848 to December 1853.

Extract from *Salmagundi* No. I, on 'Sbidlikins the Cockney. 1 (3 July 1847), 514.

"Van Corlear's Horn." 3 (19 August 1848), 568-569. From "the forthcoming" Author's Revised Edition of *History of New York*.

"The Author's Apology" and other extracts from *History of New York*. 3 (2 September 1848), 605-607. In review of the Author's Revised Edition.

Extracts from "Sunday in London." 3 (7 October 1848), 704-705. In review of the Author's Revised Edition of *The Sketch Book*.

"Gold Hunting." 3 (23 December 1848), 951. From the Author's Revised Edition of *Columbus*, "to be published shortly."

Conclusion of "Introduction" to *A Book of the Hudson*. 4 (14 April 1849), 343. In advertisement for the book, "just published."

"Goldsmith on His Travels." 5 (21 July 1849), 50-51. From "the forthcoming new Life," the Author's Revised Edition.

"Leaves from Irving's Goldsmith." 5 (15 September 1849), 221-222.

"Night Journey of the Prophet from Mecca to Jerusalem; and Thence to the Seventh Heaven." 5 (8 December 1849), [485]-487. "In advance" from Vol. 1 of *Mahomet and His Successors*.

Extracts from Vol. 1 of *Mahomet and His Successors*. 5 (22 December 1849), 537-539; continued 5 (29 December 1849), 560-561.

"Siege and Capture of Jerusalem." 6 (9 February 1850), [121]-122. "In advance" from Vol. 2 of *Mahomet and His Successors*.

"The Traitor Lover" and "The Prophet Queen Cahina." 6 (27 April 1850), 415-416. From Vol. 2 of *Mahomet and His Successors*, introduced by a few words of review.

Letter to Jessie Merwin, dated Sunny Side, February 12, 1851. 8 (8 March 1851), 193. "Has got into the papers through the *Kinderhook Sentinel*."

Testimonial for Webster's Dictionary: "I find it an invaluable *vade mecum*." 8 (17 May 1851), 407. In advertisement.

* Letter to James W. Beekman, Chairman of "The Senate Committee of Literature," State of New York, dated Sunnyside, June 25, 1851. 9 (26 July 1851), 68. In "Report of Minority of Committee on Literature in Reference to the Purchase by School Districts of Webster's Dictionary."

Extracts from letter to G. and C. Merriam, dated by them February 1849. 9 (13 September 1851), 215. In advertisement.

"The Story of the Enchanted Soldier." 9 (18 October 1851), 307-308. A summary and long extract, in review of the Illustrated Edition of *The Alhambra*.

"The Catskill Mountains." 9 (1 November 1851), 350-351. From an advance copy of *The Home Book of the Picturesque*.

* Letter to Henry R. Schoolcraft, dated Sunnyside, October 20, 1851. 9 (15 November 1851), 389. A letter on the rights of authors to keep their work unchanged by the copyright holder; with an accompanying note to the editors from Schoolcraft.

* A note to the editors, dated November 10, 1851, forwarding a letter to Henry R. Schoolcraft dated Sunnyside, November 10, 1851, correcting a misstatement about *Astoria*. 9 (22 November 1851), 408.

"The Portrait of Columbus -- Letter of Washington Irving." A letter to William C. Bryant, undated. 10 (24 January 1852), 73-74. An editorial introduction explains: "A correspondence took place, not long since, between Joseph E. Bloomfield and Washington Irving, on the subject of the different portraits of Columbus." "At his request the correspondence has been returned to him, and in the following letter he has recast, with some additions, the information and observations contained in his more hasty notes...." First published in the *New-York Evening Post*, 26 December 1851.

Littell's Living Age [Boston].

"The Catskill Mountains." 31 (29 November 1851), 408-410. Described as "a chapter from Mr. Putnam's 'The Home-Book of the Picturesque.'"

Letter to Henry R. Schoolcraft, dated Sunnyside, Monday, November 10, 1851. 32 (17 January 1852), 104. Credited to *The Literary World*.

Extracts from *Life of Washington*, in reprint of review of Bohn Vol. IV from *The Athenæum*. 55 (17 October 1857), 177-181.

The London Magazine.

"The Broken Heart." 2 (September 1820), 281-284. In review of *The Sketch Book*.

Extracts from *History of New York*. 2 (December 1820), 577-588. In review.

* "English Eating." Signed V. 4 (September 1821), 246-249. A tentative identification, based upon an apparent identification in MSS. on the magazine in NN.

* "Peter Klaus, The Legend of the Goatherd. -- Rip Van Winkle." 5 (March 1822), 229-230. Attributed to Irving in Frank P. Riga and Claude A. Prance, *Index to the London Magazine*, 1978.

Extracts from *Columbus*. N.S.10 (1 March 1828), [281]-325. In review.

The London Weekly Review.

Extracts from *Columbus*. 2 (9 February 1828); continued 2 (16 February 1828); continued 2 (23 February 1828). In review.

M

The Magnolia; or, Literary Tablet [Hudson, N. Y.].

"The Broken Heart." 1 (17 May 1834), 270-272. From *The Sketch Book*.

The Maryland Gazette [Annapolis, Md.].

Extract from *A Tour on the Prairies*. (30 April 1835), [1].

"A Bee Hunt." (28 May 1835), [1]. From *A Tour on the Prairies*.

"The Widow and Her Son." (22 October 1835), [1]. From *The Sketch Book*.

"Westminster Abbey." (17 December 1835), [1]. From *The Sketch Book*.

The Masonic Miscellany and Ladies' Literary Magazine [Lexington, Ky.].

"The Stout Gentleman." 2 (July 1822), 25-27; continued 2 (August 1822), 71-78. From *Bracebridge Hall*.

"The Bachelor." 2 (September 1822), 102-104. From *Bracebridge Hall*.

The Mirror of Literature, Amusement, and Instruction [London].

"Lines, Written on the Falls of the River Pasaic, in the United States." 2 (29 November 1823), 452-453. First published in the *Weekly Visitor*, New York.

"New York Theatre." 3 (24 April 1824), 269-271. Letter III from *Letters of Jonathan Oldstyle*.

"The Young Robber." 4 (4 September 1824), 187-191. From *Tales of a Traveller*.

"A Contented Man." 8 (16 December 1826), 396-398. From *The Literary Souvenir* for 1827.

"Discovery of America." 11 (16 February 1828), 108-111. From *Columbus*.

Extracts from *Columbus*. 11 (Supplementary Number, 16 February 1828), [129]-137.

"Spanish Scenery." 19 (19 May 1832), 307-309. From *The Alhambra*.

"Interior of the Alhambra" and other extracts. 19 (Supplementary Number, 2 June 1832), 338-342. In review of *The Alhambra*.

"Spanish Characteristics." 19 (2 June 1832), 361. From *The Alhambra*.

Extracts from *A Tour on the Prairies*. 25 (28 March 1835), 196-200.

"Character of Sir Walter Scott." 25 (Supplementary Number, 23 May 1835), 352. From *Abbotsford*.

"Robin Hood and Sherwood Forest." 26 (4 July 1835), 12-14. From *Newstead Abbey*.

"Plough Monday." 26 (18 July 1835), 42-43. From *Newstead Abbey*.

"Story of the Marvellous and Portentous Tower." 27 (23 January 1836), 59-62. From *Legends of the Conquest of Spain*.

"Legend of Count Julian and His Family." 27 (6 February 1836), 92-93; continued 27 (13 February 1836), 104-106. From *Legends of the Conquest of Spain*.

Extracts from *Capt. Bonneville*. 29 (3 June 1837), 356-360.

Extract from *Columbus*. 35 (11 January 1840), 30-31.

Extracts from "The Legend of Sleepy Hollow," to accompany an illustration of "Washington Irving's Cottage, on the Banks of the Hudson River." 38 (17 July 1841), [35]-36. From *The Sketch Book*.

Extracts from the Life of *Margaret Miller Davidson*. N.S.2 (29 October 1842), 282-284.

The Miscellaneous Magazine [Trenton, N.J.].

"Sorrow for the Dead." Anonymous. 1 (January 1824), 14-15. From "Rural Funerals," *The Sketch Book*.

"The Broken Heart." 1 (May 1824), [97]-100. From *The Sketch Book*.

Missouri Intelligencer and Boon's Lick Advertiser [Columbia, Mo.].

Letter to unnamed correspondent [Peter Irving], dated Washington City, 18 December 1832. (11 May 1833). The letter had appeared earlier in *The Athenæum*, 2 March 1832, and in other newspapers.

The Monthly Anthology, and Boston Review.

[Portrait of Wouter Van Twiller, and Picture of the Hudson]. 8 (February 1810), 123-128. In review of 1809 edition of *History of New York*.

The Monthly Register, Magazine, and Review [New York].

"Letter of Mustapha Rub-A-Dub Keli Kahn" and other extracts. 3 (August 1807), 146 (mispaged 156)-154. In review of what is described as the Longworth volume, pp. 188. The Mustapha letter is from No. IX.

The Monthly Repository [London].

[On the Indian character]. N.S.9 (1835), 288-289. In notice of *A Tour on the Prairies*, presumably the London edition.

Extracts from *Legends of the Conquest of Spain*. N.S.10 (February 1836), 81-89. In review of the London edition.

The Monthly Repository, and Library of Entertaining Knowledge [New York].

"Genius." 3 (September 1832), 140. From "Roscoe," *The Sketch Book*.

The Monthly Review [London].

Extracts from *The Sketch Book*. 93 (October 1820), 198-207. In review of London edition.

Extracts from *Conquest of Granada*. N.S.3 (July 1829), 430-445. In review of London edition.

Extracts from *Companions of Columbus*. New and Improved Series 1 (February 1831), 244-253. In review of London edition.

Extracts from *The Alhambra*. N.I.S. 2 (June 1832), 221-247. In review of London edition.

Extracts from *Abbotsford* and *Newstead Abbey*. N.I.S. 4 (June 1835), 225-240. In review of London edition.

Extracts from *Astoria*. N.I.S. 4 (December 1836), 487-498. In review of London edition.

Mount Vernon Record [Philadelphia].

"Washington as a Farmer." 1 (November 1858), [33]-34. From *Life of Washington*.

"The Last Scene of Washington's Life." 2 (August 1859), 26-27. From *Life of Washington*.

* Facsimile of note to Mary M. Hamilton, dated Sunnyside Feb 17th. 1859. 2 (extra issue, between November and December 1859), 97.

The Museum of Foreign Literature and Science [Philadelphia].

Extracts from *Columbus*, in a review reprinted from *The London Weekly Review*. 13 (May 1828), 23-35.

Extracts from *Conquest of Granada*, in a review reprinted from *The Quarterly Review*. 17 (September 1830), 253-265.

Letter to unnamed correspondent [Peter Irving], dated Washington City, December 18, 1832. 22 (May 1833), 714-716. Reprinted from *The Athenæum*.

Extracts from Theodore Irving's *Conquest of Florida*, in a review reprinted from *The Spectator*. 28 (February 1836), 130-132.

Extracts from *Astoria*, in reviews reprinted from *The Spectator* and *The Athenæum*. 30 (December 1836), 498-505.

N

National Anti-Slavery Standard [New York].

Letter to Jesse Merwin, 12 February 1851, on old times in Kinderhook. (20 March 1851). First published in The *New-York Evening Post*, 1 March 1851.

* Letter to James W. Beekman, 25 June 1851, on Webster's Dictionary. (24 July 1851). Also published in the contemporary Dictionary Pamphlets and advertisements.

The National Pilot [New Haven, Conn.].

"A Village Politician." 1 (15 August 1822), [4]. From *Bracebridge Hall*.

"Detention by Bad Weather at an Inn" and "Ancient and Modern Spain." 1 (22 August 1822), [4]. From "The Stout Gentleman" and "The Student of Salamanca," *Bracebridge Hall*.

"The Widow's Retinue." 2 (10 April 1823), [4]. From *Bracebridge Hall*.

[On England and America]. 2 (17 April 1823), [4]. From "The Author's Farewell," *Bracebridge Hall*.

National Recorder [Philadelphia].

"Love in Woman." 2 (14 August 1819), [97]-98. From "The Broken Heart," *The Sketch Book*.

"To My Books," by Roscoe. 2 (28 August 1819), 144. "Extracted from 'Roscoe,' in Mr. Irvine's 'Sketch Book, No. 1.'"

The New England Family Magazine [Boston].

"The Birds of Spring." 1 (June 1845), 205-207. From *The Knickerbocker*, May 1839.

The New Mirror of Literature, Amusement, and Instruction [New York].

"Early History of New-York." 1 (29 April 1843), [49]-51. From *History of New York*.

"The Wife." In a separate supplement with the separate title, "Mirror Library: Sands of Gold, No. 1." 1844. An advertisement in the more conventional magazine supplement following the issue of 28 September 1844: "Persons remitting $5, will receive the NEW MIRROR for one year and TWENTY NUMBERS of this beautiful LIBRARY."

The New Monthly Magazine [London].

"The Art of Book Making," and shorter extracts. 13 (March 1820), 303-308. In review of the American edition of *The Sketch Book*.

Extracts from *Columbus*. 22 (March 1828), [288]-296. In review of London edition.

The New World [New York].

Quarto Edition.

"The Early Experiences of Ralph Ringwood." 1 (8 August 1840), 154-156; continued 1 (5 September 1840), 219-220. From *The Knickerbocker*, August, September 1840.

"Don Juan: A Spectral Research." 2 (13 March 1841), 162-163. From *The Knickerbocker*, March 1841.

Account of public dinner for Charles Dickens chaired by Irving. 4 (26 February 1842), 144. This account quotes Irving's remarks. They had previously appeared in the Daily *Albany Argus*, 23 February 1842.

* "A Toast." 4 (5 March 1842), 158. Irving's toast to International Copyright on the occasion of the public dinner for Charles Dickens. "It has never, before, been correctly published." A shorter, apparently garbled, version had appeared in The *New-York Tribune*, 21 February 1842, and in The Daily *Albany Argus*, 23 February 1842.

Folio Edition.

"Pelayo and the Merchant's Daughter." 1 (25 January 1840), [1]-[2]. From *The Knickerbocker*, January 1840.

"The Knight of Malta." 1 (8 February 1840), [1]. From *The Knickerbocker*, February 1840.

"The Early Experiences of Ralph Ringwood." 1 (8 August 1840), [1]-[2]; continued 1 (5 September 1840), [2]. From *The Knickerbocker*, August, September 1840.

New-York American.

"London Literary Dinner." (26 October 1824), [1]. From *Tales of a Traveller.*

"The Contented Man." (22 December 1826), [1]-[2]. From *The Literary Souvenir* for 1827.

"Extracts from The Life of Columbus." (6 March 1828), [1]-[2].

"The Discovery of America." (25 March 1828), [1]-[2]. From *Columbus*.

* "Advertisement" of the abridgment of *The Life and Voyages of Columbus*. Dated Seville, December, 1828. (4 April 1829), [2].

Extract from *The Conquest of Granada*. (6 February 1829), [1]-[2].

Extracts from *The Conquest of Granada*. (1 October 1829), [1]-[2]. In review attributed to the London *Spectator*.

"A Visit to Palos." (17 February 1831), [1]-[2]. From *Companions of Columbus*.

* Letter addressed to "Gentlemen," dated New-York, May 24, 1832, accepting the offer of a public dinner. (2 June 1832) [2]. The letter of invitation, from James Renwick and others, is also printed. The letter appears on the same day in the account of the public dinner in The New York *Morning Courier* and other New York newspapers.

Account of the public dinner for Irving. (5 June 1832), [2]-[3]. The account had appeared earlier in The New York *Morning Courier* and other New York newspapers, 2 June 1832.

"Legend of the Rose of the Alhambra." (18 June 1832), [1]-[2]. From *The Alhambra*. Reprinted anonymously.

* Motion of regret at the death of Sir Walter Scott, passed at a public meeting. (20 November 1832), [2]. The name of Washington Irving is printed at the conclusion, among others, as a member of the Corresponding Committee. (Irving, in fact, was not in New York at the time.)

"Scraps from the Book Kept at Stratford upon Avon." (28 October 1833), [2]. Attributed here to *The New-York Mirror*.

* "The [Thomas A.] Cooper Benefit: Address to the Public." (28 October 1833), [2]. Washington Irving is listed in the address as a Trustee, and his name is printed at the conclusion, among others, as a member of the Committee of Arrangements. Repeated on subsequent days.

* Letter to Professor B. Silliman, dated New York, 17th Feb., 1836, requesting a continuation of his lectures. (12 March 1836), [2]. Signed by Washington Irving among others.

* Letter to the editor, dated Greenburg, January 4th, 1837, defending a statement in "The Creole Village." (7 January 1837), [2].

* Letter to William C. Bryant, dated February 16th, [1837], on the question of having changed a line in a Bryant poem in Irving's edition. (17 February 1837), [2]. The letter also appears in *The Plaindealer*, 18 February 1837.

* Irving's toast to Samuel Rogers. In account of the Bookseller's Dinner held on 30 March. (3 April 1837), [2].

* Letter to the Editor, n.p., n.d., on a disagreement among members of the New York Society Library. (19 April 1838), [2]. Probably by Irving. Refering to earlier letters in the newspaper, this letter concludes, "As I perceive some of my nephews are subscribing our family name to their communications, I write myself in full ... Diedrick Knickerbocker."

"To the Editor of the Knickerbocker." (16 March 1839), [2]. From *The Knickerbocker*, March 1839.

The New York *American Citizen.*

Letter to the editor of the *New-York Evening Post*, dated November 6, 1809, signed A Traveller. (7 November 1809), [2]. From the *New-York Evening Post*, 6 November.

"Literary Notice," advertising *A History of New York* "in the press." The final paragraph, "This work was found in the chamber of Mr. Diedrich Knickerbocker...," by Irving. (4 December 1809), [3]. From the *New-York Evening Post*, 29 November.

* "Is this day published," advertising *A History of New York*. The last paragraph is the same as the one in the *New-York Evening Post*, 29 November. (6 December 1809), [3]. Reprinted in the Author's Revised Edition of *A History of New York*.

* Letter to the editor, signed Christian Brinkersnuff, attesting to the existence of Diedrich Knickerbocker. (30 December 1809).

* Letter to the editor, signed Seth Handaside, enclosing a letter to Handaside from Diedrich Knickerbocker explaining his absence and assigning his books and goods left behind. (23 January 1810), [2]-[3].

The New York *Atlas.*

Extract from letter of June 9th, 1832 to Peter S. Duponceau and others refusing with thanks a public dinner in Philadelphia. (23 June 1832). The letter had appeared earlier in the *New-York Evening Post*, 13 June 1832.

The New York *Chronicle Express.*

See the New York *Morning Chronicle.*

The New York *Commercial Advertiser.*

* Account of the public dinner for Irving. (2 June 1832). The account also appeared on the same day in the *New-York Evening Post* and the New York *Morning Courier.*

Letter to unnamed correspondent [Peter Irving], dated Washington City, December 18, 1832. (April 1833?). The letter had appeared earlier in *The Athenæum*, 2 March 1833. Not located. Reported by Stanley T. Williams in the *Life*.

New-York Daily Times.

* Letter [to Rufus W. Griswold] on the death of James F. Cooper, dated Sunnyside, Thursday, Sept. 18, 1851. (25 September 1851), 2.

New-York Evening Post.

* "'We Will Rejoice!!!'" Anonymous. (14 May 1804), [2]. See the attribution by Wayne R. Kime in the *Miscellaneous Writings*.

"Plans for Defending Our Harbour," by William Wizard, Esq. (21 August 1807), [2]-[3]. From *Salmagundi* No. XIII.

* "Distressing." A report of the disappearance of Mr. Knickerbocker. (26 October 1809). Reprinted in the Author's Revised Edition of *A History of New York*.

* "To the Editor of the Evening Post," dated November 6, 1809, signed A Traveller. (6 November 1809, although the front page is misdated 5 November), [2]. Reprinted in the New York *American Citizen*, 7 November, and in the Author's Revised Edition of *A History of New York*.

* "To the Editor of the Evening Post," undated, signed Seth Handaside. (16 November 1809), [3]. Reprinted in the Author's Revised Edition of *A History of New York*.

* "Literary Notice," advertising *A History of New York* "in the press." The final paragraph, "This work was found in the chamber of Mr. Diedrich Knickerbocker...," is by Irving. (29 November 1809), [3]. Reprinted in the New York *American Citizen*, 4 December, and in the Author's Revised Edition of *A History of New York*, where it is misdated 28 November.

"This Day Is Published," advertising *A History of New York* (mistakenly described as in three vols.). The last paragraph is the same as the one in the advertisement of 29 November. (7 December 1809), [3]; repeated 8 and 12 December. A similar (but correct) advertisement had appeared in the New York *American Citizen*, 6 December.

* "Communication," signed Ludwick Von Bynkerfeldt, affirming the existence and the authorship of Diedrich Knickerbocker. (27 December 1809), [2].

* Extract from letter to Churchill C. Cambreling, dated London, 2 March 1831. (28 April 1831).

* Account of the public dinner for Irving. (2 June 1832). The account also appeared on the same day in the New York *Commercial Advertiser* and the New York *Morning Courier*.

* Letter to Peter S. Duponceau and others, dated June 9th, 1832, refusing with thanks a public dinner in Philadelphia. (13 June 1832).

* Account of the public dinner for Charles Dickens chaired by Irving. (19 February 1842). Not seen. Presumably some of Irving's remarks and toasts are quoted. See the accounts in the Daily *Albany Argus*, 23 February 1842, *New-York Tribune*, 19-21 February 1842, and *The New World*, 26 February and 5 March 1842.

* Letter to Philip Hone, 4 April 1842, refusing with thanks a public dinner of appreciation. (7 April 1842).

* Letter to William C. Macready, 9 May 1849, urging him to continue his performances despite "the outrage at the Astor Place Opera House." Signed by Irving and forty-seven others. (9 May 1849).

* Letter to Jesse Merwin, 12 February 1851, on old times in Kinderhook. (1 March 1851).

A note to the editors of *The Literary World*, forwarding a letter to Henry R. Schoolcraft, dated Sunnyside, November 10, 1851. (26 November 1851). First published in *The Literary World*, 22 November 1851.

* Letter to William C. Bryant on portraits of Columbus. (26 December 1851). The letter includes the revised version of a letter to Joseph E. Bloomfield, originally written 28 October 1851. On 1 November 1851, Irving had written Bryant to request the chance to revise his original remarks. On 20 December he sent this open letter to Bryant, with a covering letter.

* Letter to George Sumner, 4 January 1856, requesting him to lecture. Signed by Washington Irving, William C. Bryant, and four others. (10 January 1856).

The New York *Gazette and General Advertiser.*

Account of the public dinner for Irving. (4 June 1832). The account had appeared earlier in the New York *Morning Courier* and other New York newspapers, 2 June 1832.

New-York Herald.

"This Day Is Published," advertising *A History of New York*. Dated 7 December at foot of the advertisement. (9 December 1809), [3]. The advertisement had first appeared in The New York *American Citizen*, 6 December, and The *New-York Evening Post*, 7 December.

* Petition to W. C. Macready to continue his performances. Signed by 47 citizens, including Irving. (9 May 1849).

The New-York Mirror.

The heading of this weekly periodical changes during the sixteen years of Irving's occasional appearances. In 1826 it carries the subtitle, *And Ladies*

Literary Gazette. By 1831 the subtitle is dropped and a description is added, "A Weekly Journal of Literature and the Fine Arts."

"The Contented Man." 4 (30 December 1826), 178. First published in *The Literary Souvenir* for 1827, London, and republished in the *New-York American*, 22 December 1826. Here it is attributed to "the last number of Blackwood's Magazine."

"The Broken Heart." 4 (7 April 1827), [289]-290. From *The Sketch Book.*

"The Dull Lecture." 5 (26 January 1828), 231. From *The Atlantic Souvenir* for 1828.

"Phillip of Pokanoket." 6 (12 December 1829), 178-179. From *The Sketch Book.*

Dedication to Samuel Rogers from *Poems, by William Cullen Bryant.* 9 (28 April 1832), 343. In an editorial notice of the book, reprinted from *The Athenæum*, 3 March 1832.

Account of the public dinner for Irving, 30 May 1832, including Irving's address and toast, and his letter of 24 May accepting the invitation. 9 (9 June 1832), 386-387. First published in the New York *Morning Courier*, 2 June 1832, and other newspapers of the day.

Letter to Peter S. Duponceau and others, dated June 9th, 1832, refusing with thanks a public dinner in Philadelphia. 9 (23 June 1832), 407. The letter had appeared earlier in the *New-York Evening Post*, 13 June 1832, and the Philadelphia *National Gazette and Literary Register*, 14 June 1832.

"Scraps from the Book Kept at Stratford Upon Avon." ("Lines Written at Stratford" under a variant title). 11 (26 October 1833), 136. First published in *The Port Folio*, June 1825, and *The Albion*, 2 March 1833.

* "Mathews Not at Home." Anonymous. 11 (1 March 1834), 278. Headed by an editorial introduction: "A letter from an American gentleman in England to his friends in this city, dated about the first of December last...."

"A Leaf from Washington Irving's Works": "A Wet Sunday in the Country"; "An American Farm Yard"; "Women's Hearts." 11 (26 April 1834), 344. From various sketches in *The Sketch Book.*

"English Writers on America." 12 (24 January 1835), [233]-234. From *The Sketch Book.*

* "Newton the Painter." Anonymous. 12 (21 March 1835), 303.

"The Honey Camp"; "A Bee Hunt"; "The Passenger Pigeon." 12 (4 April 1835), 318. From *A Tour on the Prairies*, "in advance of publication."

"An Unwritten Drama of Lord Byron." 13 (17 October 1835), 122. First published in book form in *The Gift* for 1836. This text is probably taken from its first periodical appearance in *The Knickerbocker*, August 1835, but might be taken from an early copy of the annual.

"A Haunted Ship; A True Story -- As Far as It Goes." 13 (9 January 1836), 218. From *Heath's Book of Beauty* for 1836.

"Florinda." 13 (6 February 1836), 251. From *Legends of the Conquest of Spain*.

* Letter to William C. Bryant, dated New-York, March 31, 1836, proposing a public dinner of appreciation. Signed by twenty-six authors, artists and others, including Irving. 13 (16 April 1836), 334.

"The Widow's Ordeal: Or a Judicial Trial by Combat." 14 (22 October 1836), [129]. First published in *The Magnolia* for 1837. This text is probably taken from proofs or from a preliminary copy, since *The Magnolia* is described as "just published" in the issue of 29 October 1836.

"The Indians' Revenge." 14 (22 October 1836), 131. From *Astoria*, "previous to its publication."

"The Creole Village. A Sketch from a Steamboat." 14 (4 November 1836), [145]-146. From *The Magnolia* for 1837.

"Return of a War Party"; "Climate West of the Rocky Mountains"; "Indian Sepulchre"; "Fish of the Columbia River"; "Canadian Voyageurs"; "Antelopes." 14 (17 December 1836), 198. From *Astoria*.

"The Marvellous Tower." 14 (13 May 1837), 366. From *Legends of The Conquest of Spain*.

"The Indian Chief Blackbird." 14 (27 May 1837), 382. From *Astoria*.

"An Indian Battle." 14 (3 June 1837), 390. From Theodore Irving's *The Conquest of Florida*.

"Perilous Passage of the Great Morass." 14 (10 June 1837), 396. From Theodore Irving's *The Conquest of Florida*.

"Story of Kosato, the Renegade Blackfoot." 15 (1 July 1837), 7. From *Capt. Bonneville*. "The publishers politely forwarded to us some sheets...."

"The Uninvited Guest." 15 (29 July 1837), 34-35. From *Capt. Bonneville*.

[View from a lofty peak]. 15 (29 July 1837), 39. Brief extract from *Capt. Bonneville*.

"Washington Irving and Sir Walter Scott." 15 (21 October 1837), 134. From *Abbotsford*.

"Early Experiences of Ralph Ringwood." 18 (8 August 1840), 55; continued 18 (5 September 1840), 82-83; continued 18 (10 October 1840), 126. From *The Knickerbocker*, August, September 1840.

Extract from *History of New York*, to accompany an illustration of St. Nicholas. 19 (2 January 1841), [1]-3.

Letter to Philip Hone, dated New-York, April 4, 1842, refusing with thanks a public dinner of appreciation. 20 (16 April 1842), 123. First published in The *New-York Evening Post*, 7 April 1842.

The New York *Morning Chronicle (*and *Chronicle Express).*

The New York *Morning Chronicle* was edited by Washington Irving's brother Peter Irving from its founding in early October 1802 to some time in 1805. It was a daily paper whose political policy was to oppose Federalism and to support Aaron Burr, then vice-president of the United States, and Edward Livingston, then mayor of New York City. But it also ran lighter pieces supplied by occasional anonymous or pseudonymous correspondents, one of whom was Washington Irving. Some of the occasional pieces were political in nature, some simply concerned with the current life of the city. Of the twenty columns of the four-page paper, however, only six or seven at most were given to editorial matter. Some news was included, but a great part of the paper was composed of advertising.

On 25 November 1802 the New York *Chronicle Express* began publishing on Mondays and Thursdays as a semi-weekly version of the *Morning Chronicle*, probably aimed at wider distribution outside of the city. The first issue contains a "Prospectus" declaring that the policy of the new paper will be to "support with firmness the present administration, and to advocate with manly freedom genuine REPUBLICAN principles." It also promises, "The interests of LITERATURE will be blended with those of commerce and politics." The editorial matter was chosen from the *Morning Chronicle*. Since the semi-weekly carried considerably less advertising, generally only half a page or so, it had room to choose a good deal of the editorial and occasional matter. Perhaps the lack of advertising explains in part why the paper ran only until 7 May 1804.

Both newspapers are today quite scarce. Individual issues of the *Morning Chronicle* are scattered about various libraries, as well as reproduced on microcard by the American Antiquarian Society, but the *Chronicle Express* I have been able to discover only in an apparently complete run in the library of the New York Historical Society.

Since the *Chronicle Express* is essentially a version of the *Morning Chronicle*, both are included in the same listing here when the given piece by Irving appeared in both.

The full and exact degree of Irving's authorship in the *Morning Chronicle* will probably never be known. He and his friends and acquaintances who wrote the lighter, sophisticated, often mocking pieces for the paper carefully preserved their anonymity under various pseudonyms. It was a small and select group that had every intention of keeping the circle closed to outsiders. In keeping with that spirit, Irving never discussed his authorship in public, then or later, and left little or no direct evidence for the modern scholar -- surely a deliberate suppression. It was a game played by the young wits, and part of the game was to restrict knowledge to the few insiders who were playing and who were in the privileged know. Irving remained faithful to the rules and the spirit all of his life. Why else are there no relevant letters, no later references or reminiscences or nostalgic anecdotes? Add to the spirit of the game Irving's great reluctance all of his life to acknowledge any writing that he felt would not advance or fortify his literary reputation, and the difficulty of identifying any of his early periodical writing is understandable. He did not want it identified. We are fortune that he even allowed the *Oldstyle* letters to be attributed to him. But there must have been a great deal more.

Irving's writing in the *Morning Chronicle* is here presented in three categories. First are those pieces that are surely his: the *Oldstyle* letters, and those occasional pieces that can be traced to the Journals and Notebooks of 1803-1806, and those that are so overwhelmingly typical, so replete with parallels and repetitions of theme and content, so in keeping with all we know of the young Irving that they almost proclaim their authorship. That is not to say that Irving was necessarily the sole author. Just as he collaborated in so much of his early work, he may well have collaborated also in some of these pieces.

Second are those pieces identified as "probably by Irving." Here the probability is strong that Irving was the author or at least one of the authors. Although no tangible proof of authorship can be cited, the parallels to known writings are striking, or the subject matter and treatment are in keeping with the known facts of his life and interests and attitudes of the time. Many of these pieces are directly connected to writings in the *Morning Chronicle* or in the *Corrector* that are ascribed to Irving with more confidence. These are also the pieces, like those in the categories above and below, that were chosen to be reprinted in the *Chronicle Express* whenever appropriate.

Third are those pieces identified as "possibly by Irving." In this category, the probability of Irving's authorship is less. Identification is made on the basis of style and of general attitude and treatment. These are more of the light pieces that tend to appear when Irving was in town and sometimes refer to writings that can be ascribed to Irving more confidently. Despite the lower degree of probability, the list is conservative, reluctant to claim even the possibility of authorship without adequate reason and a strong "feel."

* "The Eccentric Man." Anonymous. # 19 (22 October 1802), [2], cols. 3-5.

* "Communication; From Ballston or Milton Springs." Anonymous. # 37 (12 November 1802), [3], col. 1.

* "For the Morning Chronicle." Signed Jonathan Oldstyle. # 39 (15 November 1802), [3], cols. 1-2. *Letters of Oldstyle # 1.*

* ""For the Morning Chronicle." Signed Jonathan Oldstyle. # 44 (20 November 1802), [2], cols. 4-5. *Chronicle Express*. "To the Editor." # 1 (25 November 1802), [1], cols. 3-4. *Letters of Oldstyle # 2.*

* "Theatrics. Communication." Signed Jonathan Oldstyle. # 53 (1 December 1802), [2]-[3]. *Chronicle Express*. # 3 (2 December 1802), [3], cols. 1-3. *Letters of Oldstyle # 3.*

* "Theatrics. Communication." Signed Jonathan Oldstyle. # 56 (4 December 1802), [2], cols. 4-5, to [3], col. 1. *Chronicle Express*. # 4 (6 December 1802), [3], cols. 2-4. *Letters of Oldstyle # 4.*

* "Theatrics. Communication." Signed Jonathan Oldstyle. #62 (11 December 1802), [3], cols. 1-2. *Chronicle Express*. # 6 (13 December 1802), [3], cols. 2-3. *Letters of Oldstyle # 5.*

* "We have received a note from our correspondent Jonathan Oldstyle." Anonymous editorial note. # 90 (15 January 1803), [2], col. 4. *Chronicle Express*. # 16 (17 January 1803), [2], col. 5.

* "To the Editor of the Morning Chronicle." Signed Jonathan Oldstyle. # 91 (17 January 1803), [2], cols. 2-3. *Chronicle Express*. "To the Editor of the Morning Chronical." # 17 (20 January 1803), [1], cols. 3-4. *Letters of Oldstyle #6.*

* "To the Editor of the Morning Chronicle." Signed Jonathan Oldstyle. # 96 (22 January 1803), [2], cols. 3-5. *Chronicle Express*. "Theatric. To the Editor of the Morning Chronicle." # 18 (24 January 1803), [2], cols. 2-4. *Letters of Oldstyle # 7.*

* "The communication ... from our highly respected correspondent, Jonathan Oldstyle...." Anonymous editorial note. # 106 (3 February 1803), [2], col. 3.

* "To the Editor of the Morning Chronicle." Signed Jonathan Oldstyle. # 110 (8 February 1803), [2], cols. 3-5. *Chronicle Express*. "To the Editor of the Morning Chronicle." # 23 (10 February 1803), [2], cols. 1-3. *Letters of Oldstyle # 8.*

*   "To the Editor of the Morning Chronicle." Signed Jonathan Oldstyle. # 173 (23 April 1803), [2], cols 4-5, to [3], col. 1. *Chronicle Express.* "To the Editor of the Morning Chronicle." # 44 (25 April 1803), [3], cols. 1-3. *Letters of Oldstyle* # 9.

*   "To the Amateur." Signed Banquo. # 375 (16 December 1803), [2], col. 5, to [3], col. 1. *Chronicle Express.* # 112 (19 December 1803), [2], col. 4.

*   "For the Morning Chronicle; To Mr. Andrew Quoz." Signed Dick Buckram. # 381 (24 December 1803), [2], col. 5. *Chronicle Express.* # 114 (26 December 1803), [2], col. 4.

*   "For the Morning Chronicle; "To Mr. Andrew Quoz." Signed Dick Buckram. # 386 (30 December 1803), [3], cols. 1-2. *Chronicle Express.* # 116 (2 January 1804), [2], cols. 1-2.

*   "Communication; Concert of Madame Deseze." Signed An Amateur. # 411 (28 January 1804), [3], col. 1. *Chronicle Express.* # 124 (30 January 1804), [3], col. 2.

*   "To the Editor of the Morning Chronicle." Signed Walter Withers. # 442 (5 March 1804), [2], col. 5, to [3], col. 1. *Chronicle Express.* # 135 (8 March 1804), [1], cols. 4-5.

*   "Bordeaux Theatre -- A letter from an American gentleman at Bordeaux." Anonymous. # 626 (11 October 1804), [2], col. 4.

*   "Extract of a Letter from Bordeaux, dated Aug. 29." Anonymous. # 655 (14 November 1804), [2], col. 5.

*   "The great dearth of Intelligence at present may render acceptable the following extract of a letter from an American gentleman now in France...dated Marseilles, Sept 5." Anonymous. # 698 (10 January 1805), [2], col. 5.

PROBABLY BY IRVING

"For the Morning Chronicle; The Petition of Pompey Caninus." Signed A Sly Dog. # 144 (21 March 1803), [2], col. 5, to [3], col. 1. *Chronicle Express.* # 35 (24 March 1803), [1], col. 5, to [2], col. 1.

"For the Morning Chronicle." Signed R. Thunderbolt. # 177 (28 April 1803), [3], col. 1. *Chronicle Express.* # 46 (2 May 1803), [2], col. 2.

"For the Morning Chronicle; A Traveller's Tale." From the journal of Shing-fu the Chinese traveller. # 185 (7 May 1803), [2], cols. 3-4. *Chronicle Express.* # 48 (9 May 1803), [2], col. 5, to [3], col. 1.

"To the Editor of the Morning Chronicle." Signed R. Thunderbolt. # 187 (10 May 1803), [2], cols. 4-5. *Chronicle Express*. #49 (12 May 1803), [2], cols. 4-5.

"For the Morning Chronicle; To Robert Thunderbolt, Esq." Signed An Actor. # 196 (20 May 1803), [2], cols. 3-4. *Chronicle Express*. # 52 (23 May 1803), [1], col. 5, to [2], col. 1.

"A Chinese Tale; Further Extracts from the Journal of Shing-fu, the Chinese Traveller." # 199 (24 May 1803), [2], col. 4. *Chronicle Express*. # 53 (26 May 1803), [2], cols. 2-3.

"To the Editor of the Morning Chronicle." Signed J. Bruiser. # 208 (3 June 1803), [2], cols. 3-4. *Chronicle Express*. # 56 (6 June 1803), [2], cols. 2-3.

"Communication." Signed Quiz-Goose. # 243 (15 July 1803), [2], col. 4. *Chronicle Express*. # 68 (16 July 1803), [3], col. 5.

"Further Extracts from the Journal of Shing-fu." # 247 (20 July 1803), [2], col. 5, to [3], col. 1. *Chronicle Express*. # 69 (21 July 1803), [3], cols. 3-4.

"Communication." Signed Quiz Goose. # 248 (21 July 1803), [2], col. 5. *Chronicle Express*. # 70 (25 July 1803), [1], col. 4.

"An ironical correspondent...." Anonymous editorial note about the previous Quiz Goose piece. # 249 (22 July 1803), [2], col. 4.

"For the Morning Chronicle." Signed An Amateur. # 368 (8 December 1803), [3], col. 1. *Chronicle Express*. # 110 (12 December 1803), [1], col. 4.

"Communication; Philharmonic Society." Signed One of the Cogniscenti. # 382 (26 December 1803), [2], cols. 4-5. *Chronicle Express*. Signed One of the Cognoscenti. # 15 (29 December 1803), [1], cols. 3-4.

POSSIBLY BY IRVING

"Philharmonic Concert." Anonymous. # 167 (16 April 1803), [2], col. 5. *Chronicle Express*. # 42 (18 April 1803), [2], col. 4.

"To the Editor of the Morning Chronicle." Signed a Traveller. # 183 (5 May 1803), [2], cols. 3-4. *Chronicle Express*. # 48 (9 May 1803), [1], col. 2.

"We have received a note from our correspondent, Jonathan Oldstyle...." Anonymous editorial note. # 190 (13 May 1803), [2], col. 4.

"To the Editor of the Morning Chronicle." Signed Traveller. # 193 (17 May 1803), [2], col. 4. *Chronicle Express*. # 51 (19 May 1803), [1], cols. 4-5.

"To the Editor." Signed Traveller. (Includes an anonymous poem, "To Julia"). # 197 (21 May 1803), [2], col. 5. *Chronicle Express*. # 52 (23 May 1803), [2], col. 5.

"Communication; Medical Hoax." Signed A. B. # 400 (16 January 1804), [2], col. 5. *Chronicle Express*. # 121 (19 January 1804), [1], col. 4.

The New York *Morning Courier*.

Account of the public dinner for Irving. (2 June 1832), [2]. The account also appeared on the same day in The *New-York Evening Post* and The New York *Commercial Advertiser*.

The New York *People's Friend & Daily Advertiser*.

"Letter from Mustapha Rub-a-dub Keli Khan ...." (10 June 1807), [2]-[3]. From *Salmagundi* Number XI.

The New-York Review.

"The Dull Lecture." 1 (October 1837), 444. In a review of *The New-York Book of Poetry*, in which this poem does not appear.

New-York Spectator.

Account of the public dinner for Irving. 35 (5 June 1832), 2-3. The account had appeared earlier in The New York *Morning Courier* and other New York newspapers, 2 June 1832.

New-York Tribune.

* Letter to Charles Dickens, dated New-York, 24th January 42, greeting him on arrival in America and proposing a public dinner. Signed by forty-one eminent New Yorkers, including Irving. (9 February 1842), [2].

* Account of the public dinner for Charles Dickens chaired by Irving. The account merely describes Irving's remarks, although it quotes his "sentiment" to Dickens. (19 February 1842), [2]. Continued (21 February 1842), [4], where a version of Irving's "sentiment" to International Copyright is quoted. For a full account of Irving's remarks, see the Daily *Albany Argus*, 23 February 1842, and *The New World*, 26 February 1842. For the full version of the toast to International Copyright, see *The New World*, 5 March 1842. A version of the account also appears in The *New-York Evening Post*, 19 February.

The New-Yorker.

"The Widow's Ordeal: or A Judicial Trial by Combat." 2 (8 October 1836), 39-40. From *The Magnolia* for 1837.

"The Creole Village. A Sketch from a Steamboat." 2 (12 November 1836), 115-116. From *The Magnolia* for 1837.

"The Crayon Papers. To the Editor of the Knickerbocker." 7 (23 March 1839), From *The Knickerbocker*, March 1839.

"Sleepy Hollow." 7 (18 May 1839), 133-134. From *The Knickerbocker*, May 1839.

"Recollections of the Alhambra. The Abencerrage." 7 (15 June 1839), 196-198. From *The Knickerbocker*, June 1839.

"Spanish Romance. Legend of Don Munio Sancho De Hinojosa." 8 (21 September 1839), 6-7. From *The Knickerbocker*, September 1839.

"The Conspiracy of the Cocked Hats." 8 (26 October 1839), 88. From *The Knickerbocker*, October 1839.

"Mountjoy: or Some Passages form the Life of a Castle-Builder." 8 (14 December 1839), 198-200; continued 8 (4 January 1840), 245-248. From *The Knickerbocker*, November, December 1839.

"A Shakespearean Research." 8 (1 February 1840), 308-309. First published as "The Bermudas: A Shakespearean Research" in *The Knickerbocker*, January 1840.

"The Grand Prior of Minorca." 8 (8 February 1840), 324-325. From *The Knickerbocker*, February 1840.

"Abderahman: Founder of the Dynasty of the Ommiades in Spain." 9 (9 May 1840), 115-117. From *The Knickerbocker*, May 1840.

"The Early Experiences of Ralph Ringwood." 9 (8 August 1840), 322-325; continued 9 (5 September 1840), 386-388. From *The Knickerbocker*, August, September 1840.

"The Seminoles." 10 (10 October 1840), 55-56. From *The Knickerbocker*, October 1840.

Extract from *Goldsmith*. 10 (7 November 1840), 116.

"Sketches in Paris in 1825": "A Parisian Hotel," "My French Neighbor," "The Englishman at Paris." 10 (14 November 1840), 131-132. From *The Knickerbocker*, November 1840.

"Parisian Sketches in 1825": "English and French Character," "The Tuileries and Windsor Castle," "The Field of Waterloo," "Paris at the Restoration." 10 (26 December 1840), 230-232. From *The Knickerbocker*, December 1840.

"Don Juan: A Spectral Research." 10 (13 March 1841), 403-404. From *The Knickerbocker*, March 1841.

The North American Review [Boston].

"The Author's Chamber" and other extracts. 35 (October 1832), [265]-282. In review of *The Alhambra*.

* Review by Irving of *History of the Northmen, or Danes and Normans* by Henry Wheaton. Anonymous. 35 (October 1832), 342-371. Reprinted in *Spanish Papers*, 1866.

"A Wild Horse of the Prairie," "Introduction," "A Buffalo Hunt," "A Republic of Prairie Dogs." 41 (July 1835), [1]-28. In review of *A Tour on the Prairies*.

Extracts from *Astoria*. 44 (January 1837), 200-237. In review.

Extracts from *Margaret M. Davidson*. 53 (July 1841), 139-146. In review.

Letter on Washington Allston from *Cyclopædia of American Literature* by E. A. and G. L. Duyckinck. 82 (April 1856), 326-330. A large part of the original letter, in review of the *Cyclopædia*.

O

The Observer, and Repertory of Original and Selected Essays [Baltimore].

"From the Whim-Whams and Opinions of Launcelot Langstaff, Esq." 1 (15 February 1807), 105-107; continued 1 (21 February 1807), 117-119. From "From the Elbow-Chair," *Salmagundi* No. I.

Extract from *Salmagundi* No. V. 1 (28 March 1807), 205-206.

The Ordeal: A Critical Journal [Boston].

["Passaic -- A Tradition," untitled]. Signed TOBINUS. 1 (13 May 1809), 298-299. In the introductory comments: "supposed to have been written by one of the authors of 'Salmagundi.'" The poem had appeared earlier in the *Weekly Visitor*, New York.

P

The Pastime (A Literary Paper) [Schenectady, N. Y.].

"Passaic Falls ... A Tradition." Anonymous. 2 (28 May 1808), 27-28. Preceded by an anonymous note: "[These beautiful lines were taken from the Album, kept at a public-house near Passaick Falls, New-Jersey.]" The poem had appeared earlier in the *Weekly Visitor*, New York, 27 September 1806.

The Philadelphia Album, and Ladies' Literary Port Folio.

Account of the public dinner for Irving. 6 (9 June 1832), 180-181. Irving's speech is given, but not his letter of acceptance; many of the other speeches are omitted. The account had appeared earlier in The New York *Morning Courier*, 2 June 1832, and other New York newspapers. This is essentially the same account that appears in The Philadelphia *National Gazette and Literary Register*, 9 June.

Letter to Peter S. Duponceau and others, dated June 9th, 1832, refusing with thanks a public dinner in Philadelphia. 6 (16 June 1832), 188. The letter had appeared earlier in The Philadelphia *National Gazette and Literary Register*, 14 June 1832, and also in The *New-York Evening Post*, 13 June.

"Legend of the Rose of the Alhambra." 6 (23 June 1832), 195-196. From *The Alhambra*.

Extracts from *The Alhambra*. 6 (7 July 1832), 214-215. Attributed to *The New-York Mirror*.

"Ponce de Leon." 6 (29 September 1832), 311-312. From *The Companions of Columbus*.

"The Young Robber." 7 (4 May 1833), [137]. From *Tales of a Traveller*.

The Philadelphia *National Gazette and Literary Register.*

"A Literary Dinner at a London Bookseller's." (11 September 1824), [1]. From *Tales of a Traveller*, Part 2.

Account of the public dinner for Irving. (9 June 1832), [4]. Irving's speech and toast are given, but accompanied only by the toast of Mr. Charles King. The account had appeared earlier in The New York *Morning Courier*, 2 June 1832, and other New York newspapers. This is essentially the same account that appears in *The Philadelphia Album*, 9 June.

Letter to Peter S. Duponceau and others, dated June 9th, 1832, refusing with thanks a public dinner in Philadelphia. Accompanied by a letter of June 6 from eight citizens of Philadelphia offering a public dinner. (14 June 1832), [1]. The letter had appeared earlier in The *New-York Evening Post*, 13 June.

Letter to the editor of *The Plaindealer*, undated, defending himself for an alteration in Bryant's poems. (4 February 1837), [2]. Reprinted.

"Extract from Washington Irving's New Work Entitled *Adventures in the Rocky Mountains*." (15 June 1837), [1].

"A Chronicle of Wolfert's Roost." (13 April 1839), [2]. From *The Knickerbocker*, April 1839.

"Sleepy Hollow." (6 May 1839), [2]. From *The Knickerbocker*, May 1839.

"The Birds of Spring." (23 May 1839), [2]. From *The Knickerbocker*, May 1839.

"Recollections of the Alhambra." (13 June 1839), [2]. From *The Knickerbocker*, June 1839.

"The Enchanted Island." (18 July 1839), [4]. From *The Knickerbocker*, July 1839.

"Communipaw." (1 October 1839), [2]. From *The Knickerbocker*, September 1839.

"Mountjoy; or, Some Passages from the Life of a Castle-Builder." (19 December 1839), [2], [4]. From *The Knickerbocker*, November and December, 1839.

"The Knight of Malta; The Grand Prior of Minorca." (8 February 1840), [4]. From *The Knickerbocker*, February 1840.

"Abderahman." (5 May 1840), [2]; continued (7 May 1840), [4]. From *The Knickerbocker*, May 1840.

"The Taking of the Veil." (13 June 1840), [4]. From *The Knickerbocker*, June 1840.

"The Early Experiences of Ralph Ringwood." (11 August 1840), [4]. From *The Knickerbocker*, August 1840.

"A Seminole Tradition." (14 November 1840), [4]. From *The Knickerbocker*, October 1840.

The Plaindealer [New York].

* Letter to the editor, undated, defending himself for an alteration in Bryant's poems. 1 (28 January 1837), 131.

Letter to William C. Bryant, dated February 16th, on the controversy over Irving's alteration in Bryant's *Poems*. 1 (18 February 1837), 186-187. An editorial introduction credits the letter to "the *American* of last evening."

The Port Folio [Philadelphia].

"A Letter from Mustapha Rub-A-Dub Kali Khan, ... to Asem Hacchem...." N.S.3 (21 March 1807), 179-181. From *Salmagundi* No. III.

"Letter from Mustapha Rub-A-Dub Keli Khan, to Asem Hacchem." N.S.3 (16 May 1807), 308-312. From *Salmagundi* No. VII.

"Letter from Mustapha ... to Asem Hacchem." N.S.3 (30 May 1807), 342-346. From *Salmagundi* No. IX.

"The Stranger in Pennsylvania," by Jeremy Cockloft, the Younger. N.S.3 (30 May 1807), 346-350.

"Lines Written at the Falls of the Passaick." Anonymous. Another N.S.3 (May 1814), 487-489. In the June issue, the editors thank "our much-admired correspondent" for his "elegant stanzas." The poem had appeared earlier in the *Weekly Visitor*, New York.

"The Stout Gentleman." 14 (July 1822), 53-60. From *Bracebridge Hall*.

"A Remark on Knickerbocker." (The beginning of Ch. 1 of Book VI of *History of New York* printed as poetry). 17 (May 1824), 422.

* "Impromptu, by Washington Irving, Esq. at the Birth-place of Shakspeare." ("Lines Written at Stratford" under a variant title). 19 (June 1825), 516. The poem was published again, in what may be a separate transcription, in *The Albion*, New York, 1833.

Q

The Quarterly Review [London].

* Anonymous article by Irving that purports to be a review of *A Chronicle of the Conquest of Granada.* 43 (May 1830), [55]-80. Incorporated in the introduction to the Author's Revised Edition of *The Conquest of Granada.*

* Anonymous review by Irving of Alexander Slidell Mackenzie's *A Year in Spain* by a Young American. 44 (February 1831), [319]-342.

R

Roberts' Semi-Monthly Magazine [Boston].

"The Wife." 1 (1 February 1841), 55-57. From *The Sketch Book*.

The Rough-Hewer, Devoted to the Support of the Democratic Principles of Jefferson [an occasional newspaper published in Albany, N. Y.].

"'A Time of Unexampled Prosperity.'" No. 9 (16 April 1840), 67. From *The Knickerbocker*, April 1840.

The Rover: A Weekly Magazine [New York].

"The Widow's Ordeal." 1 (1843), 4-7. From *The Magnolia* for 1837.

"Count Julian and His Family." 1 (1843), 59-61. From *Legends of the Conquest of Spain.*

"A Bee Hunt." 2 (1844), 166-167. From *A Tour on the Prairies.*

"Hell Gate" and " The Adventure of the Black Fisherman." 3 (1844), 401-403. From *Tales of a Traveller.*

"My First Visit to Abbotsford." 4 (1845), 111-112. From *Abbotsford.*

"The Adventure of the Mason." 5 (10 May 1845), 126-127. From *The Alhambra.*

The Rural Repository [Hudson, N. Y.].

"The Bold Dragoon." 1 (19 February 1825), 145-148. From *Tales of a Traveller.*

"Death of Columbus." 5 (5 July 1828), 23. From *Columbus.*

"Indian Sketches. Departure from the Grand Pawnees." 11 (29 November 1834), 100. From *A Tour on the Prairies;* here attributed to the *New-York American.*

"The Seminoles." 17 (5 December 1840), 100-101. From *The Knickerbocker,* October 1840.

S

The Saturday Evening Post [Philadelphia].

[Short passage on beeswax in England and bees in America]. 1 (18 August 1821), [1]. Reprinted from The Baltimore Chronicle, which had reprinted from Campbell's Magazine, attributing the anonymous piece, probably erroneously, to Irving.

"The Young Lovers." 1 (22 June 1822), [1]. From "The Lovers," *Bracebridge Hall.*

"The Storm Ship." 1 (14 December 1822), [1]. From *Bracebridge Hall.*

The Saturday Magazine [London: Society for Promoting Christian Knowledge].

"Travelling in Spain." 1 (14 July 1832), 10-11. From *The Alhambra.*

"Forest Trees." 7 (4 July 1835), 3-4. From *Bracebridge Hall*.

"Love for the Dead." 7 (21 November 1835), 199. From "Rural Funerals," *The Sketch Book*.

"A Wreck at Sea." 8 (30 January 1836), 37. From "The Voyage," *The Sketch Book*.

[Two brief passages on the fortitude of women]. 8 (13 February 1836), 60, 63. These are the first two paragraphs of "The Wife," *The Sketch Book*.

[Brief passage on nature scattering the seeds of genius]. 8 (19 March 1836), 107. From "Roscoe," *The Sketch Book*.

[Brief passage on the fortitude of women]. 8 (2 April 1836), 134. Repeat of the second paragraph of "The Wife," *The Sketch Book*.

[Brief passage on the fortitude of women]. 8 (9 April 1836), 143. Repeat of the first paragraph of "The Wife," *The Sketch Book*.

"Rural Funerals." 8 (28 May 1836), 204-207. From *The Sketch Book*.

"The Muleteer." 9 (15 October 1836), 151. From "The Journey, "*The Alhambra*.

"The Falls of the Passaic." 10 (18 February 1837), 59. From *The Atlantic Souvenir for 1827*.

Adventures of a Hunter." 11 (7 October 1837), 143. From *A Tour on the Prairies*.

A Republic of Prairie Dogs." 11 (21 October 1837), 158-159. From *A Tour on the Prairies*.

Maternal Solicitude." 11 (28 October 1837), 165. Brief extract from an unidentified source.

Saturday Museum: A Family Newspaper [Philadelphia].

Extracts from two letters to Edgar A. Poe (apparently changed to third-person form by Poe). 1 (25 February 1843); reprinted 1 (4 March 1843), [1]. In a biography of Poe written anonymously by Henry B. Hirst. These would appear to be the letters extracted in the advertisements in Poe's *Tales of the Grotesque and Arabesque*, 1840.

The Scottish Episcopal Review and Magazine [Edinburgh].

"The Stout Gentleman." 2 (September 1822), 429-436. In review of *Bracebridge Hall*.

The Scourge; or, Monthly Expositor of Imposture and Folly [London].

Two extracts from *Salmagundi*: from "From My Elbow-Chair" in No. XII, and from "To the Ladies" in No. V. 3 (2 March 1812) (also dated 1 March), 206-215. Preceded by a letter from John Lambert, dated 13 February 1812, sending a copy of *Salmagundi*, presumably his own London edition of 1811.

Southern Ladies' Book [Macon, Ga.].

"Abderahman: The Washington of Spain." 1 (May 1840), 292-301. From *The Knickerbocker*, May 1840.

"Parisian Sketches in 1835: English and French Character; The Tuilleries and Windsor Castle; The Field of Waterloo." 2 (December 1840), 316-319. From *The Knickerbocker*, December 1840.

The Southern Literary Messenger [Richmond, Va.].

* Extract from undated letter to T. W. White, the publisher, expressing good wishes to the new magazine. 1 (August 1834), [1].

"A Republic of Prairie Dogs." 1 (April 1835), 456-457. In review of *A Tour on the Prairies*.

Extracts from *Abbotsford* and *Newstead Abbey*. 1 (July 1835), 646-648. In review.

"St. Mark's Eve." 6 (June 1840), 472. From *Bracebridge Hall*. In notice of the two-vol. edition of the *Works* published by Lea & Blanchard.

The Southern Review [Charleston, S. C.].

Extracts from *Columbus*. 2 (August 1828), [1]-31. In review.

Extracts from *Companions of Columbus*. 7 (May 1831), 214-246. In review.

U

The United States Literary Gazette [Boston].

"Story of the Young Italian." 1 (15 September 1824), [161]-163. In review of Part 1 of *Tales of a Traveller*.

"Buckthorne, or The Young Man of Great Expectations." 1 (1 October 1824), [172]-173. In review of Part 2 of *Tales of a Traveller*.

V

The Vicksburg, Mississippi *Advocate & Register*.

* Letter to "Gentlemen," dated Vicksburg, November 17, 1832, refusing with thanks a public dinner. (21 November 1832).

W

The Weekly Entertainer; and West of England Miscellany [Sherborne].

"John Bull." N.S.2 (31 July 1820), 93-99. From the London edition of *The Sketch Book*.

"The Pride of the Village." N.S.3 (23 April 1821), [317]-321. From *The Sketch Book*.

"The Legend of Sleepy Hollow." N.S.4 (23 July 1821), 58-60; continued N.S.4 (6 August 1821), 83-85. From *The Sketch Book*.

[On first arriving in England]. N.S.5 (10 June 1822), 359-361. From "The Author," *Bracebridge Hall*.

"The Stout Gentleman." N.S.5 (17 June 1822), [369]-371; continued N.S.5 (24 June 1822), 387-390. From *Bracebridge Hall*.

The Weekly Visitor, and Ladies' Museum [New York].

"The Wife." 4 (17 July 1819), 184-186; continued 4 (24 July 1819), 199-201. From *The Sketch Book*.

Weekly Visitor; or, Ladies' Miscellany [New York].

* "From the Passaic Album." 4 (27 September 1806), 384 (mispaged 370). The poem is introduced by a letter to the editor by "C. W.," who writes that he had "transcribed the following handsome production of a young gentleman of this city" from "the 'PASSAIC ALBUM' at Major Godwin's." The poem was later published in various periodicals and in *The Atlantic Souvenir* for 1827.

The Western Miscellany [Dayton, Ohio].

"The American Desert." 1 (March 1849), 291-292. From *Astoria*.

The Western Monthly Magazine [Cincinnati, Ohio and Louisville, Ky.].

Extracts from *Astoria*. 5 (November 1836), [685]-687. In review.

The Westminster Review [London].

Extracts from *The Alhambra*. 17 (July 1832), 132-145. In review.

Extracts from *Astoria*. 26 (January 1837), 318-348. In review.

Y

Yankee Doodle [New York].

* Extract from a letter, undated, to the committee for an Edwin Forrest dinner regretting that he is engaged. 1 (24 October 1846), 29.

Complete
Works

TO LIST THE COMPLETE WORKS of Washington Irving published in his own lifetime would seem at first a simple matter. But in fact it raises a difficult question: what constitutes a "Collected Works of Irving"? In Paris, for instance, the Galignanis and Baudry both reprinted in English, volume by volume to 1837, all of Irving's works through *Captain Bonneville* (except for *The Letters of Jonathan Oldstyle*). And surely most if not all of the volumes could have been purchased together, particularly since the two publishers kept bringing out new impressions or new editions of the earlier volumes. Yet there is no evidence that either publisher considered the accumulating volumes as "Collected Works." They expressed no such concept, either directly by statement in the volumes nor indirectly by a common format or binding. When Baudry did bring out *The Complete Works of Washington Irving* in one volume in 1834, the prospectus for the volume makes clear that the earlier separate editions were just that: "L'éditeur de cette nouvelle réimpression a publié plusieurs éditions de chacun des ouvrages ci-dessus: la pluparte se vendent séparément...."

It might seem that a set of Collected Works, if more than one or two volumes, would be brought out together and sold together, and so could be identified easily, but that seems not to have been generally the practice. Sauerländer's set of translations appeared work by work from 1826 to 1836, and the Author's Revised Edition from 1848 to 1859; even the Carey, Lea & Blanchard Works appeared in Philadelphia over a period of two years, 1836-1837. The only workable test would seem to be the intention of the publisher to produce a set of "Complete Works," with that intention clearly expressed in the identification of the individual volume, either within each volume or on the original binding. Additionally, the different volumes in the set would generally be issued in a common binding, although a number of different common bindings might be offered. It helps too to have the set advertised as a "Collected Works." Perhaps such a definition is merely common sense. But the commercial requirements of publishing and the happy circumstance of Irving's long productive life complicates even that definition for any Complete Works of Irving. For instance, both Henry G. Bohn and George Routledge in London in 1850 brought out Irving's separate works in cheap individual editions and then bound together impressions of the individual editions in larger volumes, generally containing more than one work, and labeled them "Collected Works." When *Wolfert's Roost* and the *Life of*

Washington appeared in later years, Bohn apparently added them as "additional volumes" of the Collected Works. Similarly, George P. Putnam in New York began in 1848 to bring out new revised editions of the earlier works to constitute a final Collected Works to be called "The Author's Revised Edition." But Irving kept providing new works: *Mahomet and His Successors* in 1850 was added immediately to the set, and so identified. *Wolfert's Roost* in 1855 was published separately and eventually was added to the set in the common numbering and format. *Life of Washington* in five volumes, 1855-1859, was first published separately in octavo and then reprinted in the common duodecimo format both for separate popular sale and for use as additional volumes of "Irving's Works." What then constitutes The Author's Revised Edition, the original fifteen volumes (even then including the two added volumes of *Mahomet and His Successors*) or the twenty-one volumes that it eventually became?

At least we know the number of volumes in the various sets of The Author's Revised Edition, and the titles they include. Carey, Lea & Blanchard's Collected Works provides a more ambiguous set. In 1836 and 1837, the Philadelphia publishers re-copyrighted many of Irving's earlier works and began to bring out a set of Irving's Works, so identified on the spines of individual volumes (although not within the volumes) and in contemporary advertisements. Irving even provided revisions of *A History of New York* and *The Alhambra* for the set. But what of the three volumes of *The Crayon Miscellany* that Carey, Lea & Blanchard had published the year before, in 1835? Or what of the *Columbus* in two volumes that they had taken over in that same year? Neither has been located in the "Works" binding, and the *Columbus* is of a noticeably different size, but the publishers may nevertheless have considered them a part of the Collected Works. The resulting confusion seems to have been reflected when PP and DLC reported to the National Union Catalogue a set of Irving's Works in twelve volumes, while CtY reported a set in seventeen volumes. A case may be made for either number of volumes, but twelve would seem to better fit the definition.

With exception of the one-volume Baudry and the two-volume Lea & Blanchard Collected Works, produced and issued specifically for sale in that form, all of the other Collected Works were first produced and issued as separate editions of individual works. As such, they are included in the entries for the individual titles in the "Original Works" section. In this "Complete Works" section, accordingly, the made-up sets are given only an abbreviated, general description.

1A. *Irving's Works.* 12 vols. Philadelphia: Carey, Lea, & Blanchard, 1836-1837.

The six major works through *The Alhambra. Salmagundi* is not included. *A History of New York* and *The Alhambra* were revised for these Collected Works.

The Works volumes were advertised and sold individually and can be distinguished only by the identification of "Irving's Works" on the spines of the original cloth bindings. Each was also newly copyrighted in the name of Washington Irving. For a description, see the individual entries.

See the introduction to this section for a brief discussion of the number of works included in the set.

PP and DLC report the Works in 12 vols.; CtY, in 17 vols.

2A. THE WORKS | OF | WASHINGTON IRVING. | CONTAINING | [The works are listed in two columns, with a double vertical rule between columns. In the first column: THE SKETCH BOOK. | KNICKERBOCKER'S HISTORY OF | NEW YORK. | BRACEBRIDGE HALL. In the second column: TALES OF A TRAVELLER. | A CHRONICLE OF THE CONQUEST | OF GRANADA. | THE ALHAMBRA.] | IN TWO VOLUMES. | WITH A PORTRAIT OF THE AUTHOR. | VOL. I. [II.] | [rule] | PHILADELPHIA: | LEA AND BLANCHARD. | 1840. All within double frame lines.

(25.2×15.6): Vol. I. $[1]^4$ $[2]^6$ $3\text{-}44^6$ 45^4. The last leaf is a blank. Not reckoned: preliminary engraving from portrait by G. S. Newton. Vol. II. $[-]^4$ $[1]^2$ $2\text{-}43^6$.

Vol. I. [i]-[ii], half-title, verso blank; [iii]-[iv], title, on verso copyright (see the note below) and printer; [v]-viii, table of contents; [13]-180, *A History of New York*; [181]-350, *The Sketch Book*; [351]-534, *Bracebridge Hall*. Vol II. [i]-[ii], half-title, verso blank; [iii]-[iv], title, on verso copyright (see the note below) and printer; [v]-vii, table of contents; [viii], blank; [9]-187, *Tales of a Traveller*; [188], blank; [189]-393, *Conquest of Granada*; [394], blank; [395]-516, *The Alhambra*. Each work has its own title page, dated 1840. All pages of text in double columns. Double frame lines around each page.

Each of the two volumes carries a copyright notice in the name of Washington Irving, but without a date. Additionally, the title page for each individual work carries on the verso a copyright notice, dated 1836 in the name of Washington Irving.

Lineation: Vol. I. p. 100, will ... thwarting ; p. 200, and ... parson, Vol. II. p. 100, churchyard ... a ; p. 200, picked ... without

Printer: C. Sherman and Co.

Southern Literary Messenger, June 1840, noticed. *Knickerbocker*, July 1840, reviewed.

CtY, TxU.

3A.   *Irving's Works*. 15 vols. "Author's Revised Edition." New York: George P. Putnam, 1848-1850.

Sixteen major works through *Mahomet and His Successors*. *The Companions of Columbus* is added to *The Life and Voyages of Columbus* and treated as a unified work. *A Tour on the Prairies* is combined with *Abbotsford* and *Newstead Abbey* in one volume, titled *The Crayon Miscellany*. *Salmagundi* and *Legends of the Conquest of Spain* are not included. *Wolfert's Roost* was later added as Vol. XVI, and the *Life of Washington* as Vols. XVII-XXI.

Irving revised the original sixteen works for this edition.

Each volume was sold individually as well as in complete sets. Individual volumes were reprinted in new impressions as needed, and the complete set was kept in print through Irving's lifetime and after. For a description, see the individual entries.

The set was available in a wide variety of common bindings.

Complete sets are held by many libraries, including CtY, NN, TxU, ViU.

1E.   *Irving's Works*. 10 vols. "Bohn's Library Edition." London: Henry G. Bohn, 1850.

Eighteen major works through *Mahomet and His Successors*. *Goldsmith* is not included. Theodore Irving's *The Conquest of Florida* is added to Vol. X. At some point after 1855, *Wolfert's Roost* was substituted for *The Conquest of Florida*. Also, the *Life of Washington* was later added to the set.

Each work was first published individually in "Bohn's Shilling Series." Individual works were reprinted in new impressions as needed, and bound into new volumes of the "Library Edition." Apparently, a complete set was issued in the "Library Edition" in 1854. For a description, see the individual entries.

There is a matching set of the 10 vols. in NN.

2E.   *Washington Irving's Works*. 10 vols. "The Popular Library." London: George Routledge, 1850.

Eighteen major works through *Mahomet and His Successors*.

Each work was first published individually in "The Popular Library" series. For a description, see the individual entries.

Not seen in a complete set, and some combined volumes not located.

1Fa. THE | COMPLETE WORKS | OF | WASHINGTON IRVING | IN ONE VOLUME, | WITH A MEMOIR OF THE AUTHOR. | [cut of American eagle] | PARIS, | BAUDRY'S EUROPEAN LIBRARY, | RUE DU COQ, NEAR THE LOUVRE. | SOLD ALSO BY AMYOT, RUE DE LA PAIX; TRUCHY, BOULEVARD DES ITALIENS; THÉOPHILE BARROIS, JUN., | RUE RICHELIEU; LIBRAIRIE DES ÉTRANGERS, 55, RUE NEUVE-SAINT-AUGUSTIN; | AND FRENCH AND ENGLISH LIBRARY, RUE VIVIENNE; | SIGISMOND SCHMERBER, FRANCFORT ON MEIN. | [stylized swelled rule] | 1834.

First issued in four parts for subscribers. Not located in that form. The Prospectus (see below) specified that the engraved portrait, the titles, the table of contents, and the Memoir of Irving would be provided with the last part.

Subsequently issued in one volume in boards. (26.6 x 17.0): $[-]^2$ a^4 b^4 c^2 $[d]^1$ 1-159^4. The last leaf apparently excised. Not reckoned: preliminary portrait engraved by Blanchard.

[i]-[ii], half-title, on verso printer; [iii]-[iv], title, verso blank; [v]-xvi, "Memoir of Washington Irving," anonymous; [xvii]-xxvi, table of contents; [1]-104, *Salmagundi*; [105]-223, *A History of New York*; [224], blank; [225]-344, *The Sketch Book*; [345]-476, *Bracebridge Hall*; [477]-604, *Tales of a Traveller*; [605]-942, *Life and Voyages of Columbus*; [943]-1031, *The Companions of Columbus*; [1032], blank; [1033]-1181, *The Conquest of Granada*; [1182], blank; [1183]-1269, *The Alhambra*; [1270], printer.

Printer: Casimir, 12, Rue de la Vieille-Monnaie.

Lineation: p. 100, Thank ... ourselves ; p. 200, sweat ... ever!

Marbled paper boards with red T cloth shelfback. The cloth has a darker red design that suggests marbling. Sides blank. White paper label on spine: [double rule] | THE | COMPLETE WORKS | OF | WASH. IRVING | WITH A MEMOIR OF THE AUTHOR. | [rule] | One Volume [fancy] | EMBELLISHED WITH A BEAUTIFUL PORTRAIT. | [rule] | 1834. | [double rule]. The figure 3 in the date is difficult to distinguish from a 5 until examined under a strong glass. White endpapers.

The Prospectus promises to subscribers the first part on 1 August [1834], the second part on 20 August, the third part on 10 September, and the fourth part on 1 October. Listed in *Bibliographie de la France*: pp. 1-320 on 23 August 1834, # 4656; "Deuxième livraison" on 27 September 1834, # 5302; "Troisième livraison" on 18 October 1834, # 5684; "Quatrième (et dernière) livraison" on 8 November 1834, # 6141.

TxU (2), *BL*.

Prospectus.

A Prospectus for the edition was issued at some time before August 1834. The only copy located, in French, is bound in a copy of the edition itself in TxU, trimmed (apparently) from its original size. There it consists of a first leaf, paged [1]-2. Page [1] is headed: [cut of American eagle] | THE COMPLETE WORKS | OF | WASHINGTON IRVING | IN ONE VOLUME IMPERIAL OCTAVO, | WITH A PORTRAIT. | PARIS, BAUDRY, 9, RUE DU COQ, PRÈS LE LOUVRE. | [stylized swelled rule] | Prospectus. [fancy]. On that page, continuing onto the second, is an appreciation of Irving. On page 2 also is a description of the proposed work and its contents, and the conditions of subscription. At the foot of the page is an advertisement for Schiller's sämmtliche Werke published in Stuttgart & Tübingen by Cotta, 1834, for sale by Baudry. The imprint of Casimir, Paris, appears at the lower right. Bound after the first leaf of the Prospectus is what appears to be a second leaf. On the recto is a sample page: the beginning of "The Stout Gentleman" from *Bracebridge Hall*, paged 377. But the page is not in the same setting as page 365 of the edition itself, on which the beginning of "The Stout Gentleman" appears. The verso of the leaf is blank.

b.
(1Ga
[*The Complete Works*. In six parts. Frankfurt am Main: Sigismond Schmerber, 1834.]

Not located. Listed in Wilhelm Heinsius, *Allgemeines Bücher-Lexicon 1828-1834*, and Christian G. Kayser, *Vollstandiges Bücher-Lexicon 1833-1840*.

Heinsius and Kayser also list a "Pocket-Edition" by Schmerber in 1834. Not located. It is not clear what this is. Is it the same impression bound in thin parts? A new edition would be entirely too weighty for any pocket.

For a description of Schmerber's impression in two volumes, see the following impression of 1835.

c.
(1Gb
THE COMPLETE WORKS | OF | WASHINGTON IRVING | IN ONE VOLUME, | WITH A MEMOIR OF THE AUTHOR. | [extended swelled rule] | Francfort on the Main, [fancy] | SOLD BY SIGISMOND SCHMERBER. | [rule] | 1835. Vol. II adds above the swelled rule: [double rule] | PART II.

Despite the claim of IN ONE VOLUME on the title page of Vol. I, the work was issued in two vols. (The title was probably copied from the title of the Baudry edition of 1834.) Vol. II begins with p. 681 of the text.

(27.2 x 17.2 untrimmed): an impression of the Baudry edition of 1834. Casimir's imprint still appears on the last page of Vol. II. The same sheets? The first new title is substituted as a cancel in Vol. I and the second is inserted in Vol. II. No half-titles. The engraved portrait is retained.

Tan paper boards. Front covers missing on copy examined. On back covers, within double rules, advertisements for *Robertson's complete Works*; KUNSTREISE DURCH ENGLAND UND BELGIEN; and eight works by Maria Edgeworth. Spines blank.

TxU. Copy reported in Bayerischer Staatsbibliothek, München.

d. [Paris: Baudry, 1843.]

Not seen. Copies reported in MB, NN.

TRANSLATIONS

German.

Washington Irving's sämmtliche Werke. 74 Bändchen. Frankfurt am Main: Johann David Saurländer, 1826-1837.

Fifteen major works in translation through *Captain Bonneville*. Various translators.

The numbering of the parts is somewhat misleading, since *The Companions of Columbus* is counted twice, once as Bändchen 29-31, added at the end of the eight-part form of *The Life and Voyages of Columbus* (Bändchen 20-28) to make a twelve-part combined form, and once as Bändchen 41-43, a separate publication of the work. It should be noted also that individual works appear to have been issued by the publisher bound in various combinations of their component parts.

Each work was published and issued separately although numbered and identified as part of a Collected Works. There is some question, in fact, of whether the Collected Works were ever issued as a single set, although some of the separate titles were reprinted after first issue, presumably as demand dictated. For a description, see the individual entries.

Complete sets reported in CtY, NN, and Bayerischer Staatsbibliothek, München.

Index

THIS IS AN INDEX only of the titles of Washington Irving's writings. And it is restricted to his own choice of titles. In contemporary periodicals or books containing reprinted contributions, editors often made up their own titles for extracts from Irving. Those are indexed, however, under Irving's original title, not the editor's.

The one notable exception is those books in which Irving had an important hand as editor, major contributor, translator, or advisor, books that are not his alone but that are in some part his own: Theodore Irving's *The Conquest of Florida,* for instance, or some of the plays of John Howard Payne. A short contribution alone, even a new and original contribution, would not be enough.

For Irving's books that consist of a collection of shorter titled pieces (such as *Salmagundi, The Sketch Book, Bracebridge Hall, Tales of a Traveller, The Alhambra*) each book is indexed whenever possible and appropriate by the individual titles of its contents, except in the one principal discussion in this bibliography devoted to that book as a whole (and there the index page numbers are italicized). So when, for example, "The Wife" is reprinted in a periodical or in a book by someone else, it is indexed only under "The Wife," not under *The Sketch Book.* For Irving's books that do not consist of a collection of shorter titled pieces but are divided into chapters or present a coherent or chronological narrative (such as *A History of New York, The Life of Columbus, Oliver Goldsmith, Life of Washington*) each book is indexed simply under its own title, even though chapters or other smaller portions of the work may carry subtitles.

Irving published under many pseudonyms in addition to the "Geoffrey Crayon" so familiar by his middle years. When a book of short piece appeared initially under a name other than Crayon or Irving, the name is given here as part of the title.

Finally, I should point out that a title may, and surprisingly often will, appear more than once on an indexed page.

Abbotsford, 197, 284, 387, 388,
    393, 400, *402-409, 416-418,*
    652, 660, 684, 688, 707, 711,
    713, 721, 733, 735, 744
Abderahman, 700, 728, 731, 735
The Abencerrage. *See*
    Recollections of the Alhambra
The Abencerrages, 365
The Adalantado of the Seven
    Cities. *See* The Enchanted
    Island
The Adventure of My Aunt, 217
The Adventure of My Uncle, 217
The Adventure of Sam. *See* The
    Adventure of the Black
    Fisherman
The Adventure of the Black
    Fisherman, 218, 733
The Adventure of the Englishman,
    218, 282
The Adventure of the German
    Student, 217, 224, 685, 696,
    703, 704, 706
The Adventure of the Little
    Antiquary, 218
The Adventure of the Mason, 364,
    365, 609, 614, 692, 704, 733
The Adventure of the Mysterious
    Picture, 217
The Adventure of the Mysterious
    Stranger, 217, 240
The Adventure of the Popkins
    Family, 218
Adventures of Capt. Bonneville, 285,
    421, 422, *433-445,* 479, 550,
    621, 627, 678, 685, 687, 688,
    692, 707, 711, 721, 730, 741,
    747
Advertisement [*Salmagundi*], 8, 17
Advertisement [*Sketch Book*], 123,
    124, 147
Advertisement to Second Edition
    [*Bracebridge Hall*], 186
The Alhambra, 234, 284, *362-386,*
    343, 400, 414, 686, 713, 730,
    737, 742, 743, 745
The Alhambra by Moonlight, 284,
    364, 607, 616, 617, 666
Alonzo de Ojeda, 350-361

American Researches in Italy: Life
    of Tasso; Recovery of a Lost
    Portrait of Dante, 701
[Anecdote of "a colony of
    Patlanders"], 700
[Anecdote of Admiral Harvey], 699
[Anecdote of the French
    Revolution], 700
The Angler, 125, 126, 281, 593, 696
Annette Delarbre, 184
An Appeal...in Behalf of Lamartine,
    581-582
Aristidean Gallery of Portraits, 689
The Art of Book Making, 124, 281,
    598, 618, 695, 706, 714
Astoria, 285, *419-432,* 433, 436, 667,
    685, 690, 697, 707, 713, 721,
    729, 736, 737
The Author, 184, 608, 705, 736
The Author's Account of Himself,
    124, 691, 695
The Author's Chamber, 364, 729
The Author's Farewell, 184, 705,
    706, 714
The Author's Farewell to Granada,
    368
Autumnal Reflections, by
    Launcelot Langstaff, 11, 52,
    278, 279

Bachelors, 184, 711
A Bachelor's Confessions, 184
The Balcony, 364, 365
The Beauties of Washington Irving,
    267-285
"Being, as it were...", 9, 34
The Belated Travellers, 218, 224
The Bermudas: A Shakespearian
    Research, 475, 621, 677, 699,
    728
Beware of Imposters!!, 689
Billy Luscious, 689
Biographical Memoir of Capt.
    David Porter, 534, 536, 680
Biographical Memoir of
    Commodore Perry, 534, 536,
    537, 680
Biographical Notice of the Late Lt.
    Burrows, 534, 536, 537, 680

[Biographical sketch of Irving by the Duyckincks], 580, 581

Biographical Sketch of Thomas Campbell, by a Gentleman of New York. *See Poetical Works of Thomas Campbell*

Biography and Poetical Remains of Margaret M. Davidson, ix, *446-455*, 633, 712, 729

Biography of Capt. James Lawrence, 534-537, 679

The Birds of Spring, 285, 475, 556, 557, 617, 626, 627, 635, 647, 659, 662, 664, 668, 698, 714, 731

Boabdil El Chico, 364, 365

The Boar's Head Tavern, East Cheap, 124, 696

The Bold Dragoon; or, The Adventure of My Grandfather, 217, 282, 692, 696, 707, 733

The Booby Squire, 217

A Book of the Hudson, 456-459, 677, 693, 708

Bordeaux Theatre, 725

Bracebridge Hall, x, xii, *183-204*, 277, 282, 404, 591, 687, 691, 704, 743, 745

Broek: or, The Dutch Paradise, 476, 665, 701

The Broken Heart, 124, 281, 580, 581, 595, 600, 604, 605, 607, 617, 619, 629, 632, 640, 643, 652, 653, 659, 663, 664, 667, 694, 695, 704, 710, 712, 714, 720

Buckthorne; or, the Young Man of Great Expectations, 217, 282, 735

The Busy Man, 184, 613, 655

By Anthony Evergreen, Gent., 8, 9, 11, 26, 34, 54, 72, 86, 279

By Launcelot Langstaff, Esq., 11, 52

Card, 8, 22, 68

The Catskill Mountains, 567, 568, 655, 665, 703, 704, 709

Chap CIX of the Chronicles of the...City of Gotham, 11, 52, 86

Characteristic Portraits, Lately Added to the Shakespeare Gallery, 689

Charles the Second, 208-215, 528

The Charming Letorières. *See* The Taking of the Veil

Christmas, 125, 281, 595, 600, 608, 652, 664, 666, 694, 695

Christmas Day, 122, 125, 141, 695

The Christmas Dinner, 122, 125, 141, 281

Christmas Eve, 125, 281, 631, 638, 695

Christmas Morning, 122, 125, 141

A Chronicle of the Conquest of Granada, by Fray Antonio Agapida, 283, 284, *335-349,* 372, 412-414, 607, 608, 653, 654, 690, 691, 706, 712, 713, 715, 743, 745

A Chronicle of Wolfert's Roost. See Wolfert's Roost

The Club of Queer Fellows, 217

Cockloft Hall, by Launcelot Langstaff, 10, 49, 86, 278

Col. Blubber, 689

Communication, by Ludwick Von Bynkerfeldt, 718

Communication; Concert of Madame Deseze, by An Amateur, 725

Communication; From Ballston or Milton Springs, 724

Communipaw, by Hermanus Vanderdonk, 456, 698, 731

The Congressional Fracas, 689

The Conquest of Florida, by Theodore Irving, 437, 479, *548-550,* 684, 688, 707, 713, 721, 744

The Conspiracy of Neamathla. *See* The Seminoles

Conspiracy of the Cocked Hats, by Roloff Van Ripper, 698, 728

A Contented Man, 476, 539, 540, 687, 696, 706, 708, 711, 715, 720

Conversations with Talma, 572,
573, 668
The Count Van Horn, 476, 699
The Country Church, 124, 281, 657,
686, 691, 695, 704
The Court of Lions, 284, 364, 365
The Crayon Miscellany, 387-418,
742, 744
The Crayon Reading Book. See
Beauties of Washington Irving
The Creole Village; A Sketch from
a Steam-Boat, 475, 483, 484,
552, 604, 697, 721, 727
The Crusade of the Grand Master
of Alcantara, 367
The Culprit, 184

Dedication to Wilkie [Alhambra],
363
Defence of Fort M'Henry, 680
Description of Pompey's Pillar, 616,
652
Desultory Thoughts on Criticism,
698
The Devil and Tom Walker, 218,
242, 623, 696
Diego de Lepe and R. de Bastides,
350-361
Diego de Nicuesa, 350-361
Dolph Heliger, 184, 203, 204, 282,
456, 593, 595, 600, 610, 612,
629, 646, 652, 656, 658, 664
Don Juan: A Spectral Research,
476, 685, 692, 701, 715, 728
The Dull Lecture, 543, 580, 581,
606, 607, 720, 727

The Early Experiences of Ralph
Ringwood, 476, 483, 484, 559,
676, 700, 715, 722, 728, 731
Ebenezer, 689
The Eccentric Man, 724
The "Empire of the West," 699
The Enchanted Island; The
Adelantado of the Seven
Cities, 476, 483, 484, 553, 686,
698, 731
English and French Character. See
Sketches in Paris in 1825
English Country Gentlemen, 184

English Eating, 710
English Gravity, 184
English Writers on America, 124,
687, 691, 704, 720
The Englishman at Paris. See
Sketches in Paris in 1825
Essays and Sketches. See Beauties
of Washington Irving
An Expedition in Quest of a
Diploma, 367

Falconry, 184
The Falls of Passaic, 540, 541, 598,
611, 619, 622, 623, 625, 649,
676, 687, 688, 711, 729, 732,
734, 736
Family Misfortunes, 183, 184
Family Reliques, 184, 705
Family Servants, 184
The Farm-House, 184
Fashions, by Anthony Evergreen, 8,
20, 86
A Fete in the Alhambra, 366, 367
The Field of Waterloo. See
Sketches in Paris in 1825
The First Locomotive Again. See
To the Editor of The
Knickerbocker, by Hiram
Crackenthorpe
Flummery from the Mill of Pindar
Cockloft, Esq., 8, 22, 68
Forest Trees, 184, 592, 612, 667,
734
Fortune Telling, 184
The French Libertine. See Richelieu.
The Freyschütz, 265-266
From My Elbow-Chair, 6, 8-11, 20,
22, 26, 29, 39, 40, 42, 45, 47, 54,
55, 68, 86, 278, 279, 705, 735
From the Elbow-Chair of
Launcelot Langstaff, 7, 12, 17,
77, 729
From the Mill of Pindar Cockloft,
Esq., 9, 10, 33, 39, 45, 75, 278

General Remark, 8, 22, 68
The Generalife, 366
Gentility, 184
Gipsies, 184, 705
Government of the Alhambra, 363

The Governor and the Notary, 366, 367, 614

Governor Manco and the Soldier, 366, 367

The Grand Prior of Minorca, 475, 692, 699, 715, 728, 731

Grave Reflections of a Disappointed Man, 217, 282, 643, 652, 666, 669

The Great Mississippi Bubble, 475, 621, 700, 732

The Great Unknown, 217, 224

Guests from Gibbet-Island, by Barent Van Schaick, 456, 476, 483, 484, 559, 677, 699

The Hall, 184

The Hall of the Ambassadors, 364

Harvey's Scenes of the Primitive Forest of America, 557-558

The Haunted House, 184

The Haunted Ship: A True Story -- As Far as It Goes, 551, 560, 669, 721

Hawking, 184

Hell Gate, 218, 733

The Historian, 184

A History of New York, by Diedrich Knickerbocker, ix, x, xii, 83, 84, *87-114*, 279-281, 456, 552, 570-572, 580, 581, 592, 593, 599, 603, 608, 611-613, 619, 629, 633, 640, 644, 647, 651, 652, 654, 656, 660, 662, 664, 666-668, 686, 691, 693, 704, 706, 708, 710, 712, 714, 717-719, 722, 732, 742, 743, 745

History of the ... Arts of Design, by William Dunlap, *547-548,* 678

Horsemanship, 184

The House of the Weathercock, 365

The Household, 363, 364

"How hard it is ...," by William Wizard, 11, 55

"How now, mooncalf!" 8, 20, 68

The Hunting Dinner, 217, 224

Important Negotiations, 363

Inhabitants of the Alhambra, 364

The Inn at Terracina, 218, 609

The Inn Kitchen, 125, 281, 695

Interior of the Alhambra, 363, 364, 687, 711

International Copy-Right Law, 558-559

The Iron Footsteps, by John Waters, 559, 700

The Irving Gift. See Beauties of Washington Irving

Irving Vignettes. See Beauties of Washington Irving

Isaac, 689

The Jesuits' Library, 364

John Bull, 122, 125, 281, 691, 695, 706, 736

The Journey, 363, 733, 734

Juan Ponce de Leon, 350-361

Jusef Abul Hagiag (or Hagias). *See* Yusef Abul Hagig

Kidd the Pirate, 218, 283, 705

The Knight of Malta. *See* The Grand Prior of Minorca

The Lay of the Scottish Fiddle, 680

A Legend of Cummunipaw. *See* Guests from Gibbet Island

Legend of Count Julian and His Family, 410-415, 677, 688, 702, 711

Legend of Don Munio Sancho de Hinojosa, 367, 686, 698, 728

The Legend of Don Roderick, 410-415, 701

Legend of Prince Ahmed Al Kamel, 366, 386

The Legend of Sleepy Hollow, 126, 180, 181, 281, 282, 456, 595, 597, 695, 702, 711, 736

Legend of the Arabian Astrologer, 365

The Legend of the Enchanted Soldier, 368, 709

Legend of the Engulfed Convent, 476, 621, 687, 699

Legend of the Governor and the Notary. *See* The Governor and the Notary

Legend of the Governor and the
    Soldier, 366
Legend of the Moor's Legacy, 366,
    386
Legend of the Rose of the
    Alhambra, 366, 386, 643, 655,
    716, 730
Legend of the Subjugation of
    Spain, 410-415, 701
Legend of the Three Beautiful
    Princesses, 365, 366, 386, 707
Legend of the Two Discreet
    Statues, 366, 367
Legends of the Conquest of Spain,
    ix, 343, 372, 380, 387, *410-415,*
    685, 688, 701, 707, 711, 712,
    721, 733, 744
L'Envoy, 123, 126
Letter for The American Lycoeum,
    555
[A Letter from Bordeaux], 725
[A Letter from France], 725
Letter from Granada. *See* Public
    Fetes of Granada
Letter from Mustapha, 8-11, 20, 26,
    32, 39, 42, 49, 51, 53, 54, 72, 86,
    278, 640, 643, 652, 655, 661,
    685, 712, 727, 731, 732
Letter on *Cyclopædia of American
    Literature,* 581, 678
Letters of Jonathan Oldstyle, ix,
    205-207, 529, 605, 606, 696,
    711, 724, 725, 741
Letters, to:
    S. Austin Allibone, 576-580
    James W. Beekman, 563, 565,
        566, 709, 713
    William C. Bryant, 709, 716,
        719, 721, 731
    Edward Bulwer-Lytton, 573-
        576
    Churchill C. Cambreling, 718
    Childs & Peterson, 576-580,
        678
    L. Gaylord Clark, 700, 702, 703
    Secr. John M. Clayton, 560,
        561
    Committee for Edwin Forrest
        dinner, 737
    Charles Dickens, 676, 677, 727

William Dunlap, 547, 548
Peter S. Duponceau, 717, 718,
    720, 730
Evert and George Duyckinck,
    580, 581, 709, 729
Gentlemen (Vicksburg, Miss.),
    736
Rufus W. Griswold, 570, 694,
    718
Mary M. Hamilton, 713
Harper & Brothers, 561
Philip Hone, 719, 722
Peter Irving, 684, 712, 713, 717
William Jerdan, 569
Rann Kennedy, 538
Charles Lanman, 579, 582, 583
William C. Macready, 719
G. & C. Merriam, 563-565, 709
Jesse Merwin, 693, 709, 713,
    719
Edgar A. Poe, 554, 734
George P. Putnam, 702
James Renwick, 716
Henry R. Schoolcraft, 709,
    710, 719
Capt. Gregory Seaworthy
    (George H. Throop), 562
Prof. B. Silliman, 716
George Sumner, 719
Abdiel S. Thurston, 703
W.P. Van Ness, 703
T.H. White, 735
Andrew Wilson, 694
Joseph E. Worcester, 563, 566,
    583, 584, 688
The Library, 184
*Life and Letters of Thomas
    Campbell,* by William Beattie,
    116, 677, 694
*The Life and Voyages of Christopher
    Columbus,* x, xii, 283, *288-334,*
    353, 355, 359, 596, 600, 602,
    605, 608-610, 612, 616-618, 620,
    627, 635-640, 648, 652, 654,
    655, 666, 677, 678, 684, 685,
    687, 690, 691, 696, 705, 706,
    708, 710, 711, 713-715, 733,
    735, 742, 744, 745, 747
Life of George Washington, x, 285,
    475, *485-523,* 647, 659, 660,

665, 678, 685, 692, 707, 710,
    713, 741, 742, 744
*Life of Mahomet. See Mahomet and
    His Successors*
*Life of Margaret M. Davidson. See
    Biography...Davidson*
*The Life of Oliver Goldsmith. See
    Oliver Goldsmith*
[Lines Written in the Album at
    Stratford], 677, 697, 716, 720,
    732
Literary Antiquary, 184
A Literary Dinner, 217, 687, 696,
    705, 715, 730
Literary Life, 217
Little Britian, 125, 126, 281, 696,
    704
The Little Man in Black, by
    Launcelot Langstaff, 11, 53,
    278, 595, 610
*Lives of the Successors of Mahomet.
    See Mahomet and His
    Successors*
Local Traditions, 365, 366
London Antiques, 125
Lord Byron, 680
Love-Charms, 184, 705
Love-Symptoms, 184
The Lovers, 184, 282, 733
Lovers' Troubles, 183, 184

Mahomet and His Successors, 285,
    460-474, 677, 693, 708, 709,
    742, 744
The Manuscript, 184
Mathews Not at Home, 720
May-Day, 184
May-Day Customs, 184
Mementos of Boabdil, 364, 365
Memorandums for a Tour..."The
    Stranger in New Jersey," by
    Jeremy Cockloft, 8, 22
Micer Codro, the Astrologer, 350-
    361
Mine Uncle John, 10, 42, 86, 278
*The Miscellaneous Works of Oliver
    Goldsmith. See Oliver
    Goldsmith*
Mr. Wilson's Concert, by Anthony
    Evergreen, 7, 17

The Moorish Drum, 555, 556, 688
[Motion of regret at death of Sir
    W. Scott], 716
Mountjoy: or Some Passage Out of
    The Life of a Castle-Builder,
    475, 559, 699, 728, 731
Muhamed Abou Alahmar [or
    Mahamad Aben Alahmar],
    364, 366, 367
The Mutability of Literature, 124,
    281, 598, 695, 704
My French Neighbor. *See* Sketches
    in Paris in 1825
The Mysterious Chambers, 364

National Nomenclature, 698
New-York Assembly, by Anthony
    Evergreen, 7, 12, 278,708
The New-York Review, 533
Newstead Abbey, 197, 284, 387, 388,
    393, 400, *402-409, 416-418,* 652,
    684, 688, 707, 711, 713, 735,
    744
Newton the Painter, 720
Note [or Notes], by William
    Wizard, 33, 42, 51, 54, 279
[A note from Jonathan Oldstyle],
    724
Notice, 8, 22, 68
Notoriety, 217, 224, 705

An Old Soldier, 184
Oliver Goldsmith: A Biography, 165,
    243-264, 283, 652, 693, 701,
    702, 708, 728, 744
On Greatness, by Launcelot
    Langstaff, 10, 49, 72, 278
On Passaic Falls. *See* The Falls of
    the Passaic
On Style, by William Wizard, 9, 34,
    279
[On value of the Hudson scenery],
    702
Origin of The White, The Red and
    the Black Men. *See* The
    Seminoles
Original Pictures for the
    Pandemonian Gallery, 690

The Painter's Adventure, 218

Palace of the Alhambra, 284, 363, 610

Panorama from the Tower of Comares, 364, 711

Paris at the Restoration. *See* Sketches in Paris in 1825

A Parisian Hotel. *See* Sketches in Paris in 1825

Pedro A. Niño and Chris. Guerra, 350-361

Pelayo and the Merchant's Daughter, 621, 692, 699, 715

Peter Klaus, The Legend of the Goatherd, 710

Peter Smink, by John H. Payne, *539*

[Petition to Congress for a law of international copyright], 690

[Petition to W.C. Macready], 719

The Phantom Island. *See* The Enchanted Island

Philip of Pokanoket, 123, 125, 182, 281, 599, 612, 630, 680, 703, 720

Plans for Defending Our Harbour, by William Wizard, 10, 47, 685, 718

Poems by William Cullen Bryant, 545-546, 684, 720

The Poetical Works of Thomas Campbell, 115-121, 626, 680, 685, 686

Poets and Poetry of Moslem Audalus, 367

The Poor-Devil Author, 217

Popular Superstitions, 184, 696

A Practical Philosopher, 217, 224, 283, 652

Preface [*Sketch Book*], 124, 677, 702

The Pride of the Village, 125, 282, 686, 688, 695, 704, 708, 736

Prince Ahmed al Kamel. *See* Legend of Prince Ahmed Al Kamel

Proclamation, from the Mill of Pindar Cockloft, 8, 20

Prospectus [*Sketch Book*], 124

Prospectus for Collection of English Literature. *See Oliver Goldsmith*

Public Fetes of Granada, 365, 700

A Ramble Among the Hills, 364, 365, 366

Rare Fun!!!, 690

Ready-Money Jack, 184, 282, 647, 705

Recollections of the Alhambra, 476, 553, 686, 698, 728, 731

Reflection on the Moslem Domination in Spain, 364, 608, 686

Relics and Geneologies, 366

[Remarks upon introducing Daniel Webster], 570

A Retrospect, Or 'What you Will,' 10, 47

Review of *A Year in Spain,* 732

Review of *History of the Northmen* by Henry Wheaton, 729

[Review of *Odes* by Edwin C. Holland], 680

[Review of *The Conquest of Granada*], 732

Richelieu, 208, 286-288

Rip Van Winkle, 124, 179, 180, 281, 456, 553, 594, 598, 601, 602, 622, 640, 641, 649, 655, 664, 691, 695

The Rocky Mountains. See Adventures of Capt. Bonneville

The Rookery, 183, 184, 613, 696, 706

Roscoe, 124, 181, 281, 594, 612, 695, 706, 712, 714, 734

The Route to Fondi. *See* The Adventure of the Englishman

A Royal Poet, 124, 281, 686, 695

Rural Funerals, 122, 125, 281, 607, 609, 612, 616-618, 633, 636-638, 642, 643, 646, 648, 650, 652, 655, 656, 658, 662, 663, 665, 666, 687, 696, 704, 705, 712, 734

Rural Life in England, 124, 154, 282, 608, 618, 620, 622, 638, 639, 643, 647, 655, 666, 691, 695

St. Mark's Eve, 184, 282, 592, 596, 632, 652, 665, 735

Salmagundi, by Launcelot Langstaff, and others, ix, xv, *3-86*, 110, 111, 122, 126, 232, 278, 279, 528, 591, 593, 690, 708, 729, 743-745

The School, 184, 593

The Schoolmaster, 184, 593

The Seminoles, 476, 483, 484, 678, 692, 701, 728, 731, 733

"Sitting late the other evening," by Launcelot Langstaff, 7, 17

The Sketch Book, ix, x, xv, xvi, xviii, 88, *122-182,* 262, 277, 281, 282, 527, 691, 693, 694, 705, 712, 720, 743, 745

Sketches from Nature, by Anthony Evergreen, Gent., 10, 49, 278

Sketches in Paris in 1825, 475-477, 690, 701, 728, 735

Sketches of a Traveller. See Beauties of Washington Irving

Sleepy Hollow, 686, 698, 728, 731

Spanish Romance, 367

The Spectre Bridegroom, 125, 182, 282, 594, 622, 631, 695

[Speech at public dinner for Dickens], 676, 677, 684, 715, 719, 727

[Speech at public dinner for Irving], 546, 547, 676, 684, 686, 717-720, 727, 730

The Stage Coach, 125, 281, 593, 620, 695, 704

The Storm-Ship, 184, 282, 595, 652, 733

The Story of the Bandit Chieftain, 218

The Story of the Young Italian, 217, 598, 601, 602, 705, 735

The Story of the Young Robber, 218, 553, 692, 703-707, 711, 730

Story Telling, 184

The Stout Gentleman, 184, 282, 580, 581, 595, 609, 649, 657, 664, 678, 685, 693, 696, 710, 714, 732, 734, 736, 746

The Stranger at Home; Or, A Tour in Broadway, by Jeremy Cockloft, 10, 45, 68

The Stranger in Pennsylvania, by Jeremy Cockloft, 6, 9, 40, 41, 68, 75, 732

Stratford-on-Avon, 125, 126, 592, 593, 594, 607, 618, 632, 656, 696

The Strolling Manager, 217, 218

The Student of Salamanca, 184, 714

Style at Ballston, by William Wizard, 10, 51, 86

A Sunday in London, 124, 708

The Taking of the Veil, 621, 700, 731

Tales of a Traveller, x, 77, *216-242,* 282, 283, 373, 693, 743, 745

Tea, A Poem, from the Mill of Pindar Cockloft, 7, 11, 54, 279, 630

Theatrical Intelligence, by William Wizard, 10, 49

Theatrics, by William Wizard, 7, 9, 12, 29, 68, 86

The Three Kings of Bermuda, and Their Treasure of Ambergris. *See* The Bermudas

A Time of Unexampled Prosperity. *See* The Great Mississippi Bubble

To Launcelot Langstaff, Esq., 6, 8, 9, 17, 40, 41, 75

To Mr. Andrew Quoz, by Dick Buckram, 725

To Readers and Correspondents, 10, 48

To the Amateur, by Banquo, 725

To the Editor of *The Knickerbocker,* by Geoffrey Crayon, 456, 570-572, 697, 702, 717, 728

To the Editor of *The Knickerbocker,* by Hiram Crackenthorpe, 559, 698

To the Editor of *The Knickerbocker,* by Washington Irving, 678, 699

To the Editor of the *Morning Chronicle,* by Walter Withers, 725

To the Editor of the *New-York American,* 716

To the Editor of the New York *American Citizen,* by Christian Brinkersnuff, 717

To the Editor of the *New-York Evening Post,* by A Traveller, 717, 718

To the Editor of the *New-York Evening Post,* by Seth Handaside, 717, 718

To the Editor of *The Plaindealer,* 730, 731

To the Ladies, by Anthony Evergreen, 11, 55, 77, 86

To the Ladies, from the Mill of Pindar Cockloft, 8, 26, 76, 84, 735

To the Reader [*Tales of a Traveller*], 217, 224

To Toby Tickler, Esq., 689, 690

[Toast to Samuel Rogers at Booksellers' Dinner], 677, 716

A Tour on the Prairies, 284, *387-401,* 402, 404, *416-418,* 422, 433, 614, 616-618, 627, 632, 635, 636, 646, 652-655, 664, 677, 684, 688, 690, 693, 697, 702, 707, 710-712, 720, 729, 733-735, 744

The Tower of Comares, 363, 364

The Tower of Las Infantas, 365, 366

Traits of Indian Character, 123, 125, 182, 282, 607, 608, 612, 652, 680

Travelling, 184, 705

Travels in South American, by F. Depons. *See A Voyage to the Eastern Part of Terra Firma*

The Truant, 364

The Tuilleries and Windsor Castle. *See* Sketches in Paris in 1825

'*Twas I,* by John Howard Payne, 528, *541-542*

An Unwritten Drama of Lord Byron, 551, 688, 697, 721

Valdivia and His Companions, 350-361

Vasco Nuñez de Balboa, 284, 350-361, 609, 652, 691

The Veteran, 366

A Village Politician, 184, 692, 705, 714

Village Worthies, 184

Vincente Yañez Pinzon, 350-361

Visitors to the Alhambra, 366, 367, 386

The Voyage, 124, 281, 282, 592, 600, 612, 616, 617, 632, 634, 646, 648, 661, 667, 668, 691, 693, 695, 706, 734

A Voyage to the Eastern Part of Terra Firma, by François Depons, xii, 527, *529-533*

Voyages and Discoveries of the Companions of Columbus, 284, 289, 300-302, 305-311, *350-361,* 676, 706, 712, 716, 730, 735, 744, 745, 747

'We Will Rejoice!!!', 718

The Wedding, 184, 628, 678, 704

Westminister Abbey, 125, 126, 282, 607, 621, 622, 640, 652, 667, 668, 685, 696, 710

The Widow, 184

The Widow and Her Son, 124, 282, 592, 595, 597, 600, 601, 619, 628, 637, 640, 646, 652, 664, 667, 668, 685, 696, 702, 710

The Widow's Ordeal; or A Judicial Trial by Combat, 475, 552, 697, 721, 727, 733

The Widow's Retinue, 184, 714

The Wife, 124, 282, 595, 603, 607, 612, 614, 616, 617, 621, 630, 634, 636, 638, 640, 642, 645, 647, 648, 652, 654, 657, 662, 685-688, 695, 703, 704, 706, 707, 714, 732, 734, 736

Wives, 184, 282, 601, 652

Wolfert Webber, or Golden
    Dreams, 218, 242, 456, 643,
    702
Wolfert's Roost, 475, 483, 484, 686,
    698, 730
Wolfert's Roost, 285, *475-484*, 527,
    707, 741, 742, 744
The Wooden-Legged Ghost, by
    John Waters. *See* The Iron
    Footstep
The Works...of...Robert Treat
    Paine, 679

A Year in Spain, by a Young
    American, 527, *543-545*, 684
Yusef Abul Hagig, 364, 367